Labour and Working-Class History

in Atlantic Canada:

A Reader

Social & Economic Papers No. 22
Institute of Social & Economic Research
Memorial University of Newfoundland

Labour and Working-Class History in Atlantic Canada: A Reader

Edited by David Frank
and Gregory S. Kealey

ISER

Institute of Social and
Economic Research

Printed on acid-free paper

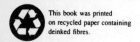

This book was printed
on recycled paper containing
deinked fibres.

Cover photographs courtesy of Provincial Archives of Newfoundland and Labrador

Canadian Cataloguing in Publication Data

Labour and working-class history in Atlantic Canada

(Social and economic papers ; no. 22)
ISBN 0-919666-78-7

1. Working class -- Atlantic Provinces -- History. 2. Trade unions
-- Atlantic Provinces -- History. I. Memorial University of
Newfoundland. Institute of Social and Economic Research.
II. Frank, David, 1949- . III. Kealey, Gregory S., 1948- .
IV. Series.

HD8109.A8L32 1995   305.5'62'0971509   C95-950217-3

Contents

Acknowledgements

We would like to thank the following authors, editors, and publishers for permission to reprint their work. For chapters 1, 2, 9 and 13, we thank the Canadian Committee on Labour History and the editor of *Labour/Le Travail*. For chapters 6, 7, 8, 10, 12 and 15, we thank the editor of *Acadiensis*. For chapters 5 and 11 we thank the Canadian Historical Association for permission to reprint from *Historical Papers*. We thank McGill-Queen's University Press for chapter 4 and the University of Toronto Press for chapter 3. Finally, we thank the *Journal of Canadian Studies* for chapter 16, Mount Allison University for chapter 14, and York University and the authors for chapter 17.

The following individuals also helped us with the production of this volume: Debra L. Coombs, now at Notre Dame, for scanning and formatting; Irene Whitfield of the Canadian Committee on Labour History for producing camera ready copy; Susan Nichol and Jeanette Gleeson of ISER for seeing the project through publication; and Sean Cadigan of Memorial University for keeping a watchful eye on the whole project.

D.F. Frank, Fredericton
G.S. Kealey, St. John's
15/02/95

Contributors

Acheson, T.W. (Bill), is a member of the Department of History, University of New Brunswick, Fredericton, N.B.

Bittermann, Rusty, teaches at the University College of Cape Breton in Sydney, N.S.

Cadigan, Sean, is currently working at Memorial University of Newfoundland, St. John's, NF on the Tri-Council Eco-Research Project on Sustainable Development in a Cold Ocean Environment.

Chisholm, Jessie, is a doctoral candidate in History at Memorial University of Newfoundland, St. John's, NF.

Connelly, M. Patricia, teaches Sociology at St. Mary's University, Halifax, N.S.

DeLottinville, Peter, is an archivist at the National Archives of Canada, Ottawa, ON.

Forbes, E.R. (Ernie), teaches in the Department of History at University of New Brunswick, Fredericton, N.B.

Forsey, Eugene, was a Canadian Senator and pioneer of Canadian labour history.

Frank, David, teaches history at University of New Brunswick and is a former editor of *Acadiensis*.

Glasbeek, Harry, teaches Law at Osgoode Hall, York University, Toronto, ON.

Kealey, Gregory S., teaches history at Memorial University of Newfoundland, St. John's, NF and edits *Labour/Le Travail*.

Little, Linda, farms near Pictou, N.S.

MacDonald, Martha, is a member of the Economics Department at St. Mary's University, Halifax, N.S.

McIntosh, Robert, is an archivist at the National Archives of Canada, Ottawa, ON.

McKay, Ian, teaches history at Queen's University, Kingston, ON.

Muise, D.A., teaches history at Carleton University, Ottawa, ON.

Reilly, Nolan, is a member of the History Department of the University of Winnipeg, Winnipeg, MB.

Sager, Eric W., teaches history at University of Victoria, Victoria, B.C.

Thomson, Anthony, is a sociologist at Acadia University, Wolfville, N.S.

Tucker, Eric, teaches Law at Osgoode Hall, York University, Toronto, ON.

INTRODUCTION

The Labour Question in Atlantic Canada

In the 1990s the Labour Question was making headlines. One week there were pictures from Arichat, Nova Scotia of angry crowds storming a strikebound lobster plant and the security staff escaping by helicopter. In St. John's, Newfoundland we watched striking municipal workers closing down the city arena and forcing the American Hockey League's Maple Leafs to leave town for part of the season. The following year the school term throughout the province was interrupted for four weeks by a dispute between teachers and the provincial government. Meanwhile, in Sussex, New Brunswick dairy workers were entering the third frustrating year of a lockout in which their jobs had been taken over by replacement workers. In Point Tupper, Nova Scotia workers were occupying a half-empty factory until the company agreed to comply with provincial law on industrial shutdowns. In Charlottetown, in one of the largest demonstrations in the Island's history, thousands of public-sector workers, armed with placards and white balloons, surrounded the legislature to protest wage reductions and broken contracts. And from Pictou County there came the tragic news that 26 miners had died suddenly in a pit explosion of the kind familiar to local miners for almost 200 years.

Although the Labour Question first appeared on the regional agenda in the 19th century, more than a century later it remains very much in the public eye. Even at a time when constitution-making and free trade dominated the headlines, it was impossible to read a newspaper or watch the news without seeing the latest report from the world of work. This is hardly surprising, since the work experience is one of the most widely shared social experiences in the region today. In Atlantic Canada today more than one million people earn their living in the form of wages and salaries, and labour force participation rates range from 53 per cent in Newfoundland to 66 per cent in Prince Edward Island.[1] Membership in unions in the Atlantic Provinces ranges from Newfoundland's 53 per cent, Canada's highest union density rate, to New Brunswick's 37 per cent, Prince Edward Island's 33 per cent, and Nova

[1]Statistics Canada, *Perspectives on Labour and Income*, 6, 2 (Summer 1994), 58-9.

Scotia's 31 per cent.[2] Yet a definition of the work experience must also include those who are deprived of regular employment due to the legacy of underdevelopment and crisis in many parts of the regional economy. Statistics reveal only a part of the story, but in 1993 the official unemployment rates in the Atlantic Provinces were far worse than the Canadian average of 11.2 per cent. Newfoundland's 20.2 per cent, Prince Edward Island's 17.7 per cent and Nova Scotia's 14.6 per cent were the highest in Canada, while New Brunswick's 12.6 per cent was outweighed only by Quebec's 13.1 per cent.[3] In addition a broad approach to the world of work must also include those — mainly women — who perform productive work in the household or in the wider economy without the benefit of formal remuneration. In short, the experience of work is as important for understanding regional society as any of the other shared identities within the region based on ethnicity, community, generation or gender.

The issues raised by the Labour Question in the 1990s are not new ones. They have been with us for the better part of two centuries. Indeed they have formed one of the permanent debates about social organization in the modern world. Every society must reach decisions about how the world of work is to be organized and how the rewards of economic life are to be distributed. And whatever success they have had in accommodating contradictory demands, none of the arrangements has proven permanent. As a result the Labour Question has remained a source of social conflict and an issue for public debate through to the present. As we look at the ways the everyday lives of people of Atlantic Canada have changed over time, the world of work provides one of the most useful ways of understanding the continuing evolution of our society.

Turning to the history of work in the region, it is worth noting that before the 1970s there was relatively little scholarly interest in this theme in Atlantic Canada. The number of academics working on the history of the region at all was limited, and labour history was not high on their list of priorities. There were studies of early unions in Nova Scotia by C.B. Fergusson and Ken Pryke, and by Eugene Forsey on Prince Edward Island.[4] In Newfoundland G.E. Panting examined the political importance of the Fishermen's Protective Union and Peter Neary discussed the social history of the Bell Island iron ore miners.[5] Richard Rice completed a

---

[2]Statistics Canada, *Annual Report of the Minister of Industry, Science and Technology under the Corporations and Labour Unions Returns Act, Part II, Labour Unions, 1991* (Ottawa 1993), Appendix 1.6, p. 25.

[3]Statistics Canada, *Perspectives on Labour and Income*, 6, 2 (Summer 1994), 58-9.

[4]C.B. Fergusson, *The Labour Movement in Nova Scotia Before Confederation* (Halifax 1964); Ken Pryke, "Labour and Politics: Nova Scotia at Confederation," *Histoire sociale/Social History*, 6 (1970); Eugene Forsey, "Some Notes on the Early History of Unions in Prince Edward Island," *Canadian Historical Review*, XLIV, 4 (1965).

[5]G.E. Panting, "The Fishermen's Protective Union of Newfoundland and the Farmers' Organizations in the West," Canadian Historical Association, *Annual Report* (1963); Peter Neary, "'Traditional' and 'Modern' Elements in the Social and Economic History of Bell Island and Conception Bay," *Communications historiques/Historical Papers* (1973).

substantial unpublished study of organized labour in Saint John in the 19th century and A.A. MacKenzie prepared a study of the Farmer-Labour Party in Nova Scotia.[6] At the national level, scholars such as Harold Logan and Eugene Forsey, both of whom had personal links to the region, did not neglect Atlantic Canada. In their general histories of Canadian labour both authors included useful coverage of Atlantic Canadian labour.[7] Yet in 1976 the editors of a collection of essays on Canadian labour history pointed out that labour historians had devoted less attention to Atlantic Canada than they had to other regions.[8]

Much of this changed in the decades of the 1970s and 1980s, as labour history in Atlantic Canada benefited both from the renaissance of regional history and from the increased attention to regional and social history generally among Canadian historians. The most notable developments took place at Dalhousie University, where several faculty and graduate students turned their attention to labour and social history themes. The journal *Labour/Le Travail*, founded by the Committee on Canadian Labour History, began its publishing history at Dalhousie University in 1976 and then moved, with the editor, to the Memorial University of Newfoundland in 1980.[9] Meanwhile, both at Dalhousie, Memorial University and the University of New Brunswick, graduate students were producing studies of various aspects of the working-class experience in the region, and this research soon found its way into the pages of journals, including *Acadiensis*, the influential new journal of regional history established at the University of New Brunswick in 1971.[10]

Outside the university there was also an increasing interest in labour history on the part of students and teachers, union members and the general public in the region. Labour history was accepted as a regular theme in the courses offered by the Atlantic Region Labour Education Centre, a residential college sponsored by the federations of labour in the four provinces. Popular local history periodicals such as *Cape Breton's Magazine* in Cape Breton included features on working-class

[6]Richard Rice, "A History of Organized Labour in St. John, New Brunswick," MA thesis, University of New Brunswick, 1968; A.A. MacKenzie, "The Rise and Fall of the Farmer-Labour Party in Nova Scotia," MA thesis, Dalhousie University, 1969.
[7]Harold Logan, *Trade Unions in Canada* (Toronto 1948); Eugene Forsey, *Trade Unions in Canada, 1812-1902* (Toronto 1982).
[8]Gregory S. Kealey and Peter Warrian, eds., *Essays in Canadian Working Class History* (Toronto 1976), 190.
[9]*Labour/Le Travail* originally named *Labour/Le Travailleur*. The title was changed in 1983 to remove an unintended gender bias. The Committee on Canadian Labour History, founded in 1971, became the Canadian Committee on Labour History in 1991.
[10]For the origins of *Acadiensis*, see the preface to Eric Swanick and David Frank, eds., *The Acadiensis Index, 1971-1991* (Fredericton 1992), which also contains a useful index of the journal's contents in its first 20 years of publication. See also the anthologies, P.A. Buckner and David Frank, eds., *Atlantic Canada Before Confederation* (Fredericton 1990) and *Atlantic Canada After Confederation* (Fredericton 1988).

themes,[11] as has the important alternative newsmagazine, *New Maritimes*.[12] In Newfoundland the Federation of Labour published a general history of labour in the province authored by a well-known journalist.[13] In Nova Scotia one union commissioned a professional historian to write its 100th anniversary history.[14] In New Brunswick researchers published a substantial guide to the published work on labour history in the province and helped organize workshops in labour history.[15] Regrettably, there was no substantial discussion of labour history in the otherwise useful guide, *Teaching Maritime Studies*, nor was the role of labour adequately represented in a well-funded high school text for Maritime Studies.[16] The latest general history of Atlantic Canada, however, published under the title *The Atlantic Provinces in Confederation*, provides a more balanced picture and includes a considerable amount of labour and social history in its contents.[17]

The strengths of the new labour history have been mainly in the discussion of the emergence of an industrial working class, especially in the factory towns and mining centres that experienced rapid growth in the late 19th and early 20th centuries before entering upon the long crisis of deindustrialization in the 1920s. These writers undertook not only to establish the presence of an industrial working class in the region, but also to explain some of the reasons for the rise and fall of the industrial economy associated with the National Policy in this period. In documenting the emergence of a working-class community, they also showed how economic crisis provoked vigorous resistance on the part of workers, most notably in the labour wars of the early 1920s.

More recently, attention has moved both backward and forward in time. Several important studies have focused on the preindustrial history of work in the region, especially in sectors such as the fisheries and the merchant marine and more recently

[11] A selection of articles from *Cape Breton's Magazine* is Ronald Caplan, ed., *Down North: The Book of Cape Breton's Magazine* (Toronto 1980), and an index is contained in issue No. 50, pp. 53-62.

[12] A fine introduction to *New Maritimes* is Ian McKay and Scott Milsom, eds., *Towards a New Maritimes: A Selection from Ten Years of New Maritimes* (Charlottetown 1992).

[13] Bill Gillespie, *A Class Act: An Illustrated History of the Labour Movement in Newfoundland and Labrador* (St. John's 1986).

[14] Ian McKay, *The Craft Transformed: An Essay on the Carpenters of Halifax, 1885-1985* (Halifax 1985).

[15] David Frank *et al.*, compilers, *The New Brunswick Worker/Les travailleurs au Nouveau-Brunswick: A Reader's Guide/Un guide au lecteur* (Fredericton 1986).

[16] P.A. Buckner, ed., *Teaching Maritime Studies* (Fredericton 1986); George Peabody, Carolyn MacGregor, Richard Thorne, eds., *The Maritimes: Tradition, Challenge and Change* (Halifax 1987).

[17] E.R. Forbes and D.A. Muise, eds., *The Atlantic Provinces in Confederation* (Toronto/Fredericton 1993). The companion volume, P.A. Buckner and John G. Reid, eds., *The Atlantic Region to Confederation: A History* (Toronto/Fredericton 1994), also devotes unprecedented attention to the world of work.

in the woods and on the farm.[18] Other studies have carried us forward into the more contemporary world, where the provincial and federal states have played a significant role, both in structuring the possibilities of development in the older resource-based industries and in providing a significant level of employment in the public sector.[19] At the same time attention has also broadened to include less formal kinds of participation in the working-class experience represented by the irregular and seasonal patterns of labour in local economies of survival throughout the region.[20] There has also been an overdue attention to the important role of women in the regional economy, both through their longstanding labour within the domestic and household economies of the region and through their increasing participation in the formal labour force.[21] Another recent development has been the increased attention to the history of work among historians of Acadian society, again an indication of the ways in which the history of work is discovering the elements of commonality in the regional experience.[22]

The situation noted in 1976 by Kealey and Warrian had changed considerably by the 1990s, and recent surveys of Canadian labour history contain numerous

[18]Important in this regard was the work of the Atlantic Canada Shipping Project at Memorial University. For example, see Rosemary Ommer and Gerald Panting, eds., *Working Men Who Got Wet* (St. John's 1980) and Eric W. Sager, *Seafaring Labour: The Merchant Marine of Atlantic Canada, 1820-1914* (Kingston and Montréal 1989). See also Rosemary Ommer, ed., *Merchant Credit and Labour Strategies in Historical Perspective* (Fredericton 1990), L. Anders Sandberg, ed., *Trouble in the Woods: Forest Policy and Social Conflict in Nova Scotia and New Brunswick* (Fredericton 1992) and Daniel Samson, ed., *Contested Countryside: Rural Workers and Modern Society in Atlantic Canada, 1800-1950* (Fredericton 1994).
[19]Gary Burrill and Ian McKay, eds., *People, Resources and Power: Critical Perspectives on Underdevelopment and Primary Industries in the Atlantic Region* (Fredericton 1987), Michael Earle, ed., *Workers and the State in Twentieth Century Nova Scotia* (Fredericton 1989), Bryant Fairley, Colin Leys and James Sacouman, eds., *Restructuring and Resistance: Perspectives from Atlantic Canada* (Toronto 1990).
[20]See especially Sandberg, ed., *Trouble in the Woods* and Samson, ed., *Contested Countryside*.
[21]Martha MacDonald, "Studying Maritime Women's Work: Underpaid, Unpaid, Invisible, Invaluable," in Buckner, ed., *Teaching Maritime Studies*, pp. 119-29, and Marilyn Porter, "'She Was Skipper of the Shore Crew': Notes on the History of the Sexual Division of Labour in Newfoundland," *Labour/Le Travail*, 15 (Spring 1985). See also Linda Kealey, ed., *Pursuing Equality: Historical Perspectives on Women in Newfoundland and Labrador* (St. John's 1993) and Janet Guildford and Suzanne Morton, eds., *Separate Spheres: Women's Worlds in the 19th-Century Maritimes* (Fredericton 1994).
[22]See Ginette Lafleur, "L'industrialisation et le travail remunéré des femmes: Moncton, 1881-1891," in Daniel Hickey, dir., *Moncton, 1871-1929: Changements socio-économiques dans une ville ferroviaire* (Moncton 1990), and Nicole Lang, "L'impact d'une industrie: Les effets sociaux de l'arrivée de la Compagnie Fraser Limited à Edmundston, N.-B., 1900-1950," *Revue de la Société Historique du Madawaska*, XV, 1-2 (avril 1987). See also the special issue, "Les syndicats au Nouveau-Brunswick," *égalité: revue acadienne de l'analyse politique*, 31 (printemps 1992).

references to the history of workers in this region.[23] Moreover labour history has played a large part in reshaping our understanding of the general history of Atlantic Canada in the 19th and 20th centuries. The present volume offers an introduction to recent work on the history of labour in Atlantic Canada. Most of the selections in this reader were originally published as journal articles or book chapters during the 1970s, 1980s and 1990s and they have been chosen from a much larger body of material which appeared during these years. The collection is designed to be useful to students who are studying the history of Atlantic Canada or the history of labour in Canada. It is divided into four sections, each corresponding to an identifiable period in the history of workers in the region. For each section there is a brief introductory note and a set of suggestions for additional readings. Although the book is mainly designed for student use, it is also our hope that the book will be useful to general readers, including working people and union members, whose needs have not been adequately met by much of the historical writing about the region in the past. The public determination to learn about our past, and especially to focus attention on the history of working people in the region, has provided a challenge which a new generation of researchers is beginning to meet.

[23]See, for instance, Bryan Palmer, *Working-Class Experience: Rethinking the History of Canadian Labour, 1800-1991* (Toronto 1992) and David J. Bercuson and David Bright, eds., *Canadian Labour History: Selected Readings* (Toronto 1994), as well as the several regional contributions to W.J.C. Cherwinski and Gregory S. Kealey, eds., *Lectures in Canadian Labour and Working-Class History* (St. John's 1985).

Part One
The World of Pre-Industrial Work

The early history of the Atlantic Region was characterized by a variety of labour systems that preceded the emergence of the working class in the 19th century. In native societies, for instance, work was organized on a communal basis, with divisions of labour based on age, gender, kinship and prestige. The division of labour among the men and boys who sailed on the early fishing expeditions was much more differentiated, and the rewards of the voyages were distributed on a complex share arrangement under which the largest returns went to the owners and captains of the vessels. Among the settled European populations in the region there was similar variety, ranging from the extended family networks among the early Acadian communities to the slaveholding households that existed in 18th century garrison towns such as Louisbourg and subsequently among the Loyalists. On the resource frontiers those who worked in the great staple industries catching fish or cutting wood were often not employees of the fish and lumber companies, but they still lived in a condition of continual dependence on local merchants for credit, supplies and access to markets. For much of the population in colonial society the world of the self-sufficient independent rural producer was thus more of an ideal than a reality. Rusty Bittermann examines the many ways in which the rural farm households of the Maritimes were drawn into the labour market, thus beginning the separation of workers from the possibilities of making a living on their own land. Linda Little studies an early instance of labour conflict in the Newfoundland outports, questioning the stereotype of a passive population and showing the ways in which the population was prepared to challenge the merchants' control of the local economy. T.W. Acheson discusses the complex world of the urban artisan, demonstrating the presence of an articulate and ambitious social group in Saint John prepared to advance its interest in progress and development; with the advent of industrialism some of these artisans would go on to become successful capitalists while others would form the basis of an urban working class. Eric W. Sager looks at the so-called golden age of sail from the perspective of the thousands of sailors who worked on board its floating workplaces; although unions did not exist in this difficult environment, he nevertheless shows that workers undertook to protect their rights by other means.

Additional Reading

Bittermann, Rusty. "The Hierarchy of the Soil: Land and Labour in a 19th Century Cape Breton Community," *Acadiensis*, XVIII, 1 (Autumn 1988), 33-55.

Cadigan, Sean T. "Merchant Capital, the State, and Labour in a British Colony: Servant-Master Relations and Capital Accumulation in Newfoundland's Northeast-Coast Fishery," *Journal of the Canadian Historical Association*, N.S. #2 (1991), 17-42.

_____. "Artisans in a Merchant Town: St. John's, Newfoundland, 1775-1815," *Journal of the Canadian Historical Association*, N.S. #4 (1993), 95-119.

_____. *Hope and Deception in Conception Bay: Merchant-Settler Relations in Newfoundland, 1785-1855* (Toronto 1995).

Fingard, Judith. *Jack in Port: Sailortowns of Eastern Canada* (Toronto 1982).

_____. "The Relief of the Unemployed Poor in Saint John, Halifax and St. John's, 1815-1860," *Acadiensis*, V, 1 (Autumn 1975), 32-53.

Hornsby, Stephen J. *Nineteenth Century Cape Breton: A Historical Geography* (Montréal and Kingston 1992).

Howell, Colin and Richard Twomey, eds. *Jack Tar in History: Essays in the History of Maritime Life and Labour* (Fredericton 1991).

Ommer, Rosemary E. *From Outpost to Outport: A Structural Analysis of the Jersey-Gaspé Cod Fishery, 1767-1886* (Montréal and Kingston 1991).

Sager, Eric W. *Seafaring Labour: The Merchant Marine of Atlantic Canada, 1820-1914* (Montréal and Kingston 1989).

Sutherland, David A. "The Stanyan Ropeworks of Halifax, N.S.: Glimpses of a Pre-Industrial Manufactory," *Labour/Le Travailleur*, 6 (1980), 149-58.

Walker, James W. St. G. *The Black Loyalists: The Search for a Promised Land in Nova Scotia and Sierra Leone, 1783-1870* (New York 1976).

Wynn, Graeme. *Timber Colony: A Historical Geography of Early Nineteenth Century New Brunswick* (Toronto 1981).

Rusty Bittermann

1

Farm Households and Wage Labour in the Northeastern Maritimes in the Early 19th Century

One of the most enduring mythologies of rural life in the temperate regions of North America has centred on the freedom resulting from easy access to land. In the New World unlike the Old, the story goes, land was plentiful, free from the encumbrances of a feudal past, and common folk might gain unimpeded access to its abundance and carve an independent niche for themselves. In the 18th and 19th centuries, the mythology was fostered by the effusions of travel accounts and emigrant manuals as well as by the writings of immigrants themselves. Since then it has been broadly sustained in North American historiography.

In keeping with the larger trend, the myth of the independent yeoman has held a prominent place in Maritime literature. It can be found in the works of such Gaelic bards as Allan the Ridge of Mabou, himself one of the many immigrants who arrived in the region from Scotland early in the 19th century. In the New World, he lyricized, "free land" gave rise to "riches and herds of cattle" for common folk: "Now that you have come across the sea/ to this fair land,/ you will want for nothing the rest of your life;/ everything prospers for us."[1] It figures in Joseph Howe's "Western Rambles." With "a wife and an axe," Howe maintained, an industrious man might carve out a handsome competence and become "truly rich and independent."[2] Thomas McCulloch's Mephibosheth Stepsure, too, sustains the contention that in

[1]Margaret MacDonell, *The Emigrant Experience: Songs of Highland Emigrants in North America* (Toronto 1982), 90-2.
[2]Joseph Howe, "Western Rambles," in *Travel Sketches of Nova Scotia*, M.G. Parks, ed., (Toronto 1973), 95-6.

Published with the permission of the editor.© Canadian Committee on Labour History from *Labour/Le Travail*, 31 (Spring 1993), 13-45.

the Nova Scotian countryside a natural abundance ensured that those with frugal and industrious habits would be rewarded with economic security and independence.[3] The theme of yeomanly independence emerges as well in the writings of these men's descendants: "Every man in Washabuckt," wrote Neil MacNeil recalling his experiences in a turn-of-the-century Cape Breton rural community, "was his own boss, for he got his livelihood from nature and did not have to work for any other man or thank any one but God for it."[4] And so it is still told to younger generations by older folk in Cape Breton: there was a time before the dependence of the contemporary era when those willing to work might combine their labour with an abundant land to derive a livelihood and secure an independence for themselves. In contemporary regional historiography it reemerges in the works of those who emphasize the insularity and self-sufficiency of rural households in the early 19th century and conceptualize the history of the countryside during subsequent decades in terms of the loss of an earlier independence rooted in the direct fulfilment of needs through access to the land.[5]

That the image of the independent yeoman was to a certain degree a reflection of a reality experienced by some rural residents in the Maritimes is indisputable. The opportunities for acquiring an independent rural livelihood were relatively greater in British North America than they were in the Old World. Many transformed these possibilities into reality and achieved a "propertied independence."[6] Those who enjoyed such circumstances, however, were but one component of a larger farming population. And many who came to enjoy a modicum of yeomanly independence only experienced this condition during a fraction of their lives. Like any powerful and pervasive mythology, the image of the independent yeoman is partly rooted in a reality. Problems arise, though, when a fragment of the rural experience becomes a characterization of the whole. It is not my intention here to consider how this mythology developed, or to unravel the various strands of peasant dream, liberal ideology, and social critique that have sustained it. Rather, I want to examine what it has obscured, indeed tends to deny: the importance of wage labour to farmfolk in the northeastern Maritimes in the first half of the 19th century.[7] The

[3]Thomas McCulloch, *The Stepsure Letters* (Toronto 1960).
[4]Neil MacNeil, *The Highland Heart in Nova Scotia* (Antigonish 1980, [1948]).
[5]Charles W. Dunn, *Highland Settler: A Portrait of the Scottish Gael in Nova Scotia* (Toronto 1953); D. Campbell and R.A. MacLean, *Beyond the Atlantic Roar: A Study of the Nova Scotia Scots* (Toronto 1974); John Warkentin, "The Atlantic Region," in R. Cole Harris and John Warkentin eds., *Canada Before Confederation: A Study of Historical Geography* (Toronto 1977), 169-231; Peter Sinclair, "From Peasants to Corporations: The Development of Capitalist Agriculture in the Maritime Provinces," in *Contradictions in Canadian Society: Readings in Introductory Sociology* (Toronto 1984), 276-93.
[6]The phrase is drawn from Daniel Vickers' superb analysis of the ideal and some of its implications. Daniel Vickers, "Competency and Competition: Economic Culture in Early America," *William and Mary Quarterly*, 3rd Series, 47:1 (1990), 3-29.
[7]The mythology is often incongruously juxtaposed with another reality. Neil MacNeil, for instance, even as he extols the independence Washabuckers achieved on the land, tells of the

survey which follows underlines the significance of wages to the farm population and highlights the profile of farm dwellers within the larger labour force.

Much of the rural population of the Maritimes began farm-making in the New World by spending part of their time as employees. In his study of rural life in Ontario, Robert Leslie Jones suggested a three-tier typology of new agricultural settlers: those with the capital (or credit) to hire others to speed construction and land clearing, those with the means to support themselves during the start-up period of farm-making, and, lastly, those who found it necessary to engage in off-farm work in order to sustain themselves while farm-making.[8] Given what we know of the economic circumstances of many of those who settled in the northeastern Maritimes in the late 18th and early 19th century, it is clear that thousands in Atlantic Canada fell in the latter category.[9] Rev. George Patterson's description of the adaptive strategies employed by the passengers who arrived on the *Hector* reflects the difficulties and possibilities available to other emigrants who came to the region under similar circumstances. Initially lacking the means to establish themselves on the land, Patterson noted, they spread out to places distant from Pictou where they could find work: "Not only men, but mothers of families, hired out, and their children, male and female, they bound out for service, till they should come of age."[10] As John Cambridge, a Prince Edward Island landlord, observed in the first years of the 19th century, those who arrived with little or no capital "generally work for others till they have acquired a little stock" and in the years that follow they "get assistance by working for the neighbouring farmers, till they have brought their own farms gradually forward."[11]

regular flow of labour southward and of his grandfather's difficult experiences commuting on foot between Washabuckt and a job many miles north in industrial Cape Breton.

[8]Robert Leslie Jones, *History of Agriculture in Ontario 1613-1880* (Toronto 1946), 60.

[9]J.S. Martell, *Immigration to and Emigration From Nova Scotia, 1815-1838* (Halifax 1942); R.G. Flewwelling, "Immigration to and Emigration from Nova Scotia," *Nova Scotia Historical Society Collections*, 28 (1949), 75-105; D.C. Harvey, "Scottish Immigration to Cape Breton," *Dalhousie Review*, 21:1 (April 1941), 313-24; Barbara Kincaid, "Scottish Immigration to Cape Breton, 1758-1838," MA dissertation, Dalhousie University, 1964; D. Campbell and R.A. MacLean, *Beyond the Atlantic Roar*, 7-75; Helen I. Cowan, *British Emigration to British North America: The First Hundred Years* (Toronto 1961), 172-227.

[10]Rev. George Patterson, *A History of the County of Pictou Nova Scotia* (Montréal 1877; rept. ed. Belleville, Ontario 1972), 86.

[11][John Cambridge], *A Description of Prince Edward Island in the Gulf of St. Lawrence, North America with a Map of the Island and a Few Cursory Observations Respecting the Climate, Natural Productions and Advantages of its Situation in Regard to Agriculture and Commerce; Together with Some Remarks, as Instructions to New Settlers* (London 1805), 8. See too John Lewellin, *Emigration. Prince Edward Island: A Brief But Faithful Account of this Fine Colony* (1832), reprinted in D.C. Harvey, ed., *Journeys to the Island of St. John* (Toronto 1955), 199. Captain Moorsom provides evidence on the process as well, though in this case viewed from the vantage point of the agricultural employer. Moorsom notes that in the Windsor region agricultural labourers were primarily recruited from among new settlers

A good account of the settlement process in Pictou County in the early 19th century is provided by Lord Selkirk. Describing the farm-making labours of a household from Perthshire, he noted that the man of the house was "obliged to work for hire" to feed his family and sustain the credit necessary for purchasing the articles needed for capitalizing his farm. This particular household had the advantage of being settled on good land adjacent to West River and its occupants had the potential, one would imagine, of escaping from the necessity of wage dependence, but in the early years of establishment, Selkirk estimated that the Perthshire man spent "full half his time employed at wages off the farm."[12]

The ledger book of Cape Breton merchant Lawrence Kavanaugh provides insights into the process as well. In 1818, Kavanaugh recorded the influx of a number of settlers from Prince Edward Island who took up lands along the eastern shoreline of the Bras d'Or Lakes. Several opened accounts in St. Peter's with Kavanaugh shortly after their arrival. James Corbit began his dealings with Kavanaugh by depositing £5 in cash and selling him a saddle for £2 10s.[13] In return Kavanaugh provided Corbit with provisions and supplies — flour, meal, codfish, tea, vinegar, rum, tobacco, a pipe, salt, cod line, shoes, and calico — as well as the financing necessary to buy out a previous occupant of the lot he had occupied. Corbit's account with Kavanaugh was a relatively modest £33 (provisions plus interest) during the next six years, suggesting — particularly given the quantities of goods and the absence of building materials and tools on the account — that he was dealing with others as well to obtain his household supplies. To meet these particular debts, Corbit worked for Kavanaugh, 2 1/2 days in 1819, 33 days repairing and building a boat in 1821, 1 day sawing planks in 1822, 24 days sawing the following year, and half a day sawing in 1824. A credit to his account by a man named McAdam for 29 shillings in 1820 probably represents yet another 12 days work performed in this case for McAdam. The survival strategies of many country-folk, as the landlord John Hill noted in the case of Prince Edward Island, commonly included temporary work for anyone who might give them "an order on the shopkeepers for cloathing and tools."[14] As well, Corbit sold Kavanaugh a couple of chickens in 1820, an ox and a small amount of fresh mackerel and chickens in 1823, and 6 shillings worth of butter in 1824, leaving him still in debt to the St. Peter's merchant for £8 at the end of the year. Lacking knowledge of Corbit's dealings with others, it is impossible to gauge how much off-farm work he in fact engaged in during these years or to calculate his progress in farm-making, though

---

who had not become established and from the younger members of poorer farm households who worked away in the summer and returned in the winter. Captain W. Moorsom, *Letters From Nova Scotia; Comprising Sketches of a Young Country* (London 1830), 207-8.

[12]Patrick C. White, ed., *Lord Selkirk's Diary, 1803-1804: A Journal of his Travels in British North America and the Northeastern United States* (Toronto 1958), 51.

[13]For Corbit's account see the Kavanaugh Account Book, 1818-1824, MG3, vol. 301, 212, Public Archives of Nova Scotia (PANS).

[14]John Hill, Memo on Quit Rents, [1802], CO 226/18/230.

the nature and scale of farm produce suggest a rudimentary, perhaps a single-cow, holding. The evidence from Corbit's account and from the other new arrivals from Prince Edward Island who appear on Kavanaugh's books reinforce, though, Cambridge's, Selkirk's, Hill's, and Patterson's observations concerning the importance of wage work to new settlers in the early stages of farm-making.

How long might immigrants such as those appearing in Kavanaugh's ledgers, or observed by Selkirk and Cambridge, engage in wage work before they could sustain themselves and their households with the returns of their farms? The answer would vary, of course, depending upon their circumstances at the time of arrival, the natural resources of their farm properties, the annual returns that could be made from wage work, and the level of their commitment to acquire a self-sustaining operation. Peter Russell's calculation of an average clearing rate in Upper Canada during the early 19th century of 1.5 acres per year per adult male probably is a reasonable estimate for the Maritimes as well.[15] At such a rate, a minimal 25 acres of fields would, when additional labour could not be hired, typically be realized only after a decade of work. Often, it would seem, this took longer. The itinerant shoemaker and missionary, Walter Johnstone, estimated that on average, the first generation of settlers on Prince Edward Island would "not clear more than 20 or 30 acres all their life."[16] Another observer noted that there were "many who have been 20 years in the colony" and "have no more than 5 acres cleared."[17] To the cost of sustaining a household while preparing the land base necessary for household subsistence were added the costs of stocking and equipping such a farm. S.S. Hill, the son of John Hill, one of Prince Edward's Island's largest landlords, advised would-be immigrants to expect costs of roughly £200 for the livestock, tools, and supplies necessary for establishing a farm of 30 cleared acres.[18] Though it was not in his interest to exaggerate the costs of farm-making on the Island, Hill's figure

[15]Peter A. Russell, "Forest into Farmland: Upper Canadian Clearing Rates, 1822-1839," *Agricultural History*, 57:3 (July 1983), 326-39. A listing of squatters on Indian lands in Middle River indicating length of settlement and the extent of their fields gives some indication of the clearing rates of Highlanders in Cape Breton. For the eleven households for which there was adequate data, the average rate of clearing was just under two acres per year. On average these households had been located on their lands for six years and had just under eleven acres of land cleared. If anything these particular rates could be somewhat inflated as the cleared acreages may include lands that natives had cleared and/or those improved by other squatters who were driven off prior to the settlement of these individuals. Nova Scotia House of Assembly, *Journals*, 1862, App. 30, Report of Indian Committee, 7.

[16]Walter Johnstone, *A Series of Letters, Descriptive of Prince Edward Island* (1822) reprinted in D.C. Harvey, ed., *Journeys to the Island of St. John*, 126.

[17]Rusticus to the editor, *Prince Edward Island Register* (Charlottetown), 29 November 1825, 1.

[18][S.S. Hill], *A Short Account of Prince Edward Island Designed Chiefly for the Information of Agriculturalists and other Emigrants of Small Capital* (London 1839), 66.

seems high.[19] What is beyond doubt is that with wages typically averaging around two and a half shillings per day, with work sporadic and seasonal, and with the needs of daily subsistence having first claim on income, raising the monies necessary to equip a farm was, typically, the product of years of labour.

The cost of land, of course, had to be factored into the farm-making process as well. On Prince Edward Island, there was little Crown land and most immigrants found it necessary to obtain land from landlords. In the 1820s and 1830s, an unimproved freehold would, typically, cost somewhere from 10 shillings to one pound per acre.[20] By leasing land, a new settler might defer these start-up costs, but in time would incur a rental cost of around £5 per year for 100 acres of land.[21] In Nova Scotia, the costs of acquiring "free" Crown land probably ran around £20 for a typical 200-acre lot.[22] With the termination of a "free" Crown land policy in the late 1820s, these costs increased as lands were sold at public auction with a base price established at 2s 3d to 2s 6d per acre.[23]

Given the costs of land, stock, and equipment, and the labour required for preparing fields, even when a household managed to acquire good lands — and many in the region did not — years and probably decades elapsed between beginning the tasks of clearing and planting and arriving at a condition where, as Neil MacNeil phrased it, one did not have to "thank anyone but God" for one's living.[24] We can multiply, then, the experiences of Corbit and his fellow Prince Edward Islanders newly arrived in Cape Breton whose wage work appears in Kavanaugh's books, the Perthshireman who Selkirk observed, or those who took passage aboard the *Hector* described by Rev. Patterson, by the thousands of

[19]Graeme Wynn's estimate of a minimal outlay of £30 to £40 is admittedly a very conservative estimate of simple start-up costs. Working farms of 100 acres with 20 acres cleared would, he notes, have fetched from £100 to £300 in New Brunswick in the 1830s. Graeme Wynn, *Timber Colony: A Historical Geography of Early Nineteenth Century New Brunswick* (Toronto 1981), 80.
[20]George Seymour to T.H. Haviland, 5 February 1837, 114 A/508/3, Warwick County Record Office (WCRO); Robert Stewart to John Pendergast, 23 April 1834, Robert Stewart Letterbooks, Ms. 2989/1, PAPEI (Public Archives of Prince Edward Island); State of Sales of Land by Sir James Montgomery, Baronet and Brothers, GD1/409/15/C14568, Scottish Record Office (SRO).
[21]Selkirk Papers, MG 19/E1/73/19302-13, National Archives of Canada (NAC); Rental of the Property of Sir James Montgomery, Baronet and Brothers, GD1/409/16/C14568, SRO.
[22]Donald Campbell to [a relative in Lewis], 7 October 1830, reprinted in the *Stornaway Gazette*, 30 September 1972, MG 100, vol. 115, #33, PANS.
[23]S.J. Hornsby, "Scottish Emigration and Settlement in Early Nineteenth Century Cape Breton," in Kenneth Donovan, ed., *The Island: New Perspectives on Cape Breton History 1713-1975* (Sydney, Nova Scotia 1990), 58.
[24]Graeme Wynn's commentary on J.E. Woolford's 1817 watercolour, *View on the Road from Windsor to Horton by Avon Bridge at Gaspreaux River*, that behind the security portrayed in this image of a farm household which had achieved a comfortable competency there lay a "half-century of unremitting work," is acute. Graeme Wynn, "On the Margins of Empire, 1760-1840," in Craig Brown, ed., *The Illustrated History of Canada* (Toronto 1987), 256.

emigrants of modest means who took up farms in the northeastern Maritimes in the late 18th and early 19th century — people who of necessity had to follow similar work strategies for many years. The ongoing process of settlement and farm-making was intimately linked with the maintenance of a vast pool of farm-based labourers in pursuit of work opportunities.

Weather conditions and the presence or absence of crop and animal diseases played a substantial part in expediting the progress of household independence or, alternatively, in dashing hopes of agricultural security. A household which enjoyed a margin of independence in a favourable year could be plunged into debt and dependence in another. The extraordinary frosts of 1816 and the 1830s, and the repeated failure of the potato crops due to blight in the 1840s in particular, forced large numbers of farm households into an increased reliance on purchased food-stuffs. Particularly vulnerable were the newer and poorer farm households with limited inventories of livestock and reliant almost exclusively on their harvest of their potato and grain crops. Such natural disasters swelled the numbers in pursuit of work and expanded the commitments many households found it necessary to make to off-farm labour. Employment was needed to pay for provisions and to meet the costs and debts incurred during years of crisis.[25]

For many, the quality of land resources available — particularly when coupled with a poverty that diverted labour and capital away from farm improvements and toward the needs of basic sustenance — precluded ever escaping the necessity of engaging in extensive wage work.[26] As the Crown surveyor in Baddeck, D.B. McNab, noted in 1857, there were "hundreds" of farms in this region of Cape Breton where ten, twenty, or thirty years after initial settlement their occupants remained heavily reliant on off-farm employment in order to "eke out the means of a scanty

[25]On the frosts of 1816, a year that became known as "eighteen hundred and froze to death" see Rev. George Patterson, *A History of the County of Pictou Nova Scotia* (Montréal 1877; rept. ed. Belleville, Ontario 1972), 286; Howard Russell, *A Long Deep Furrow: Three Centuries of Farming in New England* (Hanover, New Hampshire 1976), 136, 147-8. For discussions of those of the 1830s and government initiatives to ban exports of foodstuffs and provide relief see the *Royal Gazette* (Charlottetown), 12 August 1834, 3; 9 December 1834, 3; 26 July 1836, 3; 13 September 1836, 3; 14 February 1837, 3; 28 February 1837, 3; 7 March 1837, 1-2; 11 April 1837, 3. The impact the potato blight of the 1840s had on Cape Breton is dealt with in Robert Morgan, "'Poverty, wretchedness, and misery': The Great Famine in Cape Breton, 1845-1851," *Nova Scotia Historical Review*, 6:1 (1986), 88-104 and S.J. Hornsby, *Nineteenth Century Cape Breton: A Historical Geography* (Montréal 1992), 111-20. For discussion of the impact of the potato failures of the late 1840s on Prince Edward Island see the *Islander* (Charlottetown), 26 November 1847, 2; 24 December 1847, 3; 7 April 1848, 3; 14 April 1848, 3; 3 November 1848, 2; 12 January 1848, 3.
[26]In his study of farm-making in Upper Canada in this period, Norman Ball notes the presence of immigrants trapped by similar cycles of poverty there. Norman Rodger Ball, "The Technology of Settlement and Land Clearing in Upper Canada Prior to 1840," PhD dissertation, University of Toronto, 1979, 30-2.

subsistence."[27] In general, he contended, such settlers occupied the difficult hill lands, the backlands, of the Island and tended to be squatters rather than freeholders. The Land Commissioners taking evidence on Prince Edward Island in 1860 heard similar testimony concerning areas of Prince Edward Island, often predominantly occupied by squatters, where few settlers successfully managed to derive the bulk of their livelihood from the soil.[28]

While some households made ends meet by combining wage work with the sale of selected farm "surpluses," often enough exchanging costly foods like butter and meat for cheaper breadstuffs and fish, there were others which appear to have been exclusively, or almost exclusively, reliant on the sale of labour to meet the costs of household goods and food and to procure seed and animal provisions. The ledger books of the North Sydney trader, John Beamish Moore,[29] for instance, reveal a number of backland households whose occupants had nothing but labour to sell during the years of their dealings with him.[30] During the period 1853 to 1860, the members of Angus Link's household paid for their supplies of oatmeal, barley flour, and oats through a combination of Angus's own labour and that of his wife and daughter.[31] So, too, did the Angus McDonald household pay its debts through Angus's own labour and that of his sons and daughter.[32] The debts of the Murdoch Ferguson household as well were repaid entirely by Murdoch's labour and that of a female member of the household.[33] Moore's account book reveals something of the seasonality of the pressures on these backland households as well. Between 1853 and 1861, the accounts of those identified as backlanders in his books reveal recurrent debts for hay, barley flour, and oatmeal needed in April and May to replenish exhausted winter supplies, and seed grain (barley and oats) needed in May and June to permit planting another season's crop. Merchant ledgers reveal only a fragment of these patterns. Wealthier members of rural communities as well often took on the role, and assumed the benefits, of acting as provisioners and sources of credit to poorer households through the months of greatest scarcity. It appears to have been particularly common for those acting as road commissioners to sell

[27]D.B. McNab to Uniacke, 3 January 1857, Nova Scotia House of Assembly, *Journals*, 1857, app. 71, 421.
[28]Ian Ross Robertson, ed., *The Prince Edward Island Land Commission of 1860* (Fredericton, 1988), 136.
[29]A number of John Moores lived in and about North Sydney in the mid-19th century. Stephen Hornsby treats this account book as being that of John *Belcher* Moore. The Public Archives of Nova Scotia, though, stand by their description of it as being that of John *Beamish* Moore. Stephen J. Hornsby, *Nineteenth-Century Cape Breton: A Historical Geography*, 72, 138-9; private correspondence with J.B. Cahill, 26 October 1992.
[30]These backlanders may have been selling farm products elsewhere, perhaps closer at hand, but the fact that they routinely purchased bulky items, such as 1/2 barrels of flour and bushels of grain from Moore without ever selling farm goods seems to suggest that they had little or nothing to sell.
[31]John Beamish Moore Account Book, 1848-67, 14, Micro Biography, PANS.
[32]*Ibid.*, 22.
[33]*Ibid.*, 23.

provisions on credit during the winter and to retain the road-work returns due to these households the following summer.[34]

Backlanders such as these, though possessing or occupying considerable acreages, were yet compelled by necessity to participate extensively in labour markets near and far in order to make up for the great inadequacies of their farm returns. They were, as the Crown surveyor in Baddeck, D.B. McNab, noted, the New World equivalent of Great Britain's day labourers: they "represent[ed] this class."[35] Quantitative analysis of census data from Middle River in Cape Breton and from Hardwood Hill in Pictou County suggests that in the third quarter of the 19th century, somewhere between a quarter and a third of the households in these agricultural districts of northeastern Nova Scotia needed to earn $100 or more in off-farm income in order to secure a minimal livelihood.[36] At the common agricultural wage rate of roughly 80 cents per day, this would be the equivalent of 125 or more working days.[37] Viewed in another fashion, given an average family food requirement of roughly $200, these farms at best probably derived only half their food needs from their own resources.[38] Data from Middle River confirms as well D.B. McNab's assertion that reliance on off-farm sources of income most often occurred among those who occupied rough hill lands: 84 per cent of the households with negative net farm incomes estimated to be greater than $100 in 1860-61 were those of backlanders.[39] Physical constraints necessitated much of the pattern of adaptation that McNab and others described.

Besides new settlers requiring an income during their years of farm establishment and backlanders grappling with chronic resource problems, analysis of the Middle River census returns indicates yet another stream of rural peoples being propelled into participation in the work force in the mid-19th century and beyond. Estimates of the relationship between farm resources and household needs reveal three basic household categories. At one end of the spectrum there were households,

[34]*Spirit of the Times* (Sydney), 19 July 1842, 347; Captain W. Moorsom, *Letters From Nova Scotia*, 288.

[35]Nova Scotia House of Assembly, *Journals*, 1857, Appendix No. 72, 421.

[36]Rusty Bittermann, Robert H. MacKinnon, and Graeme Wynn, "Of Inequality and Interdependence in the Nova Scotian Countryside, 1850-1870," *Canadian Historical Review*, (forthcoming).

[37]The estimate of an average agricultural wage for Nova Scotia is drawn from Julian Gwyn, "Golden Age or Bronze Moment? Wealth and Poverty in Nova Scotia: the 1850s and 1860s," *Canadian Papers in Rural History*, 8 (1992), 195-230.

[38]Charles H. Farnham, "Cape Breton Folk," *Harpers New Monthly Magazine* (1886), reprinted in *Acadiensis*, 8:2 (Spring 1979), 100. These estimates are considered in detail in Bittermann, MacKinnon, and Wynn, "Of Inequality and Interdependence in the Nova Scotian Countryside," and Rusty Bittermann, "Middle River: The Social Structure of Agriculture in a Nineteenth-Century Cape Breton Community," MA dissertation, University of New Brunswick, 1987, app. IV.

[39]Rusty Bittermann, "Economic Stratification and Agrarian Settlement: Middle River in the Early Nineteenth Century," in Kenneth Donovan, ed., *The Island: New Perspectives on Cape Breton History 1713-1975*, 86-7.

primarily those of backlanders, where farm returns were chronically and substantially short of household subsistence needs — households that of necessity had to look for income beyond the farm across the full course of the family life cycle. On the other extreme there was a significant minority of households, the commercial core of the valley's agricultural economy, where farm production was well in excess of household subsistence needs and the returns from farm product sales were sufficient to permit substantial reinvestments in agriculture and in other pursuits. Members of such households had the option of working for themselves with their own resources or working for others. Wedged between these two strata were families whose condition more closely approximated the image of household self-sufficiency permeating so much of the literature on the rural Maritimes — farms on which the value of production roughly matched current needs. Although they possessed sufficient resources to derive a livelihood from the land, it is clear though, from the census and probate returns, that the resources of many of these households were not expanding at a rate sufficient to permit all their offspring to begin life in similar circumstances. Demographic growth was forcing, and would force, many individuals from an emerging generation within these middle strata households into participation in the labour force.[40]

Throughout the early 19th century, then, substantial numbers of the members of farm households situated in the northeastern Maritimes — new settlers, backlanders (along with others whose farm resources were chronically insufficient for household needs), and some of the offspring of middle-strata households — necessarily had to maintain a significant and regular involvement in the labour force despite the fact that they had access to extensive tracts of land. Added to the ranks of these workers of necessity were many who were drawn for one reason or another by the opportunities afforded by off-farm work, people who might move in and out of the workforce at will alternately deriving a living from farm resources or choosing to participate in the labour force.

Those seeking employment might work in many different niches of the regional economy. Some of the Prince Edward Islanders who settled along Cape Breton's Bras d'Or Lakes in the second decade of the 19th century found jobs with Lawrence Kavanaugh, the merchant from whom they obtained provisions. John Corbit made ends meet in part by sawing lumber and doing boat-carpentry work for Kavanaugh. During the period 1818 to 1824, others worked for this St. Peter's merchant building fences, mowing hay, planting potatoes, looking after livestock, driving cattle that he had purchased, rafting timber, and working in his fishing operations. Daily wages ranged from 1 shilling 4d. to the more common 2 shilling 6d. Some jobs, such as mowing, were arranged by piece work, 5 shillings per acre, while yet other workers were hired on a monthly basis. Women appear sporadically in Kavanaugh's ledger, "knitting" twine at a fixed price per length and doing washing of some sort, again being paid by the piece.

[40]*Ibid.*; Rusty Bittermann, "Middle River: The Social Structure of Agriculture in a Nineteenth-Century Cape Breton Community," 157-9.

The variety of tasks for which Kavanaugh hired labour, the different rates and means of payment, and the diverse composition of his work force — both in terms of age and gender — help suggest the complexity of the labour market in this period. The different areas of economic activity noted in his ledger — agriculture, the timber trade, vessel construction, the fishery, and general tasks associated with operating a mercantile establishment — capture much of the array of work available to the farm-based labourer of the northeastern Maritimes in the first quarter of the 19th century. Timber, ships, fishing, and trade — the listing of occupations sounds so close to T.C. Haliburton's description of the typical Nova Scotian who could be "found superintending the cultivation of a farm and building a vessel at the same time; and is not only able to catch and cure a cargo of fish, but to find his way to the West Indies or the Mediterranean" with it, that it is necessary to underline an important distinction between Haliburton's figure and those whose lives are under discussion here.[41] The occupational pluralist figuring in the *Old Judge* is an extension of the independent yeoman of other regional literature; his life is grounded in his control over a material abundance. The goods with which he loads his vessel are the "surplus" remaining from the produce of his farm, and though Haliburton does not address productive relationships, the thrust of this passage is that woods work and shipbuilding, too, are rooted in family labour which is being applied to resources over which this Nova Scotian exercises ownership or control. Certainly there were such people scattered about the Maritime countryside, although as I have argued elsewhere and will argue below, family labour alone did not typically sustain this sort of productivity.[42] I am focusing here on the property-poor farm dweller whose labour sustained the entrepreneurial pluralism of others. The capital barriers which prevented acquiring an independence in agricultural production tended to be similarly limiting in other sectors of the economy. Whereas, for instance, the household with an agricultural abundance might be in a position to send their oxen to the woods and equip a cutting crew, ultimately selling the end-product in the timber market, the participation of the capital-poor in this trade was more likely to be for the wages gained from handling an ax.[43]

Although other facets of the regional economy probably rivaled it in terms of the amount of wage employment offered, during the first half of the 19th century agriculture may well have been the pre-eminent type of wage work when measured in terms of sheer numbers of participants, even if the extreme seasonality of demand

[41]Thomas Chandler Haliburton, *The Old Judge; or, Life in a Colony*, ed. with an introduction and notes by M.G. Parks, (Ottawa 1978), xxi.

[42]Rusty Bittermann, "The Hierarchy of the Soil: Land and Labour in a 19th-Century Cape Breton Community," *Acadiensis*, 18:1 (Autumn 1988), 33-55.

[43]There were, of course, other ways by which impecunious farmfolk might participate in these economies including share systems and the acquisition of outfits on credit. In some regions, though, even the more prosperous farm households increasingly found it difficult to maintain an independent foothold in the logging business in the Maritimes. See Béatrice Craig, "Agriculture and the Lumberman's Frontier in the Upper St. John Valley, 1800-70," *Journal of Forest History*, 32:3 (July 1988), 125-37.

meant that few worked as farm hands for extensive periods. The labour requirements of agriculture in the Maritimes in the era before the mechanization of
harvesting and planting were such that not only big farms with scores of acres in
hay and crops but even many relatively small operations found it necessary to hire
seasonal help. Harvesting operations in particular required the assistance of many
hands. A small operation might hire an extra worker or two for a few days or weeks
to assist with getting in the crops, while a larger operation might add many daily
labourers to its more permanent workforce. Timber operators also sometimes
employed large crews to gather hay for their woods operations.[44]

Peter MacNutt, for instance, a merchant and farmer living near Princetown,
Prince Edward Island, harvested his crops in summer and autumn 1837 with the aid
of his "own men" — household members and long-term employees — augmented
by the daily labour of 30 workers drawn from neighbouring farms. During that
autumn, some worked for only a day, while others worked for MacNutt for ten or
eleven days, though never at a continuous stretch. The patterns point to the varied
nature of MacNutt's labour needs even during the harvest. There were some tasks
that required few or no additional hands and others for which he would hire nine
additional workers on a daily basis to complement household members and servants. The composition of his crews varied in accordance with the farm calendar
and the progress of harvesting operations. For certain tasks, such as raking hay,
bundling grain, and digging potatoes, MacNutt employed the cheaper labour of
women, girls, and boys. A few men, for instance, might begin mowing at the
beginning of the week and be joined by a growing and more heterogeneous work
force later in the week as the mowed hay began to dry and required raking, hauling,
and stacking.[45]

The patterns of wage work recorded in MacNutt's diary also reflect, one can
be sure, the needs of the rural folk recruited to work on his farm. Having to attend
to crops of their own, they moved back and forth first between hay-making on their
own farms and MacNutt's, and later between the harvesting of their own grain and
root crops and those of MacNutt. Records from the 1830s concerning the nearby
David Ross farm show Donald MacLean, a casual labourer on the farm, alternately
working on his own holding and that of the Rosses, at times spending half a day
harvesting MacLean crops and the other working with David Ross. On other
occasions he would work at the Ross farm in the evenings, though in general he,
like the workers on Peter MacNutt's farm, spent an entire day or a cluster of days
working for wages, returning, one assumes then, to the demands of the home

[44]James Yeo, for example, appears to have recruited large hay harvesting crews drawing
extensively from among the Acadian and Native populations of Prince Edward Island. See
George Seymour, "Journal of Tour of Canada and the United States (1840)," entry for 7
September, CR 114A/1380, WCRO; Robert Stewart to John Lawson, 7 October 1835, Robert
Stewart Letterbooks, Ms. 2989/2, PAPEI.
[45]Diary of Honourable Peter MacNutt, Sr., Ms. 3552, 7 August 1837 – 4 November 1837,
PAPEI.

harvest.[46] The degree of flexibility workers might have in moving between their own farm operations and that of their employer(s) varied, of course, as a function of proximity. Donald MacLean lived close to the Ross farm and might, if he could negotiate it, work on his own *and* his neighbour's farm in the course of a day. Many of the labourers appearing on the payroll of those harvesting the hay on William MacKenzie's fields in Middle River later in the century, though, had traveled greater distances to the farm. Workers such as these found it necessary to take up residence at the work site for the duration of the harvest.[47]

In the era before the mechanization of harvest operations, the demand for agricultural labourers during the late summer and autumn was extensive. Analysis of the crop returns and household composition of farm households in Middle River between 1850 and 1875 suggests that roughly one-quarter of the farms there required some help from beyond the household in order to harvest their crops.[48] The labour demands for harvesting the crops on Middle River's farms were typical of those found elsewhere in the agricultural districts of Nova Scotia and Prince Edward Island. There was, as a Nova Scotian report on labour conditions noted at mid-century, "always a great cry for field labour" at harvest time.[49] Certainly the employment of the wage labour in the agricultural sector was concentrated in these late summer and autumn months. The difficulty for the worker who was also a member of a farm household was that this too was the busiest period on the home farm. Such conflicts of interest could be solved, as Donald MacLean did, by moving back and forth between the work demands of the home farm and wage labour on the harvest of an adjacent holding or, as it would appear that some of those working for Peter MacNutt did, by dividing the total household workforce between the limited requirements of home-farm crops and the wage opportunities on more prosperous farms.

Although the bulk of wage labour was drawn into agriculture during the harvest season, some daily employment was available for men, women, and children throughout the year. The David Ross farm hired help for fencing, ploughing, harrowing, sowing, quarrying stones, cutting and sawing firewood, and slaughtering livestock as well as for harvest operations. The record books of Alex McLellan at Indian River, Prince Edward Island and Joseph Dingwell at Little River in the same colony show both purchasing labour not only for the harvest but for threshing

[46]David Ross Diary, 3-5, Prince Edward Island Collection, University of Prince Edward Island (UPEI).

[47]William MacLean versus William MacKenzie, RG 39, "C", #645, PANS.

[48]Rusty Bittermann, "Middle River," 63.

[49]Nova Scotia House of Assembly, *Journals*, 1867, Immigration Report, App. 7. See too Captain W. Moorsom, *Letters from Nova Scotia*, 206-7; *Abstract of the Proceedings of the Land Commissioners' Court Held During the Summer of 1860 to Inquire into the Differences Relative to the Rights of Landowners and Tenants in Prince Edward Island* (Charlottetown: *The Protestant*, 1862), 101, 141.

in the winter, ploughing in the spring, and for fence work and building construction at other times of the year.[50] Labourers also were hired for land clearing.[51] As well, some farmers found it expedient to maintain year-around servants. As with much daily work, the wage rates associated with these long-term contracts varied depending on age and gender. John Lewellin noted in 1832 that while "farming men-servants" were retained at 30 to 40 shillings per month, girls received 12 to 15 shillings.[52]

The use of agricultural machinery that sharply reduced the critical demands for harvest labour was not widespread until well into the second half of the 19th century. Thus the demands for agricultural labour grew at roughly the same pace as the expansion of agricultural output in the first half of the 19th century. Mechanical threshers which permitted grain to be readied quickly for market began to be used in the 1830s, but these reduced a labour demand that could, if necessary, be spread across late fall and winter. The mowers, rakes, reapers, and binders that would, when in place, reduce the enormous demands for labour during harvest season by as much as 80 per cent were not a significant presence in the region until the 1860s and afterward.[53]

For many of the Maritime-born, agricultural work probably was their first taste of wage employment. There was demand for the labour of both girls and boys in the harvest fields, and the scale and nature of the work, coupled with the manner in which it was organized, made it a relatively small step from working on the home farm. Those engaged in agricultural employment might work as a lone addition to another family's workforce, or they might be part of a crew of a dozen or more working the harvest fields. In either case, though, they were likely to be working for someone they already knew in a familiar setting among familiar faces, with a heterogeneous workforce — both in terms of age and gender — and to be performing tasks that were the common stuff of agricultural life. The work contract was likely to be informal, struck on a daily basis, and to demand a transportation commitment no more onerous than a walk.

Wage work in the timber trade and the shipbuilding industry — agriculture's great rivals for labour in the first half of the 19th century — was, in general, quite different from that in agriculture. This was male employment, and much of the work in these industries was concentrated at sites at some distance from the farms from

[50]Alex McLellan Account Book, ms. 2802/1, PAPEI; Joseph Dingwell, Ledger, Ms. 3554/1, PAPEI.
[51]*Royal Gazette*, 15 March 1836, 2.
[52]John Lewellin, *Emigration. Prince Edward Island*, 196. In 1851 John Lawson reported wages of £24 to £30 per year for farm servants. John Lawson, *Letters on Prince Edward Island* (Charlottetown 1851), 20.
[53]*Royal Gazette* 18 April 1837, 3; James Robb, *Agricultural Progress: An Outline of the Course of Improvement in Agriculture Considered as a Business, an Art, and a Science with Special Reference to New Brunswick* (Fredericton 1856), 18; Rusty Bittermann, "Middle River: The Social Structure of Agriculture in a Nineteenth-Century Cape Breton Community," 150-2.

which many came. Such employment was often for extended periods of time, for woods work was available from late fall until spring, and shipbuilding, when the market dictated, might be conducted on a year-round basis.[54] There were, of course, considerable variations in the nature of the work experience in woods work and shipbuilding. Some of the employment available within these industries was local and organized in small, perhaps primarily family-based, crews. Hired hands might be added to a cluster of brothers cutting logs for the winter or be employed casually in one of the many lesser shipyards turning out modest numbers of smaller vessels. Employment with small local operations where one might return home on a daily basis aided the integration of wage work with farm work. The Irish who settled on the backlands of Lot 29 in southwestern Queen's County, Prince Edward Island, for instance, and who worked in W.W. Lord's timber and shipbuilding operations, were said to have been able to clear their lands and hoe their crops "in spare time."[55] Looking back on his Cape Breton childhood, Aeneas McCharles recalled that his father combined working on his farm in the Baddeck valley with carpentry work at the shipyards four miles away in the port of Baddeck.[56] Labour in these pursuits, however, was also being organized by capitalists operating on a much larger scale, who relied upon recruiting labourers from beyond the immediate locality of their operations. Entrepreneurs like the Archibalds in Cape Breton and the Popes, Macdonalds, and Cambridges on Prince Edward Island hired scores of men to work at their shipyards, sawmills, and woods operations. So too did their counterparts elsewhere in the region who, even before steam vessels and rail transportation eased the burdens of travel, were drawing labourers from the farms of northern Nova Scotia and Prince Edward Island to work in their operations. By the 1820s and 1830s, farmers in significant numbers were traveling back and forth between the timber camps and shipyards of the Miramichi and their homes in northern Nova Scotia and Prince Edward Island.[57]

Many of those working in these operations were likely to spend part of their lives as bunkhouse men, living at the worksite and labouring on a regular schedule

[54]A.R.M. Lower, *The North American Assault on the Canadian Forest: A History of the Lumber Trade Between Canada and the United States* (Toronto 1938), 32-3; Graeme Wynn, *Timber Colony*, 54; Richard Rice, "Shipbuilding in British America, 1787-1890: An Introductory Study," PhD dissertation, University of Liverpool, 1977, 178-81.

[55]Mary Brehaut, ed., *Pioneers on the Island* (Charlottetown 1959), 58. On the local organization of farm-based labour for Prince Edward Island's shipyards see too Basil Greenhill and Ann Giffard, *Westcountrymen in Prince Edward's Isle* (Toronto 1967), 56-76; Malcolm MacQueen, *Skye Pioneers and "The Island"* (Winnipeg 1929), 26.

[56]Aeneas McCharles, *Bemocked of Destiny: The Actual Struggles and Experiences of a Canadian Pioneer and the Recollections of a Lifetime* (Toronto 1908), 10-11.

[57]*Prince Edward Island Register*, 20 October 1825, 3; John MacGregor, *Historical and Descriptive Sketches of the Maritime Colonies of British America* (London 1828), 168; David Stewart's Journal, 31, PAPEI, 3209/28; *Royal Gazette*, 30 May 1837, 3. See too the *Royal Gazette* 26 June 1838, 3, on the theft of £35 — a season's wages — from a lumberman returning from the Miramichi woods to his residence in West River, Pictou County.

for extended periods of time.[58] In both logging and boatbuilding, wages might be paid partly in kind — shipyards tended to be organized around a truck store — and differentially paid in accordance with a division of labour along skill lines.[59] Farmers and farmers' sons working in the large shipyards shared their workspace with greater numbers than did those in woods camps, and were engaged in work that required more complex forms of organization.[60] The experience of work in the shipbuilding yards that produced large vessels was, as Richard Rice has argued, that of a large, complexly-orchestrated manufactory.

In 1824 it was estimated that perhaps 1,000 men, drawn from a total Island population of roughly 20,000, worked in Prince Edward Island's shipyards to produce some 10,000 tons of shipping.[61] This figure excludes those working in the woods to supply materials for the shipyards, and those working in the woods to produce timber for export. If a similar worker/tonnage ratio held in Nova Scotia, the numbers employed at shipbuilding there would be roughly double those of Prince Edward Island. In both cases, the expansion of shipbuilding during the

[58]Abraham Gesner, *The Industrial Resources of Nova Scotia* (Halifax 1849), 215-7; Graeme Wynn, *The Timber Colony*, 62; Arthur R.M. Lower, *Great Britain's Woodyard: British America and the Timber Trade, 1763-1867* (Montréal 1973), 189-96. On shipyard/bunkhouse deaths due to drunkenness and violence see the *Prince Edward Island Register*, 25 September 1824, 3; *Prince Edward Island Register*, 27 February 1827, 3.

[59]Richard Rice, "Shipbuilding in British America, 1787-1890: An Introductory Study," PhD dissertation, University of Liverpool, 1977, 171, 186-92. The labour contracts from the 1840s entered in Joseph Dingwell's ledger indicate that he paid most of his labourers half in cash and half in "trade." Joseph Dingwell Ledger, Ms. 3554/1, PAPEI. Capt Moorsom's account of labour relations on the waterfront in Liverpool in the summer of 1828 suggests the reasons for Dingwell's clear indications of the mode of payment in his contracts. There were, he noted, "two scales of value, the 'cash price,' and the 'goods price,'" and "the various gradations thereof distinctly marked in all transactions between employers and labourers." Moorsom reported a rate of exchange in favour of cash at a ratio of 3 to 4. Captain W. Moorsom, *Letters From Nova Scotia; Comprising Sketches of a Young Country*, 292. For information on Joseph Pope's shipyard and truck store see John Mollison, "Prince County," in D.A. MacKinnon and A.B. Warburton, eds., *Past and Present of Prince Edward Island* (Charlottetown 1906), 86. Lemuel and Artemas Cambridge offered their ship carpenters the choice of employment by the month or payment "by the seam." *Prince Edward Island Register*, 23 May 1826, 3.

[60]According to Dougald Henry (b. 1817) the modest shipbuilding operation run by the Bells of Stanley River Prince Edward Island employed 30 or more men in the yards. Working days, he relates, began at six with a break for breakfast at 8. For Dougald Henry's account of shipyard life as compiled by Dr. Hedley Ross, see Mary Brehaut, ed., *Pioneers on the Island*, 47.

[61]*Prince Edward Island Register*, 27 March 1824, 3. Shipbuilding declined precipitously after the depression of the mid-1820s. It would be more than a decade before output on Prince Edward Island would surpass these figures. Evidence compiled by Richard Rice from 3 Québec shipyards suggest reasonably similar man/ton labour force rations there in the mid 1850s varying from 8.6 to 16.3 tons per man. Richard Rice, "Shipbuilding in British America," 179.

pre-Confederation decades took place at roughly the same pace as the growth of population in these provinces.[62] As a consequence, the percentage of those engaged in shipbuilding to the larger population probably remained more or less the same on average across these decades, while varying sharply, of course, from year to year as the tonnage under construction responded to external demand.

Despite a number of efforts, a commercial fishery based in Prince Edward Island developed slowly. Prior to 1850, the fishery conducted by Island merchants provided few job opportunities.[63] In Cape Breton, on the other hand, fishing was an enterprise of greater significance. Of particular importance were the Channel Island firms that conducted an extensive industry from their bases in Arichat and Chéticamp. Although the scale of operations was large, and the work labour-intensive, it does not appear that these firms drew substantial amounts of wage labour from among the farm population of the interior. Stephen Hornsby suggests instead that their operations were conducted by combining the independent commodity production of fisherfolk clustered in coastal communities, linked to the firms by ties of credit, with the work of a seasonal wage-labour force drawn from the Channel Islands rather than Cape Breton.[64]

The opportunities available for wage work with the American fishing fleet as it worked in Maritime waters may well have been of greater significance. Vessels working out of New England ports came by the hundreds to the small harbours of the Atlantic coast and the Gulf of St. Lawrence, where they picked up supplies of food and water, profited by smuggling, and often engaged additional hands both for fishing in Maritime waters and for pursuing the fishery off Labrador and Newfoundland.[65] At midcentury, it was estimated that perhaps 4000 Nova Scotians were working with the American fishing fleet, typically labouring aboard vessels crewed by a dozen or so fishermen. Although the majority would have been drawn from fishing communities about the coast, some of these hands traveled from interior regions to join the fleet as it moved through the Strait of Canso region. Others

[62]*Ibid.*, 15-6; John Warkentin, "The Atlantic Region," 180.

[63]John MacGregor, *Historical and Descriptive Sketches of the Maritime Colonies of British America*, 63; *Prince Edward Island Register*, 24 March 1829, 3.

[64]Stephen J. Hornsby, "Staple Trades, Subsistence Agriculture, and Nineteenth-Century Cape Breton Island," *Annals of the Association of American Geographers*, 79:3 (1989), 415. Rosemary Ommer too notes the significance of wage workers drawn from Jersey in the Gulf fishery. Rosemary Ommer, "'All the Fish of the Post': Property Resource Rights and Development in a Nineteenth-Century Inshore Fishery," *Acadiensis*, 10:2 (Spring 1981), 113. Father Anselme Chiasson, though, notes the exploitation of Acadian wage workers in the early 19th century by the Robin Company in Chéticamp. Father Anselme Chiasson, *Chéticamp: History and Acadian Traditions*, trans. by Jean Doris LeBlanc (St. John's 1986), 66-7. Certainly too resident fish merchants like Laurence Kavanaugh made use of local wage labour.

[65]John MacDougall, *History of Inverness County*, 17; Abraham Gesner, *The Industrial Resources of Nova Scotia*, 104-10; *Colonial Herald* (Charlottetown), 17 October, 1838, 3; *Colonial Herald* (Charlottetown), 5 June 1839, 4.

traveled south to the fishing ports of Maine and Massachusetts to sign on.[66] While
the labour of women was a significant component of the family-based in-shore
fishery, recruitment for the American fishing fleet, as for the timber industry and
the shipyards, and unlike wage labour in agriculture, almost exclusively tapped the
male members of farm households.[67] Workers were paid, it would appear, either
on a monthly basis or by a share in the value of the catch and were signed on for
periods ranging from weeks to months.[68] Islanders working on American vessels
in the late 1830s reportedly were paid at a rate of £6 per month.[69]

Beyond the labour required for the tasks associated with the production of
commodities from fields, forests, and fisheries, the merchants and others involved
in these trades required workers for the multitude of tasks associated with assem-
bling, transporting and managing these goods. The ledgers of merchants like
Lawrence Kavanaugh, John Munro, Joseph Dingwell, Peter MacNutt, Peter Smyth,
Robert Elmsley, and John Beamish Moore show wages paid for delivering messages, rounding up and driving livestock, hauling hay, "looking after timber,"
sorting fish, stacking deal, loading vessels, tending stock, both onshore and on
voyages to market, and a host of other irregularly-necessary tasks generated by the
uneven rhythms of mercantile activity. Work might also be obtained aboard the
vessels moving these goods between ports.[70]

Grist mills, saw mills, and other processing industries scattered about the coast
and waterways provided work opportunities for farm-based labourers too. While
most of those employed were men, women and boys as well sometimes found work
in these enterprises. In 1871 nearly 20 per cent of those working in the carding and
fulling mills of the seven northeastern counties of Nova Scotia were women.[71]
Many enterprises, either because they were reliant upon seasonally-fluctuating
water supplies for their power or because demand was irregular, were part-time

[66]For the general patterns of recruitment see Paul Crowell to James Uniacke, 10 February
1852, Nova Scotia House of Assembly, *Journals*, 1852, app. 25 and the statements of David
Bears, Nova Scotia House of Assembly, *Journals*, 1852, app. 13. On some of the folklore
arising from the involvement of Cape Bretoners in these patterns of work see John P. Parker,
Cape Breton Ships and Men (Toronto 1967), 130-1 and John MacDougall, *History of
Inverness County*, 123-4.
[67]Marilyn Porter, "'She was Skipper of the Shore Crew': Notes on the History of the Sexual
Division of Labour in Newfoundland," *Labour/Le Travail*, 15 (Spring 1985), 105-24.
[68]Harold Innis, *The Cod Fisheries: The History of an International Economy* (Washington,
D.C., 1940; rept. ed. Toronto 1978), 325, 326-7, 333-4.
[69]*Journals*, Prince Edward Island House of Assembly, 1837, 81-2.
[70]Lawrence Kavanaugh Account Book, 1817-24, MG 3, vol. 301-2, PANS; John Munro
Daybook, 1851-55, Micro Biography, PANS; Joseph Dingwell Ledger, Ms. 3554/1, PAPEI;
Diary of Honourable Peter MacNutt, Sr., Ms. 3552, PAPEI; Peter Smyth Ledger, 1833-6,
MG 3 vol. 284, PANS; Robert Elmsly Diary, 1855-89, PANS; John Beamish Moore Account
Book, 1848-67, Micro Biography, PANS; Eric Sager, *Seafaring Labour: The Merchant
Marine of Atlantic Canada, 1820-1914* (Kingston 1989), 136-63.
[71]*Census of Canada, 1870-71*, vol. 3, (Ottawa 1875), 316.

operations requiring labour for limited periods. The ledger books of John Munro of St. Ann's, Cape Breton, for instance, indicate that the labour he obtained for his grist and carding mill in 1851 and 1852 was hired on a daily basis, his employees putting in from 25 to 58 days of work over the course of the year.[72] Some coming from a distance to work for Munro, such as Alex McKenzie of Big Harbour, surely must have stayed in St. Ann's during the period when the mill was running. A similar pattern of part-time employment was followed as well by those whom Lawrence Kavanaugh hired for his sawmill operations in St. Peter's earlier in the century, and in Middle River too.[73] In 1870 one of the saw mills in the community worked for two months, the other for four. The three grist mills in Middle River operated for seven months of the year on average.[74]

In the first half of the 19th century, farm-based labourers found wages in building construction and work on roads, wharfs, canals, and the first of the region's railways. State expenditures on public buildings — such as the construction of Government House and county court houses and jails in Prince Edward Island during the 1830s — played a significant, though often short-lived, role in generating demand for construction workers. So too did projects like the Shubenacadie Canal and the Albion Mines Railway, portents of the demand for labour that bigger transportation projects would engender in the third quarter of the 19th century. On a more regular and local basis, annual state appropriations for road, bridge, and wharf improvements created a substantial amount of wage employment. Such state-generated work was, as Murray Beck has noted, central to the household economies of many of the rural poor, and its interruption could be the cause of considerable deprivation in the countryside.[75] Privately-funded rural and urban construction work also provided employment for farm-based workers. Most of this work, like the construction work associated with transportation systems, tended to be seasonal employment for males.[76] When the work was close to home, the remuneration to be gained at road work or on construction jobs might, for those who possessed draft animals, be broadened by bringing horses or oxen to the job. Many, though, took their skills further afield. By the 1840s, if not sooner, labourers

[72]John Munro Daybook, 1851-55, Micro Biography, PANS.
[73]Lawrence Kavanaugh Account Book, 1817-24, MG 3, vol. 301, PANS.
[74]*Canada*, Census, 1870/71, Schedule 6.
[75]Beck perceptively notes the differential impact of the blockage of appropriations in the revenue dispute of 1830: wealthier farmers suffered because of the deteriorating condition of the roads and bridges they used to move their goods; the rural poor suffered because of the loss of wages gained from working on the roads. J. Murray Beck, *Joseph Howe*, vol. 1, *Conservative Reformer, 1804-1848* (Kingston 1982), 72.
[76]Those working on road crews gained income from both directly from the state through the disbursement of government monies in wages (albeit through the often-sticky hands of local road commissioners) and indirectly through the performance of statutory labour requirements for wealthier rural residents. For examples of the latter see the David Ross Diary, 2, Prince Edward Island Collection, UPEI, and Lawrence Kavanaugh Account Book, 1817-24, MG 3, vol. 302, 99.

from the farms of the northeastern Maritimes were moving seasonally to construction sites in Boston and to other distant centres. Though an urban Cape Bretoner it
would seem, George Musgrave's description of employment with a crew of nine in
Roxbury, Massachusetts beginning work at dawn with breaks at six for breakfast,
noon for dinner, and supper after dark at the end of the day probably captures the
experience of many farm-based workers as well. Working and lodging with other
single young men, he set the relatively high wages he was earning, and the
expectation that he would soon accumulate enough to enable him to quit, against
the discomforts of his long days.[77]

The coal mining industry as well provided work for farm-based labourers, even
as it increasingly came to rely upon a skilled workforce for the actual mining. In
the first decades of the 19th century, few of those working the coal seams of Cape
Breton or Pictou were skilled colliers. Men more accustomed to finding their way
about fish flakes or over cutover ground might yet find work in the pit signing on
for a few months or a year. The experience of work in the Cape Breton coal fields
in this period paralleled in some ways the work in the timber and shipbuilding
industries: bunkhouse life, an entirely male workforce, and the truck store.[78] With
the arrival of the General Mining Association in the 1820s and the massive
injections of capital that came with it, coal mining became technologically more
sophisticated and corporate policy favoured reliance upon a professional core of
miners imported from the British coal fields. There remained, however, much
demand for less-skilled casual workers in and about the mines. Of the 335 employees on the payroll at the Albion mines in in the mid-1830s, only 66 were actually
colliers. Scores of others were involved in construction and transportation tasks.[79]
To meet this demand, the General Mining Association drew from the surrounding
countryside about their mines and yet farther afield.[80] As Abraham Gesner noted,
the labour force employed at the mines was divided. There was a well-housed and
well-paid professional core and then there were the others, the "labouring farmers,"
who received less-generous treatment and were paid at roughly half the rate of the
skilled miners.[81] Over time both the General Mining Association and subsequent
operators in the Nova Scotian coal fields would increasingly turn again to the
countryside for the recruitment of miners as well as general labourers.[82]

[77]George Musgrave to Ann, 7 August 1842, Micro Biography: Moore, no. 10, PANS.

[78]Richard Brown, *The Coal Fields and Coal Trade of the Island of Cape Breton* (London
1871), 70-2; J.S. Martell, "Early Coal Mining in Nova Scotia," in Don Macgillivray and
Brian Tennyson, eds., *Cape Breton Historical Essays* (Sydney 1980), 41-53.

[79]James M. Cameron, *The Pictonian Colliers* (Halifax 1974), 27.

[80]The Albion Mines ran ads for "seasonal" labourers in Prince Edward Island in the 1830s.
See the *Colonial Herald*, 4 May 1839, 4. See too Joseph Howe, "Eastern Rambles," in *Travel
Sketches of Nova Scotia*, 163; James M. Cameron, *The Pictonian Colliers*, 102.

[81]Abraham Gesner, *The Industrial Resources of Nova Scotia*, 273.

[82]Del Muise, "The Making of an Industrial Community: Cape Breton Coal Towns, 1867-
1900," in *Cape Breton Historical Essays*, 80.

Around 1,500 men found employment in and about Nova Scotia's coal mines in the 1830s. Thousands more would be recruited in the coal boom of the third quarter of the 19th century.[83] Some of these workers were young men from the farm communities of the region who were in the process of severing their ties to the soil. Some ultimately would return to the countryside with their savings.[84] Yet others continued to farm even as they worked for mining companies. In the 1860s it was reported in Cape Breton that surface workers by the hundreds "leave their work, at certain seasons, to attend to their crops."[85]

A more heterogeneous workforce found wages in employment as domestic servants and in textile work and factory work. With increasing urbanization and the growth of middle-class demand for domestic servants, both within the region and in more distant centres, many young farm men and women were drawn out of the countryside and into domestic service for at least part of their working lives.[86] Wanted "An active LAD from 14 to 16 years of age to be indented as a house servant. One from the country would be preferred," ran an ad in the Charlottetown paper.[87] By 1851, roughly 20 per cent of Saint John households employed a servant, or servants, and one out of seven Haligonian households employed at least one servant.[88] Other farmfolk found employment as domestic servants in wealthier rural

[83]Ian MacKay, "The Crisis of Dependent Development: Class Conflict in the Nova Scotia Coalfields, 1872-1876," in Gregory S. Kealey, ed., *Class, Gender, and Region: Essays in Canadian Historical Sociology* (St. John's 1988), 21, 30-4; Richard Brown, *The Coal Fields and Coal Trade of the Island of Cape Breton*, 98, 111-39.

[84]There were obviously other variations here as well. Some floated back and forth for years at a time between wage work in the mines and life on the land.

[85]Nova Scotia House of Assembly, *Journals* 1864, app. 4, 3. On the continuing linkages some mine workers maintained between country home and mine and the significance of these to social relations in the working class communities about the mines in the late 19th and early 20th centuries see David Frank, "The Industrial Folk Song in Cape Breton," *Canadian Folklore Canadien*, 8:1-2 (1986), 21-42; Danny Samson, "The Making of a Cape Breton Coal Town: Dependent Development in Inverness, Nova Scotia, 1899-1915," MA dissertation, University of New Brunswick, 1988.

[86]Faye E. Dudden, *Serving Women: Household Service in Nineteenth-Century America* (Middletown, Connecticut 1983). Claudette Lacelle's study of domestic servants in Montréal and Québec City in the second decade of the 19th century and Toronto, Québec City and Halifax in the 1870s, suggests a reasonably equal split between men and women domestics early in the century. Over the next half century, though, the numbers of women in domestic service grew and rural recruitment became increasingly important. Claudette Lacelle, *Urban Domestic Servants in 19th-Century Canada* (Ottawa 1987), 18-20, 78. John Lawson reported that women servants were receiving £9 to £12 per year in Prince Edward Island at mid-century. John Lawson, *Letters on Prince Edward Island*, 20. For an insightful early 20th-century account of a country woman's experience as a domestic servant in Charlottetown see Bertha MacDonald, *Diary of a Housemaid* (n.p. 1986).

[87]*Prince Edward Island Register*, 23 May 1826, 3. See too *Prince Edward Island Register*, 20 January 1825, 3; 21 August 1827, 3.

[88]T.W. Acheson, *Saint John: The Making of a Colonial Urban Community* (Toronto 1985), 233-4; Claudette Lacelle, *Urban Domestic Servants in 19th-Century Canada*, 81.

homes. Though putting-out work does not appear to have been conducted on a large scale in the northeastern Maritimes, some men and women were hired by merchants to weave homespun by the yard. Women were hired as well to knit and perform other hand work.[89] More significantly, by the 1840s women were being recruited from the southern Maritimes to work in the factories of New England. In July of 1849, the Saint John *Courier* reported the departure aboard the "Fairy Queen" of "upwards of 100 young women who had been engaged to work in a factory at Salmon Falls near Portland."[90]

Clearly as the nature of off-farm work varied, so too the ways in which it was integrated into the household economy differed. Daily work close at hand, such as on a neighbouring farm or for a local merchant, permitted, at least in theory, a good deal of flexibility. That farmers and merchants alike required casual labour and employed adults and children, both males and females, meant that various household members might move back and forth between work on the home farm and wage employment. John Beamish Moore's ledger from North Sydney in the 1850s, for instance, shows that the backlander Archy McDonald's household earned wages alternately from Archy's work, that of "his boys," and that of "the girl."[91] The accounts of other backlanders on Moore's ledger show a similar heterogeneity in the composition of household labour made available to the merchant for wages. The same pattern of varying daily movement of different members of the same household in and out of the local agricultural labour force is apparent in the MacNutt farm ledger as men and children, male and female, appear in varying numbers from day to day. One day a father and a couple of sons might be on the payroll, another day perhaps only the sons or only the daughters would be employed. There is no way to know whether the pattern was set by demand or by supply, or to discern how in fact those who momentarily disappear from the day book deployed their labour, but clearly local work afforded the possibility of a varied and shifting household response to the needs of the home farm. Local contract work and putting-out work offered similar flexibility. A man who had been hired to mow a field, dig a cellar, or clear land might, particularly if the work was close at hand, exercise some discretion in choosing his hours of employment and integrating such work into other tasks concerning his own resources. As well, he might flexibly use the labour of other members of his household to complete the task. Such would also be the case with the farmer/tailors contracted to sew trousers or for shirtmaking, or the farm women employed by the piece for spinning, weaving, or knitting.

Other employments permitted less flexibility. Some types of work — such as that in shipbuilding, the timber industry, employment with the American fishing

[89]For examples, see John Munro Daybook, 1851-55, Ann McLeod's account, 2 November 1852, Micro Biography, PANS; John Beamish Moore Account Book, 1848-67, 11, 13, 16, 23, and 30, Micro Biography, PANS; Lawrence Kavanaugh Account Book, 1818-24, 193, MG 3, vol. 302, PANS; Lawrence Kavanaugh Account Book, 1817-24, 228, MG 3, vol. 301, PANS.
[90]*Courier* (Saint John), 21 July 1849, 2.
[91]John Beamish Moore Account Book, 1848-67, 22.

fleet, or the construction trades — provided employment almost exclusively for adult males and often entailed working at a considerable distance from one's residence. In homes where the male head engaged in such work, women often were left to manage household and farm for extended periods. Seeking lodgings at a farm house on the Cape Breton-side of the Strait of Canso in the summer of 1831, David Stewart, a Prince Edward Island landlord, and his traveling companion Richard Smith of the General Mining Association, discovered that the man of the farm "was gone to Miramichi to cut lumber."[92] Only Mrs. MacPherson and her two children were home. At mid-century, the Crown surveyor in Baddeck, D.B. McNab, reported that there were "hundreds" of farms located on poorer lands in his region of the Island where the men of the household traveled to "distant parts of the province or to the United States" each summer and left the maintenance of the farm to "their wives and children."[93] With the boom in railway construction and coal mining in the third quarter of the 19th century, a local observer noted that Cape Breton farmers and their sons "by hundreds, nay, thousands, [were] leaving their farms to the women, and seeking employment at the collieries and railways."[94] Some, such as a Highlander born on Lewis residing in Middle River who planted his crop of oats and potatoes and then traveled on foot to Halifax to work on the railway each year, appear to have regularized their patterns of distant wage work so that they synchronized with the seasonal rounds of farming. Come harvest time, the Lewis man would be back in Middle River.[95] In other households the distant wage work of males was made possible because females and children assumed a full array of farm tasks.[96]

The types of employment possibilities available to farm-based labourers varied across place — though the mobility of labour minimized the significance of some of this — and across time as the economies of timber, ships, fish, and agriculture waxed or waned and as decisions of the state and the private sector shaped the demand side of the labour market. The possibilities for the integration of wage employment into the economies of farm households varied, too, across the cyclical passages of family time. In some households a wage supplement was obtainable only if the male household-head worked off the farm on a daily or more extended basis. In others further along in the family life cycle, younger members of the household, male and female, might take on the role of subsidizing the farm with wage work. As the Prince Edward Island Land Commissioners learned when they inquired into the survival strategies of the rural poor there, household budgets were

[92]David Stewart's Journal, 31, PAPEI, 3209/28.

[93]Nova Scotia House of Assembly, *Journals*, 1857, Appendix No. 72, 421.

[94]*Journal of Agriculture for Nova Scotia*, July 1871, 652.

[95]Francis MacGregor, "Days that I Remember," January 1962, Ms. 12/71, 31, Beaton Institute, Sydney, Nova Scotia.

[96]These different patterns of domestic life in poorer households no doubt underwrote the perception that backland women were particularly able workers. Backland girls, notes Margaret MacPhail's character John Campbell, made the best marriage partners as "They can work outside and in and keeps a fellow warm in bed. What else would you want!" Margaret MacPhail, *Loch Bras d'Or* (Windsor, Nova Scotia 1970), 84, 65.

balanced because "the boys hire out," the family had put their "children out to service," and/or wages were sent home by family members who had moved away.[97] Such possibilities were available to households only at certain points in the family life cycle. The Strait of Canso household David Stewart and Richard Smith visited — finding a woman and two children at home and the husband in the Miramichi woods — probably was a young family with limited options, but a household with older children might be sustained, in part, by the remittance of money from the earnings of children working at distant locales.[98]

Earnings gained by a younger generation working away for prolonged periods might be sent to support a home farm but might as well be saved to finance a new household.[99] For many, prolonged, and often distant, wage work, was an early phase in lives that ultimately would be lived out on the land. Young men or women might work away for years to accumulate the cash necessary to permit them to acquire the things needed to establish a household of their own. "Tell Mary MacDonald," wrote Thomas Murchison from Boston to his cousin on Prince Edward Island, "not to engage with any in marriage until my return."[100] Cousin Malcolm was instructed to look after Thomas Murchison's Island property in his absence as well. Further afield, Walter McDonald wrote home to Pictou from Melbourne, Australia concerning his impending return and his traveling companion's interest in marrying sister Marion who had remained in Nova Scotia.[101] Such requests surely must have been repeated again and again as young rural Maritimers sought to combine distant earnings with local ambitions. For many others, of course, off-farm work was the first step in lives that would ultimately be lived out elsewhere.

Although remote worksites could be attractive because of the wages being offered (and perhaps the fact that in most cases they were being offered in cash), the ability to gain continuous work was a drawing card for many as well. "It would surprise you," wrote Thomas Murchison on his arrival in Boston in January 1846, " to see all the work there is going on here. As far as I travelled I could not see an

[97]Ian Ross Robertson, ed., *The Prince Edward Island Land Commission of 1860* (Fredericton 1988), 116-9.

[98]Alan Brookes, "The Exodus: Migration From the Maritime Provinces to Boston During the Second Half of the Nineteenth Century," PhD dissertation, University of New Brunswick, 1978, 88; Bettsy Beattie, "Going Up to Lynn: Single Women from the Maritime Provinces Working in Lynn, Massachusetts, 1870-1930," paper presented to the Atlantic Canada Studies Conference, Orono, Maine, 18 May 1990. In her insightful evocation of life in mid-19th century rural Cape Breton, Margaret MacPhail relates how the MacKiels, a backland family, survived in part because an older daughter working as a domestic in Arichat sent money home as did a son working with the Grand Banks fishing fleet. Margaret MacPhail, *Loch Bras d'Or*, 7.

[99]These were not, of course, mutually exclusive endeavours. Labouring to support the home farm could affect one's inheritance and thus ultimately contribute to the ability to become established on one's own at a later date.

[100]Thomas Murchison to Malcolm Murchison, 15 January 1846, Ms. 3084/1, PAPEI.

[101]Walter McDonald to Mother, 25 December 1862, MG 100/184/13, PANS.

idle man that wished to work." He was, he reported, "in very good employment and making money fast" and intended to be back by spring.[102] George Musgrave wrote in a similar vein from Roxbury in August of 1842. Work had been easy to obtain, and though the hours were long he was making five dollars a week plus board and would not be returning to Cape Breton until the fall.[103] Such returns compared favourably to the wages offered in Prince Edward Island and Cape Breton, and the ability to obtain steady employment at cash wages meant that the migrant worker might return with substantial savings. The unusual opportunities for big wages drew others able to afford the passage monies yet further afield. A Yarmouth man working in the California gold fields wrote home in July of 1849 that labourers were receiving from eight to sixteen dollars per day. Although the cost of board was extraordinarily high and life precarious and violent, he would not, he thought, start making his way homeward until autumn because the opportunities for amassing a vast savings were unrivalled.[104]

One of the most striking things revealed by a survey of the waged work of farm-based labourers during this era is its multiformity. Employment might be on a daily basis or for extended periods of time. It might entail working with a small family unit or with a large, complexly-organized, stratified workforce composed exclusively of wage labourers. It might involve working with those of the same age, gender, and class background or with a more heterogeneous grouping. And it might be found in staples production, construction, manufacturing, transportation, or in aid of the "self-sufficient" activities of other farm households. Remuneration might be in cash, in kind, as a positive ledger entry, or in a mixture of these forms.

Insofar as the terms of contract between employer and employee were concerned, working circumstances varied across a broad spectrum of personal and impersonal relationships. Wage work might be found locally with a relative or neighbour or with a previously unknown employer in a distant locale. In the case of a local employer, who was a friend or relative, mutually advantageous terms may have been negotiable. Employee choices concerning the timing and terms of work — and employer — may have been more sharply constrained, though, in other localized working circumstances when the resident elite, particularly those possessing the power of a ledger or rent book, or perhaps holding a mortgage, sought extra hands. Did those working for merchants like Lawrence Kavanaugh, John Beamish Moore, and Peter Smyth — workers whose wages were set against ledger debts already incurred — come seeking employment, or were they summoned? And, if they lacked the cash or commodities to clear their debts, did they have the freedom to say "no"? The same question clearly applies to the many tenants on Prince Edward Island employed by land agents for road work, land clearing, construction,

[102]Thomas Murchison to Malcolm Murchison, 15 January 1846, Ms. 3084/1, PAPEI.
[103]George Musgrave to Ann, 7 August 1842, Micro Biography: Moore, no. 10, PANS.
[104]*Nova Scotian* (Halifax), 30 July 1849, 243, col. 1 & 2.

and shipbuilding whose wages were directly set against their arrears on rent rolls.[105] Although in theory they were working for wages, in practice many of these tenants came to be under a labour obligation to their landlords. At the other extreme were the farm-based labourers earning wages from strangers in distant work sites. The Cape Bretoner George Musgrave was initially put off by the long hours he was expected to work in Roxbury and in consequence quit his job. But, he wrote home, "on consideration of my employer adding a dollar per week to my wages I returned to work again."[106] Clearly, a cash nexus was at the heart of this work relationship and many others like it.

These variations in the labouring experiences of farm-based workers raise questions about the extent to which paternal or "personal" relations can be said to be broadly characteristic of the working experiences of British North Americans in this period. No doubt paternalism informed the relationship between employers and employees in many instances, and quite possibly in most. This model, however, with its emphasis on local power structures and non-economic forms of labour recruitment and control, does not effectively capture the labouring experiences of temporary workers, often originating in the countryside, who moved in and out of the workforce. As Clare Pentland admitted in his exploration of the concept, their circumstances do not fit the model.[107] The issue of numbers is, of course, important here. If workers such as these represent a relatively insignificant part of the total labouring population, perhaps there is some justification for viewing the nature of their circumstances as marginal to the broader picture. Existing research does not provide a clear answer to the numbers question. It is perhaps significant, though, that seasonal employees equaled or outnumbered permanent workers at the St. Maurice forges and at D.D. Calvin's lumber operations at Garden Island, supposedly classic examples of paternalistic labour practices in action. These enterprises in fact employed more workers who fell outside the model than within it.[108] The pattern was repeated in the Maritimes. The General Mining Association in Nova Scotia, too, had its well-paid and well-housed skilled workforce operating within locally-sustained, paternalistic structures, and a numerous body of differently-treated "labouring farmers" who moved in and out of the mining towns. Such, to varying degrees, appears to have been the case in other Maritime industries as well.

[105]The practice was widespread. Lord Selkirk's agent William Douse, for instance, had at least 80 men working off their rents at a rate of 3/6 for a 6 AM to 7 PM working day in the summer of 1838. Selkirk Papers, MG 19, E1, v. 73, 19207, PAC. See too Robert and David Stewart's notice to tenants in *Royal Gazette* 30 September 1834, 1 and the Worrell rent books, RG. 15, PAPEI.

[106]George Musgrave to Ann, 7 August 1842, Micro Biography: Moore, no. 10, PANS.

[107]H. Clare Pentland, *Labour and Capital in Canada, 1650-1860* (Toronto 1981), 45-6.

[108]The majority of the workforce at the forges appear to have been temporary. The division between permanent and temporary workers at D.D. Calvin's operations was roughly equal. H. Clare Pentland, *Labour and Capital in Canada, 1650-1860*, 42-5; Bryan D. Palmer, *Working-Class Experience: The Rise and Reconstitution of Canadian Labour, 1800-1980* (Toronto 1983), 15.

Perhaps the circumstances of a skilled fraction of the work force have assumed too great a profile in our conceptualization of labour relations, and worker consciousness, during the first half of the 19th century. Greater attention to the lives of farm-based workers may force some reassessment in our understanding of the contours of the experience of work during this period.[109]

The issue of numbers emerges again with the broader argument being presented here. While it is relatively easy to assemble data pointing to the involvement of farm-based workers in a wide variety of wage labour, establishing the breadth of this is another matter. One way to approach the issue is from the supply side, from the perspective of the household. Where data — such as census returns — permit, it is possible to estimate farm production and consumption and to calculate the numbers of farms requiring an income supplement. Applying this sort of analysis to the census returns from Middle River and Hardwood Hill suggested that roughly one-quarter to one-third of households fell into this category. Though the ratios would vary, similar analysis of data from farming communities elsewhere in the northeast Maritimes almost certainly would reveal roughly-comparable patterns. Perusal of the census returns from the region indicate the recurring presence of farms with insufficient resources to maintain their occupants. It does not require the application of a complex algorithm to discern that, given the climate and soils of this region, a family of eight would not have been able to make ends meet with five cleared acres and a single cow. But since wage work was not the only strategy for augmenting deficiencies in farm income, it is not safe to equate all farm deficits with a comparable involvement in wage labour. Moreover, there were inducements to wage work other than that of immediate necessity. Wage labourers were drawn from across the spectrum of farm types, not just from operations with annual deficits. Likely these numbers more than compensate for those who may have successfully managed to supplement insufficiencies of farm income without recourse to wages, judging from a reading of a variety of sources. What needs to be emphasized is that the analysis of farm deficits ultimately rests on a series of assumptions concerning patterns of production and consumption. No matter how carefully done, the resulting figures are estimates. Shave down the calculations for household consumption levels or increase the coefficients for livestock productivity and we arrive at new estimates for the numbers of farm households requiring income supplements. To test the accuracy of such estimates, we need close analysis of the economic behaviour of specific households.

The problems of quantifying workforce participation do not get any easier when approached from the demand side. Existing evidence concerning employee numbers, length of work, and origins is fragmentary, although there are some sectors for which we have contemporary estimates of the numbers of workers. Shipbuilding, according to the editor of the *Prince Edward Island Register*, em-

[109]For a consideration of this issue in a European context see Jean H. Quataert, "A New Look at Working-Class Formation: Reflections on the Historical Perspective," *International Labour and Working Class History*, 27 (Spring 1985), 72-6.

ployed 1000 Islanders in 1824. The Island was a relatively small place and the editor took a keen interest in developments in the shipbuilding industry. His figure is probably well-grounded. Assuming that perhaps one-quarter of the total Island population of 20,000 comprised adult males, this would mean that one-fifth of them were working at the shipyards for some period of the year. In adjacent New Brunswick two decades later, it was estimated that roughly 20,000 were employed in the timber industry.[110] Figures such as these can be set against production tallies to provide a starting point for compiling estimates of the labour force in other years and other locales. So, too, fragmentary evidence concerning the numbers of labourers employed on specific farms and in particular enterprises can permit, by extrapolation, the creation of rough estimates of the labour demands of the industry as a whole. Unfortunately, little such work has been done. The fragments of evidence concerning employment, however, suggest that a composite picture would reveal substantial numbers of farm dwellers participating in near and distant labour markets. It needs to be emphasized, though, that for many participation was brief. The percentage of farm-dwellers engaging in the wage economy is a very different figure from the percentage of the total productive time any one individual spent within the wage economy. Which is the more important figure depends, of course, on the questions we ask.

The problem of attempting to quantify the extent of farm-based wage labour in the first half of the 19th century is a difficult one. With more research into the behaviour of particular households and the circumstances of specific communities or industries for which there are good records, it will be possible to obtain a better sense of the scale of the phenomenon. At best, though, the figures will be very rough estimates, reasonable guesses based on limited evidence. What is clear, however, even given the limits of the existing state of our understanding, is that wage work needs to be carefully factored into our understandings of rural life.[111] Though an oft-noted reality, it has not always assumed the profile that it should. Too often the appealing vision of rural autonomy and insularity has nudged it aside. Drawn in by the image of the independent yeoman, we seek to explain his decline. Influenced by the mythology of the autonomous household, or by its more recent derivative, the autonomous community in which households achieved independence by equitable sharing, we examine rural life in terms of narrowly-defined geographical communities. None of this is entirely wrongheaded, but we need to recognize more explicitly that the presuppositions that are guiding these questions and approaches originate in a powerful mythology that is rooted only partly in the rural reality of the early 19th-century Maritimes.

[110]Report from the New Brunswick *Royal Gazette* cited in the *Islander*, 20 November 1846, 2.
[111]Certainly too, as Larry McCann has noted, these patterns have implications for urban development in the Maritimes as well. Larry McCann, "'Living a Double Life': Town and Country in the Industrialization of the Maritimes," in Douglas Day, ed., *Geographical Perspectives on the Maritime Provinces* (Halifax 1988), 93-113.

I am reminded of the discrepancies in the assumptions which the scholar Bernard Pares brought to his study of the Russian countryside and the reality that he encountered when he actually moved among rural folk on the eve of the Revolution of 1905. Arriving at a peasant meeting in Tver, miles from the nearest train station, he expected to find rural folk with but a dim perception of the world that lay beyond their village. He discovered instead that more than 40 per cent had worked in either Petersburg or Moscow.[112] The rural world that he found was not the insular one he had expected. Charles Farnham had a similar experience in Cape Breton in the 1880s. Traveling across the remote northernmost highlands, he encountered a young woman along the road and gave her a lift. When she asked to be put down at an intersecting cart trail, Farnham, who had come to Cape Breton to experience life in its primitive purity, inquired as to the direction she was taking. "Where does that road go to Maggie?" "It goes to the Strait of Canso, sir, and on to Montana . . ."[113] Twenty years earlier, perhaps the answer would have been Boston and half a century before, as David Stewart and Richard Smith discovered when they wandered the island, the trails led to Chatham and the Miramichi. The paths, roads, and waterways of the northeast Maritimes took countryfolk in many directions. And they brought many of them back again, weeks, months, and years later. Work in a neighbour's field or house or mill provided training for, and gave way to, work in more distant settings. With their movements, farm-based labourers continuously integrated a host of near and distant economies and experiences into the fabric of rural life. In Margaree, Marshy Hope, and Bear River, life was shaped not just by local crop returns and the relations between neighbours but by wages remitted from away and by the experiences and ideas of those who worked elsewhere.[114] Externalities visited on familiar feet.

From a rural perspective, from the hearths of these workers, there is a central commonality in many of these work experiences: their function, their integration into the economies of households that maintained a commitment to (or reliance upon) a soil-based livelihood.[115] Many worked so that they might farm. For the new settlers that Lord Selkirk and John Cambridge observed, wage work was undertaken as a temporary means by which sufficient capital might be acquired to permit an escape from the necessity of working for others. So too for the young men and women labouring to acquire a nest egg, wage work was a necessary phase in a

[112]Bernard Pares, *A Wandering Student: The Story of a Purpose* (Syracuse 1948), 127.

[113]Charles H. Farnham, "Cape Breton Folk," 97.

[114]For a splendid example of how a focus on migratory labour can deepen our understanding of change in agrarian *and* urban and industrial society, see Bruno Ramirez, *On the Move: French-Canadian and Italian Migrants in the North Atlantic Economy, 1860-1914* (Toronto 1991).

[115]For Russian peasants, the perceived importance of the functional commonality of all such off-farm work is reflected in its designation by a single word, *promysly*, meaning all those activities necessary to round out the insufficient returns gained from the soil. Theodor Shanin, *Russia as a Developing Society*, vol. 1, *The Roots of Otherness: Russia's Turn of Century* (New Haven 1985), 68.

life that it was hoped might be lived primarily outside of it. The contemporary language of praise underscores the importance of the objective. Describing the agricultural prosperity that a cousin had come to enjoy on Prince Edward Island, John McRa indicated the extent of his accomplishments by reporting that he had become "very independent."[116] Joseph Howe spoke of the same goal and perhaps beyond when he argued that the industrious Nova Scotian yeoman might with "a wife and an axe" become "truly rich and independent." The Rev. John MacLennan, on tour in the 1820s from his parish in Belfast, Prince Edward Island, lauded the condition of some of Middle River's farm households by noting that they were in "very independent circumstances."[117] Donald Campbell indicated the extent of the good fortune he had obtained in Cape Breton by saying that he was free from the impositions of factor and laird and "any toilsome work but what I do myself."[118]

These people had to some extent gained what many sought. The dream of achieving control over one's labour and its product and of acquiring "independence" was, of course, a widely shared aspiration of rural and urban dwellers alike. The language and arguments used to articulate these ideals in the Escheat struggle on Prince Edward Island in the 1830s are not dissimilar to those employed by many urban workers in this period.[119] The belief that such goals of autonomy and independence might best be achieved by securing a land-based livelihood was both widespread and persistent even among those deeply embedded in the industrial labour force. The Ohio labour commissioners who assembled the state's first annual labour report in 1877 estimated that roughly one-half the mechanics and labourers in Ohio's urban centres were working to accumulate the savings necessary so that they might acquire a farm.[120] Similarly, as Ewa Morawska has argued, the majority of East Central European peasants who traveled to American industrial centres at the turn of the 20th century engaged in wage labour thousands of miles from home so that they and their families might become more securely established on the soil; they did so with the intention of returning to their rural communities.[121] Such was the case as well, Theodore von Laue has argued, with much of the industrial work force in late-19th and early-20th century Russia.[122] For centuries peasants in the

[116]John McRa to Archibald McRa, 1 January 1817, Ms. 3363/2, PAPEI.

[117]Letter of Rev. John MacLennan, 1827, Glasgow Colonial Society Correspondence, M-1352, 129, PAC.

[118]Donald Campbell to [a relative in Lewis], 7 October 1830, reprinted in the *Stornaway Gazette*, 30 September 1972, MG 100, vol. 115, #33, PANS.

[119]Rusty Bittermann, "Agrarian Alternatives: The Ideas of the Escheat Movement on Prince Edward Island, 1832-42," *Acadiensis* (forthcoming).

[120]Cited in Peter H. Argersinger and Jo Ann Argersinger, "The Machine Breakers: Farmworkers and Social Change in the Rural Mid West of the 1870s," *Agricultural History*, 58 (July 1983), 401.

[121]Ewa Morawska, "'For Bread with Butter': Life-Worlds of Peasant Immigrants from East Central Europe, 1880-1914," *Journal of Social History*, 17:3 (Spring 1984), 392.

[122]Theodore von Laue, "Russian Peasants in the Factory, 1892-1904," *Journal of Economic History*, 21 (1961), 80.

Friuli and Saxony have "consciously" chosen, Douglas Holmes and Jean Quataert contend, to integrate wage work with agrarian pursuits on their rural holdings as a way of resisting a "propertyless working-class existence."[123]

Other farm-based workers in the northeast Maritimes, of course, may have resigned themselves to the necessity of perpetually maintaining the dual commitments of self-employment and working for others, or may indeed have embraced wage work never seeking to attain a degree of choice over their involvement in the labour market.[124] Given the sporadic and uneven nature of the demand for labour in the region in the early 19th century, life without the fall-back of an agricultural holding could be precarious.[125] Rather than working so that they might farm, some, no doubt, farmed so that they might live to work. For many, however, access to the soil held out the hope of achieving control over their time and their labour, and persistence in straddling two worlds constituted a way of resisting the imperatives and dependence of wage work.[126]

We need to look more closely at the transformation of these dreams, which had been closely associated with the myth of the independent yeoman, and at changes in the strategies adopted by working people. Few still maintain that true independence is to be gained by eschewing wage work for agricultural pursuits and by struggling to gain a toehold on the soil. The goal of a "propertied independence" that was embedded in the mythology and once held such an important position in the aspirations of working people of the North Atlantic world has long since lost its lustre. And though many rural residents in the region continue to engage in seasonal

[123]Douglas R. Holmes and Jean H. Quataert, "An Approach to Modern Labor: Worker Peasantries in Historic Saxony and the Friuli Region over Three Centuries," *Comparative Studies in Society and History*, 28:2 (April 1986), 202.

[124]Many emigrants had experience with similar work patterns before they migrated. See Barbara M. Kerr, "Irish Seasonal Migration to Great Britain, 1800-38," *Irish Historical Studies*, 3 (1942-3), 365-80; A.J. Youngson, *After the Forty-Five: The Economic Impact on the Scottish Highlands* (Edinburgh 1973), 182-4; T.M. Devine, "Temporary Migration and the Scottish Highlands in the Nineteenth Century," *Economic History Review*, 32 (1979), 344-59; William Howatson, "The Scottish Hairst and Seasonal Labour 1600-1870," *Scottish Studies*, 26 (1982), 13-36; E.J.T. Collins, "Migrant Labour in British Agriculture in the Nineteenth Century," *Economic History Review*, 29 (1976), 38-59. As Maritimers moved on, some carried these patterns of work to new locales. See Aeneas McCharles, *Bemocked of Destiny*, 28; Neil Robinson, *Lion of Scotland* (Auckland 1952, 1974), 28, 80, 99.

[125]Judith Fingard, "A Winter's Tale: The Seasonal Contours of Pre-Industrial Poverty in British North America, 1815-1860," *Historical Papers*, (1974), 65-94; D.B. MacNab to Uniacke, 3 January 1857, Nova Scotia House of Assembly, *Journals*, 1857, app. 71, 421.

[126]On the significance of agrarian strategies to working-class struggles in Great Britain and the United States in this period see Malcolm Chase, *'The People's Farm': English Radical Agrarianism, 1775-1840* (Oxford 1988); Sean Wilentz, *Chants Democratic: New York City and the Rise of the American Working Class, 1788-1850* (New York 1984), 164-216, 335-43; Paul Conkin, *Prophets of Prosperity: America's First Political Economists* (Bloomington 1980), 222-58.

work at near and distant job sites, fewer and fewer rely on farming as a means to survive periods when they are not engaged in wage work.[127] Surely these will be key themes for those who would write the environmental history of the region. The decline of the belief that the labourer's salvation was to be found on the land and the decline of agriculture as a safety net have profoundly affected our perception of the significance of arable soil, and of land more generally. For increasing numbers, even of rural residents, it is no longer a matter of importance.

[127]The terms of eligibility for unemployment benefits have played a role here in forcing some to choose between a state-based or land-based safety net and/or to define themselves as workers rather than farmers.

The author wishes to gratefully acknowledge the assistance received from the Social Sciences and Humanities Research Council of Canada, whose financial support aided this research. I am also grateful to Carmen Bickerton, Michael Cross, Margaret McCallum, Danny Samson and the participants in the Atlantic Canada Workshop (Lunenburg, September, 1990) and the Rural Workers in Atlantic Canada Conference (Saint Mary's University, October, 1990) for their comments on an earlier version of this paper. By "northeastern Maritimes" I mean Prince Edward Island, Cape Breton Island and the northernmost section of peninsular Nova Scotia. I take some liberties with the time frame indicated, occasionally drawing evidence from the late 18th century and beyond 1850. Nonetheless this essay is primarily about farm-based wage work in the first half of the 19th century.

Linda Little

2

Collective Action in Outport Newfoundland: A Case Study from the 1830s

Gibbeted corpses, ominous letters left by a stealthy arsonist, disguised vigilantes on lonely roads, and boisterous parades of aggrieved fishermen were remarkably common in the Newfoundland outport settlements of Harbour Grace and Carbonear in the 1830s. At least 30 different acts of protest ranging from a solitary cry against injustice to a parade of up to 4,000 striking sealers were recorded over the decade, each one pointing to a strong tradition of Newfoundland resistance.[1]

The home countries of England and Ireland both had active plebeian traditions. Ideas of what was right and wrong, just and unjust, were as clear to the population in Newfoundland as they had been in England and Ireland, and the island's common people were as anxious to protect their interests in the new society as were their Old World counterparts.[2] Naturally, the forms of plebeian protest common in the mother

[1]Space does not permit inclusion here of all 30 incidents. For a complete description see Linda Little, "Plebeian Collective Action in Harbour Grace and Carbonear, Newfoundland, 1830-40," MA thesis, Memorial University of Newfoundland, 1984. There is some indication that Newfoundlanders indulged in a variety of types of collective action throughout the island dating from the earliest settlements. Contemporary accounts include stories of Whiteboys, faction fights, a United Irishman rising, mumming, wrecking, and food riots. Little, 8-13.

[2]E.P. Thompson, "The Moral Economy of the English Crowd in the Eighteenth Century," *Past and Present*, 50 (1971), 78-9. The literature on protest movements and plebeian forms of protest is extensive. Outstanding works dealing with the English and Irish contexts are: Douglas Hay, Peter Linebaugh, *et al.* eds., *Albion's Fatal Tree: Crime and Society in Eighteenth Century England* (New York 1975); and Samuel Clark and James Donnelly, eds., *Irish Peasants: Violence and Political Unrest 1780-1914* (Madison 1983). See also G.C. Lewis, *Local Disturbances in Ireland* (London 1835).

Published with permission of the editor. © Canadian Committee on Labour History, from *Labour/Le Travail*, 26 (Fall 1990), 37-59.

country were transferred to the colony, as they were familiar and effective, but also because common symbolism and ritual lent the authority of longstanding custom to a relatively new society.[3] Protests were recognized for what they were by both the plebeian population and the ruling class when they embodied recognizable forms of resistance such as arson, maiming, anonymous notes, night visits, riots, and parades.

This paper is a case study of the towns of Harbour Grace and Carbonear during the period 1830-1840. The instances of plebeian collective action which occurred during this decade are chronicled and analyzed, not as isolated incidents in the history of the towns, but as a series of events in a continuing tradition of resistance. Newfoundlanders formed strong alliances within their communities. Most people identified with their own ethno-religious group; Newfoundland's Irish Catholics and the English Protestants occupied separate worlds in close geographical proximity. Social networks within these religious groupings were tight, encouraging ready organization and collective action. As strong as these ties were, however, they did not *prevent* people in the wider community from acting together to achieve a common goal. The first part of this paper recounts a number of diverse collective plebeian acts, and examines the motives and social loyalties connected with each. The second deals with election violence where the population used informal means to affect change in a formal theatre. The third section is devoted to the largest plebeian disturbance of the decade, the 1832 sealers' strike. Here fishermen transcended their various social biases to work in class ways for their common good.

The towns of Harbour Grace and Carbonear are situated about five miles apart, on the north shore of Conception Bay, 80 miles from St. John's. Economically, the Conception Bay area was a relatively vibrant region of the island, Harbour Grace being second only to St. John's as a mercantile center, with Carbonear close behind. During the 1830s, more than 4,000 people resided in each settlement. This was a new population; permanent settlement had become the norm only from the beginning of the century. In 1836 Roman Catholics comprised just over half the population of both towns. The remainder of the population was mostly Anglican in Harbour Grace, and mostly Wesleyan in Carbonear, but each town had a significant number of people of the opposite Protestant denomination.[4] Religion was an important factor, not only because of prevalent religious prejudice, but also because religion was indicative of ethnic background as well. The Catholic population was almost totally Irish, specifically from a small region of southwest Ireland, and the Protestant sects were from an equally confined region of southeast England.[5] In addition, religion had a class aspect in that the relatively even demographic balance between the two groups made Harbour Grace and Carbonear more volatile than most other

---

[3]Eric Hobsbawm, "Inventing Traditions," in Eric Hobsbawm and Terence Ranger, eds., *The Invention of Tradition* (Cambridge 1983), esp. 1-2.
[4]Census of Newfoundland and Labrador, 1836; *Journal of the House of Assembly*, 1838, appendix, 128-9.
[5]John Mannion, ed., *The Peopling of Newfoundland* (St. John's 1977).

areas of the island where settlements were predominantly of one religion or the other. Most of the population was directly involved with catching or processing fish, but there also were small upper and middle classes of merchants, agents, planters and craftsmen. The two settlements were quite similar, but Harbour Grace was slightly more prosperous with a larger mercantile community, better farming, and smaller households.

In 19th-century Newfoundland, the cod fishery was the basis of the economy. Merchants outfitted the fishermen on the condition that the fishermen brought their fish to them. After the fishing season was over, the merchant set the price of fish, tallied the amount caught by the fisherman, and subtracted the value of the supplies. The final figure, profit or loss, was registered in the merchant's account book so fishing families could draw their winter supplies from their merchant's store up to the amount earned.[6] If the family had not earned enough to keep themselves through the winter, the merchants often would see them through by advancing food supplies on credit, thus increasing the family's debt and keeping them in the service of that merchant. The system looked quite simple on the surface, but there were many wrinkles. Cod fishermen could occupy a variety of social positions.[7] There were "independent" fishing families who owned their own boat and processing facilities, and who brought finished salt cod to the merchant. Merchants also bought raw fish and had it salted at their premises. Thus, there were people who worked on shore for wages or credit, those who owned large, decked fishing vessels which delivered raw fish, and those who worked on those vessels for a share of the catch. The Conception Bay fishery was further complicated by the fact that fishing and salting could take place along the coast of Labrador as well as in Conception Bay.[8] Bay fishermen who spent the summer months fishing in Labrador and returned to their Conception Bay homes for the winter could also own property in Labrador, which allowed them to catch and salt their own fish, or they could work for others earning wages, credit, or shares.

Also important to Newfoundland's economic life in the 19th century was the seal fishery, which in the 1830s could be expected to provide about one-third of a Conception Bay fisherman's income. In contrast to the cod fishery, the seal fishery had a straightforward organization whereby men hired on board a sealing vessel and worked for a share of the catch; all sealers were essentially equal.[9] Also, the

---

[6]For an account of life at a merchant's counting house see Edmund Gosse, *The Life of Philip Henry Gosse* (London 1890), 48-51.

[7]Little, "Plebeian Collective Action," 56-65.

[8]For a description of the Labrador fishery and its social organization see Philip Tocque, *Newfoundland As It Was and Is In 1877* (Toronto 1878), 258-76; W.A. Black, "The Labrador Floater Codfishery," *Annals of the Association of American Geographers*, 50:3 (1960); Thomas Talbot, *Newfoundland* (London 1882), 2-34.

[9]Contemporary accounts of sealing can be found in Lewis Anspach, *A History of the Island of Newfoundland* (London 1819), 415-23; Richard Bonnycastle, *Newfoundland in 1842* (London 1842), 130-5; J.B. Jukes, *Excursions In and About Newfoundland During the Years*

seal fishery was not always conducted completely through the truck system, as there was a limited history of cash being used for at least partial payment in the seal trade in some areas.

I

A collective action is an act committed for the perceived benefit of a given group of people, and thus requires consensus about what *is* beneficial or just. Usually, many people are involved in such an action, but the size of such groups can vary from two or three to thousands. Acts committed by individuals are also included, provided that they involve an appeal to the community at large, or are meant to reflect the views of that community. The collective actions examined here might or might not have been illegal: their formal legal status was irrelevant to the perpetrators.

The case of Daniel McCarthy in 1830 provides an early example of a popular view of justice that transcended the law. McCarthy was a poor shoemaker who occupied an abandoned fish house with his wife and children as squatters for four or five years.[10] When the building was to be torn down as a fire hazard, McCarthy refused to leave. The magistrate assembled a large body of special constables to evict McCarthy and his family, and pull down the house. McCarthy resisted. Claiming he was armed and would defend himself to the last, he refused the bail offered him if he gave himself up peacefully.[11] Magistrate Danson was appalled at McCarthy's lack of respect and reported that he had:

Threatened revenge on all persons concerned and even myself as soon as the *Kerry Men* should arrive from the fishery who would assist him and that before the following winter was over we should have very little to call our own, and intimated that our Houses should not be safe and defied all authority.[12]

The special constables refused to obey the magistrate's order to break open the door and destroy the poor man's house.[13]

The following day the door was unlocked and two regular constables were sent to evict McCarthy. They succeeded only after a desperate struggle in which both constables were wounded. McCarthy, his wife, and stepson were jailed but the magistrate was nervous about a potential rescue by fellow Irishmen, as it was

of 1839 and 1840 (London 1842), 251-322; Talbot, *Newfoundland*, 15-21; Tocque, *Newfoundland As It Was*, 304-7.

[10]Provincial Archives of Newfoundland and Labrador (PANL), Incoming Correspondence of the Colonial Secretary's Office, GN 2/2, Petition of Daniel McCarthy, 18 March 1831; GN 2/2, Rogerson to Danson, 3 November 1830; GN 2/2, Magistrates' Report, 3 June 1831.
[11]PANL, GN 2/2, Danson and St. John to Ayre, 1 September 1830; GN 2/2, Magistrates' Report, 3 June 1831.
[12]PANL, GN 2/2, Magistrates' Report, 3 June 1831.
[13]PANL, GN 2/2, Petition of Daniel McCarthy, 18 March 1831.

something they had "often the inclination to do,"[14] and because the "Lower Order of persons" in Harbour Grace "were elated at [the] resistance to legal Authority."[15]

Although McCarthy had been evicted legally, he still felt it unjust that he should be forced to leave. His claim on the property was that he had lived there several years and had nowhere else to go. The special constables may also have seen the injustice of turning a poor man and his family out of their house in the fall of the year, and may have been intimidated by McCarthy's threats. In any case, the appeal to the cohesiveness of the Conception Bay Irish community to stand by one of its members who had been wronged had a serious effect. Whether or not the threats would have come to fruition we do not know, but it is clear that both McCarthy and the magistrate believed that they would because of strong Irish Catholic loyalties in the area.

The following spring, passions were aroused over a more directly economic issue. In May 1831, a disturbance was reported at the Harbour Grace mercantile establishment of Hugh William Danson and company.[16] A crowd was moved to action when the firm was declared insolvent, and the fishermen and sharemen Danson employed became anxious about the shares and wages owed them from the seal fishery. Apparently the trustees were unwilling or unable to meet the debts of shares and wages to the fishermen when the firm declared bankruptcy. When the news reached those concerned, fishermen retaliated by "forcibly possessing and rolling upwards of one hundred casks of oil into the street."[17] The men threatened to destroy the oil, but the step proved unnecessary, as the trustees soon assured them that the sharemen would be paid their due that evening. The act was described as "robbery," a "riot," and an "outrage," but the fishermen obtained swift and fair settlement of their grievance. Although the fishermen may have had no legal claim on Danson's oil, they had a moral claim to their wages and it was on this basis that they acted.

The largest and most radical examples of plebeian collective action in Conception Bay during this decade occurred in conjunction with the 1832 sealers' strike. Because of its significance, the strike will be dealt with separately at the end of the paper.

The years 1833 and 1834 were particularly bad ones in the cod fishery, and the demand for poor relief was especially great.[18] Hardship prompted a number of assaults upon local merchant houses. In spring 1833, Thomas Elsworth was arrested

[14]PANL, GN 2/2, Magistrates' Report, 3 June 1831.

[15]PANL, GN 2/2, Danson and St. John to Ayre, 1 September 1830.

[16]PANL, GN 2/2, Ridley to Entendant of Record, 31 May 1831; *Public Ledger*, 3 June 1831; Centre for Newfoundland Studies (CNS), Colonial Office Papers (CO) #194 vol. 95, 95, Prescott to Glenelg, 15 December 1836.

[17]*Public Ledger*, 3 June 1831.

[18]The administration of relief was a major item of business in the governor's correspondence in 1833 and in 1834. See for example, PANL, GN 2/2, Stabb to Crowdy, 28 May 1833; Harbour Grace Magistrates' Letters, Crowdy to Harbour Grace Magistrates, 25 February 1833.

for violently attacking, and breaking the counting-house door of merchant Thomas Chancey.[19] A month later, another man walked through Carbonear declaring that unless supplies were given to him and others for the summer, they would fire the stores. After assaulting almost every respectable person he met, he entered merchant Robert Pack's house and "grossly abused" Pack's wife before he was removed. Although the incident took place during the day and in the presence of many, no one attempted to interfere with the man.[20] In November 1834, Chancey's premises again were the target of vandalism when a man named Macky broke two doors and forced himself into Chancey's office where he used violent language to the merchant.[21] When Macky was charged, he refused bail and was not penitent, but instead regretted he had not "gone through the window like a horse instead of going through the doors."[22] Sensing strong public support for Macky, the constable who was detailed to escort the prisoner to Harbour Grace jail demanded an entourage of six or eight special constables.

All four direct attacks on the merchants' establishments suggest sympathy among the fishermen and a detached hostility towards the "respectable" and merchant community. Each protest suggests that principle, rather than desire for personal gain, was at stake: those who work hard all year deserve to receive enough to live on.

Burial customs and an accepted standard of respect for the dead were enforced by plebeian action when necessary in Conception Bay. Dissection and gibbeting were punishments used in Britain and her colonies for crimes considered particularly obnoxious.[23] Dissection played a dual role, supplying surgeons with cadavers for medical research while providing a dreaded punishment for the masses.[24] The mutilation and display of human bodies, regardless of the atrocities the criminal may have committed, was considered thoroughly repugnant by the plebeian population.

Public distaste for the exhibition of human corpses was no less prevalent in Newfoundland. In early 1834, a man named Peter Downing (or Downey) was convicted for the brutal murders of a school teacher, his infant son and a servant girl. For his crimes Downing was sentenced to be hanged and dissected. Whether

[19] Harbour Grace Magistrates' Letters, file #15, Chancey to Danson, 11 May 1833.

[20] *Carbonear Star*, 19 June 1833.

[21] *Carbonear Star*, 26 November 1834.

[22] *Carbonear Star*, 26 November 1834.

[23] In Hay, *et al.*, eds., *Albion's Fatal Tree*: see Hay, 50; Linebaugh, 81; Winslow, 163. Burial rights and the place of burial were also important enough to spark action. In Ireland, Whiteboys executed and buried by the state sometimes had to be buried in quicklime to prevent families from claiming the corpses. James Donnelly, "Pastorini and Captain Rock: Millenarianism and Sectarianism in the Rockite Movement of 1821-4," in Clark and Donnelly, eds., *Irish Peasants*, 132.

[24] See Linebaugh.

that dissection ever took place is not clear, but the governor arranged for the body to be displayed in chains near the scene of the crime.[25]

On the evening of 29 April 1834, a large crowd assembled in Harbour Grace to cut down the gibbeted body of the murderer.[26] In an act of defiance, the partially decomposed body was paraded through the town, past the Court House, and dropped on the doorstep of a magistrate, Dr. Stirling, along with a note which read:

Dr. S.
This is your man you were the cause of bringing him here take and bury him or Look Out should you be the cause of allowing him to be put up again we will mark you for it so do your duty and put him out of sight
truly
A friend
Anon Carbonear[27]

The body was buried immediately at the Court House, and no attempts were made to have the incident investigated or the body gibbeted again.[28]

In the nearby town of Port-de-Grave a similar incident occurred around the same time.[29] A planter named Snow was murdered by his wife, her lover, and a servant. The three were convicted and ordered to be dissected and hung in chains. They were hanged, but the obnoxious dissection and exhibition of the bodies was not carried out in this case. Although the Port-de-Grave surgeon was anxious to have the bodies for anatomical studies, the local Catholic priest interceded, claiming that the sentence of dissection and display had been remitted. The surgeon was unable to acquire them as specimens because a large and angry crowd surrounded the jail when he went to collect them. The crowd was successful in intimidating the surgeon, who made only token scratches on the necks of the bodies before giving them up to the crowd. The surgeon thus fulfilled his obligation to carry out his part in the sentence and avoided angering the large crowd. The subsequent funeral was reported as being "more like that of Martyrs than Felons," as the Port-de-Grave people celebrated their victory in preventing the display of the bodies.[30]

Widespread public disgust toward a gibbeted corpse is thus evident. The anonymous note to the Harbour Grace magistrate demanded that plebeian concepts

[25]CNS, CO 194 vol. 27, Cochrane to Stanley, 15 March 1834.
[26]PANL, GN 2/2, Stark to Crowdy, 12 May 1834. The only estimate as to the size of the crowd puts it at "at least 1000 men." Downing was hanged at the beginning of April when most of the working male population was away at the seal fishery. The body was cut down a month later when the sealing vessels were arriving back from the ice. It is reasonable to speculate that the men arrived back from sealing to find the offensive body displayed, and immediately united to cut it down.
[27]PANL, GN 2/2, Stirling and Danson to Crowdy, 30 April 1834 (encl).
[28]PANL, GN 2/2, Harbour Grace Magistrates to Crowdy, 30 April 1834.
[29]CNS, CO 194 vol. 87, Cochrane to Stanley, 15 March 1834.
[30]*Ibid.*

of justice be respected; "Do your duty and put him out of sight," the letter instructed. The people used their numbers effectively to challenge the authorities and enforce their standards of decency.[31]

An interesting contrast to these two examples of disgust about the exhibiting of corpses is found in the case of John Moxley's burial. Here religious loyalties challenged the popular beliefs regarding decent burial. On 28 February 1838, John Moxley of Carbonear died of self-inflicted wounds after "cares and afflictions of the world became too much for him."[32] An inquest was held and the family was granted a warrant to bury the body in the regular manner. Moxley, however, was a Catholic and as a suicide had died in a state of mortal sin; his body was refused interment in the Catholic cemetery. The body was to be buried in the Anglican graveyard at the direction of Stark, the coroner and magistrate, and it was carried there, accompanied by about 100 people.[33] News of the burial circulated rapidly and 30 or 40 Anglican church parishioners immediately assembled to prevent the indignity of having a Catholic body, rejected by the Catholics themselves, buried in their churchyard.[34] The body was not buried that evening, as frozen ground kept the gravediggers busy for two days, but the intent was clear. The following day, the minister could not get the people to enter the church for worship and had difficulty restraining the crowd. Tension was heightened by the continuing work of the gravediggers, but the minister was able to keep the peace by appointing a committee to deal with the matter.[35]

The law dictated that the coroner had the authority to direct the interment of anyone's body who had died of suicide in any burial ground which, looking to the religion of the deceased person, he considered expedient.[36] Anglican church parishioners were not as concerned with the laws on the books as they were with their consecrated churchyard being used for burying the corpses of Catholics, especially of sinners. The grave was finished and the body buried on 4 March, but that same night the body was dug up and carried off about three-quarters of a mile from the churchyard.[37] The coffin was badly abused and the head and shoulders of the body were visible. The constables believed, on the basis of threats and intimidation, that the people from the Anglican church had removed the body.[38] The body was retrieved and buried again by the constables according to the original warrant.

On 9 March the grave was again opened and the naked body dragged out of the coffin and off over the snow. It was believed that the corpse had been tossed

[31]PANL, GN 2/2, Stark to Crowdy, 12 May 1834; CNS, CO 194 vol. 95, Prescott to Glenelg, 15 December 1836 (encl.).
[32]*Carbonear Star*, 7 March 1838. Moxley left a widow, eight children, numerous debts, and an estate worth only £5. This may account for his slashing his own throat with his razor.
[33]PANL, GN 2/2, Collings *et.al.* to Crowdy, 4 March 1838.
[34]PANL, GN 2/2, Collings *et al.* to Crowdy, 4 March 1838.
[35]PANL, GN 2/2, Collings *et al.* to Crowdy, 4 March 1838.
[36]PANL, GN 2/1/41, Crowdy to Stark, 9 March 1838.
[37]PANL, GN 2/2, Stark to Crowdy, 8 March 1838.
[38]PANL, GN 2/2, Stark to Crowdy, 8 March 1838 (encl.).

into the sea until it was found again, five days later, at nearby Crocker's Cove.[39] A constable reported that he had met 150 men carrying the body, wrapped in mats, back to the churchyard in Carbonear.[40] Who these men were is unknown. They may have been Catholics insisting on a burial for their coreligionist. They may have been Anglicans who felt the insults to the body had gone too far and were willing to make concessions. This is possible in light of the earlier affair over the public display of Downing's body. Whatever the reasoning the corpse was dropped at the churchyard but "no person in Carbonear, for love or money would help to bury the body, either in the Churchyard or assist in carrying it back in the Woods for interment."[41] The constables had a new coffin made (for the sake of decency) and buried the body privately that night. The coroner received a threat that the body would be left at his doorstep but he continued to insist on having Moxley buried at the originally proposed site.[42] The following night the corpse was disturbed for the last time, this time by Moxley's friends. Four of them dug up the coffin and buried it back in the woods where it likely would not be interfered with again.[43]

The Anglicans were undoubtedly and understandably upset by the idea of having their consecrated ground used to bury the bodies of people rejected by their Catholic neighbours. The rumour of the burial sparked instant reaction in the crowd which assembled to intervene. They were willing to trust legal and peaceful means for redress of their grievance, but when this failed and the body was buried anyway, the Anglicans were forced into direct action. The authorities were shocked by such acts, but although the magistrates claimed a vigilant search would be made for the perpetrators, no one was ever apprehended. The retrieval of the body following the second incident may have indicated that the Protestant community regarded the discarded, exposed body as indecent treatment; however, their refusal to bury the body in the churchyard and the continuing threat of disinterment suggests the original objection was sustained. Apart from the original attempt to have the body buried, and possibly to have it brought back from Crocker's Cove, Catholic participation is not reported. No attempt was made to guard the body and it was Catholics, in fact, who ultimately dug up the corpse to have it buried elsewhere. One can only speculate, but it seems plausible that the Catholics too, recognized the injustice of burying Moxley in the consecrated ground of the churchyard.

The incident demonstrated accepted burial customs and an understanding of what was fair and decent regardless of what the laws allowed coroners to order. Disregarding these accepted customs resulted in plebeian demands for redress through legal channels; when these were denied direct action was taken.

Arson was a popular and effective means of protest, as it offered the possibility of wreaking heavy damage upon carefully selected targets with little effort or risk

[39]PANL, GN 2/2, Stark to Crowdy, 12 March 1838; PANL, GN 2/2, Stark to Crowdy, 15 March 1838.
[40]PANL, GN 2/2, Stark to Crowdy, 15 March 1838.
[41]PANL, GN 2/2, Stark to Crowdy, 15 March 1838.
[42]PANL, GN 2/2, Stark to Crowdy, 15 March 1838.
[43]PANL, GN 2/2, Stark to Crowdy, 16 March 1838.

of detection. In May 1834, a Harbour Grace merchant and planter, John Nuttall, was the victim of this form of plebeian attention. On 2 May, Nuttall received a letter advising him, "for his own good [to] drop the persecution of Michael Kief" (or Keefe), and allow him to assist his "starving Family Crying for Bread."[44] Four days later Nuttall found a less-conciliatory note wrapped around a stone thrown into his yard, "You persicuting in solvent Scounderelll... we will levell your wifes property... we put up with you to long... We are watching your movements... we will Make You Suffer For it...."[45]

The author or authors not only were offended by Kief's inability to relieve his starving family, but also by some undisclosed venture of Nuttall's to win a large amount of insurance money. After a third note warning of an impending arson attack, Nuttall's cooper came to him with the news that someone was trying to burn down his premises.[46] A hole in the side of his store suggested evidence of an incendiary's half-hearted attempt. The magistrate reporting the incident believed it was part of a plebeian conspiracy, and described it as one act in "a system of terror and alarm" instituted by "one side" of the population.[47]

The arson attempt at Nuttall's followed a similar attempt on the newly established cholera hospital in Harbour Grace. A European cholera outbreak in 1832 caused fear in New World ports almost immediately. Mobs gathered to oppose facilities to harbour cholera victims of the 1830s epidemic in Saint John, Quebec, and Niagara.[48] During epidemics in the next two decades, hospitals were destroyed by fire or vandalism by crowds in P.E.I., Saint John, Quebec City, and London, Ontario.[49] In Harbour Grace in 1834, a boat and crew were hired to operate a quarantine facility, and provisions were made for a cholera hospital. No sooner was the hospital established than someone broke one of its windows, and an arson attempt on the structure was discovered.[50] The community was dedicated to keeping the dreaded disease away from their town. By burning the cholera hospital, they hoped to force the infected victims to go elsewhere.

When cholera did hit Newfoundland in 1835, mass public opposition to the local sheltering of victims was immediate in Harbour Grace. When two people died of the disease, authorities claimed "we could not get possession of the house to

[44]PANL, GN 2/2, Harbour Grace Magistrates to Crowdy, 8 May 1834 (encl.). Michael Keefe was a fisherman who owed £35 to Nuttall. When he fell behind on his yearly £8 payment he was prosecuted and imprisoned. Peter J. Roberts, "The Harbour Grace Elections 1832-61," MA thesis, University of New Brunswick, 1969, 9. For a full text of the three notes sent to Nuttall, see Appendix A.

[45]PANL, GN 2/2, Harbour Grace Magistrates to Crowdy, 8 May 1834 (encl.).

[46]PANL, GN 2/2, Harbour Grace Magistrates to Crowdy, 8 May 1834 (encl.).

[47]PANL, GN 2/2, Stark to Crowdy, 12 May 1834.

[48]Geoffry Bilson, *A Darkened House: Cholera in Nineteenth Century Canada* (Toronto 1980), 111-12.

[49]Bilson, *Darkened House*, 111-12.

[50]PANL, GN 2/2, Parkin to Crowdy, 30 April 1834; PANL, GN 2/2, Parkin to Crowdy, 2 May 1834.

which we carried the stranger without the presence of soldiers, and now we hold it in fear of its being burnt down in the night."[51]

Maiming was a popular form of plebeian protest, often used on animals to prevent encroachment of livestock onto cultivated land. Maiming, especially in the form of ear cropping, also was used to deter humans from unpopular actions. In the spring of 1835 Henry Winton, outspoken editor of the leading Tory and anti-Catholic newspaper, the *Public Ledger*, fell victim to this ruthless sanction.

Winton was a well-known figure in Newfoundland who, through his aggressive journalism, had made many enemies, especially among Catholics. Several times he had been rewarded for his obnoxious editorials with notes and placards claiming the people "would set a mark upon him and have his life."[52] When a St. John's mob attacked his house on Christmas Day 1831, troops were needed to quell the crowd.[53]

On the afternoon of 19 May 1835, Winton was riding from Carbonear to Harbour Grace when he was ambushed at Saddle Hill by a small band of people with painted faces.[54] He was pelted with stones, knocked from his horse, and beaten about the head. Winton's attackers then filled his ears with mud and gravel, and used a clasp knife to cut several pieces from his right ear and sever the left one entirely. They then ran off into the woods, leaving their bloodied victim on the road to find his way to town as best he could.[55]

Support for this act was widespread among the plebeian population. The governor complained that it was "a matter of open triumph and rejoicing to the Catholics of low degree, even female servants and children expressing the greatest satisfaction."[56] Despite a reward-offer of £1,300, pardon for the accomplices, protection, and free passage out of the country, no one came forward with evidence against the perpetrators. No one was ever charged with the offence, and the reward remained unclaimed. Longstanding traditions of peasant violence provide against their own detection by imposing severe sanctions, often death, upon informers.[57] This element of popular culture well might have accounted for the reluctance of anyone to claim the reward despite the fact that half of the populations of Harbour Grace and Carbonear were Protestant, and supposedly Winton sympathizers.

This was not the end of the Winton affair. On 13 May 1840, five years after the incident involving Henry Winton, another man was ambushed on Saddle Hill

---

[51]Bilson, *Darkened House*, 136.

[52]Select Committee on Newfoundland, 1841, Capt. H. Geary, 99; *Public Ledger*, 2 June 1835.

[53]Select Committee on Newfoundland, 1841, R. Job, 56 and T. Cochrane, 10.

[54]Neither of the victims was certain about the number of assailants but the number five seems the most likely. PANL, GN 2/2, Harbour Grace Magistrates to Crowdy, 20 May 1835; PANL, GN 2/2, Stark to Crowdy, 19 May 1835.

[55]PANL, GN 2/2, Harbour Grace Magistrates to Crowdy, 20 May 1835, (encl.).

[56]CNS, CO 194 vol. 90, Prescott to Grant, 29 May 1835; See also PANL, GN 2/2, Brenton to Crowdy, 20 May 1835; Harbour Grace Magistrates' Letters, file #13, Danson and Buckingham to Simms, 2 June 1835.

[57]Lewis, *Local Disturbances*.

and had his ears cut off. Herman Lott worked as an overseer for Winton in his St. John's printing shop where the *Public Ledger* was published. Lott was travelling alone from Harbour Grace to Carbonear, and as he crossed Saddle Hill, four men with black crepe over their faces ran out of the woods.[58] The men knocked him down and dragged him into the woods. After a violent scuffle Lott was knocked out, and when he awoke he had been robbed of seven dollars and had portions of both ears cut off.[59]

The governor issued a proclamation offering a £300 reward for the capture of Lott's assailants as soon as he heard of the incident.[60] The magistrates examined as many witnesses as they could find in their attempt to discover the culprits. They found that on the day of the maiming, four men were seen running from Carbonear to Saddle Hill, two of them wearing hats painted green under the rim.[61]

The green hats were considered significant in light of the story publicized after the ear cropping. On 20 February 1840, Herman Lott had been abducted by a gang on the streets of St. John's, blindfolded, and taken to a room for questioning about Winton. Lott had little to say about Winton that his captors did not already know, but they issued a warning to Winton through Lott. They claimed that Winton had slandered the Irish in Newfoundland but that:

he and others like him would perhaps find out that there was a RIBBON SOCIETY in this country equally as terrible as ever it was in Ireland and that he (Mr. Winton) *would soon find his house too hot for him.*[62]

There was little doubt, at least among the authorities and the conservative press, that Lott's maiming was the result of a widespread Irish Catholic conspiracy.[63] In this case, as in Winton's, no one was approached for the crime.

The Winton and Lott maimings graphically illustrate the lengths to which the Irish Catholic community would go to avenge the insults hurled at it by the Tory press. Although substantial rewards were offered, no Catholic would break ranks to report the culprits, and no Protestant would risk revenge. To a great extent, people still associated themselves with their ethnic backgrounds and worked to maintain those ties.

Because there were strong feelings of loyalty toward religion and ethnicity, people could rally quickly and effectively when needed. Plebeian action, however, was in no way restricted to ethnic issues. The incidents of collective action examined above varied greatly in their form and purpose. Some dealt with issues

[58]PANL, GN 2/2, Habour Grace Magistrates to Crowdy, 15 May 1840, (encl.).
[59]*Carbonear Star*, 20 May 1840.
[60]PANL, GN 2/1/43, Crowdy to Danson, Power, and Stark, 18 May 1840.
[61]PANL, GN 2/2, Danson and Stark to Crowdy, 20 May 1840.
[62]*Public Ledger*, 22 May 1840.
[63]CNS, CO 194 vol. 108, Prescott to Russell, 22 May 1840; PANL, GN 2/2, Danson and Stark to Crowdy, 11 June 1840; *Times*, 27 May 1840; *Public Ledger*, 19 May 1840; *Public Ledger*, 22 May 1840.

that affected the whole community and others affected the lives of only a few. Those responsible ranged from the hundreds of people reportedly involved in the retrieval of Downing's body, to the individuals who committed token acts of protest against merchants. But what all these incidents had in common was an underlying appeal to a common idea of justice or plebeian rights. Through traditional plebeian methods of resistance, people could render the authorities impotent by non-cooperation. In this way there was a certain plebeian influence in social relations. The result was not anarchy (as the respectable community often feared) but rather the enforcement of a slightly different conception of what was just and what the duties of the authorities were.

II

Newfoundland elections provided a formal outlet for democratic expression, but this expression often assumed traditional plebeian forms. The wide franchise which allowed all male householders to vote after one year's residency helped interest the island's labouring population in politics. The form and content of electoral disturbances are significant, not only as a chapter in continuing plebeian resistance, but also in the way they demonstrate the balance between the formal institutions of the propertied classes, and the informal avenues open to working people. Although elections were held in Conception Bay in 1832, 1836, 1837, and 1840, only the election of 1836 and the by-election of 1840 were accompanied by popular disturbances.

Newfoundland had basically two political viewpoints which solidified into parties as the 1830s advanced. The Liberals were associated with the reformers, the Catholics, and the working men, while the Tories were associated with the Protestants and the old merchant élite.The Conservatives believed that the island should remain in the hands of the fish merchants, who had most to gain by the island's prosperity, and therefore were the most likely to govern well. The Liberal party, on the other hand, espoused the ideas of democracy, Catholic rights, and the development of various sectors of the economy.

In 1836 seven candidates ran to fill the four available seats. By the end of the election only the four Liberal candidates were still in the race and so were elected. When Robert Pack and James Power, the two most popular candidates, both declined the honour of standing for office, they were induced to run as representatives by more informal means. A contingent of 40 or 50 working-class men marched from Harbour Grace and Carbonear led by a "respectable" party of two priests, two merchants, and a publican.[64] The band marched to fife and drum music and carried banners through the streets to the homes of the men, and finding them, the crowd pressed them to stand as Liberal candidates in the election.[65] Both men

---

[64]*Public Ledger*, 1 November 1836; *Carbonear Sentinel*, 27 October 1836.
[65]*Public Ledger*, 1 November 1836.

addressed the crowd and agreed to the request this time.[66] The band, having been satisfied, paraded the lower street for some time and then dispersed.

Informal means were used to subtract names from the candidates' list as well as to add to it. On 2 November 1836, the *Carbonear Star* printed a notice from Thomas Newell, a Conservative candidate, declaring his withdrawal from the race due to an attack on his house. He did not describe the attack but claimed "The people of this Bay have no protection but the mighty arm of Him, who saved last night, my life and the life of my little ones."[67] After the polling began, the other two Conservative candidates, Ridley and Prowse, were also forced to withdraw because of violence.

The election was conducted by a roving poll which began in Harbour Grace on 1 November. On 31 October a large number of men and women met at Saddle Hill where they joined an "immense concourse" of people from Carbonear.[68] They marched into Harbour Grace with bands playing and, armed with sticks, paraded through the streets of the town, displaying their support for the Liberal candidates, or (according to some) intimidating the populace.[69] The following day, several hundred men, some carrying sticks and bludgeons, marched from Carbonear to escort Pack and Power to the Harbour Grace polls. They had signs and banners and one man, Roger Thomey, had a green ribbon around his hat and a green sash around his waist.[70] At the polls they met Thomas Ridley, a Tory candidate, and his supporters, who were planting their banners nearby. The Liberal supporters shouted "Down with the Tories" and, as Ridley's men answered with three cheers for the Tories, the Liberals attacked the small Tory band with their sticks. They rushed the voters, striking them, destroying flags, and dispersing them before they could vote. One man testified he was struck across the back of the neck, beaten on the head, knocked down and trampled upon. When he came to his senses, he was helped up by a shoemaker and told he should go home or he likely would be murdered, along with all others who supported the blue colours.[71] By one account, as many as 21 people were wounded.[72] Pack and Power, who had been inside the poll, returned to find the melee and were "greatly dismayed and entreated people to be peaceable."[73]

The tactics used to influence election results were not unusual. The parades, banners, bands (especially involving fifes and drums), and slogans were standard

[66]It was generally acknowledged that Pack and Power were in a coalition with the two other liberal candidates; Brown of Harbour Grace, and Godfrey of Brigus. PANL, GN 2/2, Harbour Grace Magistrates to Crowdy, 24 October 1836.

[67]*Carbonear Star*, 2 November 1836.

[68]CNS, CO 194 vol. 95, Prescott to Glenelg, 9 December 1836 (encl.).

[69]*Ibid*; CNS, CO 194 vol. 95, Prescott to Glenelg, 9 December 1836 (encl.); *Public Ledger*, 4 November 1836.

[70]CNS, CO 194 vol. 95, Prescott to Glenelg, 9 December 1836 (encl.).

[71]PANL, GN 2/2, Stark to Crowdy, 19 November 1836 (encl.).

[72]CNS, CO 194 vol. 95, Prescott to Glenelg, 9 December 1836 (encl.).

[73]PANL, GN 2/2, Court Report on King vs. Pack, Power, *et.al.*, February 1837.

political fare in Britain, and had become so in British North America. Assuming direct control of the hustings and forcing a desired candidate was the most logical, direct, and common way for those without power to exercise control over the political process.[74] When large numbers of people participated in a political event, they preferred to use informal rather than formal means to exert their powers.

There were numerous cries from the authorities about helplessness in and inability to keep the peace in these conditions,[75] but in this instance they at least were able to identify enough individuals to lay charges against eight people.[76]

The effectiveness of the plebeian society, its organization and independence, are once again made clear through the example of Roger Thomey. Thomey, a cooper employed by Robert Pack, was one of the men charged with riot and assault. A warrant was issued; the sheriff who set off for Carbonear to arrest him found him at Pack's stage. Not wanting to bring the prisoner back through town and risk a disturbance, the two men rowed across to the south side of the bay and disembarked at a wharf. They had only gone about 50 yards when a large mob of men rushed out of the neighbouring lanes, ready to attack with clubs and stones.[77] The men swore Thomey would not be taken, threw stones, and rescued him from the constables, though Thomey himself called out that he was willing to go. The scale and violence of the gathering increased and the sheriff found it impossible to retake the prisoner, and so returned to Harbour Grace without him. He claimed he had neither the manpower to take Thomey, nor the resources to keep him should a rescue be attempted.[78]

Attempts to save Thomey from prosecution continued. Shortly after his warrant had been issued, a threatening letter was thrown into Ridley's yard.[79] Ridley was advised to drop the prosecution and was threatened, "you will feel heavily the Malediction of the people/it will surely insense the publick against you." The note, written by 'a labourer,' claimed Danson was not acting in the public interest and thus, was not doing his duty as he should. The same charge was directed towards the other magistrates involved, and all were threatened with a public "reward."

The authorities felt powerless with a great proportion of the population of Carbonear being "in open opposition to the authority of the law."[80] Two men,

[74]For an example in early New Brunswick history, see Scott See, "Election Crowds and Social Violence: The Northumberland County, New Brunswick Campaigns of 1842-43," MA thesis, University of Maine, 1980.

[75]PANL, GN 2/2, Stabb to Garrett, 17 November 1836; CNS, CO 194 vol. 95, Prescott to Glenelg, 9 December 1836, (encl.).

[76]The men charged were Robert Pack, James Power, Roger Thomey, William Harding, William Saunders, Edward Haydon, John Meaney, and Andrew Quirk.

[77]PANL, GN 2/2, Sheriff's report, 14 November 1836.

[78]*Ibid.*; PANL, GN 2/2, Stabb to Garrett, 17 November 1836.

[79]CSN, CO 194 vol. 95, Prescott to Glenelg, 14 December 1836, (encl.). For complete text of the note see appendix B.

[80]CSN, CO 194 vol. 95, Prescott to Glenelg, 14 December 1836, (encl.). For complete text of the note see appendix B.

Simon Levi and Joseph Pippy, had sworn against Thomey and their names appeared in his warrant. On 15 November, a crowd which attacked Levi's house broke several windows and a door. Mr. and Mrs. Levi were not home, but a servant girl was knocked unconscious by a stone, and a minister felt he must rush in to protect the children.[81] The following night, about 100 men with blackened faces surrounded the house of Joseph Pippy in Mosquito.[82] They broke the windows and doors and then entered the house. They dragged Pippy's wife from her bed, threatened his brother with a blunderbuss, and demanded to see Joseph. He was discovered hiding under the stairs, beaten and made to promise to drop prosecution against Thomey. The men even required that Pippy obtain a statement from the magistrate to this effect, and produce it the following night when they returned.[83] Magistrate Stark reluctantly complied with Pippy's request for a retraction, but sent a constable to Pippy's to get a complaint about the outrage. Pippy had been completely intimidated and would not visit the magistrate again, nor did he want to be seen with a constable.[84]

Peter Edwards, who had also signed Thomey's warrant, likewise backed away from his statement. He was so frightened that he would be murdered along the road on his trip to St. John's that he begged the local priest to announce from the altar that he had given evidence against his will.[85]

These retractions were followed closely by a similar statement by Thomas Gosse, who had accused one Richard Lahey of assaulting him during the violence at the polls. Gosse made a second statement before the magistrates claiming that Lahey had never hit him but had, in fact, prevented an unknown assailant from continuing the attack.[86] The authorities were appalled at the situation in Harbour Grace and Carbonear, which they saw as a "reign of terror."[87] The law was no longer in their hands, but had been replaced by a system of rough justice dictated and executed by that ominous and amorphous entity, "the Mob."

Trial proceedings against the St. John's and Conception Bay election rioters were held in St. John's before a special jury.[88] Of the eight men charged with a variety of crimes, only Thomey and two other rioters, William Saunders and William Harding, were punished. All three received twelve-month sentences for

[81]CNS, CO 194 vol. 95, Prescott to Glenelg, 9 December 1836 (encl.).

[82]CNS, CO 194 vol. 95, Prescott to Glenelg, 9 December 1836 (encl.).

[83]CNS, CO 194 vol. 95, Prescott to Glenelg, 9 December 1836 (encl.).

[84]CNS, CO 194 vol. 95, Prescott to Glenelg, 9 December 1836 (encl.).

[85]Peter J. Roberts, "The Harbour Grace Elections 1832-61," MA thesis, University of New Brunswick, 1969, 42.

[86]CNS, CO 194 vol. 95, Prescott to Glenelg, 9 December 1836 (encl.).

[87]*Ibid.*; CNS, CO 194 vol. 95, Prescott to Glenelg, 14 December 1836 (encl.); *Carbonear Star*, 16 November 1836.

[88]Simultaneous elections in St. John's also were accompanied by riots and similar disturbances.

rioting, and Thomey also was fined £25 for assault.[89] When the personal petitions of the prisoners had no effect on altering these harsh sentences, a prominent liberal leader from St. John's petitioned on their behalf.[90] The Colonial Office was convinced that the sentences were excessively severe and the men were released.[91]

The trials illustrate the strength of the officially-constituted institutions of law, but also the strength of the informal plebeian methods of control in Newfoundland society. In the end it must be recognized that the law courts triumphed, and three rioters were sent to prison. On the other hand, there is evidence of a strong plebeian force. Through collective action with a combination of threat and violence, the rioters attempted to prevent the arrest and trial of a journeyman cooper who had acted violently in a crowd to ensure that a liberal candidate was returned at the polls. Colonial Office interference in sentencing indicates there was a feeling that moderation, if not tolerance, should be shown when dealing with popular disturbances.

In winter 1840, a by-election was held in Conception Bay to fill the seat of a deceased representative. Many of the tactics of 1836 recurred. This time the battle was between two dealers, Edward Hanrahan and James Prendergast. Both men were Catholics but sources vary on the differences between them. Some saw Hanrahan as a priests' candidate under the thumb of the church, and Prendergast as an independent Catholic.[92] Local priests were active in the election, joining in parades and preaching political sermons in support of Hanrahan.[93] The Tory press reported that the priests were the prime instigators in inciting the lowest and most ignorant portion of the population to violence in order to ensure Catholic hegemony.[94]

Throughout the election, there were parades and violence to prevent people from casting their votes. On the day of the largest riot, Carbonear polls opened as usual at ten o'clock, but around two o'clock, one side (it is not clear which) ran out of voters. When a boatload of voters arrived at the beach, a riot began in an attempt to prevent them from casting their ballots. A Hanrahan supporter was shot in the hand, men were beaten with pickets, and stones were thrown in the general melée.[95] While trying to contain the violence, Magistrate Ridley received a severe beating.[96] When the disturbance was reported, the returning officer closed the polls with

[89]*Royal Gazette*, 10 January 1837; CNS, CO 194 vol. 104, Prescott to Glenelg (draft), 8 October 1837.
[90]Roberts, "Harbour Grace Elections," 44.
[91]CNS, CO 194 vol. 97, Glenelg to Prescott, 31 May 1837.
[92]Roberts, "Harbour Grace Elections," 60.
[93]*Patriot*, 12 December 1840.
[94]*Public Ledger*, 15 November, 1 December, 8 December, 19 December, 29 December 1840.
[95]CNS, CO 194 vol. 109, Prescott to Russell, 10 December 1840, (encl.); CNS, CO 194 vol. 109, Prescott to Russell, 11 December 1841, (encl.); *Sentinel*, 31 December 1840; *Public Ledger*, 11 December 1840; *Public Ledger*, 15 December 1840; *Patriot*, 12 December 1840; *Times*, 16 December 1840; *Vindicator*, 16 January and 19 January 1841.
[96]There was a suggestion that the magistrate was more concerned with repressing the Hanrahan supporters than suppressing the riot in general. *Vindicator*, 9 January 1841.

Prendergast ahead. The election ultimately was declared invalid and the seat remained empty until the next election in 1842.

Once the brawl was over people continued to parade the streets of the town, intimidating opponents and breaking windows.[97] That evening, an angry mob burnt to the ground a Carbonear house owned by one Ash, a Carbonear planter.[98] Although Ash was a cousin to Hanrahan's wife he had voted for Prendergast. Not only had Ash voted for the wrong side, but he had betrayed his own people.[99] A second arson partially burnt the house of a poor man who voted for Prendergast, and then implicated many Hanrahan supporters concerned with the hustings riots.[100]

Night visits were used as a means of retribution against those who had withheld support from Hanrahan. A young schoolmaster named Talbot was dragged from his bed at midnight by three men who beat him with pickets and left him unconscious. Another individual took advantage of the growing reputation of Saddle Hill as a place of plebeian strength to threaten a magistrate's son, when late in December, a man rushed out of the woods there and brandished a stick above the head of Dr. Stirling's boy as an act of defiance against the law.[101]

Such actions had their echo in reports of district cattle-maiming. Three men of the Taylor family, important merchants in Carbonear, were approached by friends of several arrested men to become sureties for their appearance in court. Each man refused to stand up for the rioters and as a result had an animal maimed.[102] In January, John Taylor's horse was lamed by a hatchet wound below its foreknee. In mid-February, Joseph Taylor's horse suffered a large hatchet slash across the back and Richard Taylor's cow received a deep wound on the rump. The planter, Henry Watts, also reported that his cow had been hacked in the thigh later that month.[103] The magistrates promised to make inquiries, but were not surprised by the events and expected more to follow, "owing to the state of the community" in Carbonear.[104]

By mid-February 1841, the magistrates had heard rumours that a blacksmith from the North Shore was making and distributing pikeheads.[105] Although the rumour was not substantiated, it was significant in that it demonstrated the continuing fear of popular revolt among the respectable classes and the continuing tradition

[97]PANL, GN 2/2, Power, Pack, and Pack to Crowdy, 9 December 1840; *Carbonear Star*, 12 December 1840.
[98]*Star*, 12 December 1840; *Star*, 13 February 1841.
[99]*Star*, 13 February 1841; *Star*, 12 December 1840.
[100]PANL, GN 2/2, Harbour Grace Magistrates to Crowdy, 14 December 1840; PANL, GN 2/2, Emerson to Crowdy, 17 December 1840.
[101]PANL, GN 2/2, Harbour Grace Magistrates to Crowdy, 2 January 1841.
[102]PANL, GN 2/2, Danson and Stark to Crowdy, 18 March 1841 (encl.).
[103]PANL, GN 2/2, Danson and Stark to Crowdy, 18 March 1841 (encl.).
[104]PANL, GN 2/2, Danson and Stark to Crowdy, 18 March 1841.
[105]PANL, GN 2/2, Danson and Stark to Crowdy, 20 February 1841.

of Irish rebellion methods.[106] The pike was a weapon synonymous with Irish violence, having become a symbol of the rebellion of 1798. The manufacturing of pikes subsequently was outlawed in Britain.

The magistrates were appalled both by the disorder and their inability to control the situation. They requested troops and were persistent enough to get them. Once the 100 troops arrived at Carbonear and Harbour Grace, the disturbances ended and the magistrates began to search for the ringleaders. Many warrants were issued for those believed to have been involved in the election disturbances. While some were arrested, the pursuit continued for many more. Resistance to prosecution for election offenses continued quietly and the authorities saw law and order being undermined at every turn. The magistrates reported:

we are thoroughly convinced that threats, intimidation, and other unlawful devices will be resorted to by the friends of the guilty to prevent Witnesses and Jurors honestly and independently doing their duty...[107]

The silence of potential witnesses, some broken windows, and a threatening note were among the evidence which supported the magistrates' suspicions.[108] A 14-year-old boy had been slated to testify against a suspected rioter, but changed his mind after receiving an anonymous note promising, "ye Protestant buggars ... will not escape much longer."[109]

The election disturbances of 1836 and 1840 are both important in their political ramifications, namely the development of the liberal party and the direction of the government of the island. This is not their primary importance, however, for the purposes of this paper. The elections provided a framework and an opportunity for increased plebeian input into the workings of the society. The plebeians displayed cohesion among sectors of the working class population, continuity of the traditions of plebeian protest, and suggested some lines of allegiance which existed in the communities.

As in the other instances of collective action, the people demonstrated that groups within the society could recognize common goals, communicate them to others, and work effectively towards those goals. The methods they used were well established in the British plebeian tradition and their symbols were easily recognizable. They were quite, although not totally, effective in enforcing a conspiracy of silence aimed at incapacitating the law courts. Although a few men were convicted in connection with incidents during both elections, plebeian efforts to enforce the popular will through informal channels were extensive and impressive.

[106]PANL, GN 2/2, Danson and Stark to Crowdy, 18 March 1841.
[107]PANL, GN 2/2, Danson and Stark to Crowdy, 22 March 1841.
[108]PANL, GN 2/2, Harbour Grace Magistrates to Crowdy, 9 May 1841; CNS, CO 194 vol. 112, Law to Russell, 10 June 1841, (encl.).
[109]PANL, GN 2/2, Harbour Grace Magistrates to Crowdy, 9 May 1841 (encl.). For full text of the note, see appendix C.

III

In 1832, the fishermen of Carbonear and Harbour Grace staged a strike to protest the manner in which the seal fishery operated. The strike was noteworthy for the large numbers of people involved, and the cohesion displayed by the sealers. Whereas political, religious, and local divisions were stressed in the collective actions examined above, the strike demonstrates that these social divisions could be overcome. It is in 1832 that we see the strongest evidence of the class loyalties which existed in Harbour Grace and Carbonear in the 1830s.

The seal fishery was a growing industry at the beginning of the decade. Despite the short, six-week season, a fisherman could expect to make one-third of his yearly income from a good sealing voyage. The merchant's role in the seal fishery was similar to the part he played in the cod fishery, in that he outfitted men in return for the product. Economically, however, there was an important structural difference. Cash, rather than credit notes, historically had been used for at least partial wage payment in the seal fishery. Because the seal fishery held out this promise of potential cash, truck payment and tied sales were a grievance which could be easily identified and articulated. The seal fishery operated on a relatively short-term, high-pressure, and high-profit basis in comparison to the cod fishery. The fishermen were in a stronger position because of the greater demand for their labour, and the higher value of their product.

The seal fishery held a unique position in the social and economic fabric of Conception Bay. Socially, the seal fishery helped expose a more rigid and definite class structure than was evident at any other time of the year. While the complex social structure of the communities persisted, work relationships for the three months of the seal fishery were comparatively straightforward. Each sealing vessel required a supplier, a master, and a crew of sealers. Labour and management were distinct. Whereas in the cod fishery men could hold a variety of positions in relation to their merchants and their means of production, these same men were all in the same "class" in the seal fishery. In addition, men from settlements all over Conception Bay gathered in Brigus, Harbour Grace, and Carbonear to sign onto their ships. They were brought together geographically during sealing to a much greater extent than in the cod fishery.

The sealers' strike began peacefully when, on 5 January 1832, a notice was posted in the towns of Carbonear and Harbour Grace announcing that a meeting of the fishermen and sharemen of Carbonear would be held on 9 January "... fore the purpose of taking into consideration the best and most effectual method of getting clear of truck."[110] The fishermen of Harbour Grace were requested to join the struggle to "shake off the yoke they have so long and unjustly (tho' patiently)

[110]PANL, GN 2/2, Harbour Grace Magistrates to Crowdy, 21 January 1832 (encl.). Notice #1 is reprinted in appendix D.

borne."[111] The notices were written in neat, legible hand, and clear, fairly elaborate sentences. No threats, challenges, or insults were included, but rather the notice had a very official air. The meeting was to take place on Saddle Hill, which was half way between Carbonear and Harbour Grace. On the morning of the ninth, 2,000 to 3,000 men marched with fife and drums to the hill where they discussed the issue, and parted peacefully. The hill was christened "Liberty Hill" in honour of the occasion.[112] "Liberty" was a familiar watchword applied to many major democratic movements in Europe in the 18th and 19th centuries. All agreed they should receive cash rather than goods in payment for seals, and that half the amount due was to be paid on the delivery of the seals and the other half given in cash on 10 November.[113]

On 4 February a second notice was posted around the two towns calling for another Saddle Hill meeting on 9 February.[114] This notice addressed not only fishermen, but sealing masters, too, who were called to produce the agreements they held with their crews. The second notice was equally well-written, but the content was less conciliatory. Masters were summoned by name to appear. Any who did not attend were to be "delt with according to a resolution that will be entered into at that meeting and will afterwards undoubtedly be acted upon."[115]

On the appointed day, the men and some of the masters met on the hill. The meeting was systematic and orderly. Masters were called by name to present their agreements or the agreements of their merchant. The agreement was either accepted by the cheering crowd, or if unacceptable, torn up.[116]

Many, but not all, mercantile firms were represented at the meeting. The merchants either accepted or ignored fishermen's demands as they saw fit. It was only after an open attack on the property of Thomas Ridley, an important merchant of Harbour Grace, that the fishermen attracted the interest of the merchant and governing classes and the press. In the early hours of the morning of 18 February, more than 200 men armed with saws and hatchets boarded Ridley's vessel, *Perseverance*, which was lying at the wharf. They cut the masts, rigging, yards, and gaffs, causing damage estimated at £120. The ship's mate was forced back below deck and threatened by several men with guns when he tried to interfere.[117]

[111]PANL, GN 2/2, Harbour Grace Magistrates to Crowdy, 21 January 1832 (encl.). Notice #1 is reprinted in appendix D.

[112]Cochrane Papers, reel II, Stark to Cochrane, 24 February 1832.

[113]PANL, GN 2/2, Harbour Grace Magistrates to Crowdy, 28 February 1832. Statement of Thomas Dunford (encl.).

[114]PANL, GN 2/2, Harbour Grace Magistrates to Crowdy, 18 February 1832 (encl.). Notice #2 is reprinted in appendix D.

[115]PANL, GN 2/2, Harbour Grace Magistrates to Crowdy, 18 February 1932 (encl.). Notice #2 is reprinted in appendix D.

[116]PANL, GN 2/2, Harbour Grace Magistrates to Crowdy, 28 February 1832. Statement of Thomas Dunford (encl.).

[117]PANL, GN 2/2, Harbour Grace Magistrates to Crowdy, 18 February 1832. Statement of William Ewan (encl.).

Reaction to the fishermen's attack was swift and strongly worded on the part of the magistrates and merchants. The magistrates immediately notified the governor, stating that life and property might be in danger.[118] They feared the systematic organization which had resulted in "notices and threats against lives and property of those not complying with their views respecting the abolition of the barter system."[119] The governor issued a proclamation against the sealers, declaring the Saddle Hill meetings illegal; a reward of £100 was offered to anyone who would give information about the destruction of Ridley's ship, with pardon offered to informers.[120]

Constables were sent from St. John's to post the governor's proclamations in prominent places at various mercantile establishments. Within two hours all the proclamations had been torn down. Even the copy on a board by the Harbour Grace court house was broken to pieces.[121] The notices were replaced, in some cases, by another placard from the Carbonear fishermen, similar to its predecessors in style and form but cockier in tone. The uncooperative were advised to be more compliant lest they receive "what will not be agreeable from the Carbonear Men."[122]

The sealers' notice itself was removed by the authorities, and replaced by the governor's proclamations, which was immediately torn down again in turn. This defiance of governmental authority among the fishermen produced great tension in the towns. The magistrates' letters to St. John's began to take on a desperate air. One letter claimed that the merchants, "aware of their defenseless situation, felt themselves under the necessity of complying with [the sealers'] requisitions."[123]

The fishermen were careful in selecting their targets. They attacked only those who they felt were interfering with their progress. A planter named Nichole was met by three men with a pistol, a large stick, and a scythe but was released when they discovered he was not the man they were after. Seven men with blackened faces visited the home of a ship's master where a member of the household was suspected of being untrue to the cause. Amidst a great commotion the traitor was dragged from his bed and beaten.[124] A man living near Saddle Hill who claimed to know some of the ringleaders was visited during the night by more than 100 armed men and was only saved from shooting by his wife's pleading.[125] Another man, who had intended to identify the vandals on Ridley's ship, suddenly withdrew his offer of information and claimed to know nothing about the incident.[126]

[118]PANL, GN 2/2, Harbour Grace Magistrates to Crowdy, 18 February 1832.

[119]PANL, GN 2/2, Harbour Grace Magistrates to Crowdy, 18 February 1832.

[120]Governor's Proclamation, 22 February 1832. (See *Royal Gazette*, 28 February 1832.)

[121]PANL, GN 2/2, Harbour Grace Magistrates to Crowdy, 4 March 1832.

[122]PANL, GN 2/2, Harbour Grace Magistrates to Crowdy, 28 February 1832 (encl.). Notice #3 is reprinted in appendix D.

[123]PANL, GN 2/2, Harbour Grace Magistrates to Crowdy, 23 February 1832.

[124]*Public Ledger*, 13 March 1832.

[125]*Public Ledger*, 13 March 1832.

[126]PANL, GN 2/2, Harbour Grace Magistrates to Crowdy, 27 February 1832. Statement of John Stevenson (encl.). Statement of Stephen Smallcomb (encl.).

On 1 March a fourth and final notice from the men was posted, designating 3 March as deadline for settling the agreements and "all masters of vessels (were) requested to have two sides to their agreements one part to be held by the Crew and the other themselves."[127]

The magistrates prepared for the 3 March meeting by mustering more than 100 special constables in each town.[128] Guards were positioned in both Carbonear and Harbour Grace, and by Saddle Hill to inform the magistrates of any assemblage. When men began to gather at the Harbour Grace wharf, the magistrates, deputy sheriff, police, and eight specials went to town and found 500-600 men at William Innott's pier.[129] When magistrates' orders to disperse had no effect, the Chief Magistrate read the Riot Act. This had only a momentary effect as the men departed to rally again at Thomas Ridley's wharf. The magistrates and their entourage arrived at this gathering as one man was tearing up an agreement and another was being called upon to read a second agreement. The magistrate demanded the reader hand the agreement over to him, which the fisherman did despite "repeated calls and threats from those about him as well as the risk of personal violence."[130] Once the magistrate had the agreement he was quite at a loss as to what he should do with it, and finding himself the centre of attention in what seemed to him a hostile crowd, he gave up the paper and claimed to the governor that "the noise, uproar, and numbers made any attempt to stop them after this futile."[131] The men paraded through the streets stopping opposite each merchant house in turn to read their agreements, and on finding each one satisfactory, cheered and moved on. The men continued peacefully until they had visited all the merchants, whereupon they dispersed.

Three days later, the sealers repeated the parade procedure in Carbonear. This time the magistrates knew better than to interfere. The procession went smoothly with the exception of a disturbance at the quay of Best & Waterman. Waterman's agreement was not satisfactory, but despite this, sealers had signed on and boarded two of his vessels. Approximately 200 strikers went to the schooners and commanded these men to go ashore. All complied except three or four on the *Morning Star*. These men were dragged off the vessel and one man, Thomas Scalon (or Scanlon), was severely beaten with sticks and sealing gaffs. When John Snook, the master of the vessel, arrived and objected to the violence he was threatened with similar treatment. At Waterman's premises a crowd of more than 1000 demanded a new agreement from him, and threatened to cut the masts of the *Morning Star* if

[127]PANL, GN 2/2, Harbour Grace Magistrates to Crowdy, 4 March 1832 (encl.).

[128]The magistrates did not appear to have had great difficulty recruiting constables, although they promised to send the governor the names of two or three who contemptuously refused oaths. (These names do not appear in later records.) A number of merchants from both towns voluntarily stepped forward to serve. PANL, GN 2/2, Harbour Grace Magistrates to Crowdy, 4 March 1832.

[129]PANL, GN 2/2, Magistrates to Crowdy, 4 March 1832.

[130]PANL, GN 2/2, Magistrates to Crowdy, 4 March 1832.

[131]PANL, GN 2/2, Magistrates to Crowdy, 4 March 1832.

he did not comply. Out of fear he drafted and posted a new agreement which was found to be acceptable.[132]

In the final parades, the sealers managed to settle with all the merchants and they now prepared to leave for the ice. By 14 March all but three sealing vessels had sailed and peace was restored.

In 1832 Conception Bay conditions were right for a strike. Sealing was an expanding industry; the demand for labour was high, and the markets for seal oil expanding. The industry was generating extra cash in the economy and the sealers were in a sufficiently strong position to demand some of that cash. The nature of the seal fishery as an intense, high-pressure, short-term, high-profit pursuit made it conducive to such a protest. The simple class organization of sealers, masters, and merchants, and the close physical proximity of those involved, encouraged the development of class cohesion and facilitated collective action among the plebeians. The relative poverty and precarious existence of most Newfoundland fishermen and the lure of cash profits clarified the sealers' real grievances. In this industry a simpler opposition of capital and labour occurred, unlike the cod fishery, in which personal ties, a divided workforce, and varying individual circumstances complicated the picture.

The people of Harbour Grace and Carbonear were able to conduct a powerful strike because they had developed both the requisite social cohesion and the sophistication to understand their interests and advantages. The understanding of the plebeian population can be seen through their mass participation, the methods used, and the general level of consciousness displayed. Attendance at the Saddle Hill meetings was very high. Estimates of participation vary from more than 1000 to 4000 persons, but it is obvious that most fishermen were involved, as the combined number of men in Carbonear and Harbour Grace between the ages of 16 and 60 was approximately 1800 in 1836.[133] Even the lowest attendance estimates of 1000 to 2000 indicate that a large percentage of the active fishermen were present from the two major towns, and possibly from surrounding settlements.

The methods of protest used were those common to plebeian disturbances in England and Ireland. The sealers posted anonymous notes and used violence selectively and collectively, playing on their strengths and avoiding the more middle-class modes of protest such as petitions or litigation.

Probably the most important feature of any grassroots movement is the level of consciousness demonstrated by the protesters. The sealers' strike illustrated extensive popular awareness. The solidarity of the sealers is the most obvious and impressive display of their community cohesiveness. The sealers' strongest weapons were their numbers and their anonymity, two factors reliant on strong solidarity. No one was brought to trial in connection with any incident arising out of the seal strike, as none could be apprehended. Enquiries disclosed few clues as to who the

---

[132]PANL, GN 2/2, Harbour Grace Magistrates to Crowdy, 7 March 1832. Statement of William Waterman (encl.).
[133]Census, 1836.

ringleaders, or even the participants, were. Harbour Grace and Carbonear each had populations near 4000, and sealing brought in men from neighbouring settlements, so it is certainly plausible that a participating sealer would have seen many people whose names he did not know. On the other hand, it hardly was possible for anyone at the meetings to know no one present. Yet, the enquiries of the magistrates and the constables yielded very little. It is particularly strange that no one who attended the Saddle Hill meetings could (or would) identify any of the men who read out agreements. Although the data are somewhat tenuous, estimates of even the most basic literacy skills run around 25 per cent for that time.[134] Surely the few fishermen competent enough to read aloud sealing agreements would have been easily identified by the fishing population. If the constables made any reasonable effort to find those involved, there was a strong conspiracy of silence among the sealers. When the governor had the proclamation posted, he offered a reward of £100 and pardon to anyone who would point out a leader, but no one came forward to claim the reward. In order to maintain solidarity, the sealers required each merchant to present his agreement before the entire crowd of men, rather than attempt to make individual contracts. Breaches of the law were committed in gangs, whose members were thus using their numbers and anonymity to the best advantage.

While the men could not have been successful unless their solidarity was for the most part voluntary, there is also the suggestion that compliance was forced in some cases. The reports of the night visits illustrate this. A fisherman was attacked for being suspected of being untrue to the cause. Another man received a visit when he threatened to report the names of those who instigated the Saddle Hill meetings. The witness to the vandalism on Ridley's ship suddenly reversed his position and would not name names. A planter accosted on the road would not point out his assailant to the magistrates. Probably the best example of forced solidarity was the incident at the Best & Waterman wharf. The men who had boarded their ship while there were outstanding agreements to be ratified were chased away, and those who resisted were attacked. The extensive solidarity (both spontaneous and forced) demonstrated during the strike testifies to the strong cohesion among the plebeian population and to a fairly elevated level of consciousness.

The strike was highly organized and had very successful communication lines despite a divided community. The message put forward by organizers was obviously one readily understood, agreed upon, and passed on by the sealers. The local, ethnic, religious, educational, and social divisions did not interfere with the goals and actions of the conflict. Besides pointing out the efficiency of informal communication networks, the apparent mass agreement of the grievances and desired ends illustrate a fairly homogeneous understanding and a basic level of class consciousness. The sealers focused their antagonism on merchants and planters. They understood who was working in their interest and who was on the other side. While

[134]David Alexander, "Literacy and Economic Development in Nineteenth Century Newfoundland," in David Alexander, *Atlantic Canada in Confederation*, Eric Sager, Lewis Fischer, and Stuart Pierson, eds., (Toronto 1983), 118.

some merchants and planters were conciliatory and the sealers did not treat all merchants with hostility, they were firm in their demands with all. While all sealers did not necessarily recognize their position in relation to their superiors as inimical or necessarily conflictual, they did recognize their own interests and were prepared to force the merchant to make concessions.

The sealers' strike was a progressive movement in the sense that the sealers were demanding concessions rather than resisting encroachments on previously existing benefits. Exactly how much cash had been given and how widespread the idea of free sale was before 1832 is unknown. It is clear that in 1832 the sealers were either demanding new benefits or more of the old ones. Sealing only recently had become an important industry in Newfoundland, and so customs regarding the operation of the industry had yet to be established. The strike was one event in the ongoing struggle to establish customary rights which would protect the interests of the plebeians. This protest demonstrates that the plebeian population was an active force, not simply reacting to stimuli presented by the ruling class, but working to forge a decent place for themselves in society. In the dynamic economic environment in Conception Bay the plebeians strove to influence their own positions.

Because of the uncommon success of this protest, it is easy to overstate the level of the consciousness of the sealers. It must be remembered that this was an isolated incident in the routine of labour. The protest was not repeated regularly or expanded. Most importantly, the cod fishery was run entirely on the truck system and no concerted effort was made to oppose these abuses. The cod fishery was mentioned in the first sealers' notice, but never after that. The sealers were successful, but this success was never used to improve the conditions of the fisherman on a large scale. The cohesion attained in the seal fishery was not sufficient to be expanded to the working class in general, but only to operate within the specific, particularly conducive circumstances of sealing.

Although the strike was primarily a plebeian movement, it received some support from the higher levels of society and this may have contributed to its success. Some merchants and members of the middle class appear to have given tacit support to the sealers. Although it is not impossible that the four anonymous notes were composed and written by a sealer, the low literacy rate and the fine composition and penmanship of the notes would suggest otherwise. The sealers received local support in editorial letters to the *Conception Bay Mercury*. James Prendergast, a dealer, refused to have a governor's proclamation posted on his store, and his campaign as a liberal candidate in 1840 suggests some sympathy with the fishermen. Clerks, publicans, and especially sealing captains, could have identified individual strikers to the constables but no one did. Of course, lack of opposition does not necessarily imply support or even sympathy. There is a question of the practicality of active opposition in such a movement. There was little chance of military support as the governor was reluctant to spare even six St. John's constables to help out.[135] The lockup in Harbour Grace was incapable of holding any sizeable number of people, and there was the real threat of violent, open retaliation against anyone who interfered with the strikers.

Although some masters and merchants complied with the sealers because they had no choice, it appears that some supported the cause. The merchants were in a difficult position in Carbonear and Harbour Grace in that there was a degree of competition among them. The cod fishery was the most important economic pursuit and thus it was most important that merchants kept control over their own fishermen. With the great surge in the prosperity of the seal fishery at the beginning of the 1830s, the fishermen demanded fairer remuneration. If all the merchants could agree not to give anything extra to the sealers, then the united front would be successful. If, however, one merchant was willing to make concessions, the others stood to lose not only their sealers, but also their cod fishermen. A merchant who gave in to the sealers stood to gain in popularity as well as in the security of his workforce. A merchant could be seen to be supporting the industrious fisherman in his fight for justice, and by paying cash, he could encourage him to save and to strive to get ahead. The demands of the sealers were restricted enough not to undermine the real power of the merchants or threaten the status quo in any significant way. Merchant Robert Pack of the major firm Fryer, Gosse & Pack gave in to the sealers' demands immediately and gladly, and he was followed promptly by a number of other merchants. Once the sealers' demands were accepted by some, others had little choice but to follow suit. Ultimately all merchants gave in, although some, like Thomas Ridley and William Waterman, did so under duress.

It is difficult to ascertain the extent of middle- and merchant-class support, as opposition also existed and appears much more prominent and vocal. The two magistrates who wrote most of the correspondence to the governor, Danson and Buckingham, greatly feared the mass of sealers. They were afraid of anarchy, mob violence, and riot. The panic-stricken reports of these two individuals provide the most prominent source of information about the unfolding events. The surviving newspaper data also favour the reactionary position, stressing the lawlessness of the populace and the atrocities committed.

Sealing was a profitable industry in Conception Bay in the first half of the 19th century, and one which offered an environment conducive to collective action by the workers. The class structure, in terms of work relationships, was simpler in the seal fishery than in the cod fishery as men of varying positions fell into the three classifications of sealer, master, or merchant. The strike was a success, primarily due to the cohesion and dedication of the sealers of Carbonear and Harbour Grace, and perhaps to the support they received from the liberal-minded members of the middle class. Opposition to the men was disunited and relatively weak. The 1832 strike is a rare opportunity to view the people of 19th-century Conception Bay acting in class ways. The sealers were able to overcome social and cultural divisions to further their collective interests. They attempted to deal with the ships' masters

[135]PANL, GN 2/1/41, Crowdy to Harbour Grace Magistrates, 22 February 1832.

whenever possible, asking them to present agreements and using them as targets
for intimidation and threats. In this way they minimized their contact with the
merchants whom they preferred to keep distant. Through a mixture of traditional
methods and more progressive demands and ideas, the sealers succeeded in increasing their control of the limited cash flow within the local economy.

IV

The extent of collective action during the decade is testimony to the organization
which existed among the plebeian population. Lines of organization, communication, and mobilization were well developed, with ethno-religious, local, and class
loyalties being the basis of plebeian action. The people had similar conceptions of
what was just in society, what was to be considered acceptable and what was not.
Plebeian standards were dynamic rather than static, which meant that the population
could be mobilized to achieve rights which had not existed previously in Newfoundland, to increase plebeian input, to establish customs, and to create traditions.

People variously mobilized to defend their identity as in the case of Winton's
maiming, their religious pride as in the burial and disinterment of Moxley's body,
their common sensibilities as in the rescuing of the gibbeted corpse, and their class
as in the sealers' strike. Different situations brought different loyalites to the fore.
The ethno-religious divisions in Conception Bay society were great, but the loyalties which formed along the lines of these divisions could and did aid community
organization. The sealers' strike demonstrated that, when called upon, the plebeian
population was able to overcome the deep divisions in society and act together in
their class interest.

When acting in concert, the plebeian population was successful in influencing
the workings of their society. They used the symbols, rituals, and methods of
plebeian resistance from Europe, transplanting the whole tradition to Newfoundland. The fishermen of Harbour Grace and Carbonear were not the silent, pliable
workforce which often has been portrayed. The plebeian population was vibrant
and active, attempting to influence their environment to their advantage through
their own actions, by their own means, and according to their own standards.

Appendix A

Three anonymous notes sent to Nuttall

South end, Harbour Grace, May 1, 1834
Sir —
I mearly advise you and request you will *take it* for your own good and drop the persication of Michael Kief he is long a nuf deprived from assisting a starving *family* Crying for Bread You should of taken the advise of the partner of your bosom and let him out You may i dare Say find use a nuf for the Six (pence a day)? that you are throwing away Recolect you have a family of your own which i hope will never feel the same misfortunes or the want of common nourishment as they do i tell you the Publick Voice is against you crying *Shame* i hope you will consider over this as it is my wish for your own good or _____
i am yours truly _____a Friend

Nuttall
You Persicuting in *solvent* Scounderell let the Poor Man oute of Prison to relive his family that is starving _____or we will level your wifes propperty _____ this will be done before Saturday Night, we put up with you to long_____and you shant consume us a gain to get £2500____ in Surance_____We are watching your movements_____we No well what you got this amount_____in Surd for _____take this as a Warning if Not we will Make You Suffer For it

Guirls beware and take care / for this night we mane to take your masters life / so disapare / The family need not fear / Mr. Chancy come from Carbonear / and take his sister home, / for she is not no longer Nuttall's Wife i own / Margaret Chandler and Elen Shay / be ware and take care / for this night We Mane to take your Masters life / so disapare

Appendix B

Note sent to Thomas Ridley

Thomas Ridley Esq[r]

Understanding that you are taking steps to the persecution of some few individuals. in the event of any process so as to lead to the conviction of any person or persons as a friend I advise you to discontinue those proceedings, otherwise you will feel heavily the Maladiction of the people it will surely insense the publick against you
they waited on you and you treated them with contempt they took you by the hand and you dispised them know then if you do not take an advise from a friend then you will certainly Rue the Day on which you appeared on the hustings. You may charge all your disappoint-ments to a few of your Bosom friends namely Stark Mayne and a few others so I beg you will desist I fear these two persons will be amply Rewarded
a Labourer

Appendix C

Note Sent to a Potential Court Witness

Notice
Mrs. Jackman
If you allows your Son to swear against Kily mark
the consequence ye Protestant Buggars
depend on it it shall be a damnd sore swear for him
for his life we will depend the young scoundrell
and you as bad as him to allow it he will not escape much longer

Appendix D

Three Notices Posted by the Striking Sealers

Notice
A Meeting of the fishermen and sharemen of Carbonear will take place on Saddle Hill next Monday the ninth day of January at half past eleven o'clock in the forenoon fore the purpose of taking into consideration the best and most effectual method of getting clear of truck the ensuing spring the fishermen of Harbour Grace are earnestly requested to co-operate with their Carbonear Brethern in this truly worthy and momentous affair — and shew by their compliance that they are both willing and able to shake off the yoke they have so long and unjustly (tho' patiently) borne
Carbonear January the fifth 1832

Notice
Is hereby given that the fishermen of Carbonear and Harbour Grace are requested to meet on Saddle Hill on thursday next the ninth day of February at 11 o'clock. All Masters of vessels bound on a sealing voyage are hereby required to be in attendence and to produce their several agreements with their crews to the Meeting Any person or persons who do not comply with this Requisition Shall be dealt with according to a Resolution that will be entered into at that meeting and will afterwards Undoubtably be acted upon

Harbour Grace 4th february 1832

Since we last advertised we find that our instructions were adhered to tho we have been told unwillingly by the Willy Scot and his cunning colleague they it seems doubted its authenticity and we hope they do not request practical proofs - we have also had a peep at the St. John's newspaper and are very much obliged to the agents of the Express packet for the praise he so very liberally bestows upon us - it is not unknown to us how secretly they dispatched the Express to St. John's and the intended combination about to be entered into to reduce the price of seals we trust the understrapping in a certain Mercantile Establishment will find other employment than traducing us and shewing how finely they can write a newspaper of quality
    Otherwise they shall have what
    will not be agreeable from
                                        the Carbonear Men

T.W. Acheson

3

Bone and Sinew: The Artisans and the Social Order

If merchants and merchant leaders were able to dominate the community agenda, particularly before 1840, the opposition to this domination came not from the manual labourers dependent on their system but from the producers' interest. That interest bound together a number of status groups, ranging from apprentice artisans to shopkeepers to established small manufacturers, led by a petite bourgeoisie of small masters. It is an interest that Michael Katz described as a class in his early work on mid-nineteenth-century Hamilton; in his later study of Hamilton and Buffalo he argued that the journeymen and masters were members of competing classes.[1] Other historians have been more tentative in judgement. All agree that an

[1] See M.B. Katz, *The People of Hamilton, Canada West* (Cambridge, Mass. 1975), 27, 311, and with M.J. Doucet and M.J. Stern, *The Social Organization of Early Industrial Capitalism* (Cambridge, Mass. 1982), ch. 1. In his second work, Katz argues that all nineteenth-century urban societies were divided into a business class and a working class and these corresponded to those who owned the means of production and those who sold their labour in return for money. Membership in the class, then, has nothing to do with class consciousness or class awareness; one is a member of a class because of one's relationship to the means of production. It is difficult to quarrel with any objective statement of classification. However, Katz destroys the objectivity of his model by insisting that the business class contains not only "those individuals who owned the means of production" but also "those whose interests and aspirations identified them with the owners" (44). Using this definition Katz assigns entire categories of men to the business class: all professionals and even the meanest clerk or school teacher become a capitalist. It is not improbable that a majority of members of the business class did not own the means of production unless it is defined in terms of skills or hand tools. Leaving aside the question of how the historian measures the aspirations of each member of a society — a concept that, in any event, seems very akin to class consciousness — why does Katz assume that no artisan or labourer possessed any aspiration to become a proprietor or at least to better his material lot in life? And if that possibility is admitted, is it possible to assign artisans en masse to the working class?

Published with permission of University of Toronto Press, from T.W. Acheson, *Saint John: The Making of a Colonial Urban Community* (Toronto 1985), 67-91.

artisanal interest existed in the eighteenth century and that it was gradually eroded in the face of nineteenth-century industrialism. In her study of nineteenth-century Newark, Susan Hirsch argues that artisan deference to the merchant élite had waned by the time of the American Revolution and that a significant artisanal system in which most journeymen were able to become masters by the time they were forty flourished until at least 1830. A similar community of interest among Kingston artisans is described by Bryan Palmer.[2] British studies suggest that even in the late nineteenth century the aristocracy of labour and a petite bourgeoisie of small proprietors remained closely linked.[3] The experience of the artisan group in Saint John demonstrates that it was not just an economic interest but a politically self-conscious social group.

Tentative and episodic evidence abounds for class perceptions on the part of those occupying the lower and middling social strata within Saint John society. The late eighteenth-century debate between residents of the Upper and Lower Coves in the city, which erupted into near violence in the 1785 elections, had as its basis an intense antagonism between an élite of prominent Loyalists who had received many favours and offices of high status and who had asked for considerably more, and a large number of Loyalist commoners who resented the pretensions of their social betters.[4] Echoes of the 1785 contest could be heard periodically in the nineteenth-century debates of the Common Council. Similarly, much of the denominational antagonism of the early nineteenth century contained the seeds of class conflict. The leadership of the early Wesleyan movement was almost entirely drawn from the tradesmen and labourers of the city, in sharp contrast to that of the churches of England and Scotland. Comparison of the social origins of Wesleyan and Church of England clergy reveals the same kind of social gulf that existed between the leading laymen of the two institutions.[5]

[2]Susan Hirsch, *Roots of the American Working Class: The Industrialization of Crafts in Newark 1800-1860* (Philadelphia 1978), 8, 11, 12, 41; Bryan Palmer, "Kingston Mechanics and the Rise of the Penitentiary, 1833-1836," *Histoire Sociale/Social History* (May 1980), 7-32.

[3]See, for example, Robert Gray, *The Labour Aristocracy in Victorian Edinburgh* (Oxford 1976), and Geoffrey Crossick, *An Artisan Elite in Victorian Society: Kentish London 1840-1880* (London 1978). For useful discussions of the nineteenth-century petite bourgeoisie see Crossick, "Urban Society and the Petty Bourgeoisie in Nineteenth-Century Britain," in Derek Fraser and Anthony Sutcliffe, eds., *The Pursuit of Urban History* (London 1983), 306-25.

[4]J.S. MacKinnon, "The Development of Local Government in the City of Saint John 1785-1795" (unpublished MA thesis, University of New Brunswick 1968), 21-4; W.S. MacNutt, *New Brunswick: A History 1783-1867* (Toronto 1963), 60-2; James Hannay, *History of New Brunswick I* (Saint John 1909), 154-6.

[5]Biographical details of these clergy groups may be found in E.A. Betts, *Bishop Black and His Preachers* (Sackville 1976), appendix II; A.W.H. Eaton, *The Church of England in Nova Scotia and the Tory Clergy of the Revolution* (New York 1891); G. Herbert Lee, *Historical Sketches of the First Fifty Years of the Church of England in the Province of New Brunswick, 1782-1833* (Saint John 1880).

Yet to view denominations simply as manifestations of class can be a treacherous undertaking. The characteristic attitude of leading Wesleyans toward their social superiors during the period of lower-status domination was deference. It was precisely at the point that Wesleyans came to occupy and to perceive themselves as entitled to occupy positions of higher status that their antipathy toward the colonial élite burst forth. But if the concept of Wesleyanism as a class movement encounters difficulties, the social groups from which the Wesleyans draw most heavily — the artisans — do provide the most distinctive and persistent example of class behaviour in colonial Saint John.

Artisans composed nearly half the original Loyalist freemen of 1785.[6] Throughout the first half of the nineteenth century they rather consistently composed about a third of freeman admissions, a proportion confirmed by the 1851 Census. Comprising a wide variety of occupations and wide range of incomes, the artisans were always a powerful interest and on a number of important issues they did act as a class. By mid-century they perceived themselves, and were perceived by observers of the scene, as the "bone and sinew" of the community. In terms of economic function, artisans were distinguished from those of higher and lower status in one important way: other groups were concerned with the provision of services, but craftsmen produced all the goods made in the city apart from the simple mechanical process of sawing deals.

In no way did the early city so faithfully reflect the late medieval origins of its institutions as in the means through which the townspeople organized themselves for the production of goods. Production was equated to craft and each craft was structured around a trade, which in turn was organized on the traditional triad of apprentice/journeyman/master. The importance accorded the trades in the city's constitution, which attempted to restrict both the franchise and the benefit of the trade to those who had served a satisfactory apprenticeship under a master who was a freeman of the city. The apprenticeship process was central to the trades system.[7] Not only did it provide a critical form of educational and skills development, but it instilled the pride, confidence, and sense of apartness that distinguished the training of professionals. This formation of the artisan usually began in early adolescence when the youth was bound over by his parents to a master craftsman. The standard indenture of apprenticeship was a legal document formally assented to by a magistrate binding the young man to a life of servitude in his master's household for a period of from four to eight years. *The Courier* editor, Henry Chubb, "voluntarily and of his own free will," was bound to a master printer for seven years at the age of fifteen. The contract, borrowed from traditional English models, provided board, lodging, washing, and a new suit of clothing for his apprentice. In

[6]Freemen's roll of the city of Saint John 1785-1862, New Brunswick Museum, Saint John [NBM].
[7]A point made by Hirsch in her study of Newark. Palmer, however, sees it as an exploitative arrangement after 1800. See Hirsch, *Roots*, 6, and Bryan D. Palmer, *Working-Class Experience: The Rise and Reconstitution of Canadian Labour 1800-1980* (Toronto 1983), 28-9.

return Chubb was required to serve faithfully, keep his master's secrets and commands, neither to damage nor waste his master's goods. He was further forbidden to commit fornication, contract matrimony, play at cards or dice, buy or sell goods without his master's permission, or frequent taverns or theatres.[8]

The control that masters were given over their charges was an attractive feature to civic authorities since it played an important role in the maintenance of order and good discipline among a large segment of the city's male population during the sometimes difficult passage from adolescence to manhood. The exercise of this authority by the masters was encouraged by Common Council, which placed responsibility for the public misdemeanours of apprentices clearly on the shoulders of the masters.[9] The rigorous control was frequently not appreciated by the apprentices and the search for fugitives became a regular feature of the daily press before 1850. By 1817, Henry Chubb, now Master Chubb, was beset by problems with his own apprentice, "Peter James Wade, 16, smart but a drunkard," who had fled his master's service.[10] Chubb offered 5*s.* for the return of the apprentice and £5 for information leading to the conviction of those harbouring him. The complaint was not uncommon, but as the law made the harbouring of a fugitive apprentice a hazardous undertaking, most fled the city.[11] As late as 1841, Sam Wilson was arrested for absconding from his master, the sailmaker and assistant alderman Robert Ray, and sentenced to two months at hard labour for assaulting the city marshal who made the arrest.[12]

Despite these commotions, and restrictions, the apprentice system had a good deal to offer young men.[13] In the short run, there was promise of a skill and a paid series of night courses. In the long run, there was a respectable status, admission to the freedom of the city, and the possibility of becoming a master with ownership of a shop.[14] Among a number of Loyalist families, the artisan's status became a tradition that engendered a native tradeocracy comprising an intricate pattern of fathers, sons, grandsons, nephews, uncles, and cousins. Many young second-generation natives could combine a respectable trade with their father's freehold and shop, a

[8]Indenture of Henry Chubb, Chubb Family Papers, NBM.

[9]See, for example, the firecracker ordinance of 1819 that provided a 20*s.* fine against the master of the offender (*City Gazette*, 11 August 1819).

[10]*The Courier*, 15 January 1817.

[11]See, for example, *The Courier*, 18 January, 25 September, and 15 November 1817.

[12]*Ibid.*, 12 June 1841.

[13]Despite Katz's contention that few nineteenth-century journeymen became masters, Bruce Laurie has demonstrated that over half the Methodist and Presbyterian journeymen in 1830 were masters or small retailers by 1850. Hirsch found that most Newark artisans over the age of forty were masters. See Bruce Laurie, *The Working People of Philadelphia 1850-1880* (Philadelphia 1980), 48.

[14]See the Mechanics Institute School in *The Courier*, 28 December 1839 and the petition of Peter Cougle for release from his apprenticeship after 3 years, 9 months of service with H. Littlehale, a house joiner. Common Council supplementary papers, Vol. 4, 30 June 1842, Provincial Archives of New Brunswick [PANB].

sure guarantee of becoming both master and burgher. The Bustins, the Hardings, and the Olives provide characteristic examples of the great trades families of the city. Fifteen Bustins, sixteen Hardings, and sixteen Olives were admitted as freemen between 1785 and 1858. The Bustin clan included five carpenters, four butchers, three harness makers, two masons; the Olives, six ship carpenters, three carpenters, two shipwrights, and a joiner; the Hardings, four tanners, two shoe-makers, and a blacksmith.[15]

Only toward mid-century did the ranks of this tradeocracy begin to break as young third-generation members began to move toward commerce and the professions. The Hardings were particularly successful in this: three became medical doctors, two were merchants, and one entered the law. This mid-century shift out of the trades on the part of young natives is confirmed by the 1851 Census. A sample of 732 east-side households reveals 23 apprentices almost equally divided between natives and Irish arrivals in the 1840s. By contrast the ranks of the young merchants' clerks expanded rapidly in the 1840s and by 1851 their members rivalled those of the apprentice artisans. More than two-thirds of the clerks were natives. Confirmation of the trend out of the crafts, particularly on the part of young natives, is found in the late 1850s in the complaints of *The Courier* editor who bewailed the abandonment of the crafts by young men of artisan families and scolded their parents — particularly their mothers — for denying the dignity of manual work and for placing a premium on any occupation that permitted its occupant to wear a white collar.[16] The decline of the crafts among native families was probably a reaction against the admission of Irish tradesmen who depressed the wages and reduced the importance of the status of artisans. The native-Irish tension was reflected in the matching of masters and apprentices. Native masters accepted only native apprentices, a fact which meant that almost all journeymen boat and coach builders would be natives while the shoemaking trade was given over to the Irish.[17] The native preferences doubtless reflected a traditional pattern of fathers apprenticing their sons to friends and acquaintances in the fathers' craft or in other similar crafts.

The purpose of the apprentice system was to train an exclusive body of skilled workers dedicated to the craft and determined to restrict its practice to those of like formation. The journeymen craftsmen constituted a broad and influential cross-section of the city's population. Together with the masters, they comprised about 35 per cent of the freemen and 35 per cent of all employed males in the city.[18] Thus they easily formed the largest electoral group in the city, outnumbering all commercial freemen by a ratio of two to one.

[15] These examples are drawn from the Roll of Freemen.
[16] *The Courier*, 28 October 1858.
[17] These data are drawn from the 1851 Census manuscript sample. See T.W. Acheson, *Saint John: The Making of a Colonial Urban Community* (Toronto 1985), ch. 12.
[18] On the relative strength of the artisan group in other British North American cities see Palmer, *Working-Class Experience*, 31, and Katz, *The People of Hamilton*, 70.

In 1851, more than three of every four artisans were family heads living in tenements or freeholds of their own. A very small number — about one in fourteen — were single men living with their parents, and the remainder — about one in six — were lodgers, one-third of whom lived with employers. Although all were legally required to be freemen to practise their trade, only about two out of five of those in the sample did so. Virtually every master was a freeman but journeymen, particularly in the lesser trades, frequently failed to acquire their freedom. The proportion of freemen rose to half among the native tradesmen, fell to two in five among the Irish, and to little more than one in five among the other groups. It was remarkably low among those of English, American, Nova Scotian, and Islander origins — doubtless indicating a view toward a temporary residence in the city on the part of members of these groups.

The most important crafts were those relating to the use of wood. Domestic carpenters — a group embracing carpenters, joiners, and cabinet-makers — accounted for 27 per cent of the east-side artisans in the 1851 Census. When combined with the shipbuilding trades (13 per cent of the census sample) and the furniture and coach-making crafts, the woodworkers composed some 42 per cent of the total artisans found in the 1851 Census. Another 18 per cent were employed in the leather trades, including tanners, cordwainers, and saddlers, and another 14 per cent in the metal trades — blacksmiths, whitesmiths, tinsmiths, machinists, and foundry men. Together these six categories accounted for 70 per cent of the city's artisans, the remainder being scattered through dozens of skills, the largest of which related to the production of clothing and food.

There were significant differences in the wages received for service within the various trades. These ranged from the 45s. a week that a millwright could command in 1841 to the mere 15s. paid to a baker, who received little more than the day labourer. In terms of remuneration there were three general categories of trades. The aristocrats were the wood craftsmen (carpenters, joiners, shipwrights, cabinet-makers), the tailors, and the painters, all of whom could expect 40-45s. a week when work was to be found. A second group were the smiths, butchers, masons, and shoe-makers, whose wages ranged between 29s. and 34s. Finally, there were the bakers and wheelwrights. Artisans' wages, of course, like all others, fluctuated in response to the demands of the local market. The year 1846 was a period of recession. Donaldson's figures for 1831, while not easily comparable because of the categories used, would indicate a weekly wage of about 45s. for a good journeyman carpenter or joiner, compared with 43s. eleven years later; a common labourer received 18s. compared with 15s. in 1841.[19] Wages of Saint John carpenters appear to have been comparable to those received by their counterparts in Upper Canada.[20]

---

[19] Based on CO 188/41, 306; CO 188/75; New Brunswick, *Journals of the House of Assembly* (1847).

[20] See Palmer, *Working-Class Experience*, 22.

Most wages declined after 1841. By 1846 average wages were probably not more than 75 per cent of those in 1831, although, since prices also fell, living standards were probably not notably lower. The differences in wages were important but since the suffering seemed to be general, the wage declines in any one craft were probably not viewed as the results of discriminatory treatment.

More significant than the rise or decline of wages generally was the relative position enjoyed by a particular skill within the economic hierarchy of trades. In good times, journeymen joiners and ship carpenters employed servants and ate salt beef, fresh pork, and bread made from American wheat flour; they enjoyed an income comparable to that of most small business men and non-conformist clergymen of the period. By contrast the shoe-maker kept no servant and mixed a good deal of fish with his meat, while the baker, like the common labourer, fed his family on fish and potatoes.[21] Three pennies would buy the working man two pounds of fish and three pounds of potatoes at most times of the year, as compared with a third of a pound of salt beef, or a quarter-pound of butter, or one pound of oatmeal, or a half-pound of sugar, or three eggs, or one pint of milk. Certainly the evidence suggests that a journeyman carpenter enjoyed an income closer to that of a master carpenter than to that of a journeyman shoemaker.[22]

Still another dimension to the artisan movement was stratification based on ethnicity. The 1851 Census revealed sharp ethnic patterns among particular trades. The proportion of artisans from each ethnic origin corresponded closely to that which the ethnic group bore among the heads of households as a whole, the sole exception being Irish arrivals after 1840. Native artisans, for example, accounted for 27 per cent of all craftsmen in the city. Their proportions, however, varied sharply from trade to trade. The natives were usually strong in all of the wood trades and among painters. They equalled the Irish in the domestic carpentry trades, outnumbered them almost two to one in the shipbuilding trades, and comprised all the coach and furniture makers in the city. By contrast, the leather trades, particularly shoemaking, were an Irish preserve by 1851, where Irish outnumbered natives almost eight to one. The same Irish predominance characterized the metal, clothing, and food trades, and the workers in stone. Significantly, the trades dominated by natives were also those that provided the largest remuneration, while those providing the poorest remuneration, such as shoemaking, were largely staffed by newer Irish arrivals whose presence made impossible the regulation of the trade by the city masters.[23]

Sharp differences in size and organization existed not only among the trades but also within them. The 1851 Census required master shoemakers to give information on the number of workers employed and on the value of output. While

[21]CO 188/41, 306.

[22]Katz has argued that journeymen and master artisans should be in different classes because the differences between them are greater than the differences among either journeymen or masters. This conclusion was reached on the basis of the Hamilton assessment records.

[23]An experience common to Newark as well. See Hirsch, *Roots*, 47.

the answers to the latter question doubtless grossly undervalued the product, they do provide a clue to the variations present in this trade. Most shoemaking shops were small, consisting of a master, one or two journeymen, and perhaps an apprentice. Masters admitted to values of from £75 to £1000. The same differences were found throughout most other trades. It is impossible to determine with any accuracy either the status or income of a master. Donaldson indicated in 1831 that master carpenters and joiners, who worked for supervisor's wages in the construction industry, received about 20 per cent more than did a first-class journeyman. It is likely that comparable differentials existed between journeymen and the minor master shoemakers and tailors, but it is clear that the greater masters in some trades were in the process of developing independent means that enabled them to meet smaller merchants on equal terms.

The traditional and emerging trades structures were both plainly visible in 1851. A significant number of master artisans, particularly in the footwear and clothing trades, maintained households that contained both their journeymen and their apprentices. At the other extreme, some individual firms had grown so large that the enterprises might more accurately be described as small factories. Most notable among these were the iron foundries. The Portland blacksmith James Harris had expanded his operations to include a block of buildings employing more than seventy men and boys. Within the city Thomas Barlow employed another sixty-five, and the city's other founders employed comparable numbers. The wage spread between the blacksmith and the foundry-engineers in the metal trades was no greater than that between the small master cabinet-makers employing a few journeymen in their shops and a leading furniture maker like J.W. Lawrence, who employed sixteen men and boys in making furniture to the value of £2250.[24]

Expanding local markets brought about a rapid change in the structure of the traditional trades. Master tradesmen responded to these opportunites in a variety of ways. Immigration produced large numbers of shoemakers and tailors. These trades required only limited capital — in some cases artisans even owned their own tools — and the result was a profusion of small shops and small masters.[25] By contrast, those trades permitting the application of steam-generated energy tended to remain concentrated in the hands of relatively few masters who added to their shops and employed an increasingly sophisticated technology.[26] Thus, while the shoemaking shops increased in number, offering numerous opportunities for ambitious young tradesmen to possess their own shops, the tanneries were concentrated in the hands of a few masters who came to employ more men in a more structured fashion and to play increasingly important roles in the life of the city. Daniel Ansley, who entered the trade as freeman tanner in 1809 at the age of eighteen and became a leading master tanner, finally classified himself as a merchant in the 1851 Census. Already possessing substantial shops in the early 1830s, four of the tanners greatly

[24]Saint John 1851 Census manuscript, Kings Ward, 238, PANB.
[25]As was the case in Newark. See Hirsch, *Roots*, 8.
[26]*Ibid.*, ch. 2.

increased their capacity after 1840 by the installation of steam engines.[27] The same development occurred in the flour trade. Grist-mill owners had constructed sixteen plants by 1840, each costing between £3000 and £5000 and each capable of grinding between 7000 and 12,000 barrels annually.[28] The most important elements in the city's industrial activities were the sawmills and iron and brass foundries, which became increasingly capital intensive as steam engines largely replaced water-driven mills.

The principal masters of that trade provide a useful insight into the successful trades leadership of the city. James Harris came from Annapolis as a young man and began to practise his blacksmith's craft. He gradually added machine, pattern, and fitting shops to his blacksmith's enterprise. In 1831 he added a blast furnace. Over the next few years a stove shop, a car shop, and a rolling mill completed the New Brunswick Foundry. His partner was a Scottish machinist, Thomas Allen, who completed his apprenticeship in Glasgow and settled in Saint John in 1825. Allen's son Thomas apprenticed as a machinist in his father's foundry, and a second son, Robert, became a moulder through the same process; a third son, Harris, studied as a brass founder. All three came to be owners of Saint John foundries by the early 1860s.[29] The Saint John Foundry was established in 1825 by Robert Foulis (a Scottish scientist and inventor and graduate in medicine of Aberdeen University) and was later taken over by a Fredericton merchant, T.C. Everitt, and two Saint John men, John Camber, a blacksmith, and James Wood, a machinist. George Fleming established the Pheonix Foundry in 1835. Fleming had served as a machinist's apprentice at the Dumferline Foundry in Scotland and then had worked as a journeyman in Glasgow, Cork, Pictou, Saint John, Boston, and Baltimore. His partners included a local carpenter, Thomas Barlow, an iron moulder, John Stewart, and later a long-time clerk with the firm, Thomas Humbert.[30] The city's ten iron and brass foundries in 1860 were thus distinguished by their Scottish and native ownership, by their structure as multiple partnerships that enabled them to bring together the necessary capital resources, and by the size of their producing units.

The foundries were the largest producing units in the city by the end of the colonial period. Three hundred journeymen and apprentices worked in them in 1850;[31] by 1873 the New Brunswick Foundry alone possessed a workforce of 300. The foundries were clearly operating on the factory system. In these, as in the bakery, carriage and cabinet-making, tanning, and milling trades, the application of steam power and new technology to create a more efficient system of production was well under way by 1840. The founders, of course, were using steam power before 1830. Barzilia Ansley first brought steam power to a tannery in 1838. Thomas Rankine, a product of a Scottish baker's apprenticeship, introduced hand

[27]RLE/834, pe. 91; RLE/845, pe. 208; PANB.
[28]RLE/828, pe. 42, 43; RLE/840, pe. 122; RLE/850, 418; *The Chronicle*, 22 March 1839.
[29]*St. John and Its Business: A History of St. John* (Saint John 1875), 124, 128-9.
[30]*Ibid.*, 125-6.
[31]RLE/851, pe. 412, PANB.

machinery to his business in 1844 and steam power eight years later. G.F. Thompson did the same in the paint trade in 1850. Four years later, Joseph and George Lawrence introduced steam power to the furniture-making firm their father had established in 1817. That same year Jeremiah Harrison applied steam to the carriage-making trade.[32]

The application of newer techniques to the traditional trades and the consequent growth of the firms between 1830 and 1860 certainly led to the growth of a group of prosperous masters having less and less in common with their journeymen and, conversely, limited the opportunities for those journeymen to acquire their own shops.[33] Yet the effect of this should not be overplayed. The growth of larger producing units was a slow process and in most firms involved a master artisan who had been a long-time resident of the city. Most important, apart from the iron foundries and a few sawmills, none of the producing units before 1850 could be described as factories in the sense that they employed more than twenty-five people in a plant powered by steam engines or water paddles. Most Saint John artisans in 1851 worked either in artisans' shops employing no more than five people or in the shipyards.[34] Moreover, the trades represented as much a social as an economic status. James Harris, Daniel Ansley, and the baker Stephen Humbert might become prominent, prosperous burghers, might even hold the Queen's Commission of the Peace with the right to style themselves "Esquire." Yet they remained artisans, married the daughters of artisans, and expressed the attitudes and biases of artisans, were perceived as tradesmen by their social superiors, and supported the interests of artisans. Throughout the colonial period — despite the changing structure and work relationships within some trades — that ethos remained a powerful source of identification binding most elements of the trades into a common interest.

This is not to suggest that loyalty to that interest was not sometimes divided or that elements of the interest did not war among themselves. The masters' use of the law to enforce obedience upon the apprentices has already been mentioned. Richard Rice has demonstrated the presence of Friendly Societies of carpenters, joiners, cabinet-makers, and painters as early as 1837, but no evidence that any of them took action against the masters.[35] Confrontations between masters and journeymen,

[32]*St. John and Its Business*, 101, 103, 105, 137.

[33]This is what Katz assumed in his work on Hamilton and Buffalo. Crossick, too, has reservations about the closeenss of small masters and men in mid-nineteenth-century Birmingham. Hirsch, however, found that small masters in Newark paid fairer wages and kept their firms operating longer in times of adversity than did larger operations. See Crossick, "Urban Society and the Petite Bourgeoisie," 322, and Hirsch, *Roots*, 89-90.

[34]A useful comparison and discussion of work place forms is found in Bruce Laurie, *Working People of Philadelphia 1800-1850* (Philadelphia 1980), ch. 1.

[35]J.R. Rice, "A History of Organized Labour in Saint John, N.B., 1815-1890" (MA thesis, University of New Brunswick 1968), ch. I. Rice suggests that collective action by shipwrights and carpenters may have begun in 1799, but it is probable that the "principal shipwrights" who composed the organization were the masters, not the journeymen. The earliest active unions were among shop clerks, the semi-skilled and unskilled sawyers, and ship labourers.

usually over rates of pay or slow payment, occasionally occurred. As early as 1830 the journeymen tailors of the city threatened to withhold their labour until the masters agreed to make payment of wages within three days of the completion of their work and to charge no more than 12*s.* board each week. No further evidence of confrontation occurred until 1841 when a mechanic wrote to the smiths and moulders of the city in the columns of *The News* calling for a one-hour reduction in the workday.[36] In 1856 journeymen printers at *The Courier* withdrew their services because their employer had taken an extra apprentice into the office.[37] Significantly, although Eugene Forsey has provided evidence of a ship carpenters organization, there is no evidence of any confrontations in the shipyards of Saint John.[38]

But incidents of this nature, although indicating an underlying tension within the interest, were relatively few. More important, they were short-lived and left few permanent scars. For the deeply alienated journeyman, Boston lay near and emigration provided a final solution when insoluble problems arose. By contrast, the activities of masters and journeymen, whether working alone or in concert with other groups within the city, revealed something closely resembling a genuine class consciousness.

In the 1830s the artisan leadership erected and attempted to erect a number of distinctive tradesmen's institutions. Throughout the period 1830-60, this leadership maintained a clear and strongly worded program designed to defend the social and economic interests of the artisan. The enemy was perceived to be the great merchant, and in these artisans' organizations the merchants found the most organized and persistent opposition to their domination of the colonial economy. The leadership of the crafts varied, depending on the point at issue. The most persistent spokesmen for the artisanal interest were the small masters whose families had enjoyed a long residence in the city, such as the Blakslees who for three generations had operated a candle and soap-making shop, and the sail-making Rays and Robertsons, the baking Rankins, and the woodworking Nesbits and Lawrences. Many were families with deep roots in the rocky soil of Saint John whose credentials as founding fathers were as respectable as those of the patricians. Like their followers, they were active supporters of the evangelical and temperance causes in the city. In sharp contrast to their mercantile opponents, they represented a localist emphasis that had the city at the centre of its world-view. They were unfailing in their resolve to employ the

---

The first documented instance of artisans taking action against masters occurred in 1864 when the caulkers struck for several months (ch. II).

[36]*The Courier*, 29 May 1830. Tailors were usually paid half in board and half in cash; *The News*, 17 May 1841.

[37]*The Courier*, 20 December 1856.

[38]Eugene Forsey found evidence of organizations among sawyers, ship carpenters, carpenters and joiners, tailors, and cabinet-makers between 1835 and 1849. Yet there is no indication of any activity directed against their employers. See Forsey, *Trade Unions in Canada* (Toronto 1982), 9-10.

authority of the state to protect the economic interests of the "bone and sinew" of the colony and to provide the kinds of development that would eventually lead to the relative self-sufficiency of the province.

Between 1835 and 1839 serious efforts were made to create three artisan institutions, followed in the late 1840s by a fourth. The reasons for this sudden discovery of occupational community cannot be accurately determined, although it was doubtless associated with the rising fortunes and expectations of most craftsmen in the heady days of the mid-1830s. Certainly the idea of the unity of the crafts and of the necessity to band together to further the interests of artisans closely paralleled the rising tide of religious dissent that culminated in the rejection of all social inequalities in the 1840s. Since the leadership of the two movements involved much the same personnel, they may well have shared similar perceptions and values.

The first of these co-operative efforts was the creation of a joint stock company to undertake the hunting of whales. Exploitation of the great southern whale fishery was just well under way. The combination of imperial and provincial tariffs provided 100 per cent protection on black oil and 30 per cent on sperm oil in the British and colonial markets. Saint John possessed the marine personnel capable of such long and arduous marine undertakings. A petition to establish a joint stock concern to be known as the Mechanics Whale Fishing Company was forwarded to the legislature and enacted into law in 1835. The act provided for the creation of a corporation possessing authority to raise a £50,000 capital through sale of 5000 shares of stock each with a par value of £10.[39]

The firm was an artisanal concern at the beginning. The original petition had been signed by 162 men, 71 of whom can be identified.[40] Two-thirds of these were tradesmen and most of the remainder were shipbuilders, grocers, and merchant mechanics. Among the petitioners was John Grey, first vice-president of the House Carpenters and Joiners Society of Saint John.[41] Its directors included the shipbuilder John Duncan, the hatter C.A. Everitt, the newspaper editor Henry Chubb, and the merchant John Wishart; its long-time president, Thomas Nesbit, was a master cabinet-maker. In 1837 the company was owned by 160 individuals drawn mainly from the trades most concerned with the making and outfitting of vessels and the processing of whales — most, but by no means all, masters. In addition, there was a sprinkling of grocers and other small business men, and a few merchants and professionals.

The enterprise was a financial success. Once the initial voyages were completed, the investment proved both profitable and safe. That very success proved its undoing as an artisan's enterprise. The merchant community began to invest heavily in the stock after 1840 and artisans, particularly in the financial crisis of 1841-42, were often forced to sell their holdings to merchants at prices well below their

[39]RLE/835, 2nd session, pe. 1.
[40]New Brunswick, *Journals of the House of Assembly* (1838), appendix 1, Mechanics Whale Fishing Company.
[41]*The Courier*, 4 March 1837.

normal market value.[42] By 1846, only 53 of the 160 stockholders of 1838 remained
in the company. They had been joined by a number of great merchants and banking
institutions. The tradesmen each generally owned between four and thirty shares of
stock, each valued at about £10 in 1847. The stock held by the newcomers was much
more substantial. For all practical purposes the company had ceased to be a
"mechanics" enterprise by that time.[43]

The second trades institution developed from the top down. Mechanics institutes had by 1835 become the most fashionable organization among leading British
artisans.[44] Dedicated to progress and the enlightenment of the working man, the
institution was viewed with some scepticism by the more conservative elements of
British society. The movement for the institute actually began as part of a more
general interest in the nature and possible applications of new scientific knowledge.
In Saint John, as in England, the leadership in promoting this interest in scientific
theory was taken by a group of professionals led by several judges, clergymen, and
physicians. In June 1836 they formed the New Brunswick Philosophical Society.
Five months later they capped their success by enrolling sixteen "of the most
respectable master mechanics [a term used for artisans in the metal crafts] in the
city" in the society.[45] From this point onward, there was persistent talk of the
educational advantages that a proper mechanics institute, with its lecture series,
library, and museum, could provide for the tradesmen of the city. The impetus for
the institute certainly came from the society and when the decision was finally made
to create an institute late in 1838 the society members, under the leadership of
patricians like Chief Justice Chipman, Mr. Justice Parker, and Beverley Robinson,
decided to continue their guidance of the new organization by merging the society
with the institute. It was a curious and unequal marriage. Forty-two members of the
Philosophical Society joined 175 tradesmen to create the new organization.[46] A
10s. entrance fee and annual dues of 15s. ensured that the institute would be
restricted to the aristocracy of labour. None the less, the institute found strong
support among the large numbers of craftsmen in the city. Within fourteen months
its membership was approaching 400, and by 1851 it reached 1250.[47]

[42]See the merchants' letters in *The Courier*, 26 December 1840.

[43]Details on operations of the company between 1838 and 1847, including financial statements and lists of shareholders and directors, may be found in the *Journals of the House of
Assembly.*

[44]The Saint John development closely paralleled the English. See Mabel Tylecote, *The
Mechanics Institutes of Lancashire and Yorkshire* (Manchester 1957), chs. 1, 2, and 8. The
Halifax Mechanics Institute predated that of Saint John and suffered from many of the same
early problems. See Patrick Keene, "A Study in Early Problems and Policies in Adult
Education: The Halifax Mechanics' Institute," *Histoire Sociale/Social History*, 16 (Novem-
ber 1975), 255-74.

[45]*The Courier*, 5 November 1836.

[46]*Ibid.*, 1 December 1838; 2 March 1839.

[47]*Ibid.*, 20 April 1839; 17 May 1851.

The institute initially suffered an identity crisis. At heart was the question of whether it was to provide broad scientific instruction for the city at large or a specialized technical instruction for the benefit of the tradesmen. Leadership in the organization was taken at first by former Philosophical Society members who dominated the early executive committees and mounted lecture series on geology, ethics, and astronomy — much to the chagrin of many artisans who demanded instruction in practical mechanical principles.[48] The debate between the social leaders of the city and the practical mechanics continued for the next three years.[49] One *Chronicle* correspondent argued as early as December 1838 that the gentlemen who were running the institute thought the mechanics a mass of semi-barbarians incapable of making any kind of responsible decision. He demanded that all propositions the executive wished to implement be presented in writing to the general membership, discussed, and voted on by secret ballot.[50] The debate continued into the spring of 1839 with demands for executive responsibility to the general membership and threats that artisans would withhold their subscriptions.[51] The bill to incorporate the institute was a particularly controversial issue because it had been prepared by the provisional directors and its contents were not revealed to the membership at large before being sent to Fredericton.[52] Rumbles of discontent were heard as late as 1841, but any hope Chipman had of being able to direct the affairs of the organization were soon dashed.

The institute remained a forum for public discussion and education, but after 1840 its leadership passed more and more to the tradesmen, particularly the master tradesmen, of the city. By 1842 the directorate contained the iron founders T. Barlow, G. Fleming, J. Harris; the cabinet-makers Thomas Nesbit and Alex Lawrence; the shipbuilders John Duncan and J. Lawton; the druggists S.L. Tilley and J. Sharp; the printer and editor Henry Chubb; and the merchant tailor William Robertson; together with a doctor, a lawyer, and two merchants.[53] As the decade progressed, its leaders became more and more involved in the important social and economic issues of the day. The final break with the city's patricians occurred in 1844 when the directors opened their hall for Sunday services by the Scottish cleric and Evangelical Alliance leader W.T. Wishart, against the express wishes of Chipman.[54]

[48]See, for example, the letter from "Mechanic" in *The Chronicle*, 28 December 1838.

[49]A similar debate conducted among artisans, white-collar workers, and the gentry occurred within the London mechanics institutes at mid-century. See Crossick, *An Artisan Elite*, 137-9.

[50]*The Chronicle*, 28 December 1838.

[51]See the correspondence from A.R. Truro in *The Courier*, 2 March 1839, and from "Mechanic" and "Member of the Water Company" in *The Chronicle*, 4 and 18 January, 8 March 1839. The motion to give control of institute funds to the executive committee had apparently been passed at a meeting attended by fourteen members.

[52]See "Member of Mechanics Institute" in *The News*, 26 November 1841.

[53]*The Courier*, 16 April 1842.

[54]E.P. Costello, "A Report on the Saint John Mechanics Institute 1838-1890" (unpublished MA report, University of New Brunswick 1974), 9-10.

The institute served a number of purposes apart from arranging public lectures series. Day and night schools were offered from the beginning, the latter designed particularly for the benefit of apprentices and masters. By 1845 many institute leaders, imbued with much of the evangelical ideology associated with the temperance movement and the Evangelical Alliance, succeeded in attaching the British school to the institute. In 1855, masters and journeymen combined to form the Mechanics Charitable Association to aid distressed tradesmen and to "elevate" labour.[55] The strength and unity of the artisans was most impressively displayed in 1840 on the occasions of the opening of the Mechanics Hall and the arrival of the governor general. On the first of these, about 1200 craftsmen paraded the streets of the city in military formation, each craft marching en bloc, its members arrayed in the traditional insignia and symbolism of the trade. First, in point of honour, came the blacksmiths, followed by the founders, the hammermen, carpenters, tailors, painters, bakers, and shoe-makers.[56] Two months later, the arrival of the governor general was heralded by more than 1500 artisans marching under the banner of the Mechanics Institute.[57] In addition to the crafts present in May, the procession included the riggers, coopers, and shipwrights.

It is very doubtful that these parades can be seen as evidence of trade-union activity. Master and journeymen certainly marched together under the common banner of their trade and some apprentices may have done so as well.[58] Led by the city's master artisans, the institute remained the most obvious symbol of the views and interests of the masters and most respectable journeymen artisans throughout the remainder of the colonial era. Its only competition for the artisans' allegiance was the short-lived Chamber of Trades, which in the early 1840s attempted to play the same role among craftsmen that the Chamber of Commerce played among merchants. Again, if the list of 1841 officers is any indication, the Chamber of Trades was composed of both masters and journeymen.[59]

The remaining two efforts to create distinctive artisanal institutions were both destroyed by political powers against which the artisans could not prevail. The creation of a Mechanics Whaling Company and the Mechanics Institute was followed in 1839 by the demand for a mechanics bank based on the Scottish banking system. The reasons for the demand are not hard to find. The inability or unwillingness of the Bank of New Brunswick directors to make available sufficient accom-

[55]*The Courier*, 5 May 1855.
[56]*Ibid.*, 30 May 1840. These parades were similar to the craftsmen's independence day parades in Newark before the community divisions of the 1830s. See Hirsch, *Roots*, 6.
[57]*Ibid.*, 25 July 1840.
[58]*The Courier* account of 25 July makes this point clear: "The members of the Mechanics Institute assembled in the following order: carpenters, *members not in the trades*, riggers, shoemakers, ..."
[59]See *The News*, 24 April 1841 and *The Courier*, 6 November 1841. The president of the Mechanics Institute, a 34-year-old Irish-born joiner, John Wilson, was also vice-president of the Chamber of Trades.

modation to satisfy many business men had led to the formation of the City and Commercial banks in the 1830s. Master tradesmen had played a role in both of these formations, yet, for a second and third time, they found their expectations frustrated. All three institutions proved to be unwilling to serve the needs of the trades. In the financial crisis of 1839, the banks strongly discriminated in favour of the merchant community, which controlled the bank stock.

In January 1839, a public meeting of mechanics was held at the Albion House for the purpose of discussing the possibilities of establishing a bank in which "the property of the working and middle class of society [would] be represented." Arguing that these classes had been disregarded in the operation of the existing banking establishments and that "the greatest portion of the wealth of this Province [is] owned by the operatives of this country," many of whom were stockholders in the existing banks, the meeting proposed to create a Mechanics Property Bank with a capital of £150,000 to £500,000, to be operated on the Scottish system.[60] The meeting concluded when 199 artisans petitioned the legislature for the creation of a non-mercantile bank with an initial capital of £100,000, which they proposed to raise.[61] Not surprisingly the list of petitioners was dominated by artisans with strong support from the master mariners, the grocers, and the Baptist clergy of the city.

The problems faced by the tradesmen in dealing with the provincial political establishment were reflected in the handling of the petition. It was introduced to the assembly by Isaac Woodward, a Saint John member, merchant, and long-time spokesman for the Chamber of Commerce, who moved that it be referred to the Committee on Colonial Banking. That committee, chaired by Woodward, brought back a negative recommendation arguing that compliance would "increase the difficulty and embarrassment of monetary affairs" by increasing the number of banks in the province.[62]

The fourth attempt at creating trades institutions occurred in 1848-50 when the city's leading shipbuilders, arguing that Carleton was largely populated by trades-men, proposed to create a joint stock company to contract the building and sale of sailing vessels. The proposal had important implications for the shipbuilding industry of the province. Its organizers included virtually every leading citizen of Carleton, headed by William Olive and six members of his shipbuilding clan, George Bond, Thomas Coram, John Littlehale, R. Stockhouse, Henry Nice and four members of his family, William and Joseph Beatteay and three members of that family.[63] The Olives were among the earliest shipbuilders in the province and, together with the smaller yards of the other builder clans of Carleton, constituted an important element in the provincial shipbuilding industry. Supported by 258 Carleton artisans, a bill to incorporate the Carleton Mechanics Shipbuilding and

[60]*The Courier*, 2 February 1839. Hirsch noted the same problem among Newark masters in the 1840s. See Hirsch, *Roots*, 92.
[61]RLE/839, pe. 203, PANB.
[62]New Brunswick, *Journals of the Legislative Assembly* (1839), 330, 434.
[63]RLE/849, pe. 295, PANB.

Navigation Company passed the Legislative Assembly at its 1849 sitting but was defeated in an 8 to 6 division in the Legislative Council.[64] Undeterred, the petitioners returned in 1850 only to repeat the same process, this time suffering a decisive defeat in the council.[65]

The expressions of occupational community that gave rise to distinctive institutions devoted to the interests of craftsmen in the 1830s were only a forerunner of the demands for protection made by artisans in the 1840s. Only freemen could legally carry on a craft in the city. About two of every five artisans were freemen, including virtually all masters. Although the law was frequently broken or occasionally even misapplied — as when the mayor admitted Americans as freemen in 1810 — that right remained a legal whip that could be (and frequently was) used against Americans and other non-freemen operating within the city.[66]

The extent to which this threat was used depended upon the diligence of the mayor and the willingness of artisans to bring complaints. Robert Hazen, for example, was sympathetic to the interests of artisans in the late 1830s. His city inspector regularly reported the tailors, painters, carpenters, and other non-freemen craftsmen working within the city. Hazen apparently regularly tried and fined the offenders, a practice that had the effect of forcing British immigrants to purchase their freedom and of driving the Americans out or at least into less conspicuous positions.[67]

In times of economic difficulty, the freemen artisans were more likely to act as their own police, reporting offenders and in some cases mounting public protests against aliens. Americans, sometimes operating with the co-operation of the masters, sometimes in competition with them, were the principal culprits. The situation was particularly acute within the building trades. The major problem for local journeymen was the arrival in the city of numerous American craftsmen seeking temporary employment at wages below that normally paid to members of the trades. So many Americans arrived at the height of the building boom following the fire of 1839 that the journeymen gathered in public meeting in the autumn to prepare a petition to Common Council asking that their rights of citizenship be protected.[68] If the prayers of that petition were granted, it was only a temporary respite. The following summer, a "Carpenter" complained that house carpenters were denied employment and that merchants and other townspeople were giving preference to "a gang of Yankees who flock to the city in summer and work for less and are free from taxes, road work etc."[69] As the depression of 1841 began the situation became

[64]New Brunswick, *Journals of the Legislative Assembly* (1849), 35, 61-62; New Brunswick, *Journals of the Legislative Council* (1849), 428.

[65]RLE/850, pe. 103, PANB; New Brunswick, *Journals of the House of Assembly* (1850), 120; New Brunswick, *Journals of the Legislative Council* (1850), 725.

[66]Rice, "A History of Organized Labour in Saint John," 4, 6.

[67]City inspector's report, 25 July and 8 August 1838, R.L. Hazen Papers, folder 2, NBM.

[68]*The Courier*, 9 November 1839.

[69]*Ibid.*, 18 July 1840.

still more tense. In early April, some 2000 journeymen gathered in Queens Square demanding that all foreign journeymen be prohibited from entering the city.[70] The meeting was held at 4:00 p.m. on a weekday and the lack of public comment on this act would seem to indicate that it was held with the consent of most masters. Despite public fears raised by the size and nature of the meeting, the journeymen proceeded to the St. John Hotel where they organized an executive to accomplish their purpose.[71]

The artisans were not without allies in this crusade. A large proportion of the men concerned were freemen and, despite a determined effort on the part of many within the city's merchant community to remove all restrictions on trade and labour within the city, the protectionists were able to elect a strong contingent of supporters to Common Council and to bring considerable pressure to bear on the mayor. The long-time Sydney Ward alderman Gregory Van Horne and his assistant, John Hagarty, were particular champions of the artisans' position, and the support of George Bond and artisan councillors Robert Ray and Ewan Cameron was usually assured. In the spring of 1840, Hagarty and Van Horne succeeded in carrying a resolution in Common Council to prevent foreigners from taking contracts or from doing work in the city that was in any way injurious to freemen mechanics.[72] After a challenge to their authority to prosecute non-freemen was successfully beaten back in the Supreme Court, the mayors of the city quite regularly prosecuted any offending American artisans in the 1840s. The results of these efforts were reflected in the 1851 Census, which revealed that not many more than 2 per cent of the city's artisans had been born in the United States. None the less, the struggle continued. Liberal reformers like Henry Chubb were scandalized by the economic restrictions imposed on Americans and argued that the capital and skills that American business men and manufacturers had to offer the city would do much to advance its interests. And this contention was strongly supported by a substantial part of the merchant community in a petition to the House of Assembly in 1850, but to no avail.

The efforts toward the maintenance of the traditional economic privileges of freemen paled by comparison with the struggle after 1840 to protect the products of city tradesmen from those of their American counterparts. This question, more than any other, divided the society of Saint John into clearly identifiable classes.[73] Protection of goods was never a simple matter in colonial New Brunswick. The principal competitor of the colonial tradesman was not the American but the British producer, and the mercantilism of the empire admitted no defence against the free importation of British goods. Only the modest transportation costs and a very small revenue tariff served as protection for the colonial tradesmen.

[70]*The News*, 9 April 1841.

[71]'Hobshot' to the editor in *The News*, 5 May 1841.

[72]*The Courier*, 16 May 1840.

[73]Bryan Palmer argues that in Upper Canada such protest involved an alliance of manufacturers and merchants. Hirsch notes that any distinctions among masters and journeymen in the early nineteenth century were overridden by their commitment in keeping prices up and markets stocked. See Palmer, *Working-Class Experience*, 57, and Hirsch, *Roots*, 8.

As early as 1827, the "mechanics of Saint John," complaining of competition from American manufactured products, petitioned for an increase in the provincial tariff on a broad range of commodities. A similar request was made in 1834.[74] Further demands were made by a number of particular trades: the leather makers in 1835 and the millers and bakers in 1828, 1835, and 1840.[75] Despite these sporadic protests, however, the combination of imperial and provincial duties provided a margin of protection for most commodities sufficient to prevent the American producer from posing a serious threat to his Saint John counterpart.[76]

The situation changed rapidly after 1840. The confluence of the 1841-42 commercial collapse with the decision of the Peel government to abandon the imperial tariff produced the kind of economic chaos and social despair that added greatly to the sense of group consciousness evident among the growing body of artisans in the 1830s. The depression produced a devastating effect on the artisanal community of Saint John. Masters and journeymen alike were involved in the common ruin as local markets largely disappeared. Between 1840 and 1842, the number of tailors in the city decreased from 400 to 60 and shoemakers from 300 to 60.[77] The decline in membership in the Mechanics Institute was so severe that the institution was threatened with bankruptcy.

Yet, while numbers of artisans joined most of the labouring classes on the dole in the terrible winter of 1841-42, and many others took their skills to the urban centres of New England, craftsmen as a group displayed a high degree of cohesiveness in the face of the general ruin. Lieutenant-Governor Sir William Colebrook was approached by a number of 'respectable mechanics' who offered to mortgage their homes to obtain funds to settle on wilderness land. With Colebrook's encouragement and the assistance of Gesner and Perley, the artisans formed themselves into associations and proceeded to petition for block grants of crown land in the counties surrounding Saint John. The initial association of twenty-three craftsmen under the leadership of Azor Betts, a housejoiner, was settled on the Pollet River in Westmorland County in early September. A second group headed by the saddler David Collins and totalling 108 associates were placed in Kings County.[78] The Mechanics', Teetotal, and Eel River settlements were almost entirely created by Saint John artisans. The settlements so made were not particularly successful.[79] The problem was not too serious, however. The provincial economy revived by 1844 and the city was capable of absorbing a large number of its erstwhile citizens.

[74]RLE/827, pe. 117; RLE/834, pe. 1.
[75]RLE/828, pe. 142; RLE/840, pe. 122; RLE/835, pe. 124.
[76]Duties on American manufacturers averaged 10 per cent in 1842. New Brunswick, *Journals of the Legislative Assembly* (1842), appendix ccxxix.
[77]RLE/844, pe. 163; RLE/844, pe. 84; RLE/842, pe. 84.
[78]Colebrook to Stanley, 29 March 1842, CO 188/76; Colebrook to Stanley, 27 September 1842, CO 188/79; *The Courier*, 22 December 1842.
[79]*The Courier*, 15 April 1843.

The crisis of 1841-42 was compounded in 1842 by the decision of the British government to begin dismantlement of the great instruments of imperial economic policy. For most Saint John artisans, this shift in imperial policy posed a threat and offered a rare opportunity. On the one hand, their local markets lay exposed to American produce, which could, in most cases, enter duty free. On the other hand, by 1846, there was a clear possibility that the provincial legislature would be able to protect colonial craftsmen even from their British competitors.

The tensions between the artisans and the governing élites that had underlain much of the artisans' protests and institutions in the 1830s were heightened by the crises of the 1840s. The first shot in the war for the tariff was fired at the 1843 sitting of the provincial legislature when 299 protectionists petitioned for the imposition of a high provincial tariff aimed at the protection of local goods against "inferior American manufactures." The document was important not only for the force of its argument but for the strong united front of artisans that it represented. It was accompanied by an even more radical proposal from the city's iron founders. Arguing that they were capable of supplying all castings for ships, mill machinery, stoves, and ploughs needed in the province, and pointing to the sufferings they and their journeymen had endured the previous few years, they asked the legislature to impose a duty on British manufactured goods.[80]

The 1843 protectionist petition was not a large one, but what it lacked in numbers was compensated for in quality. Its signatories included an impressive contingent of leading masters from virtually every trade in the city. When these efforts failed to produce the desired concessions, the leaders of the movement moved to create a formal organization that could be used as a common front behind which rural and urban producers from across the province could be organized. Using the Mechanics Institute as their base, leading protectionists attempted to weld craftsmen, fishers, and farmers into an alliance against the common enemy.

In January 1844, shipbuilder John Owens and miller and flour dealer J.W. McLeod convened a meeting of "people friendly to protection of agricultural and domestic manufacturers." Some 500 supporters attended the meeting. The organizers enunciated an explicit class purpose: "our interests we have much reason to believe have been neglected in the Halls of Legislation. The time, it is hoped, will come when the industrious classes will be able to send men from among themselves who have a community of feeling with them and an identity of interests."[81] To fulfil this aim, the meeting formed the Provincial Association, elected an executive committee for the new organization, and passed resolutions denouncing all free-trade proposals. The association authorized its executive committee to petition the legislature for a scale of duties to protect the economic interests of all classes.

The committee lost no time in printing and distributing circulars outlining the association's program. Within a month, branch associations were formed at Kingston and Hampton. Among the first recommendations made by the executive

[80]RLE/843, pe. 143, 149, PANB.
[81]*The Courier*, 20 January 1844.

committee were proposals to impose a substantial duty on cordage and canvas, to bonus farmers for growing hemp and flax, to construct model farms, and to organize mechanics' fairs. Members of the association were also encouraged to bind themselves to use, consume, and wear only New Brunswick products. The strength of the new producers' common front was reflected in the mammoth petition presented by the Provincial Association of New Brunswick to the 1844 sitting of the legislature. More than 2500 association supporters in Saint John, Kings, and York counties prayed that the legislature provide protection for the farmers, fishers, and manufacturers of the province.[82] This show of strength accomplished what the smaller group of 1843 petitioners had been unable to do: the legislature agreed to impose tariffs of 10-20 per cent on a number of products, including castings, footwear, cut nails, bricks, furniture, and agricultural implements, and specific duties on cattle, oxen, horses, and apples. Of the major Saint John trades groups, only the tailors and bakers and millers were denied any significant protection.[83] The issue did not lie there. The free traders struck back the following year and managed to restore most of the lower 1843 tariff. It was only after the 1846 general election that the protectionists were able, finally, to secure a policy of moderate protection.

The issue of protection divided the city in the 1840s just as thoroughly as did that of prohibition in the following decade. Indeed, the personnel of both groups frequently coincided. Most of the feeling generated against the mercantile free traders was tinged with a strong sense of group consciousness, a sense on the part of many urban tradesmen that the enemy had in some way abused them for its own ends and that it was an enemy that felt itself to be masters of the society. This hostility broke forth in a seemingly trivial incident in spring 1841 when a prominent patrician and merchant, G.D. Robinson, made the public comment that "the mechanics of Saint John had more wages than mechanics at other places, and that in consequence their wives were dressed in furs and silks and that they looked more like xxxx than decent women." The comment became the focus of heated debate in the city, meetings of tradesmen were held, a committee was established to investigate the case, and the *News* editor, George Fenety, felt constrained to defend the dignity and respectability of the city's mechanics, noting that, like "mechanics in all places," those of Saint John carried their heads higher than most men because "they are the bone and sinew of every land."[84]

The sense of injustice intensified in 1844 at the height of the public debate over the Provincial Association and its program. *Courier* editor Henry Chubb plainly sided with the merchants in this debate. One commentary in his paper denounced the association as a group of tradesmen who, instead of attending to their business, proposed a tariff that would enable "them to live in a style far above their station." It was commerce that must suffer for this — "that commerce which pours its wealth into our laps" and "which cannot be advantageously maintained unless our ship

[82]*Ibid.*, 10 February 1844; RLE/844, pe. 239, PANB.
[83]New Brunswick, *Journals of the House of Assembly* (1844), 152-7.
[84]*The News*, 19, 24 April 1841.

owners be permitted to buy their supplies and materials in the cheapest market and to procure their labour at the lowest possible price."[85] The attacks on the protectionists by *The Courier* were mild, however, compared to that mounted by *Loyalist* editor Thomas Hill. Hill saw in the leaders of the protectionists all the elements of Saint John society he so much despised: prohibitionists, Evangelical Alliance supporters, malcontents who would threaten even the imperial connection in their pursuit of their own material gain. Early in 1845 he wrote a play entitled *The Provincial Association*, which parodied a number of well-known Saint John mechanics and two of their wives. The play, in the words of *The News*, was "intended to bring contempt not only on the respectability of the gentlemen in question but upon their moral rectitude and the virtue of certain ladies in St. John." After initial performances in Fredericton, the play was brought to Saint John in April. The first performance occurred without incident, although the satire was so obvious and so telling that *The News* was astonished when the mayor did not close the theatre after the first night. The following evening a large number of tradesmen led by "persons whose standing in society should have caused them to respect themselves" filled the theatre, while another mob, estimated at 300 strong, gathered outside.[86] In the ensuing riot, the doors of the theatre were torn off and the interior literally torn to pieces, while the mayor and police stood by helplessly. *The Courier* thought the play was all in fun and Mayor Donaldson, long a spokesman for the timber interests, permitted another performance during work hours for the benefit of those citizens who were prepared to pay 5*s.* and sign a requisition.[87]

Hill's attack was certainly the most provocative made upon the Saint John artisans. As prosperity returned in 1845 and 1846, tensions between craftsmen and merchants lessened. Even so, strong feelings remained that were reinforced in the provincial election of 1846 in which protection and religious equality were the crucial issues. John Owens and J.W. McLeod ran on behalf of both the Provincial Association and the Evangelical Alliance. They were defeated, as was their Free Presbyterian counterpart. Ultimately, among the Saint John protectionists, only R.D. Wilmot secured election and soon became spokesman for the protectionist movement. The movement, though less intense and focused on specific industries rather than on the principle of protection, remained a potent force throughout the remainder of the decade.

The rain of petitions by individual crafts that began in 1843 continued unabated throughout the colonial period. The shoemakers petitioned in 1844 for reciprocal duties with those in the United States. They repeated the petition in 1846 and the following year returned with the support of a large body of tanners, merchants, and other tradesmen.[88] Their prayers were only occasionally heard. At the 1847 sitting of the assembly, their petition was laughed out of the chamber by a group of

[85]*The Courier*, 10 February 1843.
[86]*The News*, 4 April 1845; *The Courier*, 5 April 1845.
[87]*The News*, 9 April 1845.
[88]RLE/844, pe. 84, PANB; RLE/846, pe. 208; RLE/847, pe. 367.

anti-protectionist assembly men led by Isaac Woodward, a Saint John member and Chamber of Commerce officer. Woodward replied to the shoemakers by proposing that the assembly act on a petition from the Chamber of Commerce that would remove the tariff from every commodity with the exception of beans. The treatment meted to the shoemakers was repeated with the tailors, who also asked for reciprocity of duties with the Americans. Iron and brass foundry owners, the bakers, the leather manufacturers, the carriage makers, and the millers all made similar demands.[89] As a result of these repeated representations, the legislature imposed a modest level of protection on a limited range of consumer products made in the city. Footwear, leather, furniture, machinery, iron castings, agricultural implements, wagons and sleighs, veneers, hats, cigars, and pianos were all subject to a 15 per cent tariff.

The recession of 1849-50, occasioned in part by the final demise of British mercantilism, resulted in the migration of hundreds of artisans and labourers from the city and sparked a revival of the protectionist cause. In February 1850, a series of meetings organized by leaders of the Provincial Association were held in St. Stephen's Hall. Advertised as meetings of the Friends of Protection to Home Industry and Domestic Manufacturers, the meeting convened under the chairmanship of Thomas Allen, Esq., and heard J.W. Lawrence urge a partial withdrawal from the timber industry and the development of an extensive manufacturing capacity within the province. The petition, demanding "a higher and more decidedly protective tariff" for manufactured and farm produce, was signed by 1234 men headed by the traditional trades leadership.[90]

When the city mobilized in 1851 to press the provincial government for construction of a railway system for the province, artisans met apart from the commercial groups to present their views. At a meeting in the Mechanics Institute chaired by the mayor, they offered to take stock in the rail line provided they were offered employment on it.[91]

The sharp divisions of opinion between merchant and artisan interests evident in economic issues were manifest in other areas as well.[92] Perhaps the most obvious

[89]*The News*, 15 March 1847, "Debates on the Tariff" (by electric telegraph); RLE/844, pe. 155, 163, 168, PANB; RLE/845, pe. 298; RLE/848, pe. 178, 310, 378; RLE/850, pe. 343, 357, 358, 414, 415; RLE/851, pe. 412.
[90]*The Courier*, 23 February 1850; *The Observer*, 19 February 1850; RLE/850, pe. 416, PANB.
[91]*The Courier*, 22 February 1851.
[92]The data upon which these generalizations were drawn were produced by computer analysis of the city freemen with the signatories to 106 petitions and other documents that played some significant role in the life of the community between 1830 and 1860. Common names (i.e. John Smith), names held by two or more freemen of different occupations, and names that could not be clearly identified as belonging to a particular freeman were eliminated. This process removed about half those who were probably freemen. The remainder — those who can be clearly identified as freemen who signed some public document between 1820 and 1860 — included 207 merchants and 581 artisans. It is this group that forms the basis for these statements.

were the attempts in 1835 and 1843 to restrict admission to the freedom of the city
to the prosperous. This issue was somewhat confused because the sons of freemen
who served an apprenticeship in the city would still have been admissible on
payment of the fees of office. None the less, the response of freemen merchants,
artisans, and labourers to the 1843 proposal reflected marked differences of opinion.
Eight out of ten merchants supported the restriction while more than two-thirds of
the artisans and twenty-one of the twenty-two freemen labourers were opposed. The
artisans who opposed the proposal were drawn almost equally from native and Irish
backgrounds.

Among other matters on which numbers of freemen artisans expressed an
opinion were temperance and protection. However, both of these issues received
considerable support from the merchant interest and it is difficult to speak of a clear
division based on occupational interest. The concerns that provoked the most
reaction among freemen artisans in the colonial period were those related to secret
societies and to education. A large number of artisans opposed efforts to prohibit
secret societies in 1844 and a decade later supported incorporation of the Orange
Order. Given the length of time between the two petitions and their differing
purposes, it is not surprising that few names appeared on both. More striking is the
fact that while support for religious but non-sectarian schools in 1858 was as high
as for Orange incorporation, only 17 per cent of the petitioners signed both petitions.
In contrast, merchants appear to have played a much less significant role in efforts
either to prevent the prohibition of secret societies or to ensure passage of the 1858
schools bill. They played virtually no part in the attempts to incorporate the Orange
Order. Superficially it would appear that such differences in behaviour and attitude
were largely class based. However, since a majority of freemen artisans were
Irish-born and the great majority of merchants were not, these differences may well
have been the result of ethnic factors.

The evidence of the period suggests that there was an artisans' interest in the
city from at least 1820. As it grew in size and influence, it took on many of the
manifestations of a class. The strength of the interest lay in the persistence and
proprietorial attitudes of its leadership toward the community. They shared with the
patricians and leading merchants a place in the Loyalist myth. They played dominant roles within the Irish cultures. Many of their number were small freeholders
and many more were freemen. By 1840, much of their leadership could claim both
respectability and three generations of residency in the city; a handful of masters
even aspired to the magistracy. Although they were found in all cultures, the artisans
were concentrated in that tightly knit evangelical tradition in which were found so
many of the city's respectable artisans, masters, and small proprietors who played
such an important role in shaping the values of the mid-nineteenth-century community. Coupled with this strong cultural base was the considerable political influence
that the producers' interest enjoyed. Because of the distribution of constituencies,
the interest could often control the Common Council and the election of city
assemblymen. Finally, as they demonstrated on a number of occasions in the

colonial period, artisans could act in a concerted and self-conscious fashion in defence of their economic interests. Altogether, they alone possessed the influence, the status, and the numbers to challenge patrician and merchant interests for control of the community.

Eric W. Sager

4

Seafaring Labour: Struggles for Protection and Control

The sailor was not trapped within a culture of poverty, but he was constrained by authority and by law. In the third quarter of the nineteenth century the structure of authority in the workplace was confirmed and reinforced by laws that gave some protection to the sailor, but even greater powers to his master. In Britain these laws were intended to protect capital invested in domestic shipping and to maintain a native labour force in seafaring. In Canada, as Judith Fingard has pointed out, neither mercantilist traditions nor the presence of a domestic navy encouraged laws to protect and preserve the seafarer. Instead the interests of efficiency and profit dictated the denial of habeas corpus and the denial of the right of appeal to sailors who broke the law.[1] In Canada little was done to encourage or protect the occupation of seafaring, and merchant shipping legislation differed somewhat from British precedents as a result. At sea, however, British legislation applied in Canadian vessels. The law was being applied not to ignorant, illiterate, and brutal men, but to calculating and literate men who possessed some understanding of their customary and legal rights. In these circumstances paternalism often disappeared. Its passing was hastened when fewer deckhands were known personally to masters or mates and when fewer spoke English as their native tongue. This was a pre-industrial workplace employing skilled mechanics at the onset of industrialization. The conflict that occurred in the workplace must be understood in this context.

It would be tempting, but misleading, to assume that workplace conflict occurred as a direct result of falling rates of return in an obsolescent industry. The steep decline in ocean freight rates after the mid-1870s was an obsession to shipowners, and it certainly contributed to severe pressure on profits by the 1880s (see Graph 1). The decline in freight rates was clearly the result not of a short-term

[1] Judith Fingard, *Jack in Port: Sailortowns of Eastern Canada* (Toronto 1982), 187-93.

Published with permission of McGill-Queen's University Press, from Eric W. Sager, *Seafaring Labour: The Merchant Marine of Atlantic Canada, 1820-1914* (Kingston 1989), 164-200.

Graph 1

Tramp Shipping Freights and Selected North Atlantic Sailing Ship
Freights, 1855–99

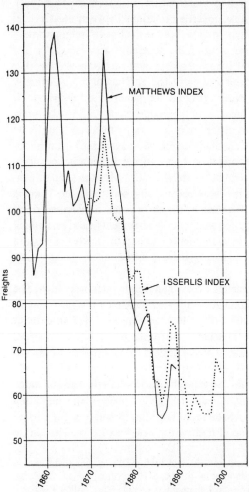

Sources: L. Isserlis, "Tramp Shipping Cargoes and Freights," *Journal of the Royal
Statistical Society* (1938), reprinted in B.R. Mitchell and P. Deane, *Abstract of
British Historical Statistics* (Cambridge, 1962), 224; Keith Matthews's index was
constructed from the following rates given in the *New York Maritime Register*:
cotton, New York-Liverpool; grain, New York-Liverpool; cotton, New Orleans-
Liverpool; deals, Saint John-Liverpool. For each of these the average of monthly
highs and lows was calculated; the annual rate is an unweighted average of the
monthly figures. The index is simply an unweighted average of the annual rates.
The method is crude, but the result is close to the Isserlis index.
Note: 1869 = 100.

trade cycle but of technological changes and an increasing supply of tonnage in a period of relatively slow growth in the volume of international trade. The pressure on masters to over-work vessels and men must have intensified. But to attribute increases in conflict to these conditions alone would be to misunderstand the genesis of discontent in the proto-industrial workplace. Conflict arose from the workplace itself and the structure of authority that governed relations between masters and wage-paid workers. Thus conflict began long before the decline in freight rates.

Although one available measure of conflict, desertion rates, suggests that conflict intensified as freight rates fell, other measures indicate that master-worker conflict was endemic even in the 1860s and early 1870s. Thus dismissal of crew into jail, and other "dishonourable" discharges, did not increase as time passed. It is impossible to derive a satisfactory measure of the frequency of conflict over time, however. Although official logs note disciplinary actions by masters, there is no complete collection of such logs for Canadian vessels. Most available logs were for voyages in the 1860s and early 1870s, and these logs indicate that conflict occurred over many issues, even before the decline in freight rates. More important than falling rates of return was the rise of the large ocean-going square-rigger. There is a striking contrast between the small vessels of the early years, or even the small vessels in the later nineteenth century for which crew agreements survive, and the larger ocean-going vessels whose crew agreements and logs are analyzed here. In the former, evidence of conflict is relatively scarce; in the latter, the evidence suggests that conflict was endemic.[2]

There was intense pressure on masters even when freight rates were high. The increasing ease of telegraphic communication allowed managing owners to maintain the pressure for speed and economy. Sailing to Argentina in 1871, Annie Butler confided to her diary the anxiety of her husband, the master of a two-masted vessel that was not rigged for speed. Day after day she prayed for favourable winds and lamented the slow progress of the vessel, for fear that the owners would blame her husband: "John is heart sick about this voyage; he knows he will sink so much money but we must try and be patient ... Last evening I felt pretty blue when I thot how matters were and John seemed so bothered. I hope things will turn out all well in the end. John knows he will be found fault with but I wish his owners had to

[2]Between 1863 and 1914 529 sailors departed from Saint John vessels of 250 tons and less; of these, none departed because of "dishonourable" discharge (discharge into jail, discharge following demotion, discharge because of refusal to proceed, and the like); only 8.1 per cent deserted. Of sailors leaving vessels of 250-499 tons, 0.5 per cent were "dishonourably" discharged and 18.4 per cent deserted. Of sailors leaving vessels of 500-999 tons, 0.5 per cent were "dishonourably" discharged and 26.8 per cent deserted. Of sailors leaving vessels of 1,000 tons and more, 0.7 per cent were "dishonourably" discharged and 21.2 deserted. The proportion of ABs who were "dishonourably" discharged changed little from one decade to the next and actually declined in the 1890s. This analysis is from the Saint John Crew List File, which contains 54,147 cases.

worry through matters as he does every day."[3] Annie's fears were justified: the owners, George and Samuel Ryerson, did not pay John Butler wages owed him after his voyage, and two years later he had still not been paid.

Speed was directly related to economy, especially in port, since the longer a vessel remained in port the higher the disbursements were likely to be. A saving in time could even compensate for a loss in freight rate, as James Duncan of Charlottetown told a master in 1872, when freight rates were high: "Do not lose one hour that can be avoided as we find it is delay which in nearly every instance loses money, and when chartering you must bear in mind that quick dispatch is very important and is worth a small concession in rate of freight."[4] In page after page of correspondence with masters the creed of parsimony is repeated: "Hold things up as cheaply as possible and make all you can of it."[5] Even when freight rates were high, shipowners kept up the pressure: "Some of the richest shipowners in our city, who have made splendid fortunes out of their ships, were you to judge by their conversation, you would fancy had difficulty in making ends meet, and however high the freights are, you are met with the terrible bug-bear of the heavy expenses."[6]

By the 1880s pressure for speed had often given way to panic: "Shipowning is not what it was in 1870, and things must be worked on a different basis altogether," wrote an enraged managing owner whose master had put back into port in Ireland because of a storm.[7] Speed and economy meant taking risks, as Robert Quirk of Charlottetown was clearly prepared to do. Quirk also argued for increased deck loads and advised his partner to ignore their master's objections: "It will be as well not to listen to the advice of a captain, as I have found out that they begin crying out long before they are hurt."[8] Even in the early 1870s the Moran family of New Brunswick was making severe, if not risky economies. W.H. Moran wrote about the *Crown Prince* in 1871: "I am doing my utmost to keep down disbursements and tending on the ship day & night. I am going to sea this time without many things which are actually necessary such as iron water tanks, plates for forecastle rail, davits, etc., etc. I am doing so to keep down expenses in Liverpool."[9]

Pressure on the master led to pressure on his crew. Of course masters had always driven sailors hard, and of course the threat and the use of force had been part of the master-crew relationship long before the 1860s and 1870s. But merchant shipping legislation now made a critical difference: it had given new legal sanctions to the master's customary use of force and to the sailor's defence of customary and

[3]Diary of Annie Butler, 3 April and 12 April 1871, in the brig *Daisy* of Yarmouth. This diary is held by Mr. Raymond Simpson of Merigomish.
[4]Letter of 5 March 1872 from James Duncan to Captain Murchison, Duncan Letterbook, Provincial Archives of Prince Edward Island, Charlottetown [PAPEI].
[5]Clement Crowell, *Novascotiaman* (Halifax 1979), 153.
[6]James Kelso of Glasgow to L.C. Owen, 28 April 1874, Owen Letterbooks, PAPEI.
[7]Robert Quirk to R.M.C. Stumbles, 5 May 1881, Duncan Letterbooks, vol. 362, PAPEI.
[8]Robert Quirk to R.M.C. Stumbles, 23 March 1881, Duncan Letterbooks, vol. 362, PAPEI.
[9]W.H. Moran to James H. Moran, 10 August 1871, Moran Papers, New Brunswick Museum, Saint John [NBM].

legal rights. The result was an escalation of conflict and of bargaining through the use of both legal and extra-legal methods. A commonplace instance will suffice to illustrate the change. In 1884 an able seaman in the *Zebina Goudey* of Yarmouth refused to obey the orders of his master on a voyage to the East Indies; the seaman was subdued by force, and on arrival in Sourabaya he spent several days in gaol. In the early nineteenth century the story would have ended there; the dispute might never have involved a gaol sentence at all, for the master might have felt obliged to settle the matter himself. In 1884, however, the master resorted to the police in Sourabaya and deducted the cost of police action and gaol expenses from wages owed to the AB at the end of the voyage. The AB, cognizant of his legal rights, charged the master for non-payment of wages, and the charge was heard in a court in Greenock. The superintendent of mercantile marine in Greenock testified that the entries in the official log were not properly signed and witnessed. The magistrate would not accept the log in evidence and ordered the arrears of wages to be paid.[10] Such appeals to the courts increased in frequency after mid-century, until court and prison officials complained that their premises were filled with seamen.[11] The resolution of disputes was often non-violent, but it was conflict nevertheless, sanctioned and encouraged in law.

The pressure on the master was often reflected in frustration with his crew and with the laws that appeared to protect sailors. George Murray, master of the *J.L. Wickwire* of Windsor, in the North Atlantic in 1870 found himself "nearly broken down from being on deck night and day" and recorded in his official log a protest on behalf of all masters: "For us there is no redress ... The Law will punish us as and brand us as tyrants, take from us our certificates our means of livelihood. if we to protect the property committed to our care drive lazy ignorant impostures to their duties when it is required ... One half of the wrecks in the Western Ocean is the fault of such crews as I have now got."[12]

But hard-pressed masters sought and found means of protecting their interests. One such protection was the provision that a deserter forfeited his claim to unpaid wages, and in the late nineteenth century we read of masters who drove men to desertion in order to make savings in wage costs. "To sail in a Nova Scotian vessel was one of the hardest experiences one could be involved in," remembered a Norwegian sailor. "I sailed in one called the *Grenada*, of Windsor. She was a proper hard case. The captain was proud of the fact that he had not paid off the crew in the course of twenty years. He was a boxer. He came on deck at six o'clock each

[10]"Action against a Yarmouth Captain," *Yarmouth Times*, 25 June 1884.

[11]Fingard, *Jack in Port*, 140. In 1854 the inspector of prisons in the Southern and Western districts reported to the Home Office in London that nine of every twelve prisoners were sailors who had refused to continue their voyages: Tony Lane, "'Philosophical Anarchists': British Merchant Seamen and Their Attitudes to Authority," typescript of a paper published in French in *Enragés* (Paris), 11-12 (1983-4), 6-7.

[12]*J.L. Wickwire* of Windsor, Official No. 52098, 1869-70, Maritime History Archive, Memorial University of Newfoundland, St. John's [MHA].

morning just looking for a chance to get into trouble with one of the men."[13] A simpler method of cutting wage costs was to hire fewer men upon departure. But in the late nineteenth century even that tactic could lead to bargaining and conflict, for sailors could now claim that an undermanned vessel was unseaworthy and seek legal redress.

In the official accounts, undesirable behaviour by sailors often appears to be motiveless, the result of drunkenness, laziness, or the inferior quality of the worker himself. But confrontations with authority, either in the vessel or on shore, were usually purposeful actions designed to effect improvements in working conditions. Long before seamen were organized in trade unions they had learned how to bargain. Their most obvious weapon was withdrawal of labour — a formidable tool at sea, where the employer could not dismiss workers and hire replacements.

Withdrawal of labour took various forms. Sailors could refuse to work, either individually or in groups. In a workplace where labour was usually applied by the co-ordinated action of men working in groups, the co-ordinated withdrawal of labour occurred naturally and frequently. Failing to join a vessel after signing the articles was also a form of withdrawing labour, and a costly one to the vessel if the sailor had been paid in advance. Desertion was also a means of withdrawing labour.

As Judith Fingard has pointed out, the sailor's confrontations with authority in port had more to do with working conditions than with motiveless disorderly behaviour.[14] The use of judicial or criminal records is fraught with problems, and criminal statistics may say more about the activities of police than the activities of sailors. Two conclusions may be drawn, however, from the sources that Fingard used, and from other late-nineteenth-century material: non-violent withdrawal of labour was far more important than other causes of court appearances by sailors; and withdrawal of labour became relatively more important as time passed. The annual reports of the Quebec and Montreal harbour police report the number of arrests of sailors in each year. This source does not state the port or nationality of vessels in which sailors were working, and so it is not possible to focus on sailors from Atlantic Canadian ships. The source is useful, however, because it states the reasons for arrests on an annual basis. In the five-year period 1870-4, 37 per cent of arrests in Quebec were the consequence of refusals to work (desertion, refusal to proceed, refusal of duty, failing to join a ship).[15] Another 29.8 per cent were absence without leave — another form of withdrawing labour, and a protest against the master's denial of shore leaves.

At Quebec, as elsewhere, masters often attempted to deny shore leave for fear that sailors might not return. Where shore leave was granted, the hours of leave

---

[13]Samlet av Svein Molaug, *Sjofolk Forteller: Hverdagshistorier fra seilskutetiden* (Oslo 1977), 33. The translation is that of Capt. W.J. Lewis Parker, USCG (Ret), to whom I am grateful for this reference.

[14]Fingard, *Jack in Port*, 140 and *passim*.

[15]Reports of the Chief Constable, Québec River Police, Canada *Sessional Papers*, 1871, no. 5; 1872, no. 5; 1873, no. 8; 1874, no. 4; 1875, no. 5.

were fixed in advance, and all too often the master expected his men to return in the early hours of evening. When they did not return they were liable to arrest. The frequency of this crime says something about the vigilance of the police, something about the fears of masters, and a great deal about the concern of masters to retain firm control over their labour force in a high-wage port.

Arrests in Quebec for assault or other types of violence were much less common (10.8 per cent), and arrests of masters and mates for assaults on crew were more frequent (16.6. per cent of crimes of violence) than were arrests of crew for assault on masters or mates (11.9 per cent of crimes of violence). Arrests for drunkenness or for the purpose of "protection for the night" were only 14.6 per cent of all arrests.

It is risky to draw conclusions about changes in crew behaviour over time from these records, since the number of policemen and their methods changed over time. The total number of arrests certainly declined over time: from an annual average of 548 by the Quebec police in the early 1870s to a mere 95 in 1889; from an average of 802 in Montreal in the early 1870s to 610 in 1888.[16] As time passed, arrests for violations of maritime law, or for withdrawal of labour, became relatively more important. Either the police or employers took such activities more seriously, or the withdrawal of labour was becoming relatively more frequent.

In her analysis of sailors' appearances before the magistrates in Quebec in 1854, Fingard found that a third had been charged with desertion or refusal to work; over half with "drunk and disorderly" offences.[17] The Quebec harbour police reports suggest that arrests for desertion or refusal to work increased relatively, to 37 per cent of all arrests by the 1870s and to 38 per cent by 1888. If we include absences without leave, withdrawal-related offences had increased from 41 per cent in 1854 to 67 per cent in the early 1870s. By the late 1880s arrests for drunkenness, assault, and other forms of violence had declined sharply in both absolute and relative terms. These changes reflect the more rapid turn-around of vessels, particularly steam vessels, which decreased total time spent in port and opportunities for arrest for such petty crimes as drunkenness. But the changes reflect also general trends in British and colonial shipping: they reflect the sailor's increasing resort to bargaining, to litigation, and to withdrawal of labour as means of protecting his rights.

Why did sailors withdraw labour? In the absence of formal organization among sailors, and in the absence of many records that allow the sailor's voice to be heard, it is difficult to assess the reasons. The motives in Atlantic Canadian vessels were unlikely to be very different from those of sailors appearing in court in Canadian ports (discussed by Fingard) or in British ports. During the campaign against unseaworthy ships led by Plimsoll and others in the 1870s, the British government attempted to keep more detailed records on vessels alleged to be unseaworthy and

[16]Reports of the Montréal Harbour Police; Reports of the Chief Constable, Québec Harbour Police, Canada *Sessional Papers*. The Montréal Harbour Police were disbanded in 1889 and the Québec Harbour Police in 1893; see Fingard, *Jack in Port*, 30-2.
[17]Fingard, *Jack in Port*, 140.

on sailors who refused duty in merchant vessels. For most of the sailors committed to prison in the 1870s for refusing to proceed to sea from a port in the United Kingdom there exists a brief statement of the reasons for refusing work. Table 1 summarizes these reasons for sailors convicted in 1870, 1871, and 1872 (excluding the large number of cases where the reason was not given). The stated reasons may conceal the real reasons, of course, and shipowners often protested that "unprincipled seamen" used unseaworthiness "as an excuse for being relieved from their engagements, more especially in cases where they have received a payment of wages in advance, or where they have thought they could improve their position."[18]

Table 1
Reasons for Refusal to Proceed in Vessels
Leaving British Ports, 1870-2

Reason Given by Sailors	No.	%
Vessel unseaworthy/leaky	284	36.5
Vessel overladen	24	3.1
Vessel under-manned	57	7.3
Inadequate provisions	52	6.7
Gear or pumps not working	6	0.8
Inadequate crew accommodations	51	6.6
Wages or advance too low	11	1.4
Other complaint about vessel or work conditions	22	2.8
Did not like master/master violent	48	6.2
Did not like mate/mate violent/dispute with mate	34	4.4
Did not like crew	6	0.8
Refusal to act as scabs	11	1.4
Drunk at the time	69	8.9
Arrived late	39	5.0
Personal illness	23	3.0
Illness in family	4	0.5
Unexplained desertion/other	37	4.7

Source: "Return of the Crews of Merchant Ships, which have been committed to Prison in the Years 1870, 1871 for Refusing to Proceed to Sea," *British Parliamentary Papers*, 1873, vol. LIX, 245ff. Nationality of sailors is not given, but probably most were British.

Concern over unseaworthy ships had preceded Plimsoll by many decades, of course. Since 1855 law officers of the crown had advised the Board of Trade that sailors did have the right to refuse to serve in unseaworthy vessels. This left the onus of proof on the sailors themselves, but from 1864, if not before, British

[18]W.S. Lindsay, *History of Merchant Shipping and Ancient Commerce* (New York 1965), vol. III, 472.

magistrates were advised to order surveys of vessels where allegations had been made. This encouraged sailors in their resort to litigation or to consular authority in foreign ports. Possibly the opportunity of better wages in other vessels or of spending an advance were reasons more common than sailors would admit in court. But this does not mean that allegations of unseaworthiness may be dismissed as spurious. In 1877 the Board of Trade ordered over 200 vessels to be detained because they were overladen. In the mid-1870s over 2,000 sailors in British vessels died each year; one estimate suggests that 36,000 seamen perished between 1872 and 1884.[19]

If sailors frequently complained about unseaworthy vessels, they had reason to do so.[20] As Table 1 suggests, most convictions followed from sailors' complaints about their vessels or working conditions: almost two-thirds fall into this category. Another 13 per cent of refusals to work followed from complaints about the master, mate, or crew of a vessel (in one vessel the crew refused to work when it discovered the previous crew on board, on strike for higher wages). In a small minority of cases, conviction followed from the vices commonly attributed to seamen in the British and colonial merchant marine: drunkenness and dilatoriness. The sailor's refusal to work was part of a struggle for control over working conditions. The struggle to improve working conditions at sea was not merely a campaign by humanitarian reformers at the parliamentary level.

It is possible to focus on the vessels of Atlantic Canada, but to do so the historian must use the official logs for those vessels, even though the logs do not allow the precision of statistical analysis. An extensive survey of these logs suggests that the pattern reflected in Table 1 was repeated in Canadian vessels: refusal to work and refusal to obey orders were the most common reasons for entries in logs relating to misdemeanours by sailors.[21] Most disputes resulted from apparent attempts by owners to minimize operating costs and concerned manning of the vessel, hours of work, victualling, cargohandling, or seaworthiness. Statutory regulations in these areas were usually voluntary — matters of custom — rather than compulsory. Working conditions were governed by a contract, and the sailor could refuse to sign the contract, but he had no right to bargain formally over its content. This situation ensured that customary practice, and practices that sailors now claimed as tradition, would collide with the interests of owners determined to minimize costs.

[19]Returns of causes of deaths of seamen, *British Parliamentary Papers*, 1873, vol. LIX, 221; 1874, vol. LX, 219; 1875, vol. LXVIII, 331; 1876, vol. LXVI, 157; 1877, vol. LXXIV, 213. In 1873-4, 506 lives were lost on or near British coasts, and 4,034 on the high seas and abroad; of the latter, 1,440 were passengers. See Neville Upham, *The Load Line — A Hallmark of Safety* (Greenwich 1978), viii-ix; A.G. Course, *The Merchant Navy: A Social History* (London 1963), 245, 247.

[20]Samuel Plimsoll, MP, *Our Seamen: An Appeal* (London 1873).

[21]When crew lists were coded, an entry was made to record the presence of an interesting official log. The following section is based on the reading of several hundred official logs for vessels registered in Saint John, Yarmouth, Windsor, and Halifax, MHA.

Undermanning was a common cost-cutting tactic. Protests occurred as a result, both during and at the beginning of a voyage. There was no statutory regulation of the minimum number of men required in a vessel, although an act of 1835 (5 and 6 William IV, cap 19) had specified a minimum number of apprentices to be carried in vessels of different tonnages. Various recommendations about proper manning levels followed, as well as humanitarian outcry that served to legitimize protest by seamen. And there was legal compulsion in cases where an undermanned vessel was judged to be unseaworthy because of the undermanning.[22] In Tinby Roads, South Wales, on 5 December 1866, an AB named George Harris refused to proceed to sea on the grounds that the vessel was short one man; a magistrate found in his favour and the master hired another seaman.[23]

Outside the United Kingdom, faced with a ruthless master, the crew might not so easily win its case. In July 1871 the *Beau Monde*, a vessel owned by the Moran family of Saint Martin's, New Brunswick, was lying in Honolulu. Seven ABs refused to man the windlass to heave the anchor: "They said there was not sufficient men on board" and they went into the forecastle. The master, a Scotsman named John W. Ross, stated in the official log that the vessel was fully manned: "The Ship has got her full number of crew 24 all tole & one passenger." The crew list indicated that only 20 crew members were employed in a three-masted ship of 1,047 registered tons. And on this same day the chief mate, an Englishman with previous experience in the *Beau Monde*, was discharged and advised the crew not to proceed in the vessel.

But Ross would not be delayed: together with his mates and petty officers and the passenger, he raised the anchor and made sail. The crew members went on deck to find the vessel under way. They said that "they would go to work if they got the pay for men that is short." The master declared that the matter would have to be settled in court on arrival in England. There is no report of a court case upon arrival in Liverpool, and the master paid off the crew. But it had not been an easy passage, for the official log records several subsequent instances of refusal to work, as well as cases of scurvy. Compared to other ships of her size in the early 1870s, the *Beau Monde* had gone round the Horn short two ABs; the crew had not been able to do anything about it.[24]

Disputes over seaworthiness often occurred before the voyage began but could also occur at sea. When a vessel was damaged at sea the master often had a difficult choice to make: should he proceed to his intended destination or put into the nearest port for repairs? Proceeding with the voyage often required repairs at sea, extra work for the crew, long hours at the pumps, and increased risk. While seeking to avoid the loss of cargo or vessel, the master was under great pressure to complete the voyage as quickly as possible. Often he would decide to proceed, but his decision

---

[22]Lindsay, *History of Merchant Shipping*, vol. III, 472-3.
[23]Barque *Suffolk* of Glasgow, Official No. 46210, 1866-7, MHA.
[24]*Beau Monde* of Saint John, Official No. 35237, 1870-2, MHA.

required the co-operation of his crew, which did not have the same interest in a speedy passage.

In 1871 the barque *Newcastle* of Windsor was five days from Greenock bound for New Orleans when she met a gale and sprung a leak. On 20 April the master reported that he had found no less than seven feet of water in the hold, and the crew manned the pumps for 16 hours. Eventually the men reduced the water to three feet eight inches, but "when turning all hands to pump ship, the[y] refused to proceed any further unless I hove up to England." The master went into the hold, found the source of the leak, but could not "get at it" to make repairs. In these circumstances the crew had its way, and the master returned to port in Britain.[25]

A similar problem occurred on board the *Pomona* of Saint John when she went aground in fog in the St Lawrence in 1868. The crew managed to get the vessel off the rocks after eight days of heavy work but refused to work unless the master put back to Quebec for repairs. In such circumstances refusing to work could result in lengthy bargaining, and in the *Pomona* bargaining continued for four days. The master argued that they could not reach Quebec because the vessel would not beat to windward. The crew argued for the nearest port, and finally they agreed on St. John's, Newfoundland.[26] In this case, several circumstances had led to bargaining and consensus: the mutual recognition of danger, a degree of mutual respect, and the recognition that both sides had power with which to back up any threats.

More often, however, the complaint of unseaworthiness would lead to a court decision or to a confrontation at sea. On leaving Montevideo in 1869 the *Alexander* of Saint John struck a reef. The men refused to proceed unless the vessel was surveyed, and they struck work for 24 hours. The master judged that it was safe to proceed and that repairs could not be effected in Montevideo. He was supported by his mates. He put the three "ringleaders" in irons and so persuaded the rest of the crew to set sail.[27]

The log books suggest that disputes over hours of work were very frequent in Atlantic Canadian vessels. Here the conflict between custom and the interests of owners was very clear. Canadian vessels followed the pattern of watch above and watch below. Neither the official logs nor the crew articles made formal note of a common violation of this tradition in Canadian vessels: no afternoon watch below. Masters who ordered both watches on deck in the afternoon often heard the following response: "Seamen refused to come on deck to assist in setting up Rigging and various other jobs of work to secure the Rigging told the mate they would not stop on deck in the afternoon."[28]

By the 1870s crews serving in ocean-going vessels appear to have lost the battle over afternoon watch, and most would expect work in that watch, but there were still occasional protests and references to past custom. In the *John Barbour* of Saint

[25]*Newcastle* of Windsor, Official No. 52087, 1871, MHA.
[26]*Pomona* of Saint John, E.T. Irvine, master, Official No. 35051, 1868, MHA.
[27]*Alexander* of Saint John, Henry Stinchcomb, master, Official No. 1421, 1869, MHA.
[28]*Gertrude* of Saint John, I.W. Doane, master, Official No. 35178, 1870-1, MHA.

John, sailing from Montreal to Montevideo in 1873, the master attempted to begin the morning work 10 minutes before custom allowed. At 5:50 a.m. he "ordered the watch to muster buckets to wash decks down." The sailors "murmured" and replied that "it was not 4 Bells (6 o'clock)." The master chose to make an example of one sailor, whom he put in irons. Later the same watch challenged the master on behalf of its colleague and cited the custom of afternoon watch below. At half past noon on 4 January, with drawn sheath knives in their hands, the men "refused to do any more work until W. Lewis was released and that they should not be kept up in the afternoon watch." The master went "to considerable trouble" (meaning, likely, that a fight ensued or that he employed a revolver) and "got them driven into the forecastle & confined them there without food until they were willing to go to their duty." The men did not return to work until noon of 7 January: they had been without food for three days. William Lewis held out for five days and then returned to work.[29]

Disputes also occurred over work on Sunday and other holidays. Here, too, custom collided with the impatience of masters determined to lay on sail or to see port times reduced. Tradition held that on Sunday necessary work about the sails and rigging would be done but that other tasks about the vessel would not occur. In vessels where David Perley Crowe was master, for instance, "the men were free to sleep, to mend or wash clothing, to engage in games or to spend the time as they saw fit."[30] But when in 1867 the master of the *David G. Fleming* of Saint John wanted to move his vessel from its anchorage into the inner harbour at Aden, his crew refused to proceed "as it was Sunday." Before the consul the master argued that "it was absolutely necessary to move the ship as she was lying in a dangerous position." Such an argument was well calculated to impress a British consul, and even tradition obliged that work be done on Sunday if a vessel were at risk. If the deckhands denied that the vessel was in danger, the consul would heed the master's judgment. The men were ordered to work, their only alternative being a jail sentence.[31]

Where the dispute could not so easily be referred to a consul or magistrate, the crew might win the dispute. On the *Peter Maxwell* of Saint John, in mid-Atlantic bound for Saint John, George Sulis ordered his crew to stitch the fore sail, which had been split in heavy weather. The crew refused this task on the grounds that it was Sunday. Sulis argued not only the need for safety but the need for speed: "It was impossible to get the Ship to the Westward without canvass." The crew was not persuaded, and the first mate and a boy stitched the sail.[32]

Very often it appears that the religious convictions of masters encouraged them toward traditional Sunday observance. But at least one Nova Scotia master, M.P.

[29] *John Barbour* of Saint John, Robert H.A. Ivey, master, Official No. 34742, 1872-3, MHA.
[30] John Congdon Crowe, *In the Days of the Windjammers* (Toronto 1959), 104.
[31] *David G. Fleming* of Saint John, Robert Sully, master, Official No. 24197, 1866-8, MHA. A similar case occurred in the *War Spirit* of Saint John, Official No. 10900, in Pensacola on 29 March 1871.
[32] *Peter Maxwell* of Saint John, Official No. 34938, 20 March 1870, MHA.

McElhinney of Windsor, took Sunday observance too far. He insisted not only that all crew members attend his "Divine Service" on Sundays but that washing clothes was a violation of the sabbath. He fined men who commited this offence, and we do not know whose will prevailed in the subsequent conflict.[33] There were few formal holidays in this industry, but Christmas Day was usually observed by the avoidance of nonessential work. When Thomas Trefry tried to insist that his crew wash decks on Christmas Day, all refused. Since his vessel was in port, Trefry had an option: he could and did hire shore workers to do the work and charged the cost to his seven ABS.[34]

Disputes also occurred over the hours of work in port, again because tradition often contradicted the needs of the master and because the practice of cargo-handling varied from one port to another. In Atlantic Canada sailors were gradually replaced in major ports by shore workers, but in many ports throughout the world sailors took a major part in the tasks of loading and discharging cargo.[35] Sailors were required to do such work, and the laws about refusing work or disobeying the command of the master would apply. But there was considerable room for interpretation and dispute.

At many ports work proceeded from 6 a.m. to 6 p.m. Dispute often arose in ports where such hours were not observed, and where (as in South American guano ports) lighters carrying cargo might come alongside in the evening. In July 1870 the *Tasmanian* of Saint John was loading guano in the Guanape Islands when the crew struck: "The whole of the crew refused to take in about a ton of Guano because it was 6 o'clock. I told them 6 oclock had nothing to do with them when there was cargo alongside. I explained to them of the risk and value of it but they still refused to work Ephraim Waters and Israel Francis being ringleaders."[36] Waters and Francis were taken to the consul who told them "they must take the Guano in whenever it came alongside." The men appear to have returned to work, under the threat of being put in irons. In August 1865, the crew of the ship *Zambesi* of Saint John struck work in the Chincha Islands for the same reason. The master, John Cameron, argued that "there are no regular hours at Chinchas" and put six ABs in irons when they continued to refuse work. A British consul came on board to hear the men's complaint: he stated that "the rules of the port were to work at all hours that Cargo could be got"; the men insisted that they would not work before 6 a.m. or after 6 p.m. The consul ordered them "into confinement with bread and water for food until such time as they should turn too." Within five days the men had returned to work, but three weeks later they all struck again, refusing to sail the vessel from Callao. Only after further visits to the consul (we do not know what occurred at this time)

[33]*David McNutt* of Windsor, Official No. 48436, 1868-9, MHA.
[34]*Salus* of Halifax, Official No. 48137, In Savannah, 25 Dec. 1867, MHA.
[35]Judith Fingard, "The Decline of the Sailor as a Ship Labourer in 19th Century Timber Ports," *Labour/Le Travailleur*, 2 (1977), 35-53.
[36]*Tasmanian* of Saint John, Official No. 35076, July 1870, MHA.

did the vessel proceed.[37] Disputes over loading after 6 p.m. also occurred in American cotton ports and in the West Indies.[38]

Attempts to economize in the provision of food led to confrontations in which the resistance of workers had a clear purpose. Complaints about grub were inevitably more common on longer voyages, when vessels were more likely to run short of provisions, or when food was spoiled and bread was stale. Disputes over victuals were also frequent because by the 1860s crew articles stated the amount that the crew was promised on a daily or weekly basis, and so the crew had prior knowledge and a clear basis for argument if the scale was violated.

Disputes over victualling often involved threats and violence, and here violence was clearly directed toward the improvement of conditions of service. Only a few days out of Liverpool, Charles Curry, master of the *Juno* of Windsor, found himself faced by an enraged crew which had discovered that, faced with a long voyage to Rio de Janeiro, the bread was already stale. "The remainder of the crew came aft and threatened to take our lives. I then went on deck and told them I would give them better bread," but the problem was not solved. On the next day the crew "armed themselves with belaying pins and clubs," and the master forced the men back toward the forecastle by brandishing his revolver. Upon arrival in Rio the crew demanded to see the British consul, and when the master refused to allow more than two of them ashore, most deserted.[39]

Sometimes complaints over victualling were resolved in favour of the crew, when the quantity promised in the crew list had not been given, or when the quality was so bad that the food was inedible. In Rangoon on 18 September 1872, a British consul examined samples of biscuit from the ship *S. Vaughan* after six ABs had refused duty. "The samples produced and admitted by the Master and officer to be the ships' bread were decidedly bad." The master agreed to remove all stale bread from the vessel and was ordered to pay the crew "compensation for the number of days during which it was issued to them."[40] At other times the crew of a badly provisioned vessel had no option but jail or desertion. When Edward Baxter, master of the Saint John ship *Ann Gray*, ordered his vessel under way from the Clyde to Saint John via Belfast, his 12 ABs and one OS refused to proceed on the grounds that "they wanted to be better fed" and that "the stove would not keep the forecastle warm at sea" because of inadequate fuel (the date was 1 December). All these deckhands were sent to jail for six weeks, and Baxter hired another crew, all of

[37]*Zambesi* of Saint John, Official No. 35207, 1865-6, MHA.
[38]On 2 December 1870, the crew of the *Maud* of Saint John, loading bales of cotton in Savannah, quit work at 6 p.m., leaving four bales of cotton on the wharf. It appears that the master hired others to load the remaining bales (*Maud*, Official No. 41890, 1870-1). In Belize on 24 January 1874 Henry Taylor ordered the crew of the *Fair and Easy* of Windsor to "take in some logs of mahogany that were chafing against the ship." The crew refused on the grounds that it was 9 p.m., and the sailors were sent to jail until the vessel sailed (*Fair and Easy*, Official No. 61487, 1873-4, MHA).
[39]*Juno* of Windsor, Official No. 48477, 1873, MHA.
[40]*S. Vaughan* of Windsor, Official No. 61466, 1872, MHA.

whose members deserted in Belfast. A third crew took the vessel to Saint John and promptly deserted.[41]

In theory sailors knew in advance what food they would receive. In practice, however, they did not know what stores the vessel carried. The list of provisions may be deceptive. Underneath the scale of provisions on the front of most crew lists were the words "Equivalent substitutes at Master's option" — which left the matter open to interpretation. Samuel Hughes, master of the *William Carvill*, sailing in 1869 from Liverpool to Rangoon, agreed to provide something less than the Board of Trade-recommended scale of 1868, but nevertheless a fairly common diet: 1 1/2 pounds of beef or pork daily; a pound of bread a day; 1 1/2 pounds of flour weekly; peas three times a week; and sugar, coffee, water, and lime juice. It is very unlikely that the crew received even this minimal diet, because after six months at sea five men, including the cook, had scurvy.[42] In a letter accompanying his official log, the master blamed the scurvy on "bad Aden water" and the refusal of the men to drink fresh rain water at sea.

When victualling was clearly inferior, crews might obtain some relief by appealing to a magistrate or consul, but neither the likelihood of redress nor the penalties imposed constituted an effective deterrent. The ship *Athenais* of Saint John set sail for Callao from Aden on 29 August 1866. She was so badly provisioned that on arrival in Callao on 10 December most crew members, including the first mate, were suffering from scurvy. The consul ordered a doctor to investigate, and the doctor ordered 12 seamen and the first mate into hospital. On 17 December the consul advised the master, William Birch, that his vessel would not be given clearance until a full investigation had been carried out.

A naval court inquiry into the causes of scurvy found "the Beef and Pork has been of very inferior quality, and the Lime juice quite useless as an anti-scorbutic, which we consider to have been the sole causes of the sickness of the crew and consequently we deem the owners of the ship highly reprehensible and adjudge them to pay the hospital expenses, as well as the expenses for the surveying of the proceedings." The court stated further that the master "has shown a culpable want of attention to his crew while sick, and who we consider highly to blame for leaving Aden knowing the inferior quality of the Provisions with so small a supply of livestock." After this reprimand the vessel was allowed to sail, which she did on 19 December. Birch had been delayed only a few days. On his next voyage we find Birch making his own silent protest: he recorded in his official log what food was issued to the crew on almost every day of the voyage.[43]

There is evidence that seamen in Canadian vessels were sometimes ordered to perform work not normally associated with their ranks. Many disputes arose in such circumstances, when interpretations of custom differed. In the *Beau Monde*, passing through the Red Sea in 1868, the mate ordered both the cook and the steward to

[41]*Ann Gray* of Saint John, Official No. 34844, 1867-8, MHA.
[42]*William Carvill* of Saint John, Official No. 35168, 1869-70, MHA.
[43]*Athenais* of Saint John, Official No. 35141, 1868-9, MHA.

assist in reefing the fore topsail. The cook refused on the grounds that, since it was noon, he was "going to make the men's dinner." The master attempted to resolve the dispute by putting the cook in irons: he clearly expected that the cook must assist in working the sails at any time of day. After two days in irons the cook returned to his galley, but he had not forgotten his disagreement with the master and he refused to do any extra work. A few weeks later he served the master pea soup "quite covered on the top with small flies and a quantity of large maggots," and the master gave up the struggle, noting in his log that "acts of dirtiness are of frequent occurrence with the Cook."[44]

Sailors were sticklers for routine, and they could use the ship's routine as grounds for "working to rule." Isaac Doane, master of the *Gertrude* of Saint John, discovered an entire crew of "sea lawyers" after he refused to give them coffee at 6:30 a.m., when they were accustomed to it. "They all made answer and said they would not work half so hard as they had done." The protest continued with the crew protesting about late breakfasts and refusing to work unless breakfast were served promptly at 6 a.m.[45]

Crew articles, as they became more detailed and comprehensive, could also serve as the basis of working to rule. In December 1869 the *William Carvill* of Saint John was at sea from Moulmein to Liverpool when the crew demanded that butter and bread be weighed out individually to each man, instead of being weighed out once for the whole watch before the men divided it among each other. The dispute arose not between deckhands but from conditions in the ship: several crew members had previously refused to work and had requested their discharge in Moulmein, which the master denied them. When the master refused to order that butter be weighed individually, the crew refused to take it. On 1 January the master "sent to the men three bottles of wine being new year's day," but they returned [it] saying it was not on the articles." On 2 January the men were served a half-pound of rice each (presumably in lieu of potatoes), but "they returned it saying it was on the articles only as a *substitute*. They were offered Preserved Potatoes they also refused to take them." On 11 January the men were demanding individual weighing of their quarter-ounce of tea, their bread, their three ounces of molasses, and their lime juice and sugar. On 19 January Thomas Clarke, AB, "refused to have his sugar saying it was too much weight saying the Steward wanted to Rob the owners." Other ABs refused their lime juice and sugar on the same grounds. The sarcastic defence of the owner's interest was a pointed rebuke of master and officers.[46]

Sailors knew that the master was the servant of shipowners, and they understood that by contract they were doing no more than selling labour power in return

[44]*Beau Monde* of Saint John, James Linskill, master, Official No. 35237, Nov.-Dec. 1867, MHA.

[45]*Gertrude* of Saint John, Official No. 35178, 1868-9, MHA. For another instance of "sogering" or working to rule see Richard Henry Dana, *Two Years before the Mast* (New York 1946), 87.

[46]*William Carvill* of Saint John, Hugh Seeds, master, Official No. 35168, 1869-70, MHA.

for wages. The universal use of a formal contract legitimized sailors' protests, and this was what so infuriated masters and owners: the sale of labour power by contract had legitimized informal bargaining over all conditions of employment. Now the sailor raised issues that masters thought trivial or picayune. The master of a New Brunswick barque, shortly after leaving Saint John, discovered that his starboard watch "refused to work, on a/c of the bread, it is good but the fellows having seen some of the fresh, are not content till they get some of it." Later in the same voyage, "the men all came aft and requested molasses in their Barley soup, & said the beef & bread was bad, the infernal scoundrels all they want is to get some hold of us."[47]

Such complaints were not a simple response to hunger nor even a defence of established custom. First one watch, and then an entire crew, were claiming a right grounded in their view of natural justice and a "moral economy of provision."[48] The presence of fresh bread, only a few days from port, proved that it was possible to provide fresh bread; therefore nothing inferior was acceptable. The uncontrollable fury of sailors in particular instances suggests not a simple, unreasoning response to deprivation, but rather a sense of moral outrage at the violation of assumed rights. In 1873 the master of a Saint John ship infringed upon his second mate's right to spend more shore leave as he chose, and the second mate responded in violent rage, attacking the master with his fists and with a boathook: "I found the 2nd mate in a Rum Shop drinking and a good deal the worse for liquor, I called him out and told him I wondered at him drinking that way, and he said what I drink I pay for, I dont want you or any other Buger to pay for my drink I suppose I can come and drink as well as you ... On the way to the ship he was very impudent, saying it was all my fault, I did not know the way to handle men, I told him I would treat him as he deserved, he said ... you starve gutted animal, you can only give me the law and no more."[49] It was not only drink but also pride and moral outrage that moved this sailor to violence.

In the last half of the nineteenth century it was possible to charge masters with assault and to obtain convictions. There were definable limits to the use of punitive force, and sailors took advantage of this fact. On many occasions crews acted together to attempt to remove one of their fellows from irons when they felt an injustice had been done, or when the punishment caused the victim to become ill. Moral outrage against an excess of force often led to further violence, as occurred in Aden in 1866 when the master of the *Henry* of Saint John was summoned before the magistrate on a charge of criminal violence against six of his seamen. When the magistrate dismissed the charge and the triumphant master ordered the men back to the ship, the six plaintiffs were so enraged at the failure of justice that they attacked and thrashed the master in the courtroom, whereupon they were sentenced

---

[47]Journal of James N. Smith (supercargo), in the Barque *Susan*, 9 May and 15 July 1850, NBM.
[48]E.P. Thompson, "The Moral Economy of the English Crowd in the Eighteenth Century," *Past & Present*, no. 50 (Feb. 1971), 136.
[49]*Tasmanian* of Saint John, George B. Willis, master, Official No. 35076, 1872-3, MHA.

to three months in prison.[50] Violent as they often were, seamen were moved by a moral consensus that law and contractual obligations seemed to sanction: "You can give me the law and no more."

How effective were seamen in this primitive bargaining process? It is impossible to know precisely how many court actions resulted in decisions favourable to sailors, but the evidence of the official logs suggests that where sailors refused duty they rarely won their case. Most disputes were settled at sea, however, where withdrawal of labour could be a potent weapon. Provided a vessel was not in danger, the crew could cease work at less cost to itself than to the master, and of course master and officers were always outnumbered.

Nevertheless, master and officers always possessed superior power, even at sea. The master was usually the only person in a vessel who possessed firearms. Occasionally one reads of able seamen with firearms, and in one very leaky New Brunswick vessel in 1855 a crew demanded extra food for extra work, and, according to the master, "they are firing pistols ocationaly to intimidate and force ther demands."[51] Seamen usually possessed only sheathknives; masters kept pistols and sometimes shotguns in their cabins. Rarely was a master confronted by an entire crew at the same time, and well before violence was threatened a cautious master attempted to isolate "ringleaders" from the rest in order to divide and weaken his opponents. If all else failed, the power to withdraw food would usually force men into submission. Faced with such powers even a united crew had difficulty in winning concessions from a determined master.

The crew of the *Brenda* of Halifax was overpowered even by a weak master in 1869. George Tilley appears to have had frequent troubles with his crews: on his previous voyage the entire crew refused to work until Tilley replaced the steward (the men believed that the steward was trying to poison them); and on that voyage Tilley's wife had been assaulted by the second mate.[52] Now, on 28 March 1869, Tilley's crew refused to work. The *Brenda* was lying at the South-West Pass, near the mouth of the Mississippi, and Tilley had given orders to heave the anchor and set sail for Pensacola. The crew first objected to setting sail on a Sunday. But there were other issues at stake, for on the next day the crew had still not touched the anchors and was insisting on a survey of the vessel, believing it to be unseaworthy.

[50]*Henry* of Saint John, A. Van Norden, master, Official No. 34891, 1866-7, MHA.

[51]*Perekop*, Simon Graham, master, quoted in R.J. Cunningham and K.R. Mabee, *Tall Ships and Master Mariners* (St John's 1985), 95. John Froude fired a revolver during a fight on deck in the 1890s: *On the High Seas: The Diary of Capt. John W. Froude* (St. John's 1983), 68. William Henry Sulis of Saint John, master of the *Africana*, kept both a revolver and "1 Double Bar Gun" in his cabin: *Africana* of Saint John, Official No. 37160, 1868-9, MHA. John Spain, master of the *Favourite* of Saint John, also carried both revolver and double-barrelled shotgun and allowed his carpenter to use and to fire the latter during a confrontation with an AB in July 1863 (*Favourite*, Official No. 2332, 1863, MHA).

[52]*Brenda* of Halifax, Official No. 42385, 1867-8, from Cardiff to Madras, MHA.

The master answered that no surveyors were available in South-West Pass; the men would have to sail to Pensacola before a survey could be made.

The crew continued to refuse work, but the master still had options open to him. First he threatened to put the spokesmen for the crew in irons; the men, "cursing and using the most fearful language," went toward the forecastle. The master went to his cabin and took out his revolver; thus equipped, and accompanied by his two officers and bosun, he went toward the forecastle. Having identified two men as "ringleaders," he called them out. The two men came out of the forecastle with knives in hand and dared the master to shoot them. The master hesitated, thinking that "if I went to any stringent measures there might be trouble."

At this point Tilley ordered the cook and the steward to give no food to the crew. At 5 p.m. on the 29th, having had no food all day, the men were in a mood to negotiate. They offered to sail to Pensacola if the master would discharge them there. The master, "having to make any kind of promise to get the anchors hove up agreed to let the consul in Pensacola settle the matter. By this combination of force, withdrawal of food, and the promised intervention of the consul, the master had his way. The men were fed, and the vessel proceeded to Pensacola. There, on 5 April, a surveyor appointed by the consul declared the vessel to be "fit for any service." By 9 April, ten seamen, having failed to win their case, had deserted.[53]

The master possessed other means by which to enforce work-discipline at sea. He was physically removed from the crew, and he could use this distance to separate the men from each other and to exercise his authority over each man separately. The master remained on the poop or in his cabin: if he chose to speak directly to a seaman, it was always on his terms, following a summons to come aft. And every sailor had his "trick at the wheel," when he stood for hours, alone with the master on the poop. There, while his eyes passed from compass to vessel to the sea, the sailor could see the master standing a few feet away, a silent figure of authority. One did not speak to him, except to acknowledge an order. The master said nothing, unless the vessel were off course, and then uttered whatever advice or insult he chose. One did not enter the master's cabin, except to receive a reprimand, to witness one's misdemeanours recorded in the log, or to receive medical treatment. Authority in the vessel was visible but remote, but the master could impress and even intimidate by his silent presence.

The final guarantee of the master's superior power at sea was his possession of nautical instruments and his knowledge of their use. The first mate might possess these things as well, but it was unlikely that any other person in the vessel did so. There are remarkably few stories that tell of a master who had so lost all his other powers that his knowledge was his only remaining weapon. In a British ship, the *Berwickshire*, sailing from London to India, the master used his knowledge to overpower a crew — and the story, or others like it, would have travelled through forecastles around the world, among the many yarns of masters and men. The master wanted normal work on Sunday; the crew went to work, grumbling; a violent

[53]*Brenda* of Halifax, Official No. 42385, 1868-9, MHA.

"bucko" mate set off a brawl, and a united crew forced the master and mates to hide in the master's cabin. The bosun took charge of the deck, "but having no nautical instruments at his command it was not long before the crew were out of their reckoning ... Recognizing their helplessness they commenced to parley with the skipper and eventually they offered to release him and the other officers if he would let bygones be bygones. To this he agreed." In Bombay the master summoned the police and charged his crew with mutiny.[54] For a few hours the crew thought that it had control of the vessel, but the illusion was short-lived. Such was the power that the art and science of navigation had bestowed on the master of large sailing ships.

Against the formidable powers of the master the crew did have means of bargaining and of protection, as we have seen. It also possessed rights under common law, and men could bring charges of assault against master and officers. Convicting a master of assault usually required proof that the use of force had been unprovoked and that the crew had committed no prior violation of disciplinary provisions in the Merchant Shipping Acts. If a master were convicted, the penalty was usually a fine (in Aden in 1866 the master of a Saint John vessel was convicted of assault on members of his crew and fined 30 shillings). In Hong Kong in 1894 the master of a Halifax vessel was convicted of murdering a crew member, and there were other cases where British masters were convicted of murder.[55] The sentences were usually light, however. Certainly the possibility of charging a master with assault did little to alter the balance of power in a ship.

Official logs and court records can give the misleading impression that violence was unusually chronic in sailing vessels. But there is no way to know whether violence and corporal punishment were more common at sea than in mines and factories. Masters and foremen on land were not required by law to record all disciplinary actions. And even official logs themselves suggest that the incidence of violence should not be exaggerated. Most entries in the logs relate to non-violent incidents, to illness, to accidents, or to damage to vessel or cargo. Most pages in

---

[54]James Evans, *Recollections: or Incidents Culled from the Lives of Some of Our Seafaring Men* (Berwick-on-Tweed 1908), 74-5.

[55]*David G. Fleming*, Robert Sulley, master, Official No. 24197, 1866-8. James Crowe, master of the *Selkirk* of Halifax, was arrested and convicted of murder, but a petition to the governor was successful after further evidence was heard, and Crowe was released. The story is told in letters from Crowe and from his wife to Martin Dickie, in Martin Dickie Papers, PANS, MG 7, vol. 93. The master and first mate of the British vessel *Lady Douglas* were convicted of murdering a seaman in 1887. The death penalty was commuted to five years' imprisonment for the master and 18 months for the mate: *Nautical Magazine* (Aug. 1887), 617. See also the trial of a master and mate who beat a 13-year-old boy to death with a boat-hook in 1847. The defence argued that the "punishment administered to the deceased was the usual and ordinary mode of treating skulkers on ships, however rough it might appear to landsmen." The master was convicted of manslaughter and sentenced to two years in prison: Aled Eames, *Ships and Seamen of Anglesey* (Llangefori 1973), 387.

most official logs are blank — silent testimony to the fact that nothing occurred to disturb the routine of work at sea.

But even if violence were infrequent, conflict was endemic, The power of the master, and the stringent legal framework governing work at sea, were designed in part to contain that conflict. One measure of that conflict is the frequency with which men sought to escape from their workplace. Although the crew of the *Brenda* was overpowered by the master in 1869, and took the vessel to Pensacola as he wished, it did have an option apart from further submission. It could, and did, leave the vessel, withdrawing labour permanently from that employer.

Taking leave of a vessel was not the same as taking leave of other workplaces: here the manner of one's going was far more a matter for decision by both employer and employee, and the process was governed by statutory law. One did not simply pick up one's tools, or give notice, and leave. The sailor signed a contract to serve in particular places and for specified periods of time. To leave without permission of the master, and before the terms of the contract were fulfilled, was desertion — an offence punishable by the forfeit of wages earned and 12 weeks' imprisonment. Desertion was at one level an expression of discontent, and it was inherently an act of conflict between employer and employee. For sailors, as for workers in other industries characterized by isolation and high turn-over rates, quitting was a "demonstration of freedom and independence of the employer."[56] In the smaller sailing vessels of Atlantic Canada, making short coastal runs or passages to Britain and back, such expressions of discontent were relatively rare. By the later nineteenth century they were very common.

The master's stated reasons for the departure of his crew are not a perfect guide to motives or circumstances. There were many reasons for leaving vessels, and the crew lists miss some. Very often, as log books make clear, a mutually agreed discharge conceals dissatisfaction on both sides. Any analysis of reasons for leaving a vessel based on entries in crew agreements is likely to underestimate the number of escapes or discharges resulting from discontent. The entry "failed to join" offers no guide to the reasons for not joining, which may have nothing to do with the vessel.

There were ways to leave a ship at sea, and one suspects that these were not always reported accurately. Sailors sometimes threatened to jump overboard, and occasionally they carried out the threat.[57] Suicide was rare in sailing vessels, but it may be underreported. The main problem with the reporting of discharges in the crew lists is that the entries were made by the master and so reflect his interpretation

[56]A.J.M. Sykes, "Navvies: Their Work Attitudes," *Sociology*, III (1969), 26; Richard A. Rajala, "The Rude Science: Technology and Management in the West Coast Logging Industry 1890-1930," MA thesis, University of Victoria, 1986; Edmund Bradwin, *The Bunkhouse Man* (Toronto 1972), 58-60, 74.
[57]A Greek sailor repeatedly threatened to jump from the *Gertrude* of Saint John, Official No. 35178, 1865-6, MHA. The cook in the *Margaret Rait* jumped overboard after being beaten by the third mate and master: Captain James Doane Coffin, *Journal of the Margaret Rait 1840-1844* (Hantsport, N.S. 1984), 26-7.

of events. Leaving a vessel was an act defined by laws that the sailor did not write. If sailors had given their reasons for leaving a vessel, the record would look very different. But the crew agreements remain an indispensable guide, if not to the motives of sailors, to relations between the sailor and authority upon departure.

For virtually all who signed crew agreements in our four fleets there is an entry under "Date, Place, and Cause of Leaving this Ship." Almost half (49.4 per cent) were discharged by mutual consent at the end of the voyage. Only a very small number (1.9 per cent) remained with the vessel at the end of the voyage, and most of these were officers. There were other reasons that make no formal statement of conflict with authority: sailors were discharged by mutual consent during voyages (10.3 per cent); were discharged because of illness (1.0 per cent); died at sea (0.8 per cent); or were discharged because the vessel was sold, wrecked, or condemned, or because the voyage was abandoned (1.1 per cent). In a majority of cases, therefore, sailors left vessels without placing themselves in conflict with law or authority. What is surprising is the number of departures that involved conflict because the sailor was departing before the terms of his contract were fulfilled. About 35.5 per cent of departures fell into this broad category. They included desertion (25.4 per cent), either before or during a voyage; failure to join (9.3 per cent); discharge before sailing (0.3 per cent); discharge by court order or into jail (0.4 per cent); and discharge following demotion or refusal to work (0.1 per cent).

Departures involving conflict or discontent increased over time. Desertions were slightly under 20 per cent of all discharges in the 1860s. By the years 1879 to 1890 desertions had risen to 28.7 per cent in all four fleets. The proportion failing to join increased from less than 6 per cent in the 1860s to 11 per cent in the 1880s. In the same decades the proportion remaining at the end of the voyage fell, and so did the proportion discharged by mutual consent at the end of the voyage. The pattern is the same in all four fleets. There is no more telling measure of the increase of conflict in the workplace than this: by the 1880s two in every five sailors ran afoul of both their masters and the law in the course of the average voyage by the manner of their leaving their ships, and their departure made them liable to prison sentences. In the 1860s the proportion had been one in four; in the 1840s, at least in the vessels of Atlantic Canada, much lower.

Sailors had many opportunities to leave before their voyage was completed, and many personal, economic, and other factors could persuade a man to leave his ship. It is possible, however, to say something about the conditions in which desertion occurred and in which it increased. The timing of the increase in desertion affords a first indication of those conditions. Graph 2 plots the proportion of desertions and failure to join on an annual basis for the Saint John fleet, in those years for which data are adequate. The desertion rate was already high in the 1860s, but the upward trend is slight before 1877. The proportion of desertions then rose: it was higher in the mid-1880s than ever before, and higher again in the late 1890s. A comparison with Graph 1 — the freight rate indices suggests an interesting coincidence. The desertion rate increased when freight rates fell, and there is a

Graph 2

Discharge Reasons by Year, Saint John Fleet, 1863–1910

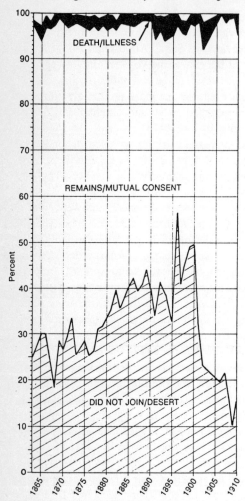

Source: Crew Agreements for Saint John-registered vessels, MHA.
Note: These figures are percentages of all stated reasons for leaving ships or for
terminating the crew agreement.

strong negative correlation (the coefficient is -0.81) between the two series. The
coincidence is unlikely to be accidental, for there is other evidence to suggest that
desertion was a response to the pressure on wages and other cost-cutting measures
that followed from declining rates of return.

Those who deserted were usually in the lower ranks and hired at the lowest
rates of pay. Table 2 indicates the percentages of discharge reasons by rank. This

table is based on discharges of sailors in four fleets, but it matters little which fleet we choose, and in most of the analysis that follows the Saint John crew file will be used. Very few officers failed to join or deserted, but a large proportion of ABs and OSs ended their service in a vessel before a voyage began or by deserting during the voyage. Most of the increase in desertion rates over time was accounted for by the increasing propensity of ABs to desert and, to a lesser extent, by the increase in deckhands as a proportion of the total labour force.

Table 2
Discharge Reasons (%) by Rank, Four Fleets, 1863-1914

Discharge Reason	Officer	Petty Officer	AB	OS	Other*
Did not join/desert	8.0	15.1	41.5	36.4	20.9
Dishonourable Discharge	0.2	0.2	0.5	0.3	0.2
By mutual consent	83.7	79.1	54.3	58.0	69.3
Remains with vessel	5.0	2.7	1.0	2.2	6.9
Death/illness	1.5	1.7	1.8	2.1	1.8
Other	1.6	1.2	0.9	1.0	0.9

Source: Crew Lists, MHA.
*Other includes boys and apprentices and a number of engineers and trimmers in the handful of steamers in the sample.

Desertion rates increased across time for all sailors, whatever their rank, so there were certainly many other factors at work. The longer the voyage, in space and time, the greater the proportion of the crew that deserted. A longer voyage offered more opportunities to desert and increased the likelihood of disputes over victualling and other working conditions. It also increased the likelihood of arrival in ports where labour was relatively scarce, and where the wage differential between those in the ship and those on shore, or in other ships, would tempt men to desert. Many other conditions of work and of conflict accompanied the longer voyage and increased the frequency of desertion. But time was certainly a factor in the process, for it was relatively easy to sign on for a West Indian passage and know that whatever the conditions might be, and whatever disputes might develop, one would have to endure them for only a few weeks before obtaining one's discharge.

Table 3 offers a comparison between discharges in a few broad types of voyage. The first three routes involved coastal or short-distance voyages; the next three were longer voyages and trans-oceanic passages. On the longer voyages, more than a third of sailors signing on deserted during the voyage or failed to join. Following a long voyage the crew was very unlikely to remain with the same vessel. The proportion of voyages in the latter categories increased by the 1880s and 1890s and these longer voyages were one important condition of increasing conflict and desertion. One reason for the fall in desertion rates after 1896 (see Graph 2) was that voyage duration declined and the proportion of shorter coastal voyages increased again, as the large ocean-going sailing vessels went off registry more quickly than did smaller vessels.

Table 3
Discharge Reasons by Trade Route (%), Four Fleets, 1863-1914

Trade	Did Not Join/ Deserted	Remained at End	Discharge by Mutual Consent
West Indies	23.7	3.3	69.4
Europe/Britain	9.2	4.9	84.3
East Coast North America	26.2	6.6	60.9
North Atlantic	37.0	2.3	59.2
South America	34.5	0.7	60.7
Pacific/Far East	37.1	0.7	58.6

Source: Crew Lists, MHA.

Frequency of desertion also increased with the size of vessels. So did the number of "dishonourable" discharges. In the Saint John fleet, as in the others, a small proportion of crews in our sample served in vessels under 250 tons. But in those that did, no sailor received a "dishonourable" discharge (meaning discharge into jail, discharge following demotion, and the like), and only 12.5 per cent failed to join or deserted. In vessels of 500 tons and more no less than 31.3 per cent failed to join or deserted (see also Table 4, limited to North Atlantic voyages in the 1880s). Illness and death were much more frequent in large vessels than in smaller ones (in small vessels 1.1 per cent of those signing crew lists left through illness or death; in vessels over 500 tons, 2.5 per cent). There is a connection, of course, between size of vessel and length of voyage; but the larger vessel was also the workplace in which the older paternalism and localism had weakened or disappeared. In larger vessels fewer sailors were associated with the master or the vessel by past experience, family connection, language, or the ties of a common homeland.

Certain factors having to do with the personal characteristics of sailors do not help to explain the rise in desertion rates. Those born in certain places were more likely to desert than to be discharged by mutual consent. Europeans, Scandinavians, and Americans deserted more often than did those born in British North America or Britain.[58] But this fact is unhelpful: a larger proportion of Canadians and British

[58] The proportion in the Saint John sample who deserted (excluding those who did not join), including all ranks and all cases after 1863, was as follows: Nova Scotians — 15.3 per cent; New Brunswickers — 15.0 per cent; English — 19.1 per cent; Scots — 16.5 per cent; Welsh — 18.4 per cent; Irish — 21.1 per cent; Scandinavians — 31.2 per cent; Germans — 29.7 per cent; French — 23.4 per cent; other Europeans — 28.1 per cent; Americans — 25.5 per cent.

held officer rank, where desertion was least likely; and a larger proportion of Europeans and Scandinavians served in the 1880s and 1890s, when desertion rates had risen for all nationalities. The nationality of the sailor offers no guide to his behaviour on leaving a vessel.[59] There is no source that allows a statistical measure of the relationship between nationality and misdemeanours during work at sea, but no national group was unusually prone to "dishonourable" discharge, and a relationship between nationality and conflict with authority at sea seems unlikely.

Did the increasing average age of deckhands have anything to do with desertion? It is possible that older sailors may have engaged more readily in conflict when freight rates fell and owners and masters demanded more of both vessels and men. But age explains little: older sailors were slightly less likely to desert, and less likely to receive "dishonourable" discharges, than were sailors in their twenties.[60] Did literacy contribute to the desertion rates, by providing a better-educated and more litigious labour force, which was more likely to enter into disputes with masters? There is in fact no statistical relationship between literacy and reason for discharges, when we look at particular ranks and time periods.[61] Literate seamen were neither more nor less likely than the others to desert or to receive "dishonourable" discharges.

Table 4
Desertions, North Atlantic Voyages, Saint John Fleet, 1880s

Tonnage Class	% of Starting Crew Members Who Desert
100-249 tons	15.0
250-499 tons	19.9
500-999 tons	36.7
1,000-1,499 tons	36.1
1,500 + tons	44.1

Source: Saint John Crew Lists, MHA.

[59]Including only ABs signed on between 1891 and 1912, Canadian-born sailors were more likely to desert than others, but again the statistical relationship is weak: 47.2 per cent of British North America-born ABs deserted or failed to join in this period, compared to 41.1 per cent of Scandinavian ABs, 43.9 per cent of other Europeans, and 47.6 per cent of Americans.

[60]In the Saint John fleet, 25.5 per cent of sailors aged 20-29 deserted; 0.8 per cent were discharged "dishonourably." Of those aged 35 or over, only 17.4 per cent deserted; 0.5 per cent were discharged "dishonourably." Selecting only ABs produces comparable differences.

[61]In the Saint John fleet, selecting ABs only, the cross-tabulation of reason for discharge with literacy produces Cramer's $V = 0.02$. Of all ABs who were literate, 29.5 per cent deserted; of illiterate ABs, 27.7 per cent. Literate Canadians in the Yarmouth fleet were somewhat more likely to receive discharges by mutual consent or to remain with the vessel: see David Alexander, "Literacy among Canadian and Foreign Seamen," in Rosemary Ommer and Gerald Panting, eds., *Working Men Who Got Wet* (St. John's 1980), 27.

Desertion was a consequence not of the personal characteristics of the sailor but of the relationship between worker and employer and between worker and workplace. The worker was pressured to leave his vessel by conditions on board, or he was tempted to desert by the prospect of better opportunities on shore or in other vessels. In any particular instance, desertion was likely to result from some combination of these "push" and "pull" factors. Certain masters seem to have had an unusual number of deserters, and there is evidence to suggest that masters from British North America were more likely to experience a high rate of desertion and of dishonourable discharges. In the 1880s, for instance, almost 31 per cent of the crews hired by masters residing in Nova Scotia or New Brunswick deserted. Where the master of a Saint John vessel stated his residence to be the United Kingdom, his desertion rate was only 21.6 per cent.

More impressive evidence follows if one asks this question: if there was a high rate of desertion from a vessel, what were the chances that the master was from Nova Scotia or New Brunswick? The probability was, in fact, very high. Of those masters in the Saint John file who experienced a desertion rate of 30 per cent or more among their crews, over 90 per cent resided in Nova Scotia or New Brunswick. Of those masters who experienced a low desertion rate (less than 20 per cent) a large proportion (42 per cent) gave as their residence a place outside British North America. Even more striking is the evidence that masters residing in British North America were more likely to discharge their crews into jail: in the period from 1879 to 1890, sailors working for a Canadian master were more than four times as likely to receive a "dishonourable" discharge as were sailors working for a master who resided in Britain.[62]

Part of the reason for the differences noted here is that Canadian masters frequented those places and trade routes where desertion was likely, for reasons that had nothing to do with the master himself. But there were other reasons for the higher desertion rate among "Bluenose" masters: the reputation for harsh discipline, imposed as much by force as by law, was not entirely undeserved. Canadian owners and masters were determined to cut costs in their industry. They tended to sail their vessels with fewer men than did British owners and masters, for instance.[63] There can be little doubt that the high desertion rate was in part the result of the costcutting pressures imposed by British North American owners and masters, and the conflict that often resulted.

One other condition helps to explain the rising desertion rate: the growing disparity between wage levels in a vessel and wage levels elsewhere. To some extent this was a long-standing cause of desertion: wages for sailors signing on in British and European ports had long since been lower than wages in North American ports.

[62]Of crew members hired by masters who gave their residence as a place in British North America, 0.36 per cent were given "dishonourable" discharges; of those hired by masters residing in Britain, 0.08 per cent received "dishonourable" discharges.

[63]See Eric W. Sager, *Seafaring Labour: The Merchant Marine of Atlantic Canada, 1820-1914* (Kingston 1989), ch. 7.

To the sailor who signed on in Britain for a few pounds a month, the knowledge that wage levels in his North American port of call were several times as high was a strong temptation to desert. By the last decades of the nineteenth century the disparity between wages in sailing ships and wages on land had increased. And there was now another difference: steamers were also hiring crews, and they offered higher wages for deckhands than did sailing vessels, particularly on the western side of the Atlantic. Sterling wages paid to ABs in sailing vessels did not increase; after the 1870s they declined slightly. By the 1880s and 1890s a larger number of sailors were entering ports on the western coasts of North America, where the labour market for sailors was small and wages tended to be very high in relative terms. Falling rates of return in the sailing ship industry increased conflict between employer and employee by encouraging the sailor to desert in search of better opportunities.

There is a relationship between the reason for leaving a vessel and the port where the sailor left. Ports in Canada and the United States accounted for only 23.4 per cent of all discharges from vessels in the Saint John fleet. But the majority of departures in those North American ports were desertions. The result is that Canadian and U.S. ports accounted for no less than 64.4 per cent of all desertions.[64] The increase in the overall desertion rate resulted partly from the fact that by the 1880s a larger proportion of sailors was entering North American ports. Even more important, of all crews leaving in North American ports by the 1880s, a larger proportion left by deserting. Thus, in the 1860s, 59.9 per cent of departures in North America were desertions; by the 1880s, this proportion had risen to 70 per cent.

Table 5 lists the major desertion ports in North America. The propensity to desert in a port must be measured by reference to the total number of desertion opportunities, or the number of man-entrances into port. No less than a third of man-entrances into U.S. ports resulted in desertion (the only other region near to this rate was Australia, with 30 per cent).[65] On an average passage from Britain or Europe to New York, the master could expect to lose almost half his crew.

Table 5 suggests something of the experience of the able seaman who signed on for the return voyage from Liverpool to the United States. He might earn £3 a month from Liverpool. He arrived in the United States to find that unskilled general labourers on shore were earning more than he was. If the AB from Liverpool could desert and find a berth in another vessel putting out from the American port, his monthly wages could increase by 40 per cent or by as much as 110 per cent.

---

[64]If we aggregate reason for discharge into four categories (remains with the vessel, discharge by mutual consent, dishonourable discharge, and desertion) and if we aggregate place of discharge into five regions, the cross-tabulation of reason with place yields Cramer's $V = 0.52$; lambda with reason dependent $= 0.33$. The relationship strengthens if we include only ABs: lambda with reasons dependent $= 0.45$.

[65]Lewis R. Fischer, "A Dereliction of Duty: The Problem of Desertion in Nineteenth Century Sailing Vessels," in Ommer and Panting, *Working Men Who Got Wet*, 58.

Table 5
North American High-Desertion Ports, 1863-1914

Port	Desertions as % of All Man-entrances	Average AB Wages ($) from the Port
New York	49.0	23.11
San Francisco	45.8	21.25
Baltimore	39.0	23.12
Portland, OR	39.0	31.50
Saint John	37.6	21.49
Portland, ME	37.5	21.35
Philadelphia	35.2	25.27
New Orleans	31.9	22.03
Boston	30.9	21.29
Port Townshend, WA	30.3	25.00
Pensacola	29.4	17.79
Charleston, SC	27.5	25.41
All US ports	33.0	23.18
Quebec City	21.2	18.00
Liverpool AB sterling wage		14.87

Source: Saint John Crew Lists, MHA.

Such wage disparities may appear to shift the emphasis from the vessel itself to alternative opportunities on land. But "push" factors remain important in the explanation of desertion rates. One of every three desertions occurred outside North America. One in every five occurred in continental Europe, the West Indies, South America, Africa, India, or Asia, where local opportunities were less likely to be attractive. And even where high American wage levels played a part, it was the contrast between wage levels in most vessels and wage levels outside the vessel that created the incentive to desert.

We can see the "push" factor of low wages operating very clearly to encourage desertion: desertion occurred where wages were significantly below average. In this analysis, only able seamen's wages are included; all wages are converted to dollars (at $4.86 per pound sterling). In the Saint John fleet, the average monthly wage for the AB who remained in a vessel at the end of the voyage was $19.56. The average wage for the AB who received an "honourable" discharge was $18.59. But the average wages for ABs who deserted was only $15.83. The average wage for those receiving a "dishonourable" discharge was even lower ($15.10). Analysis of variance confirms that these averages are significantly different.[66]

[66]The Scheffe multiple range test denotes means significantly different at the 0.05 confidence level. For AB wages broken down by four aggregated discharge reasons, discharge by mutual consent and remains were significantly different from desertion and "dishonourable" discharge.

The effect of low wages was particularly dramatic among sailors who left vessels in North American ports. Table 6 compares by levels of wages ABs who left in selected North American ports (Quebec City, New York, Philadelphia, Baltimore, New Orleans, and San Francisco). Where wage levels were low (less than $12.99 or the sterling equivalent) over 81 per cent of those leaving were deserters. Ninety-six per cent of all desertions were accounted for by those in the lowest wage category.[67]

Table 6
Wage Levels and Discharges of ABs Entering Selected
North American Ports, 1863-1914

AB Monthly Wages	% of Crew Remaining Or Receiving Honour- able Discharge	% of Crew Deserting	% of Crew Leaving for Other Reasons *
$12.99 or less	17.6	81.5	0.9
$13.00-$14.99	11.4	52.3	36.4
$15.00-$16.99	54.7	41.1	4.2
$17.00 or more	75.2	18.1	6.7

Source: Saint John Crew Lists, MHA.
*Did not join, discharge before sailing, discharged into jail, and other "dishonourable" discharge.

Desertion was an illegal action that resulted in part from differential wage levels. It was a form of conflict originating within the capitalist labour market and within the wage relationship between labour and employer. For the sailor it was nothing more than a means of self-improvement and a form of bargaining, although the sailor did not use such words. Wages were low and conditions poor in one place; desertion might offer a remedy. As a bargaining tactic, desertion affected wage levels, not only for individual deserters but throughout the industry. Where the destination of a vessel was a known high-desertion port or area, the master often paid higher wages to his ABs. Thus if a vessel were sailing for the United States and paying sterling wages, average wages would be 8 per cent higher than if the destination were the United Kingdom, and 10 per cent higher than if the destination were Africa, India, or Asia.

A more refined analysis requires that we look at departures from specific ports and in specific time periods. Such analysis confirms that masters were persuaded to offer higher wages when sailing to high-desertion areas. If we look at wages for ABs hired in Liverpool in 1872 and 1873, there is a significant difference between mean wages by the intended destination of the vessel. The mean wage where the destination was British North America was slightly under £4. Where the destination was the United States, the average was about £3-17-0. But where the destination

[67]Chi square = 1218.4 with 6 degrees of freedom; Cramer's $V = 0.36$.

was any other part of the world, the average wage was about £3-3-0.[68] There was a difference here of more than 20 per cent between average wages to North America and average wages to other places.

These higher wages were certainly not offered because of a shortage of sailors wishing to travel the passage to North America. There is instead evidence that masters could be more selective in their choice of crew on these routes. Harris Barnes of Halifax states in his "Reminiscence" that in 1863 he could not find work at all in a vessel from Liverpool to North America: "The end of all was I did as many others had to do, I paid my passage to New York in one of the large packet ships about ready to sail."[69] In 1884, Cephas Pearl of Tancook, Nova Scotia, signed on a vessel in Liverpool for Boston: he used an alias — "George Smith" of London — because, he said, if you hailed from "America" the master would not hire you, for fear you would jump ship in the United States.[70] Masters tried to select their crews carefully, and there was no shortage of sailors willing to make the Atlantic crossing. The higher wages must therefore be an inducement of another sort: either an attempt to reduce the wage disparity upon arrival in North America or an inducement designed to allow greater selectivity in the choice of men.

There is other evidence that masters were compelled to respond to the threat of desertion. Trying to locate and apprehend deserters was difficult and costly. Prevention was a better cure, and so masters attempted to place restrictions on crews sailing for high desertion ports. The most common restriction was the denial of shore leave at a foreign port, or the denial of any advance of wages in a foreign port, or both of these restrictions together. The former was applied more often as time passed, until, by the 1890s, 79 per cent of Saint John vessels sailed with this restriction applied to the crew.

Even before workers were organized and before the term *strike* was known, withdrawing labour was commonplace as a means of protection and as a bargaining tactic. Its frequency is suggested not simply by the ratio of desertions to port-entrances, but even more by the ratio of desertion to time worked. We know for each sailor the number of days worked in each vessel, and for entire fleets the total man-years worked by crews between 1863 and the early 1900s. For the Saint John fleet there were, over this period, 0.6 desertions per man-year worked (the rate went up from 0.44 in the 1860s to 0.81 in the 1890s): sailors deserted on average once for every year and eight months worked. This form of withdrawal was certainly more frequent than any other. It was also much more frequent than the rare "dishonourable" discharge. In the Saint John fleet there were only 1.7 "dishonourable" discharges for every hundred man-years worked.

[68]The calculations were done in dollar equivalents, and the results were: $19.26 where the destination was British North America; $18.68 where the destination was the United States; $15.46 where the destination was other.
[69]Reminiscences of Harris Barnes, Public Archives of Nova Scotia, Halifax [PANS], MG 108, no. 9.
[70]Diary of Cephas Pearl, Feb. 1884, PANS, RG 7, no. 14A.

Conflict with authority was endemic in sailing vessels, but violent confrontations were less frequent than official records and the reminiscences of sailors might
suggest. Conflict took the form of non-violent litigation and withdrawal of labour,
and it increased when the state sought to protect capital invested in shipping by
extensive regulatory measures relating to the labour supply and work-discipline at
sea. Sailors sought to use the law to their advantage and to use the vessel's
dependence on their labour as a means of bargaining with their masters. When
bargaining was impossible they withdrew their labour by desertion, and desertion
itself became part of the bargaining process.

To the struggle with employers and with authority sailors brought the capacity
for adaptation and survival of men who were literate, migratory, self-reliant, and
tenacious in defence of assumed rights. They were not enfeebled and brutalized by
their workplace, but they had learned, as James Doane Coffin put it, "to be content
with what you have and use all the means of getting more."[71] From their mutual
dependence on each other and on the skills necessary for work and survival, they
learned a simple moral creed which informed their view of social norms and
obligations in the workplace:

So when one has proved his friendship
Cling to him who clings to you
Those who stand amid the tempest
Firm as when the skies are blue
Will be friends while life endureth
Cling to those who cling to you[72]

And in the recurring conflict with their employers they believed what John Froude
of Twillingate had learned in his seafaring career — that human ingenuity and the
lottery of good fortune were greater than the power of the state:

All things eant done
By mite but by prvdence which is
Present with us all as we travell threw the
Changing scens of life oer land and sea[73]

[71]*Journal of the Margaret Rait 1840-1844* (Hantsport, N.S. 1984), 48.
[72]*On the High Seas*, 168.
[73]*Ibid.*, 122.

Part Two
Industrial Revolution

The coming of the industrial revolution had a major impact on the working life of people in the region, whether they lived in the towns and cities or in the countryside. One significant influence was the pull of labour markets from adjacent areas, especially from the milltowns and urban centres of New England, an influence which accounts for one of the major population movements of the period. Similar pulls existed within the region as well, as opportunities for industrial employment developed in railway, factory, and mining towns across the region. One of the classic industries associated with the National Policy was the cotton industry, and Peter DeLottinville traces the impact of the arrival of this industry on the social life of a small lumber town on the St. Croix River in New Brunswick. The recruitment of labour for industry drew principally on the local population within the region, a factor that helps account for some of the strength of the new working-class communities. New groups drawn into employment by the demands of industrial and urban development included two groups of particular interest. Robert McIntosh introduces the young men and boys who worked in the coal mines of Nova Scotia, while D.A. Muise analyzes the presence of young women who worked as clerks, teachers and factory operatives in urban centres.

Additional Reading

Babcock, Robert H. "Labour and Industrial Capitalist Development in the North Atlantic Region, 1880-1920," in Deian R. Hopkin and Gregory S. Kealey, eds., *Class, Community and the Labour Movement: Wales and Canada, 1850-1930* (St. John's 1989), 21-48.

Beattie, Betsy. "'Going Up to Lynn': Single, Maritime-Born Women in Lynn, Massachusetts, 1879-1930," *Acadiensis*, XXII, 1 (Autumn 1992), 65-86.

Crawley, Ron. "Off to Sydney: Newfoundlanders Emigrate to Industrial Cape Breton, 1890-1914," *Acadiensis*, XVII, 2 (Spring 1988), 27-51.

Fingard, Judith. *The Dark Side of Life in Victorian Halifax* (Halifax 1989).

Guildford, Janet. "'Separate Spheres': The Feminization of Public School Teaching in Nova Scotia, 1838-1880," *Acadiensis*, XXII, 1 (Autumn 1992), 44-64.

Hickey, Daniel, dir. *Moncton, 1871-1929: Changements socio-économiques dans une ville ferroviaire* (Moncton 1990).

Kealey, Gregory S., ed. *Canada Confronts Industrialism: The Royal Commission on the Relations of Labor and Capital, 1889* (Toronto 1973), Parts 4 (New Brunswick) and 5 (Nova Scotia).

Léger, Raymond. "L'industrie du bois dans la Péninsule acadienne, 1875-1900," *La revue d'histoire de la société historique Nicolas Denys*, 16 (mai-août 1988).

McCann, Larry. "'Living a Double Life': Town and Country in the Industrialization of the Maritimes," in Douglas Day, ed., *Geographical Perspectives on the Maritimes* (Halifax 1988), 93-113.

McKay, Ian. "'By Wisdom, Wile, or War': The Provincial Workmen's Association and the Struggle for Working-Class Independence in Nova Scotia, 1879-97," *Labour/Le Travail*, 18 (Fall 1986), 13-62.

_____. "Capital and Labour in the Halifax Baking and Confectionery Industry During the Last Half of the Nineteenth Century," *Labour/Le Travailleur*, 3 (1978), 175-96.

_____. "Class Struggle and Merchant Capital: Craftsmen and Labourers on the Halifax Waterfront, 1850-1902," in Bryan D. Palmer, ed., *The Character of Class Struggle: Essays in Canadian Working-Class History, 1850-1985* (Toronto 1986), 17-36.

Maynard, Steven. "Between Farm and Factory: The Productive Household and the Capitalist Transformation of the Maritime Countryside, Hopewell, Nova Scotia, 1869-1890," in Daniel Samson, ed., *Contested Countryside: Rural Workers and Modern Society in Atlantic Canada, 1800-1950* (Fredericton 1994), 70-104.

Myers, Sharon. "'Not to be Ranked as Women': Female Industrial Workers in Turn of the Century Halifax," in Janet Guildford and Suzanne Morton, eds., *Separate Spheres: Women's Worlds in the 19th-Century Maritimes* (Fredericton 1994), 161-83.

Peter DeLottinville   5

Trouble in the Hives of Industry: The Cotton Industry Comes to Milltown, New Brunswick, 1879-1892

The national policy of John A. Macdonald was the most significant economic strategy in nineteenth-century Canadian history.[1] Not only did it stimulate industrial growth in the fledgling Dominion but, with the construction of a national railway and settlement of the West, it shaped Canadian society into its regional economic zones. The folly or wisdom of the National Policy has been vigorously debated ever since 1879.[2] A prosperous, powerful Central Canada feeding on a dependent West while ignoring Maritime protests for a fair deal have become common themes in Canadian historical writing. For the most part, these national and regional studies have concentrated upon the general impact of tariff reforms on single industries or regional economies. The large scale of such studies, however, sometimes forces historians to overlook the specific impact that industrial change has upon social structure. While census returns may accurately portray the increases in invested

[1]This paper is based upon research undertaken for my Master's thesis, "The St. Croix Cotton Manufacturing Company and Its Influence on the St. Croix Community, 1880-1892," (Dalhousie University 1979). Acknowledgements for my thesis also extend to this paper and I would specifically like to credit my thesis supervisor, Gregory S. Kealey, for his valuable advice and assistance.

[2]A complete list of such works is unnecessary here, but my research was influenced by T.W. Acheson's "The National Policy and the Industrialization of the Maritimes, 1880-1910," *Acadiensis*, (Spring 1972), 3-28; John Dales, *The Protective Tariff in Canada's Development* (Toronto 1966); V.C. Fowke, "The National Policy — Old and New," in W.T. Easterbrook and M.H. Watkins, eds., *Approaches to Canadian Economic History* (Toronto 1967); and Simon J. McLean, *The Tariff History of Canada* (Toronto 1895).

Published with permission of the Canadian Historical Association from *Historical Papers* (1980), 101-15.

capital, consumption of raw materials, and the value of finished products, such information does little to explain the effects of industrialization in human terms.

This paper attempts to illustrate the impact of one National Policy industry upon a single community. The St. Croix Cotton Manufacturing Company, situated along the Maine-New Brunswick border in the town of Milltown, New Brunswick, operated as an independent company from 1880 until 1892. In many ways, the St. Croix company typified the intentions of the National Policy. Milltown was a lumber town whose timber resources had been largely depleted by the late 1870s. Its young residents were migrating to the United States in search of employment. Using foreign capital, local entrepreneurs built the cotton mill to ensure that their community would have an economic future. Since the factory continued to manufacture cotton until the 1950s, Milltown appeared to be one of the successes of the National Policy. On closer examination, however, the history of the St. Croix mill was less impressive. The first twelve years of Milltown's industrial transformation illustrated a community struggling with the disruption of established economic and social structures. The local business élite was replaced by outside directors and managers. Industrial unrest pitted worker against manager, and neighbour against neighbour. Local politicians found they had little influence over their town's economic affairs. Everyone in Milltown had to adjust to living in the shadow of the St. Croix mill. In one sense, Milltown can be seen as a microcosm of the cotton industry and perhaps other single industry towns as well. The general problems which confront a community trying to preserve its traditional social values and still adjust to current economic realities has relevance to all Canadian communities.

In order to appreciate the significance of the St. Croix mill's history, one must remember that this cotton factory, was a single example of the transformation of the Maritimes from a staple to an industrial economy. The 1880s saw Saint John grow faster than the industrial centre of Hamilton, Ontario. New Glasgow, Moncton, Marysville, and Halifax, all witnessed dramatic growth in their industrial sectors as the eastern provinces equipped themselves to battle with the manufacturing power of Ontario and Québec.[3] When looking at Canadian industry as a whole, it should be stressed that by 1890 there were over one hundred villages comparable to Milltown. These small towns contained over 4,500 industrial establishments representing over $2.5 million of invested capital and almost 25,000 jobs. While this was only one fourteenth of the industrial capacity of the forty-six major Canadian cities, the social transformation of such villages deserves consideration.[4]

The Milltown experience may be represented in three general stages. Brief background sketches of Milltown before the cotton mill and of the national developments in the cotton industry show the merging of local and national interests. The original expectations about the mill will be compared to the actual conditions to show the general scale of community disappointment. Finally, a bitter

---

[3]T.W. Acheson, "National Policy and the Industrialization of the Maritimes," *Acadiensis*, 4-5.

[4]*Census of Canada*, (1891), IV, 368-75.

strike, law suits, and environmental pollution provide benchmarks to gauge the shifts in local attitudes.

Milltown was a community of sixteen hundred settled on the banks of the St. Croix River which served as the international boundary between Canada and the United States. Over one-half of the inhabitants of this tightly knit community were of Irish origin, with another 30 per cent of English and 13 per cent of Scottish origins.[5] The excellent water power of the river at Milltown provided power for its saw mills which processed the timber harvested in the St. Croix valley. Directly across the river from Milltown, New Brunswick, the clutter of saw mills and small wooden houses continued, forming the aptly — but unimaginatively — named community of Milltown, Maine. Common ethnic backgrounds, family ties, and mutual interests made the local acknowledgement of border restrictions rather carefree, much to the vexation of customs officials.

Neither of the two Milltowns were self-contained communities. The New Brunswick town relied upon the neighbouring settlement of St. Stephen, one mile downstream at the head of navigation. With a population twenty-three hundred, St. Stephen acted as a shipping point for the St. Croix timber as well as a retail and financial centre for upriver communities. Calais, Maine, directly across the river from St. Stephen, fulfilled a similar function for American timber, and maintained a small shipbuilding industry. Although locally thought of as two separate communities, Calais and Milltown, Maine, shared a common municipal government. Together the two Milltowns, Calais, and St. Stephen made a comfortable, if not prosperous, living on the local timber and maritime trade. The working men of the two Milltowns allowed the middle class residents of St. Stephen and Calais to enjoy their more picturesque neighbourhoods, far from the sawdust and lumberyards.

Considering the location of Milltown, the prosperity of the New England textile centres naturally attracted interest and admiration. Like those towns, Milltown possessed good water power, a tolerable climate, transportation links by rail and sea, and an available source of labour. The selection of a suitable new industry was made easier with the National Policy tariff changes introduced in 1879. Almost overnight, the small domestic cotton industry looked ripe for expansion as Canadian producers tried to fill the gap made by the higher tariff on imported cottons. What looked like a good investment to the St. Croix entrepreneurs, however, appeared equally lucrative to several other Canadian investors. The resulting expansion in cotton manufacturing was dramatic. In 1879 there were only seven Canadian cotton mills, but by 1881 there were four more in operation and another nine mills under construction. Between 1879 and 1883, capital invested in cotton mills jumped from $2.1 million to $8.5 million. Cloth production increased from 38 million yards to 115 million yards.[6]

[5] *Census of Canada*, (1881), I, 222-3. For additional information on the St. Croix valley economy and social history, see Harold A. Davis' excellent local study, *An International Community on the St. Croix* (Orono 1950).
[6] *Monetary Times*, 31 August 1883, 235.

This rapid increase in industrial capacity was due almost entirely to the tariff restrictions. During the early 1880s, cotton mills became symbols of the new, prosperous, industrial Canada. Unfortunately, once all the production came on the market, the bubble burst. The orders were cancelled, prices slashed, and cotton stocks plummeted. With the October 1883 failure of Montréal's David Morrice and Sons, which acted as distributing agent for most of the Canadian cotton factories, a sense of panic ensued. Cut-throat competition became the hallmark of the cotton market. These acute problems prompted leading cotton manufacturers to form voluntary associations in an effort to regulate market practices, prices, and production. The Canadian Cotton Manufacturers Association formed in 1883, and its successor the Dominion Cotton Manufacturers Association established three years later, both had very short term influence. Member companies frequently broke the Associations' regulations to gain a temporary advantage over their competitors. Stock prices remained low throughout the 1880s. As it became clear that the industry could not continue in this way, the largest cotton manufacturers, A.F. Gault and David Morrice of Montréal, bought out almost all of their competitors. Using English capital, Gault and Morrice created the Dominion Cotton Company in 1889 from all the grey cotton mills. Three years later, they organized all coloured cotton mills into the Canadian Coloured Cotton Company.[7] Between them, Dominion Cottons and Canadian Coloured Cottons monopolized the industry. While they could not immediately solve the problem of over-production, these companies did maintain better control on prices and distribution.

The 1880s had witnessed so many changes in the Canadian cotton industry that Liberal critic, James D. Edgar, MP, remarked that the industry, "has been the most spoilt, it is the most saucy and it is certainly the most dangerous"[8] of all the new "infant" industries. Critics charged that the National Policy, rather than creating a healthy domestic cotton industry, had allowed the manufacture of cotton goods to fall into the hands of a few Montréal monopolists. In the process, the hopes of the Milltown entrepreneurs and other investors for a share in the new industrial future had been shattered.

In light of these national developments, the transformation of Milltown's economy from timber to cotton was not an easy one, particularly when none of the local major capitalists had the slightest knowledge of the textile trade. The local lumber economy was almost exclusively under the control of four local families —

[7]The Dominion Cotton Company included the Hudon, Coaticooke, Craven, Kingston, Chambly, Moncton, Nova Scotia, Windsor, Ste. Anne, Merchants and Magog cotton mills, all of which specialized in the production of grey and uncoloured cottons. The Canadian Coloured Cotton Company included the Lybster, Dundas, Canada, Stormont, Hamilton, Ontario, Merriton and Gibson mills. The only remaining independent mills were the Montréal, Yarmouth, Cornwall, Montmorency, New Brunswick, and Saint John mills. See *Monetary Times*, 9 September 1892, 277-9.

[8]*House of Commons Debates*, 17 February 1893, 807. Edgar's speech details the Liberal charges that the National Policy was responsible for the monopolization of the cotton industry.

the Eatons, the Todds, the Chipmans, and the Murchies. These families were related by marriage and common business ventures and possessed much of the wealth made from the exploitation of the only major natural resource. The leading men of these families controlled not only their own personal fortunes, but the economic future of the entire St. Croix valley as well. An inability to transfer the capital made from the timber industry into more profitable channels would permanently cripple the local economy. There was a considerable amount at stake, therefore, when the lumber barons, Henry F. Eaton, James Murchie, and Freeman H. Todd, showed interest in an article published in the local Conservative organ, *The St. Croix Courier*, about the activity in A.F. Gault's Montréal cotton factories. At a private meeting on 1 February 1880, these three men, along with the local shipper, Zechariah Chipman, and several other community leaders, decided to build a twenty-thousand-spindle cotton mill at a cost of $300,000. Technical aspects of the business would be handled by an experienced manager and outside capital gladly accepted once local investors had a chance to get in on the enterprise.[9]

During the following months these leading capitalists waged a public-stock campaign, aided by the talents of the *Courier*'s editor, David Main, who saw the erection of a cotton mill as concrete proof for the merit of the Conservatives' tariff policy. Public meetings were held in Milltown, St. Stephen, and Calais where the proposal was outlined with references to the prosperous nature of the New England cotton centres. The campaigners stressed that the new mill would be a secure place for local capital, provide jobs for local workers, increase the trade of merchants, and create healthy rises in real estate values. They painted a picture of the best of all possible worlds. Several commentators were adamant that the plan could not possibly fail. After receiving a petition from many of the town's property holders, the Milltown Town Council bought $30,000 stock in the venture.[10] By May local stock subscriptions had reached $80,000. While much of the risk was taken by the leading capitalists, many residents bought small amounts of stock. For them, the cotton factory was a public project designed to launch their community into a new era of prosperity. If the community's improvement also meant private gain, then the small stockholder was doubly glad to contribute. When total subscriptions reached $90,000 in July, the local organizers decided to look outside the St. Croix valley for additional support.

Inquiries to Saint John capitalists and the famous lumber baron of Marysville, Alexander Gibson, received attention but no firm commitments since new cotton mills were also being talked about in those communities. The first definite proposal

[9]*St. Croix Courier*, 5 February 1880, 2.
[10]Provincial Archives of New Brunswick, Fredericton, New Brunswick (hereafter PANB), Hill Collection, George F. Hill Political Correspondence, 1880, folder 522-71. When the 126 petitioners were traced through local business directories and assessment books, it was discovered that all were property holders and 10 per cent merchants, 14 per cent professionals, 4 per cent lumber mill owners, 33 per cent artisans, 18 per cent saw mill employees, 9 per cent labourers and 6 per cent farmers, with 6 per cent of the petitioners unidentified.

for additional capital came from a Waterville, Maine, cotton manufacturer, Amos D. Lockwood. Lockwood promised $200,000 and also put the Milltown organizers in touch with Lewis Dexter of Providence, Rhode Island. Both Dexter and Lockwood had considerable experience in the American cotton industry and no doubt eyed the protected Canadian market with interest. The local enthusiasm for a cotton factory, combined with the technical knowledge and financial connections of the Americans, appeared to be mutually advantageous.[11]

The involvement of Lewis Dexter and Amos Lockwood, however, greatly increased the scale of the project. In finalizing the initial Act of Incorporation for the St. Croix Cotton Manufacturing Company, local capitalists had called for a total capitalization of $400,000, which was an unprecedented amount in local terms.[12] Dexter and Lockwood insisted that the capitalization for the mill be increased to one million dollars. In return, the Americans asked for the ten-year tax exemption previously granted to local investors plus a $30,000 bonus. In March 1881, the Milltown Town Council showed their approval of the deal by offering half of their $30,000 stock to the American investors. This move was unanimously endorsed by local property holders. The remaining $15,000 of the bonus was collected privately from both Canadian and American residents of the St. Croix towns.[13] Once negotiations were completed in May 1881, local stock subscriptions jumped to $200,000.

Despite the success of the local organizers in raising the capital for the cotton mill, the eventual structure of the St. Croix company was radically altered from the original idea. Instead of being a locally controlled company, only 20 per cent of the stock was held by St. Croix residents. The lumber barons of the valley were very much junior partners in the operation. With no technical knowledge of cotton manufacture, the local investors, who were represented by James Murchie on the Board of Directors, were simply expected to maintain good relations with the local community. This alteration in plans, however, did not dampen local enthusiasm. If a large factory would ensure future prosperity, then many residents felt that the larger the factory, the greater the prosperity. Construction of the mill got underway quickly. The cornerstone ceremony took place in June 1881 with full Masonic ritual. Large crowds attended the ceremony and several received half holidays to celebrate the event.[14] Local eagerness to have the mill in production prompted Milltown's mayor, James Murchie, to read the riot act to construction workers who downed

[11]*St. Croix Courier*, 30 September 1880, 2; 25 November 1880, 2; 28 October 1880, 2.
[12]*Ibid.*, 4 March 1880, 2.
[13]PANB, Milltown Council Minutes, 16 March 1881, 250-1; 18 March 1881, 281; *Calais Advertiser*, 23 March 1881, 2. The *Advertiser*'s list of private contributors revealed that of the $15,000 bonus, 38 per cent came from merchants and grocers, 20 per cent from professionals, 10 per cent from lumber mill owners and manufacturers, 7 per cent from artisans, and 1 per cent from labourers. The remaining 24 per cent came from unidentified sources.
[14]*St. Croix Courier*, 30 June 1881, 2.

tools to protest a cut in wages.[15] Such municipal interference in private disputes was uncommon on the St. Croix and certainly indicated a darker side to local enthusiasm.

When the thirty-four thousand spindles of the St. Croix mill began to turn in June 1882, the rhythms of factory life slowly became the rhythms of Milltown. The symmetry of the four-storey, red brick factory located next to Salmon Falls dwarfed all other buildings in the valley town. The size of the factory was so novel that during its erection a police constable had to keep curious onlookers from interfering with construction. For most residents, the change in the landscape was a source of pride. One observer wrote that the new mill "will convert one of the lowest, most squalid parts of the village into a neat and tidy hive of industry."[16] When the mill's bell summoned workers to the factory at 6:00 a.m., some residents complained at being awakened at such an early hour, but the community soon grew accustomed to the regularity of the shift changes. The mill's bell became a familiar time check for all residents as they began to assess the changes this new enterprise had upon community living.

The new mill affected most residents by offering a new place of employment. With five hundred new jobs, the pattern of emigration among the young residents was temporarily reversed. The lack of a skilled labour force, however, meant that initially most of the skilled jobs went to outsiders. All the managers, overseers, and second hands were imported from the New England mills, particularly from those around Waterville, Maine, where Amos Lockwood had his factories. Several skilled workers were local residents who had spent years in the New England mills and took this opportunity to find work closer to home. This group of new residents did not include any of the numerous French Canadians working in the American textile centres. R.E. Patterson, contractor for the St. Croix mill, refused to hire French Canadians whom he described as "a very inferior class of men"[17] and this policy was continued by the mill superintendent, J.W. Brown. Such discrimination drew no complaints from local observers who regarded the new jobs as a return on their bonuses and tax exemptions.

Those residents who did find work in the mill had to adjust to long, monotonous hours in hot, noisy, gas-lit rooms. Along with learning how to spin, weave, and dye cotton, the mill hands had to contend with fines for substandard work and the discipline imposed by the overseers. For most hands it was their first experience with industrial conditions. Two-thirds of the positions were filled by women who had had few employment opportunities in the old lumber economy. In 1891, 371 women and 31 girls under sixteen years of age were employed at the St. Croix mill. Some were employed in the relatively easy job of ring spinning, others in the finishing rooms or as unskilled workers. A few women, however, became weavers

[15]*Calais Times*, 3 February 1882, 2; *St. Croix Courier*, 2 February 1882, 2.
[16]*Canadian Biographical Dictionary and Portrait Gallery of Eminent and Self Made Men* (Chicago 1881), 674.
[17]*Calais Times*, 20 January 1880, 1; 10 February 1880, 2.

and in this job female workers could make a wage comparable with their male counterparts. The low wages paid to women was a crucial factor in remaining competitive on the depressed Canadian market. Daily wages of 65 to 80 cents for female ring spinners compared very favourably, in the eyes of cost-conscious managers, to the $1.25 to $1.50 paid to male mule spinners.[18]

Work at the St. Croix mill continued uninterrupted throughout the 1880s. While its managers avoided the temporary shutdowns which occured at many of the Canadian mills, the St. Croix's production did fluctuate with market conditions. As a result the total number of workers needed in the mill varied from month to month. Slow periods inevitably caused the dismissal of employees. Young female hands returned to their families in town or surrounding countryside to await better times. The uncertainty of steady employment, however, also created a very mobile labour force. Statistical information on this question for the St. Croix mill is limited, but it appeared that over 27 per cent of male employees stayed only a year or two in the mill.[19] The new mill did not, therefore, permanently stop the emigration of young locals, but rather taught these residents a marketable skill to take to other cotton centres.

Outside the factory, the mill hands' lives were still closely involved with the company. The large increase in the local work force created severe pressures on the housing market. In part, this problem was alleviated by company houses. Eight houses were built for the mill's supervisory staff and a boarding establishment, known as Corporation House, provided accommodation for eighty workers.[20] These measures still left a good deal of the housing demands to be filled by local property owners. In a few years, land prices rose dramatically and in some cases sold from five to ten times above 1880 prices. Two commercial boarding houses were started and several householders took in one or two boarders. While such a development pleased local landowners, a shortage of housing continued throughout the 1880s. The lack of adequate working-class housing pushed the percentage of propertyless residents from 38.4 in 1880 to 46.8 in 1890. Most of those without property were cotton mill workers. In 1886, almost 70 per cent of male cotton mill workers did not own property. Among saw mill employees, who were long-time residents, only one-third did not own property. Three years later, however, the percentage of propertyless male mill hands dropped to 46.7 suggesting that the highly mobile, propertyless worker was more common to the early years of the

[18] *Census of Canada*, (1891), IV, 119; *Report of the Royal Commission on the Relations of Capital and Labour* (Ottawa 1889), New Brunswick Evidence, 178.

[19] Data on mobility was obtained by comparing the seventy-two employees listed in the *1886 McAlpine Charlotte County Directory* (Saint John 1886); and the fifty-four employees listed in the *1889 McAlpine New Brunswick Directory* (St. John 1889); with the Milltown Assessment Books for the 1880s. Assessment Books listed all property owners and British males over twenty-one years of age.

[20] PANB, Milltown Valuation and Assessment Book, 1883, Ward 2, n.p.; *Calais Times*, 11 May 1883, 2.

mill.[21] By 1889, almost all of the workers came from within twenty miles of the factory.

Indeed, the gradual integration of the cotton mill workers with other segments of the community can be seen throughout the 1880s. Early references to the "cotton mill folk" were soon replaced by individual names. The St. Croix mill superintendent, Lewis Dexter, sat on the local schoolboard towards the end of the decade. The loom-fixers' ball became a social highlight of the year. Baseball games between the weavers and the mulers were a popular summer-night entertainment. These minor items knit together the everyday lives of the mill workers and the townsmen. This growing familiarity with life in a cotton mill town, however, made residents aware that many of the predictions made by the original supporters of the mill were not coming true.

The St. Croix mill did bring a great deal of money into town. Average monthly wages totalled approximately $18,000, but this could fluctuate from $10,000 during a slow month to $30,000 during peak periods.[22] These wages, of course, kept many of the local retailers in business. Not only the Milltown merchants, but those of St. Stephen and Calais as well, were heavily dependent upon the patronage of the mill's workers. For them, the local bonuses had been justified, as they had been for the local property owners. There was a key group within the community, however, whose initial investments did not pay off — the local stockholder.

Because the St. Croix's managers and overseers were not from the Milltown community, the local stockholders were needed to keep alive that co-operative spirit prominent during the first year of the company's existence. The owners of the major lumber mills, such as James Murchie, Freeman Todd, or Henry Eaton, were well-qualified to deal with any local problems because of their intimate knowledge of the community and its members. Events soon transpired, however, which made these men less than eager for such a task. Large dividends are the quickest way to a stockholder's heart, but unfortunately the St. Croix mill never paid anything upon its stock. As soon as the mill opened, the Canadian market showed signs of being overstocked. In October 1883, David Morrice and Son, a large Montréal dry goods firm and selling agent for most of the Canadian cotton mills, failed. By giving generous financing to Canadian mills during 1882, the Morrice firm accumulated $1.75 million in unsecured liabilities. When the 1883 fall season proved very sluggish, Morrice and Son defaulted on its payments and was ordered to stop lending money to cotton mills. Among these mills was the St. Croix factory.[23] When the Morrice failure was announced, the St. Croix directors were selling company stock in Providence, Rhode Island. The panic which followed the Morrice failure halted these stock sales and the St. Croix mill found itself short of funds. Since most of

[21]Figures on home ownership were obtained by comparing residents listed in the local directories for 1886 and 1889 (see note 19) with the Milltown Assessment Books from 1880 to 1892.
[22]*Calais Times*, 2 March 1883, 2; 20 October 1884, 2; *St. Croix Courier*, 9 June 1892, 3.
[23]*St. Croix Courier*, 25 October 1883, 2.

the money advanced to the mill came from Rhode Island banks, these banks issued strict financial guidelines in order to protect their investment. The St. Croix operation was thought to have a good long-term future, and the creditors pressured the mill's management to increase production and reduce operating costs to meet payments on their debts.[24]

Such matters were handled exclusively by the American textile experts and the local directors soon found themselves cut off from most management decisions. Many measures taken to increase production, such as reductions in wages and speed-ups of machinery, drew increasing criticism from local employees. In the face of such complaints many smaller stockholders became less vocal in their support of the mill. Still, local lumber mill owner, James Murchie, remained active on the mill's behalf, possibly because his other business interests declined. The *St. Croix Courier*'s editor, David Main, also remained faithful to the only example of National Policy effectiveness in his constituency. Most other stockholders, however, regarded the local money invested in the mill either as a bad debt or a public-spirited investment which would never be personally rewarding.

The cooling of relations between the American managers and the local business élite was accelerated by lawsuits over the water power of the St. Croix River. In 1885, John D. Andrews, a local axe manufacturer, successfully took the cotton mill to court for interfering with his water power.[25] In August 1888, the St. Croix managers launched an action against F.H. Todd and Sons' lumber mills for the obstruction of water power. Freeman Todd found himself in the odd position of being sued by a company which he had helped to create.[26] In both cases, the St. Croix's managers made the most of their economic muscle by arguing that the older, but smaller, companies had no right to jeopardize such a large investment. This line of reasoning won few allies among local manufacturers.

The deterioration of good will between the local élite and the mill managers was not in itself the critical factor in reversing community support. Yet once these influential citizens no longer saw their interests as identical to those of the cotton mill, they looked much more sympathetically upon complaints of the local mill hands. It was among the mill workers that the first signs of discontent appeared. The attitude of the mill hands was important because Milltown residents were predominantly working-class people. As one prominent citizen remarked, "A man who wears a clean collar in Milltown is taking upon himself undue dignity."[27] In an open clash between mill hand and manager, the Milltown community would naturally side with the workers.

The discontent of the St. Croix mill hands finally erupted in late January 1886. Four years after the mill started production, it was evident to all workers that the

[24]*Ibid.*, 15 November 1883, 2.
[25]*Calais Times*, 26 November 1885, 2; 3 December 1885, 2; *St. Croix Courier*, 8 September 1887, 3.
[26]*St. Croix Courier*, 9 August 1888, 3; 30 May 1889, 2.
[27]*Calais Times*, 27 August 1885, 2.

promises made to them during the stock campaign of good, permanent jobs would remain simply promises unless they took action. In early January, Superintendent Lewis Dexter announced a 5 to 10 per cent reduction on the piece rate paid to mule spinners and weavers. No previous notice of this reduction was made and the customary price lists, which allowed workers to see the extent of the wage cut, were not posted. The highly skilled mule spinners gave their two weeks' notice. Failure to do so could have resulted in a heavy fine. The weavers took no action, but two weeks later they received a second reduction and immediately left their looms. The mule spinners joined them. On the following day three hundred strikers met in Milltown's People's Hall to plan strategy. The strikers, headed by the Milltown band, marched on the St. Croix offices and demanded their pay. The company paid them off the next day.[28] Milltown was about to experience its first cotton mill strike.

Initially, local reaction to the strike was one of surprise and unease. The community newspapers had frequently reported on New England strikes and lamented these unprofitable clashes between capital and labour. These distant disputes did not really prepare the local residents for the confrontation between the only major source of income and the welfare of their friends and neighbours. In taking advantage of the fruits of industrial development, Milltown now had to come to terms with its antagonistic elements. Rumours circulated that the strikers had smashed machinery and many wondered if a long strike would be the final blow which closed the St. Croix mill.

Confident in his power to make workers return to work without granting any concessions. Superintendent Dexter refused to hear the strikers' demands. Undaunted, the striking hands continued to meet daily. By the weekend, their number increased to seven hundred. Committees were formed to raise funds, distribute relief, and organize the strikers. The female hands took an active part in these committees and all other strike activities. On Saturday afternoon, all strikers assembled at the People's Hall in Milltown. Once again led by the Milltown band, the strikers marched through the streets of Calais where they reassembled at the local skating rink. The strikers' position was explained to those in attendance. The marchers then crossed the bridge to St. Stephen and returned to Milltown. This demonstration of strength and organization, "elected the sympathy of the entire community,"[29] according to one commentator. Another witness wrote,

We doubt if ever a prettier scene ever gladdened the eyes of any people than the handsome girls and boys who paraded Saturday afternoon and asked by their presence in the streets of Calais and St. Stephen that all fair-minded people would hasten the day when justice would come to all alike and labor troubles and strikes would be unnecessary and gladly forgotten by poor and rich.[30]

[28] *Calais Advertiser*, 3 February 1886, 3; *Calais Times*, 4 February 1886, 2.
[29] *Calais Advertiser*, 3 February 1886, 2.
[30] *St. Croix Courier*, 11 February 1886, 2.

The local residents gave more than sympathy. Aid in money and favours came from several influential citizens and even some of the St. Croix mill's stockholders contributed to the strike fund.

Surprised at the strikers' ability to rally community support, Superintendent Dexter agreed to meet with the strikers on Monday morning. They had four demands: a ten-hour day, a 10 per cent wage increase, a standardization of piece work to prevent further speed-ups of machinery, and the right for all strikers to return to work.[31] Along with the well-organized nature of the strikers, these demands prompted Dexter to complain that the strike was being formented by a "foreign element" engaged in similar disturbances in the United States.[32] The strike leader, John Danily, had indeed only been in town two weeks before the strike. He spoke highly of the efforts of the Knights of Labor to improve the condition of the working man. During the strike, two Knights' locals were formed in Calais and Milltown, Maine, and the Knights' philosophy clearly showed its influence during the dispute.[33] But there were no direct links between the strikers and the Knights of Labor; the local mill hands were simply responding to the harsh treatment they had received at the factory. On Monday afternoon, the superintendent rejected all of the strikers' demands.

Even as Dexter was meeting with the strikers, his supervisor, H.H. Shumway, was searching Milltown, St. Stephen, and Calais for workers to replace the strikers. Shumway found no volunteers among local residents and eventually had to travel to Eastport, Maine, to find new hands. Word of the importation of strike-breakers soon leaked out. The section hands, who helped oversee the looms, refused to teach "nobsticks" how to weave and joined the strikers. This walkout forced the mill to close completely. On 9 February, the mill's representative began his journey back to Milltown and the strikers took to the streets to show their strength. The Milltown Town Council, fearing a confrontation between the strike-breakers and the mill hands, summoned seventy-six special constables from among the local residents. Billie clubs were turned out on the mill's lathes for the men, but when the time came to swear in the constables only ten appeared.[34] Most of these were employed by the mill. As far as the Milltown residents were concerned, the strike-breakers did not deserve protection.

On Tuesday night, the train carrying the new hands arrived. The company's representative had managed to hire only forty girls from the Eastport sardine factories. They were accommodated in the company boarding house and on their daily journeys to the mill were protected by armed guards. Strikers continually harassed and ridiculed the strike-breakers, but carefully remained within the law. The mill windows were boarded up and armed guards posted at entrances. Such

[31]*Ibid.*, 4 February 1886, 2.
[32]*Ibid.*
[33]*Ibid.*, 18 February 1886, 2; *Calais Times*, 25 February 1886, 3.
[34]*Calais Advertiser*, 17 February 1886, 3; PANB, Milltown Town Council Minute Book, 10 February 1886, 452-3.

measures by the management alarmed local residents who expected a violent confrontation any day. To head off the threat of violence, three respected citizens tried to arbitrate the dispute.

Calais mayor George M. Hanson and two Milltown residents, barrister W.J. Fowler and general dealer S.D. Pineo, worked for four days before they persuaded Dexter to submit a proposal to the strikers. According to this agreement, the piece rate would be standardized and the increase in wages and reduction of hours referred to the Rhode Island creditors.[35] On the twentieth day of the strike, the mill hands decided to return to work under these conditions. The speed-up of machinery, which had triggered the strike, had been resolved and the other matters postponed until later. It was a modest victory for the strikers. The local press was highly laudatory over the results of the arbitration proceedings. Such positive action seemed to indicate that Milltown could settle industrial disputes reasonably and avoid the constant struggle between capital and labour which characterized larger cities.

This hopeful illusion was destroyed once the hands returned to work. A few months after the strike, one-third of the work force was fired. Those dismissed included the hands active in the strike.[36] Such actions suggest that the superintendent's acceptance of the arbitration proceedings was merely a pretext to resume production. Community influence in regulating matters of mill production was non-existent. Market conditions would not allow the managers to improve working conditions and still pay their creditors, and the creditors came first. The dismissal of so many employees, however, left the mill short of skilled workers. To solve this problem, the St. Croix managers imported 116 Scottish textile workers in September. Though powerless to save the jobs of the strikers, Milltown residents did their best to make the new arrivals uncomfortable. The Scots were ostracized from the normal social functions of the mill hands.[37] This type of community pressure proved so effective that most of the Scots left by late November. This incident signalled the changed attitude of local residents and indicated an awareness that the St. Croix managers were more interested in their investment than the Milltown community.

By the end of 1886, the community's attitude towards the St. Croix mill was one of restrained hostility. Despite its indifference to local sensibilities, however, the cotton mill was still the only major industry in town. Its wages paid the bills and kept the merchants solvent. Even its most vocal critics respected the economic importance of the mill in the local economy. Although none of the promises made during the original stock campaign had materialized in an agreeable form, local residents shouldered part of the blame by inviting the Rhode Island investors into the project. This realization, however, did not prevent periodic outbursts of anger towards the St. Croix mill.

The cotton factory had given the Milltown community a secure economic base, but in the process divided that community as never before along class lines. Direct

[35]St. Croix Courier, 18 February 1886, 2.
[36]Calais Advertiser, 30 June 1886, 3; St. Croix Courier, 1 July 1886, 2.
[37]St. Croix Courier, 9 September 1886, 3; Calais Times, 25 November 1886, 2.

confrontations did not occur after the 1886 strike, but one incident did reveal the suspicions that management had towards local workers. In 1889 a series of unexplained fires broke out at the factory and Superintendent Dexter suspected arson. He hired a Boston detective to pose as a mill hand and discover the incendiary. The detective singled out seventeen-year-old Henry McIntee and eventually persuaded the boy to burn down the mill. One night, the detective and McIntee started some cotton waste on fire and, by a prearranged signal, McIntee was caught in the act. During the trial in late October, the detective presented his evidence, but the jury remained undecided with six voting for conviction and six for acquittal. At a second trial, the judge told the jury that the McIntee case was the strongest case of circumstantial evidence he had ever seen. The *Calais Times* reported the trial's outcome with obvious approval:

In the Country Court in St. Andrews, last week, [the St. Croix cotton mill] failed to secure a conviction of Henry McIntee of Milltown, who was tempted by a hired detective to pretend to commit a crime. After three days trial the verdict was 'not guilty,' and the boy's acquittal causes almost universal pleasure in the community.[38]

There was certainly nothing surprising about the community's joy in the acquittal of a seventeen-year-old native. Still, the suspicions of the mill superintendent were never really resolved. If McIntee was innocent, was there someone else with a grudge to settle?

The sharpest criticism of the St. Croix mill was touched off by damage to the local environment. Nineteenth-century lumber towns such as Milltown could hardly be described as clean places to live, but whatever unspoiled nature remained in the area was highly valued by local residents. The St. Croix River's salmon population received careful assistance from local conservationists. The St. Croix mill was not the neat and tidy hive of industry originally envisioned, since the waste water from its dyeing process proved fatal to local fish. Periodic complaints about the destruction of the local fish population had no effect upon the mill's operation. In August 1887, the *Calais Advertiser* grew tired of the constant criticism and asked, "Would it not be just as judicious to look after the sporting fraternity and let the mill grind cotton?"[39] The economics of the situation made the *Advertiser*'s comment a reasonable one, but the *Calais Times* took this opportunity to let off some stream. In a long editorial, the *Times* reviewed the "extraordinary license" allowed the mill and pointed out the paltry returns on the investments in the factory:

When the St. Croix Cotton Mill Company serves notice that it will treat with contempt all complaints against its illegal measures, and will denounce as 'irresponsible' all those who

[38]*Calais Times*, 31 October 1889, 2; *St. Croix Courier*, 20 June 1889, 2; 14 July 1889, 2; 31 October 1889, 2.
[39]*Calais Advertiser*, 31 August 1887, 2.

oppose its high handed proceedings, then the time has come to remove its conceit through vigorous fight.[40]

This outburst was the first unqualified attack upon the St. Croix mill for its disregard of community values, but no action followed these words. The mill continued to pollute the St. Croix River. Only after repeated complaints by Dominion Fisheries Inspector Pratt and the insistence of the Fisheries Department did the factory reduce its pollution.[41]

These incidents demonstrated the growing disillusionment of certain segments of the local community. It was not until December 1891, however, that the full extent of the community's dissatisfaction became evident. In December the ten-year tax exemption granted the cotton mill expired. Directors of the company asked for a continuation of the exemption since other mills across Canada enjoyed similar privileges. In order to remain competitive, the St. Croix mill needed the same advantage. This was a common plea of local industries dealing on the national market and usually the local government agreed readily to the exemption, expecting indirect benefits to offset lost tax dollars. In January 1892, a public meeting was held in Milltown, but no decision was reached. The company directors sent circulars to each ratepayer asking for their support. Because of the local feeling about the mill, the Town Council refused to make the decision. It decided to canvass the ratepayers and agreed to abide by the consensus. Once the ballots were counted, the decision was very clear. No one voted to renew the exemption. Ballots fixed the average assessment for the mill at $225,000. Considering the depressed state of the cotton market and the local assessed value on other properties, this figure represented a fair tax burden on the factory. On that assessment, the company would pay $5,000 annually in taxes.[42]

This refusal to extend special privileges to the St. Croix mill was not in itself a great blow to the company. The significance of this decision has more to do with community values than economics. During the 1886 strike, in the law suits over water rights, and throughout the pollution of the St. Croix River, Milltown found itself unable to effect any changes in the mill's operation. The cotton factory was simply too powerful to be influenced by community pressure. Taxes, however, were entirely within the community's power. This was perhaps the only channel through which the local residents could express their hostility towards the mill. As "Milltowner" explained the tax question to the *St. Croix Courier*,

Milltown has about paid dollar for dollar what it has received during the past ten years of exemption ... if the mill needs any further fostering care as an infant industry, then let Calais and St. Stephen which receive three quarters of the benefit, come forward with a helping

[40]*Calais Times*, 1 September 1887, 2.
[41]*Ibid.*, 2 October 1890, 2.
[42]*St. Croix Courier*, 14 January 1892, 3; *Calais Advertiser*, 17 February 1892, 2.

hand and not ask Milltown to beat the bush and catch the bird any longer. It looks like too much crow to Milltown.[43]

After ten years of difficulty between the company and the community, Milltown residents decided that the community came first.

If the Milltown residents had come to terms with their own "infant industry," national opinion still remained uncommitted. The "infant" cotton mills proved unprofitable as single companies but, with the merging of these mills into the Montréal combinations, renewed hopes were expressed about the future. One month after the Milltown tax issue, the owners of the St. Croix mill sold out to the Canadian Coloured Cotton Company. This company combined almost all of the independent mills which were still outside the Dominion Cotton Company. These two combinations gave the Montréal manufacturers an undisputed monopoly over the industry. Questions of production, price, and marketing affecting the St. Croix mill would now be decided in Montréal. For Milltown, the rules of the game had changed overnight. In future, if Milltown did not want to give concessions to the company, new production and jobs could be located in Marysville or Cornwall. The contest between community and company was one-sided while the St. Croix mill was an independent concern, but the Montréal directors could play one town against another in a never-ending shell game to decide which community prospered and which declined.

Milltown's experiences with the St. Croix mill between 1880 and 1892 clearly demonstrated that industrial growth created as many problems as it solved. There was more money in town, but housing prices soared. There were more jobs, but the working conditions created dissatisfaction among local workers. Those characteristics of single industry communities present during the lumber economy actually intensified with the increased scale of the cotton factory. The new mill marked the end of an economy controlled by local businessmen. Decisions affecting Milltown were increasingly made in Rhode Island and later Montréal. And just as residents disliked the American management, they would grow to mistrust the Montréal directors who made decisions on a national scale without much consideration of local impact.

By focusing on the dynamics of the community itself, one can see in Milltown's history an illustration of the local élite's role in shaping the attitudes of residents. At first, its co-operation made the company's position an easy one but, once community leaders became detached from the day-to-day operations of the mill, problems occurred. In the end, the conciliatory role of the local élite between the community and the company was futile, since the company would not compromise its competitive position to placate local sensibilities. The mainspring of local discontent was the community's working class. The mill hands had first-hand knowledge of the mill, and the realities of cotton manufacture forced them to attempt improvements. The behaviour of the mill hands can be partially linked to

[43]*St. Croix Courier*, 31 December 1891, 2.

the working-class tradition of Milltown. As a lumber town, Milltown was no stranger to strikes and work stoppages. Local experience, however, was only part of the situation. When the New England textile workers taught locals to weave cotton, they also gave them a familiarity with the opinions and character of American cotton hands. The 1886 strike and the formation of Knights of Labor locals under the Maine District Assembly illustrated the influence of outside forces. Taking their tactics from other places, but preserving the local spirit, the mill hands forced all local residents to face realities.

For the St. Croix mill, these realities were harsh, and community influence over them very slight. Still, within these limitations, the local residents asserted their own community values. They refused to be cowed by the managers' economic strength. In this attempt to bite the hand that fed them, Milltown residents were not displaying any conservative, backwoods fear of change. Their decision to end the tax exemption was a practical assessment of their situation. In 1892, it was too early to feel nostalgic over the rough and hard life in the saw mills. For all its shortcomings, locals accepted the fact that cotton had come to Milltown.

Robert McIntosh

6

The Boys in the Nova Scotia Coal Mines, 1873-1923

A correspondent of the *Scottish American Journal*, who visited the Albion Mines in Pictou County in 1880, could not help but be struck by a sharp division in the mine labour force: "The boys seem(ed) happy enough, and were bright little fellows from 11 to 15 years of age; the men were respectful and small in stature, but they appeared dull and phlegmatic by contrast with the younger generation." Unfortunately, colliery boys have not caught historians' attention as they did this Victorian correspondent's. While the relatively "dull and phlegmatic" older Nova Scotian miners have been the subject of an extensive amount of recent historical research, the boys have been virtually ignored.[1]

The boys were by no means a homogeneous group. In the provincial Mines Act, the term "boy" was taken to refer to anyone under 18; within the mining community, it was often applied to anyone not yet meriting the use of the handpick — in other words, one who had yet to attain the position of coal cutter, or miner proper. "Boy" described individuals aged from eight to 21, engaged in a variety of occupations within the mine. From 1880 to 1890 the proportion of boys in the

[1]*Trades Journal*, 15 September 1880. Recent theses on the miners include David Frank, "Coal Masters and Coal Miners: the 1922 Strike and the Roots of Class Conflict in the Cape Breton Coal Industry," MA thesis, Dalhousie University, 1974; "The Cape Breton Coal Miners 1919-1925," PhD thesis, Dalhousie University, 1979; Don Macgillivray, "Industrial Unrest in Cape Breton 1919-1925," MA thesis, University of New Brunswick, 1971; Ian McKay, "Industry, work and community in the Cumberland coalfields, 1848-1927," PhD thesis, Dalhousie University, 1983; Robert McIntosh, "A Community Transformed: The Nova Scotian Coal Miners 1879-1925," MA thesis, Carleton University, 1985; Sharon Reilly, "The Provincial Workmen's Association of Nova Scotia 1879-1898," MA thesis, Dalhousie University, 1979. A recent exception to general inattention to mine boys is Ian McKay's article "The Realm of Uncertainty: The Experience of Work in the Cumberland Coal Mines, 1873-1927," *Acadiensis*, XVI, 1 (Autumn 1986), 3-57.

Published with permission of the editor. From *Acadiensis*, XVI, 2 (Spring 1987), 35-50.

provincial colliery workforce rose from 17.1 to 21.5 per cent, but they failed to participate fully in the large expansion in the mine workforce after the turn of the century. Their relative strength in the mine workforce fell steadily during the early 20th century as their average age increased and by 1910 they comprised only 8.8 per cent of the mine workers (see Table One). In 1923, legislation virtually excluded boys from the province's coal mines.[2]

Table 1

	No. of Boys in Workforce	Total Colliery Workforce	% of Boys in Workforce
1874	555	3939	14.1
1876	565	3510	16.1
1878	510	3017	16.9
1880	519	3041	17.1
1882	627	3455	18.1
1884	768	4565	16.8
1886	722	4379	16.5
1888	740	4312	17.2
1890	1102	5119	21.5
1892	882	5659	15.6
1894	844	5826	14.5
1896	699	5704	12.3
1898	686	5127	13.4
1900	735	5500	13.4
1902	792	7606	10.4
1904	877	10624	8.3
1906	826	10712	7.7
1908	921	12087	7.6
1910	1063	12059	8.8
1912	922	12504	7.4
1914	831	13632	6.1

Department of Mines *Reports* give no separate figures for boys after 1915. These figures exclude those engaged in construction work at provincial collieries.

Boys were in the mines for a number of reasons. The state of technology in the late 19th century required that individuals under a certain size be employed for particular tasks. Wage levels have also to be stressed: the labour of boys was cheaper than that of their fathers and older brothers. The presence of young workers in the

[2]Nova Scotia, Department of Mines Reports, in *Journals and Proceedings of the House of Assembly*, for 1880, 1890, and 1910; Nova Scotia *Statutes*, 1923, 13 Geo. V, c. 54, sect. 1.

mine had further advantages for older workers: by equating "boys" with low-skill, poorly-paid work, the status of the "skilled" collier was safeguarded. At the same time, the boys' employment was welcomed within mining families, since they could then contribute to the family income and since their early initiation into the Victorian coal mine was expected to lead eventually to the most highly skilled positions.

One important factor determining the number of boys employed was the method of late 19th- and early 20th-century coal mining. The technique used over this period, labelled "room and pillar," had been introduced into Nova Scotia by the General Mining Association in the middle third of the 19th century.[3] A variety of levels were driven outward from the core shaft in the mine; balances were cut up into the coal seam from these levels. In each balance, "rooms" from which coal was mined in an initial cutting alternated with the "pillars" of coal left to buttress the mine ceiling. This technique of extraction gave the mine a characteristic "honeycomb" appearance. Popular with the miners — the disparate workplaces within the mine allowed them a good deal of autonomy — it persisted in the province against the in-roads of more modern mining techniques. Notwithstanding minor 19th century experiments, the more regimented "longwall" system of mining did not first appear in a major Springhill pit until 1924; "room and pillar" endured into the 1920s and beyond on Cape Breton and not until 1930 did longwall begin to replace "room and pillar" in Pictou County.[4] Loading continued to be undertaken by hand at least as long.[5] Although improvements in haulage continued to be introduced over this period, horses had yet to be displaced by 1923. While the introduction of mechanical cutters transformed facework between 1873 and 1923, boys' work was substantially unchanged.

Two early 19th-century innovations in mining greatly increased the demand for child labour. Pioneered in Great Britain, these and other state of the art mining techniques were subsequently introduced into Nova Scotia by the General Mining Association. In Great Britain, the introduction of horses and some wheeled vehicles underground had gradually displaced women, the traditional "beasts of burden." As the burden of work became lighter, women were replaced by the less expensive labour of boys. By mid-century the task of hauling coal generally fell to 14 to 17 year old boys, called drivers, and the horses they led. Where seams were too narrow to permit the passage of horses (or adults), coal continued to be moved manually

[3]Donald MacLeod, "Miners, mining men and mining reform: the changing technology of Nova Scotian gold mines and collieries, 1858-1910," PhD thesis, University of Toronto, 1982, 308.
[4]McKay, "Industry, work and community," 243; Frank, "Coal Masters and Coal Miners," 220; James M. Cameron, *The Pictonian Colliers* (Halifax 1974), 120.
[5]At the more technologically advanced U.S. bituminous mines, the first successful mechanical loader was not introduced until 1922. See Alexander Mackenzie Thompson, "Technology, Labour and Industrial Structure of the United States Coal Industry: A Historical Perspective," PhD thesis, Stanford University, 1979, 61.

by boys on all fours dragging sledges. A second technologial innovation early in the 19th century encouraged the employment of even younger children. As mines extended deeper underground, problems of ventilation became more pressing. Under the compound system of mine ventilation developed by John Buddle, doors known as "traps" were introduced into mines. Generally closed so as to channel air throughout the mine, these doors had to be frequently opened to allow the passage of drivers, their horses and material. "Trappers," often less than 10 years old, were employed to perform this task. These boys worked long days relative even to the miners, since they were the first down the shaft and the last to leave the mine at the end of the shift. At Victorian mines where "expansion and technical progress" were most pronounced, child labour was most extensive.[6]

The child's experience of work in the mine, shaped by the technology of the day, changed as he grew older. The boy, introduced to the mine by his father, would likely be employed in various odd jobs on the surface, if he were not immediately placed by a trap. Surface employment might include running errands, cleaning lamps or distributing picks. Far less pleasant work involved the sorting of coal; perched above a belt carrying the recently-mined coal, it was the boys' responsibility to remove any stone inadvertently brought up with the coal. The work of trapper boys was no more appealing. Labouring "under conditions which were very like solitary confinement in darkness," these boys almost welcomed the bullying of passing drivers as a relief from tedium.[7] The contrast between the frightened trapper boy and the self-confident driver is captured in two mid-19th century colliery songs from Great Britain. In one the following verse is found: "Father! must I go down with you/ Into that dark and dismal hole,/ And leave the sky above so blue,/ Buried amidst the blackest coal?" And in the other song, this verse: "What a merry gay life is that of the Driver/ And what if I scarce see the sun,/ I can sing in the dark, and spend my last stiver/ In sweeties, and frolic, and fun."[8] The trapper was a novice in the mine; the driver was familiar with its rhythm.

The variety of tasks a boy might perform in the course of his education in "practical mining," as the miners called it, was described to the 1888 Labour Commission by a number of Springhill mine workers. William Terrace, a veteran of the mine at 15, had first worked at the age of ten turning a fan and had recently started driving. Murdoch McLeod, a 29-year old miner, had entered the pit at nine as a trapper; he had "worked [him]self up," spending many years as a driver before becoming a miner. Elisha Paul's path to coal cutter was even more varied. Employed

---

[6]See J.S. Martell, "Early Coal-Mining in Nova Scotia," *Dalhousie Review*, XXV, 2 (July 1945), 156-72; D.A. Muise, "The GMA and the Nova Scotia Coal Industry," *Bulletin of Canadian Studies*, VI, 2/ VII, 1 (Autumn 1983), 70-87; Neil K. Buxton, *The Economic Development of the British Coal Industry* (London 1978), 27, 131; Angela V. John, *By the Sweat of Their Brow: Women Workers at Victorian Coal Mines* (London 1980), 23, 33.

[7]Sir Llewellyn Woodward, *The Age of Reform* (Oxford 1962), 153; John Benson, *British Coalminers in the Nineteenth Century: A Social History* (Dublin 1980), 49.

[8]J.R. Leifchild, *Our Coal and Our Coal-Pits* (London 1968 [1856]), 151, 155.

first as a trapper, Paul graduated to the position of driver within a few months. His next occupation was on a balance, supervising the movement of empty boxes up to the miners' workplaces and the passage of boxes full of coal down to the levels. By 16 he was a cage runner; he removed full boxes from the balance and replaced them with empty ones for the return trip back to the miners. Later he was employed as a loader; he filled the boxes with the coal freshly cut by the miner. At 19, Paul became a cutter.[9] The experience of these boys was not untypical of the late 19th century Nova Scotian colliery; the hierarchy of tasks was not rigid and boys who aspired to the handpick could follow a variety of routes to the position of cutter.

A handful of miners enjoyed even greater upward mobility, despite their early introduction to mine work. The establishment of mining schools in the coal towns, long a goal of the Provincial Workmen's Association (PWA), the first miners' union in Nova Scotia, aided the ambitious miner. The career of J.R. Dinn provides one of the more spectacular examples of mobility within the mine workforce. Dinn started work in the "Caledonia" mine, Dominion Coal #4, in 1900. Sixteen years old at the time, his first job was as a loader. Attending night school during the winter months, Dinn passed the examination for overman in 1906 and was appointed to this minor underground supervisory position. Five years later he was appointed assistant underground manager; in 1919, underground manager; and finally, in 1921, Dinn became manager of the mine he had entered two years earlier as a labourer. Indeed, by the turn of the century all Nova Scotian colliery managers had risen from the position of "practical miner."[10] These individuals were, of course, exceptional; the typical boy had a much different experience of the mines. In accordance with an expression current in the turn of the century Pennsylvania anthracite fields, "twice a boy and once a man is a poor miner's life," the miner's working life would usually end above ground, where he would engage in light work similar to that of boys.[11]

A boy's experience of the mine might end yet another way: in death or disability. The youngest workers, less attentive and knowledgeable, nonetheless shared the dangers of the mine with older miners. Like them, the boys fell victim to the great mine disasters. The explosion in the number one mine at Springhill in

[9]Royal Commission on the Relations of Capital and Labor, *Nova Scotia Evidence* (Ottawa 1889), 302, 288; Gregory S. Kealey, ed., *Canada Investigates Industrialism (The Royal Commission on the Relations of Labor and Capital, 1889)* (Toronto 1973), 402-3.

[10]E.H. Armstrong papers, MG2, Box 686, F2/17830, PANS; Donald MacLeod, "Colliers, Colliery Safety and Workplace Control: The Nova Scotian Experience, 1873-1910," *Historical Papers* (1983), 251. The PWA congratulated itself in 1888 that promotions from its ranks to those of management included five former Grand Masters and two Assistant Grand Masters. See the *Trades Journal*, 11 April 1888. This pattern of spectacular upward mobility was found in fiction also. See Ian McKay's introduction to C.W. Lunn's "From Trapper Boy to General Manager: A Story of Brother Love and Perseverance," *Labour/Le Travailleur*, 4 (1979), 211-40.

[11]Harold W. Aurand, *From the Molly Maguires to the United Mine Workers: The Ecology of an Industrial Union 1869-1897* (Philadelphia 1971), 37.

1891 killed 125 — 17 of them boys 16 years of age and younger.[12] Although far less striking, the daily small accidents in the colliery were in fact the greater killers. Death or disability could occur in a variety of ways. A roof fall, a common accident, killed a boy at Little Glace Bay in 1882. George Jones, approximately 14 years old, died in an explosion in 1889 while hauling timber on the nightshift; his brother James was badly burned at the same time. That same decade a boy lost his arm in an accident in the blacksmith shop at the Drummond colliery in Westville.[13] Only the fortunate survived to enjoy what PWA leader John Moffatt described as the goal of the respectable miner: "a good, comfortable home, education, music, good literature, [and] insurance with sufficient wages to lay by to help out in old age."[14]

The circumstances of boys' work in the mine changed little over the turn of the century. Boys continued to occupy the same kinds of positions and to receive the same levels of pay relative to adult mine workers. C.O. Macdonald estimated that in 1880 the average pay of a boy employed in a Nova Scotian colliery was 65 cents per day. An adult labourer received 50 per cent more than a boy; a cutter, nearly 2½ times as much.[15] These differential wage rates remained intact as long as boys were employed in the mines. At Sydney Mines, boys had closed the wage differential somewhat by 1920, likely because the youngest children had been excluded from the Nova Scotian mines by then, but a mine worker classified as a boy could still expect to receive approximately 60 to 70 per cent of a man's pay. Boys, limited to tasks designated for them, continued to be paid at a discriminatory rate.[16]

From these observations, it should be clear that neither changes in the techniques of mining nor a substantial narrowing of differential wage rates can fully explain the boys' gradual exclusion from the mine. In fact, a change in social attitudes was the most important single cause of the boys' dwindling place in the colliery workforce. This crisis of legitimation, as it will be labelled here, was expressed in a series of amendments to the provincial Mines Act, which raised the minimum age required for work in the mine from 10 in 1873, to 12 in 1891, and to 16 in 1923.[17]

The 1842 outcry in Great Britain against female and child employment provides a useful entry into the question of legitimation. The Children's Employment Commission (whose purview was later extended to include women) was established

[12]Roger David Brown, *Blood on the Coal: The Story of the Springhill Mining Disasters* (Windsor, N.S. 1976), 13.
[13]*Trades Journal*, 11 October 1882, 26 June 1889, 10 June 1885.
[14]Quoted in Robert Drummond, *Recollections and Reflections of a Former Trades Union Leader* (n.p. c. 1926), 184-5.
[15]C. Ochiltree Macdonald, *The Coal and Iron Industries of Nova Scotia* (Halifax 1909), 45.
[16]See the schedule of wages recommended by the Board of Arbitration under Judge G. Patterson for the Nova Scotia Steel and Coal Corporation, in the *Labour Gazette* (April 1920), 394.
[17]In 1947 the minimum age for underground employment became 17; in 1954, 18. Nova Scotia *Revised Statutes*, 1873, c. 10, sect. 4; *Laws* of Nova Scotia, 1891, 54 Vic., c. 9, sect. 3; 1923, 13 Geo. V, c. 54, sect. 1; 1947, 11 Geo. VI, c. 39, sect. 7; 1954, 3 Eliz. II, c. 56, sect. 14.

in the autumn of 1840 to probe conditions in the British coalfields. It was among the first in the English-speaking world, and followed an earlier inquiry into child millworkers. Although the commissioners and their public may have been morally outraged at the conditions within British mines, no problem of legitimation existed within the isolated mining communities, where child labour was not only needed; it was expected.[18] Indeed, one of the more poignant aspects of the history of legislation restricting child labour is the extent to which working-class parents resisted such laws. This resistance has to be appreciated in light of what has been labelled family "survival strategies."[19] The child worker had a significant role to play in contributing to the family income; state efforts to limit his potential for employment struck directly at the family's struggle to resist poverty. The economic importance of child labour collided with new social attitudes emerging over the Victorian age, which idealized childhood and the family. This ideal, aspired to but not necessarily practised by male trade unionists, defined the male as the sole family wage-earner; along with the related "cult of domesticity," it enhanced his status within the family.[20] When abhorrence of child labour was allied with the contemporary call for universal schooling, legislative restrictions on the employment of children began to appear.

In Nova Scotia the crisis of legitimation was more subtle than in Great Britain. Having developed its coal industry at a later date, Nova Scotia was able to avoid to some extent the controversies which emerged in Britain. For instance, as the conflict developed anew in Britain in the 1880s over the employment of women as surface workers, Nova Scotian mine workers could congratulate themselves that neither

[18]Neil J. Smelser, *Social Change in the Industrial Revolution* (Chicago 1959), esp. ch. 9.

[19]Survival strategies took numerous forms. Miners in Scotland traditionally kept a garden; when the British Empire Steel Company pushed wages down to a starvation level, company president Roy Wolvin criticized miners for spurning his 1921 offer of free plowing and fertilizer, with seed potatoes at cost. (The [Duncan] Royal Commission Respecting the Coal Mines of the Province of Nova Scotia *Minutes of Evidence*, 2743, Labour Canada Library, Hull.) Other 19th century survival strategies are discussed in Bettina Bradbury, "Pigs, Cows, and Boarders: Non-Wage Forms of Survival among Montréal Families, 1861-91," *Labour/Le Travail*, 14 (Fall 1984), 9-48; Joy Parr, *Labouring Children: British Immigrant Apprentices to Canada 1869-1924* (Montréal 1980); Bettina Bradbury, "The Fragmented Family: Family Strategies in the Face of Death, Illness and Poverty, Montréal, 1860-1885" in Joy Parr, ed., *Childhood and Family in Canadian History* (Toronto 1982), 109-28. Benson, *British Coal Miners*, 139, notes that in Great Britain children handed over their pay to their parents as long as they lived in the family home. The testimony of Robert McTagarth before the 1888 Labour Royal Commission provides evidence of this practice in Canada. See Kealey, ed., *Canada Investigates*, 423.

[20]Walter E. Houghton, *The Victorian Frame of Mind 1830-1870* (New Haven 1957), 344; Heidi Hartmann, "Capitalism, Patriarchy, and Job Segregation by Sex," *Signs*, 1, 3, part 2 (Spring 1976), 137-69; Barbara Taylor, *Eve and the New Jerusalem*, (London 1983), esp. ch. IV, "'The Men are as Bad as their Masters...': Working Women and the Owenite Economic Offensive, 1828-34."

women nor girls had ever been employed in provincial collieries.[21] The burden of supporting the family therefore fell to the principal male breadwinner and as many of his sons as were employed. In the provincial coalfields, miners took steps to safeguard their employment by attempting to control the market for mine workers. In 1879, when they formed the Provincial Workmen's Association, miners sought to establish a system of "apprenticeship" to protect the integrity of coal mining as skilled labour. The PWA strove to enforce, not only in practice but also to some extent by law, the prolonged process such as that by which Elisha Paul, the miner from Springhill, had received the pick. Legislative provisions for the certification of colliery employees, largely the result of PWA intimacy with the provincial Liberal government under W.S. Fielding, bear witness to partial PWA success in protecting this pattern of apprenticeship. An 1881 amendment to the Mines Act required the certification of colliery officials by a provincially-constituted board of examiners and by the end of the decade cutters themselves needed provincial accreditation.[22]

The struggle over employment in the coalfields, whereby the miners attempted to restrict and management fought to broaden access to the picks, was closely tied to the question of child labour. Because they were "apprenticed" to the craft of mining, the boys would have been given priority over newcomers to the mine by the PWA. It was never able to accomplish this objective. At a meeting of the PWA Grand Council in 1884, a delegate announced indignantly that "at one of the mines lads verging on manhood and who had been brought up in the mine and were capable of mining were denied the picks, while those about whom the officials knew nothing were given them."[23] While the PWA protested that "coal smashers fresh from the back woods" were being employed as cutters, a "prominent colliery manager" criticized PWA efforts "to make as it were a guild and prevent the employment of strangers at a time when labor below may be required."[24] On the question of control of the labour market, the interests of the miners clashed continually with those of management.

In the clash between workers and mine management the participation of boys was also evident. Indeed, the boys' response to mine work was noteworthy for its vigour: the small, frightened trapper boy matured rapidly and mine boys consistently demonstrated resilience and self-reliance. An early editorial in the *Trades Journal,* the official PWA newspaper, remarked on the boys' general lack of respect for their elders and on their readiness to abuse verbally mine officials — in the

[21]*Trades Journal*, 18 March 1885.
[22]H.A. Logan, *Trade Unions in Canada* (Toronto 1948), 172-4, provides a succinct overview of provincial legislation passed at PWA instigation during the 1880s and 1890s. The term "apprenticeship" is used loosely here, in terms of initiation to mine work.
[23](Semi-) Annual Meeting of (PWA) Grand Council, *Minutes* (April 1884), 59, Labour Canada Library, Hull.
[24]*Trades Journal*, 11 May 1887; *Canadian Mining Review*, 15, 2 (February 1896), 30.

expression of the day, their "saucing."[25] In Springhill in 1887 a boy was ordered, and refused, to travel through a section of the mine he considered dangerous. "Harsh words passed between them," reported the *Trades Journal*, "the boy using the harshest it is said."[26] Their brazenness was more than merely verbal: boys' strikes over the turn of the century were a continual irritant to mine management — and, occasionally, to older mine workers.

Boys demonstrated repeatedly their willingness to quit the mine; in fact, they may have struck more often than older mine workers. Former PWA Grand Secretary and *Trades Journal* editor Robert Drummond remarked that for two years after the Dominion Steel Company gained control of Dominion coal in 1910 there was "not even a boy strike."[27] In 1925 A.S. MacNeil, General Superintendent of the British Empire Steel Corporation mines, testified to the Duncan Royal Commission that "a boy if he was disciplined in any way, or did anything wrong, he was liable to go home and would cause a strike in that part of the mine, or the whole of the mine, or two or three mines."[28] A variety of motives prompted the boys to strike. Even verbal clashes with mine officials could lead to a general walkout of boys.[29] Recreational strikes — the lure of a circus or a game of baseball — also occurred periodically.[30] As well, boys struck in defence of traditional patterns of work. Dominion Coal drivers walked out to resist the replacement of contract pay by a daily rate in 1904.[31] More importantly, boys and officials consistently disputed what constituted a fair day's work and a just level of pay. Boys struck a pit at New Waterford in 1921, for instance, over hours of work — whether horses were to be stabled on the company's or the boys' time.[32] One of the earliest strikes recorded by the *Trades Journal* stemmed from a dispute over pay at Stellarton.[33] The boys' frustration at the restrictions placed on their access to promotion also gave rise to strikes. The boys at the Drummond colliery in Westville walked out for a day in June 1887 in protest against their obligation to perform boys' work — at a maximum of 75 cents per day — until the age of 18. Although mine boys were unable to graduate to the position of loader, mine neophytes — "greenhorns" — were taken on for this task. Although

---

[25]*Trades Journal*, 11 August 1880. See as well the *Trades Journal*, 15 February 1888 for miners' complaints regarding a pick boy "having a tendency to be a boss."

[26]*Trades Journal*, 17 August 1887.

[27]Robert Drummond, *Minerals and Mining Nova Scotia* (Stellarton 1918), 243.

[28]Duncan Commission, *Minutes*, 2555.

[29]This occurred, for example, after the altercation in Springhill mentioned above. The boy was sent home, at which time the rest of the boys in the slope struck, closing it down. *Trades Journal*, 17 August 1887.

[30]Ian McKay refers to instances of boys at the Joggins mines foregoing work in favour of baseball in "Industry, work and community," 608; *Halifax Herald*, 15 August 1905, 7 June 1906.

[31]*Halifax Herald*, 30 January, 2 February 1904; *Maritime Mining Record*, 10 February 1904.

[32]"Strikes and lockouts" file, RG27, vol. 327, no. 171, Public Archives of Canada (PAC).

[33]*Trades Journal*, 2 June 1880.

the *Trades Journal* believed the boys to have "acted a little rashly," it acknowledged their "just cause of complaint."[34]

The qualification in this editorial reflects the ambivalence of adult miners regarding independent action on the part of boys, and suggests that tension existed between boys and older mine workers. Although employment enhanced the boy's status within the family and may have been welcomed by the boy for that reason, the boy whose father carried him to the pit, "the little fellow being unable [to manage] the long journey," probably entered the workforce unwillingly.[35] At the Reserve Mines (Cape Breton), one observer reported in the 1880s, the "parents generally ask for the work."[36] At the same time, adult miners, while condoning their boys' entry into the workforce, balked at their assumption of adult roles. Reports of drunken colliery boys on mine pay days were not uncommon: a couple of "drunk and disorderly" Stellarton boys, aged 12 and 14, found themselves jailed in the course of a particularly boisterous evening in 1888. Adult miners found intoxicated boys, in the expression of the day, "a hard-looking sight."[37]

Although only those at least 17 years old qualified for membership in an adult lodge, the PWA constitution made provision for the establishment of boys' lodges with the sanction of the existing adult lodge at a given pit. "Junior" lodges, as they were called, tended to be short-lived and presumably failed to meet the interests of the boys, since they appear to have played no part in boys' strikes.[38] Indeed, PWA officials as a rule discouraged strikes; their commitment to various kinds of arbitration was reinforced when written contracts were introduced into the Nova Scotian coalfields after the turn of the century.[39] With the introduction of the federal Industrial Disputes Investigation Act in 1907, which provided more legal penalties for spontaneous strikes, the PWA redoubled its efforts to avoid them. On occasion, adult unionists would even act themselves to break a boys' strike. In July 1887 drivers were on strike for four days over wages at Bridgeport, Cape Breton. Because "the parents of the fractious youths considered that the step was ill-chosen they took

---

[34]*Trades Journal*, 8 June 1887.
[35]See McKay, "Industry, work and community," 598; Annual Meeting of Grand Council, *Minutes*, 1890, 221.
[36]Macdonald, *Coal and Iron Industry*, 57.
[37]*Trades Journal*, 21 November 1888, 2 January 1889.
[38]Eugene Forsey, *Trade Unions in Canada 1812-1902* (Toronto 1982), 348, mentions two such lodges: Garfield, founded in March 1884 at Westville and Springhill Juvenile, formed in January 1891. The *Trades Journal*, 26 October 1887, referred to "Stedfast" lodge, organized that year at the Reserve Mines. The *Labour Gazette* (February 1905), 878, noted two boys' lodges on Cape Breton shortly after the turn of the century: Standard, at Dominion #3, and Redpath, at New Aberdeen. King George (Sydney Mines) was represented at the PWA Grand Council Meeting in 1911. See Annual Meeting of Grand Council, *Minutes*, 1911, 676.
[39]The first PWA contract was signed with the Dominion Coal Company in December 1904. See the *Labour Gazette*, May 1905, 1222-3.

the culprits in hand and sent them to work."[40] Nonetheless, the boys' agenda differed from that of adult miners and they struck frequently.[41] After 1919 the United Mine Workers represented Nova Scotia miners, but even UMWA District 26, noted for its radicalism, did not condone spontaneous boys' strikes. "So far as I can foresee," wrote ex-PWA Grand Secretary John Moffatt in 1924, "there will be no major labour troubles this year. There are nearly always small incipient strikes among the boys but they don't last long and are frowned down by the Unions."[42] Cape Breton drivers, in particular, contested regularly and independently of adult miners their conditions of employment.[43] With neither the PWA nor the UMW did the boys see their interests completely served by the adult unionists.

Certainly miners' unions in Nova Scotia sanctioned discrimination against those labelled "boys" in terms of tasks and pay. Recent research in Great Britain has underlined the role of nominally industrial unions in maintaining hierarchies of status and wages in the labour process not only by enshrining hierarchical wage scales in collective agreements with management, but also by a union commitment to subcontracting, whereby high skill workers would supervise their helpers, paying them directly.[44] Both practices were employed in the Nova Scotian collieries. Although trapper boys and coal sorters were generally on the company payroll, at times, particularly in the 19th century, drivers and loaders were paid directly by the

[40]*Trades Journal*, 20 July 1887.
[41]The following is certainly an incomplete list of boys' strikes during the PWA years, 1897 to 1917. Only those strikes not noted elsewhere in this paper are listed here. The year of the strike, its location, and the persons striking (if known) are given: 1883, Pictou Co.; 1887, Reserve Mines, drivers; 1888, Thorburn; 1889, Springhill; 1905, Springhill; 1906, Springhill (2); 1907, Westville; 1907, Acadia colliery; 1909, Springhill, drivers; 1909, Westville. See *Trades Journal*, 20 June 1883, 22 June 1887, 27 June 1888, 31 July 1889; "Lacelle" file, RG27, vol. 143, file 611:04.10, PAC; *Labour Gazette* (August 1906), 174; (October 1907), 468; "Strikes and lockouts" file, RG27, vol. 296, no. 2998, PAC; Halifax *Herald*, 10 March 1909; *Labour Gazette* (July 1909), 124.
[42]"Strikes and lockouts" file, RG27, vol. 332, no. 2, PAC. Moffatt made his remark in a letter to federal Deputy Minister of Labour H.H. Ward, dated 26 April 1924.
[43]These include those during October 1920 at Dominion #1 and #9, two strikes at New Waterford in July 1921, and strikes at Dominion #1 and #9 in June 1922. See "Strikes and lockouts" file, RG27, vol. 323, nos. 361 and 364; vol. 327, nos. 171-2; vol. 327, no. 4, PAC.
[44]See, for instance, Roger Penn, "Trade union organization and skill in the cotton and engineering industries in Britain, 1850-1960," *Social History*, 8, 1 (January 1983), 37-55; William Lazonick, "Industrial relations and technical change: the case of the self-acting mule," *Cambridge Journal of Economics*, 3, 3 (September 1979), 231-62; "Production Relations, Labor Productivity, and Choice of Technique: British and U.S. Cotton Spinning," *Journal of Economic History*, XLI, 3 (September 1981), 491-516. Miners could however act to improve the levels of pay of those they "employed." This occurred, for instance, in Pictou County in November 1887, when the Acadia Coal Co. put a ceiling of $1.20 per day on the sum it would deduct from a miner's pay for his loader. This practise was of sufficient concern to Drummond that he raised it in his testimony before the 1888 Labour Commission. (*Trades Journal*, 9 November 1887; Kealey, ed., *Canada Investigates*, 438.)

miners. The failure of the PWA to implement satisfactorily its system of apprenticeship — as a result of the access of 'greenhorns' to the mine — and thus protect the job market led to discontent among the boys who were subject to discriminatory wage levels, especially since boyhood apprenticeship did not directly involve the acquisition of the skills of the handpick miner. Nonetheless, the pattern of initiation into mining which the PWA sought to safeguard had relative advantages. Many of the occupations available to children at this time were barred to them when they reached maturity.[45] By entering the mine, in contrast, a boy could expect to acquire the handpick eventually, and to remain a miner throughout his working life.

One of the consequences of this practice was a low level of formal education among miners. In the late 19th century the mining community made "practical mining" the focus of a boy's education; although schooling could be combined with work in the mine, this made school attendance irregular and to some extent seasonal. In Cape Breton in the 1880s, attendance was relatively good over the winter when mines were closed. At other times of the year, colliery boys attended school on the days when the pit was idle.[46] Commitment within the mining community to this customary, casual approach to children's education was eroded over the turn of the century, due partly to pressure from the province, which continually raised the minimum acceptable level of formal education and established the means to enforce this minimum. The impact on the colliery boy of this evolving provincial position on education was profound.

By virtue of successive provincial school acts over the turn of the century an increasingly greater proportion of Nova Scotian children attended school to a greater age for a greater portion of the year.[47] Contemporary changes in the way childhood was defined, aspects of which emerged as early as the mid-19th century, reinforced ideas about the need for universal and compulsory children's education. When the child became defined as dependent on adults and at the same time in need of protection from adults, the door was opened to extensive interference with the manner in which parents raised their children.[48] In tandem with the emergence of

[45]Gareth Stedman Jones, *Outcast London: A Study in the Relationship between Classes in Victorian Society* (Harmondsworth 1971), 68-70.
[46]Macdonald, *Coal and Iron Industry*, 48.
[47]Measured as the percentage of those enrolled in daily attendance in the winter term, attendance figures rose slightly over the late 19th century, from 53.2 in 1878 to 55.8 ten years later. Attendance in the second quarter (November through January) stood at 63.7 in 1900, 70.2 in 1910, and 74.4 in 1922. These figures are taken from the "Annual Report on Schools" for the relevant year, found in Nova Scotia, *Journals and Proceedings of the House of Assembly*. Averages in mining counties such as Cumberland or Cape Breton do not differ significantly from the provincial average, but county-level figures will obscure to some extent those from mining communities.
[48]A useful introduction to the extensive literature on education is Chad Gaffield, "Back to School: Towards a New Agenda for the History of Education," *Acadiensis*, XV, 2 (Spring 1986), 169-90. Early research on childhood dated the emergence of modern ideas on childhood at the turn of the century. See Neil Sutherland, *Children in English-Canada:*

this modern notion of childhood appeared the outlines of a universal system of schools.

In Nova Scotia, the "Free Schools Act" of 1864 established the framework for a common school system and an 1865 act guaranteed this system's viability by providing for compulsory assessment of property owners for the upkeep of schools. A child's formal education was not necessarily ensured by the mere existence of a school system and no provision was made in the 1860s for compulsory attendance. In 1883, however, local school boards were permitted to oblige children between seven and 12 to attend school for at least 80 days per year and to fine parents who did not send their children to school. In 1895 the "Towns' Compulsory Attendance Act" was passed by the province; at local option, school boards could compel every child aged between six and 16, resident in an incorporated town, to attend school at least 120 days per year. At the same time provision was made for truancy officers who were empowered to arrest children absent from school. Their parents were subject to fines; the child, in certain circumstances, to imprisonment. Exemptions from school were, however, granted to children over 12 with at least a grade seven common school education and any child over 13 whose income was indispensable. Because many mining communities remained unincorporated until well into the 20th century their school boards were subject to the provisions of the Education Act pertaining to rural areas; the stipulations of 1883, which compelled children from seven to 12 to attend school at least 80 days per year, remained in force. In 1915 the urban upper age limit was raised to 16; the House of Assembly did not inaugurate province-wide compulsory school attendance (for those seven to 14) in rural areas until 1921. In 1923 rural school boards were given the discretion to require six to 16 year olds to attend school and the framework of a modern primary system of education was established in Nova Scotia.[49]

Concern for children's education was reflected not only in school legislation, but also in mines legislation. Although age restrictions on Nova Scotian mine workers had been in place since the first provincial Mines Act of 1873, which had

---

Framing the Twentieth-Century Consensus (Toronto 1976). Subsequently, a case has been made for an earlier, mid-19th century change in public attitudes towards children. See Patricia T. Rooke and R.L. Schnell, "Childhood and Charity in Nineteenth-Century British North America," *Histoire sociale-Social History*, XV, 29 (May 1982), 157-79. In neither instance is consideration given to the changing role of children in the workplace in shaping our notion of childhood.

[49] P.L. McCreath, "Charles Tupper and the Politics of Education in Nova Scotia," *Nova Scotia Historical Quarterly*, 1, 3 (September 1971), 203-24; William B. Hamilton, "Society and Schools in Nova Scotia" in J. Donald Wilson *et al.*, eds., *Canadian Education: A History* (Scarborough 1970), 86-105. 46 Vic., c. 17, "An Act to Secure Better Attendance at Public Schools"; 58 Vic., c. 1, sect. 4; 5 Geo. V, c. 4, "The Cities' and Towns' Compulsory Attendance Act"; 11-12 Geo. V, c. 59, sect. 7; 13 Geo. V, c. 52, sect. 11. A synopsis of much of this legislation is found in Department of Labour, *The Employment of Children and Young Persons in Canada* (Ottawa 1930), 98.

prohibited the employment of boys under ten in or about the mines, amendments in 1891 were the first in Nova Scotia to place educational restrictions on boys entering the mines. Legislation passed in 1908 prohibited from the mine any boy between 12 and 16 who had not completed grade seven.[50] A general concern for the child's welfare and concern specifically for his education began to push the boy from the workforce.

The role of the Nova Scotian mining community regarding legislation restricting the employment of its boys was ambivalent. Robert Drummond, in his submission before the Royal Commission on the Relations between Labour and Capital in 1888, pressed for a minimum age of 12 for work underground in the mines. Other witnesses stressed to the commissioners the need within the mining community for the boys' income.[51] Even with Drummond, the question of child labour held a low priority. In 1882 the *Trades Journal* had reported that an eight-year-old labourer, "a very precocious little chap," was employed at the Halifax Company colliery in Pictou County. The newspaper did not note that his employment brazenly contravened existing provincial statutes, but stressed that the child was foregoing "a fair chance of education."[52] Drummond was very reluctant to sanction interference with parental control of children in areas apart from education. When disturbing reports of child abuse at J.M. Fortier's Montréal tobacco factory arrived in Nova Scotia in 1888, Drummond maintained that it was more important to protect the worker than his child. Although he acknowledged that some protection in law was desirable for both parent and child, he insisted that "the parent, or the guardian of the child has surely certain rights which should not be interfered with."[53] Although the question of child labour was of limited importance to Drummond, he was concerned that a child receive a minimum level of schooling.[54] This concern, as an examination of PWA activity shows, was also limited.

PWA efforts on behalf of formal schooling focused on protecting the integrity of the miners' trade. At a meeting of the PWA Grand Council in October 1890, Drummond stressed the desirability of keeping uneducated boys out of the mine, because they were a threat to safety within the mine and they demeaned the status of the mining community generally. The Council, acknowledging the importance

[50]*Revised Statutes of Nova Scotia*, 1873, c. 10, part 1, Nova Scotia, *Laws*, 1891, 54 Vic. c. 9, sect. 3; 1908, 7 Edward c. 8, sect. 19. The principle requiring a minimum level of formal education before children were permitted to work was adopted in British collieries in 1860, when legislation was enacted stipulating that ten- and 11-year-old boys could only be employed if they had earned an educational certificate or if they attended school at least two days a week for at least three hours per day. See Frederic Keeling, *Child Labour in the United Kingdom* (London 1914), xiv.

[51]Kealey, ed., *Canada Investigates*, 440; Labour Commission, *Evidence*, 294, 301, 303, 351, 414.

[52]*Trades Journal*, 6 December 1882.

[53]*Trades Journal*, 14 March 1888.

[54]The minimum age Drummond recommended, 12, was well below that recommended by the royal commissioners, 14. See also the *Trades Journal*, 24 April 1889.

of schooling for miner certification, instructed the PWA legislative committee to propose to the province a minimum age of 12 for colliery workers; in addition, a boy was not to be permitted to work "unless he be able to read, write and count as far as fractions." The Fielding government acquiesced and the desired amendment to the Mines Act passed without debate in 1891. Although the PWA Grand Council continued to discuss child labour intermittently, the initiative for delayed entry into the collieries in order to acquire an extended formal education passed from the miners' unions in Nova Scotia to a larger community.[55]

PWA interest in children's schooling was limited to the youngest and confined to the rudiments. Even so, it appears to have been more concerned than the mining community as a whole. The *Trades Journal* reported regularly on school activities, and just as regularly berated parents for their lack of interest.[56] As late as 1908, the provincial director of technical education, F.H. Sexton, singled out the mining community for criticism, charging that boys remained ill-educated in mining towns owing to their early entry into the mine.[57] School attendance improved steadily over the turn of the century, bolstered not only by heightened provincial requirements for education but also by improved wage levels which reduced the mining family's dependence on boys' pay.[58] Nonetheless, given the entrenched sanction within the mining community for child labour, the income it brought the family, and the promises held out by formal education, the decision to send a boy into the mine or to school — or to continue school — must often have been anguished.[59]

In 1923, when the Mines Act was amended to exclude from colliery work everyone under 16, the employment of individuals who would be unhesitatingly labelled children came to a close. A variety of factors prompted the 1923 amendment. Following World War One a crisis occurred in the coal industry and there was a general rise in unemployment. Adult miners could no longer afford the luxury

---

[55]Annual Meeting of Grand Council, *Minutes*, 1890, 221-2; Nova Scotia, House of Assembly, *Proceedings and Debates*, 1891; see the Annual Meeting of Grand Council, *Minutes*, 1906, 532, for a debate on child labour in the context of the night shift. One delegate argued with passion that "it is unfair and almost inhuman to have a boy of tender years go into the coal mine to be stunted in physical growth and in intellect, or else be injured, possibly fatally as sometimes occurs." The PWA showed much greater interest in adult education. See Donald MacLeod, "Practicality Ascendant: The Origins and Establishment of Technical Education in Nova Scotia," *Acadiensis*, XV, 2 (Spring 1986), 68-9.

[56]See, for instance, *Trades Journal*, 4 November 1885, for Drummond's complaints about poor parental attendance at school examinations.

[57]See the "Annual Report For the Public Schools, 1907-08," in Nova Scotia, *Journals and Proceedings of the House of Assembly*, 1908, 81.

[58]Wages in the provincial collieries improved significantly after the turn of the century. See Ian McKay, "The Provincial Workmen's Association," in W.J.C. Cherwinski and G.S. Kealey, eds., *Lectures in Canadian Labour and Working-Class History* (St. John's 1985), 130.

[59]McKay, "Industry, work, and community," 598, discusses this in reference to the Cumberland County mines.

of apprenticed boys. By excluding boys from the mines, jobs were created for family heads. Nova Scotia also lagged seriously behind the rest of Canada with respect to legislation restricting child employment within the mine; Ontario, for instance, had prohibited the employment of boys under 15 in 1890 and in 1912 set the minimum age at 17.[60] Finally, in 1923 Nova Scotian rural school boards also received approval to raise the school-leaving age to 16. Provincial sanction had been won for a new status for children, who were universally now defined as school children. This particular amendment simply capped a lengthy process whereby the traditional sanctions for the employment of children collapsed. Social attitudes changed slowly, childhood was redefined, and new means of educating children were instituted. By this process, traditional notions of apprenticeship and collective contributions to the family budget were succeeded by state-enforced provisions for a universal, minimum level of formal education. The colliery boy gave way to the school child.

[60]Québec had set the age for male underground employment at 15 in 1892; Ontario had raised the age to 18 by 1919; Saskatchewan to 14 in 1917; Alberta to 16 in 1908; and British Columbia to 15 in 1911. See Department of Labour, *Employment of Children and Young Persons in Canada* (Ottawa 1930), Table C.

Special thanks to Del Muise for reading an earlier draft of this paper. Research was assisted by an MA fellowship from the SSHRCC.

D.A. Muise

7

The Industrial Context of Inequality: Female Participation in Nova Scotia's Paid Labour Force, 1871-1921

Eighteen-year-old Marie LeBlanc was typical of the largest category of working women of her generation in Nova Scotia.[1] In April 1901 she was employed as a servant in the household of Amherst merchant Samuel Geddes. Like most servants (77 per cent in 1901) Marie came from the countryside. Though a Roman Catholic, she worked in a Methodist household; here, too, her experience proved typical in an era when the middle classes were predominantly Anglo-Protestant and servants often Catholic. Marie reported earnings of $140 the previous year, which did not include board and was based on twelve months' employment. The Geddes' household comprised 43-year-old Samuel, his wife Alice, who did not work outside the home, two sons of six and two years and Marie. It was a comparatively small household in 1901, especially in "Busy Amherst" where boarders and working children more than equalled the numbers of householders in the workforce.

In contrast to Marie, yet like numerous other working women in the province, 22-year-old Georgina Willard taught grade school in the bustling coal town of Sydney Mines. She lived at home with her parents, three teen-aged sisters and a younger brother, in a large frame house on Oxford Street, in the mine town's fashionable "Upper Town." No servants lived in the Willards' house; however, teen-aged girls were expected to assist with normal housework and the family may have employed help that did not live in, for many servants and cleaning ladies lived at home. As Baptists, the Willards were a minority in the predominantly Presbyte-

[1]Pseudonyms are used for all these individuals, who are drawn from the 1901 manuscript census. This census is available to researchers under the provisions of the Access to Information Act.

Published with permission of the editor. From *Acadiensis*, XX, 2 (Spring 1991), 3-31.

rian, Anglican and, increasingly, Catholic town. But they would not have felt out of place among the town's almost exclusively Anglo-Protestant professional and managerial élite. While Georgina's annual earnings of just under $200 totalled less than half the mean salary reported by the town's male teachers, her modest income was almost double the average reported by servants, by far the largest group of employed women in Sydney Mines, where there were very few other opportunities for paid employment for women.

Thomas Willard, her father, was a clerk at the offices of the General Mining Association. Fifty-one years old in 1901, he reported an income of $600, which, while not a management-level salary, was well above the mean income of $455 reported by miners heading their own households that year in Sydney Mines. Still, the combined family income of father and daughter did not match that of many miners with one or two sons working underground.[2] Enjoyment of a family income for at least parts of a family's life-course was becoming common, as Nova Scotia's bustling urban economy provided a variety of new opportunities for employment.

Surplus rural workers such as Daisy Miller, also took advantage of these new opportunities. Daisy, who came from the nearby rural community of Hebron, lived in a boarding house on Gardiner Street in north-end Yarmouth and worked in the massive spinning room of the nearby Yarmouth Duck and Yarn cotton mill. Her experience typified that of yet another large group of young working women whose employment in factories and lives as boarders in households, to which they were not connected by family, marked a new departure for the provincial society. Half of the 150 workers employed in the mill in 1900 were female. Daisy's move to Yarmouth was part of a massive demographic shift occurring throughout rural Nova Scotia. All five of her fellow lodgers were young country-born women who, like 17-year-old Daisy, worked as spinners for Yarmouth Duck and Yarn. The six cotton girls shared two large rooms and, in 1901, reported suspiciously identical annual earnings of $167. While it is unlikely that, given the very high turn-over rate at the mill, all six would have worked the entire previous 12 months, a time-pay book for the previous decade shows that, for six full 10-hour days, spinners and doffers earned wages of $3.00-$3.25 per week.[3] Room and board was advertised in Yarmouth that year for between $2.00 and $2.50 per week. After paying board, Daisy and her fellow cotton workers may have had little left over. But, as elsewhere, young women were prepared to endure low wages and difficult working conditions to escape the drudgery of household labour.[4]

[2]Robert McIntosh, "'Grotesque Faces and Figures': Child Labour in the Canadian Coalfields, 1820-1930," PhD Thesis, Carleton University, 1990. Chapter 4.
[3]Cosmos Cotton Collection, Paybooks, 1887-1897, Yarmouth County Historical Society.
[4]Many such women migrated from rural to urban areas. See Alan Brookes, "Out-Migration from the Maritime Provinces, 1860-1900: Some Preliminary Considerations," *Acadiensis*, V, 2 (Spring 1976), 26-55. Patricia Thornton, working from the demographic evidence of those who remained behind, has argued that women were among the most mobile in the migration from the country-side. See "The Problem of Out-Migration from Atlantic Canada, 1871-1921: A New Look," *Acadiensis*, XV, 1 (Autumn 1985), 3-30.

Lizzie Williams, the 51-year-old widow who owned and operated Daisy's boarding house, had yet another earning experience typical of women during that period of transition. She had no children living at home, but cared for her 70-year-old mother. From the $700 she reported as her earnings from rentals that year, Lizzie provided the food and other services that went with maintaining a boarding house, including $90 paid in wages to her young servant girl.

Though much has been written about the nature, structure and significance of the industrialization of the Maritime provinces, women's participation in the new workforces created in the course of industrialization remains little understood.[5] Scholars dealing with the history of women during the period have highlighted the twin drives for suffrage and educational equality by middle class women, both of which aimed to expand women's sphere of activity in the public realm.[6] While "Working Girls" became objects of enquiries into urban life's potentially unwholesome consequences, their working and living experiences remain largely unex-

[5]Useful surveys of recent trends in women's history are Bettina Bradbury, "Women's History and Working-Class History," *Labour/Le Travail*, 19 (Spring 1987), 23-43; and Gail Campbell, "Canadian Women's History: A View from Atlantic Canada," *Acadiensis*, XX, 1 (Autumn 1990), 184-99. Most studies deal with the experience of women in larger centres and focus on systemic inequalities faced on entry into the labour force. All focus on increases in participation by women and increased diversity, a process characterized by Marjorie Griffin Cohen as "the modernization of inequality," which failed to change relative positions of men and women in a patriarchal system reinforced under capitalism. See *Women's Work, Markets and Economic Development in Nineteenth Century Ontario* (Toronto 1988), 152. Notable as well are B. Bradbury, "Women and Wage Labour in a Period of Transition: Montréal, 1861-1881," *Histoire sociale-Social History*, XVII (May 1984), 115-31; Joy Parr, *The Gender of Breadwinners: Women, Men and Change in Two Industrial Towns, 1880-1950* (Toronto 1990). Five recent studies centred in the Maritimes are Sheva Medjuck, "Women's Response to Economic and Social Change in the Nineteenth Century: Moncton Parish, 1851 to 1871," *Atlantis*, XI (Fall 1984), 5-19; Ginnette Lafleur "L'industrialization et le travail remunéré des femmes, Moncton, 1881-1891," in Peta Tancred-Sheriff, ed., *Feminist Research: Prospect and Retrospect* (Kingston 1988), 127-40; Margaret McCallum, "Separate Spheres: The Organization of Work in a Confectionary Factory, Ganong Bros., Saint Stephen, New Brunswick," *Labour/Le Travail*, 24 (Autumn 1989), 69-90; and Shirley Tillotson, "The Operators Along the Coast: A Case Study of the Link Between Gender, Skilled Labour and Social Power, 1900-1930," *Acadiensis*, XX, 1 (Autumn 1990), 72-88, and "'We Will all soon be "first-class men"': Gender and Skill in Canada's early twentieth-century urban telegraph industry," *Labour/Le Travail*, 27 (Spring 1991), 97-126.
[6]Judith Fingard, "College, Career and Community: Dalhousie Coeds, 1881-1921," in Paul Axelrod and John G. Reid, eds., *Youth, University and Canadian Society: Essays in the Social History of Higher Education* (Montréal 1989), 26-50; E.R. Forbes, "Battles in Another War: Edith Archibald and the Halifax Feminist Movement," in *Challenging the Regional Stereotype: Essays on the 20th Century Maritimes* (Fredericton 1989), 67-89; and John Reid, "The Education of Women at Mount Allison, 1854-1914," *Acadiensis*, XII, 2 (Spring 1983), 3-33.

plored in the scholarship dealing with the regional transition.[7] Knowledge of the changing patterns of female participation in paid labour remains limited as well.[8] This paper explains the changing nature of women's paid work during Nova Scotia's industrial transition. It contributes to a literature on the gendered dimensions of class formation in the context of the specific realities of given communities. A primarily quantitative probe, this article describes the major trends during the transition, locating women workers within the new workforces in three selected towns: Yarmouth, Amherst and Sydney Mines.

Nova Scotia's urban population grew from under 20 per cent of the provincial total in 1871 to just under 50 per cent by 1921.[9] Yet the province's over-all population hardly increased at all. In fact, Nova Scotia's share of Canada's population declined sharply during this period, exacerbating a political crisis that was reducing the Maritime region's political clout in Ottawa.[10] At the same time, the unprecedented growth of the Canadian economy involved Maritime towns increasingly in nation-forming exchanges, as the resource enclaves which had characterized the pre-industrial period were replaced by a set of interlocking dependencies

[7]Margaret McCallum, "Keeping Women in their Place: The Minimum Wage in Canada, 1910-25," *Labour/Le Travail*, 17 (Spring 1986), 29-58; Janet Guildford "Coping with De-industrialization: The Nova Scotia Department of Technical Education, 1907-1930," *Acadiensis*, XVI, 2 (Spring 1987), 69-84; Christina Simmons, "Helping the Poorer Sisters: The Women of the Jost Mission, Halifax, 1905-1945," *Acadiensis*, XII, 1 (Autumn 1984), 3-28. An example of women coping in an industrial setting is offered in David Frank, ed., "The Miner's Financier: Women in the Cape Breton Coal Towns, 1917," *Atlantis*, VII (Spring 1983), 137-43.

[8]Although this study will not focus on participation rates, preliminary evidence seems to confirm hypotheses presented by the more general literature. Prior to the 1920s at least, the general trend was for women to leave the labour force by their mid-20s: dropping from a maximum participation rate of about 40 per cent between the ages of 17 and 25 to less than 15 per cent for those over 25. The basic study of female participation rates in Canada remains Sylvia Ostry, *The Female Worker in Canada* (Ottawa 1968); more contemporary is Patricia Connelly, *Last Hired, First Fired: Women and the Canadian Workforce* (Toronto 1978). American women's experience is treated in Lynn Y. Weiner, *From Working Girl to Working Mother* (Chapel Hill 1985). Some analysis is found in Canada, *Sixth Census of Canada, 1921* Volume IV (Ottawa 1929), Table 5, which depicts high rates at younger age levels and a decline after the mid-20s. Participation rates rose steadily over the past century.

[9]L.D. McCann, "Staples and the New Industrialism in the Growth of Post-Confederation Halifax," *Acadiensis*, VII, 2 (Spring 1979), 47-79. Definitions of "urban" vary somewhat, but by the end of World War I, a population shift favoured Pictou, Cumberland and Cape Breton counties where the heavier industrial towns absorbed more and more of the population, at the expense of the rural parts of the province. On intra-regional population shifts see Thornton, "The Problem of Out-Migration from Atlantic Canada"; and Brookes, "Out-Migration from the Maritime Provinces."

[10]E.R. Forbes, "'Never the Twain Did Meet': Prairie-Maritime Relations, 1910-1927," *Canadian Historical Review*, LXI, 1 (March 1978), 18-37.

tying the provincial economy to the steam-based technologies that were coming to dominate North American life.[11]

Located at Nova Scotia's southern, northern and eastern extremities, Yarmouth, Amherst and Sydney Mines responded to the challenges of an integrated national economy with intensive capitalization and extensive physical growth. New railroad construction linked the three towns to each other and to the rest of the province. Public construction brought the trappings of a modern state, with the establishment of new institutional structures, ranging from post offices and fire halls to a variety of churches and educational institutions. In a spirit of "Boosterism" common to the age, the local governments acquired the technological means to service their rapidly increasing populations. Publicly and privately funded electricity and street railways, telephone exchanges, sewerage and water works proliferated, adding a new dynamic to town growth. To carry out such projects the towns sought incorporation under Nova Scotia's new municipal legislation: Amherst and Sydney Mines incorporated in 1889, Yarmouth in 1890. The established élites controlling these new local governments, sought, through the provision of local services, to attract more industry to their communities.[12]

At the beginning of the period, in 1871, Yarmouth, Amherst and Sydney Mines ranked as Nova Scotia's second, third and fourth urban centres. By 1921, their populations, which ranged in size from 2,000 to 3,000 in 1871, had climbed to between 7,000 and 10,000. Reflecting various dimensions of the province's social and ethnic construction, each offers a distinctive window into community responses to the challenges of this period of unprecedented growth. Yarmouth's population surge coincided with the massive redeployment of mercantile capital towards manufacturing in the 1880s. Amherst's growth surge occurred in the 1890s and early 1900s; in Sydney Mines, the establishment of a primary steelmaking complex in 1902-3 initiated a surge in population growth (see Figure 1). In the three towns taken together, the number of women in the workforce rose from just over 300 (10 per cent) in 1871 to almost 2000 (22 per cent) by 1921, a rate of increase half again as fast as that of the male workforce. But that growth was unevenly distributed,

[11]The seminal discussion of the economic transition is T.W. Acheson, "The National Policy and the Industrialization of the Maritimes, 1880-1910," in P. Buckner and David Frank, eds., *The Acadiensis Reader, Volume II: Atlantic Canada After Confederation* (Fredericton 1985), 176-201. An assessment of recent writing is provided in Eric Sager, "Dependency, Underdevelopment, and the Economic History of the Atlantic Region," *Acadiensis*, XVII, 1 (Autumn 1987), 117-36. See also Ian McKay, "The Crisis of Dependent Development: Class Conflict in the Nova Scotia Coal Fields, 1872-1876," in Gregory S. Kealey, ed., *Class, Gender, and Region: Essays in Canadian Historical Sociology* (St. John's 1988), 9-49.
[12]D.A. Muise, "The Great Transformation: Changing the Urban Face of Nova Scotia, 1871-1921," *Nova Scotia Historical Review*, 11, 2 (Autumn 1991), 1-42; and L. Anders Sandberg, "Dependent Development, Labour and the Trenton Steel Works, Nova Scotia, c. 1900-1943," *Labour/Le Travail*, 27 (Spring 1991), 127-62.

reflecting significant differences in patterns of development among the three towns (see Table 1).[13]

Yarmouth, metropolitan centre of the southwestern counties for the previous century, had been Nova Scotia's most dynamic "Wood, Wind and Sail" community. Because of its very active mercantile sector, it was often referred to as the province's most "American" town, a view reinforced by the fact that it was made up almost entirely of descendants of pre-Loyalist American migrants to the area.[14] Its merchants, along with those of the Pictou area,[15] were among the province's most astute in responding to opportunities presented by the 1878 National Policy. Two major community-based industries emerged there in the 1880s. Both were connected to the "Wood, Wind and Sail" era and controlled, initially at least, by local entrepreneurs. The expanded and diversified Burrill-Johnson Foundry, which had originated in the 1850s as a supplier of iron knees and fastenings for Yarmouth's large shipbuilding and outfitting industry, built stoves and other housewares, as well as watermain piping, steam engines and pumps, which were sold regionally, nationally and internationally. In the 1880s the company added a boat-building yard where small steam-powered vessels were constructed. At full production, the expanded foundry employed over 150 workers, none of them women. The second industry, Yarmouth Duck and Yarn, was formed following a meeting in 1883 of a few of Yarmouth's most prominent merchants. Importing the necessary technology and managerial skills from neighbouring New England, it quickly developed into a major sailcloth factory. The number of employees grew steadily to over 200 by 1900 and to more than 300 by 1921, almost half of them women. These two factories, along with a woollen mill and a shoe factory on the northern outskirts at Milton, gave Yarmouth the province's most concentrated industrial workforce south of Halifax. Because of the nature of its expansion, Yarmouth offered women the greatest variety of opportunities for paid work. And women responded: the proportion of women in the workforce rose from a low of six per cent in 1881 to a high of 31 per cent by 1921 (see Table 1).

Amherst, located on the edge of the pasturelands of the Tantramar Marsh, also has a rich lumbering and agricultural hinterland in Cumberland County. Although disadvantaged by its lack of immediate access to tide water, the town performed most of the usual local metropolitan functions. When the Intercolonial Railway

[13]Figure 1, Table 1 and all subsequent Figures and Tables are based on data bases created for the "Maritime Communities in Transition" project. They include all census attributes for the entire workforce as recorded in the manuscript census returns for the towns of Yarmouth, Amherst and Sydney Mines for each of the six national censuses between 1871 and 1921. Together, all the data files comprise upwards of 40,000 cases. All data for this paper has been analyzed using SPSS PC+ and Microsoft Chart.

[14]Robert Aitken, "Loyalism and National Identity in Yarmouth Nova Scotia, 1830-1870," MA thesis, Trent University, 1975, Chapter 3.

[15]L.D. McCann, "The Mercantile-Industrial Transition in the Metal Towns of Pictou County, 1857-1931," *Acadiensis*, VIII, 2 (Spring 1979), 47-79.

Table 1
Workforces in Transition, Female/Male Ratios

		1871	1881	1891	1901	1911	1921
		F/M	F/M	F/M	F/M	F/M	F/M
Yarmouth	#	136/1447	93/1200	424/1291	500/1650	709/1752	863/1907
	%	9/91	6/94	25/75	23/77	28/72	31/69
Amherst	#	112/709	144/659	355/1078	322/1516	732/2733	707/2620
	%	13/87	18/82	25/75	18/82	22/78	22/78
Sydney Mines	#	54/581	14/720	14/704	50/950	265/2417	370/2254
	%	9/91	2/98	6/94	5/95	10/90	14/86
Total	#	302/2737	251/2579	793/3073	872/4116	1706/6902	1940/6781
	%	10/90	9/91	21/79	17/83	20/80	22/78

Figure 1
Population Growth in Three NS Towns, 1871-1921

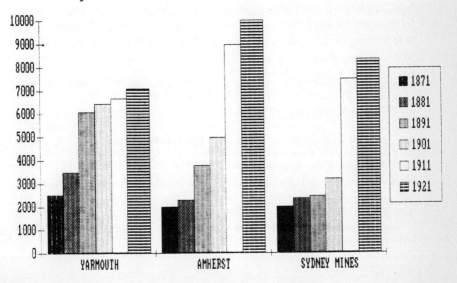

passed through in the 1870s, possibilities for industrial development emerged, especially after Saint John and Amherst based investors succeeded in having a spur line constructed to tap the rich coal resources of nearby Springhill.[16] With a supply of coal assured, Amherst entrepreneurs set out to expand their town's industrial base.[17] Rhodes-Curry began as a construction and manufacturing firm taking advantage of opportunities in public construction and railway expansion. Eventually it successfully contracted to build everything from wooden railway rolling stock and mine cars, supplied in the thousands to both regional and national markets, to housing developments and public buildings. After 1909, however, as steel cars replaced wooden-bodied ones, the massive car plant was gradually shut down. The construction end of the firm's business collapsed with the recession in the region's building boom after 1911, and the firm shut down altogether early in the 1920s. Robb Engineering, the town's second major industry, began when the son of a small local foundry operator returned from New England to expand the family's operations. By the 1890s Robb's manufactured its own line of steam engines and boilers which sold throughout Canada and internationally. Eventually, the firm would assemble railway locomotives as well.[18] Clearly, women would find no opportunities for paid employment in the town's major industries. But Amherst was also home to Hewson's, one of the province's largest woollen mills, and to the huge Amherst Boot and Shoe factory, both of which employed large numbers of women. Women had, in any case, always represented a significant proportion of Amherst's paid workforce, comprising 13 per cent as early as 1871. By 1911, when the town's workforce reached its peak for the period, the proportion of women stood at 22 per cent (see Table 1). Although Amherst's factories collapsed after World War I, for a time they made "Busy Amherst" the region's most intensely developed industrial town of its size, with an integrated capitalist class which coordinated community development.

Following the arrival of the General Mining Association [GMA] in the 1820s, Sydney Mines had come to occupy a central place in Nova Scotia's coal mining industry. In 1901 it was probably Nova Scotia's most "British" town, primarily due to its continuing domination by paternalistic Richard H. Brown, whose father had run the GMA's operations in Cape Breton for its first 40 years. The Browns'

[16]Ian McKay, "The Realm of Uncertainty: The Experience of Work in the Cumberland Coal Mines, 1873-1927," *Acadiensis*, XVI, 1 (Autumn 1986), 3-58.
[17]The major study of Amherst's emergence as an industrial community is Nolan Reilly, "The Emergence of Class Consciousness in Industrial Nova Scotia: A Study of Amherst, 1891-1925," PhD dissertation, Dalhousie University, 1982, Chapters 1 and 2; and "The General Strike in Amherst, Nova Scotia, 1919," *Acadiensis*, IX, 2 (Spring 1980), 56-77. See also McKay, "The Realm of Uncertainty."
[18]A survey of the *Amherst Daily News* (1900-1911) revealed the link between the town's rise and the expansion of other Maritime industrial communities. Almost daily its reports included announcements of contracts or orders awarded Rhodes-Curry or Robb Engineering for public construction, railroad rolling stock, or the supply of equipment to industries and communities throughout the region.

preference for Scots and English miners helped maintain the dominance of British mining systems, along with the social organization of the community that it implied. The takeover of the GMA, in 1901, by the Pictou- and Halifax-based Nova Scotia Steel and Coal Company, was followed by massive new investment in a primary steel plant.[19] The new owners turned to the United States for their technology, as well as for coal mining machinery and many of the key steel-makers. The bulk of the workers remained local, however, and continued to live in company owned housing and to buy their goods at the company store. With its occupational base narrowly confined to mining and related trades prior to 1902 and commercial opportunities limited by company control over trade, the town lacked the leadership and capital that drove Yarmouth and Amherst to diversify their economic bases. Its expansion was troubled by the uncertain corporate history of the Nova Scotia Steel Company and ended abruptly with its absorption by Dominion Steel in 1921. Within weeks, the Sydney Mines plant was dismantled and Sydney Mines reverted to its role as a coal town.[20] None of its industries ever employed women, save for a few clerks in the post-1900 period. As a result, women's participation in the paid workforce remained limited: just two per cent of the workforce in 1881, they had risen to 14 per cent by 1921 (see Table 1).

Generally speaking, Nova Scotia's industrial moment was brief. Yarmouth, Amherst and Sydney Mines all ceased to grow by 1911 and would contract thereafter. Yet the transformation wrought by the industrial process remained, both in the physical structures put in place to enable towns to deal with their dramatically increased populations and, even more significantly, in the experience and memories of the people who flocked to and through the towns. As Yarmouth, Amherst and Sydney Mines responded to their varied industrial opportunities, the size, the sex and the structure of their workforces were transformed. Their new industries depended on thousands of new workers, including hundreds of women, whose arrival dramatically affected the household and social structures of the three communities.

While all three attracted new workers from outside the region and country, they depended on their immediate hinterlands for most of their new recruits.[21] In

[19]McCann, "The Mercantile Industrial Transition"; and Kris Inwood, "Local Control, Resources and the Nova Scotia Steel and Coal Company," Canadian Historical Association, *Historical Papers* (1986), 254-82.

[20]D.A. Muise, "The General Mining Association and Nova Scotia's Coal, 1827-1857," *Bulletin of Canadian Studies*, X (1983), 23-40; "The Making of an Industrial Community: Cape Breton Coal Towns, 1867-1900," in Brian Tennyson and Don Macgillivray, eds., *Cape Breton Historical Essays* (Sydney 1980), 76-95; McCann, "The Mercantile-Industrial Transition"; Craig Heron, *Working in Steel* (Toronto 1988), Chapters I-II and "The Great War and Nova Scotia Steelworkers," *Acadiensis*, XVI, 2 (Spring 1987) 3-34; and W.J.A. Donald, *The Canadian Iron and Steel Industry: A Study in the Economic History of a Protected Industry* (Boston 1915).

[21]In 1901 census takers asked respondents if they had been born in an urban or rural location. While Yarmouth workers and householders were almost even in terms of rural/urban birth,

Amherst a rise in the numbers of New Brunswick born, at least half of whom were Acadian, changed forever the ethnic composition of the town. Yarmouth remained the most uniformly Nova Scotian in terms of its residents' birthplaces, but, like Amherst, it acquired a large Acadian minority, most from surrounding rural communities. Sydney Mines remained relatively homogeneous as well, though a small cadre of British born miners and a larger throng of young Newfoundland labourers, clustered at opposite ends of the occupational ladder, helped define the more central place occupied by the Cape Breton majority.[22] All in all, foreigners remained a very small portion of the workforce in all three towns, though some Italians and Poles were recruited to Sydney Mines. Few immigrant women entered the paid workforce during the pre-1920s period, probably because few women accompanied men on the initial voyage to Canada. Large numbers of country-born women did, however, find their way to the jobs becoming available in the towns.

The experiences of Marie, Georgina, Daisy and Lizzie represent aspects of the impact of the industrial transition on women's opportunities for paid work. Although Nova Scotian women had long participated in the household economies of fishing and farming, their contributions were subsumed within the male dominated family unit and characterized as supplementary or incidental to the production of staples.[23] Most women working for remuneration had been concentrated in jobs associated with home-making and child rearing, chiefly as servants in middle and upper class households, or as producers of goods or services for other women, as milliners or dressmakers. As teachers of very young children in the emerging educational institutions of the pre-Confederation period, numerically they were coming, by the 1870s, to dominate a profession notorious for discriminating against them.[24] Even so, women had been largely absent from waged work before the arrival of cotton and woollen mills and shoe factories. And though they had previously figured hardly at all in clerical occupations, women would also come to dominate this sector after 1900, as towns acquired more complex social and

---

the other two towns were quite different. Immediately prior to the major expansion of the steel industry, 71 per cent of the workers in Sydney Mines were urban born; in contrast, just 32 per cent of Amherst's workers reported urban origin.

[22] On the migration of Newfoundlanders to industrial Nova Scotia see Peter Neary, "Canadian Immigration Policy and Newfoundlanders, 1912-1939," *Acadiensis*, XI, 2 (Spring 1982), 69-83; Ron Crawley, "Off to Sydney: Newfoundlanders Emigrate to Industrial Cape Breton, 1890-1914," *Acadiensis*, XVII, 2 (Spring 1988), 27-51; Mary-Jane Lipkin, "Reluctant Recruitment: Nova Scotia Immigration Policy, 1867-1917," MA thesis, Carleton, 1982.

[23] See Cohen, *Women's Work* for a discussion of the main contours of the role of rural women in staples producing economies. For the Atlantic region, a broad range of scholarship deals with women as part of a family economic strategy in resource zones like the fishery. See, for example, Marilyn Porter, "She Was Skipper of the Shore Crew: Notes on the History of the Sexual Division of Labour in Newfoundland," *Labour/Le Travail*, 15 (Spring 1985), 105-23.

[24] Janet Guildford, "'Separate Spheres' and the Feminization of Public School Teaching in Nova Scotia, 1838-1880," unpublished paper presented to the Atlantic Canada Studies Conference, Orono, Me., May, 1990.

economic structures. By 1900, as never before, women's labour was becoming a factor in the province's economic development. And the number of women in the workforce continued to grow until, by 1921, in Yarmouth, Amherst and Sydney Mines at least, women comprised over 20 per cent of paid workers (see Figure 2).

Figure 2
Workforce Growth (By Gender) Yarmouth, Amherst and Sydney Mines*

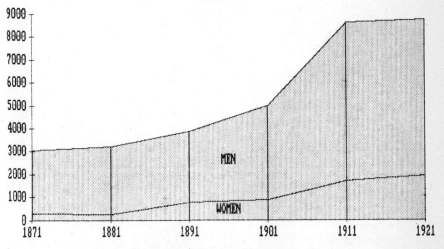

*This graph combines the workforces of all three towns.

The first striking increase in the numbers and occupational range of women in the paid workforce under review occurred between 1881 and 1891, with the establishment of Yarmouth's cotton mill; then, between 1900 and 1911, the number of women in the workforce almost doubled again, increasing from 872 to 1706 as job opportunities further increased and diversified (see Table 1). But this over-all trend must be understood in the context of the zones of women's employment, for there were sharp contrasts. In the coal and steel centred economy of Sydney Mines, women's participation remained confined to the service sector, while in Yarmouth upwards of 20 per cent of the female labour force worked in factories by the turn of the century, and close to a third by the end of World War I. The sharp decline in the number of women factory workers in Amherst following closure of the woollen mill and shoe factory there offers mute testimony to the narrow range of industrial occupations open to women. There, as elsewhere, many women who worked in factories during the war lost their jobs soon afterward. After 1901, stenographic, clerical and secretarial occupations, along with such new trades as telephone and telegraph operators, brought larger numbers of women into new areas of the workforce.[25]

[25]Graham S. Lowe, "Women, Work and the Office: The Feminization of Clerical Occupations in Canada," *Canadian Journal of Sociology*, 5 (1980), 361-81; "Class, Job and Gender

Even as the occupational profile of women workers became more complex, the most prominent feature of their participation in paid work continued to be their concentrations in the personal service sector (see Figure 3).[26] Only in Amherst, and

Figure 3
Female Workers (By Sector), 1901-21
(Yarmouth, Amherst and Sydney Mines)

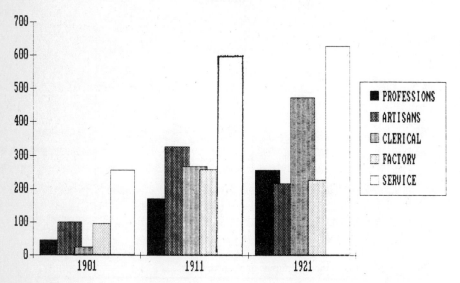

then not until 1921, were household servants ever eclipsed in numbers, in that case by the increasingly diversified group of clerical workers. Yet, the places where women did housework for pay changed over the 50-year period. In 1871, servants

---

in the Canadian Office," *Labour/Le Travail*, 10 (Autumn 1982), 11-37; and "Mechanization, Feminization and Managerial Control in the Early Twentieth-Century Canadian Office," in Craig Heron and Robert Story, eds., *On the Job: Confronting the Labour Process in Canada* (Kingston/Montréal 1986), 177-209.

[26]To assist analysis women's occupations have been divided into five categories: PROFES-SIONS (teachers, nurses, etc.); CLERICAL (clerks, stenographers, secretaries and tele-phone/telegraphic operators); ARTISANS (milliners, dress-makers, seamstresses, etc); FACTORY (spinners, weavers, factory hands etc.); and SERVICE (servants, washerwomen, maids etc). The scale implied by this structuring of workers includes independent producers who may have been a part of the service area and the denigration of women who controlled their own economic destiny, such as the small number of female boarding-house keepers, who were in fact petty-proprietors who often employed servants. It also excludes those involved in various types of household production that may not have been included in the census categories. On the problems inherent in any attempt to build occupational scales see Michael B. Katz, Michael J. Doucet, and Mark J. Stern, *The Social Organization of Early Industrial Capitalism* (Cambridge 1982).

were employed mostly in middle class households; after industrialization, servants and those in related occupations, such as washerwomen, became more involved in reproducing the labour power of their fellow workers in a wide variety of boarding houses and hotels. At various times, over half of all male and female workers boarded or lived as dependent relatives in houses headed by others. Such a volatile young workforce, as well as contributing to the malleability of households, demanded expansion of boarding-house keeping, an occupation dominated by widows.

Yarmouth and Amherst's middle classes had supported large numbers of seamstresses, dressmakers and milliners through the turn of the century; Sydney Mines had always lagged behind in providing opportunities for waged work in traditional women's artisanal areas, a consequence of the absence of many middle-class spenders, as well as its proximity to the more developed service and commercial sector in nearby North Sydney, where most of the needs of the tiny group of middle-class women could be met. But integration with an emerging consumer-oriented economy and rapid urban development brought dramatic increases in the availability of ready-made clothing, a corollary of which was a decline in artisanal production. As more of the local market was absorbed by the expansion of regionally and nationally organized retail outlets, more women came to work as clerks selling clothing and other consumer goods than were ever employed producing those sorts of items in artisanal shops.[27]

Studies of the demographic attributes of female workers during the early stages of industrialization focus on their comparative youth and fractional earnings relative to their male counterparts. Relative earnings of male and female workers reflect the basic disparities faced by women, although any comparison of individual earnings or occupational mobility is problematic unless individuals can be linked over time through successive censuses or in some other fashion.[28] Some limited observations are made possible by considering the relationship between age and earnings at 10-year intervals and subjecting the findings to a gendered analysis. Figure 4 provides age profiles for male and female workers in 1921. The downward trend of women in the workforce beyond the age of 21 contrasts significantly with the comparative stability and upward trend among male workers after the age of 30.

[27]Mercedes Steedman, "Skill and Gender in the Canadian Clothing Industry, 1890-1940," in Heron and Story, eds., *On the Job*, 152-76. An enduring theme in both Amherst and Yarmouth newspapers following the turn of the century was the complaint that workers and others were buying goods produced outside their community, particularly from central Canadian chains or mail order houses being established during the period. Maritimers, it was argued, should spend their money where they had earned it so that it could recirculate to prompt more employment. On the extension of Canadian businesses, including some discussion of retail chains to the region see L.D. McCann, "Metropolitanism and Branch Businesses in the Maritimes, 1881-1931," *Acadiensis*, XIII, 1 (Autumn 1983), 112-25.

[28]Linkages have not yet been attempted with this data, though such a strategy is likely to be more useful when focusing on male workers, who tended to stay in the workforce for more extended periods. Women were seldom in the workforce for a 10-year period, so are difficult to trace in successive censuses.

The relatively short time women spent in the workforce reinforced wage differentials, further inhibiting the achievement of wage parity.[29]

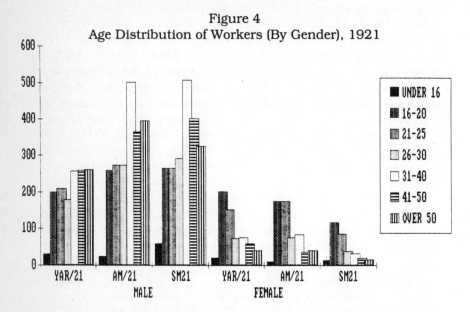

Figure 4
Age Distribution of Workers (By Gender), 1921

A comparison limited to single workers provides further insight into the changing nature and structure of the workforce. In post-1900 Yarmouth, for instance, single female workers outnumbered single male workers. On average, these women were one to two years older than their male counterparts. Obviously, the presence of a cotton mill with its specific requirements for both male and female youth could have a decisive impact on the demographic composition of the workforce. In Amherst and Sydney Mines, where the proportion of single women *vis à vis* single men was never as large, this relationship was reversed, although the mean ages of single male and female workers remained quite close.[30] Marriage, of course, changed matters

[29]Fluctuations in the age structure of the workforce occurred for a variety of reasons. For example, in 1901 a large in-migration of younger men, many of them day-labourers employed in construction trades, drove the average age of male workers to all-time lows, though their mean age rose gradually to a high of 38.5 by 1921. The mean age of working women tended to be under rather than over 25, but also rose to a new high of 29 by 1921.

[30]In both cases the number of single men employed declined by a third, while the number of single working women remained stable or actually increased. With so many young miners in its workforce, Sydney Mines had a much different profile than the other communities. In 1911 and 1921, single males averaged just over 25 years while females averaged 24.5. In Amherst, men and women both averaged 24.5 years in 1911; the average age of single women had risen to 26 ten years later while that of their male counterparts remained unchanged. Though these increases may not seem dramatic, they reflected the fact that women were remaining spinsters for longer periods and were also remaining in the workforce.

significantly, for males were expected to retain their jobs after marriage while women were socially and culturally barred from doing so.

Cultural norms limiting women's participation in paid work to the years between childhood and marriage prevented them from progressing to more responsible, and therefore more lucrative, positions within those sectors they occupied. In the main, earnings were a function of age, which is a rough surrogate for years in the workforce no matter what the area of the economy or the gender of workers (see Figure 5). But most industrial jobs, virtually all skilled trades not specific to women, such as seamstress or milliner, and all management positions, were controlled by males throughout the period. Male earnings rose sharply after 20, peaked between 31 and 40 and, in most instances, declined somewhat after 50. Women's earnings, as well as being far below those of men at all ages, rose more gradually, peaking by about age 30 and generally declining thereafter. Though primary earning years differed somewhat across communities and for different occupations, the earning curves were remarkably similar in all three towns.[31]

Figure 5
Mean Earnings (By Age and Gender), 1921

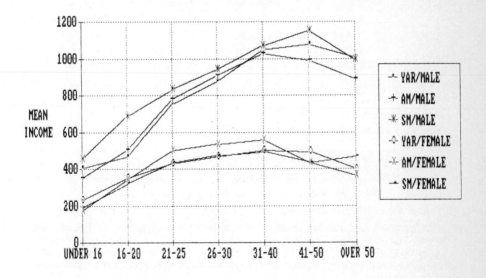

[31]Similar curves drawn for 1901 and 1911 reveal identical relationships, with the slightly higher earnings of Amherst women and Sydney Mines men equally apparent. The reason for the former lies with the more diverse nature of its female workers, particularly in the artisanal and later in the clerical areas. Higher earnings for workers in Sydney Mines reflect the concentration of mining and industrial jobs and the general absence of common labourers, whose earnings tended to lower the averages for younger men.

But while the general patterns proved similar, women's actual earnings fluctuated widely from town to town and across occupations. Table 2 captures some of
that variation through a comparison of Amherst and Yarmouth in 1911 and 1921.[32]
The experience of Sydney Mines was similar, although the numbers and varieties
of occupations were much smaller. While professional and new white-collar workers generally out-earned their working-class sisters, there was significant variation
from town to town. In Amherst, rapid expansion in the clerical sector contributed
to the comparatively higher average earnings there by 1921, though the strong male
labour movement in the town may also have influenced the women's wages.
Yarmouth's cotton workers were hierarchically structured, with weavers among the
highest paid blue-collar workers. The relatively poor performance of artisanal
workers, such as tailors, may have reflected a more intermittent involvement in the
workforce. But who were the tailors and weavers as opposed to the clerks or
teachers?

Table 2
Mean Annual Wages for Women in Selected Occupations, 1911-1921

	1911		1921	
	Yarmouth	Amherst	Yarmouth	Amherst
Teachers	$412 (31)	$320 (31)	$697 (32)	$656 (48)
Nurses	$344 (7)	$345 (10)	$576 (18)	$745 (12)
Stenos.	$304 (32)	$374 (34)	$503 (38)	$604 (85)
Clerks	$166 (14)	$286 (43)	$430 (23)	$642 (42)
Teleph. Op.	$192 (5)	$377 (7)	$510 (9)	$450 (14)
Tailors	$272 (19)	$250 (23)	$394 (9)	$446 (30)
Weavers	$357 (19)	$354 (11)	$565 (57)	$447 (14)
Servants	$168 (100)	$235 (136)	$224 (154)	$238 (152)

Religion and ethnicity have held a certain primacy in analyses of factors in the
formation of Nova Scotia's communities, though their intersection with class
formation in the industrial period is less developed in the literature.[33] Yet the
convergence of religion, ethnicity and class in shaping both individual and community experience can readily be illustrated through a comparison of British and

[32]The figures in Table 2 include only those who reported earnings of at least $100, thereby
eliminating casual workers. Occupations that were not represented across both censuses were
also excluded, as were occupational categories which included fewer than five individuals.

[33]The Scots experience in eastern Nova Scotia is assessed in R.A. MacLean and D. Campbell,
Beyond the Atlantic Roar: A Study of the Nova Scotia Scots (Toronto 1974). An example
dealing with urban formations is Elizabeth Beaton, "Religious Affiliations and Ethnic
Identity of West Indians in Whitney Pier," *Canadian Ethnic Studies*, XX, 3 (1988), 25-45;
for a more contemporary analysis asserting a basic equality in French/British attainments see
E. Hugh Lautard and Donald J. Loree, "Occupational Differentiation Between British and
French in the Atlantic Provinces, 1951-1971," in *Labour in Atlantic Canada* (Saint John
1981), 32-41.

Acadian workers in Amherst and Yarmouth. Recent arrivals on the urban scene, Acadian workers were the least prepared, either socially or educationally, to compete for those professional or clerical sector jobs where English literacy or higher levels of educational achievement were a precondition of employment. In 1891, for instance, 38 per cent of Yarmouth's Acadian female workers reported that they were unable to read, while only five per cent of non-Acadians were so disadvantaged. Reduced language and literacy skills helped restrict women's employment options in cases where contact with the public or literacy was required. Acadian women, as demonstrated in the 1911 census, were all but excluded from clerical and professional positions in Yarmouth and Amherst. In both towns, over two-thirds of Acadian women were employed either as servants or as hands in the shoe or textile factories (see Figure 6).[34]

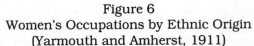

Figure 6
Women's Occupations by Ethnic Origin
(Yarmouth and Amherst, 1911)

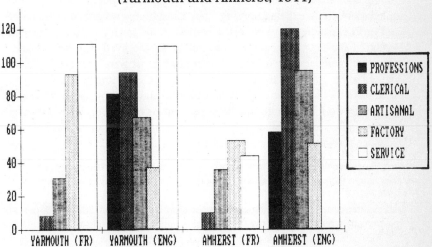

Most of these Acadian women were migrants from the countryside, and their experience typified that of other rural migrants. Recruitment of surplus labour from rural communities was a strategy for filling less attractive jobs for women as well as men. In Amherst and Yarmouth, upwards of 80 per cent of all servants were country-born; and in Yarmouth 90 per cent of female cotton mill workers described themselves as rural-born. Clerical workers and teachers, on the other hand, were much more likely to be urban-born and included no appreciable number of Acadians or Catholics in their ranks. Educational opportunities in town were undoubtedly greater than those in the countryside, though probably as important were the

[34]The only group lower on the occupational ladder was the smaller contingent of black women, who were invariably servants.

contacts established while growing up within the social and cultural milieus that conditioned the transformation of communities.[35]

Cross-gender case studies of Yarmouth's cotton workers and of teachers in all three towns further illustrate the relative importance of gender, age, ethnicity and birthplace in understanding women's experience of waged work. From the moment it entered production in 1884, Yarmouth's cotton mill needed a workforce to tend and feed its giant machines; and, in an industry in which success was dependent on exploiting the willingness of younger workers to endure harsh conditions and low wages, the workforce required constant replenishment.[36] While the more technical jobs were filled by experienced New England workers, most production jobs at the new mill could be performed by relatively inexperienced young men and women.[37] By 1901, 20 per cent of Yarmouth's working women were employed at the mill. Unlike Milltown and Marysville in New Brunswick, or the much larger mills of Québec or New England, neither corporate owned housing nor company sponsored boarding houses were provided in Yarmouth. Most recruits were drawn either from surrounding communities or from within the town itself, and appear to have found accommodation within existing housing stock close by the waterfront location of the plant or in expanding working class districts in the town's burgeoning south end. A small hand-drawn sample of those mill girls who lived at home indicates that they were members of working-class families; most were daughters of men who worked either in the cotton mill or at the nearby iron foundry.[38] Obviously, the need for a family wage was an element in the decision taken by numerous young women to go to work in the mill. But the large numbers of boarders among women mill workers indicates that country girls were also attracted on an individual basis by the chance for waged employment and limited 'independence.'

[35]Sydney Mines' small number of female workers were mainly from urban backgrounds (77 per cent), though there, as elsewhere, women workers were almost universally daughters of the working class.

[36]A brief qualitative analysis of cotton company time/pay books for the 1880s-1890s period reveals a dramatic turn-over in employees in the basic spinning and weaving jobs, particularly among female employees and among young Acadian workers of both sexes. Cosmos Cotton Collection, Paybooks, vol. I, Yarmouth County Historical Society.

[37]For a comparative perspective on the employment of young women in cotton mills, see Peter DeLottinville, "Trouble in the Hives of Industry: The Cotton Industry Comes to Milltown, N.B., 1879-1892," CHA *Historical Papers* (1980), 100-15; Gail Cuthbert-Brandt, "Weaving it Together: Life Cycle and the Industrial Experience of Female Cotton Workers in Québec, 1910-1950," *Labour/Le Travail*, 7 (Spring 1981), 113-26. The more family-centred practices of some American mill towns do not seem to have been the norm in Yarmouth. See Tamara Hareven, *Family Time and Industrial Time: The Relationship Between Family and Work in a New England Industrial Community* (Cambridge, Mass. 1982).

[38]One of the strategies of capitalists during this period was to blend the industrial formations within communities to provide employment for a variety of different types of workers in order to encourage development of a family wage among the numbers of operatives within the town and thereby ensure a wider series of opportunities for workers of either sex and at various stages of their working lives.

Cotton mill workers can be readily identified in the 1911 and 1921 censuses, since individuals were required to report their places of employment. In 1911, 108 men (47 per cent) and 124 women (53 per cent), from the manager down to the lowest ranking operative, identified the cotton mill as their place of employment. The vast majority of women employees were under 25, with over half concentrated in the 16-20 age cohort. Male workers, more evenly spread across the age spectrum, were also older on average (28), more likely to be of British origin (65 per cent) and more highly paid ($449 per annum). Women were younger (20 on average), more likely to be Acadian (70 per cent) and less well paid ($267 per annum). Though comprising just 23 per cent of Yarmouth's population, Acadians made up 54 per cent of all cotton mill employees in 1911. Acadian women earned marginally less than English women ($256 vs. $275), but they were also younger on average (19 vs. 25). Like their sisters, Acadian males, the third largest group after Acadian females and English males, tended to be younger than male anglophone workers (23 on average vs. 30) and were more likely to be single. They reported mean earnings of $343 as compared to an average of $509 for their anglophone counter-parts. Most single Acadian males at the mill worked alongside their sisters in production areas. The more skilled and higher paying loom-fixing or supervisory roles were invariably occupied by married English males. Multivariate analysis of declared earnings suggests the link between gender, age and ethnicity in determining wage rates. Those reporting yearly earnings above $300 were concentrated in the over-20 group confined mostly to males (see Figure 7). There was little gendered distinction in earnings between workers under the age of 20 doing the same jobs.

The mill's workforce grew by 40 per cent between 1911 and 1921 (from 232 to 372 workers). The male-female ratio reversed: 221 (60 per cent) males to 151 (40 per cent) females; the proportion of single workers fell to 56 per cent of all workers as compared to 72 per cent in 1911. The number of Acadian women remained virtually the same as in 1911 (88); English women increased from 29 to 51. The mean age of single women workers was a full two years higher than that of single males (22 vs. 20). Overall, males averaged 32 years in 1921, females 23, a significant increase in both cases. Although women's mean earnings had risen to $539 by 1921, mean earnings for men had risen to $859. Married males averaged $1995, single men $573, and single women $532; single Acadian men averaged $569 and single Acadian women $525. As in 1911, Acadian males proved much more likely to be single and, like Acadian women, continued to be ghettoized in weaving, spinning, spooling and carding jobs on the shop floor. British males, who tended, on average, to be older, continued to hold down the most lucrative and responsible jobs. Age, gender and ethnicity continued to play a significant role in determining earnings and job hierarchy. The gap in earnings between women and men, Acadians and British, and married and single workers had not narrowed appreciably, even though men were now performing many jobs previously done by women. Discrepancies are most clearly illustrated in the earning curves for men and women workers. By 1921 women had caught up with the earning levels of men in

1911. But by 1921, men above the age of 25 were earning far more than any woman (see Figure 7).

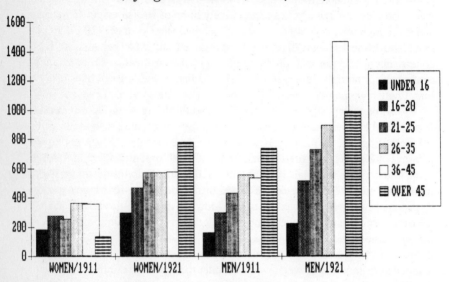

Figure 7
Mean Earnings of Yarmouth Cotton Workers
(By Age and Gender, 1911/1921)

Throughout the period, Yarmouth Duck and Yarn recruited a high proportion of its workers from among rural youth displaced by the over-population of subsistence farms. In earlier periods such surplus workers might have left the province in search of employment. But now, given an opportunity to remain in Nova Scotia, some, at least, chose to accept work closer to home, despite harsh conditions and low wages. For young single women, the promise of a pay packet almost as large as that earned by their unmarried brothers (93 per cent of male counterparts' in the 16-25 age cohorts in 1921) may have made mill employment especially attractive. These young recruits contributed to the formation of a broad new urban proletariat, regularly replenished from the countryside in a situation that saw a constant turnover among operational staff, while management and those highly skilled workers who maintained or repaired the machines remained relatively stable.

The case of the Yarmouth cotton mill provides a concrete illustration of the significant intersection of gender, class and culture; the relatively low status of women and Acadians was critical to the restructuring of the town's workforce. The cotton industry initiated into waged labour young women and men who might not otherwise have had the opportunity for waged work locally. But significant disparities between women's and men's earnings persisted and were reflected in job ghettoization based on gender, ethnicity and age. If female workers sometimes

reported earnings as high as those achieved by male workers performing the same
or similar tasks, the men in question were often young Acadians, who, like their
female counterparts, found fewer opportunities for advancement within the industry. Like Acadian males, women were denied the prospects for upward mobility
accorded to non-Acadian males. Resistance to the inequities imposed by the
industry did occur and, during the war, when the demand for labour was high and
rich war contracts resulted in increased production, workers' committees succeeded
in negotiating a number of wage increases.

Not all women workers were as immediately affected by the process of
urbanization and industrialization as the new class of factory girls. But the changes
brought by urbanization revolutionized community life and no worker could
completely escape their impact. To some extent, each town's approach to the
provision of public education was a function of its socio-cultural profile. Yarmouth
and Amherst had very active local middle classes committed to the commercial and
industrial advancement of their communities. They took pride in providing their
children with extensive educational opportunities at public expense and borrowed
heavily to construct new school buildings, which were discussed in glowing terms
in the local press. Sydney Mines' less notable educational accomplishments reflected the coal industry's failure to value universal literacy for its workforce. But
the coal town, which sent its sons into the workforce at earlier ages than was
common elsewhere, had almost no resident middle class to push for the implementation of educational reforms.[39] And because the coal company owned the majority
of homes, the proportion of privately owned property was too small to provide a
tax base to support the school system. Hence, town incorporation in 1889 brought
little change.

Whatever different attitudes toward provision of educational facilities may
have prevailed within each community, gender balances among teachers proved
remarkably similar as feminization rose from just under 70 per cent in 1871, to over
90 per cent by 1921.[40] School boards composed of middle-aged, largely middle-
class men hired young women as teachers because they were readily available. In
the process, women experienced a type of ghettoization similar to that of their sisters

[39]Robert McIntosh, "The Boys in the Nova Scotia Coal Mines, 1873-1923," *Acadiensis*,
XVI, 2 (Spring 1987), 35-50; Kate and John Currie, "A History of Education in Sydney
Mines, 1828-1900," unpublished paper, Beaton Institute, University College of Cape Breton,
1980.
[40]Central Canada as well as New Brunswick underwent a similar shift during this period.
Alison Prentice, "The Feminization of Teaching in British North America and Canada,
1845-1875," *Social History/Histoire Sociale*, 8 (1975), 5-20; Marta Danylewycz, Beth Light
and Alison Prentice, "The Evolution of the Sexual Division of Labour in Teaching: A
Nineteenth Century Ontario and Québec Case Study," *Social History/Histoire Sociale*, 16
(1983), 81-109; and Marta Danylewycz and Alison Prentice, "Teacher's Work: Changing
Patterns and Perceptions in the Emerging School Systems of Nineteenth and Early Twentieth
Century Central Canada," *Labour/Le Travail*, 17 (Spring 1986), 59-82. For the Nova Scotia
experience see Janet Guildford, "'Separate Spheres.'"

in the cotton mill, even though their ethnic and religious traits differed sharply. A tendency to British Protestant dominance and underrepresentation of Catholics reflected a bias against full access to education for minority groups and the lack of higher academies in rural areas where most Catholics had lived prior to industrial transformation. Daughters of the middle and lower middle classes for the most part, these young women worked for much lower wages than their male colleagues, or even than their female counterparts in factories or offices. They did so because they could afford to and because they shared a missionary attitude towards their profession that permitted them to accept low wages, even while remaining in the workforce for longer and longer periods.

Women teachers were older, on average, than other groups of female workers but they were still significantly younger than their male colleagues. In 1901 the mean age for women teachers was less than 23, while the mean age for men and women taken together was 25. In 1911, only three of the 19 male teachers, as compared to 51 of the 77 female teachers, were under 25. In 1921, all 10 male teachers were over 25, but the largest number of women (47) were over 30 and less than half were under 25. By that time, the overall mean age had risen to 33 (44 for males and 31 for females). As in the cotton mill, age variance reflected a bias against employing married women. But the rise in the mean age of women teachers between 1901 and 1921 indicates that women were remaining spinsters and in the workforce for longer periods.

Jarring discrepancies typified earnings of male and female teachers. In 1921, for example, male teachers averaged over $1200 per annum, compared to women's mean earnings of $667. Moreover, the earning curve for female teachers remained flat, while that for males rose sharply with age (see Figure 8). Gendered bias in teachers' salaries reflected the notion that married male teachers with families to support required higher salaries than did single women living at home. To some extent, this perception was accurate. Virtually all male teachers headed their own households, while over 90 per cent of female teachers were single, living at home or as boarders in households headed by others. Even so, the few widowed women who headed their own households were unable, either by virtue of their status as family heads or their longer experience, to earn what might have been considered a 'family wage' of the sort that male teachers were able to command. Gender-based licensing systems reinforced these inequalities.

Although the number of teachers rose dramatically as local school boards expanded their services, the increase, from just 50 in 1871 to 133 by 1921, did not match the rate of population growth in the towns. Student/teacher ratios increased over the period as the schools adopted a strict grade system and increased the numbers in each classroom. With the division of students into age specific grades, female teachers became ghettoized in the lower grade levels. In classrooms, the introduction of industrial-like modes of organization led to a division of labour similar to that of the factory. As in factories, males dominated all supervisory positions, which were thought to require higher qualifications and the male qualities

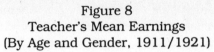

Figure 8
Teacher's Mean Earnings
(By Age and Gender, 1911/1921)

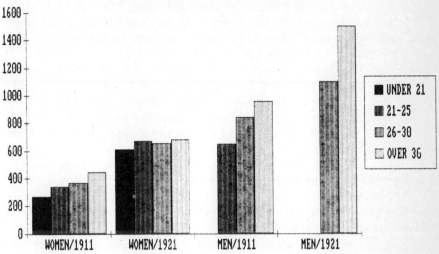

of leadership and discipline. Prior to World War I, the jobs available in the new high schools, except for a few home economics teachers, were invariably staffed by men. There, men commanded higher salaries while instructing fewer students, a system that would not change very much over the following half century.

Until further investigation into women's direct experience of paid work in Nova Scotia has been completed, any conclusions concerning the impact of industrialization or women's part in the transformation of communities must remain tentative. However, this analysis of their involvement in paid work provides the basis for a number of observations. Women workers tended to be younger, almost invariably unmarried, and to stay in the workforce for shorter periods than their male counterparts. While this general pattern persisted throughout the period, significant changes did occur between 1911 and 1921, probably as a consequence of the war. Though the most common field of employment for women continued to be the service sector, the places where servants worked came to vary considerably over time. And, like their male counterparts, women faced discrimination based on their ethnic and religious backgrounds. Thus, servants were often Catholics and factory workers often Acadian. And both groups were drawn largely from the countryside. In contrast, jobs requiring literacy or communication skills, such as teaching and clerking, went mainly to British-stock Protestant women emerging from the lower middle classes within the towns.

While men and women may have experienced migration somewhat differently, new women workers, either by themselves or in the company of kin, participated actively in labour force expansion. Paralleling the diversification of work opportunities was a change in the ethnic composition of urban Nova Scotia, the result of large scale migrations of Acadians, rural Scots and Newfoundlanders from the countryside into towns. In Yarmouth, Amherst and Sydney Mines, Roman Catholics who came to dominate the lower rungs of the occupational ladder transformed predominantly Protestant towns. At this stage we can only speculate on the cultural impact of this major shift on institutions and social structure.

Everywhere, the most striking characteristic of women workers was their youth relative both to male workmates and to the remainder of the adult female community. Women's participation in the workforce was effectively limited to the years between childhood and marriage. Culturally determined responsibility for child rearing and household maintenance precluded continuing participation in the labour force by married women. Those widows not dependent on earnings of kin were generally confined to menial occupations, although those who owned property could convert their homes into boarding houses. Those with skills, such as teachers, could occasionally re-enter the workforce, but not usually at a level appropriate to their age or experience. It is quite likely that many married women participated in hidden economies of production not recorded by the census taker and it is evident that artisanal production specifically directed towards serving the needs of other women continued for some time and was probably dominated by women in the older age ranges.

Wherever they worked and whatever their backgrounds, women earned less than their male counterparts, though in some cases that may have been as much a function of the relatively short time they spent in the workforce as of their gender. The more diverse a town's economic base, the wider the choices for prospective women workers. After 1891, Yarmouth and Amherst provided many new opportunities in industrial and commercial sectors, including clerical jobs in stores and businesses, which Sydney Mines only began to match by 1921. Disappearance of the female equivalent of the honest artisan, who might have controlled some of her own means of production and regulated work processes in her own home, was as pronounced for women as it was for men during the same period. Indeed, in many ways, Nova Scotia women's experience of work degradation mirrored that of their male counterparts.

Although conclusions remain speculative, understanding how women experienced capitalism can also shed light on community economic development through these years when manufacturing and urban development reoriented the regional economy. Women in the forefront of that transition were subject to all the frustrations of working in factories controlled by machines and processes foreign to any of their prior experiences. Yarmouth and Amherst, which attracted the largest and most diverse group of women workers, were exposed to the vicissitudes of the new competitive system into which the region had been thrust following Confederation. When deindustrialization replaced the expansiveness of the 1880-1910 period, women, as well as men, faced enormous dislocations as consolidation of production resulted in over-production. The only way to make machines pay for themselves was to eliminate interruptions. The cut-throat competition, in which Maritime producers were disadvantaged by distance and concentrations of capital, made the region particularly vulnerable to the inroads of central Canadian companies determined to eliminate them. Such competition not only suppressed earnings but also threatened the very existence of the region's industrial base and the urban structures dependent upon it.

In the end, women became as marginalized as men by the new dependence on capitalist consumer-oriented economies; deindustrialization threatened their new jobs as much as it did those of male workers. Those unskilled and semi-skilled women who remained in the workforce, finding their job options reduced or eliminated, were trapped in dependent relationships, often as servants of those middle-class groups who were managing this latest process of transformation. Teachers and nurses remained ghettoized at the bottom of systems unable or unwilling to meet their expectations, and continued to receive very low pay despite their demonstrably higher educational attainments. Ironically, a dramatic rise in opportunities for women in clerical work, where they were often employed by some of the same central Canadian businesses that were engineering the consumer-oriented revolution overtaking the region, reflected a broader social submission to a central Canada dominated economy. Nova Scotia's passage from colonial dependence on staple exports, through capitalist transformation, industrialization and urbanization to dependence and deindustrialization was as much a female as a male experience. Women's place in the process can begin to be understood now that we are coming to know more about who they were, where they worked and some dimensions of their labour and their lives.

This study has been assisted by grants from the Social Sciences and Humanities Research Council for the project: "Communities in Transition: Maritime Towns and the National Policy, 1870-1921." Students in my research seminars at Carleton between 1986 and 1989 helped its early conceptual development as did my colleague Carman Bickerton. Bob McIntosh created some of the Sydney Mines data bases as part of his PhD thesis on child labour in the coal fields. Carleton and SSHRCC funded research assistants to code and re-code census manuscripts: Kerry Badgley, Barbara Clow, Daniel Yee, Sue Jenkins, Sean Purdy, Mike Bernards, Keith Hodgins, Tom Matheson, Sheila Day, Fulton Rhymes and Dorothy McGrath. Data assembly and initial analysis was assisted by Carleton's Computer and Communications Service Group — Bruce Winer, Greg Morrison, Jane Wilson and Jane Miller. An early version of this paper was presented to the Atlantic Canada Workshop at Saint Mary's University in Halifax in September, 1989. This version has benefited from the reading and comments of Carman Bickerton, Alison Prentice, Gillian Creese, Suzanne Morton and by Acadiensis' *ever vigilant anonymous readers.*

Part Three
Labour's War

The Labour Question took shape as a widespread public issue in Atlantic Canada in the late 19th century, at a time when the relations between workers and employers were changing rapidly under the impact of industrialism and urbanization. The rise of unionism was one outcome of the effort to establish a balance of power between workers and employers in this new world of work. Ian McKay's chapter provides a broad discussion of the new conditions facing both workers and employers at the beginning of the 20th century: the political and economic integration of the Maritimes into Confederation linked local business conditions, including labour markets and labour organization, to the broader developments of the continent. Although unions were accepted as legal entities by this time, they had no special rights under the law, and efforts to establish union recognition usually proceeded by a test of force. Jessie Chisholm examines the emergence of a remarkable Newfoundland union of the era that not only established a strong labour presence on the waterfront but also rendered assistance to other groups of Newfoundland workers. Nolan Reilly's case study of Amherst, Nova Scotia in 1919 establishes that this small factory town generated some of the same conflicts and solidarities as the more famous Winnipeg General Strike of the same year. The most dramatic events in this era of labour conflict were those fought out in the coalfields, where a variety of factors converged to accelerate the urgency of the struggle; in the case of J.B. McLachlan, a radical union leader who expected a revolutionary outcome to the labour wars, the labour movement was checked not only by corporate resistance but also by the intervention of the provincial state and an unsympathetic international union.

Additional Reading

Babcock, Robert. "Saint John Longshoremen During the Rise of Canada's Winter Port, 1895-1922," *Labour/Le Travail*, 25 (Spring 1990), 15-46.

_____. "The Saint John Street Railwaymen's Strike and Riot, 1914," *Acadiensis*, XI, 2 (Spring 1982), 3-27.

Busch, Briton Cooper. "The Newfoundland Sealers' Strike of 1902," *Labour/Le Travail*, 14 (1984), 9-46.

Earle, Michael and Gamberg, H. "The United Mine Workers and the Coming of the CCF to Cape Breton," *Acadiensis*, XIX, 1 (Autumn 1989), 3-26.

Fillmore, Nicholas. *Maritime Radical: The Life and Times of Roscoe Fillmore* (Toronto 1992).

Forrestell, Nancy. "Times were hard: The Pattern of Women's Paid Labour in St. John's Between the Two World Wars," *Labour/Le Travail*, 24 (Fall 1989), 147-66.

Forestell, Nancy and Jessie Chisholm. "Working-Class Women as Wage Earners in St. John's, Newfoundland, 1890-1921," in Peta Tancred-Sheriff, ed., *Feminist Research: Prospect and Retrospect* (Kingston 1988), 140-8.

Frank, David. "Contested Terrain: Workers' Control in the Cape Breton Coal Mines in the 1920s," in Craig Heron and Robert Storey, eds., *On the Job: Confronting the Labour Process in Canada* (Kingston and Montréal 1986), 102-23.

Frank, David and Donald MacGillivray, eds. *George MacEachern: An Autobiography* (Sydney 1987).

Frank, David and Nolan Reilly. "The Emergence of the Socialist Movement in the Maritimes, 1899-1916," *Labour/Le Travailleur*, 4 (1979), 85-113.

Heron, Craig. "The Great War and Nova Scotia Steelworkers," *Acadiensis*, XVI, 2 (Spring 1987), 3-34.

Manley, John. "Preaching the Red Stuff: J.B. McLachlan, Communism, and the Cape Breton Miners, 1922-35," *Labour/Le Travail*, 30 (Fall 1992), 65-114.

McCallum, Margaret. "Separate Spheres: The Organization of Work in a Confectionary Factory — Ganong Brothers, St. Stephen, New Brunswick," *Labour/Le Travail*, 24 (Fall 1989), 69-90.

McDonald, Ian D.H. *"To Each His Own": William Coaker and the Fishermen's Protective Union in Newfoundland Politics, 1908-1925* (St. John's 1987).

Morton, Suzanne. "Women on their Own: Single Mothers in Working-Class Halifax in the 1920s," *Acadiensis*, XXI, 2 (Spring 1992), 90-107.

Ryan, Shannon. *The Ice Hunters: A History of Newfoundland Sealing to 1914* (St. John's 1994).

Seager, Allen. "Minto, New Brunswick: A Study in Class Relations Between the Wars," *Labour/Le Travailleur*, 5 (Spring 1980), 81-132.

Winsor, Fred. "'Solving a Problem': Privatizing Workers' Compensation for Nova Scotia's Offshore Fishermen, 1926-1928," *Acadiensis*, XVIII, 2 (Spring 1989), 94-110.

Ian McKay

8

Strikes in the Maritimes, 1901-1914

As James Pender sat at his desk on 6 November 1912, he was thinking about the traumatic events of the last few months and their ominous implications. Just one month before, the machinists in his nail factory in Saint John had presented a request for a wage increase and the nine-hour day, and they later refused to work on a Saturday afternoon at the rate normally paid during the week. On 7 October, three machinists, including two who had represented the workers in negotiations with Pender, were dismissed, and the remaining men went on strike in support of their shop mates. Like so many other employers in the Maritimes, Pender found himself in the middle of a difficult industrial conflict.[1]

Pender exemplified many of the features of the age of consolidated capitalism. He doubtless saw himself as the Saint John *Sun* described him, as a "progressive business man" and a "most excellent citizen." He had responded with anger to attempts by the U.S. Steel Company to force Canadian wire nail manufacturers into dependence, pledging his support instead to the Dominion Iron and Steel Company and its new rod mill in Sydney. Predictably Pender supported protection for the wire industry, and he also supported the Liberal Party, whose policies toward the steel industry had allowed it to reap the benefits of protectionism without formally rejecting its free-trade heritage. When he ran as a candidate for the party in 1908, 55 workers in his factory signed a letter praising him as "the friend of labor and the unswerving and outspoken advocate of everything pertaining to the welfare of our city." Sixteen of these workers had been employees of Pender for more than 15 years. Pender at once represented both the old competitive capitalism, for the nail

[1]*Standard* (Saint John), 8 October 1912, *Eastern Labour News* (Moncton), 12 October 1912. An earlier version of this paper was delivered to the Atlantic Workshop in Halifax in 1981. Since that time I have received support and criticism from many colleagues, for which I am very grateful. I thank Doug Cruikshank for sharing his own research on strikes with me, and Linda Baggs and Pat Burden for research assistance.

Published with permission of the editor. From *Acadiensis*, XIII, 1 (Autumn 1983), 3-46.

industry in Saint John had been one of the conspicuous triumphs of the National Policy, and the new monopoly capitalism, for the Pender enterprise was soon to be little more than a bookkeeping entry in the consolidated balance sheet of the Dominion Steel Corporation.[2]

Perhaps he had been stung by the attacks upon his use of "Homestead tactics" and upon his rudeness to the men's committee. (A poem in the labour press on this strike noted, "Next day he sent for the committee,/ said he dident [sic] give a damn,/ He would'nt [sic] be dictated to/ by any union man").[3] Whatever the reason, Pender took the unusual step of writing a heartfelt polemic on the subject of strikers and labour organizers to the Department of Labour, denouncing labour organizers and the foolish workers who listened to them:

We think it an outrage on Canadian Industries that lazy adventurers from the United States should be permitted to come into this country & organize Unions & collect dues from Confiding dupes who Know little or nothing about the way their dues are wasted by these loafing promoters who bask in the sunshine of these dues contributed by their confiding dupes who thus loaf a soft & easy living and live in affluence on the mischief they create between men & their employer by playing on the feelings & prejudices of the men & who make them believe that they are abused & badly used when such is not the case We think they should be jailed or deported whenever they show their mischievous presence in Canada & we hope to see legislation ere long that will deport them same as lepers.[4]

From Pender's point of view, the strike was the result of foreign agitators who had somehow undermined the relations of men and employers by appealing to irrational feelings. (In fact, the "lazy adventurer" in question was the Canadian vice-president of the International Association of Machinists, and Pender's solution of erecting a protective barrier against foreigners would not have stopped him.) Pender thought the vital nucleus of the problem was the contamination of his naive workers, those confiding dupes who just four years before had pledged they would forever be "willing and anxious to fight the battles of our generous employer." Now they seemed to be fighting against him. The workers thought the problem stemmed from the impact upon Pender of his dependence upon the growing monopoly in the steel industry. Noted the *Eastern Labour News*: "Mr. Pender is not altogether to blame for this matter. He has generally been fair, but the heads of the great steel trust at Sydney, who own the Pender Plant with one Douglas as chief executive, are the people to blame for the present trouble in a usually peaceful house."[5] Monopoly capitalism, this analysis seemed to suggest, had created a new type of employer. What is so fascinating about these comments is that both sides thought that a previously peaceful situation had been transformed by the new structures of

[2]*Sun* (Saint John), 7, 8 April 1904, 19 September 1908.
[3]*Eastern Labour News*, 23 November 1912.
[4]Strikes and Lockout Files, Vol. 300, file 3605, Department of Labour Records (RG 27), Public Archives of Canada [PAC].
[5]*Eastern Labour News*, 26 October 1912.

Canadian capitalism. Their angry responses brought out the bewilderment and uncertainty felt by men in a difficult new situation.

Recent studies have illustrated the strength and significance of working-class movements in the Maritimes during the late 19th and early 20th centuries. Other work has emphasized the organization of local and international unions and the emergence of the socialist movement in the region.[6] A study of strikes in the Maritimes can help provide a regional context for such work, and also help correct the regional imbalance in national historiography. Strikes themselves were crucial events, and no historical interpretation of the region in this period can safely overlook them. By studying the vigorous response of the region's workers to the new political economy of the early 20th century, we can start to understand the human implications of economic change. For these reasons, it is worth our effort to describe and analyze the general pattern of strikes, often in quantitative terms. This general pattern can then be related to the region's economic structure and help broaden our understanding of the economic revolution which transformed the region from the 1880s to the 1920s. In particular, two major themes emerge from this analysis: the transformation of the labour market and the revolution in the workplace. In important ways, then, this study can help us grasp the complex and profound changes taking place in the Maritimes, a society too often written off as a peripheral backwater where deferential and isolated workers were sporadically aroused by organizers for international unions. A history of the strikes of 1901-1914 helps us replace this condescending approach with a more complex understanding of the strengths and weaknesses of the working-class movement in the Maritimes in a decisive period of class awakening. It shows us how widespread was the movement of resistance which had so shocked and offended Pender.

The Maritime Provinces were dramatically transformed in the years between 1870 and 1914. Initially dependent upon exports of timber, lumber products, ships and fish, the Maritimes experienced rapid industrial growth in the decade following the introduction of the National Policy in 1879. In the first phase of industrialization, the region was characterized by locally-controlled secondary manufacturing located in widely-dispersed centres. In the 1890s and early 20th century, a widespread

[6]Recent publications in Maritime working-class history include Robert Babcock, "The Saint John Street Railwaymen's Strike and Riot, 1914," Acadiensis, XI (Spring 1982), 3-27; Peter DeLottinville, "Trouble in the Hives of Industry: The Cotton Industry Comes to Milltown, New Brunswick, 1879-1892," Historical Papers 1980, 100-15; Judith Fingard, Jack in Port (Toronto, 1982); David Frank, "Company Town/Labour Town: Local Government in the Cape Breton Coal Towns, 1917-1926," Histoire sociale/Social History, XIV (May 1981), 177-96; Donald Macgillivray, "Military Aid to the Civil Power: the Cape Breton Experience in the 1920s," Acadiensis, III (Spring 1974), 45-64; Nolan Reilly, "The General Strike in Amherst, Nova Scotia, 1919," Acadiensis, IX (Spring 1980), 56-77; Allen Seager, "Minto, New Brunswick: A Study in Class Relations Between the Wars," Labour/Le Travailleur, 5 (Spring 1980), 81-132. See David Frank and Nolan Reilly, "The Emergence of the Socialist Movement in the Maritimes, 1899-1916," Labour/Le Travailleur, IV (1979), 85-113, for an article which parallels the present study in periodization and regional focus.

movement of economic consolidation brought most of these consumer-goods industries under the control of Montréal finance capital, the major seaports into the Canadian transportation system, and the separate communities of the Maritime provinces into closer association with each other and with Montréal, the metropolis. A second phase of industrialization, focused on the coal and steel industries, emerged strongly in the same period. The advent of monopoly capitalism coincided with both the industrialization and subordination of the region. The consequence was highly paradoxical, for while the rapid loss of control over the regional economy by its indigenous capitalists accentuated underdevelopment in the long term, its short-term effect was to help overcome the problem of fragmentation and enable Maritimers to build more coherent class and regional traditions.[7]

Throughout the period 1901-1914 workers in the Maritimes faced an economy and society of striking variety. The greater part of the region was dominated by the rhythms of rural life, whether this was the agriculture of Prince Edward Island and the Annapolis Valley or the fishing economy of the coastal villages from Passamaquoddy to Cape North. If we remove the metal and coal towns of the region's north-east (the band of communities from Moncton to Glace Bay) and the two large seaports, we find in the remainder of the region only three communities with more than 5,000 people in 1911: two capital cities (Fredericton and Charlottetown) and the venerable old port of Yarmouth. In the remaining 20 centres in this zone, the average population was 2,469. Here was a zone of slow growth and outright population losses. The first, dispersed phase of industrial growth had left its mark; there were still cotton factories in Windsor, Milltown and Marysville, among other legacies of the National Policy. But the greater part of this area was dominated by primary production. Working-class life took place in small towns or villages, and only a few of these developed large labour movements. Paternalism could find its natural habitat here, in communities small enough to permit the personal sway of the capitalist to carry into many spheres of life.

Halifax and Saint John were different places altogether. Retaining many industries founded during the National Policy, they also faced the massive restructuring required by the growth of a national transportation system. The redevelopment of both cities as the winter ports of the Dominion suggested the consolidating logic of the new age. Workers here lived in variegated urban centres. In the early 20th century both cities were undergoing rapid changes which tended to conflict with their modest growth of population. In Saint John 5,270 employees worked at

[7]See T.W. Acheson, "The National Policy and the Industrialization of the Maritimes, 1880-1910," *Acadiensis*, I (Spring 1972), 3-28; Larry McCann, "Staples and the New Industrialism in the Growth of Post-Confederation Halifax," *Acadiensis*, VIII (Spring 1979), 47-79; Robert Babcock, "Economic Development in Portland (Me.) and Saint John (N.B.) During the Age of Iron and Steam, 1850-1914," *The American Review of Canadian Studies*, IX (Spring 1979), 3-37; David Frank, "The Cape Breton Coal Industry and the Rise and Fall of the British Empire Steel Corporation," *Acadiensis*, VII (Autumn 1977), 3-34; Elizabeth W. McGahan, *The Port of Saint John*, Vol. I, *From Confederation to Nationalization 1867-1927* (Saint John 1982).

177 major establishments in 1911: in Halifax-Dartmouth 4,490 workers found employment at 123 establishments. These estimates do not include the many men who found employment on the waterfront and who formed the natural core of the labour movement in both cities.

Finally, in the region's eastern and northern section, was found the belt of heavy industry and the coalfields, which from Moncton to Glace Bay formed the dynamic heart of the second wave of industrialization. The coalfields posted a 93 per cent increase in production in the first decade of the 20th century, and the number of employees rose from 9,184 to 14,977. Even more impressive were the huge population increases in Amherst and Sydney. Unified by the railway system, dominated by the bankheads belching smoke and by dirty duff banks, and dotted with the heavy industry spawned by the age of the railway — from car works at Trenton and Amherst, to the new steel mills themselves at Sydney and Sydney Mines — this zone had an ambience quite different than that of Halifax or the rural Maritimes. Workers here lived in the front ranks of the great economic transformation, and they experienced its opportunities and difficulties at first hand. Often they lived in instant communities, built for the sole function of servicing the great empire of steel and coal whose conquests were the pride of the local boosters. This was the heartland of monopoly capitalism.

Speaking in round figures — it would be pretentious, given the highly flawed statistics, to do anything else — of the region's 45,000 industrial workers in 1911, 61 per cent lived in the highly industrialized zone from Moncton to Glace Bay, 22 per cent in the great seaports, and 18 per cent in the semi-rural remainder of the region.[8]

Where do we find significant working-class protests in this period? Almost everywhere. In Halifax and Saint John, workers increasingly supported international unions and resurrected trades and labour councils; labouring men mounted campaigns for political representation; labour issues were debated in the churches and in the newspapers. Labour movements here were often divided. Longshoremen, because of the enduring effects of casualism, often fought each other as strenuously as they fought their employers; only after the International Longshoremen's Association installed itself on the docks did a degree of unity replace division. Skilled craftsmen might well regard unskilled workers as potential enemies who stood ready to help employers undermine their position. The many women who found employment in the two major cities were generally left outside the ranks of organized labour (although there were significant exceptions) and little effort was made to organize the juveniles who delivered messages and performed countless other functions in the urban economy. Trade unionism in the two major cities had made important and decisive gains, and the "foreign agitators" so roundly de-

[8]The data in the preceding paragraphs are drawn from the *Census of Canada, 1911*, Vol. III, Tables XI, XII, XXXV. It should be noted that census statistics are approximate because establishments with fewer than five employees were not counted, and many seasonal industries were also missed.

nounced by Pender had effected a shift towards international affiliation — but it did not challenge the traditional divisions within the working class nor the political order very aggressively.[9]

It was a far different story in the railway, metal and coal towns of the industrial core. There one found many powerful and cohesive trade unions which within their communities exerted an impact far beyond the workplace. The most important union of all was the Provincial Workmen's Association, perhaps the most misunderstood and misrepresented of all Canadian trade unions. Frequently labelled a "company union" by its critics, the PWA united workers in the coalfields throughout Nova Scotia and made significant and controversial inroads into the transportation sector. Because the PWA had changed its structure at the end of the 19th century to one in which many important powers were wielded by district sub-councils, the workers within the union were rarely discouraged from going on strike. More strikes were waged by the PWA in this period than by any other union. Decentralization aided local militants, who in many cases sympathized with socialism. Much of the rhetoric of the local activists was tinged with a syndicalist spirit, in stark contrast to the moderate language of the union's leadership. The PWA absorbed many of the energies unleashed by the "new unionism" of the 20th century, and like many of the trade unions discussed by David Montgomery, this aggressive local pursuit of workers' power coexisted with a moderate provincial leadership. International unionism made headway in Moncton, Sackville and Sydney, but until 1908 the PWA exerted an unquestioned sway over the coalfields. Only when a conservative rump attempted to undermine a majority decision to affiliate with the United Mine Workers of America did the PWA lose its credibility as the fighting arm of the miners.[10]

The rest of the region is something of an enigma. International unions were influential in St. George, Fredericton, the Hants County gypsum district, and elsewhere. Local organizations surfaced in surprising places. Pugwash had its own longshoremen's union, and the workers of Sussex, New Brunswick, united behind a local Nine Hours League. From some sectors of the rural Maritimes there is silence: whether because of the partial nature of our sources or a genuine absence of working-class mobilization, there is next to nothing indicating organization in the lumber camps, the great majority of the fishing communities, or in agriculture. Fishermen in Nova Scotia belonged to the Fishermen's Union of Nova Scotia, which was a union in name only.[11] However, sardine fishermen in Charlotte County

[9]See Robert Babcock, *Gompers in Canada: A Study in American Continentalism Before the First World War* (Toronto 1974), 119-23, for a description of the activities of the American Federation of Labor in the Maritimes: earlier organizational history may be found in Eugene Forsey, *Trade Unions in Canada 1812-1902* (Toronto 1982).

[10]The union's early history is described by Sharon Reilly, "The History of the Provincial Workmen's Association, 1879-1898," MA thesis, Dalhousie University, 1979.

[11]L. Gene Barrett, "Underdevelopment and Social Movements in the Nova Scotia Fishing Industry to 1938," in Robert Brym and R. James Sacouman, eds., *Underdevelopment and*

and lobster fishermen at Gabarus and Main-a-Dieu in Cape Breton organized active protests against canneries which suggest something more than spontaneous, unorganized outbursts. Many small communities of the rural Maritimes witnessed serious strikes by workers who, at least formally, had no organization. In Shelburne, Bridgetown, Woodstock, and Parrsboro — to name only a few places — we find strikes organized by men who made coherent demands and fought in an organized way. The many ties of kinship and community binding workers together in these centres may have helped them fight successfully without formal union organization. In the rural Maritimes, supposedly dominated by an ancient paternalism and an absence of class conflict, we find instead a number of interesting experiments in purely local working-class mobilization.

The workers of the Maritimes faced a wide variety of conditions and created an astonishing diversity of organizations, but certain things were commonly experienced. No one stood completely apart from the dynamic expansion of the economy. Throughout the record of strikes, we find navvies and construction labourers, from the new sewers of Springhill and Amherst and Fredericton, the buildings of Dalhousie University in Halifax and the churches of Sydney, to the waterworks extension in Saint John and railway construction near Campbellton. The new economy entailed a massive expansion in the physical capital of the state apparatus. Everywhere we find the same complaint: "Labour is scarce." There are no reliable unemployment statistics for this period, but the consistency with which the scarcity of labour is referred to suggests that the workers' movement faced no great shortage of jobs. Although no studies of the standard of living have been completed of the calibre of those for other regions, it appears that Maritime workers all faced an economy in which wage increases did not keep pace with inflation. The record of the strikes brings to the fore the pervasive fear that earnings were slipping beneath what workers thought an acceptable level. Prices of food, fuel and other necessities in Maritime cities rose between 31 and 43 per cent, and rents from 36 to 56 per cent: lower increases than reported elsewhere in Canada, but enough to make the workers of the Maritimes very anxious. Local construction booms, such as the one in Sydney between 1901 and 1904, sent prices and rents skyrocketing.[12] Everywhere we find evidence that the region was increasingly being unified by the railway system and the emergence of much larger employers. The rail yards of Halifax gave work to men from Memramcook, unemployed fishermen found work in Halifax and Saint John, and the great building boom in Sydney caused a shortage of skilled workers in Halifax and a reorientation of agricultural production in the surrounding countryside. Coal strikes were regarded with utmost seriousness because they could

---

Social Movements in Atlantic Canada (Toronto 1979), 127-160, provides the essential background for fishing.

[12] As the *Chronicle* (Halifax), 18 June 1901, remarked during a strike of steamer firemen in 1901: "There is a scarcity of firemen here, and in consequence the men are very independent". For the cost of living, see Canada, Department of Labour, Board of Inquiry into the Cost of Living, *Report* (Ottawa 1915), Vol II, 76-7, 377, 382, 1063.

bring to a halt industries throughout the region. A strike in Springhill caused real fears of fuel shortages in Saint John, Amherst, and Moncton. Longshoremen were reminded of the wide ramifications of their militancy by no less a personage than Israel Tarte, who warned Saint John longshoremen that their excesses would drive their port into the same ruin which had befallen Québec, all to the benefit of Montréal and Halifax.[13]

There were isolated strikes in this period, strikes waged by men whose actions had little possible bearing on workers elsewhere in the region. But such isolated strikes loom less large than the strikes which affected parts of the region far removed from the site of the conflict. In an economy dependent on coal, railways, and steamships, workers derived tremendous power from the interlocked character of production. A 19th-century coal strike was a nuisance; a large coal strike in the 20th century was a calamity. A new dynamism could be found in this economy, and here lies the key to the militancy of these years. Workers enjoyed the unusual position — in the Maritimes, at any rate — of being able to take advantage of their scarcity value in the labour market. The rapid expansion of the economy masked serious structural weaknesses and allowed contemporaries to confuse growth with genuine development. But it did give workers a rare chance to make their power felt in this society, and this chance was seized with real enthusiasm.

Workers in the Maritimes fought at least 411 strikes from 1901 to 1914, accounting for 1,936,146 striker-days. It is difficult to place this statistic in national context, because it is derived from sources different than those customarily cited. (The official data for the Maritime region are highly defective.) The highly ambiguous statistics we do possess hint that this level of militancy was comparatively high.[14] It is also not altogether easy to place this finding in temporal perspective.

[13] *Chronicle*, 5 June 1901, 30 May 1903, *Herald* (Halifax), 17 June 1904, *Sun*, 24 October 1907, 24 November 1905.

[14] The number of striker-days is calculated by multiplying the number of strikers by the working days involved. All strike statistics in this paper are drawn from a computer file compiled from three sources: (1) the published works of the Department of Labour, notably the *Labour Gazette* and the *Report on Strikes and Lockouts in Canada 1901-1916* (Ottawa 1918), (2) unpublished reports on strikes prepared by the Department of Labour in the strikes and lockouts files, and later departmental revisions [RG 27, PAC], (3) newspapers of the region, notably daily newspapers in the two major cities throughout this period (the *Sun, Standard* and *Globe* in Saint John and the *Herald* in Halifax), supplemented by the *Eastern Labour News*, the *Maritime Mining Record*, and a wide variety of local papers which were consulted if other sources indicated industrial unrest. The official strike statistics compiled by the Department of Labour are highly unreliable. According to *Strikes and Lockouts in Canada* there were 153 strikes in the Maritimes from 1901 to 1914; our evidence suggests this estimate is based on only 37 per cent of the strikes known to have occurred in the region. Moreover, the departmental estimates of individual strikes generally had to be recalculated. Inter-regional strikes are excluded from this analysis. The grave problems associated with official statistics suggest that inter-regional comparisons will have to wait until historians recalculate the strike statistics for other regions: there is at present no sound statistical base

Only a few places have been researched on the same level from the 19th to the early 20th centuries. In Halifax from 1901 to 1914 there were more strikes (54) than in the half century before 1900 (42), and in the two Cumberland coalfields there were more strikes in the first 14 years of the 20th century (37) than in the preceding 21 years (36). Impressionistic evidence from Saint John in the 1880s suggests that the high level of militancy in the early 20th century might also be seen as a break with the past.[15]

There is an abundance of evidence which suggests that contemporaries perceived the strikes of the early 20th century as a departure from tradition. In Lunenburg, the workers of the Smith and Rhuland shipyard launched in November 1910, what the local correspondent called "the first strike in the era of our commercial enterprizes ...." The strike of workers at the Eastern Hat and Cap Company in Truro was reported under the headline, "Truro Has Had Its First Taste of a Real Genuine Strike With Modern Accompaniments," and after enumerating such signs of local progress as paved streets and a new railway station, the writer concluded, "Now the sight of strikers on our streets gives the finishing touches to all that goes to make up the daily routine of the biggest city in the world." The general strike of skilled and unskilled workmen in Shelburne, which in 1912 closed down the shipyards, boat shops and other establishments of the town, was thought to be the community's first major strike. It was believed that the workers of the Hartt Boot and Shoe Factory in Fredericton had launched the factory's first strike when they walked out in 1907.[16] Even in the coalfields and major ports, where large strikes had been noted since the mid-19th century, contemporaries noted a new intransigence. In Springhill, a town which more than any other symbolized the class polarization of the age, it was said that "wars and rumours of wars are practically our daily portion in this town." The Halifax *Chronicle* conveyed the same sense of alarm when it commented in 1901, "Local labor circles are agitated just now and it is not known where the end will be."[17]

The strikes were found throughout the region. The greatest number were found in the seaports (198), followed by 143 strikes in the region of heavy industry and 70 in the widely-dispersed industrial and resource communities elsewhere. Table

---

for such an enterprise. For seminal work on strike patterns in other countries, see Edward Shorter and Charles Tilly, *Strikes in France, 1830-1968* (Cambridge 1974), James E. Cronin, *Industrial Conflict in Modern Britain* (London 1979), and Michelle Perrot, *Les ouvriers en grève: France 1871-1890*, 2 tomes (Paris 1974), probably the best study to date.

[15]See Ian McKay, "The Working Class of Metropolitan Halifax, 1850-1889," Honours Thesis, Dalhousie University, 1975; Babcock, "Saint John Street Railwaymen," 10, and James Richard Rice, "A History of Organized Labour in Saint John, New Brunswick, 1813-1890," MA thesis, University of New Brunswick, 1968 — although this last work reminds us of the more militant period in Saint John of the 1870s.

[16]*Herald*, 22 November 1910; *Colchester Sun* (Truro), 23 October 1912; *Evening Mail* (Halifax), 14 May 1912; *Globe* (Saint John), 4 July 1907 and *Daily Gleaner* (Fredericton), 11 July 1907.

[17]*Herald*, 7 August 1907; *Chronicle*, 3 June 1901.

1 lists the Maritime centres which recorded more than 10,000 striker-days in the period 1901-1914. Of these 11 locations, five were dominated by the coal-mining industry. Other important strike locations included Sydney Mines (8 strikes), Moncton (5), Fredericton (19), Amherst (11), and Newcastle/Chatham (8). One may read the evidence in two ways. If one is anxious to stress the peculiar militancy of the coal miners, one should note that 69 per cent of the striker-days in the region can be placed in Glace Bay and Springhill. More than half the total striker-days can be attributed to the coal miners' strikes in Inverness, Glace Bay and Springhill in 1909-11 for recognition of the United Mine Workers of America. On the other hand, Saint John was by far the regional leader in the *number* of strikes, and the two port cities together accounted for 48 per cent of the region's strikes. An approach to the region's workers, such as that championed by Stuart Jamieson, which emphasizes the "low incidence of strikes or other overt expressions of industrial conflict," outside the coal mining industry, falls wide of the mark. The coal miners were exceptional not because they decided to go on strike more often than other workers but because their strikes were far larger in terms of numbers and duration.[18]

The strikers could be found in a wide range of occupations. Messenger boys, waitresses, actors, professional hockey players, attendants at bowling alleys, paid members of church choirs, and firemen comprised some of the less usual strikers, whose 24 strikes are classified under "miscellaneous." Coal miners waged 82 strikes, unskilled labourers 140, factory workers 62, and skilled craftsmen 103. These data are somewhat startling, because they disagree sharply with the pattern in central Canada, where skilled craftsmen dominated both the labour movement and the history of industrial conflict. The most active single group were the labourers — including longshoremen, haypressers, freighthandlers, construction labourers — and if we add to their number the factory workers, men who rarely were considered skilled, we arrive at the surprising conclusion that close to half the strikes were waged by those without generally recognized skills. As soon as we examine striker-days, however, the coal miners once again assert their dominance, accounting for fully 74 per cent of the striker-days (as compared with 3 per cent for unskilled labourers, 14 per cent for factory workers, 7 per cent for skilled craftsmen, and 2 per cent for other workers).

Particular groups within each occupational category emerge from the analysis as leaders of strikes. A surprising number of strikes (18) were fought by boys who worked in the coal mines, an indication of the power wielded by these young workers who minded ventilation doors, drove the horses, and often helped load the coal. More than half the craft strikes were found in the building trades, centred in such places as Halifax, Saint John, Sydney and Fredericton, and more than two-fifths were concentrated in the metal trades. Sackville, Moncton, and Amherst stand out particularly in this revolt of the skilled metal trades, a battle made all the more bitter by the intransigence of such employers as the Record Foundry in Moncton

[18]Stuart M. Jamieson, *Times of Trouble: Labour Unrest and Industrial Conflict in Canada, 1900-66* (Ottawa 1968), 100.

Figure 1
Location of Strikes in the Maritimes, 1901-1914

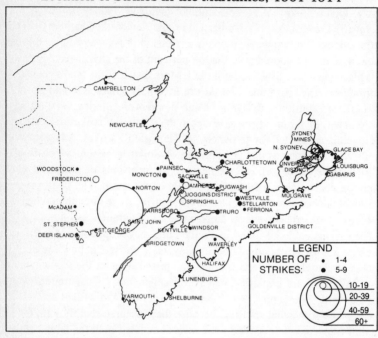

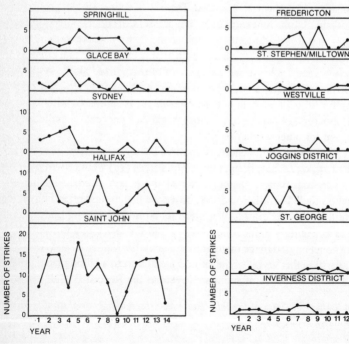

Figure 2
Striker-Days in the Maritimes, 1901-1914

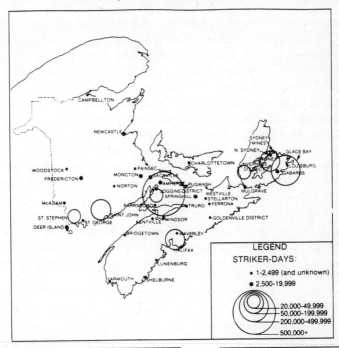

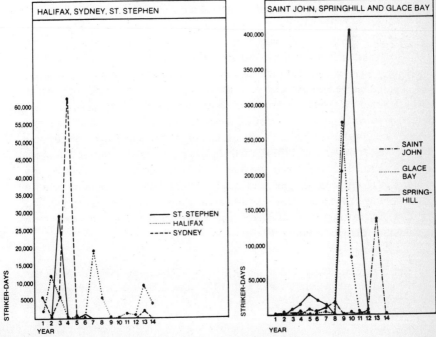

and the Fawcett Foundry in Sackville. The strikes of craftsmen were concentrated in the two economic spheres most closely integrated with the new capitalism — construction and heavy industry. There were very few strikes to be found among other craft groups, although such ancient trades as printing and caulking accounted for a few. The labourers are perhaps the most interesting group. Some of them, such as the longshoremen of Saint John and Halifax, were in the process of creating controls over the waterfront that stood comparison with the exclusivism of the crafts. Other labourers, such as the civic labourers in Saint John, were able to count on the old traditions of patronage and the political benefits of winning favour with a visible component of the working-class movement. These labourers, while they had few marketable skills, could use other means to defend their interests in the labour market. Many others were not so fortunate. A surprisingly large amount of the heavy construction work was done by foreigners. Hungarians and Italians helped build the Sydney steel mill, and Italians laid new sewers in Fredericton and built the railway in northern New Brunswick. Such men, provided to local contractors through intermediaries in Québec or the United States, had only the most rudimentary ways of defending their interests. Isolated from the rest of the society, and confronted with contractors who always seemed on the verge of bankruptcy, these foreigners faced problems quite different in scope from the unskilled labourers of the cities. Twenty-six strikes were fought exclusively by foreign workers, whose most common fate was to be immediately replaced by another gang.

Although many critics of the working-class movement placed the blame for insurgency on the shoulders of meddling organizers, the record of the strikes does not support their contention. Out of 384 strikes for which information on union status is available, 164 involved non-unionized workers, 112 members of international unions, and 108 members of regional or local bodies. The PWA alone accounted for 65 strikes, many waged by local lodges without central approval. Of course the workers of the Maritimes did not live in isolation, and ideas and methods of both American and British trade unions were followed with interest. But few strikes can be blamed on the relatively infrequent visits by American organizers, and local workers lacked neither the will nor the reasons for going on strike.

The decision to go on strike was influenced by many factors. Table 2 summarizes the annual strike record for the region, and suggests the impact of the business cycle. In the boom years of 1901-1907 there was a tight labour market and about 32 strikes a year. The recession of 1908 reduced the number of strikes, and only in 1912 and 1913 did strikes regain previous levels. By 1914 an economic reversal and the coming of the war brought strikes to their lowest point in this period. The pattern evident in the number of strikes supports the classic view that strikes were most common in times of prosperity.[19]

[19]Compare with Craig Heron and Bryan D. Palmer, "Through the Prism of the Strike: Industrial Conflict in Southern Ontario, 1901-1914," *Canadian Historical Review*, LVIII (December 1977) 425-6.

Table 1
Strike Centres in the Maritimes, 1901-1914

Place	Number of Strikes	Striker-Days	Active Workers
Springhill	19	978,664	Coal miners, railwaymen, trapper boys
Glace Bay	20	363,382	Coal miners
Saint John	144	199,025	Longshoremen, construction labourers, civic labourers, building trades, metal trades
Sydney	26	80,487	Building trades, steelworkers, construction labourers
Halifax	54	64,185	Longshoremen, building trades, metal trades
Inverness District	9	39,970	Coal miners
St. Stephen/Milltown	6	29,800	Cotton factory workers
St. George	4	24,278	Granite cutters, pulp mill workers
Joggins District	18	20,223	Coal miners
Westville	7	18,760	Coal miners
Sackville, N.B.	5	16,948	Metal trades

Table 2
Yearly Levels of Strikes in the Maritimes, 1901-1914

Year	Number of Strikes	Striker-Days	Largest Strikes
1901	26	16,489	Pictou coal miners
1902	41	37,303	Moncton moulders
1903	39	56,449	Milltown cotton workers
1904	37	96,065	Sydney steelworkers
1905	39	58,696	Springhill coal miners
1906	38	41,015	Springhill coal miners
1907	44	190,418	Springhill coal miners
1908	20	47,501	St. George granite workers
1909	21	543,320	Glace Bay coal miners
1910	14	479,689	Springhill coal miners
1911	21	164,281	Springhill coal miners
1912	32	17,339	Moncton moulders
1913	32	172,324	Saint John mill workers
1914	7	15,257	Amherst machinists
Totals	411	1,936,146	

If we look more closely at the individual communities, as Figures 1 and 2 allow us to do, we discover a more complex picture. Each community had its own pattern. The most violent fluctuations were evident in Saint John, where no fewer than 18 strikes were fought in 1905 (the peak of any location in the Maritimes in a single year) and where no strikes have surfaced in 1909. In Halifax where the peaks were lower, the city's maximum totals were found in 1902 and 1907 (nine strikes). In both cities, there was a drastic reduction in the years 1908-1910, and recovery afterwards, with Saint John experiencing a major wave of strikes in the years 1911-1913 in response to the expansion of the port. These cities most closely resembled the Ontario pattern described by Craig Heron and Bryan Palmer. In Sydney, strikes were concentrated in the first four years of the period, and were sharply reduced after the defeat of the steel strike waged by the PWA in 1904. The coalfields possessed their own pattern. The years leading up to 1909 were exceptionally militant; there were no fewer than five strikes in Springhill in 1905 alone. In 1909 to 1911 the coal miners went against the regional trend by waging the region's largest strikes, and they fell almost silent after their defeat. Were one to rely on the statistics of striker-days, one would discover a positive correlation between economic recession and militancy — because the coal miners were counter-cyclical, waging their most impressive struggles in the depths of recession.

Table 3
Strike Issues

Category I	
For higher earnings	204
Against wage reductions	22
Category II	
For recognition of union	14
For shorter hours	46
Defence of trade unionism	7
Sympathy	7
Apprenticeship control	2
Objection to new system of work	12
Change in conditions of work	31
Objection to employment of particular persons	36
Adjustment of procedures of wage payment	44
Against dismissal of worker or supervisor	43
Improvement in housing conditions	3
Political demands	2
Other/Unknown	21

Table 4
Strike Issues

	Improved Earnings	Control	Not Classified
1901	20	6	0
1902	29	11	1
1903	28	10	1
1904	21	16	0
1905	26	11	2
1906	29	8	1
1907	29	12	3
1908	14	6	0
1909	12	9	0
1910	8	4	2
1911	16	4	1
1912	21	7	4
1913	23	9	0
1914	4	2	1
Totals	280	115	16

Workers went on strike for a wide variety of reasons, and there are a number of ways of analyzing the general pattern. Adopting the categories used by Heron and Palmer, with minor additions for the regional context, Table 3 suggests the importance of wage struggles in the working-class movement. (Because a strike involving two issues is counted twice, the total of issues raised does not correspond with the total number of strikes.) About 46 per cent of the issues raised in strikes focused on the level of wage payment, while strikes in Category II, which turned broadly on questions of control, made up 50 per cent of the issues raised. It might be objected, however, that this minimizes the impact of economic issues involved in strikes by counting as demands for "control" essentially economic issues. By dividing the strikes between economic and non-economic on the strict criteria of whether or not the strikers would obtain immediate economic advantages if they won the strike, we find 280 "economic" strikes, 115 "control" strikes, and 16 which cannot be classified. Table 4 outlines the yearly fluctuations of these strictly demarcated "control" strikes. Both estimates of the issues raised in strikes make the same point. It would be misleading to present the strike as a simple response to "bread- and-butter" issues. Whether we define control broadly, as in Table 3, or very narrowly as in Table 4, we find control strikes accounting for between 28 and 54 per cent of the total. By either measure, we find workers were determined to defend certain basic controls over their jobs, such as the right to control the discharge of individuals and the character of supervision. David Montgomery's pathbreaking work on American control strikes suggests that such strikes at the turn of the century generally involved craftsmen seeking a firm hold within the congealing structure of monopoly capitalism.[20] The experience of the workers of the Maritimes may have been somewhat different, for the craftsmen did not account for most of the control strikes, nor did traditional craft issues (such as limitation of the number of apprentices) loom very large. The heartland of the control strike was the coalfields. Of the 115 "pure" control strikes, 41 were fought in the coal fields, 30 involved labourers, 13 factory workers, 22 craftsmen, and 9 other workers.

Table 5
The Results of the Strike

Year	Workers Succeed	Employers Succeed	Compromise	Indeterminate	Unknown
1901	4	4	8	5	5
1902	12	11	8	2	8
1903	8	11	8	0	12
1904	13	14	4	1	5
1905	12	17	3	0	7
1906	11	12	7	1	7
1907	12	17	8	2	5
1908	5	11	1	2	1
1909	2	8	2	0	9
1910	2	4	2	2	4
1911	8	4	2	0	7
1912	7	8	8	1	8
1913	9	8	7	1	7
1914	1	3	2	0	1
Totals	106	132	70	17	86

Finally, some assessment should be made of the success rate of the strikers. Table 5 outlines the essential data on a yearly basis. The strike was clearly something of a gamble, and the chance of winning varied with the business cycle. The bottom had fallen out of the workers' movement in the recession of 1908, for example, when 55 per cent of the strikes were defeats. When we analyze the successes of workers by occupation, we find two distinct patterns. For the coal miners and the skilled craftsmen, the strike often paid off. Coal miners won 35 per cent of their strikes outright, and lost 23 per cent; the corresponding statistics for craftsmen were 34 and 26 per cent respectively. For less well-protected workers,

[20]David Montgomery, "The 'New Unionism' and the Transformation of Workers' Consciousness in America, 1909-22," in *Workers' Control in America: Studies in the History of Work, Technology and Labor Struggles* (Cambridge 1979), 98.

however, the failure rate was crushing. Labourers lost 38 per cent of their strikes, winning only 19 per cent outright; factory workers lost 37 per cent and won 19 per cent; and miscellaneous workers lost 41 and won only 17 per cent. However, these estimates may be somewhat misleading, because they do not register variations over time. The most dramatic change was experienced by the most powerful workers, the coal miners. Before 1907 the coal miners endured only eight defeats, a failure rate of just 15 per cent; after 1907 they lost 19 strikes, including the 22-month strike in Springhill, for a failure rate of 55 per cent. These strikes illustrated the rapid ebb and flow of working-class power, especially in an age in which the state aggressively restructured labour relations and capital mobilized with resolute swiftness to keep the coal mines working.

The workers of the Maritimes clearly responded with tremendous force to the new realities of monopoly capitalism. Apart from places where no large proletarian population existed, the strike was at home everywhere: in the mines, on the docks, in the factories. The statistics reveal a differentiated working class making a wide range of demands. In order to grasp their full meaning and the structures underlying them, we need to consider closely the transformation of the labour market and the revolution in the workplace which were the preconditions for this pattern.

Economic historians have established that a marked consolidation of capital took place in the late 19th and early 20th centuries, evident in the "nationalization" of Maritime banks and the "internationalization" of stock promotions. It has been less frequently observed that the same period witnessed a consolidation of the labour market of equal scope and significance. The capitalist labour market, whose emergence in central Canada in the 1850s and 1860s was analyzed so brilliantly by H.C. Pentland, had not really demolished regional and national barriers between various local labour markets in the 19th century.[21] The massive expansion of the economy in the early 20th century demanded just such a demolition of barriers to the free circulation of labour power. Employers might debate the exquisite intricacies of incidental protection and unrestricted reciprocity with great enthusiasm, but on the subject of the need for a free labour market they were united to a man.

Centralized production and the interpenetration of finance and industrial capital made it possible for employers to gain access to far larger labour pools, within the region and outside it. This creation of a much larger labour market destabilized the working-class world, but at the same time it created new opportunities for mobilization. In the new economy, workers were informed about the going rate in the region and the country as a whole and were quite prepared to demand it. The broadening of the labour market provided them with a rapid education in the new "rules of the game," and employers were soon complaining, with perennial

[21]For economic consolidation see James Frost, "The 'Nationalization' of the Bank of Nova Scotia, 1880-1910," *Acadiensis*, XII (Autumn 1982), 3-38, and Christopher Armstrong, "Making a Market: Selling Securities in Atlantic Canada Before World War I," *Canadian Journal of Economics*, XIII (August 1980) 438-54. Pentland's major work is *Labour and Capital in Canada, 1650-1860* (Toronto 1981).

inconsistency, that the workers were playing very capably in the impersonal world of the capitalist labour market. One of the most important victories of the workers was the large increase in wages secured in the major coalfields in this period — a wage increase which took account of the rising price of coal. What was most impressive about this was that for the first time the PWA had bargained for a wage increase in a unified way, a dramatic break with the somewhat uncoordinated activities of the union in the 19th century.[22]

Workers could use the new structure to their own advantage. Many of the defeats of unskilled construction labourers have to be placed in the context of the high international demand for their services. Like 19th-century Irish railway navvies, the Italian labourers who worked at Loch Lomond near Saint John on the city's new waterworks extension endured conditions of unimaginable hardship — often they worked with cold water up to their knees and lived in primitive shanties — and they fought, along with "Galicians" and other unskilled labourers, many unsuccessful strikes. But while their situation was one of dire helplessness in some respects, it in fact provided them some power. As the *Globe* reported, the labourers believed themselves to be "masters of the situation" because of the project deadlines and the contractor's concern that rains might jeopardize the project. Even more to their advantage was the existence of many jobs throughout North America in a period of rapid urban development. After one strike, the Italians were reported to be bound for "Boston, Montréal or any other place at which they have reason to believe work may be obtained," and the project was left looking for more workers. Such labourers would come, go on strike (often with a hint of violence), and leave: the "defeats" of their strikes were spurs to their rapid departure. Austrians and Italians at work on the Fredericton sewers merely returned to the immigrant "colony" in Québec or to Boston; as they informed the *Gleaner*, there would be no trouble in obtaining work elsewhere. These foreigners embodied the ambivalence of the international labour market, which brought them harsh conditions but also opportunities for direct action. But emigration was not the prerogative of itinerant workers alone. St. George granite cutters left for employment in Newfoundland during their strike in 1902; Halifax moulders, from the anti-union Hillis Foundry, emigrated to Haverhill, Massachusetts, during a strike in 1905; when Sackville moulders emigrated to the United States, a reporter lamented that Sackville would thereby lose "a number of good citizens," thanks to the participation of Enterprise Foundry in an open-shop drive. For many skilled workers, one of the great attractions of holding a card from an international union was the flexibility it allowed in such times of trouble. Coal miners found employment in other coalfields during strikes; miners in the Joggins coalfield complained during the long strike of 1909-11 in Springhill that Springhill

[22]The wage struggles of the PWA are documented in the *Amherst Daily News*, 4 January 1901, *Sun*, 1 January 1901, *Chronicle*, 1, 2, 4, 7 January 1901; J.R. Cowans to M.R. Morrow, 17 April 1900, Exhibit H/33, Record of Proceedings, Rex v. Cowans and Dick, vol. 328, Series "A," RG 21, Public Archives of Nova Scotia; John Moffatt, *Coal Cutting Rates in Nova Scotia* (Stellarton n.d.).

miners were flooding the local labour market. Many coal miners went west when big strikes shut down the Nova Scotia industry.[23]

The new conditions of the labour market gave the workers advantages as well as undermining their traditions of local protection. In a minority of strikes the working class can be seen trying to restore such local protection by means of excluding workers of other races and nationalities, or by aligning with other classes against "outsiders." Maritimers faced daunting problems of fragmentation, and it would be unrealistic to believe that class allegiance automatically overcame deeply-rooted ethnic and religious divisions. Blacks were not proportionately represented in the crafts, and it is probable that the practice of the closed shop served to perpetuate their exclusion. Saint John machinists, for example, went on strike at one foundry in the city to force the discharge of a black man, who later commented that "he was a British subject and proud to live under the Union Jack, but ... the action of the foundry hands had made him almost ashamed that the Union Jack floated over St. John." A later strike of woodworking employees in Saint John in 1913 raised the same issue of ethnic division, although in a different way. The city's carpenters were faced with the problem of whether they would work with non-union materials coming from the woodworking factories. Although some of them supported this act of solidarity, and the international union gave its blessing to a sympathy strike, the local carpenters demurred and the woodworkers' strike was subsequently broken. As the local correspondent of the *Labour Gazette* saw it, one weakness of the strikers had been ethnic division: "The strike was not popular with native workmen. The leaders were principally new commers [sic] to the city (englishmen) labor agitators."[24] The waterfront was particularly prone to this kind of division. The divisiveness of the Saint John waterfront was legendary: divided along geographical, religious and economic lines, the city's longshoremen typified the survival of localism. Labour struggles in Pugwash pitted unionized full-time longshoremen against non-union farmers who were supplementing their normal income. The workers of the Miramichi responded with violence to the incursions of millmen and other labourers from Saint John.[25]

Even in the coal and steel centres one finds strikes which suggest ethnic and other divisions. About 300 Italian labourers went on strike in Sydney in March 1903 against the Dominion Iron and Steel Company, alleging that they were not treated as well as native workers and that the latter were given the preference in the allocation of work. The labourers also charged that they had been brought from Montréal on the understanding they were to receive $1.50 per day; their actual pay had been reduced to $1.35. A crowd of agitated foreigners armed with heavy clubs,

[23]*Globe*, 7 September 1905, 11 July 1905, 23 May 1905; *Gleaner*, 18 June 1906; *Sun*, 17 June 1902; *Herald*, 2 November 1905; *Amherst Daily News*, 21 September 1905; *Herald*, 28 August 1909; *Herald*, 15 September 1909.

[24]*Sun*, 25 April 1907; report of Fraser Gregory, vol. 302, File 13 (67), RG 27.

[25]McGahan, *Port of Saint John*, 180-187; *Amherst Daily News*, 16 August 1907; *Sun*, 17 May 1904.

picks, shovels, and iron bars assembled at both the open hearth and coke oven entrances. As native workmen passed the strikers, the Italians began to shout and lift their weapons threateningly: "The police waited no longer and started to disperse them by force. After the police did considerable clubbing and arrested one or two they succeeded in quelling the crowd." Some Hungarians and Newfoundlanders had joined the agitation, but the majority of the native workers did not take part. Nor did they protest when the Italian ringleaders of the strike, who had waved a red flag and claimed membership in an "Italian union," were dismissed.[26] Ethnic divisions also surfaced in the mines: when Newfoundlanders demanded the same pay as experienced miners but failed to get it; when coal miners in Dominion No. 6 mine complained that longwall positions were unfairly given to outsiders in preference to native workmen; when the miners of Reserve complained that "Old Country" miners had been given all the best places in the mine; and in the separate strike waged by Newfoundlanders against an increase of board for the "big shacks" of the Dominion Coal Company. When the miners of Golden Rule Lodge attempted to secure the closed shop for the PWA in Bridgeport, they encountered serious resistance from the "old countrymen" and Newfoundlanders, in surprising contrast with immediate support from the Italians.[27]

But there was another aspect to the growing prominence of immigrant workers. The immigrant often helped to bring Maritimers in contact with new ideas. At the most modest level, immigrants (or Maritimers returning from a stint outside the region) imported standards for jobs and wages. When Halifax electrical workers, during their strike of 1907, reported themselves to be in touch with "Toronto, Ottawa and Montréal," where standards were far better than in Halifax, they merely confirmed a pervasive regional pattern. Coal miners were fond of comparing their wage rates with those of the western coal miners (not always mentioning in the same analyses the higher western cost of living). The strike of Halifax boilermakers in 1907 provided a classic instance of the unintended consequences of importing workers. Confronted with a determined union anxious to enforce shop rules, the employers turned to England for a foreman and some new workers. John O'Toole of the boilermakers gave as the reason for the strike, "Men being imported from England to break our rules ...." But the English workers, discovering that Halifax rates and standards were lower than those in England, promptly joined the union and fought to bring Halifax standards up to an English level.[28]

It would probably be a mistake to insist too strongly on the divisive consequences of ethnic divisions. Acadian workers from Memramcook and other points in New Brunswick aroused considerable public sympathy when they went on strike in the Halifax rail yards in Richmond in 1912, and they fought side by side with

[26]*Daily Post* (Sydney), 3 March 1903; *Amherst Daily News*, 3 March 1903; *Chronicle*, 3 March 1903; *Herald*, 5 March 1903.
[27]*Maritime Mining Record*, 27 April 1904; *Herald*, 13 June 1906; *Herald*, 2 May 1906; *Maritime Mining Record*, 17 April 1901; *Herald*, 21 March 1907.
[28]*Herald*, 4 July 1907; vol. 295, file 2997, RG 27.

local men. The case of the Scottish girls brought to work for the Christie Fish Company in Dartmouth became a *cause célèbre* in reform circles in Nova Scotia. A reporter for the Halifax *Daily Echo* found that the girls (who were required to gather seaweed, periwinkles, and cord wood, nail boxes, and perform other tasks from 7 a.m. to 6:30 p.m. for $4.00 per week) lived under close supervision and were forced to do without coal. The Chief of Police and the Society for the Prevention of Cruelty managed to win somewhat better conditions for them. Immigrants also became members of the PWA, and Scottish, Belgian and Welsh miners distinguished themselves in the long struggles for the UMW. It would appear that the "vertical" consciousness of some workers, who defended their position in the labour market by erecting barriers to strangers, was of less significance than an emergent "horizontal" consciousness based on a common class position.[29]

Perhaps the most visible sign of the new economy of labour was the pervasive influence of strikebreaking, which represented the forceable breaking down of barriers to a free labour market. The emergence of mass strikebreaking presupposed a certain consolidation of employers, who could blacklist employees, oppose restrictions to the hours of labour, and collaborate in setting prices. Strikebreaking represented a logical outcome of the consolidation of capital, because the massive scale on which it was practised in this period required both companies big enough to have access to large pools of labour, and the active involvement of the state. The recruitment of strikebreakers was not altogether a new phenomenon; at least as early as the 1880s one reads of the importation of men for the purpose of taking strikers' jobs. But there is nothing in the 19th century to compare with the scope of the strikebreaking drive in the early 20th century.[30]

For many unskilled workers, of course, automatic replacement by others in the course of a strike was an unavoidable fact of life. The gas-house employees who went on strike in Saint John in 1905 for a modest wage increase included employees of 31 years standing. The management had no qualms about replacing such old employees by unemployed labourers thoughtfully recruited by the Saint John police department. Countless strikes could be given the epitaph of a Saint John labourers' strike of 1902: strikers fired, "men hired indiscriminately." "Others have taken their places and the work continues without any interruption," was the description of the termination of a railway labourers' strike near Sydney Mines. Such strikers faced the brutal dehumanization of the capitalist labour market.[31]

But the new mass strikebreaking represented an effort to generalize their condition to all the workers and remove the worker's proprietary interest in his job. In this age it was systematized and perfected, not "naturally," but by an active

[29]*Herald*, 30 August 1912; *Daily Echo* (Halifax) 30 April, 2 May 1910; for the admission of immigrants to the PWA, see Minutes of Holdfast Lodge of the PWA, Joggins, 29 August 1896, Dalhousie University Archives.
[30]For an example, see Robert Drummond, *Recollections and Reflections of a Former Trades Union Leader* (n.p. [Stellarton] n.d. [1926]) 39.
[31]*Sun*, 27, 31 May 1905; *Sun*, 22 April 1902; *Daily Post*, 3 May 1902.

process in which the key element was physical force. Systematic, mass replacement of a striking workforce was attempted in 23 strikes. No strata of the working class were protected: the skilled were as jeopardized as the unskilled, and may indeed have sustained heavier losses. Thus the record of strikebreaking includes threats of replacement against Saint John ship carpenters, the replacement of Halifax carpenters by men from outside districts during a strike in the summer of 1903, and the replacement by American strikebreakers of Saint John tailors in 1904. The printers of the two port cities faced tough employers, and Montréal strikebreakers were used against Saint John printers of the *Telegraph* and *Times*; advertisements for strikebreakers were inserted in newspapers as far away as London and Manchester. Fredericton plumbers were replaced with men imported from Québec, Saint John machinists by renegade craftsmen from Amherst, and Halifax plumbers by English plumbers who came to the city via Montréal.[32] Workers in the mills and factories suffered the same fate. Employers were generally attracted to recruitment of foreign or Québécois workers, because such men would be desperate enough to agree and because they could not easily communicate with the strikers. This tactic was not foolproof. Italian strikebreakers brought in to break the Sydney steel strike in 1904 were met at the gates by Italian members of the PWA. Given the past record of the Sydney Italians, who earlier had posted notices that anyone going to work would be killed, one imagines many spirited conversations at the entrance. The management of the pulp mill in St. George, New Brunswick enjoyed greater success in recruiting strikebreakers ("anything and everything ... that might pass for a man," wrote the spokesman for the union), particularly from Weymouth, Nova Scotia.[33]

Throughout the region strikebreaking threatened militant workers and brought home the lessons of the new labour market. But the coalfields and the docks were in a league by themselves. Strikebreaking on the waterfront was facilitated by the presence of crew members, who could be coerced or cajoled into doing the work of the longshoremen themselves. Longshoremen in Saint John in 1905 derived a certain amount of enjoyment from watching the awkward efforts of crew members unloading a valuable cargo of bricks:

The Longshoremen who were on the McLeod wharf yesterday morning when the crew of the Alcides were trying to get some bricks unloaded were much amused when one after another the contents of three tubs were emptied into the harbor, owing to the awkward manipulation of the unloading apparatus. These bricks were worth seven cents apiece, and about forty-five dollars' worth went over the side of the vessel. The longshoremen are talking of making information against these men for throwing refuse into the harbor.

[32]*Sun*, 17 March 1902; *Labour Gazette*, August 1903, 106; *Sun*, 24 May 1904; *Sun*, 6, 9 April 1908; vol. 299, file 3507, RG 27; *Standard*, 28 October 1912; *Chronicle*, 27 June 1914 and vol. 303, file 14 (17) RG 27.
[33]*Herald*, 4 June 1904, *Chronicle*, 2 March 1903; Christopher Wren to F.A. Acland, 9 September 1912, vol. 298, file 3341, RG 27, and *Standard*, 8 June 1911.

This was a light-hearted moment in an otherwise difficult war. Like all other employers, the steamship lines could exploit ethnic divisions in strikes on the waterfront (although Halifax blacks refused to play along in 1902 and Italians were to prove difficult in Saint John in 1905). But they enjoyed additional advantages thanks to the integration of the Canadian transportation system, which allowed them easy access to the vast casual labour market of Montréal. This was the key factor in the smashing of the Saint John strike in 1905. The Shipping Federation, with its headquarters in Montréal, used the services of The General Labor Company, Limited, a professional strikebreaking outfit, and this company recruited men for a period of two weeks or longer. Since the negotiations were generally carried out in English, many of the foreigners were not fully aware of the function they were really performing. The Saint John longshoremen were highly creative in their response, putting up many of the strikebreakers as guests and encouraging many others to quit work, but the strikebreaking tactic ultimately did succeed in defeating them.[34]

The coalfields provided the most unforgettable instances of the new economy of labour. There was no precedent for the importation of 3,000 strikebreakers into Cape Breton and several hundred into Springhill. Once again Montréal-based companies secured the services of a strikebreaking outfit, this time the Reliance Labor Exchange, housed, appropriately enough, on St. James Street. Once again the employers advertised far and wide for men, and company recruiting agents scoured Newfoundland. One was unwise enough to look for recruits in Cumberland County, and was relieved of 25 strikebreakers in Amherst by UMW sympathizers and encouraged to leave Springhill by a crowd of between 200 and 300 men. Further problems were presented by English miners who balked at living in prison conditions behind the barbed-wire fences provided for the strikebreakers in Cape Breton. The general manager at Springhill, J.R. Cowans, had rhapsodized about the wonderful future his company would face if only he could get rid of his rebellious workers and replace them with Europeans or Chinese; his strikebreakers, who arrived in 1910, proved to be disappointingly preoccupied with fighting among themselves.[35]

Strikebreaking involved such difficulties and problems, and it was a tactic guaranteed to escalate labour disputes into miniature civil wars. Like the Saint John longshoremen, the Cape Breton miners commented on the shoddy work of the men who had replaced them. When Dan McDougall, president of the United Mine Workers of America in Nova Scotia, was asked how he thought the imported

[34]For a discussion of the 19th-century pattern, see Judith Fingard, "The Decline of the Sailor as a Ship Labourer in 19th Century Timber Ports," *Labour/Le Travailleur*, 2 (1977) 35-53; *Sun*, 25 November 1905; *Herald*, 3 April 1902; *Sun*, 29 November 1905; *Sun*, 24, 25 November 1905.
[35]*Herald*, 13 July 1909; *Herald*, 27 July 1909; *Herald*, 18 August 1909; *Herald*, 4 July 1909; *Sun*, 10 December 1909 and *Herald*, 21 April 1910. For disturbances among the strikebreakers, resulting in the death of one man, see Peter Owen Carroll, *Life and Adventures of Detective Peter Owen Carroll* (n.p., n.d. [c.1924]) 68.

workmen compared with the striking miners, he replied, "I don't consider them in the same class with our men, either physically or morally. The men on strike, by the company's own admission, comprise the pick of skilled Cape Breton miners, and it is practically impossible to duplicate them anywhere." Such men would fight strikebreakers with determination. One report from Cape Breton in 1909 dramatized the battle for control over the labour market:

There is a steady tug of war between the Dominion Coal Company and the U.M.W. as to who is to control the new-comers looking for work. Tonight the U.M.W. rounded up one hundred men for a Moncton contractor and shipped them off to Sydney in a special car. The car had just left the big town when a special train from Louisburg came in over the company's road with over one hundred men who are ready to work at daylight. The U.M.W. pickets claim that they will have half of these by tomorrow night and it is only a matter of time until they get the others. U.M.W. pickets are stationed at all points and it is practically impossible for a stranger to enter town without being held up, and once it is learned he is looking for work the U.M.W. and the company representatives both endeavour to get control of him and it is a case of the best men winning.

Besides such mass mobilization in the streets, the UMW sent representatives to Newfoundland to counteract the recruiting efforts of the company and published advertisements (later the subject of criminal proceedings) in the Montréal French-language press. J.B. McLachlan of the UMW even wrote to Samuel Gompers of the American Federation of Labor to persuade him to write to the leaders of Belgian labour to stop strikebreakers from leaving that country.[36]

Workers also appealed to the law. Saint John printers appealed to the Alien Labour Act, which had been passed in 1897 in retaliation against American alien labour legislation. The city's longshoremen attempted to take advantage of the labour licensing system which imposed a tax of $7.50 on outsiders who came to the city to work. Had this embodiment of local protectionism served their purposes, mass strikebreaking would have been expensive indeed. In the 1907 longshore-men's strike, however, the shipping companies managed to have their investment in the labour licences returned. Against the efforts of the Canadian Shipping Federation, the Trades and Labour Council and the *Eastern Labor News* continued to fight for the licensing system, seeing in it an element of protection against the new labour economy, but that system had clearly failed to protect the longshoremen from the army of strikebreakers the shipping companies held in reserve. Similarly, Halifax electrical workers cited municipal bylaws governing the certification of wiremen, and plumbers reported to the Board of Health those strikebreakers lacking proper qualifications. There were really very few laws, however, which could stand

[36]*Herald*, 28 March 1910; *Herald*, 9 July 1909; for attempts to stop Belgian strikebreaking, see Gompers to Bergmans, 30 March, 1 April 1910, Gompers to J.B. McLachlan, 1 April 1910, National Union Files, Reel No. 7, AFL-CIO Library, Washington, D.C.

against mass strikebreaking, and the trend of legislation was running strongly in the other direction.[37]

Strikebreaking was very successful, and all the workers' efforts to combat it failed. From the pacific tactics of the PWA in the 1904 steel strike, during which union sentinels were posted in Truro, Halifax, Saint John and other points to watch stations and report upon incoming labourers,[38] to the legal challenges mounted by the Saint John longshoremen and the Halifax craftsmen, the record of failure was consistent. Strikebreakers were given the protection of the militia and police, and in the four great strikes dominated by hundreds of strikebreakers, nothing could match the combined force of capital and the armed servants of the state.

Monopoly capitalism entailed far-reaching changes in the labour market, but it also entailed a dramatic transformation of the labour process. Tables 3 and 4 have already suggested the broad range of issues which sparked strikes, and established that by both liberal and conservative measures, strikes over questions of job control were central to the pattern as a whole. Such "control" struggles took place in the context of dynamic new philosophies of work, which might broadly be subsumed under the heading "scientific management."[39] As a specific ideology and practice associated with F.W. Taylor and his disciples, scientific management had very limited relevance to the Maritimes, where so many workers were employed in such unsuitable industries as longshore and coalmining. But taken in its broadest sense, scientific management — a systematic effort to obtain greater productivity from workers by exerting greater managerial discipline — had great relevance to the region, and its impact can be seen in many of the workers' struggles. We can explore the struggle for control more fully by examining several crucial dimensions of such control struggles, particularly hiring, discharge, supervision, and production techniques, as well as more general issues of control.

The ability of workers to influence the labour market through placing limits on hiring was possibly the most crucial. In the 19th century the vital battleground for this kind of struggle was the enforcement of apprenticeship rules. Although the painters of Saint John were able to defend apprenticeship traditions in 1903, one has the distinct impression that apprenticeship had long since ceased to be an effective safeguard against the dilution of the crafts. The experience of the moulders of Sackville is instructive. The moulders of the Fawcett Foundry failed to win any of their demands regarding shop management, and their employer filled the shop

[37]*Sun*, 18 July 1908; *Sun*, 9 January 1902, 29 July 1904, 26 December 1906, 10, 20 February 1908; *Sun*, 4 December 1907; *Eastern Labor News*, 12 August 1911, 26 October 1912; *Eastern Labor News*, 27 May, 28 October 1911; *Herald*, 5 July 1907.

[38]*Herald*, 4 June 1904.

[39]For discussions of scientific management, see Harry Braverman, *Labor and Monopoly Capital: The Degradation of Work in the Twentieth Century* (New York 1974), and Richard Edwards, *Contested Terrain: The Transformation of the Workplace in the Twentieth Century* (New York 1978), among many other titles. Michael Burawoy provides an exciting analysis of the literature concerning the workplace in "Towards a Marxist Theory of the Labour Process: Braverman and Beyond," *Politics & Society*, VIII (1978), 247-312.

with apprentices. On the other hand, coal miners managed to enforce a form of apprenticeship through safety legislation which imposed a waiting period on new miners before they could advance "to the picks" and become fully-fledged miners. They were not able, however, to impose effective legal restrictions upon the new machine runners who played an important role in the Cape Breton mines.[40]

A second sort of control over entry to the labour market was the demand for union recognition and the related (but not identical) insistence upon the exclusive employment of union members (the "closed shop"). The craftsmen of the Maritimes were rather surprisingly not prone to press closed-shop demands. Such strikes were mounted by Truro painters in 1904, Saint John painters in 1905, and the Halifax building trades in 1914 (in sympathy with plumbers faced with strikebreakers), but with mixed results. The most dramatic failure occurred in the Halifax printing trades, when the composing room staff of the Halifax *Chronicle* and *Echo*, from the foreman to the boys, went on strike to protest the employment of a non-union machinist on their monolines. This strike failed, as did an attempt by Saint John carpenters to enforce the city-wide closed shop in 1907. This record seems to correspond with other evidence suggesting a weakening of the craftsmen's position in the region during this period.[41]

By contrast, both longshoremen and coal miners made significant advances. In 1907, Halifax longshoremen scored a signal victory when they went on strike to lend some weight to a "distinct understanding" that non-union men were not to be employed. Their success in this strike marked the culmination of a sporadic campaign to control hiring that went back to 1884. The coal miners in the PWA staged an impressive province-wide struggle for the closed shop from 1905-1907 — a campaign which strengthened the union immeasurably after its defeat in Sydney in 1904. In Westville, for example, the coal miners simply posted notices about the works to the effect that they would not work with non-union men after 5 November 1906. As a result of the notice, 100 non-union men joined Ladysmith Lodge of the PWA. A similar struggle in Chignecto (which began as a wage dispute but escalated into a demand for the closed shop and union recognition) forced the resignation of the general manager, James Baird.[42]

Secondly, workers defended their rights to job control by limiting management's right to dismiss employees. Some of these strikes were poignant reminders of the helplessness of many organized and unskilled workers in the face of arbitrary employers. The boys who worked at the Victoria Bowling Alley in Saint John went

[40]*Sun*, 23 April 1903; *Amherst Daily News*, 3 May 1902; *Herald*, 12 July 1902. For an analysis of the weakening of the miners' resistance to the employment of machine runners without the training period, see Donald Macleod, "Miners, Mining Men and Mining Reform: Changing the Technology of Nova Scotian Gold Mines and Collieries, 1850-1910," PhD thesis, University of Toronto, 1981, 538-45.

[41]*Herald*, 19 July 1904; *Sun*, 1 June 1905; vol. 303, file 14 (28) RG 27; *Sun*, 6 August 1902; *Sun*, 28 March 1907 and vol. 294, file 2838, RG 27.

[42]*Herald*, 7 August 1907; vol. 295, file 2989, RG 27; *Herald*, 5, 12 February 1907; *Herald*, 7 November 1906; *Herald*, 11 April 1906.

on strike to protest the dismissal of another boy who had had the misfortune to get sick. About 300 workers at the Nova Scotia Car Works in Halifax went on strike in 1911 after the management fired their unofficial representative, who had tried to interview the employer about new rules being enforced by the company. Gold miners at the Boston-Richardson mine in Goldboro were incensed when the management fired miners who had had the temerity to take time off to vote in an election, but the workers were not reinstated. In such situations, the unorganized workers were at the mercy of the employers.[43]

Once again, the heartland of control lay in the coalfields, the antithesis of the authoritarian world of the unskilled labourer. It seemed, to weary newspaper editors and irate mine managers, that the coal miners would protest if anyone was ever discharged from a coal mine. There was criticism of the miners of Westville, for example, who tied up their mine from 3 April to 25 April 1905 over a discharge of a man accused of improperly grooming the horses. Should a major industry be tied up by so trivial an issue? But for the miners the issue concerned not only whether the hostler involved should be fired but whether the union could claim him as a member. As the men's committee explained its position: "The company say there must be discipline, the men say granted, but let it be tempered with mercy." The employee was reinstated.[44] So often in the coal mines of this period we find the clash of two irreconcilable rights, the right to independence and work, and the right to discipline and fire. As the press noted with regard to a strike of boys in Springhill in 1906, "With the company it is a question of regulation, and with the boys it is a question of upholding the right of a person to keep his own job if he so desires provided there is no breach of discipline." But where did the boundaries of just discipline lie? In 1906, according to the coal boys of Springhill, they did not enclose such vital issues as dismissal or the allocation of work within the mine. In November of that year they went on strike because a trip runner formerly on the 2,600-foot level was moved up to the 3,200-foot level, and the runner from the latter level placed at inferior employment. This was considered unjust. They also insisted on the reinstatement of a loader who had been dismissed for loading boxes without the proper weight. The strike ended in a compromise which suited the boys, and prompted the general manager to comment, "We own the works, we pay the wages: we have some right to say where and how our employees shall work." These strikes by the lowliest workers of the mine suggest the industrial freedom its other workers must have enjoyed, in marked contrast to the harsh discipline of so many factories and construction sites.[45]

[43] *Eastern Labor News*, 5 February 1910; *Eastern Labour News*, 9 September 1911; *Evening Mail* (Halifax), 19, 22, 25 March 1904.
[44] *Herald*, 10, 12, 25 April 1905.
[45] *Herald*, 29, 30 November 1906; see also *Amherst Daily News*, 7 December 1906; and *Herald*, 15 December 1906.

The question of supervision surfaces with frequency in the record of the strikes. The selection of foremen was generally conceded to be the exclusive prerogative of management, and only in the case of the printers and a few very minor officials in the coal mines were supervisors included within the union. But workers occasionally influenced the selection process. The Intercolonial trackmen of Saint John and district forced the resignation of their sub-foreman as an act of solidarity with their brothers on the Canadian Pacific system. This sub-foreman had worked as a strikebreaker during a recent strike, and the unionized trackmen described his appointment as an insult. There was something of a tradition of this in Charlotte County. Workers in Milltown appealed to an entrenched local hostility to the foreign owners of the cotton factory when they fought the selection of a new foreman in 1902. Since the arrival of the new foreman, an American, a number of local overseers had been discharged and their places filled with newcomers from other mills. The community and employees were outraged. The community felt that the company was betraying an informal agreement that it would give preference in promotion to citizens of Milltown, an offence which seemed particularly heinous in light of the large tax concessions made to the company. Workers urged that the Alien Labour Law be applied against the "small army" of men and women who worked in the New Brunswick mill from Calais, Maine. The upshot of this agitation was the resignation of the "Arrogant Yankee Cotton Mill Superintendent" and his replacement by a native of Milltown, whose elevation was said to have given "very general satisfaction among all classes." Two months later, however, weavers at the same mill went on strike against the dismissal of a popular overseer in the weave room, which suggests the debate over foremanship had not been completely resolved. Even in Ganong's candy factory in St. Stephen, that fortress of paternalism, women workers fought against the appointment of an unpopular supervisor.[46]

Workers throughout the region fought a surprising number of strikes against the dismissal of popular foremen, and this suggests the pivotal (and ambiguous) role the foreman was asked to play in the transformation of work. Sydney machinists went on strike on behalf of a foreman who had merely had a fistfight with the superintendent. Cotton factory workers in Saint John, car workers in Amherst, and coal drivers in Glace Bay all fought strikes on this issue. Workers in fact did influence the foremen whose day-to-day supervision placed them on the front lines of any transformation of work. The way in which supervision was carried out was often cited as an issue in strikes. Halifax boilermakers cited the constant "nagging" of supervisors in the Halifax Graving Dock Company as one of the primary reasons for the strike of 1907; they were continually being told to hurry up and hated what they called the "continual fault-finding" with their work. The pipefitters in the employ of the Nova Scotia Steel and Coal Company at Sydney Mines went on strike for overtime on Sundays, but they cited the quality of supervision as an important

[46]*Sun*, 11 September 1901; *Sun*, 12 January, 9 February, 14 March 1903; *St. Croix Courier*, 13 April 1911.

contributing factor. "The men also claim that there were too many bosses over them, the majority of whom did not understand their business," noted the Sydney *Daily Post*. The coal mines provided the classic location for such foremanship struggles. Coal mines could be thrown into an uproar by an official who disregarded long-standing traditions or treated colliers in an offensive manner. A strike at Dominion No. 2 in Glace Bay was caused by the peremptory decision to change the basis on which drivers had been paid, a case, noted the *Herald* correspondent, "of dissatis-faction among employees that on the appointment of a new official, sweeping changes may be looked for, and which are generally so distasteful to them as to result in a strike ...." Similarly, the abrasiveness and lack of courtesy of supervisory staff at the Springhill mines were a crucial factor in the town's many labour battles.[47]

Often the workers' dissatisfaction with working conditions crystallized in attacks upon individual foremen, and the more general debate over the nature of work was thereby overshadowed. Yet there were such general debates. While no major figure in the Maritimes came forth to advocate a fully-fledged programme of scientific management, the creation of Dominion Coal in 1893 was based on the assumption that local coal producers would attain American standards of efficiency. Local mining men, faced with the pressures of high demand and growing concen-tration in their industry, had every incentive to reduce their costs of production and increase productivity. While they could turn to mining machines and greater efficiency in the bankhead, most of the classic solutions of scientific management theory were wholly inappropriate for the mining environment. Many of the strug-gles over authority in the workplace were related to "scientific management," and stemmed from a largely frustrated attempt to make the mines into efficient facto-ries.[48] In Springhill, for instance, coal miners and management fought each other implacably over such issues as the proper weight of a box, how much the company should penalize workers for loading stone in the boxes, whether the amount of coal produced by the worker should be measured at the top of the chute or on the surface — all issues which detailed investigation shows were connected with a broadly-conceived modernization programme. Nobody outside the coal mines really grasped why the town was so frequently engulfed in conflicts over such arcane issues, but both labour and capital realized their importance for the miners' wages and the management's development programme. When labour legislation required

[47] *Herald*, 23 October 1902; *Globe*, 4 December 1902; *Amherst Daily News*, 14 January 1904 and *Herald*, 15 January 1904; *Maritime Mining Record*, 18 June 1902; *Herald*, 24 October 1907; *Herald*, 23 September 1905 and *Daily Post*, 21 September 1905; *Herald*, 11 February 1904; *Herald*, 17 June 1905. The question of foremanship is discussed effectively in Joseph Melling, "'Non-Commissioned Officers': British Employers and Their Supervisory Work-ers, 1880-1920," *Social History*, V (May 1980) 183-221.

[48] See Hugh Archbald, *The Four Hour Day in Coal* (New York 1922), Carter Goodrich, *The Miner's Freedom: A Study in the Working Life of a Changing Industry* (Boston 1925), and Keith Dix, *Work Relations in the Coal Industry: The Hand-Loading Era, 1880-1930* (Morgantown, W. Va. 1977).

the intervention of third parties, the imbroglio was complete — mystified judges were hardly able to catch up on the intricacies of coal mining in a few days. Coal miners knew the mining context inside out, and nothing could be more comprehensive than their critiques of past mismanagement and their programmes for reform. A good example is provided by the coal miners of Inverness, who outside the heroic years of 1909-11 were relatively quiet. Yet pushed into a strike by the institution of a new dockage system in 1906, they produced an impressive ten-point programme for the reform of their mine, which included new rates for track-laying, pushing boxes, shovelling down coal in heads and balances, brushing roof, and shot-firing. It was a "bread-and-butter" strike, but the mine management correctly interpreted it as an attempt to tell them how they should run the mine.[49]

The coal miners were in the vanguard of such general assaults on managerial authority. Much of this had to do with the particular circumstances of their work. Safety strikes loomed far larger in the coal mines than elsewhere. Coal miners were convinced that their own safety standards were at least as rigorous as those of the state or management. The miners of Chignecto, for example, refused to go down into their pit unless the company agreed to send down their picks together in the morning instead of leaving it up to each man to take down his own. Middle-class commentators thought this was a prime example of mindless militancy, the demand being "so trivial ... that outsiders cannot believe a settlement will be long delayed." Such comments reflected ignorance of mining conditions in Cumberland, where steeply-pitching coal seams made carrying picks a tricky and sometimes even fatal business. The miners of Joggins were equally stubborn in waiting to re-enter their mine until they were guaranteed that a recent fire had been extinguished, and those of Port Morien in refusing to go back unless ventilation was improved. Since the miners had a written code of safety regulations and a secure trade union, they could more often wage struggles for safety that lay beyond the reach of other workers — who were left struggling, with some effect, for workmen's compensation and factory inspection.[50]

Scientific management is a sub-text of the history of strikes in this period, and rarely surfaces explicitly, either in resistance to new time-keeping measures or mechanization. Workmen at Cushing's Mill at Union Point fought against a new time-marking machine in 1903, principally because it caused such crowding and crushing of men that the "strong got ahead of the weak"; it was noted that "dislike of the scheme has grown intense." J.B. Snowball told his mill workers in Chatham that they could easily be replaced by a new carrier system, and hod men were replaced with a steam carrier in a Saint John dispute in 1907. Far more common were new methods of calculating wages which entailed speeding up the performance of work. A classic instance of this was the strike at the Hartt Boot and Shoe Company in Fredericton, sparked by the attempt of an American manager to

[49]*Chronicle*, 3 December 1903; *Amherst Daily News*, 2, 3 December 1903; *Sun*, 4, 7 December 1903 detail one such Springhill dispute; *Herald*, 19 March 1906.
[50]*Herald*, 14 January 1904; *Herald*, 1 February 1904; *Chronicle*, 24 January 1903.

introduce piece work for the cutters. It appears that this "reform" was successfully resisted. A new bonus system was the cause of a strike at Pender's nail factory in 1911, and nailworkers also protested the adoption of the system at the Maritime Nail Works in 1914.[51] Other workers were incensed by production speed-ups, which often contradicted well-established notions of "a fair day's work." In Chatham workers refused to work in gangs of six instead of seven, arguing that "the work is heavy enough as it is with seven." Perhaps the most interesting struggle against intensified working schedules — and incidentally the one documented case of a "strike on the job" in this period — comes from the workers of a cotton factory in Saint John:

The weavers state that they are paid by the piece, or cut, as it is technically called, getting from 37 to 45 cents per cut. A cut, in the past, was sixty yards, and on this basis the men were paid. Some time ago the manager of the mill increased the cut to sixty-five yards, and as no action was taken by the men, a further increase of five yards was made more recently. The weavers state that they were thus expected to make seventy yards of cloth for the same money as they had previously received for sixty yards ... They say that they objected to this increase in the length of the cut, and complained, but as no remedy was provided, they of their own accord cut the cloth at the old sixty yard mark. This was discovered, and the men were warned to desist.

The strike resulting from this conflict lasted only one hour, but it was obviously part of a protracted struggle through which the workers had sabotaged the company's speeding up of production.[52]

We find a general attempt to change old rhythms of work, to speed things up and get more effort from workers. Steelworkers in Sydney, ferry engineers in Dartmouth, coal miners everywhere suggested that this was the new reality they faced. In a rare attempt to spell out the general implications of this question, a commentary on a strike of Springhill coal boys against dockage linked this very particular struggle to more general debates over the intensity of labour: "The men, and many of the most thoughtful ones too, consider that a workman should do a fair day's work and make a fair day's pay, but when he works early and late, and slaves between to produce big pay, they consider him unreasonable, and an enemy to his fellows, because he has created conditions which an average steady worker, who properly respects the constitution God has given him, cannot produce the amount he should receive."[53]

David Montgomery has observed that the struggles waged by workers in the United States in the early 20th century to establish collective control over their

[51]*Globe*, 6 March 1903; vol. 294, file 2913, RG 27; *Labour Gazette*, VII (1905), 951; *Daily Gleaner*, 13, 31 May 1909; *North Shore Leader* (Newcastle), 4 June 1909; vol. 298, file 3436 and vol. 303, file 14 (36) RG 27; *Sun*, 28 May 1907 (Chatham).
[52]*Sun*, 7, 8 March 1905.
[53]*Chronicle*, 2 October 1903; *Evening Mail*, 24 June 1908; *Amherst Daily News*, 29 March 1901; *Herald*, 4 July 1906.

conditions of work were less richly rewarded in their long-term effects than such general campaigns as that for the eight-hour day. Workplace issues were hard to generalize. Only in some of the coal strikes did workers take their demands for workplace reforms and transform these into demands for workers' control of industry. Such writers as Carter Goodrich have recognized the distinction between "negative" responses to new systems of work and "positive" demands for general workers' control.[54] Most of the control struggles of this period were defensive. Many were sparked by the workers' dislike of bad manners, highhanded autocracy and favouritism. Among the many items on the indictment brought against J.R. Cowans of Springhill by his workmen were his absolute lack of tact and his inability to "receive a committee of men in a gentlemanly manner." As one Halifax bricklayer explained in a strike for the eight-hour day: "What we object to ... is the autocratic way in which the bosses grant the eight-hour day when they like and refuse to grant it when they don't like." There was a general social critique in such remarks. As the miners of Springhill argued: "The manager in charge at Springhill cannot appreciate that a man working in his mines at Springhill is STILL A MAN, and after 18 years of experience has not yet learned that the miners are rational, intelligent, human beings, with more than ordinary amount of general information, and education, and while they are amenable to reason, will not be dogged or driven." "It's not money they want," James Pender wrote of his militant workers in 1911, "they want to browbeat us, in other words, want to run the show." Not many employers would have shared his alarm, but in the coalfields some would have agreed with him. Struggles for job controls, if conducted in a certain way and in a disciplined manner, did carry the risk of developing into battles for workers' control. As one Springhill miner urged in 1909, the struggle for the workplace could be expanded into a critique of all autocracy: "[A] time comes in the life of nations, it comes in the life of communities, and in the life of organizations when THEY CANNOT ENDURE ANY LONGER THE IMPOSITIONS FORCED ON THEM BY AN AUTOCRATIC AND OVERBEARING SPIRIT."[55]

The questions remain, what difference did the strikes of 1901-1914 really make to the evolution of regional society? Did they really represent a moment of possibility for critics of capitalism? Why was the system able to contain them? What do they tell us about the working class of the region and the level of working-class consciousness?

There can be no doubt that workers struggled against heavy odds and suffered crushing defeats. The coal miners, after nearly two years and expenditures nearing a million dollars, were denied the union of their choice and returned to work under humiliating conditions. Millmen in Saint John and moulders in Moncton and Sackville had suffered reverses. No strong regional labour movement emerged and

[54]Montgomery, "New unionism," 98; Carter Goodrich, *The Frontier of Control: A Study in British Workshop Politics* (London 1975 [1920]), 258.
[55]*Herald*, 2 November 1909; *Herald*, 6 May 1908; *Herald*, 22 August 1907; vol. 298, file 3436, RG 27; *Herald*, 17 August 1909.

workers were still without political representation. If the strike movement could be seen as a social challenge, this challenge was contained.

But we need to examine more closely the way in which this containment took place. This means looking more closely at the place of politics, and at the measures taken by the state. It must be remembered that workers enjoyed certain natural advantages in struggles with capital. A crowd of strikers could be assembled in a picket line that could stop production; sympathizers could make life intolerable for strikebreakers; workers could go on strike without warning to obtain redress for their grievances — which in many industrial contexts, particularly coal mining, meant that the companies either gave in or ran the risk of losing their investment. Nothing had happened in the labour process which had destroyed many workers' capacity for autonomous action. All of these considerations lead us to the state as the crucial new force which contained labour's challenge to capital.

The strike was frequently represented as a threat to public order and civilization itself, but violence was extremely rare and confined to very particular circumstances. Of the 22 strikes which were reported to involve some physical force (fist-fights, stone-throwing, riots), 15 involved foreign workers. No one was killed as a direct consequence of labour disputes, which suggests the generally peaceful character of strikes in the region as compared with many parts of the United States. The Saint John *Sun* "explained" the foreigners' violence by referring to the "passionate and unreflecting races from southern and southeastern Europe," but it is more plausibly viewed as the logical response of isolated construction workers, who saw forceable action as the only means of negotiating with contractors. "Collective bargaining by riot," to use E.J. Hobsbawm's useful phrase, was a predictable consequence of their conditions of employment.[56] At Hubbard's Cove in 1902, Italians employed on the Halifax and South Western Railway surrounded the house occupied by the timekeeper and started to burn it down, but were discouraged by their foreman. Later the same day the workers, armed with revolvers and axes, approached the house and began to demolish it. Once they obtained the timekeeper's books and confirmed their suspicion that they had been cheated of their wages, they dispersed, having been promised the wages due them. New Brunswick rang with large disturbances mounted by railway labourers in this period. Near Moncton, Italian, Austrian and Bulgarian workers demanded a wage increase. They paraded behind a "huge red flag," carrying clubs and firearms. They marched to the offices of the Grand Trunk Pacific in Moncton, where three were arrested. More than 800 Italians near Campbellton mounted a similar protest, also flourishing weapons and a red flag. Railway labourers working near Windsor Junction sent their foreman to hospital in 1904, and Hungarians labouring at the steel mill demolished the residence of a strikebreaker.[57] Apart from these construc-

[56]*Sun*, 3 June 1904; E.J. Hobsbawm, "The Machine Breakers," in *Labouring Men: Studies in the History of Labour* (London 1974), 16.
[57]*Herald*, 24, 29 December 1902; *Sun*, 3, 4 August 1908, and *Amherst Daily News*, 5 August 1908; *Sun*, 12 August 1908; *Herald*, 9 August 1904; *Herald* and *Sun*, 3 May 1904.

tion disturbances, so reminiscent of the 19th century, disorder was found in the two major tramway strikes in Halifax (1913) and Saint John (1914), the Sydney steel strike of 1904, and the three large strikes in the coalfields in 1909-11. In Cape Breton in 1910 company police and UMW supporters clashed, shots were fired, and two men were injured. Ten arrests were made, five on a charge of unlawful assembly and five for carrying concealed weapons. The front porch of Robert Simpson, manager at Reserve Mines, was blown up; responsibility for this act was never fixed. There were also clashes between strikebreakers and strikers in Springhill.[58]

Condensed in this way, it may appear that the record of strikes was highly violent, but given the much larger number of peaceful strikes, the absence of fatalities, and the presence of armies of detectives and militia, one is left wondering why so few disturbances occurred. Part of the reason appears to have been labour's consistent policy of non-violent protest. The PWA in 1904, facing the mass mobilization of Sydney steelworkers, hastened to reassure Nova Scotians that the strike would bear no resemblance to strikes in Europe and the United States, where "lawlessness, growing out of ignorance and vindictive spite, reign supreme." When non-unionized Italians attacked a policeman, the PWA appointed a committee to assist the city police in maintaining order among the immigrants living near the steel plant. The union dramatized its devotion to law and order by giving the militia hearty cheers on its return to Halifax, and "soldiers just as heartily returned the cheers." The PWA was pleased to announce that it had done "all they could to save the country the disgrace of having the riot act read," and the *Herald*, drawing the intended moral, remarked that "Such behavior is certainly not that of men imbued with the spirit of lawlessness and brute force."[59]

For a strike lasting 22 months and broken with troops and strikebreakers, the great Springhill strike of 1909-11 was a triumph of law and order. The strikers knew the propaganda value the company would extract from a show of disorder. (Four years earlier J.R. Cowans had described the beginning days of a strike as an "orgy" and the "biggest drunk ever witnessed in Springhill," although nobody else seems to have noticed any disturbance.) The UMW collaborated with the mayor to protect the town against fire, and urged members not to give the company "a point against them, but still maintain the same silent and determined struggle they have carried through for over a year." Victory would come only through endurance, patience and self-control. The records of the local UMW document the union's preoccupation with keeping the peace.[60]

The labour movement advocated non-violent and passive strikes. But both the state and capital championed far more aggressive and forceful approaches. Troops,

[58]*Herald*, 11 January 1910; *Herald*, 17, 28 July 1909; *Sun*, 1 March 1910.
[59]*Herald*, 28 June 1904; *Sun*, 16 June 1904; *Herald*, 12 July 1904.
[60]*Herald*, 21 June 1905; *Herald*, 12 August 1910; minutes of UMW Local Union 469, Springhill, entry for 6 January 1910, Angus L. Macdonald Library, St. Francis Xavier University, Antigonish, indicates the miners' active interest in suppressing drinking and disorder.

detectives, spies, special constables: on a scale never before imagined, these were the *dramatis personae* of these years. Employers used spies in Halifax in 1907 during a longshoremen's strike, and detectives and company police were every-where in the coalfields. It was difficult to tell where the public police stopped and capital's private army began. Saint John police refused to arrest strikebreakers who attacked strikers in 1905, and even helped to recruit strikebreakers on another occasion. Such modest efforts paled beside the great show of force brought to bear upon the strikers in the coalfields. Those who watched the scene thought instinc-tively in military metaphors, as we find in one sensitive portrait of Glace Bay's deserted company houses:

When a man is evicted from his house by the Dominion Coal company, because he has refused to work, no time is lost by the officials in putting their mark upon the empty dwelling. White boards are nailed tightly over the glass. No pains are taken to do the job artistically. All that is wanted is to make the job secure. So all over town are seen those windowless houses, not the sign of martial encounters, but the mark of an industrial struggle unparalleled in the determination of the contending armies to fight to a finish and which, tho' bloodless, is no less fierce than if the march of warlike men were seen and the roar of artillery heard.

Nobody could quite understand why the troops had been brought in, nor why they came with such fire-power. Nearly a quarter of Canada's fighting men were in Cape Breton by July 1909. Puzzled citizens wondered at the necessity of a "force which is of greater dimensions than many a punitive expedition against African tribes," combined with seven or eight hundred special constables. If all this were primarily an "aid to the civil power," it seemed odd that the representatives of civil power most concerned, the mayors of Springhill and Glace Bay, were against the coming of the troops.[61]

The troops were not required to preserve public order, but they were needed if the strikebreakers were to continue to keep the mines open. They were the embodi-ment of the new economy of labour, the free labour market carrying a gun. The state, through violence, safeguarded the achievement of the new consolidated economy of labour and prevented workers from erecting effective barriers against it. It also moved decisively to change the terms of power within the workplace.

Trade unions of this period enjoyed few formal rights, and many doubts existed as to what they could or could not do. Incorporation of trade unions, legislation on arbitration, and their daily participation in local communities, all provided trade

[61]John Bell, ed., "On The Waterfront: A Glimpse into Company Espionage," *Bulletin of the Committee on Canadian Labour History*, I (1976), 8-9, documents the use of spies in Halifax; *Sun*, 28 November 1905; *Herald*, 20 October 1909; *Herald*, 14 July 1909. For the use of local spies at Acadia Coal, Westville, see John Higston to C. Evans, 30 May 1913, RG 21, series "A," vol. 39, No. 38, PANS. The company was kept abreast of developments within the UMW by the Thiel Detective Agency. For a general interpretation, see Desmond Morton, "Aid to the Civil Power: The Canadian Militia in Support of Social Order," *Canadian Historical Review*, LI (1970), 407-25.

unionists with a certain legitimacy, but without many guaranteed legal rights. The dominant trait of Canadian labour law was an emphasis on "fire-fighting," that is, asserting "the public interest" strictly at the point of actual or apprehended conflict (and not at the point of maintaining trade-union rights in bargaining nor making sure the bargain was kept once arrived at). The Industrial Disputes Investigation Act (1907), the most important piece of federal legislation in this period, was intended to operate in utilities, railroads and coal mines, and required compulsory investigation before a strike or lockout began. The terms of employment would be frozen, and an attempt to reach an agreement was to be made by a conciliation board; if this didn't work, the board's report became public and both workers and employers were restored to their common-law rights and duties. No protection was given to unions, and even a collective agreement reached under the Act had no status in law.[62]

The IDIA is often seen as a fairly mild act, which may even have narrowed the possible scope of state intervention by hiving off a particular sector of the economy for special treatment. From the point of view of the Maritimes, however, the IDIA appears to have been a major revolution in the region's most militant workplaces, the waterfronts and the coal mines. The Act must be placed within the context of the state's use of massive displays of force to crush strikes. The Act provided no guarantees that employees would not be dismissed before or after the period of compulsory investigation, and thus ensured that employees could be victimized with impunity. Especially in the coal mines, the results were dramatic: miners could no longer conduct their swift strikes on control issues, which had won them so much direct power in the period 1901-1907; instead, they had to wait and give management as much time as it required to undermine dissidents by any number of means. Workers lost the advantages of speed and surprise, but employers lost no real power whatever. Ideologically, the IDIA was a heaven-sent weapon for capital. Manipulating the near-universal respect for the law, which the non-violent character of the labour movement reveals so well, the Act cast a suspicion of illegality and unreason over the pursuit of collective rights. The long history of conciliation in Springhill from 1907 to 1909 confirmed the usefulness of the Act for management, as board after board tried to understand mining issues, contradicted one another, issued confusing judgments, and muddied the issues beyond belief. The management broadcast far and wide the decisions of boards in its favour, but when one board (for once including some knowledgeable mining men) criticized the treatment of the coal miners, the company treated its finding as a joke. When a conciliation board ruled that the miners of Springhill had no right to affiliate with an international

---

[62]A.W.R. Carrothers, *Collective Bargaining Law in Canada* (Toronto 1965), 32; the emergence of the IDIA is described by Paul Craven, *'An Impartial Umpire': Industrial Relations and the Canadian State 1900-1911* (Toronto 1980).

union because this would imperil local interests, its ruling was popularly seen as an edict based on the law itself, and not the verdict of a few opinionated individuals.[63]

The example of the dispute in Inverness, the second of the three great strikes of 1909-11, highlights the effects of the new legal structure. The mine at Inverness was controlled by those archetypal creatures of the new age, Mackenzie and Mann, and employed 600 men. In a referendum leading up to a split within the PWA, supporters of the UMW numbered only 96, but the international union gradually won over three-quarters of the mineworkers. The PWA had negotiated a check-off of union dues with the company in 1906, and the company refused to stop the collection of dues for the PWA even after a majority of the miners turned against the old union. Then the company circulated typewritten cards to individual miners, which ostensibly allowed individuals to stop the deduction of PWA dues from their pay, and many miners signed these cards. Then, one by one, the company discharged every miner who had done so. Despite appeals from the UMW, it refused to change its policies, and on 9 July 1909 the coal miners came out on strike. Two days later the troops arrived, to protect new strikebreakers and the small number of "loyal" workers. Now the real genius of the IDIA was revealed. Although the miners had been individually fired and the "strike" called by the union was very much only a formal recognition of their dismissal, the union had not taken the precaution of consulting with the Department of Labour and going through the conciliation procedure. The coal miners' strike was therefore illegal. The UMW could be prosecuted for providing food for the strikers' families, since under Section 60, Chapter 20 of the Act, supplying provisions to a striker prior to reference of a dispute to a Board of Conciliation and Investigation was illegal. The Supreme Court of Nova Scotia, which heard the case on appeal, thought it self-evident that giving food to hungry strikers fell within the sphere of prohibited support under the Act. "It is difficult to conceive any more effectual means of aiding strikers than those found in the present case," noted the Court. "It is of course precisely the aid wanted to enable tthe [sic] strikers to live during the pendency of the strike, and it hardly needs comment to show that the defendant as an agent of the United Mine Workers of America so gave the aid with the express and sole purpose of enabling the strikers to stay out until their demands were complied with." The "conciliatory" legislation of 1907 had revealed its coercive essence: under the IDIA the company was allowed to train the physical weapon of starvation and distress against its employees and their children. It was small wonder that coal miners despised the Act.[64]

[63]For the confusion surrounding conciliation in Springhill, partly caused by a complex decision by a judge who interpreted his own ruling differently than everybody else — and announced his revision after a strike of two and a half months — see *Amherst Daily News*, 20 October 1907; criticisms of the conciliation process were made by workers (*Herald*, 7 October 1907) and newspaper editors (*Sun*, 24 October 1907); for the use of the conciliation board reports by the company for propaganda, see the *Herald*, 23 October 1909.
[64]*Herald*, 10 July 1909; "Rex v. Neilson" (1910), *Eastern Law Reporter*, Vol. IX (1910), 210-13.

The IDIA was only one aspect of the legal offensive against labour. Great progress was made in the art of issuing injunctions against picketing and in applying the doctrine that trade unions could be held liable for economic costs imposed on employers. In another case, defendants against whom no evidence had been brought, were nonetheless forbidden to "watch and beset," because the "balance of convenience" dictated that "No injury surely can be suffered by defendants by being restrained from committing alleged illegal acts which they deny." Canadian labour law was profoundly influenced by such cases as "The Cumberland Railway and Coal Co. v. McDougall *et al.*," which helped place the injunction at the centre of reactions to strikes.[65]

As a force for labour peace, the IDIA was a disaster. As a response to the dependence of an increasingly interconnected economy upon fossil fuels, and as a fillip to the emergence of an aggressively authoritarian state apparatus, the Act was a stroke of genius. Combined with the existing laws against combination and disorder, and the para-military paraphernalia of barbed-wire compounds and armed strikebreakers, the IDIA served to guarantee the preservation of the free labour market. At the same time it removed most important direct powers from the coal miners. It thus represented a victory for capital in both the new labour market and in the subordination of labour in the workplace.[66]

In Springhill and Cape Breton, the limits beyond which the pursuit of conciliation and consensus no longer applied were unforgettably exposed. On 31 July 1909, large numbers of UMW men and their supporters gathered at the Athletic Grounds in Glace Bay. They were about to march to Dominion to protest against the coal company. They marched peacefully, carrying the Union Jack. As they neared a Catholic church at the boundary of Glace Bay and Dominion, they were startled by something new: a machine gun nest and a group of artillerymen, who seemed ready to mow them down if they tried to proceed to their destination. As they returned to Glace Bay, the marchers must have reflected on the new realities of state power and the limitations these imposed upon public assembly and freedom

[65]"Dominion Coal Co. Ltd. v. Bousfield *et al.*," *Eastern Law Reporter*, Vol. VIII (1909), 145-149; "Cumberland Railway and Coal Co. v. McDougall *et al.*," Nova Scotia *Reports*, Vol XLIV (1909-1910), 544. The importance of this latter case was underlined by A.C. Crysler, *Labour Relations and Precedents in Canada: A Commentary on Labour Law and Practice in Canada* (Toronto 1949), 32. For a less famous court case, in which a PWA lodge was held to have violated the rights of an individual by insisting upon the closed shop at Westville, see *Maritime Mining Record*, 26 August 1903.

[66]The dramatic regional impact of the IDIA is revealed in the estimate of F.A. Acland of the Department of Labour, that three-fourths of the miners of Nova Scotia in 1909 were working under terms recommended by a conciliation board, or arranged while a conciliation board was being established: Department of Labour, *Report of the Deputy Minister of Labour on Industrial Conditions in the Coal Fields of Nova Scotia* (Ottawa 1909), 32. The IDIA was also used to settle disputes of Halifax freighthandlers, Halifax plumbers, and Saint John longshoremen.

of speech. Whatever William Lyon Mackenzie King's impenetrable doctrines of conciliation amounted to, they barely concealed the crucial fact that, in defence of capitalism, the state was prepared to kill.[67]

However we evaluate the social challenge represented by the strikes of these years, we should remember that the state regarded them with utmost seriousness. Maritime workers failed to remake their society, but they faced very powerful enemies at a time when their awareness of themselves was only just developing. The system did not survive only through the creative response of the state. Workers themselves were not prepared to endorse a coherent alternative to the system. In the great coalfields' strikes women turned out *en masse*, but only a small minority of women workers ever fought strikes, and there was little challenge to traditional family roles in the working class. Only occasionally did strikers make connections between industrial actions and politics. Many pointed critiques of bonusing, for example, were made during the course of strikes, and sharp words were directed against state subsidies by the men who fought the steamship lines. Local politicians were subject to sharp criticisms during some strikes, but only in Cape Breton in 1904 (when a labour party was formed immediately in the wake of the defeat of the steel strike) and in the coalfields in 1909-11 (that "harvest time for socialists"), can we make a direct connection between strikes and radical ideological shifts. Part of the ambiguity was the ability of the mainstream politicians to absorb radical rhetoric and even concede working-class demands. There could be no better example of this responsiveness than the progressive policies followed by the Nova Scotia Liberals, who constructed an alliance with the PWA to help consolidate their long hold on provincial political power.[68]

If we measure class consciousness solely by the number of socialist ballots cast, the workers of the Maritimes appear to have made only slight gains in this period. Yet this pessimistic view is too static, especially in any description of something as fluid and dynamic as consciousness. The evidence of the strikes reveals a more complex portrait. One of its most interesting aspects is the evident interest taken by workingmen in religion. It is a commonplace of Canadian social history that the first decades of the 20th century witnessed the emergence of the "social gospel" as a theological response to industrialism, but from the evidence of the strikes one

[67] See Danny Moore, "The 1909 Strike in the Nova Scotia Coal Fields," unpublished research essay, Carleton University, 1977, 97, for a good description of this incident.

[68] For the aggressive tactics of women in coal strikes, see the *Herald*, 7, 13 July 1909; for an attack on steamship subsidies by a supporter of the longshoremen, see the *Herald*, 29 May 1907; the political impact of the 1904 steel strike is discussed by Ronald F. Crawley, "Class Conflict and the Establishment of the Sydney Steel Industry 1899-1904," MA thesis, Dalhousie University, 1980, 121-2; the PWA/Liberal relationship is explored by Joe Mac-Donald, "The Roots of Radical Politics in Nova Scotia: The Provincial Workmen's Association and Political Activity, 1879-1906," BA thesis, Carleton University, 1977; Frank and Reilly, "Socialist Movement," 99-101, discuss the political impact of the strike of 1909-11 in Springhill.

gains an impression of workingmen themselves fighting for the social gospel and bringing pressure to bear against their churches. The *Eastern Labour News* covered the emergence of the new theological positions with energy and competence. Maritime workers were adamantly Christian, notwithstanding the heroic efforts of Marshall Govang, the region's first labour historian, who lectured car workers in Moncton on the benefits of Free Thought.[69] When Cape Breton mining families withdrew their children from Sunday School classes taught by company officials, or when the Salvation Army chaplain denied use of the church to strikebreakers in Springhill, they were taking important and dramatic steps. Letters to the *Herald* bristled with quotations from John Bunyan and Isaiah and demanded the Presbyterian church denounce the system of modern industry and its selfishness of spirit. We find clergymen taking emphatic steps to support local strikes. That a minister who sided with capital faced mixed reviews was illustrated by Rev. R.W. Norwood of Springhill, who denounced workers of Springhill for listening to revolutionary socialists. Not coincidentally, it was his valedictory sermon. He was attacked mercilessly by workingmen in the press. We confront a large array of evidence which suggests that workers were seeking a reconciliation of their religious beliefs with the realities of industrial conflict. In 1909 the *Herald* carried a dramatic story which illustrated this difficult situation. When a number of the wives of the strikers in Cape Breton were prevented from "interfering" with the strikebreakers and had no other way of manifesting their opposition, "they knelt down on the road and appealed to God with genuine fervour to cause the rocks in the pit to fall upon the objects of their hatred." Everywhere we find indications like this, of men and women looking for something — some confusedly, others entirely lucidly — a theological framework suited to the changed conditions of social life.[70] It is not a portrait of religious stagnation that emerges from this evidence, nor can we infer political stagnation from the continuing hold of old parties without knowing more about the concessions they offered and the political imagery that they used.

The record of strikes cannot give us a portrait of the class, for there is a vast amount of additional evidence to consider before any definitive judgements are made about the general contours of Maritime working-class history. But insofar as this partial evidence allows us to reach some initial hypotheses about class consciousness, one can easily see that it undercuts the stereotype of "regional conservatism." The slow development of regional labour historiography denies us the pleasure of criticizing a "traditional interpretation" of Maritime workers. But one can well imagine what such a "traditional interpretation" might amount to. Denied large-scale immigration and demoralized by high levels of unemployment, the

[69]Colin McKay, the region's first radical sociologist, published important essays on the social gospel in the *Eastern Labour News*. See, for example, his study of new theology in the issue of 1 February 1913; for Govang and the Moncton Truth Seekers Association, see *Eastern Labour News*, 24 April, 1, 8 May 1909.
[70]*Herald*, 31 July 1909; *Herald*, 15 April 1910; *Herald*, 17 July 1909; *Herald*, 4 September 1909; *Herald*, 31 July 1909.

argument might run, Maritime workers inhabited small, isolated worlds, where paternalist employers provided the focus of life. Growing up in the isolated and stagnant communities of a traditional region, workers would not demand many changes in a time-honoured way of life. Cut off from the main traditions of North American trade unionism by their own isolation and the domination of the PWA, that "company union," the workers of the Maritimes lived in a social as well as economic hinterland, and only a few immigrants or peripatetic organizers helped to alleviate the "feudal" conditions of their oppression.[71]

The interpretation of working-class mobilization in 1901-1914 offered here contradicts such analysis. Nothing seems backward about the workers of the Maritimes in this period — not their struggles for job control, their eagerness to press for such general objectives as nine (or even eight) hours, their rethinking of religious traditions. Most of the issues raised in the workplaces of the Maritimes could as easily have been raised in England. Whatever the scope of paternalism in the 19th century, it was a waning force in this period. Living in a dynamic region with an abundance of jobs in construction, coal mining, and manufacturing, workers were making new contacts with their brothers in North America. Even more crucially, they were painstakingly developing a regional framework of class awareness, as seen in the new regional labour press, the work of Maritimes-based organizers in other parts of the region, and the inspiration drawn by workers from other regional strikes. When pulp workers in St. George, New Brunswick tried to justify their three-year struggle to themselves, they thought of the long battles waged by the miners of Cape Breton and Springhill.[72]

One comes away from the strikes of 1901-1914 with two conflicting impressions. The first is that of monopoly capitalism reshaping the region and the working-class world, of a remorseless and inexorable process of consolidation. The second is that of a dynamic working-class movement, posing a real challenge to capital and to the traditional ruling classes of the Maritimes. It was a period of both defeat and awakening, a period in which both capital and labour were attaining greater strength. Perhaps this evidence suggests that working-class traditionalism in the Maritimes, like many other regional traditions, is of relatively recent vintage — a product of the economic collapse of the 1920s.

In Springhill in 1910, the workers displayed all the contradictory features of the new age. On 10 August 1910, a parade and picnic were held to mark the end of the first year of the Great Strike. It was a sign of the harsh defeats faced by workers in this new situation: on the very day of the parade, the company hoisted 641 tons of coal by using strikebreakers protected by the state. It would take another ten months to break the strike completely, but already the workers were fearing the

[71] An interpretation which comes close to this stereotype is that of John Mellor, *The Company Store: James Bryson McLachlan and the Cape Breton Miners, 1900-1925* (Toronto 1983); see the effective critique by Don Macgillivray, "Cultural Strip-Mining in Cape Breton," *New Maritimes* (September 1983), 16.

[72] Christopher Wren to F.A. Acland, 9 September 1912, Vol. 298, file 3341, RG 27.

worst. But was it not also a sign of the new consciousness and new discipline of labour? The procession formed up at Pioneer Hall, which had once rung to the mass meetings of the PWA, and then started down Main Street. First came the town band and a body of miners, then the band of the 93rd regiment, and then the children from the Socialist Sunday School, carrying small red flags. They were followed by another delegation of socialists, numbering about 100, who carried a large red flag. As the parade wound through Springhill, it passed house after house bedecked with red flags and banners. The parade finally reached the picnic grounds, where more than 4,000 people were gathered.[73] We know the marchers were also moving toward defeat, but their parade suggests the hopes of men and women, high in one colliery town, for a new social world. By raising high the banner of the modern enlightenment, they live on in our minds, symbols of an age of struggle and aspiration.

[73] *Herald*, 11 August 1910.

Organizing on the Waterfront: The St. John's Longshoremen's Protective Union (LSPU), 1890-1914

In 1890 the city council in St. John's voted to increase the wages of its municipal labourers to $1.00 per day. The decision prompted a local reporter for the *Daily Colonist* to interview three dockworkers about wages and working conditions on the wharves. Why were earnings so low, only 70 to 80 cents a day? Why was organization so difficult?

"Were the men always satisfied with the four shillings (80 cents) a day up to now?"
"No ... there have been strikes on one or two wharves where cargo was being discharged and on one occasion men got an increase of 10 cents for a while, but the old rates were soon resumed."
"How do you account for this?"
"The men were too poor to stick it out ... and the absence of anything like a combination among the men, account for the low wages they have been receiving ...."[1]

The labourers complained that the wages were further reduced by the autumn influx of "strolling outport men" from Conception and Trinity Bays, fishermen "willing to work for less money than eighty cents, aye, and even 'take it up' in the shops."[2] Commonplace in rural Newfoundland, the practice of paying wages in truck or in kind by certain city firms was deeply resented by St. John's labourers.[3]

[1]*Daily Colonist* (St. John's), hereafter *DC*, 20 September 1890.
[2]*DC*, 22 September 1890.
[3]*Evening Telegram* (St. John's), hereafter *ET*, 10 August 1899; *Evening Herald* (St. John's), hereafter *EH*, 23 January 1895; *EH*, 12 February 1895.

Published with permission of the editor. © Canadian Committee on Labour History. From *Labour/Le Travail*, 26 (Fall 1990), 37-59.

Dock labour in St. John's was seasonal, its rhythms determined by the ebb and flow of maritime traffic and the fluctuating patterns of the fish trade. Union organization of waterfront workers was impeded by the seasonal nature of port employment, by a diversity of hiring practices and wage schedules, and by the determined resistance of the city's mercantile interests. Yet a remarkably successful labour organization was established in 1903. Initially organized by steamboat labourers, the Longshoremen's Protective Union (LSPU) extended its membership to all dockworkers, including juveniles. Within ten years, membership had increased more than ten-fold, from 200 in the spring of 1903 to 2,600 in 1914. The LSPU stabilized employment on the waterfront through the exclusion of non-unionized and transient labour and by a uniform schedule of wages and hours. A successful strike in May 1903 forced concessions from reluctant employers; these concessions were upheld by a series of disciplined strikes in subsequent years.

This essay details the emergence of the LSPU and its organizing activities among St. John's workers. It explores select themes: the conditions of dock labour and patterns of worker resistance prior to unionization; the establishment of the LSPU in 1903 and its consolidation across the waterfront; and the involvement of the LSPU in the organization of the city's common labourers and juvenile workers. I intend to place the LSPU within the context of a rich international historiography on dock activism, indicating that Newfoundland longshoremen have also possessed a vibrant tradition of collective resistance.

I

"The most dramatic battles, triumphs and defeats of the 'new unionism' of the late nineteenth and early twentieth centuries," maintained Eric Hobsbawm, "occurred on the British waterside."[4] Escalating strikes on the St. John's docks in the 1890s and the establishment of the LSPU in 1903 were part of the international emergence of waterfront organization between the years 1885 and 1914.[5] In many major ports longshoremen possessed traditions of dockside unionism and strike activity which had pre-dated the late 19th-century insurgence. The most resilient of the dockworkers' associations had existed in maritime cities dominated by a specialized export trade, such as the ship labourers' unions in the timber ports of Quebec City and Saint John, or they were labour organizations which represented the most highly-experienced and deft of the longshore labourers.[6] The difficulties in organizing

[4]E.J. Hobsbawm, *Labouring Men: Studies in the History of Labour* (London 1986), 204.
[5]Hobsbawm, *Labouring Men*; see also David Montgomery, *The Fall of the House of Labor: the Workplace, the State and American Labor Activism, 1865-1925* (Cambridge 1987), 96-110; Eric Arneson, "To Rule or to Ruin: New Orlean Dock Workers' Struggle for Control, 1902-1903," *Labor History*, 28 (Spring 1987), 139-166; Philip J. Leng, *The Welsh Dockers* (Ormshirk, UK 1981), 3-71; P.J. Donovan, "Australia and the Great London Dock Strike: 1889," *Labour History*, 23 (1972), 17-26.
[6]J.I. Cooper, "The Quebec Ship Labourers' Benevolent Society," *Canadian Historical Review*, 30 (1949), 336-43; Judith Fingard, "The Decline of the Sailor as Ship Labourer in

labourers across the waterfront were legion, however, for dock work was characterized by intermittent employment and irregular earnings, seasonal variation, and
a fluctuating labour demand. Dockworkers were casual employees, hired by the day
or by the hour, frequently for an eighteen-hour stretch, and paid an hourly rate based
on the task performed.[7] Despite the tendencies of observers to categorize dock
labour as unskilled, the waterfront workforce was stratified by experience and
expertise.[8]

The international character of longshore activism reflected the ascendancy of
a maritime steam technology which affected the structure and pace of dock labour.[9]
The steamship intensified the irregular nature of employment on the docks. British
historians Philipps and Whiteside concluded that "pressure was put on dock
companies, wharfingers and contractors to increase labour output and they were
compelled ... to deploy their men in large numbers and short intensive bursts of
activity at whatever cost to regularity of employment."[10] While steamship stevedoring created a small cohesive group of specialized labourers, it also heightened
the casual nature of port work by encouraging a large pool of surplus labour.
Ironically, it allowed waterfront employees a degree of autonomy because steamship agents were prone to concede limited worker demands rather than risk delay,
while it intensified those variables which made dock unionism difficult — sporadic
employment, a stratified workforce, and an oversupply of labour.

In St. John's, as in other maritime cities, dockworkers were ill-paid and
erratically employed. In 1914 only 500 men in the 2,600 member LSPU (19 per
cent) were permanent employees of mercantile firms; they were generally older,
familiar hands, employed ten hours a day, and paid weekly ($6.00 to $8.00).[11] The
majority of city wharf labourers were hired by the day or by the hour; they seldom
secured more than nine months work, probably averaging six months yearly.[12] In
1890 the dockworker interviewed in the *Colonist* complained that for many years

the 19th Century Timber Ports," *Labour/Le Travailleur*, 2 (1977), 35-54; Ian McKay, "Class
Struggle and Merchant Capital: Craftsmen and Labourers on the Halifax Waterfront 1850-
1900," in Bryan Palmer, ed., *The Character of Class Struggle* (Toronto 1986), 30.
[7]For contemporary descriptions of dock work, see Charles Barnes, *The Longshoremen* (New
York 1916) based on first-hand investigations in New York 1910-1911; J.S. Woodsworth,
On the Waterfront (Ottawa 1928); ILWU Local 500 Pensioners, *Man Along the Shore: the
Story of the Vancouver Waterfront* (Vancouver 1975), especially 32-40.
[8]Concerning sectorial unionism on the docks, see Montgomery, *Fall*, 99-101; James Conley,
"Class Conflict and Collective Action in the Working Class of Vancouver, British Columbia
1900-1919," PhD dissertation, Carleton University, 1986, 472, 502; Robert Babcock, "Saint
John Longshoremen during the Rise of Canada's Winter Port, 1895-1922," *Labour/Le
Travail*, 25 (Spring 1990), 20-2.
[9]McKay, "Class Struggle and Merchant Capital," 31-2; Montgomery, 103-4.
[10]Gordon Philipps and Noel Whiteside, *Casual Labour: the Unemployment Question in the
Port Transport Industry 1880-1970* (Oxford 1985), 18.
[11]*ET*, 16 May 1914.
[12]*ET*, 16 May 1914.

he had not worked more than 100 days (four months); his yearly earnings were less than $100.[13] In 1914, the annual wages of waterfront employees ranged from $200 to $250; the minimum budget for a working-class family of seven in St. John's was estimated at $420 per year.[14] The St. John's waterfront attracted transient workers: rural handymen and labourers, outport fishermen in the off-season, the crews of fishing schooners. These "strolling outport men" competed for employment, driving down the wages of dock labour.[15]

Despite the erratic character of employment, however, there was a regular workforce attached to the harbour, city labourers who thought of themselves as dockworkers, and who resented the influx of other labourers willing to work at lower wages. The most skilled of these dockworkers were the steamboat labourers, longshoremen who discharged and loaded the steam vessels:

Their work is arduous and often dangerous and can be done only by those who are well experienced in the proper handling of goods of a breakable nature and skilled in the manipulation of special tackle required for the hoisting of heavy packages from ship to pier. Men engaged at this line of work are sought after...and come to be regarded in time as attaches [sic] of premises where steamers discharge so that they engage rarely at other work and rely on the handling of freight for a living....[16]

Although small gangs (eight to ten men) worked the hatches, large numbers of labourers (200 or 300) were required to sort and pile cargoes, and to truck them by barrows from the quays to the warehouses. Steamship stevedoring in St. John's had increased in importance over the pre-war years as the number of steamers entering and clearing port increased almost three-fold and the volume of their cargoes tripled.[17]

St. John's was a fishing port as well as a shipping centre, its wharves crowded by small fishing schooners. Cullers assessed and graded the fish; fish handlers

[13]*DC*, 19 September 1890.
[14]Estimates by LSPU President, James McGrath, *ET*, 16 May 1914. In New York, the average yearly earnings of longshoremen were estimated at $500 to $600; the family budget for a "family of normal size" was calculated at $800 to $900. Barnes, *Longshoremen*, 92.
[15]*DC*, 19, 20, 22 September 1890; *EH*, 9 July 1900.
[16]*ET*, 16 May 1903.
[17]The ascendancy of the steamer and the decline of the sailing vessel is clearly indicated in the statistics of vessels and tonnage entering and clearing port at St. John's.

Year	Vessels entering port (tonnage)	Vessels clearing port (tonnage)
1890	516 sail (75,000)	423 sail (65,000)
	175 steam (169,000)	179 steam (171,000)
1914	136 sail (25,000)	126 sail (23,000)
	305 steam (462,000)	291 steam (449,000)

Statistics compiled by Ann Coady, "Total Number, Tonnage and Crews of Steamers and Sailing Vessels entered and cleared at the Port of St. John's in the years 1880-1930," unpublished student paper, April 1974. Filed at Maritime History Archives, MUN.

employed during fine weather packed it in barrels, often under the direction of master coopers. Large numbers of boys were employed on the fish wharves and by the merchant firms, favoured by employers for their agility.[18] Handling fish was commonly viewed as unskilled and untaxing; when it was rumoured in 1903 that dry fish handlers were demanding higher wages, the *Trade Review* responded impatiently: "This class of work is not very hard .... Most of the men employed in handling dry fish are steady-going old pacers, who don't rush themselves to death, and are perfectly content with their pay and work."[19]

In earlier decades women had worked on the wharves in St. John's. The Earl of Dunraven, who visited the city in the 1870s, left a vivid description of fish handling on the waterfront and the place of the women in the labour process:

The fish ... are brought to St. John's on small schooners and thrown into heaps upon the wharves .... There they are culled over, sorted into three or four piles according to their quality by experienced cullers .... Women with hand-barrows attend upon the cullers, carry the fish into an adjoining shed and upset their loads beside barrels. A couple of boys throw the fish into a cask ... [and] roll the barrels under a screw-press where two men stand ready. Grasping the ends of the long arms of the lever, the men run quickly around ... [and] bring down the stamp with a dull thud .... The cask is then rolled out from under the press and handed over to two coopers. In a trice the hoops are driven on, the cask is headed up, and then trundled ... into the hold of some vessels .... The rapidity with which the whole process is managed is remarkable.[20]

The custom of women barrowing fish persisted in outport Newfoundland into the 20th century: in 1906 American tourist Bertha Arnold complained to the *Trade Review* of the "hard and unnatural work ... (of) women carrying barrows over slippery and uneven stages ... (and) crawling on hands and knees all day striving in the hold of a close and stuffy boat."[21] The editor of the *Trade Review* noted that the employment of women on the St. John's wharves had been halted some years

[18]For interesting descriptions of fish handlers, see terms "cullers," "tally-man" and "yaffle" in G.M. Story *et al.* eds., *Dictionary of Newfoundland English* (Toronto 1982), 129-30; 556-57; 621-22. Fish-handlers were sometimes referred to as "yafflers" in the daily press [from yaffle "to gather up an armful of dried and salted cod..."]. It is impossible to calculate the number of men employed at various tasks on the wharves as the Newfoundland census provided no breakdown of these labourers.
[19]*Trade Review* (St. John's), hereafter *TR*, 22 May 1903.
[20]Windham Thomas Wyndham-Quinn, 4th Earl of Dunraven, *Canadian Nights: being Sketches and Reminiscences of Life and Sport in the Rockies and the Canadian Woods* (London 1914), 196-7. On women employed on St. John's wharves, see Philip Tocque, *Kaleidoscope Echoes, being Historical, Philosophical, Scientific and Theological Sketches from the Miscellaneous Writings*, ed. Annie S.W. Tocque (Toronto 1895), 46; "Long-shore-women in Newfoundland," *The Youth's Companion* (19 September 1878), n.p.
[21]*TR*, 1 September 1906.

previous because of a fatal accident involving two female employees.[22] By 1890 longshore work and fish handling were "male" occupations in the capital.

"Unlike so many other trades during the age of monopoly capital changing technology was not a critical variable at the longshoreman's workplace," observed historian Robert Babcock of the Saint John waterfront; "the longshoremen carried, wheeled or trucked goods in the early Twenties in much the same manner as their fathers and grandfathers had done."[23] He noted that the shipping companies relied on hard-driving foremen to get the work done as quickly and cheaply as possible.[24] Although there were no dramatic technological changes, St. John's longshoremen complained that the installation of larger winches on the cargo vessels forced the men to work more quickly and reduced actual employment. In a series of letters to the *Evening Telegram* LSPU President James McGrath protested:

Under the old conditions with a different type of ship the work of landing was a much slower process. Now coal is handled more quickly; the present day carriers are fitted with larger winches, [and] a larger drum ... as a natural consequence the men have to work more lively .... All we want is a just share in the saving which present day conditions have brought about by lessening the hours of labor and accomplishing more work per hour.[25]

Occasionally St. John's longshoremen refused employment at certain premises which had acquired a reputation for driving their gangs of labourers. On 9 June 1910 city steamship agents met at the Board of Trade rooms to discuss a shortage of longshoremen; the meeting was in response to the labour difficulties encountered by Shea and Company in discharging the SS *Mongolian*. The LSPU quickly replied: Shea and Company had problems in obtaining longshoremen because "attempts are made to make them work harder and do more work than any other employer of labor."[26] James McGrath claimed:

When Shea & Co. have a steamer to discharge they always make it a point to employ a less number of men to handle cargo than any other steamboat agent ... when two derricks are working in the hold, eight men are employed at the two derricks; on other premises twelve men are employed .... Longshoremen, in consequence, are not at all anxious to work ... [at] Shea & Co.'s premises and would rather not go to work there at all ....[27]

Workers expressed their resistance to "speed-ups" by withholding their labour.

[22]*TR*, 1 September 1906. For responses, see *TR*, 8 September 1906.
[23]Babcock, "Saint John Longshoremen," 19-20.
[24]Babcock, "Saint John Longshoremen," 20.
[25]*ET*, 12 May 1914. See also 13, 16 May 1914.
[26]*ET*, 10 June 1910.
[27]*ET*, 10 June 1910.

II

Twenty years earlier, on 8 October 1890, longshoremen employed by Shea and Company struck work to protest a reduction in their wages and to demand higher pay. The men had been hired earlier that morning to discharge 500 tons of freight from the steamer *Caspion*. A striker explained:

We had been getting ninety cents per day up to this present work, when the pay was cut to eighty cents. This we resented, but as the majority fell into line, the rest had to follow suit. However, there has been considerable grumbling and today ... a number of the men 'kicked' but, as usual some were willing to work and 'fell-too.' By dinner time, however, the men were talked over and ... those who were willing to work in the morning now refuse to work for less than a dollar a day.[28]

After refusing to pay the strikers more than the 80 cents promised in the morning, Shea and Company induced the ship's crew, firemen and passengers to unload the cargo at a dollar a day. By evening a compromise was effected; the longshoremen resumed work the following morning for 90 cents a day.[29]

Prior to the establishment of the LSPU, there had been at least 25 strikes on the city docks in the years 1890 to 1903 (Table 1); strikes by dockworkers represented 30 per cent of work stoppages in St. John's.[30] Almost all dock strikes had been initiated by longshoremen discharging steamers and focused on higher wages and overtime rates. The pattern of strike activity was typical of non-unionized workers: ad-hoc strikes for immediate gains. On the surface, they were quite successful: 70 per cent of strikes ended in at least partial victory for the workers.

These optimistic statistics are misleading, however. Without institutional structures to protect gains or to extend concessions across the waterfront, dockworkers were forced to strike repeatedly to exact minimum concessions of little lasting value. An analysis of pay rates and wage demands (Table 2) indicates the discouraging trends. Wage schedules were not uniform from company to company, nor constant from year to year. In 1890 longshoremen at Shea's were paid 90 cents and demanded a dollar a day. Three years later, they received only 80 cents and successfully struck for $1.00; by 1896 their wages had been reduced to 70 cents and they were again forced to strike to obtain a dollar per day.[31] In 1902 dockworkers at several important mercantile firms were paid 80 cents per day, the common rate in 1890, and were striking for $1.00, the scale accorded municipal labour twelve

[28]*DC*, 8 October 1890.
[29]*DC*, 8, 9 October 1890.
[30]The data on strikes was compiled from the local newspapers; in the years 1890 to 1914 there were 181 strikes in St. John's. For an analysis of city strikes see Jessie Chisholm, "'Hang Her Down': Strikes in St. John's 1890-1914," paper to Seventh Atlantic Canada Studies Conference, University of Edinburgh, 4-7 May 1988.
[31]*DC*, 8, 9 October; *ET*, 14 June 1893; *EH*, 12 May 1896.

years previously,[32] in marked contrast with other port cities where waterfront wages were often 40 per cent higher than those of common labourers.[33]

Table 1
Strikes by Non-unionized Dockworkers, 1890-1903

Year	Number
1890	4
1893	3
1896	4
1897	1
1898	1
1899	1
1900	2
1901	1
1902	7
1903	1
Total	25

Source: Table 1 and subsequent tables based on data compiled from the daily press.

In July 1900, when the new fish from the summer fishery began arriving at St. John's, labourers employed at two fish premises struck for higher wages. The *Evening Herald* reported that "laborers are forming a combine and it is said will try to make all the laborers on wharves east of Goodridge's quit work, unless paid the amount asked."[34] The following day the strike collapsed when men employed at the neighbouring wharves refused to join the strikers; they were fearful to gamble on a strike, "prefer(ring) what they receive at present to nothing."[35] The strikers were replaced by outport men from the fishing schooners. The leaders, men "who for years had been (employed) there," were fired and blacklisted.[36] The strike illustrated neatly the difficulties in organizing across the waterfront, and the personal risks involved in strike activity: the competition of outport labour and the threat of dismissal and blacklisting. In a city marked by seasonal unemployment, meagre savings and limited labour demand the loss of a job meant misery and destitution for a blacklisted worker and his family. After an abortive strike by longshoremen in 1902, the *Evening Telegram* commented:

[32]*ET*, 21 August 1902.
[33]Philipps and Whiteside, *Casual Labour*, 6.
[34]*EH*, 31 July 1900.
[35]*Daily News* (St. John's) hereafter *DN*, 1 August 1900.
[36]*EH*, 31 July, 2 August 1900.

The man who makes himself conspicuous as a strike leader and who then fails is...a doomed man. He is marked and will get no more work. Men who look for better times at the wharves, offices, fisheries, trains, steamers are not wanted...and are driven off to Canada and the U.S.[37]

Table 2
Wage Demands by Non-unionized Dockworkers, 1890-1903

Year	Current Rate	Rate Demanded	Company	Outcome
1890	70¢ day	80¢ day	Murray	Failure
	90¢ day	$1.00 day	Shea	90¢ maintained
1893	90¢ day	$1.00	Pitts	Success
	90¢ day	$1.20 day	Harvey	$1.00 given
	80¢ day	$1.00 day	Shea	Success
1896	70¢ day	$1.00 day	Shea	Success
1898	$1.50 night	$2.00 night	Bowrings	Success
1899	$1.20 night	$2.00 night	Harvey	
1900	80¢ day	$1.00 day	Bennett	Success
1900	80¢ day	$1.00 day	Rendell	Failure
1900	80¢	$1.00 day	Goodridge	Success
1902	15¢ hour	20¢ hour	Franklin	Failure
1902	80¢ day	$1.00 day	Thorburn	90¢ given
1902	80¢ day	$1.00 day	Job	90¢ given
1902	$1.00 day	$2.00 day	Pitts	Failure
			Harvey	
1902	80¢ day	$1.00 day	Rendell	Failure
			Goodridge	

Strike activity on the St. John's docks escalated in 1902; longshoremen struck work on at least seven occasions to demand increased wages. Heightened militancy on the city wharves reflected the sense of grievance widespread among the Newfoundland labouring classes; in 1902 alone, city workers were involved in twenty strikes.[38] Outport labourers also struck to gain concessions. In 1900 over 1,600 miners struck for higher wages at Bell Island, a mining community less than twenty

[37]*EH*, 17 April 1902. See *EH*, 14 June 1902 concerning the blacklisting of strikers: "The ones with families who were led into this strike have lost...their prospects of the future." In the May 1903 strike by city longshoremen, the strikers demanded the reinstatement of leaders as part of the settlement negotiated with employers. See *EH*, 19 May 1903.
[38]Chisholm, "'Hang Her Down,'" 8.

miles from the capital;[39] in 1902 outport sealers, 3,000 men strong, paraded the streets of St. John's, determined to secure a greater return from the annual hunt.[40] The intensification of strikes by city and outport workers alike reflected the convergence of several developments: the easing of the financial crisis of the 1890s, which resulted in widening employment opportunities in the Colony; a steady increase in the rate of inflation; and the dynamic expansion of the Maritimes' economy which created a regional labour market, especially for unskilled workers.[41] After 1900 local newspapers frequently complained of the difficulty in retaining young men in the fisheries because of job opportunities elsewhere.[42] Newfoundland workers who emigrated to the coal and steel works of Cape Breton, many on a seasonal basis, often returned dissatisfied with wages and conditions at home.[43]

Dockworkers in St. John's were well aware of the rates paid longshoremen and wharf labourers in Canada; strikes in port cities, particularly Montreal, Saint John and Halifax, were extensively covered in the local press. The strike by Halifax longshoremen in April 1902 was widely publicized, both because the day rate paid Halifax workers, twenty cents an hour, was well above wages paid locally and because Halifax strikers appealed directly to Newfoundland labourers to "stay away" from the Halifax docks.[44] Amid reports of the Halifax strike, a second organizational effort by St. John's longshoremen was noted: "Many of the men who usually work discharging steamers have formed themselves into a committee and a general strike amongst the laborers associated with them is in the process of

[39]The Bell Island strike, involving 1600 miners in a six-week struggle for increased wages, has not been adequately treated. City newspapers reported that urban labourers collected funds to assist the striking miners and that some of the miners sought employment on the city docks. The press blamed the influence of the Bell Island strike for strikes on the docks: "The spirit of unrest created by the Bell Island trouble, broke out among the labourers on the docks." *EH*, 31 July 1900. For a discussion of Bell Island miners, see Peter Neary, "'Traditional' and 'Modern' Elements in the Social History of Bell Island and Conception Bay," *Historical Papers*, 1973, 105-36.
[40]Briton Cooper Busch, "The Newfoundland Sealers' Strike of 1902," *Labour/Le Travail*, 14 (Fall 1984), 73-102. Busch provided an excellent narrative of the strike. However, he treated the strike as an anomaly. Although exceptional in size, the strike of 1902 was within a tradition of collective protest; there were 42 outport strikes recorded in the city press in the years 1890 to 1914, 37 between 1901 and 1914, 16 involving sealers and fishermen (data compiled from newspapers).
[41]On rising prices, see George Cornelius, US Consul at St. John's. "Annual Report 1906," in US Consular *Despatches*, Microfilm 374, Despatch no. 9. On the regional labour market, see Ian McKay, "Strikes in the Maritimes, 1901-1914," *Acadiensis Reader*, Volume 2 (Fredericton 1985), 21-2.
[42]*EH*, 17 April 1902.
[43]*TR*, 15 March 1902. See Ron Crawley, "'Off to Sydney': Newfoundlanders Emigrate to Industrial Cape Breton 1890-1914," *Acadiensis*, 17 (Spring 1988), 27-52.
[44]*ET*, 18 April 1902.

organization."[45] Again the strike failed; dockworkers were hesitant to unite because of the presence of many needy outport men anxious for employment:

They decided to await a better opportunity. They say that there are a great many out harbour men around who would not join the strike and who would take their places at the low wages offered.[46]

III

That better opportunity arose in May 1903. On the 14th, after the commencement of the fishing season, all the longshoremen in the east end of the city struck. The strike was well organized and well-timed; the men had quit work "by a sort of pre-concerted arrangements" during a month when complaints about a shortage of labour were commonplace.[47] The longshoremen demanded twenty cents an hour, the rate conceded striking Halifax longshoremen the previous year. The following day the strike spread to the west end of the city when men discharging the Reid steamers struck work.[48] The dockers remained united for the duration of the strike; waiting cargoes were slowly unloaded by firemen, sailors and office personnel, but only a handful of city labourers accepted work as strikebreakers.[49] The crew of the SS *Siberian*, a mail steamer, were employed discharging 350 tons of inward cargo, but the men "not being used to the work, could only do it slowly." The vessel was so delayed that it boarded no outward freight, leaving 400 tons of goods behind on the docks.[50]

A meeting of the strikers, an estimated 300 men, was held at the British Hall on 16 May, organized by James Kavanagh, an experienced steamboat labourer.[51] The meeting was chaired by Michael Fleming, a strike leader, later elected as the first secretary of the labourers' union and subsequently appointed their first "walking delegate." The strikers were addressed by Michael Gibbs and William Howley, St. John's lawyers sympathetic to the workingmen's cause[52] and by Kavanagh,

[45] *EH*, 16 April 1902.
[46] *ET*, 17 April 1902.
[47] *EH*, 15 May 1903.
[48] *EH*, 15 May 1903.
[49] *EH*, 15 May 1903; *ET*, 16 May 1903.
[50] The crew of the *Siberian* had signed articles to assist in the discharge of the vessel if required. *EH*, 15 May 1903; see also 16 May for departure of *Siberian*. Another vessel in port was the SS *Regulus*; "there was a complete shutdown, her cargo being coal, a hard one to handle." *EH*, 15 May 1903.
[51] *EH*, 18 May and *DN*, 17 May 1903.
[52] Michael Gibbs (1870-1943) born St. John's, called to bar 1896; elected MHA St. George's 1897; elected mayor of St. John's 1906 as the "working man's friend"; outspoken trade union lawyer; solicitor for LSPU 1903-1943. See Melvin Baker, "Michael Patrick Gibbs," *Newfoundland Quarterly* (Spring 1986), 48. William Howley (1875-1941) born St. John's, called to bar 1898; elected MHA St. George's 1900; Commissioner of Justice 1934-1938. *Encyclopedia of Newfoundland and Labrador*, vol.2, 1097. During the years 1900 to 1904 Howley

whose speech was warmly received: "He believed that the men in the holds of the
steamers in St. John's had to work as hard as the men in Montreal and they were
worth as much pay. They had worked for starvation wages too long and it was time
for them to call halt."[53] The strikers resolved to establish a union "for the purpose
of securing to ourselves just and reasonable wages and of protecting ourselves in
the continuance of said wages and for other purposes that may be of benefit and
protection to us."[54] The union was named the Steamboat Labourers Union of St.
John's and 100 men joined that evening, each paying membership dues of 10 cents.
The strikers appointed a committee — Kavanagh, Fleming and newly-elected
President Courtney, along with Gibbs and Howley — to confer with the employers.

Three days later, union members ratified their first agreement. Wages were
fixed at 15 cents an hour for a twelve-hour day (6 a.m. to 6 p.m.); after 6 p.m.
overtime was paid at 20 cents an hour. Overtime was guaranteed for six hours, or
until the entire cargo had been discharged. Time lost by men already hired, because
of weather or delay, was remunerated. Strike leaders were reinstated.[55] Although
the wages were below those demanded initially by strikers, St. John's dockworkers
had made important gains: they had secured a uniform schedule of wage rates from
the major merchant houses on the waterfront, and they had established a formal
labour organization to consolidate gains. The accomplishments are striking, especially when contrasted with Halifax; despite the concessions won by longshoremen
in the 1902 strike, a permanent union organization was not achieved until 1907.[56]
Johnny Burke, the "Bard of Prescott Street" wrote a song in celebration of the
Steamboat Labourers Union:

Oh, we are the men today, that struck for higher pay
For we are the bone and sinew of this land
For our rights we did uphold and like men
We struck out bold
And determined all to take a manly stand

---

actively supported labour legislation and acted as solicitor for several city unions. By 1905
he had disassociated himself from the labour movement. See *EH*, 21 May 1904 for an
expression of his earlier views.

[53] *DN*, 17 May 1903. The reference to wages in Montreal reflected local press coverage of
the dock strike in that city. Terms of the Montreal settlement were summarized in *EH*, 15
May 1903.

[54] *DN*, 17 May 1903.

[55] Terms of settlement noted in *EH*, *ET* and *DN*, 18 May 1903.

[56] Catherine Waite, "The Longshoremen of Halifax 1900-1930: their Living and Housing
Conditions," MA thesis, Dalhousie University, 1977, 138. Waite writes [116] that payment
for waiting time was not secured by Halifax dockworkers until 1920.

We are the Steam Boat Labor Union
We got the terms that we did like
For to help the working man we were
Foremost in the van
The Steam Boat Labor Union Strike.[57]

Initially, the settlement affected only steamboat labourers. Yet it is clear from the newspaper coverage that the union leaders intended from the outset to press for the expansion of the Steamboat Labourers Protective Union to the wharf labourers.[58] By September, wage scales had been negotiated for fish-handlers, barrowmen and packers.[59] Membership increased steadily from 1903 to 1914, when it exceeded 2,600 men, 30 per cent of the male labour force in St. John's.[60] Again, the success of the LSPU was in marked contrast with Halifax, where membership in the Halifax Longshoremen's Association expanded modestly from 500 in 1907 to 840 in 1913, declining to 600 in 1914.[61] In April 1904, the name of the Newfoundland union was changed to the St. John's 'Longshoremen's Protective Union' to reflect the broadening of the membership base, although the daily press commonly referred to it simply as the Labourers Union.[62]

The pattern of strikes after the formation of the LSPU contrasted sharply with strike activity before 1903; strikes were disciplined, well-organized actions which successfully upheld concessions obtained in the settlement. The determination of the LSPU to impose stability on the waterfront through the exclusion of transient labour and the imposition of uniform wages and hours is reflected in Table 3.[63] The largest number of strikes (over 40 per cent) occurred over the employment of non-union labour. Union men refused to work with labourers whose union dues were in arrears; they objected to outport men barrowing and packing fish in the holds of the schooners; and they protested the employment of ship crews in the discharging of vessels.[64] Just over 30 per cent of strikes focused on contract terms: remuneration for time lost after men were hired on; payment of union rates; and the curtailment of overtime. LSPU members struck to protest deductions for time lost

[57]Quoted by Bill Gillespie, *A Class Act: an Illustrated History of the Labour Movement in Newfoundland and Labrador* (St. John's 1986), 32. Johnny Burke (1851-1930), St. John's actor, singer and poet wrote many ballads immortalizing local events and characters. See *Encyclopedia of Newfoundland and Labrador* (St. John's 1981), vol. 1, 295.

[58]*TR*, 22 May 1903; *EH*, 19 May 1903.

[59]*ET*, 16 September 1903.

[60]Membership figures quoted in annual report of the LSPU, *ET*, 16 May 1914. The potential male labour force in St. John's, aged 15 to 65 was 9858 as calculated from the Newfoundland census in 1911.

[61]Waite, "Longshoremen of Halifax," 140.

[62]*DN*, 13 April 1904.

[63]Contrast the number of strikes to uphold contract clauses in St. John's with the number (3) recorded in Halifax during the years 1902 to 1914. Waite, 176.

[64]*DN*, 31 July 1903; *ET*, 19 October, 16 November 1903; *EH*, 15, 29 April 1904, 6 March 1906; *Evening Chronicle* (St. John's), hereafter *EC*, 24 November 1908.

because of poor weather, or delays caused by the transfer of vessels from one pier to another; they quit work to protest efforts to undercut union wages or to reduce the wages of older workers.[65]

The most contentious issue was the definition of overtime. Union men insisted that they be given a minimum of six hours work if hired after 6 p.m. Employers resisted, arguing that it was their prerogative to determine closing time. The *Evening Herald* voiced the management viewpoint. "While considerable sympathy had been expressed for the men who struck for better wages as all knew they were deserving, there was no sympathy for those who presume to dictate to their employer how long they shall work."[66] The presumption of the LSPU that it regulate both waterfront manpower and the labour process was typical of the struggle between workers and employers on the docks in the early decades of the 20th century.[67]

Table 3
Strikes by Unionized Dock Workers, 1903-1914

Strikes by Year (38)	Cause of Strike
1903: 6	Employment of non-union: 16
1904: 10	Curtailment of overtime: 6
1905: 1	Higher wages: 5
1906: 5	Payment of union rates: 4
1907: 5	Unreasonable demands: 3
1908: 2	Sympathy strikes: 3
1909: 2	Time lost by hired men: 2
1910: 3	Union recognition: 2
1911: 2	
1912: 2	
1913: -	
1914: -	

The strength of the LSPU on the waterfront lay in its organization. Former strike leader Matthew Fleming was appointed "walking delegate" in September 1903 to monitor the implementation of union rules and to mediate grievances.[68] The union executive annually selected members as guards at the principal firms to

[65]*EH*, 5 May 1904; 15 February 1906; 17 September 1907; *ET*, 19 November 1910.
[66]*EH*, 3 June 1903.
[67]John B. Foster, "On the Waterfront: Longshoring in Canada," in Craig Heron and Robert Storey, eds., *On the Job: Confronting the Labour Process in Canada* (Kingston 1986), 281-308; Babcock, "Saint John Longshoremen."
[68]*ET*, 8 September 1903. On some occasions it is clear that Fleming acted as a hiring foreman. Unfortunately, hiring practices in the pre-war period were not detailed and union jurisdiction over hiring remains unclear.

enforce contract stipulations; badges were distributed to distinguish union and non-union labour.[69] By the threat of boycott, the LSPU extended its jurisdiction beyond the steamship agencies and the fish exporters with whom it had directly negotiated. The union intimated that it would strike any city premises which shipped fish or freight discharged or stacked by non-unionized labour. An irate G.L. Fearn complained in the *Trade Review*:

Upon two separate occassions when I was shipping fish by Messrs. Pitts' steamers, it was expedient to cart the fish from the railway station and pile it on Messrs. Pitts' wharf .... To do this piling, I employed labor outside of the Labor Union and, as a result, Messrs. Pitts were warned by the Union that if they allowed me to do this again they would not load the steamers ....[70]

Despite friction within the LSPU over political affiliations, the union presented a solid front at the workplace. In the many strikes described in the press, there were no union men who broke ranks to return to work before a strike settlement. There were no recorded wildcat strikes; only one strike action was not authorized by the LSPU, a brief strike by young dockers over the interpretation of Union rules.[71] Waterfront unionism increased the wages of common labourers in the city, even those outside the LSPU. American consul George Cornelius observed: "Formerly laborers earned but 80 cents to $1.00 per day of 10 hours but now these figures have been increased 30 to 50 per cent ... The betterment has been brought about by a series of 'strikes' ..."[72]

In 1890, the city dockworker interviewed in the *Colonist* had complained bitterly about the seasonal influx of outharbour men onto the St. John's wharves:

In the fall of the year when the fisheries is over, hundreds of outport men, mostly from Conception and Trinity Bays, flock into St. John's looking for work on the wharves. They are willing to work for less money than eighty cents, aye and even 'take it up' in the shops ... it is not out of meanness that they act so; many of them have starving families at home, for whom they almost starve themselves ....[73]

Tensions existed between city and rural workers, particularly in the competition for employment in the capital, but the LSPU attempted to accommodate outport labourers when possible. Determined to exclude cheap labour from the water-front,[74] the LSPU extended union membership to outport workers. As early as

[69]*ET*, 1 June 1903. Union badges and rule books were given to men upon their initiation into the union.

[70]*TR*, 22 October 1904; see also *ET*, 9 September 1903.

[71]*EH*, 14 May 1907.

[72]George O. Cornelius, American Consul at St. John's 1901-1906. Annual Report, 25 November 1906, Despatch 34/9 Microfilm 594 in US Consulate, St. John's. Despatches [microfilm series].

[73]*DC*, 22 September 1890.

[74]The LSPU were actively involved in opposing the immigration of the Chinese to Newfoundland in 1906; they petitioned the House of Assembly requesting legislation to prevent

September 1903 the *Trade Review* observed that "outport men, coming to town to work, are dropping into the Union without difficulty and paying the entrance fee."[75] Outport members were employed at union rates and received their wages in cash, in contrast with the outharbours where labourers were frequently paid in truck.[76]

When labour was scarce on the waterfront, it is possible that the hiring foremen favoured the St. John's hands, thus curtailing the employment once available to the outport labourers on the city wharves.[77] When labour was plentiful, however, outport men and city dockworkers worked side by side. After the close of the seal fishery, men brought from the north shore of Conception Bay to discharge the seals from the steamers were initiated into the Labourers Union.[78] Although a St. John's faction controlled the Executive of the LSPU, a large percentage of the membership were fishermen. President McGrath observed in 1912:

... nearly 1000 of the 2300 members on the roll of the Union are fishermen ... many hundreds of fishermen from Trinity and Conception Bays will find employment in this city this year at the rate of wages which the Union has been able to obtain for them.[79]

On occasion the LSPU waived the union dues of fishermen who were handling fish from their own schooners as long as they were paid union rates. The *Fisherman's Advocate* informed its readers in 1911:

The Laborers are busy and the supply of men does not meet the demand. At many premises ... crews of schooners are engaged by the merchants to work on the wharves .... The Labor Union is permitting this ... the crews engaged so are not required to join the Union ... to work temporarily, but we ask that crews so engaged to refuse to work unless they receive the regular wages paid to Laborers ....[80]

---

the Chinese influx: "Let cheap Chinese labor enter into competition with petitioners and decrease the present rate of wages, then there is nothing left but us to emigrate or live in a state ... intolerable." Quoted by Robert Hong, "'To take action without delay': Newfoundland's Chinese Immigration Act of 1906," Honours dissertation, Memorial University, 1987, 50.

[75]*TR*, 12 September 1903.

[76]*ET*, 9 September 1903; *FA*, 6 May 1911.

[77]For the practice of hiring familiar hands see *ET*, 16 May 1903 and 4 November 1912. There was probably tension between the outport fisherman-farmer turned dockworker and the city labourer whose dock work was his sole source of earnings. See *ET*, 17 April 1917.

[78]*EH*, 30 March 1906. On at least two occasions the LSPU successfully negotiated wage increases for the seal labourers. See *ET*, 4 April 1907; *ET*, 28 March 1910.

[79]*EC*, 24 April 1912. These figures for outport membership appear high. In 1908 when LSPU membership was estimated at 2100, the outport contingent approximated 300. *EC*, 3 October 1908.

[80]*Fisherman's Advocate*, 26 August 1911.

The LSPU was unique among longshore unions in Atlantic Canada, in successfully organizing outport fishermen and city workers within a common association and in uniting transient rural labourers and city dockers in a common cause.[81]

IV

Labourers were the largest single group of workers in St. John's. Unlike the conventional image of the dockworker as young, transient and unattached, the majority of the city's labourers were married men with dependents.[82] Our *Colonist* reporter in 1890 had been astonished by the low wages of the city dockworkers; how had their families survived on so little? One of the labourers responded in a manner which illustrated the occupational pluralism of the urban worker and the household economy of the city's poor: "... formerly the seal fisheries were good ... this, with nurse-tending by my wife got me through till some of the family were grown up. I have two sons in the States and they send money ... a daughter who lives with us is a tailoress ...."[83] The wives of the dockworkers frequently worked at waged labour, but at tasks unnoticed by the census enumerator: child tending; laundering; knitting nets and twine; sewing or finishing garments as home workers for the city's tailoring and clothing firms.[84] Addressing a delegation of longshoremen in May 1903, politician T.J. Murphy commented on the inability of dockworkers to secure a family wage:

You earn $3 per week unloading steamers ... but you do not get the work in the winter months. You have a family to support, clothe and school. Under these conditions your wife must go out and work. Your children will grow up without a mother's care; you cannot afford to pay for education; you cannot get clothes sufficiently decent to send them to school.[85]

It was the plight of the dockworkers' children which attracted notice and created unease.

In the fall of 1911, thirty boys employed at Harveys, aged ten to sixteen years, struck for a dollar a day; they had been hired at eight cents an hour to assist in the discharge of 27,000 barrels of flour from the steamships *Bonavista* and *Britannic*.

[81]In Halifax, for example, effective dock unionism was limited to longshoremen discharging and loading steamers; although units of fish handlers were organized, longshoremen and wharf men were not integrated.

[82]Calculated from *McAlpine's Newfoundland Directory: containing an Alphabetical Directory and Street Directory of the City of St. John's and of the Districts of the Island 1904* (Halifax). Directories generally under-counted labourers and domestic servants. See Gareth Shaw, "Nineteenth Century Directories as Sources in Canadian Social History," *Archivaria*, 14 (Summer 1982), 117-8.

[83]*DC*, 19 September 1890.

[84]See Nancy Forestell and Jessie Chisholm, "Working-Class Women as Wage Earners in St. John's, Newfoundland 1890-1921," in Peta Tancred-Sheriff, ed., *Feminist Research: Prospect and Retrospect* (Kingston 1988), 140-8.

[85]*ET*, 19 May 1903.

Their demands refused by management, they demonstrated, parading to the King's Wharf with a large banner. The following day the strike collapsed; strikers had been replaced by other youngsters desperate for employment. "There were plenty of boys to be had elsewhere to fill their shoes and the strikers had to go back for the usual eighty cents a day."[86] A delegation of boys was selected, however, to confer with solicitor Gibbs about the establishment of a Juvenile Branch of the LSPU.[87]

Child labour was common on the St. John's waterfront. William Coaker, founder of the Fishermen's Protective Union, recalled leaving school unwillingly as a youngster of eleven in 1881 to work on the south side wharves, tending the cullers and yaffling fish.[88] In 1890 a correspondent to the *Daily Colonist* worried about the vulnerability of juvenile labourers on the docks, some of whom were only ten or twelve years of age. These boys, he noted sympathetically, "were generally the children of very poor parents who cannot afford to send them to school ... because they require the few shillings the boys earn to keep the wolf from the door."[89] Boys were favoured by the merchant firms for specific tasks, for their quickness in conveying light packages and their agility in discharging barrels.[90] They were also employed as cheap labour in backbreaking toil, working alongside men for sixteen or seventeen hours a day; boys were paid 50 to 80 cents a day during the period 1890-1914 — 33 to 50 per cent of the adult rate.[91]

The strike by child labourers in 1911 was not singular. Perhaps the most famous of strikes by boys on the St. John's wharves was that of juvenile fish handlers in early September 1883, organized and led by Coaker, then thirteen years old. He and his companions struck Job Brothers, demanding 40 cents a day (a ten-cent increase) and parity with wages paid boys at other premises. Although the wharfinger Pa Parsons "got into a rage and ordered every boy off the premises, declaring that he never wanted to see their faces anymore," the boys persisted, posting pickets at all the entrances to Jobs to prevent the hiring of replacements. After two days the wharfinger relented, conceding the ten-cent increase and reinstating all the strikers. "To undertake such a task in those days required courage," a colleague remembered, "for boys to unite in such demands endangered their being boycotted for the rest of the Fall season."[92] Although the risk of dismissal and blacklisting remained

[86]*ET*, 15 November 1911.

[87]*DN* and *EC*, 14 November 1911; *ET*, 14, 15 November 1911.

[88]Speech by William Coaker, quoted in *Proceedings of the House of Assembly* (Government of Newfoundland), 1914, 172 and cited by John Feltham, "The Development of the F.P.U. in Newfoundland (1908-1923)," MA thesis, Memorial University, 1959, 18. Coaker stressed the necessity of free, non-denominational schools and night schools for the labouring classes in Newfoundland.

[89]*DC*, 10 October 1890; see also 18 November 1890.

[90]*EH*, 18 October 1907.

[91]For rates paid boys on the wharves, see *ET*, 25 September 1907; *EH*, 9 November 1909; *DN*, 14 November 1911.

[92]There is a wonderfully detailed account of the strike by James M. Carberry in "A Strike of Forty Years Ago," *Evening Advocate* (St. John's), formerly *FA*, 19 December 1923. The

constant in the pre-war decades, boys working on city wharves were involved in at least eight strikes; strikes by boys discharging cargoes of flour were most common, but juvenile coal trimmers, fish handlers and winch tenders also struck work.[93] All but one stoppage centred on wage increases; only one was successful — a walkout at Harveys in 1909 for wage parity with the Shea and Pitts premises.[94] Without formal union organization, children were vulnerable workers.

Child labour on the wharves alarmed the LSPU executive. As early as September 1903 boys had expressed an interest in unionization. The *Evening Telegram* noted that "the boys working on the merchants' wharves are forming themselves into a protective union and will likely become a branch of the Steamboat Laborers' Union."[95] The SLU discussed the formation of a Juvenile Branch for several weeks, but apparently abandoned this, perhaps in favour of organizing adult labour across the waterfront.[96] In 1913 the idea revived; the LSPU executive recorded their concerns in the annual report:

The necessity for organizing a Juvenile Branch of the Union has ... become very urgent for the purpose of preventing the exploitation of child labour in this city. One of the most pitiful conditions noticed by your officers was that a large number of boys under the age of 14 years are employed on the same steamships and on the mercantile premises, working upwards of 15 hours a day, some of them engaged in the most arduous tasks.[97]

A week later, an organizational meeting of boys employed on the wharves and at manual labour in the city was convened; its goals were to ensure minimum standards governing wages and working conditions for youths, and to press for legislation prohititing child labour. Seventy-five members were enrolled at the initial meeting; 30 per cent were unable to read or write.[98] A schedule was submitted to employers stipulating minimum age (fourteen years), maximum hours (ten-hour day), and wage rates (ten cents per hour discharging cargo; nine cents per hour handling fish).[99] On 4 June 1913 the first executive of the Juvenile Branch of the

story is repeated in Ian McDonald, *"To Each his Own": William Coaker and the Fishermen's Protective Union in Newfoundland Politics, 1908-1925*, ed. J.K. Hiller (St. John's 1987), 15.
[93] *ET*, 9 June 1893; *EH*, 25 September 1907; *ET*, 25 September 1907; *EH* and *ET*, 17-18 October; *EH*, 9-10 November 1909; *EJ*, 14-15 November 1911; *ET*, 27 November.
[94] The strike by boys discharging coal was for "more favorable conditions"; the strikers stated that their wages were satisfactory. *ET*, 27 November 1911. The outcome of four strikes is known; for the successful strike, see *EH*, 17-18 October 1911.
[95] *ET*, 15 September 1903.
[96] The discussion continued throughout September; see *ET*, 16, 23 September 1903. No reason was given for shelving consideration of juvenile labour.
[97] *EH*, 23 May 1913. See also *ET*, 30 May 1913 for a letter by James McGrath describing a visit to various mercantile premises. He noted the number of boys employed discharging steamers, "some of these boys had only just turned 10 years."
[98] *Ibid.*, 29 May 1913. Twelve boys were refused membership because they were under 14 years of age.
[99] *ET*, 31 May 1913.

LSPU was elected; by then membership exceeded ninety.[100] In January 1914 the LSPU opened a night school for its juvenile members, several union men acting as assistant teachers. Although night schools for working children existed throughout the period, generally under church auspices, the LSPU was the first city union to organize and finance such an institution.[101]

In St. John's the LSPU successfully intervened to secure minimum protection for children employed on the wharves. Although regretting the necessity of child labour, the union recognized that many city families depended on the income of its working boys; its goal was to "ensure for boys ... at work ... a decent living wage and to obviate labour of a character beyond their physical powers ...."[102] Few Canadian unions organized juvenile workers; an exception was the Provincial Workmen's Association (PWA) in Nova Scotia, which established separate juvenile lodges for coal pit boys.[103] Indeed, Robert McIntosh's and Ian McKay's richly detailed accounts of child labour in the Nova Scotia coal mines offer useful analogies; like the pit boys, St. John's juvenile dock workers were both exploited and enfranchised by their work, developing patterns of resistance and collective action usually associated only with adult workers. Their work "gave these juvenile workers a fighting strength unique among the thousands of children who were swept up by the industrial revolution."[104]

V

Although the LSPU concentrated on the organization of dock workers, it included labourers employed elsewhere in St. John's. It is difficult to estimate the number of common labourers organized by the LSPU, as no membership lists for the pre-war decades survived.[105] It was only when unionized labourers struck that LSPU

[100] *ET*, 5 June 1913. Although the Juvenile Branch was subordinate to the parent organization, it met independently and conducted its own affairs.
[101] *ET*, 14 January, 6 February 1914. The average nightly attendance was eighty; the night school also conducted a class for adult members unable to read or write. See *LSPU Minute Books*, 12 January 1914, Centre for Newfoundland Studies, Memorial University of Newfoundland.
[102] *ET*, 28 May 1913.
[103] Ian McKay notes in his "Strikes in the Maritimes, 1901-1914," *Acadiensis* XIII, 1 (Autumn 1983), 220, that city unions did little to organize juvenile labour in Saint John or Halifax. In his article, "The Realm of Uncertainty: the Experience of Work in the Cumberland Coal Mines, 1873-1927," *Acadiensis* XVI, 1 (Autumn, 1986), 26-33, McKay details the work experience and strikes by coal pit boys. Robert McIntosh differs from McKay in emphasizing the tensions between juvenile and adult mine workers; see his "The Boys in the Nova Scotian Mines 1873 to 1923," *Acadiensis* XVI, 2 (Spring 1987), 35-50, especially pages 42-6. Unfortunately, our sources say little about the implications of dock labour for youthful wharf labourers themselves.
[104] McKay, "Realm of Uncertainty," 26.
[105] There are lists in the back of the LSPU minute books but these are undated and fragmentary, encompassing less than ten per cent of union members. Although total mem-

organization attracted public notice and comment. In 1908, for example, twelve men hired to repair the King's Wharf quit work; members of the Carpenters' Union and LSPU respectively, they struck to protest the employment of three non-union labourers. Althought the men in question agreed to join the LSPU, "one of the foremen employed on the work intervened and refused to permit them to join the organization."[106] When the strikers refused to resume work with the non-unionized labourers, they were replaced. The foreman's actions caused considerable controversy, as repairs to the public wharf was a government contract. The LSPU passed resolutions condemning the "action of the Government in permitting the work to be done with non-union labor,"[107] and several sympathizers wrote angry letters to the newspapers, arguing that unionized labour and union rates be stipulated in government projects. "A Union Man" commented bitterly:

Working men to-day the world over must recognise that the protection and remuneration they receive is due to organization, and no man or body of men must be permitted to turn back the hands on the dial of a fair living wage and the right to organize ... the most curious feature [in Newfoundland] ... is that whenever the Government has control and the taxes of the workmen are utilized in defraying the cost, the scab or the non-union workman is invariably employed....[108]

However, the campaign for a fair wage clause in government contracts and for the employment of unionized labour on public projects was unsuccessful.

On 13 May 1910 unionized labourers hired at the union rate (fifteen cents an hour) to clean sealing steamers complained to LSPU president James McGrath that the Reid Company foreman had taken on non-union labour and had arbitrarily cut wages to twelve cents. When McGrath visited the Dry Dock to investigate, he was ordered off the property by a Reid manager: "He told me to leave dock premises or he would have me arrested. He also said you can take your union men with you."[109] McGrath then pulled the union men, 60 labourers in all, from the sealing steamers, *Beothic* and *Diana*; the Reid Company retaliated by hiring a schooner's crew to discharge the SS *Bonaventure*.[110]

The impasse became critical on 16 May 1910 when the LSPU executive convened an emergency meeting and the union members voted unanimously to "make the strike general as far as the Reid Newfoundland Co. is concerned i.e. no

---

bership figures are noted in the Annual Reports of the LSPU, no breakdowns are provided, presumably because members shifted tasks as seasonal demands and labour requirements fluctuated.

[106]*EC*, 1 September 1908; see also, 22 August 1908; *EH*, 21 August 1908; *ET*, 3 September 1908.

[107]Resolutions adopted by the LSPU; quoted in *EC*, 3 September 1908.

[108]"A Union Man," *EC*, 1 September 1908.

[109]Letter to editor, *ET*, 16 May 1910. For varying accounts of the dispute, see *ET*, 10 May; *EC*, 14, 17 May; *EH*, 14, 17 May 1910.

[110]*ET*, 16 May 1910.

Union man is to perform any work for the Co. whatsoever, if any material comes
over the line to be transhipped, Union men will not be allowed to handle it."[111] The
Reid Newfoundland Company was a major player in the Newfoundland economy,
reportedly "the biggest paymaster in the Island, bigger than the Government
itself."[112] However, the LSPU was obviously reluctant to call a general strike across
the waterfront; the LSPU minutes laconically noted "the dock business was settled
and any member wish to go to work on the dock could go [sic]."[113] Lacking strike
funds, the LSPU was most effective in quick ad-hoc strikes against individual
companies and most vulnerable in a concerted general strike. The Reid Newfoundland Company remained the only major firm on the waterfront outside the LSPU
sphere. The Newfoundland experience had counterparts in 19th-century America.[114]

    One group of urban labourers organized by the LSPU had no connection with
the St. John's waterfront. These were the sanitary workers, municipal employees
who carted away the garbage and refuse and swept the city streets. In May 1904 the
sanitary employees joined the LSPU.[115] Seemingly their situation contrasted favourably with casual waterfront labourers, as sanitary men were permanent employees paid weekly; many of the city's 30-man sanitary staff in 1910 had worked
for council 20 or 30 years.[116] In 1890 the wages of the municipal carmen and street

[111]Centre for Newfoundland Studies Archives, *LSPU Minute Book* (Volume 1), 16 May
1910; *EH*, 17 May 1910. See also *LSPU, Minute Book*, Special Meeting, 9 September 1910.
[112]P.T. McGrath, *Newfoundland in 1911* (London 1911), 24 cited in Peter McInnis, "Newfoundland Labour and World War I, the Emergence of the Newfoundland Industrial Workers'
Association," MA thesis, Memorial University, 1987, 24. Awarded the lucrative Newfoundland Railroad contract in 1898 (the infamous "Reid Deal"), the Reid Newfoundland Company secured control of the island's coastal steamship and telegraph system and the right to
purchase the publicly owned Dry Dock. By 1914 Reids were dominant in the transportation
and heavy industry sectors of the local economy. See J.K. Hiller, "The Railway and Local
Politics in Newfoundland, 1870-1911," in J.K. Hiller and Peter Neary, eds., *Newfoundland
in the Nineteenth and Twentieth Centuries: Essays in Interpretation* (Toronto 1980), 123-
147; J.W. McGrath, "R.G. Reid and the Newfoundland Railway," unpublished paper,
Newfoundland Historical Society. St. John's, 8 December 1971.
[113]*LSPU Minute Book*, 27 December 1910.
[114]David Montgomery, in describing capitalist power on the US waterfront, focused on the
steamship lines and the railroad companies which operated many of the state coastal vessels.
In New Orleans and New York, the railroads smashed the transport unions. Steamship
companies, in contrast, were much less interested in holding down the hourly wages of
longshoremen than they were in ensuring the quick discharge and dispatch of their steamships. See Montgomery, *The Fall of the House of Labor*, 103. For a Canadian equivalent,
see Conley, "Class Conflict," 517.
[115]*ET*, 26 May 1904.
[116]Letter by Patrick English, a sanitary employee for 31 years, in *ET*, 12 May 1910. See also
ET, 23 April 1907.

sweepers had been increased to $1.00 per day, a rate higher than dock labour.[117] By 1906, however, their wages lagged behind union schedules.[118] Sanitary workers had other complaints as well: the exhausting and unhealthy nature of their employment; the rigid discipline exercised by supervisory personnel; the deductions from weekly pay packets for job-related illness; the flagrant favouritism displayed by foremen.

The sanitary employees began work at midnight, the teamsters and their assistants collecting and depositing the night soil. When this task was finished, usually at 3 a.m., the workers returned home or slept on the floors of the sanitary stables until daylight. They then resumed work, gathering the ashes and household garbage and sweeping the streets until noon; during the winter months, where sweeping was impossible, they drained the cesspools. On Sundays the men were allowed to quit work at 3 a.m. to rest for morning church services.[119] In 1910 the LSPU petitioned City Council to allow sanitary employees ten minutes grace at midnight for "whenever the men are a few minutes late others are immediately sent out in their place."[120] The men were subjected to strict discipline when on the job. They were forbidden the use of tobacco in any form and they were "warned against speaking on the street to any other person than the bosses."[121] During outbreaks of infectious diseases, the sanitary workers removed the garbage and the night soil from the afflicted households; in January 1911 a sanitary employee died of typhoid and his son was reported gravely ill.[122] The LSPU complained that the wages of the sanitary employees were withheld when they were sick even when they "were injured or contracted infectious diseases while doing duty."[123] In 1910, Patrick English, a 31-year veteran of the city's sanitary services, wrote a bitter letter to the *Telegram*:

In the sanitary service there are other men who have spend 31 years in work similar to mine. When they are sick their wages are stopped even when they get a certificate from the doctor ... I ought in my years to be retired with full pay and this would only be a just recognition of my past services.[124]

[117]*DC*, 19 September 1890. Wages of street sweepers were increased from $5.60 to $6 per week. Carmen's (teamsters') rates were raised from $6.50 to $7.00; "this will give them $1 per day, the carmen working 7 days a week."

[118]*DN*, 11 August 1906.

[119]The description of the sanitary men's daily routine was taken from letters in the *ET* and *DN* on 23 May 1912. In 1899 the *ET* claimed that sanitary employees are "at work sixteen hours out of the twenty-four," 18 April 1899. See also *DN*, 27 May 1912.

[120]*EC*, 17 December 1910.

[121]These regulations were adopted in 1899. The penalties for the use of tobacco were 50-cent fine for first offence (one-half day's pay); one dollar fine for second offence (one day's pay) and dismissal for the third offence. The penalty for conversing with the public was one week's suspension.

[122]*ET*, 9 January 1911.

[123]*ET*, 1 February 1908.

[124]*ET*, 12 May 1910. Patrick English was a spokesman for the union in the sanitary department. See *EC*, 2 September 1911.

Feelings were not eased by the arbitrary practices of sanitary supervisors. In 1907 wages were raised for "men who only went to work during the past week (novices at the work) ... while several of the most reliable and trustworthy are snubbed."[125] It was the erratic enforcement of regulations by supervisors that provoked a major strike by sanitary employees in 1908, an embarrassing labour dispute for the city's mayor, Michael Gibbs, who was also solicitor for the LSPU. A sanitary employee had been dismissed for removing garbage from private property "without orders." The *Telegram* noted that "when a Sanitary man performs such a service without orders from the Supervisor he is in the wrong, whereas if he performs such with orders he is in the right."[126] The other sanitary workers struck in sympathy with the dismissed man and they were replaced by non-union workers. After several meetings between Municipal Council and the LSPU executive, the city reinstated the strikers and ordered an investigation into the grievances of the fired sanitary employee; the man was later rehired.[127]

The interventions of the LSPU on behalf of boy labourers and municipal employees were significant. Descriptions of labourers' unionism at work, as historian David Montgomery has observed, "offer fleeting glimpses of the remedies that laborers advanced for their own problems. All of them ... created some framework of stability ... and encouraged concerted action and programmatic thinking."[128] Like the labourers' unions Montgomery describes, the LSPU sought not only to raise wages, but also to moderate the grinding pace of work and to reduce the arbitrary powers of foremen and supervisors. In the case of child workers and sanitary employees, perhaps the most poignant examples of the brutalization of waged labour, the LSPU reasserted their claims to redress, to the self-respect and dignity denied them within a class-based society.

Conclusion

It is only by the establishment of an absolute monopoly of the Labor supply of a particular kind that a Union can hope to raise wages and to ameliorate the conditions under which its members work and live.[129]

Steamship stevedoring created a cohesive group of dock workers who spearheaded the unionizing drives on the waterfront in the late 19th century. Dock unions imposed a uniform schedule of wages and hours, excluded transient and non-union labour and attempted to spread available work among union members. While the

[125] *ET*, 23 April 1907.
[126] The regulation allowed supervisors to discriminate among householders. *ET*, 29 June 1908. "There is a discrimination exercised ... the rule is radically wrong and is prolific of trouble."
[127] The sanitary employees' strike received wide coverage. See *DN*, 29-30 June, 3 July; *EC*, 27-30 June, 1-7 July; *EH*, 27, 29-30 June, 1, 2, 7, 8, 11 July 1908.
[128] Montgomery, *Fall*, 96.
[129] Anonymous, "Labor Organizations in Newfoundland," *Christmas Echo*, 2 (1917), 16.

ascendancy of the steam vessel allowed a degree of autonomy to steamboat labourers it also intensified the pace of work on the docks, heightened the irregular and casual nature of port employment, and deliberately created a surplus of labour, variables which impeded unionization. In Maritime Canada, the ambiguities inherent in maritime steam technology were complicated by the persistence of traditional wharf labour associated with the fish trade and merchant capital. In Halifax, argued Ian McKay, the casual labour system and the diffuse nature of the port created social fragmentation: "Labourers ... built unions that failed either to change the system or to achieve a secure status on the waterfront."[130]

The pattern of unionization on the St. John's docks is in striking contrast to Halifax, the Maritime port it most resembled. The LSPU was successful, precisely because it was able to establish that "absolute monopoly of the Labor supply," to integrate longshoremen and fish handlers, and to accommodate casual and transient labour. The LSPU was unique among longshore unions in Atlantic Canada in successfully organizing outport fishermen and city workers within a common association and in uniting casual labourers and permanent employees in a common cause. The success of the LSPU indicates that there were more possibilities for class solidarity within merchant capital than initially suspected.

[130]Ian McKay, "Class Struggle and Merchant Capital," 35.

The author gratefully acknowledges the assistance of a SSHRC Doctoral Fellowship in researching the history of the working-class community in St. John's, 1890-1914.

Nolan Reilly

10

The General Strike in Amherst, Nova Scotia, 1919

On 19 May 1919 news of the Amherst general strike spread throughout Nova Scotia. "So far as it can be learned," the Sydney *Record* declared, "it is on practically the same lines as the one which has been paralyzing the city of Winnipeg for several days past."[1] Another editor worried that this eastern "replica of Winnipeg labour troubles" might spread to other towns in the Maritimes.[2] Strike leader Frank Burke did little to alleviate these fears when he "championed the One Big Union idea" before a large meeting of local workers the next evening and predicted that "the time would be here speedily when the Union would have full power from the Atlantic to the Pacific."[3] By the time of this speech, striking workers in Amherst had already closed the town's eight largest industries and local mechanics and civic workers had also joined the strike. For the next three weeks the life of the community was dominated by the general strike. Throughout Amherst, "the new 'One Big Union' buttons" became "conspicuous not only on the streets, but also in many establishments, worn by the employees ... in sympathy with the men."[4] Most of the town's workers and their families attended daily union meetings to discuss the progress of the strike. In speeches and petitions the strikers advanced their demands: recognition of the Amherst Federation of Labor — popularly known as the One Big Union — improved wages and working conditions, and a shorter working day. At first the employers refused "to deal in any way or form with the One Big Union as a whole," but after several weeks of often bitter negotiations they granted some, although certainly not all of their employees' demands.[5]

[1]*Record* (Sydney), 21 May 1919.
[2]*Post* (Sydney), 20 May 1919.
[3]*Daily News* (Amherst), 21 May 1919.
[4]*Eastern Federationist* (Pictou), 31 May 1919.
[5]*Daily News*, 22 May 1919.

Published with permission of the editor. From *Acadiensis*, IX, 2 (Spring 1980), 56-77.

Vying for public attention with the more dramatic episodes of class conflict that occurred in western Canada in 1919, the Amherst events received scant notice outside the Maritimes. Most contemporary commentators viewed the Amherst strike either as a sympathy strike to support Winnipeg workers or as a spontaneous protest against low wages and poor working conditions. Historians have treated the general strike in much the same manner.[6] In part, this disinterest stems from the highly specialized regional interests of Canadian historians. While there have been a number of studies of western Canadian radicalism, the writing of Maritime and central Canadian working-class history has lagged behind.[7] But recent work suggests that what David Bercuson and others have seen as western exceptionalism in the early twentieth-century history of Canadian working-class radicalism may well have been a more generalized phenomenon. The political and organizational form of this activity varied from region to region and the tendency to divide the country into radical and conservative groups of workers perhaps misses the variety of working-class responses to post-war industrial capitalism.[8]

The Amherst general strike resulted from the interaction of two broad historical processes which began prior to the First World War. First, the impact of the de-industrialization that accompanied the centralization of power and wealth in central Canada affected Amherst's working class in immediate terms as working conditions, wages, and living standards fell behind those of other Canadian workers. Particularly ominous for local workers were the signs pointing toward the complete

[6]David J. Bercuson, *Fools and Wise Men: The Rise and Fall of the One Big Union* (Toronto 1978); Ernest R. Forbes, *The Maritimes Rights Movement, 1919-1927: A Study in Canadian Regionalism* (Montréal 1979).

[7]See, for example, David Frank and Nolan Reilly, "The Emergence of the Socialist Movement in the Maritimes, 1899-1916," *Labour/Le Travailleur*, 4 (1979), 85-113; David Frank, "The Cape Breton Coal Miners, 1917-1926" (PhD thesis, Dalhousie University, 1979); Don Macgillivray, "Industrial Unrest in Cape Breton, 1919-1925" (MA thesis, University of New Brunswick, 1971); Robert Brym and James Sacouman, eds., *Underdevelopment and Social Movements in Atlantic Canada* (Toronto 1979). For an assessment of Canadian working-class historiography, see David Bercuson, "Through the Looking Glass of Culture: An Examination of the New Labour History in Canada" (unpublished paper delivered at the Conference on "Class and Culture: Dimensions of Canada's Labour Past," Montréal 1980); Gregory S. Kealey, "The Working Class in Recent Canadian Historical Writing," *Acadiensis*, VII (1978), 116-35; Gregory S. Kealey, "Labour and Working-Class History in Canada: Retrospect and Prospect" (unpublished paper delivered at the Conference on "Class and Culture: Dimensions of Canada's Labour Past," Montréal 1980).

[8]David J. Bercuson, *Fools and Wise Men: The Rise and Fall of the One Big Union* (Toronto 1978), and "Labour Radicalism and the Western Frontier: 1897-1919," *Canadian Historical Review*, LVIII (1977), 154-75. For other studies of western Canadian radicalism, consult Gerald Friesen, "'Yours in Revolt': The Socialist Party of Canada and the Western Labour Movement," *Labour/Le Travailleur*, 1 (1976), 139-57; A. Ross McCormack, *Reformers, Rebels, and Revolutionaries: The Western Canadian Radical Movement, 1899-1919* (Toronto 1977); Martin Robin, *Radical Politics and Canadian Labour, 1880-1930* (Kingston 1968).

economic collapse of the town. Second, the local labour movement, partly because of previous failures, began to move toward a more radical response to these economic developments. In 1919, the merging of these two forces forged a new working-class solidarity in Amherst, which found expression in the rise of the Amherst Federation of Labor, the renewed interest in socialist ideas and, of course, the three-week general strike.

In 1919 Amherst's economy was in crisis. Like the rest of the Maritimes, the town was confronting the final effects of its integration into the national economy. Throughout the early years of the twentieth century, Amherst thrived on a manu- facturing economy that produced railway rolling stock, steam engines and boilers, woollen goods, boots and shoes, enamel ware, furnaces, pianos, and home and office furniture. The largest manufacturer in town, Rhodes-Curry & Co., employed 2,000 men to build railway cars and to meet the demands of its construction business. Robb Engineering, known nationally for its engines and boilers, hired 500 workers, and the shoeworks and woollen mill each had 200 employees.[9] Between 1901 and 1906, Amherst's total value of production soared from $1 million to $4.5 million and the population doubled to reach almost 10,000.[10] The town bore the distinction of being one of the region's most important and rapidly growing manufacturing centres, and became known throughout the Maritimes as "Busy Amherst." Following the 1907-1908 recession, however, Amherst entered a period of decline that intensified over the next 15 years. The flood of central Canadian manufactured goods into the region and the extension of metropolitan financial control over the region's economy spelled disaster for the town.[11] In 1909, in the first and most important of a series of industrial mergers in Amherst, the million dollar Rhodes-Curry & Co. was linked with two Montréal concerns to form the Canadian Car & Foundry Co. The serious 1913-1914 depression signalled yet a further weaving of local manufacturing into the national economy. Industries severely reduced staff and at least one factory in Amherst closed permanently. Although this pattern was repeated across the country, few towns faced the total ruin of their manufacturing sector that was confronting Amherst.

[9]Employment statistics are compiled from a variety of newspaper and government sources. See, for example, Nova Scotia, *Journals of the Assembly*, 1911, Appendix no. 15. Historical accounts of Amherst's two largest industries are available in *The Busy East* (March 1911) and Norman Ritchie, *The Story of Robb's* (Amherst, N.S. n.d.).
[10]Canada, *Census*, 1911, vol. III, Table XI, "Manufactories of Cities having 5,000 inhabitants and over compared for 1891, 1901, 1911 by provinces."
[11]A number of recent writings provide a general introduction to the economic history of Atlantic Canada: Brym and Sacouman, *Underdevelopment and Social Movements in Atlantic Canada* (Toronto 1979); T.W. Acheson, "The National Policy and the Industrialization of the Maritimes," *Acadiensis*, I (1971), 3-28; David Alexander, "Economic Growth in the Atlantic Region, 1880-1940," *Acadiensis*, VIII (1978), 47-76; David Frank, "The Cape Breton Coal Industry and the Rise and Fall of the British Empire Steel Corporation," *Acadiensis*, VII (1977), 3-34.

The demands of the First World War brought an artificial buoyancy to Amherst's economy. Unemployment declined as men enlisted in the army and factories shifted to wartime production. The railway carworks concentrated on munitions, Robb Engineering built marine boilers and manufactured shells, the piano factory provided shell boxes, and the woollen mill and shoeworks thrived on government contracts. The armistice of November 1918 brought an abrupt halt to this activity. Manufacturers warned of a prolonged "readjustment period" and prepared to lay off staff, as unemployment again became a serious problem with the return to Amherst of 500 war veterans. While many local residents worried about the ability, and in some cases, the desire of local business to make the transition to peace-time production, the most heated debates were reserved for speculation over the future of the crucially important carworks.[12] Before the war Canadian Car & Foundry had suspended operations at the Amherst Malleable Iron Co. and, in 1919, it announced the closing of plants in Halifax and New Glasgow. These actions were integral aspects of Canadian Car & Foundry's policy to concentrate production in central Canada. Supervised by Nathaniel Curry, former president of Rhodes-Curry, this policy threatened the existence of the Amherst carworks. As one observer remarked, "the days of the wooden cars" built in the Amherst works were passing as surely as the days of "wooden ships and iron men" had slipped into a bygone era. If Amherst was to remain an important centre of the rolling stock industry, it needed modernization, especially equipment to construct pressed steel rolling stock. But while Canadian Car & Foundry modernized its Montréal facilities and constructed a new plant in Fort William, it retreated from car building in Amherst.[13]

In 1919, the declining importance of the Amherst shops within Canadian Car & Foundry's corporate structure created three pressing problems for local workers: irregular employment, poor working conditions, and wage differentials favouring the company's Montréal employees. Finding steady employment was a serious concern for Amherst carbuilders. During the winter of 1918, the company operated with fewer than 200 men. Although this number increased to 800 in the spring months, this was still far below the 2,000 workers employed in 1905. Given the erratic employment practices of the company, even the men hired in 1919 had few prospects for steady work. Canadian Car & Foundry often raised the hopes of Amherst workers with announcements of massive hirings, followed several months later by equally impressive layoffs. Persistent rumours of one department or another being removed to Montréal further heightened the workers' anxieties.[14] Working conditions in the carworks also created tension. In 1919 moulder William Rackham complained to the Royal Commission on Industrial Relations of high gas levels in the foundry and claimed that the factory inspector refused to heed his complaints. The commissioners were urged to tour the plant and discover for themselves that

---

[12] Amherst *Daily News*, 4 January 1919; Town of Amherst, *Urban Renewal Study*, prepared by Norman Pearson and Canadian-British Engineering Consultants (Amherst 1965), 12.
[13] *Daily News*, 20, 21 June 1919; *Monetary Times, Annual Review for 1913*, 79.
[14] *Daily News*, 21 June, 6 May, 17 June 1919.

conditions "were far from being what the law demanded."[15] Although such conditions were common, Canadian Car & Foundry's decision not to direct new investment into its Amherst facilities undoubtedly aggravated the problem. The most contentious issue in 1919 was Canadian Car & Foundry's decision not to extend to Amherst the agreement it reached with its Montréal employees. The Montréal contract recognized the International Brotherhood of Railway Carmen, and adopted the "Whitley Advisory Council idea," the nine-hour day with 10 hours pay, five-day week, overtime pay, and layoffs by seniority. Considered a "fair and reasonable settlement" by the Amherst press and most local workers, all agreed that the contract should be extended to the eastern carmen, but the company refused to grant any concessions to its Amherst employees, except the nine-hour day with no provision for 10 hours pay.[16]

The marginality of the Amherst shops to the financial health of the Canadian Car & Foundry strengthened significantly the company's negotiating position. Concentration of railway car production in Montréal made it easier, and probably necessary, given the relative decline in productivity in Amherst, to resist the contract demands of eastern workers. Management believed that the long layoffs of the previous year and the threatened closure of the carworks, which finally occurred in the 1920s, would make the carmen reluctant to strike. Canadian Car & Foundry's successful attempts to curtail union organizing in the years preceding the war, especially the 1914 defeat of the International Association of Machinists, further bolstered its determination to bargain hard in 1919.[17] But the carmen were equally determined to win a contract consistent with that of Montréal workers and partly because of their previous failures at union organizing, they began to move toward a broad based industrial unionism.

The same pressures that prodded the railway carmen toward a new form of union organization also affected other Amherst working-class families. In 1919 none of the town's eight major industries appeared to have a particularly stable future. Managerial attitudes toward the employees of the Toronto controlled Dominion Manufacturing Co. and the Truro, Nova Scotia dominated Stanfield's Co. varied little from those of Canadian Car & Foundry. Both Dominion Manufacturing's 1914 purchase of Amherst's Christie Woodworking Co. and Stanfield's takeover of the Amherst Woollen Mill during the war were mergers to improve profits through reduced competition and were followed by a rationalization of productive capacity that detrimentally affected Amherst and brought the eventual

[15]*Daily News*, 10 June 1919; *Eastern Federationist*, 14 June 1919.
[16]*Daily News*, 13 May 1919. For information on the Whitley Council concept in Canada, see Bruce Scott, "'A Place in the Sun': the Industrial Council at Massey-Harris, 1919-1926," *Labour/Le Travailleur*, 1 (1976), 158-92.
[17]"Strikes and Lockouts File," Strike #1914 (15), RG27, vol. 303, Public Archives of Canada [hereafter PAC].

closing of the facilities.[18] Next to Canadian Car & Foundry, Stanfield's was the most aggressive company in the pursuit of this policy. Stanfield's resisted any attempts to improve working conditions which were easily the most deplorable in Amherst and wages among the lowest in town. The employees' response was predictable, and between 1918-1920 they fought three bitter strikes and they were the last employees to return to work during the general strike.[19] In 1919 a number of important Amherst industries, including Amherst Boot & Shoe, Amherst Foundry, and Robb Engineering remained ostensibly locally owned and managed. These companies continued to struggle against the forces that had pushed other local industries into mergers, although Robb Engineering was already heavily financed by Montréal interests and the Amherst Foundry had proposed, but failed to complete, a union with a Port Hope, Ontario company. After the war, competition with central Canada's large scale "specialized factories" and a freight rate structure that was beginning to push local manufacturers even from traditional regional markets worried Amherst businessmen. During the general strike, local owners resisted the demands of their workers with the same determination as Amherst's absentee employers.[20]

In one way or another, the impact of regional underdevelopment touched the members of all classes in Amherst. For some individuals of the business class, like Nathaniel Curry, it brought participation in a financially attractive industrial merger and the continuation of a lucrative business career in Montréal.[21] Other manufacturers, like David Robb, who lacked Curry's shrewdness in the ways of high finance and probably retained some commitment to the region, faced the collapse of their industries before fierce central Canadian competition. Underdevelopment also posed a threat to the livelihood of many small businessmen, since factory closings and a declining population represented lost business to local merchants. Finally, the working-class families attracted to Amherst during the 1898-1908 boom faced a most uncertain future, since local industries offered little long term security and few immediate benefits.[22]

Amherst's deepening economic crisis prompted a remarkable upsurge of local working-class activity in the immediate post-war years. In November 1918, while the Amherst Board of Trade sponsored armistice celebrations, labour spokesmen made their first public appeals to "workers of every grade" to join in the building of a new labour council. They argued that collective working-class action won

[18]Dunn and Bradstreet, *Gazetteer for the Maritime Provinces* (July 1915), 370; A. Robson Lamy, "The Development and Decline of Amherst as an Industrial Centre," Honours thesis, Mount Allison University, 1930.
[19]*Daily News*, 22 May, 10 June 1919.
[20]For an analysis of the problems facing Maritime capitalists in 1919, see Forbes, *Maritime Rights Movement*, esp. 54-72.
[21]*Monetary Times Annual Review for 1913*, 79: *Who's Who in Canada, 1919-1920* (Montréal 1920).
[22]*Daily News*, 21 June 1919.

industrial disputes and predicted "that so long as the employers can keep you [workers] in your unorganized condition, just so long will you be at their mercy."[23] This call for organization struck a responsive chord among Amherst's working-class population. In late November they formed the Amherst Federation of Labor, which by the end of the year had 700 members, making it the largest labour organization in the town's history. By April 1919, its ranks had doubled and, in the early days of the general strike, its membership must have numbered over 3,000.[24] Although it drew its leadership from among the town's skilled workingmen, the Amherst Federation of Labor's organization diverged significantly from that of the short-lived 1904 and 1913 labour councils chartered by the Trades and Labor Congress of Canada. The Amherst Federation of Labor rejected the exclusivism which had characterized the craft orientated pre-war movement and emphasized the organization of unskilled workers, the majority of whom had little trade union experience prior to 1919. The commitment to the unskilled went beyond union membership to include a genuine effort to reduce the wage gap between skilled and unskilled workers. In essence, the Amherst Federation of Labor was an independent industrial union that grouped the employees of Amherst's eight largest manufac-turing concerns into one organization. The union also included building trades and civic workers, tailors, garage mechanics, the unemployed, especially the veterans, and even a restaurant owner, boarding-house proprietor, and a local doctor. As former member Lester Doncaster recalls, it "was supposed to be One Great Union, just one Great Union of all the factories in Amherst."[25]

The initial structure of the Amherst Federation of Labor was relatively simple. Workers paid a "one dollar fee," which brought them the right to participate in the election of officers and all other affairs that came before the union.[26] Membership gave the workers, at least theoretically, an equal hand in setting contract demands, initiating strike action, and the ratification of all agreements reached with individual manufacturers. During a general strike the approval of all union members was required before any one group of employees could return to work. Yet, while the Amherst Federation of Labor functioned as a single body, special units were established in several of the factories. Dane Lodge, the first and largest of these units, was organized early and may, in fact, have been organized simultaneously with the larger body. This lodge served as a workplace unit, giving special attention to the problems of union members employed in the carworks.[27] In May 1919 the Textile Workers' Union, a committee similar in purpose to Dane Lodge, was organized among the predominately female workforce in the Amherst Woollen Mills.[28] It is not surprising that these units emerged first among the textile and

[23]*Ibid.*, 20 December 1918.
[24]*Ibid.*, 3 January 1919.
[25]Interview of Lester Doncaster by the author, Amherst 1977.
[26]*Daily News*, 20 December 1918.
[27]*Ibid.*, 31 March 1919.
[28]*Eastern Federationist*, 17, 24 May, 1919.

carworkers since conditions in these shops made them the most militant in Amherst. In late summer 1918, before the formation of the Amherst Federation of Labor, both factories had experienced strikes of several days duration.[29] The presence of such organizations also accounts, in part, for the cohesiveness of these employees throughout the general strike. In June 1919 they were the last workers to reach settlements with their respective employers. Neither lodge, of course, had any independent status and they were bound by the decisions of the larger organization.

Although the Amherst Federation of Labor was the largest trade union organization in the town there were several locals of national and international unions. The railway freight handlers belonged to the Canadian Brotherhood of Railway Employees and some tradesmen supported the International Association of Machinists, Iron Molders' Union of America, and the International Brotherhood of Boilermakers' and Helpers' Union. The relationship between these unions and the Amherst Federation of Labor remains ambiguous. In the carworks, for example, most metal workers joined the Amherst Federation of Labor, probably while maintaining membership in their respective internationals. Throughout the general strike these skilled workers participated in the deliberations of Dane Lodge and other Amherst Federation of Labor activities.[30] A different situation existed in the Amherst Foundry where the moulders continued to support a strong I.M.U. presence. First organized in the 1890s, these moulders enjoyed the longest and most successful history of any Amherst union and, as recently as April 1919, had emerged victorious in a struggle over wage schedules. But although the Amherst Foundry moulders did not join the Amherst Federation of Labor, they struck in sympathy with the union.[31]

On the other hand the metal-workers at Robb Engineering showed less support for the Amherst Federation of Labor. Robb's employed the largest concentration of metal-workers in Amherst, approximately 350 workers, perhaps one-half of whom were machinists and the remainder largely moulders and boilermakers. During the months leading up to the May confrontation, these workers gave what appeared to be lukewarm support to the Amherst Federation of Labor. Though they participated in the initial stoppage on 19 May, the men broke ranks with other workers and returned to work the following day. The reluctance of the Robb employees to follow the lead of the Amherst Foundry moulders and maintain a sympathy strike was influenced by several factors. First, and most significantly, the company's history of paternalistic management fostered at the very least the grudging loyalty of the work force into the 1920s. In fact, until 1919, Robb Engineering could boast that the company had never experienced a strike since its organization in 1891. This was a remarkable achievement since elsewhere metal-workers struggled against technological change and managerial reorganization of the work process. As early as

---

[29]*Daily News*, 31 August, 9, 11 September 1918.

[30]Interview of Lester Doncaster by the author, Amherst 1977.

[31]Amherst *Daily News*, 1 May 1919; "Strikes and Lockouts File," Strike #19 (92), RG27, vol. 311, PAC; *Eastern Federationist*, 14 June 1919.

1909, the metal trades journal, *Canadian Machinery*, carried reports on Robb's experimentation with piece-work and the premium system, two important components of a managerial programme condemned by labour as "making of men what men are supposed to make of metals: machines."[32] Robb's dependency on shell contracts during the war also should have created workplace tensions, since munitions work often brought new initiatives by the employers in the areas of mechanization and the introduction of semi-skilled workers into positions controlled previously by tradesmen. This process of skill dilution generated numerous confrontations between management and labour in Canadian, British, and American metal shops. But at Robb Engineering these tensions never gave rise to a strike.[33]

David Robb embodied the paternalism that guided the company's industrial relations policies. Son of the industry's founder, active in local political and social affairs, and manager of Robb's for almost 20 years, David Robb was Amherst's most respected businessman. While guiding the company, Robb was reputed by some of his former employees to have "paid a fair day's wage," sponsored a sick benefit association, and maintained an apprenticeship program that "gave local boys a chance to get a skill and stay at home."[34] The company's economic problems were also important in keeping the men at work. Pushed from its traditional steam engine markets by large central Canadian suppliers of electric motors, Robb Engineering faced financial ruin in the pre-war years. After 1914, generous munitions contracts from the Borden government "gave 'Robbs' a new lease on life," but the company's problems returned with the war's end and David Robb embarked on a new "staple line of production to fill the gap that must naturally follow the cancellation of shell orders." The Robb-Baker tractor was expected to be the industry's new source of riches and in 1919 it was ready for production.[35] The message for the employees was simple; only an immediate shift to tractor building could avert bankruptcy. This situation was well known to the workers because, as Robb told the Royal Commission on Industrial Relations, he "showed his men his accounts, and demonstrated to them ... the urgency of the contracts upon which it [the company] was working."[36]

The relatively harmonious state of industrial relations at Robb Engineering contrasted sharply with conditions at the Canadian Car & Foundry shops. To many Amherst residents, Robb's situation demanded the co-operation of management and labour to avoid the collapse of the company, which everyone feared. In the carworks

[32]*Labour News* (Hamilton), 1 March 1912, as cited in Craig Heron, "The Crisis of the Artisan: Hamilton's Metal Workers in the Early Twentieth Century" (paper presented to the Annual Meeting of the Canadian Historical Association, Saskatoon 1979).
[33]See Craig Heron, "The Crisis of the Artisan"; Craig Heron and Bryan Palmer, "Through the Prism of the Strike: Industrial Conflict in Southern Ontario, 1901-1914," *Canadian Historical Review*, LVIII (1977), 423-58; James Hinton, *The First Shop Stewards' Movement* (London 1973); David Montgomery, *Workers' Control in America* (New York 1979).
[34]Interview of Robert McKay by the author, Amherst 1976.
[35]*Daily News*, 13 July, 29 August 1917, 9 October 1918, 4 January 1919.
[36]*Ibid.*, 10 June 1919.

the crisis seemed to be the creation of corporate policy makers, not uncontrollable economic forces, as the relatively financially secure Canadian Car & Foundry was preparing for a possible flight from Amherst in search of profits elsewhere. Such a program did little to instill any sense of loyalty among the company's Amherst employees and the carworks' history was dotted with bitter confrontations between management and labour, especially after the 1909 merger, when the general improvement in economic conditions gave rise to an upsurge in labour organizing. In the autumn of 1910 the carworkers formed Fair Play Lodge, International Brotherhood of Railway Carmen of America (I.B.R.C.). While over 500 workers were brought into this industrial union, company hostility and internal strife brought its demise in early 1911.[37] After the I.B.R.C.'s collapse conditions in the carworks steadily worsened, as Canadian Car & Foundry used the recession of 1913 to introduce significant wage reductions for the workers. The rolling mill and sheet-metal workers struck on separate occasions but were successful only in limiting and not reversing wage reductions of almost 30 per cent.[38] Buoyed by these victories, the carworks' management prepared for a major confrontation with its machinists, the company's only unionized workers, and in 1914 announced a 5 to 15 per cent wage reduction for one-half of the company's 33 machinists. Rather than accept these changes, the members of the International Association of Machinists (I.A.M.) struck in a dispute that lasted for more than a year and that was never formally settled because the company continued production with non-union workers, forcing the I.A.M. to call off the strike.[39]

The growth of conflict in the carworks during the pre-war years represented more than "simply conflicts over the size of the pay packet."[40] After the turn of the century, it was the railway and metal-working industries in North America that sought to maximize profits through the assertion of greater control over the labour process. Management perceived the deeply held artisanal culture of their craftsmen and skilled workers as the major obstacle to the success of these plans and, in response to the artisans' resistance to the erosion of workplace autonomy, tried to introduce efficiency schemes and mechanization programs to weaken the power of craft unions. The railway companies spearheaded this drive in North America and some of these changes were introduced into Amherst's railway carbuilding shops at least as early as 1913. It is significant that the earliest strikes occurred in the metal-working divisions, which bore the brunt of management's new assertiveness. Sheetmetal workers struck in August 1918 to protest working conditions, and the firing of a moulder in early May 1919, for protesting the assignment of his helper to another job, almost sparked a general strike.[41] It was not only the metal-working trades in the carworks that felt these pressures. Writing to the *Industrial Banner* in

[37]*Eastern Labor News* (Moncton), 18 February 1911.
[38]"Strikes and Lockouts File," Strike #1914 (15) and 1914 (2), RG27, vol. 303, PAC.
[39]*Ibid.*, Strike #14 (23); *Eastern Labor News*, 9 August 1911.
[40]K.C.T.C. Knowles, *Strikes — A Study in Industrial Conflict* (Oxford 1952), 219.
[41]*Daily News*, 31 August 1918, 2, 3, 5 May 1919.

1914, painter Irvin McGinn asserted that attempts by Amherst employers to "mix-in
... tradesmen and labourers of all classes" had turned many craftsmen "to the great
and noble cause of unionism."[42] Unfortunately for these workers, their rate of
organizational success was no better than that of the metal-workers.

The almost continuous conflict in the carshops, and the workers' inability to
maintain an effective craft union presence were important factors behind the growth
of industrial unionism. Clashes with management prior to 1914 had demonstrated
the ineffectiveness of craft unions in a factory employing as many as 25 different
types of tradesmen and hundreds of semi-skilled workers and labourers. Appearing
before the Mathers Commission in June 1919, Frank Burke told the commissioners
that the "all-grades principle" of the Amherst Federation of Labor was adopted
precisely because "craft unions were too easily dismissed by the employers."[43]
Another prominent labour activist in Amherst, C.M. Arsenault of Pictou County,
agreed that "craft unionism clings to the old ideas which are not keeping abreast of
economic lines and advanced ideas."[44] Tradesmen in the carworks responded
enthusiastically to calls for a broad-based industrial organization. Eleven of the 13
men holding executive rank in the Amherst Federation of Labor between November
1918 and July 1919 worked for Canadian Car & Foundry; five of them were
carpenters and four others metal-workers. The president of the Amherst Federation
of Labor, Frank Burke, a carpenter in the carworks; the vice-president, William
McInnis, a moulder; and the recording secretary, Alfred Barton, another carpenter,
had held executive positions in Fair Play Lodge, International Brotherhood of
Railway Carmen prior to the war. This continuity of leadership in the Amherst
labour movement was a crucial influence on the emergence of the Amherst
Federation of Labor and it was not limited to the carworks. Others among the
leadership cadre, like tailors Dan McDonald and John McLeod, had even longer
records of involvement in local labour activities.[45]

The conditions that pressured workers towards new organizational forms were
reinforced by a renewed interest in socialist ideas. Before the First World War,
Amherst socialists maintained locals of the Socialist and Social Democratic parties,
offered socialist candidates in civic elections, and joined other trade unionists in
sponsoring a labour candidate in a 1909 provincial by-election.[46] The fracturing of
the international socialist movement during the war discouraged many Amherst
socialists, but by 1919 they had started once again to distribute radical literature,
conduct street corner debates, and sponsor public forums. In February, a group of
S.P.C. supporters invited Roscoe Fillmore, a prominent local socialist, to speak on

[42]*Industrial Banner* (London), 1 May 1914.
[43]*Daily News*, 10 June 1919.
[44]*Ibid.*, 2 June 1919.
[45]These biographies are compiled from town directories, the daily press, and various labour
newspapers.
[46]David Frank and Nolan Reilly, "The Emergence of the Socialist Movement in the
Maritimes, 1899-1916," *Labour/Le Travailleur*, 4 (1979), 98-101.

"The Truth About Russia." In two lectures Fillmore accused the "capitalist press" of misrepresenting the revolution "because it was a purely working class movement" that meant "capitalist downfall everywhere if it succeeded in Russia."[47] This Amherst audience knew "little or nothing of the Russian situation," Fillmore observed, "and they drank it in like milk." Convinced that this "Amherst bunch contains the best blood of any part of the Maritime movement," Fillmore committed himself to organizing a new S.P.C. local among the "about 40 young energetic Reds" already in Amherst. This socialist presence was strongest in the carworks, where Fillmore found little difficulty in selling "a roll of *Red Flags* and *Soviets*."[48]

In April 1919, the sudden explosion of daylight saving time into a class question and the Amherst Federation of Labor's attempts to affiliate with the One Big Union reflected the increasingly militant mood of the working class. Daylight saving first came to Canada in 1918 as a federal war measure. When the question of continuing the practice was left to the municipalities the next year, Amherst's town council convened a public meeting in April to discuss the issue. While merchants and manufacturers championed the idea, many workers, increasingly suspicious of any initiatives from the business people, opposed it. To demonstrate their opposition, 300 Amherst Federation of Labor members marched to the public meeting and "hooted down" daylight saving proponents. Roscoe Fillmore charged angrily that daylight saving was a capitalist plot to lengthen the working day. Other workers complained bitterly that because business people did not have to rise early in the morning, they were "not in a very good position to understand what the earlier time actually meant in the average workingman's home." As a result of this confrontation, and despite the best efforts of daylight saving proponents to revive the question, the issue, the *Daily News* reported, was squashed "flatter than the proverbial pancake."[49]

It was during this debate that the leaders of the Amherst Federation of Labor established contact with the western One Big Union movement. In a telegram to Victor Midgley, secretary of the O.B.U. Central Executive Committee, the Amherst workers inquired "as to what steps we should take to unite with the One Big Union."[50] Midgley replied two weeks later that the Maritimes had jumped the gun. The Central Executive Committee was only authorized to conduct a referendum among western trade unionists to determine if they wished to leave the Trades and Labour Congress of Canada (T.L.C.) and form the O.B.U. Until then, the O.B.U.

[47]*Daily News*, 24 February 1919.
[48]R.A. Fillmore to Victor Midgley, 25 February 1919, Winnipeg Strike Trials Collection, The King vs. R.B. Russell, Provincial Archives of Manitoba [henceforth PAM]. The *Red Flag* and *Soviet* were S.P.C. publications.
[49]*Daily News*, 16, 17, 21 April 1919.
[50]Alfred Barton to C. Stevenson, 10 April 1919, One Big Union Collection [henceforth O.B.U. Collection], PAM. Correspondence between the Amherst Federation of Labor and the O.B.U. is reprinted in Nolan Reilly, "Notes on the Amherst General Strike and the One Big Union," *Bulletin of the Committee on Canadian Labour History*, 3 (Spring 1977), 5-8.

technically did not exist and had no "authority to issue or accept affiliations," although Midgley promised to keep his Amherst supporters in good supply with O.B.U. "leaflets and other propaganda."[51] In the western referendum held in May, approximately three quarters of the votes cast favoured replacing the T.L.C. with the O.B.U., whose supporters convened the new organization's founding convention on 4 June in Calgary. Several weeks later, the Amherst Federation of Labor voted 1185 to 1 to join the O.B.U.[52] This decision in favour of the O.B.U. marked the final rejection of affiliation with the T.L.C., which had been offered to the Amherst Federation of Labor in March 1919.[53]

The presence in Amherst of S.P.C. sympathizers may have provided the Maritimers with a link to the O.B.U. In the pre-war years Amherst socialists sustained an active S.P.C. branch that included such prominent Amherst Federation of Labor organizers as moulders William McInnis and Arthur McArthur, and Clarence Joise, a carpenter. Although it is not clear whether these men remained S.P.C. members, the S.P.C. did experience a revival in Amherst after the war and its activities gave the town direct contact with events in western Canada, where a number of S.P.C. activists such as Victor Midgley, R.B. Russell, and W.A. Pritchard, were involved in organizing the O.B.U.[54] The overlap in S.P.C. and O.B.U. personnel in the west was apparent to Amherst socialists and undoubtedly influenced them in the direction of the O.B.U. Yet, although this relationship may explain the Amherst socialists' interest in the O.B.U., it does not explain why the majority of Amherst union members followed suit. In fact, the decision of these Maritime workers to throw their lot in with a labour organization centred in western Canada is not as surprising as it may appear. First, similar to much of the west, Amherst lacked a strong craft union tradition. Except for the I.M.U., craft unions had been unable to protect skilled workers against the employers' assaults on their working conditions. Thus, in Amherst, the weakness of craft unions among skilled workers encouraged them to explore different forms of working class organization.

Another factor in the Amherst Federation of Labor's decision to affiliate with the westerners was the initial ideological eclecticism of the O.B.U. Because no single political position dominated the O.B.U.'s early activities, various socialist and syndicalist tendencies found a home in the union. Although this would change over the next few years, in the spring of 1919 the union's flexibility on political and industrial strategies opened the O.B.U. to many workers who otherwise might have rejected it. This was important in Amherst where the Amherst Federation of Labor's leadership was not influenced by the syndicalist tendencies popular in the west. In March 1919, Frank Burke headed the Amherst delegation attending a Halifax meeting of provincial labour leaders, which established a provincial federation of

[51]Victor Midgley to Alfred Barton, 21 April 1919, O.B.U. Collection, PAM.
[52]O.B.U. Vertical File 213, Special Collections, University of British Columbia.
[53]*Daily News*, 22 March 1919.
[54]David J. Bercuson explores the relationship between the S.P.C. and the founding of the O.B.U. in *Fools and Wise Men*.

labour and discussed forming an independent labour party to contest the next provincial election.[55] C.M. Arsenault, Pictou County labour spokesman and editor of the *Eastern Federationist*, also advocated independent labour politics. In 1919, Arsenault spent many days in Amherst assisting in the Amherst Federation of Labor's organization and campaigning for the building of a labour party.[56] The industrial rather than craft emphasis in the O.B.U. also attracted local support to the union because the Amherst Federation of Labor was already an industrial union organized along the principles of One Big Unionism.

In the spring of 1919, local workers exhibited in their actions a solidarity that was unique in Amherst's history. Relatively minor issues exploded into hotly contested disputes. When a man was accused of stealing tools from his employer he was acquitted even though the judge in his charge to the jury "had no hesitation in saying that the accused was 'not a desirable citizen in the community.'"[57] This episode and events like the daylight saving time dispute worried the editor of the *Daily News* because "though class consciousness has never been one of the particular manifestations of the workingman [sic] of this community, there is no question that it is showing a greater strength among them today than it ever did before."[58] On 1 May, events at the Canadian Car & Foundry almost precipitated a general strike when moulder Fred Reid was fired for protesting the assignment of his helper to another job. At a hastily convened meeting of the Amherst Federation of Labor, some members demanded a general strike to force the company to reinstate Reid. Although a majority of the workers at the meeting sympathized with Reid's plight, they decided to delay strike action since many of them had just returned to work after long layoffs. Another consideration of the membership was that Frank Burke and William McInnis were scheduled to leave shortly for Montréal to open negotiations with Canadian Car & Foundry officials and many Amherst Federation of Labor workers felt that strike action should be delayed until the results of these general bargaining sessions were known.[59]

The two Amherst Federation of Labor leaders travelled to Montréal on 15 May and, after several days of fruitless negotiations, climbed aboard an east bound train for Amherst, where a delegation of workers met them at the station to protest recent measures adopted by the carworks' management. While Burke and McInnis negotiated in Montréal, the company directors had instructed their Amherst manager to introduce the nine-hour day without a provision for ten hours pay. The company's unilateral action particularly infuriated the Amherst Federation of Labor officials because they perceived it as an attempt to circumvent the union.[60] On Monday, 19 May, the carworkers milled around the gates to the Canadian Car & Foundry shops.

[55]*Eastern Federationist*, 8 March 1919; *Daily News*, 3 March 1919.

[56]*Daily News*, 30 May 1919.

[57]*Ibid.*, 11, 12 October 1918.

[58]*Ibid.*, 21 May 1919.

[59]*Ibid.*, 2, 5 May 1919.

[60]*Eastern Federationist*, 24 May 1919.

The employees refused to begin the day's shift and "formed in parade marching through the principle [sic] streets" of Amherst to their meeting hall.[61] As the meeting commenced, many workers vented their frustrations with management but it was Burke who focused their anger onto two issues: union recognition and wage differentials between eastern and central Canadian workers. Burke argued that the company precipitated the crisis by refusing to recognize that the Amherst Federation of Labor had "a right to be consulted on any changes of hours, or rules of wages, affecting the men."[62] Burke also demanded that the company extend to Amherst its agreement with Montréal employees for fewer hours with no decrease in take-home pay. After listening to Burke and several other Amherst Federation of Labor officials, the carworkers dispersed with a call for an emergency meeting of the union that evening.

News of the trouble at the carworks spread quickly throughout Amherst and the evening meeting was crowded with workers who "decided that employees of all industries in the town, including town employees cease work on Tuesday morning."[63] Although the strike was called to support Dane Lodge members, the employees of each industry were directed to meet separately to prepare additional demands to be presented to the town's employers along with the basic proposals for recognition of the Amherst Federation of Labor and the eight-hour day. On Tuesday morning, every factory remained closed, building trades workers struck, and the town's outside workers left their jobs. In the evening, the Amherst Federation of Labor staged the largest working-class rally in Amherst's history. "Between two to three thousand workers met at the Labour Hall," reported the *Eastern Federationist*, "formed in a line and paraded to the square."[64] After speeches by local and visiting labour spokesmen, Frank Burke recounted some of the background to the dispute and proclaimed the union's determination to stand firm until its demands were accepted by the manufacturers.[65]

The Amherst Federation of Labor's swift action caught many employers by surprise. After recovering from their initial "shock," they gathered at the Marshlands Club to evolve a common strategy and agreed unanimously to "absolutely" refuse "one and all to deal in any way or form with the 'One Big Union' as a whole." Throughout the first two weeks of the strike, this position remained firm except for one minor and very brief incident. Late in the first week of the strike, the owners of the Victor Woodworking Co. expressed their willingness to give a wage increase to their 75 employees and recognize the Amherst Federation of Labor. Pressure from other manufacturers, however, forced Victor's to reverse its stand. The small, locally owned business explained this change of policy as a decision not "to be the first squealor [sic]" among the employers and promised it would take direction from

[61]*Ibid.*
[62]*Ibid.*
[63]*Ibid.*
[64]*Ibid.*
[65]*Daily News*, 20 May 1919.

"the big fellows," Amherst's largest employers. In order to improve its tarnished image among other manufacturers, Victor's claimed to have installed a "new system" that required only five men to operate.[66]

Although the employers agreed that union recognition was unacceptable, each industry used different tactics to get its employees back to work. Frank Stanfield, a principal owner in the Amherst Woollen Mill and director of the family's Truro textile mills, championed the intimidation technique. He refused to discuss the employees' demands, laid off his salaried staff, and announced that the Amherst plant was "closed down." Canadian Car & Foundry officials chose to ignore the strike, while the shoeworks and foundry managements agreed to meet with their workers, but not Amherst Federation of Labor negotiators. At Robb Engineering, David Robb appealed to his employees to return to work and promised to meet many of their grievances. Across the street from Robb's, the Amherst Piano Co. tried to entice its employees to return to work with a profit sharing proposal. Manager J.A. McDonald proposed that once the company achieved a seven per cent net profit on capitalization all additional profits would be divided among the shareholders and employees. The workers rejected the scheme because, as Frank Burke pointed out, the company had never turned a seven per cent profit in its six-year history.[67]

The first crack in the solidarity the Amherst labour movement had enjoyed over the previous months occurred when the employees at Robb Engineering returned to work on the second day of the strike. But, despite the company's serious financial situation and David Robb's stature as a community leader, the strike ended only when Robb agreed to negotiate a new wage schedule and a shorter working day. The next week, when these negotiations bogged down, the workers threatened to strike until their demands were met. This announcement jolted David Robb into an agreement with "a committee representing employees," granting higher wages, a nine hour day, and the "Whitley Council principle."[68] In the final analysis, it was Robb Engineering's dire economic straits that kept its employees working throughout most of the general strike. Other factories with a history of relatively harmonious industrial relations and owners with a community stature that equalled that of David Robb could not persuade their employees to abandon the general strike. To attribute the actions of the predominantly skilled workforce at Robb's simply to some tradition of craft exclusivism also seems to miss the point. The Amherst Federation of Labor won solid support from the town's other skilled workers and there is no reason to assume that Robb employees were unusually craft conscious. After their return to work the Robb employees did not abandon the Amherst Federation of Labor, as the machinists, moulders, and boilermakers made important contributions to the union's strike fund.[69]

[66]*Daily News*, 22, 31 May, 10 June 1919; *Eastern Federationist*, 31 May 1919.
[67]*Eastern Federationist*, 31 May, 7 June 1919; *Daily News*, 22, 26, 29 May 1919.
[68]"Strikes and Lockouts File," Strike #19 (144), RG27, vol. 313, PAC; *Eastern Federationist*, 31 May, 14 June 1919.
[69]*Eastern Federationist*, 14 June 1919.

Several events cushioned the effect of the Robb employees' return to work on the morale of the Amherst Federation of Labor. Most important was the town council's decision to give "full recognition" to the union and to implement the eight-hour day with ten hours pay.[70] The town council's concession to the civic workers was its attempt to find a solution to the continuing confrontation between the Amherst Federation of Labor and the employers. A majority of the councillors were small businessmen: a contractor, merchant, realtor, farm implements agent, two lawyers, and a foreman with shares in the Amherst Foundry Co., who were suffering from the decline in business precipitated by the general strike. In fact, the councillors and other small businessmen expressed some cautious support for the strikers, especially those employed by the carworks. Many felt that, as the *Daily News* editorialized, the "unpleasantness in the town was due almost altogether to the uncertainty that has prevailed at the Car Works."[71] Lawyer and former Liberal M.P. Hance Logan chided Canadian Car & Foundry "with its head office and Directorate in Montréal" because it was "naturally more interested" in its central Canadian operations "than [in] our own local industry."[72] Thus, at the end of May when the Amherst Federation of Labor approached the council to arbitrate the strike, the council immediately appointed a committee to try and resolve the dispute.[73] After several days of separate meetings with the union and employers, the committee announced that the employers were prepared to bargain with committees of their employees, including a member of the Amherst Federation of Labor executive. Furthermore, the employers conceded that the employee committees with whom they would meet did not have "the power to accept or refuse any proposition without the sanction" of the Amherst Federation of Labor general executive.[74] This in effect recognized the Amherst Federation of Labor because executive decisions required membership sanction. Elated by the decision, the union committees met with the employers, expecting a quick end to the strike, but the manufacturers retracted their offer without explanation.

The employers probably hoped that the desperate economic circumstances facing many of the strikers would force them to return to work. Apparently the union officials shared a similar concern, for they launched a major fund raising drive. A relief committee solicited funds from the Robb employees and local merchants, and sent delegations to labour meetings in Moncton, Joggins, and Springhill. The best response came from the Springhill miners who collected $537 in a house-to-house canvass.[75] The Amherst Federation of Labor also organized a "patronize those who patronize us" campaign and advertised that "electrical workers" and "employees of

[70]*Ibid.*, 31 May 1919.

[71]*Ibid.*, 20 June 1919.

[72]*Ibid.*, 21 May 1919.

[73]Amherst Town Council *Minutes*, 26 May 1919, 5, Amherst Town Hall.

[74]*Daily News*, 26, 27, 3 May 1919.

[75]United Mine Workers of America, Local 4514, Springhill, Nova Scotia, *Minute Book*, 31 May, 5 July 1919, Springhill Miners' Museum.

different industries" affected by the strike would accept odd jobs around Amherst.[76] Moral support came in the form of a continuous flow of labour leaders into the town. C.C. Dane and C.M. Arsenault of Pictou County; Silby Barrett of Cape Breton; W.N. Goodwin of Truro, formerly of the Winnipeg T.L.C.; and a number of Cumberland County United Mine Workers of America officials addressed the various union evening meetings.[77] As the general strike continued through the first week of June, support for the Amherst Federation of Labor remained strong. By this point in the dispute, picketing was unnecessary. Early in the strike Victor Woodworking had attempted to re-open with non-union staff, but the Amherst Federation of Labor members had marched to the plant and frightened away the employees. After the initial excitement of the first few days of the strike, the daily routine of many working-class families centred around putting in their gardens, perhaps spending the afternoon at the labour hall, and attending the evening union meeting.[78]

On 9 June the federal government's Royal Commission on Industrial Relations opened hearings in Amherst, bringing together representatives from both sides in the general strike. Several hundred Amherst Federation of Labor members greeted "with hearty" laughter D.W. Robb's report to the commission, especially his assertion that rents in Amherst were low. On the other hand, the workers "warmly applauded any statement that appeared to favour them," until Justice Mathers, the chairman, "threatened to adjourn the meeting if quiet was not maintained." Over the afternoon, Mathers and his fellow commissioners heard Amherst's most prominent businessmen condemn the Amherst Federation of Labor for leading a strike "similar to that in Winnipeg." They also endorsed international unions in preference to "local organizations" and committed themselves to the eight-hour day, if it was adopted universally across Canada. Labour spokesmen used the commission's hearings as another opportunity to catalogue their list of grievances against local employers. Although the session did not settle the strike, the opportunity to vent its frustrations with conditions in Amherst to an apparently neutral body boosted the union's morale.[79]

Throughout the strike, attacks were made on the integrity of the union's leadership. Frank Burke felt the brunt of most of these individual attacks, although C.M. Arsenault, as an outside "labour agitator," faced considerable criticism. When the Amherst Federation of Labor's leadership was accused of transferring union funds to the local Catholic Church, Burke replied that these "rumours" were attempts "to split the organization through the creation of religious strife." When some employers pronounced that international unions were preferable to "local organizations," many workers saw this as yet another ploy to weaken the Amherst Federation of Labor. In one particularly bitter report *Daily News* editor, A.D. Ross,

[76]*Eastern Federationist*, 7 June 1919.
[77]*Daily News*, 7 June 1919.
[78]Interview of Thaddie Gould by the author, Amherst 1977.
[79]*Daily News*, 10 June 1919; *Eastern Federationist*, 14 June 1919.

one of the strongest exponents of craft unionism, criticized the Amherst Federation of Labor for disregarding "regular trade union principles" and for adopting "the Western One Big Union program." Concerned by the effectiveness of the general strike, Ross worried that "force" would be the "only medium to be applied in the settlement of future industrial disputes in the community."[80]

The most serious attack on the union's credibility came when the *Daily News* reported on 6 June that at the previous evening's meeting, employees from Victor Woodworking had tried to raise the question of a return to work, but "failed to get a complete hearing." After witnessing these events, disgusted employees of another woodworking company also interested in ending the strike decided to "retire from the hall." Frank Burke quickly challenged the story's accuracy, insisting that the appeal presented by six employees of the Victor Woodworking Co. had been aired fully at the meeting. When their position was put to a general membership vote, he pointed out that almost 1,400 strikers voted "in favour of leaving the matter in the hands of the general executive."[81] The principle of maintaining the general strike until all workers had acceptable agreements with their employers had been confirmed earlier in the week, when the Amherst Boot & Shoe Co. had offered its employees a settlement weighted heavily in favour of its skilled workers. When several of these skilled workers had brought the offer to an Amherst Federation of Labor meeting, the shoeworks' largely unskilled women workers, with the support of the majority of the company's skilled employees, had strenuously opposed it. Not surprisingly, the proposed settlement had been defeated soundly and the strike at the shoeworks continued.[82]

At the end of the strike's third week, the town council's strike committee managed to bring the two sides together. With the union's strike fund depleted it was only the strikers' determination to wring concessions from the manufacturers that kept them away from work. On the other hand, the employers recognized that their factories would not re-open until a number of union demands were met. Who was to make what compromises remained the crucial question. At the Amherst Federation of Labor's meeting on 12 June, Frank Burke announced that the labour situation had "changed materially" over the past few days. The Amherst Boot & Shoe, Amherst Foundry, Christie Bros., and the Victor Woodworking Co. had offered to meet with Amherst Federation of Labor committees from their factories and had conceded the nine-hour day with wage increases that ensured that the workers' weekly pay remained at pre-strike levels. Similar agreements with the Canadian Car & Foundry and Rhodes-Curry Woodworking also appeared likely. Burke informed his audience that "after long deliberation" the Amherst Federation of Labor executive had decided to recommend that the union accept these offers; the alternative was to "continue a deadlock to the bitter end," which, given the financial circumstances of many members, seemed pointless. Union members,

[80]*Daily News*, 9 June, 21 May, 6 June 1919.
[81]*Ibid.*, 6, 7 June 1919.
[82]*Eastern Federationist*, 7 June 1919.

wearied by the long strike, agreed and "adopted unanimously" the executive's position.[83] Workers in the four factories with new wage scales scheduled an immediate return to work and the others planned to follow suit as soon as agreements could be finalized with their employers. In the case of Canadian Car & Foundry and Rhodes-Curry, wage schedules similar to those of the other four factories were agreed to the following day.[84] The woollen mill and a local garage remained on strike for several days longer until the garage mechanics called off their strike. The dispute at the woollen mill proved more complex, as Stanfield continued to ignore the strike, but the factory gradually re-opened.

How did Amherst workers assess the results of their three-week general strike? Some workers, like textile worker Albert St. Peter, were embittered and accused Burke of the misuse of union funds.[85] But this was not the opinion of the majority of Amherst Federation of Labor members, who in July re-elected the union's executive for another year. They must have agreed with the *Eastern Federationist's* assessment of the May events: "We heartily congratulate the Amherst union workers on their victory for no matter what may be said to the contrary it was a victory for their recognition and [sic] raise in pay. Not bad for beginners."[86] But while the majority of workers did win a shorter working day and higher wages, the victory was not all they had hoped for. Through their resistance to the union, the employers managed to stop the Amherst Federation of Labor short of the eight-hour day and at the woollen mill they defeated the union on all counts. Coupled with the events at Robb Engineering, these employer initiatives weakened the union and it never recovered the momentum it had enjoyed in the months prior to the strike.

The energy of the Amherst labour movement did not suddenly dissipate after the general strike. In the months ahead, the Amherst Federation of Labor continued to represent local workers and remained especially strong in the carworks. Although its leadership changed little over the next several years it seems unlikely that they maintained any formal contact with the O.B.U. beyond 1919. In 1920 local events continued to consume the union's attention as the women employees at Stanfield's led their third strike in as many years; the principal issue once again was working conditions.[87] At the Canadian Car & Foundry and at Robb Engineering, metal workers struck over demands for wage parity with central Canadian workers and for better working conditions.[88] The 1920 provincial election also attracted the attention of the Amherst labour movement as they helped elect Springhill miner Archie Terris, Cumberland County's Independent Labor Party candidate. Yet, despite all this activity, by the middle of the 1920s the formal presence of a trade union movement in Amherst had all but disappeared. In 1923, the Amherst Federa-

[83] *Daily News*, 13 June 1919.
[84] *Ibid.*, 16 June 1919; *Eastern Federationist*, 21 June 1919.
[85] Interview of Albert St. Peter by the author, Amherst 1977.
[86] *Eastern Federationist*, 5 July, 23 August 1919.
[87] "Strikes and Lockouts File," Strike #20 (103), RG27, vol. 320, PAC.
[88] *Ibid.*, vol. 321, Strike #20 (200); vol. 322, Strike #20 (245).

tion of Labor dissolved and the locals of international unions among machinists, moulders, and boilermakers struggled to survive in a time of declining memberships. Although in the 1920s trade union activity declined nationally for a variety of political and economic reasons, it was above all the depressed state of Amherst's economy which explains the downturn in the fortunes of the local labour movement.[89] The worst fears voiced for Amherst's future in 1919 had become a reality as the carworks, woollen mill, shoe factory and several smaller companies closed permanently, and Robb Engineering, now a division of Dominion Bridge Co., employed fewer than 100 workers. The collapse of the town's industries left almost 3,000 residents unemployed and many of them began the trek "down the road" to Canada's other regions and the New England states. Between 1921 and 1931, Amherst's population declined from 10,000 to 7,500.[90]

The Amherst general strike was the response of the local working class to the post-World War One crisis of industrial capitalism at home and abroad. In Amherst, as elsewhere in the Maritimes, intensifying regional disparities gave the situation a special urgency. In shaping their reaction to this crisis, local labour leaders drew on their pre-war trade union and political experiences, which when combined with the ideas of industrial unionism and socialism, were institutionalized in the Amherst Federation of Labor. Seeking protection in the workplace and wage parity with other Canadians, Amherst's skilled and non-skilled workers alike created the town's largest, most militant and, at least temporarily, most successful labour organization. On the other hand, it was these same regional economic and social forces that eventually destroyed the Amherst Federation of Labor and that have severely weakened the local labour movement through to this day.

[89] A discussion of the problems facing the Canadian labour movement in the 1920s can be found in Stuart Jamieson, *Times of Trouble, Labour Unrest and Industrial Conflict in Canada, 1900-66* (Ottawa 1968), 192-213.
[90] Town of Amherst, *Urban Renewal Study*, 12-3.

For their critical comments on an earlier draft of this paper, the author would like to thank David Frank, Greg Kealey, Sharon Reilly, and David Sutherland.

David Frank   **11**

The Trial of J.B. McLachlan

Shortly after two o'clock on the afternoon of 17 October 1923 the jury returned to
pronounce its verdict in a trial in the Supreme Court of Nova Scotia in Halifax. The
charges consisted of three counts of seditious libel under Section 132 of the Criminal
Code, each punishable by up to 20 years' imprisonment. The case had attracted
national attention, for the charge was an unusual one and the proceedings involved
several prominent figures in Nova Scotia. Appearing for the Crown was the
province's attorney general, Walter J. O'Hearn. In his address to the jury he declared
the case to be "the most important that had come before the courts of Nova Scotia
in recent years"; the identity of the prisoner was less important than "the principle
involved, the principle as to whether or not the doctrines of Soviet Russia should
flourish in Nova Scotia." O'Hearn had entered the provincial government only a
few months earlier, in December 1922, and added, "I determined when I assumed
the office I now hold that I would lock horns with men of this nature." Appearing
for the defence was Colonel Gordon S. Harrington, a former mayor of Glace Bay
and a leading figure in the provincial Conservative party. He told the jury that the
trial had been "a nauseating, abominable fizzle"; in the alleged seditious remarks,
the accused was "only voicing the opinions of the thousands he represented among
the miners of Cape Breton"; if the prisoner was "red" then so too were those who
elected him annually to union office. Harrington concluded by referring to the
famous trial of Joseph Howe in the same city on similar charges almost a century
earlier, and reminded the jury that Howe had won an acquittal, which was, he noted,
"the fate the prisoner in this case deserved."[1]

    Sedition trials are not common events in Canadian history; yet the charge has
been used more frequently than is commonly realized, and Kenneth McNaught has
suggested there is sufficient evidence to reveal a tradition of political trials in

[1]*Sydney Post*, 18 October 1923.

Published with permission of the Canadian Historical Association. From *Historical Papers*
(1983), 208-25.

Canada.[2] What defines a political trial, McNaught has noted, is the overt confrontation between the forces of change and the forces of continuity, an approach which underlines the significance of historical context in the study of legal questions. To know the law one must read it, but to know the uses of the law, an historical approach is essential. The trial of J.B. McLachlan on charges of seditious libel has never received close scrutiny, despite its intrinsic interest as one of the more dramatic events in Canadian labour history in the 1920s. Moreover, as an episode in the history of Canadian law, the case of The King vs. James B. McLachlan clearly demonstrates the very broad applications of a loosely defined offence such as sedition.[3]

Like J.S. Woodsworth, who was charged with seditious libel during the Winnipeg General Strike in 1919, McLachlan was arrested in the midst of turbulent events in Canadian labour history. The origins of the case were closely bound up with the events of the early 1920s in industrial Cape Breton. At the time of his arrest in July 1923, McLachlan was secretary-treasurer of District 26, United Mine Workers of America, a position he had occupied almost continuously since the establishment of the district in 1909. A veteran of the Scottish coalfields and of the early days of the UMWA in Nova Scotia, a longtime socialist and later Communist, by the 1920s McLachlan had become the symbol of radical trade unionism in Nova Scotia.[4]

During 1922, the year of the first great confrontation between the Nova Scotia coal miners and the British Empire Steel Corporation, a significant change took place in the leadership of District 26. Delegates to the annual convention in Truro in June 1922 had adopted spirited declarations denouncing the capitalist system: "we proclaim openly to all the world that we are out for the complete overthrow of the capitalist system and capitalist state, peaceably if we may, forcibly if we must." This was followed in August by the election of an executive in which the key

[2]Kenneth McNaught, "Political trials and the Canadian political tradition," in M.L. Friedland, ed., *Courts and Trials: A Multidisciplinary Approach* (Toronto 1975), 137-61.

[3]For an account of the history of seditious offences in Canada, see M.L. Friedland, *National Security: The Legal Dimensions*, [a study prepared for the Commission of Inquiry Concerning Certain Activities of the Royal Canadian Mounted Police], (Hull 1980). See also Mark MacGuigan, "Seditious Libel and Related Offences in England, the United States, and Canada," *The Report of the Special Committee on Hate Propaganda in Canada* (Ottawa 1966), Appendix I, and Peter MacKinnon, "Conspiracy and Sedition as Canadian Political Crimes," *McGill Law Journal*, 23 (1977), 622-43. Some general issues are considered in F.R. Scott, *Civil Liberties and Canadian Federalism* (Toronto 1959) and D.A. Schmeiser, *Civil Liberties in Canada* (London 1964).

[4]General surveys of labour history in industrial Cape Breton are available in Paul MacEwan, *Miners and Steelworkers: Labour in Cape Breton* (Toronto 1976), and Don Macgillivray, "Industrial Unrest in Cape Breton, 1919-1925" (MA thesis, University of New Brunswick, 1971). On the background of J.B. McLachlan, see David Frank, "The Making of a Labour Leader: The Early Years of J.B. McLachlan," paper presented to the Atlantic Canada Studies Conference, Halifax, 1980.

positions were won by men associated with the "red" declarations. McLachlan, re-elected by a two-to-one vote, was the only member of the old executive to be re-elected; president Robert Baxter was defeated by a Westville miner, Dan Livingstone, by a vote of 7,170 to 1,695. Present at the June convention had been a representative of the Workers' Party of Canada, Tim Buck, and during the following year speakers such as "Red" Malcolm Bruce and "Moscow" Jack MacDonald, as they were nicknamed locally, made speaking tours of the coalfields. McLachlan and other leaders joined the WPC, and McLachlan attended the party's convention in Toronto in February 1923. A party organizer from Toronto and Winnipeg, Tom Bell, was appointed editor of the union-backed *Maritime Labor Herald*. By the time the union leaders led a parade through the streets of Glace Bay on 1 May 1923, following a red banner with the slogans "Workers of the World, Unite" and "Long Live Communism," there were ample anxieties about the spread of radical influences in industrial Cape Breton.[5]

Those concerned included the international office of the UMWA, who objected to the district's plan to affiliate to the Red International of Labour Unions, an idea endorsed at the June convention. It had been a flamboyant, largely symbolic gesture, and the union leaders in fact pursued a cautious policy, writing to request a ruling from President John L. Lewis on the district's right to join the Red International. When the UMWA issued an extensive report stating that the Red International was "an outgrowth of the One Big Union" and ordering District 26 to withdraw its application, the district executive voted to comply; explained McLachlan, "we are prepared to retreat from almost any position, rather than give anybody the opportunity to smash our solidarity." This retreat failed to satisfy the international union, which continued to cast doubts on the legitimacy of the policies pursued by District 26. When a committee of investigation visited in May 1923, they reported not only "a splendid feeling of loyalty to the United Mine Workers" but also "ample evidence of the machinations of the red outfit of Moscow."[6]

The struggle for union recognition at the large steel plant in Sydney proved the most explosive development of 1923. Despite the longstanding labour traditions in industrial Cape Breton, the steelworkers had repeatedly failed to win recognition of their unions, but by the fall of 1922 a new organizing campaign on behalf of the Amalgamated Association of Iron, Steel and Tin Workers of America was underway in Sydney. In December 1922 the steelworkers voted to reject a company proposal for a plant council, and in February a walkout closed the plant for five days. Neither show of strength was sufficient to establish union recognition, and the steelworkers braced for the next confrontation. Increasingly, the coal miners' leaders saw the fight for union recognition at the steel plant as an opportunity to take joint action against a common employer. When an official from the federal

[5]David Frank, "Class Conflict in the Coal Industry: Cape Breton 1922," in G.S. Kealey and P. Warrian, eds., *Essays in Canadian Working Class History* (Toronto 1976), 161-84.
[6]*Maritime Labor Herald*, 13 January 1923; *The Worker*, 1 March 1923; *United Mine Workers' Journal*, 1 and 15 February, and 22 June 1923.

Department of Labour visited Sydney in March 1923, he was intrigued to find that
the steelworkers' leaders appeared for his meeting accompanied by the miners'
officers; indeed, he reported, they appeared to have formed "something like a local
One Big Union"; McLachlan and Livingstone both spoke at length and declared
that "the miners were determined to support the steelworkers, and if necessary that
they would come out in sympathy with them."[7] Meanwhile, worried by the progress
of labour organization at the steel plant and by the presence of radical influences in
local unions, Besco president Roy Wolvin sounded the alarm at a meeting of the
Sydney Board of Trade, urging members to "drive the radicals out of Cape Breton";
the board subsequently produced a resolution denouncing "Cape Breton Bolshevism."[8]

The Liberal provincial government of E.H. Armstrong soon adopted strong
measures. At the time of the miners' strike in 1922, the cabinet had authorized the
creation of a special provincial police force. Although the force was not used in
1922, the provincial police were mobilized in March 1923 and stationed in Sydney
in expectation of an imminent confrontation at the steel plant. These actions won
the premier a variety of congratulations, including an encouraging message from
his predecessor, George H. Murray, who was also prone to attribute industrial
difficulties to radical influences: "I am glad to see you are taking no nonsense from
the 'reds.' That is the proper attitude, even if a political issue were created."[9]

The steel strike did not materialize as expected, but before their departure from
Sydney in May "Armstrong's Army" embarked on a series of raids in quest of what
was described as "literature of a seditious nature." Riding into Glace Bay on the
evening of 14 May, a squad of provincial police performed a hurried search of the
offices of District 26; they failed to uncover any literature of the desired type, but
did seize the red flag which had been used in the May Day parade two weeks earlier.
Returning the following night, the police also searched the homes of several radical
leaders and union officers; at McLachlan's house they retrieved a copy of the
constitution of the Red International. This reading matter was soon forwarded to
Attorney-General O'Hearn, who by this stage was clearly contemplating legal
action against local labour leaders: "Book found possession McLachlan filled with
sedition," he telegraphed Premier Armstrong. "Will peruse 1919 amendment and
King vs. Russell in Ottawa before advising you."[10]

The attorney-general waited to proceed. The opportunity came at the end of
June 1923, in stormy events precipitated by the long-expected renewal of conflict

[7]Public Archives of Canada (hereafter PAC), Records of the Department of Labour, RG27,
vol. 143, file 611.04:10, memorandum by E. McG. Quirk, 26 March 1923.
[8]PAC, W.L. Mackenzie King Papers, MG26 J1, 76159-60, Paul McNeil and J.B. McLachlan
to King, 29 March 1923.
[9]Public Archives of Nova Scotia (hereafter PANS), E.H. Armstrong Papers, vol. 11A, file
15, 3828, G.H. Murray to Armstrong, 10 April 1923.
[10]*Sydney Post*, 15 and 19 May 1923; PANS, Armstrong Papers, W.J. O'Hearn to Armstrong,
20 May 1923.

at the Sydney steel plant. When the Besco board of directors once more rejected the union's request for recognition, the steelworkers launched a strike and began to shut down the plant on the morning of 28 June. For several days there were tumultuous scenes at the plant gates as crowds of pickets blocked traffic and attempted to prevent non-strikers from entering the plant; masked men broke into the plant and forceably removed maintenance men from the boilerhouses and coke ovens; attempts to read the Riot Act were met with howls of derision and well-aimed stones. As on previous occasions in Cape Breton, military aid to the civil power was invoked, and the first soldiers arrived from Halifax on 30 June and erected machine guns at the plant gates. The provincial police were also reassembled and arrived in Sydney on Sunday 1 July. That evening at about 7:30 p.m. a squad of sixteen mounted provincial police, led by Colonel Eric McDonald, charged through the pickets at the plant gates, swinging their clubs and driving the crowd before them into an underpass and up Victoria Road into Whitney Pier, attacking all who came in their path. The day would be remembered as Sydney's Bloody Sunday, or Sydney's Peterloo. As the news spread to the surrounding district, the coal miners crowded into protest meetings to proclaim support for the steelworkers and to demand the withdrawal of troops and police. There was a 24-hour delay while the union officers presented the demands to company officials; then the sympathetic strike was underway. Throughout the coalfield, work stopped at midnight on 3 July and some ten thousand coal miners were on strike.[11]

The following morning McLachlan composed the document which was to be the central piece of evidence in his prosecution. It was a circular letter to the local unions of District 26:

To officers and members of Local Unions:

Brothers: This office has been informed that all the Waterford, Sydney Mines and Glace Bay sub-districts are out on strike this morning as a protest against the importation of Provincial Police and Federal troops into Sydney to intimidate the steel workers into continuing work at 32¢ per hour. On Sunday night last these Provincial Police in the most brutal manner rode down the people at Whitney Pier who were on the street, most of whom were coming from Church. Neither age, sex or physical disabilities were proof against these brutes. One old woman over seventy years of age was beaten into insensibility and may die. A boy nine years old was trampled under the horses' feet and his breast bone crushed in. One woman was beaten over the head with a police club and gave premature birth to a child. The child is dead and the woman's life is despaired of. Men and women were beaten up inside their own homes. Against the brutes the miners are on strike. The Government of Nova Scotia is the guilty and responsible party for this crime. No miner or mine worker can remain at work while this

[11]*Sydney Post*, 28, 29 and 30 June and 3 and 4 July 1923; *Maritime Labor Herald*, 7 July 1923. A useful selection of interviews and documents is presented in "The 1923 Strike in Steel and the Miners' Sympathetic Strike," *Cape Breton's Magazine*, 22 (1979). On the use of the police and armed forces see Don Macgillivray, "Military Aid to the Civil Power: The Cape Breton Experience in the 1920s," *Acadiensis*, III (Spring 1974), 45-64.

Government turns Sydney into a jungle; to do so is to sink your manhood and allow
Armstrong and his miserable bunch of grafting politicians to trample your last shred of
freedom on the sand. Call a meeting of your Local at once and decide to spread the fight
against Armstrong to every mine in Nova Scotia. Act at once. Tomorrow may be too late.[12]

At once a report from the secretary-treasurer and a call to arms, the letter was an
attempt to explain the causes of the sympathetic strike and to spread the protest to
the other coalfields in Nova Scotia. As usual with district correspondence, a stencil
was prepared and copies of the letter, over McLachlan's signature, were placed in
the mail to various locals in the district. Another copy was taken by district president
Dan Livingstone, addressed to Besco vice-president D. H. McDougall, the senior
company official resident in Cape Breton, and hand-delivered to the coal company
offices in Glace Bay.[13]

The arrests came the following evening, 6 July 1923. Sydney police chief J.B.
McCormick received a telegram from Attorney-General O'Hearn informing him
that warrants had been issued in Halifax for the arrest of McLachlan and Livingstone. The charges were described by O'Hearn as "unlawfully publishing false tales
whereby injury or mischief was likely to be occasioned to a public interest, namely
the government and provincial police of Nova Scotia, contrary to Sec. 136 of the
code." Following these instructions and trailed by a carload of provincial police,
Chief McCormick and his deputy drove to Glace Bay and found their quarry at the
union offices. When they learned the policemen's mission, McLachlan and Livingstone were reported "greatly surprised," but agreed to accompany the police to
Sydney. The following day Chief McCormick drove the two men across the island
to the Strait of Canso; they boarded the train for Halifax, where they were lodged
in the county jail.[14]

The arrests had the effect of removing the principal union leaders from Cape
Breton at the height of the industrial crisis. As vice-president Alex S. McIntyre had
departed for the mainland coalfields, the *Sydney Post* commented that as a result of
the arrests, "it is not now known who will direct the strike campaign." Indeed it
soon became obvious that O'Hearn hoped the prisoners would be absent from the
scene for a lengthy period of time. In Halifax an intense legal battle developed over
the question of bail for the union leaders. When they appeared for a hearing before
Halifax stipendiary magistrate M.B. Archibald on 8 July, Andrew Cluney, K.C.,

[12]PAC, Records of the Department of Justice, RG13 C2, vol. 1233, The King vs. James B.
McLachlan, 4-5 [transcript of the case in the Supreme Court of Nova Scotia sitting as a
Criminal Court of Appeal, 1923]. I am grateful to James M. Whalen of the Public Archives
of Canada for his assistance in gaining access to this document.
[13]The King vs. McLachlan, 45-7. A more abbreviated, but similar, report was contained in
the RCMP's secret weekly report on radical activities, 12 July 1923: "on Sunday night the
Provincial Police charged the crowd through the subway and Victoria Road, with the result
that quite a number of strikers and other people were injured ....": see PAC, King Papers,
MG26 J4, vol. 89, 68755.
[14]*Sydney Post*, 7 July 1923.

appearing on behalf of O'Hearn, argued that the prisoners were men of considerable public influence and "opposed allowing these men to be at large at the present time to go back to Cape Breton and continue to do acts to the injury of the public." On behalf of the prisoners, John A. Walker, a young lawyer and an associate of Harrington, argued that the stated offence was a relatively minor one and that bail should be granted as a matter of course; he also argued that the weight of evidence apparent against the accused should be taken into account: while the warrant stated the offence was committed in Halifax, it was a matter of common knowledge that the accused were both three hundred miles distant from the scene of the alleged crime. Bail was denied, but Walker persisted, and after applying for a writ of *habeas corpus* placed the argument before Justice J.A. Chisholm of the Supreme Court of Nova Scotia. Attorney-General O'Hearn appeared in person to oppose the petition, but Justice Chisholm allowed bail and the men were released on 11 July.[15]

Having won their first legal battle, the union leaders returned from jail in time to participate in an extraordinary episode which almost changed the outcome of the 1923 strike. As the events of the strike unfolded, the Governor-General, Lord Byng of Vimy, was wending his way by train on an extended tour of the Maritimes, timed to coincide with the 150th anniversary of the landing of the *Hector* at Pictou. Prime Minister William Lyon Mackenzie King was sufficiently embarrassed by the turbulent labour scene and the presence of federal troops to cancel his own plans to participate in the Pictou celebrations, but the Governor-General himself soon became involved in the industrial dispute. Together with Mayor Dan Willie Morrison of Glace Bay, a labour member of the provincial legislature, Livingstone and McLachlan requested an interview with Byng, who, after consulting the cabinet member in attendance, Pictou MP and Minister of National Defence E.M. Macdonald, agreed to meet them in his private railway car. The interview took place on 17 July, and at the end the four men shook hands; the two union leaders, teetotallers both, watched while the Governor-General and the mayor of Glace Bay shared a drink. The outcome of the discussion was later a matter of dispute. Mayor Morrison claimed that an agreement had been reached that the provincial police would be withdrawn within twenty-four hours of the miners' return to work and that a royal commission would be appointed to investigate the steelworkers' grievances. Macdonald insisted that the Governor-General had merely clarified the union's position and had no authority to conclude any agreement with the union leaders. Although the evidence suggests a minor constitutional crisis may have been in the making, the Prime Minister was prepared to overlook the ambiguities. King telegraphed Macdonald that he was prepared to offer the appointment of a royal commission in

---

[15]*Sydney Post*, 7 and 9 July 1923; *Dominion Law Reports*, 4 (1923), 1047-9. At O'Hearn's insistence, the issue of bail for the prisoners was considered by a panel of supreme court judges on 24 July 1923, who confirmed the actions of Justice Chisholm.

exchange for a return to work, and the following day he added that if the strike could be ended on such terms, "no time should be lost in agreeing to them."[16]

Before any action could be taken, the delicate situation was upset by other developments. Like Attorney-General O'Hearn, UMW President John L. Lewis had also been waiting to take action against the radical leadership in District 26. Before the strike, he had already ordered that new elections be held in the district, a step which did not greatly alarm the leadership, as elections were already scheduled for the month of August. Responding to an appeal from Besco officials at the outbreak of the sympathetic strike, Lewis issued a warning that a sympathetic strike was in violation of contract and against union policy, and that the withdrawal of maintenance men from the mines was also indefensible. After some delay, vice-president McIntyre replied on behalf of the executive, stating "our international must understand that its jurisdiction does not give it authority to prohibit workers in Canada waging a political struggle against use of armed forces which are being used to smash our labour movement." Lewis was unconvinced, and on the evening of 17 July he released a long telegram suspending the district's autonomy. The executive officers were ordered removed from office and the membership were instructed to return to work. Silby Barrett, the former international board member defeated at the August 1922 elections, was appointed provisional president of District 26. Lewis' letter to Livingstone concluded with formidable charges:

I am familiar with the constant intrigue between yourself and your evil-genius, McLachlan, and your revolutionary masters in Moscow.... No doubt the present strike in Nova Scotia corresponds to your idea of a revolution against the British government and is in pursuance thereof.... You may as well know now as at any time in the future that the United Mine Workers is not a political institution and cannot be used to promote the fallacious whims of any political fanatic who seeks to strike down the established institutions of his government.

The arrest of the union leaders had failed to break the coal miners' solidarity, but Lewis' intervention was the blow that defeated the sympathetic strike. The coal miners gradually returned to work during the remainder of the month, and the steel strike was formally ended on 2 August.[17]

Meanwhile the legal charges against McLachlan and Livingstone made their way through the Nova Scotia courts, and were forwarded for trial at the fall criminal term of the Supreme Court of Nova Scotia in Halifax. On 24 September Walker attempted to have the trial removed to Sydney, where the court would also be sitting to consider criminal cases; he argued that a trial in Halifax imposed heavy expenses on the defendants and that it was proper for the trial to be conducted in the locality

[16]The episode may be followed in PAC, King Papers, E.M. Macdonald to King, 16, 17, 21 and 22 July 1923; King to Macdonald, 17, 18 and 22 July 1923 and F.A. MacGregor to Macdonald, 20 July 1923. See also C.B. Wade, "History of District 26, United Mine Workers of America, 1919-1941," (unpublished manuscript, 1950), chapter IV, where the account is based on interviews with D.W. Morrison.

[17]*Sydney Post*, 12 and 18 July 1923; *United Mine Workers' Journal*, 1 August 1923.

where the alleged offence was committed. O'Hearn appeared in court to oppose this motion, stating that Halifax was the appropriate venue since the initial charges had been based on the appearance of McLachlan's letter in the Halifax *Morning Chronicle*. It had not been shown, he argued, that a fair trial was not to be had in Halifax, whereas in the Sydney district juries had recently brought in at least 18 "no bills" in looting and assault cases arising from the industrial conflict.[18] He might also have noted that his own attempt to try Malcolm Bruce for making seditious utterances at a public meeting in Glace Bay in May had failed disastrously when the charges were dismissed by a local court in June.[19] O'Hearn prevailed, and on 2 October the grand jury returned true bills in the charges against the two men.[20]

During this time there had been a subtle shift in the nature of the charges in the case. Originally McLachlan and Livingstone were charged under Section 136 of the Criminal Code for "publishing false news," but the indictment presented in court in October referred instead to "a seditious libel concerning His Majesty's Government of and for the Province of Nova Scotia and the Provincial Police established under the laws of the Province." The indictment then cited the "seditious matter" in full, namely the text of McLachlan's circular letter. The indictment also stated that the offence had been commited on three separate occasions — in Glace Bay, in Halifax, and in Thorburn, a mining town in Pictou County.[21] The revision of the charges made the offence a substantially more serious one. Offences under Section 136 were punishable by a term of one year's imprisonment, whereas each charge of seditious libel was punishable by up to 20 years' imprisonment, a penalty which had been increased from two years under the Criminal Code amendments of July 1919.[22]

The amended charges also implied a change in the nature of the case against the union leaders. Initially, the focus was on the veracity of McLachlan's letter, but under the revised charge, attention was focused on the intentions of the author. In his opening remarks at the trial on 15 October, O'Hearn confirmed this view of the case with the following explanation of the significance of McLachlan's circular letter: "the issue is not whether the statement published is false or true. There are

[18] *Sydney Post*, 17 August and 22 and 25 September 1923.

[19] On the case of Malcolm Bruce, see *Halifax Chronicle*, 8 May 1923; *Sydney Post*, 30 May 1923; *Sydney Record*, 7 June 1923, and the account by Dawn Fraser, *Echoes from Labor's War: Industrial Cape Breton in the 1920s* (Toronto 1976), 60-5. The search of McLachlan's house in May 1923 had been carried out on the strength of a search warrant for Bruce.

[20] *Sydney Post*, 3 October 1923. By this stage it was also determined to proceed separately against the two men. Livingstone's case was held over to February 1924, and subsequently to October 1924, but the case was never prosecuted.

[21] The King vs. McLachlan, 4.

[22] *Revised Statutes of Canada*, 1906, vol. III, 2453-4; *Statutes of Canada*, 1919, Chapter 46, 307-10. The 1919 amendments also created a new section of the Criminal Code, Section 97A, which like the repeal of Section 133, also broadened the scope of seditious offences. See also J.B. Mackenzie, "Section 98, Criminal Code and Freedom of Expression in Canada," *Queen's Law Journal*, 1 (1972), 469-83.

many things which are true but cannot be published. It is not the question of the truth of the statement, but a question of whether it was said with the intention of creating dissatisfaction and disturbance."[23] "Away false teachings of my youth," commented Dawn Fraser. "It's now a crime to speak the truth!"[24]

Nevertheless, the Crown's case relied heavily on detailed descriptions of the events at the steel company gates. Several witnesses described the disorderly scenes at the steel plant in some detail. Captain D.A. Noble, head of the Besco police force, stated that rioting had continued at the steel plant continuously from Thursday when the strike began until Sunday night; Colonel Eric McDonald, commissioner of the provincial police, described the scene on his arrival on Friday, 29 June: "the crowd outside the gate seemed to have control of all that part of the town, and the local police or steel company's police were not able to appear on the street." The witnesses went on to describe the efforts of the provincial police to, in McDonald's words, "send the crowd home," and Sydney police chief J.B. McCormick reported there was "practically no trouble" at the plant gates afterwards. Mining engineer Walter Hurd underlined the importance of company efforts to control access to the plant, stating that if left unattended the potential damage to the coke ovens would involve a cost of $2 million to repair.[25]

The remainder of the prosecution's case focused more closely on McLachlan's opinions and actions. The book which had been taken from McLachlan's house in May was entered as an exhibit, as was a copy of the published minutes of the 1922 district convention; excerpts from the radical resolutions of that meeting were read into the record. Colonel McDonald reported also that in a meeting with company officials on 3 July, in negotiations to avert the sympathetic strike, McLachlan had stated the following words: "to hell with the property of the British Empire Steel Corporation." By calling the union's office secretary, it was established that McLachlan had indeed authored the circular letter of 4 July, a point confirmed by Canadian Press correspondent Andrew Merkel, who had verified the authenticity of the document with McLachlan. Two union members from Pictou County were called to testify to the receipt of the letter by union locals in that district. The news editor of the *Morning Chronicle* testified that he had published the document under the headline "Miners are duped by the circulation of false statements" in the 6 July edition of the Halifax newspaper.[26]

The prosecution called a total of twelve witnesses; the defence called none. When witnesses began to give evidence regarding events in Sydney, Harrington objected to testimony on this subject; if the truth of McLachlan's statement was not an acceptable defence, then evidence of the events should not be allowed. O'Hearn replied that the purpose was to show "general industrial disorder in Cape Breton," since "seditious intention shall be judged from the times in which the thing was

[23] *Sydney Post*, 16 October 1923.
[24] Fraser, *Echoes from Labor's War*, 70-1.
[25] The King vs. McLachlan, 9-14, 22-6, 28-34, 38-42 and 51-2.
[26] *Ibid.*, 33, 45-7, 53-4, 58 and 60-4.

done." Judge Mellish ruled that the evidence was to be allowed. Harrington then objected that some thirty witnesses would be required to present the defence's view of the events. As the defence was financially unable to bring witnesses from Cape Breton, he would be bound to move for a change of venue. Judge Mellish in response noted simply, "you are objecting to the evidence on the ground that you have not witnesses to meet it; I rule that is a bad ground; that is the short end to that." At the end of the trial Harrington placed a formal motion for a change of venue, on the grounds that "there is no possibility of the defendant getting witnesses here."[27]

Despite the lack of defence witnesses, Harrington and Walker were able to draw out some relevant evidence in their cross-examination of the Crown's witnesses. It was established that the proposal to join the Red International had been subsequently withdrawn by the district. In cross-examination of Colonel McDonald, Harrington was able to offer a corrected version of the statement attributed to McLachlan on 3 July: "if you put the women and children of the miners in one scale and the property of the Dominion Coal Company in the other, then I say if it is between the two, it is to hell with the property of the Dominion Coal Company." It was established as well that McLachlan had not been present at the riotous scenes in Sydney, but that there was subsequently "quite a bit of talk" about the actions of the provincial police and the Sydney police commission had held hearings on the behaviour of the police. In his questioning Harrington was thus able skilfully to suggest that McLachlan's account was not without foundation; indeed he was able to introduce into the proceedings the name and address of the pregnant woman assailed by the provincial police in one of the incidents referred to in McLachlan's letter. Harrington also elicited evidence that conditions at the steel plant gates had appeared relatively peaceful for most of Sunday, 1 July, and he alleged that the provincial police were determined to, in words he attributed to Colonel McDonald, "put on a show about eight that night at No. 4 gate." He implied also that the police might well have "passed the rum jar copiously around" before taking to the street.[28]

Perhaps the most significant testimony was brought forth on Walker's cross-examination of Andrew Merkel, the CP correspondent. Merkel explained the rather indirect route by which McLachlan's letter had reached Halifax and appeared in the press there, thus providing the original basis for his arrest on charges of "publishing false news." Arriving in Sydney on 4 July, Merkel went to the offices of the *Sydney Record*, a daily newspaper known for its sympathies for the Liberal government and the steel company. There F.W. Gray, the assistant to Besco vice-president D.H. McDougall, handed him a typewritten copy of McLachlan's letter, which had apparently been prepared from the copy Livingstone delivered to company offices earlier in the day. This was the first time Merkel had seen the document, and, he recalled, "Mr. Gray suggested I put it on the wire and distribute it." After speaking

---

[27]*Ibid.*, 10-1 and 65. In the course of the trial the defence also presented objections to the form of the indictment, an irregularity in the selection of the jury, and the admission in evidence of the book found in McLachlan's home.
[28]*Ibid.*, 15-22, 26-8, 34-8, 42-4 and 62-3.

with McLachlan to confirm the authenticity of the letter, Merkel then filed his report, and the document appeared the following day in the Halifax *Morning Chronicle* and other newspapers. O'Hearn re-examined the witness, but Merkel firmly maintained that the document was not published in the press until after it was released by F.W. Gray. Harrington later emphasized the significance of this evidence in his final address to the jury: "if McLachlan is guilty for sending this letter to the locals of his union, why is not F.W. Gray of the steel company not also guilty for having it published? ... Why aren't there more people in [the] dock besides McLachlan?"[29]

The most remarkable aspect of the trial, however, was the muted behaviour of the prisoner. Those who attended must have been disappointed to experience none of the legendary platform abilities which had made him such an effective performer at union meetings and conciliation boards. Instead McLachlan sat in uncharacteristic silence, arms crossed, pipe clenched firmly in his mouth, maintaining what one reporter described as "an air of sang froid" through the proceedings: "the worse [sic] he looked for, apparently, was disagreement by the jury."[30] McLachlan spoke only once during the trial. This was to interrupt O'Hearn's final address to the jury; when the attorney general claimed that a red flag had been seized at McLachlan's home, he interjected briefly, "there was no red flag; he never said it." A trivial point perhaps, but one that seemed to sound a note of frustration on McLachlan's part in the final hours of the trial. The powerful use of language was one of the strongest weapons in the labour leader's personal arsenal, yet McLachlan was never called as a witness nor invited to address the court. It is difficult to imagine him intimidated by lawyers or silent against his will; indeed one of the defence lawyers has recalled that McLachlan did not speak in court because he did not want to.[31] In a trial in Cape Breton McLachlan would undoubtedly have insisted on a vigorous, personal defence; in Halifax, however, if not reconciled to a guilty verdict, he was doubtful enough to entrust his fate to the judgement of his lawyers.

The role of the trial judge, Justice Humphrey Mellish, had also affected the conduct of the case. The decision to admit evidence regarding "general industrial disorder in Cape Breton" apparently surprised the defence, yet Mellish supported this line of inquiry, on several occasions putting direct questions to witnesses regarding the Sydney disturbances. In Harrington's view, the refusal to allow a change of venue prevented the defence from presenting the witnesses necessary to refute the Crown's case. Also, although several items of evidence offered by the Crown were not accepted, Mellish did allow the Crown to introduce the copy of the constitution of the Red International collected at McLachlan's home in May.

The judge's charge to the jury was particularly important. In a marvelous circularity, Section 132 stated: "seditious words are words expressive of a seditious intention. A seditious libel is a libel expressive of a seditious intention." Nowhere

[29] *Ibid.*, 54-5.
[30] *Sydney Post*, 19 October 1923.
[31] Interview with John A. Walker, Halifax, 23 September 1976.

in the Criminal Code was the crime of sedition actually defined. For the benefit of the jury Mellish quoted also the accepted authority of the day, Stephen's *History of the Criminal Law of England*: sedition embraced

all those practices, whether by words, deed, or writing, which fall short of high treason, but directly tend to have for their object to excite discontent or dissatisfaction; to excite ill-will between different classes of the King's subjects; to create public disturbances, or to lead to civil war; to bring into hatred or contempt the sovereign of the government, the laws or constitution of the realm, and generally all endeavours to promote public disorder.

Mellish qualified this sweeping definition by reading Section 133 of the Criminal Code, a section which specified the permissible scope of social criticism not to be considered seditious, beginning with the words: "no one shall be deemed to have a seditious intention only because he intends in good faith, (a) to show that His Majesty has been misled or mistaken in his measures; or, (b) to point out errors or defects in the government or constitution ...." Mellish need not have offered this qualification; he was apparently not aware that this section had been removed from the Criminal Code in the amendments of 1919. He was, however, aware of the "more modern" penalty for sedition — up to 20 years' imprisonment — enacted at the same time.[32]

Mellish then turned to the case at hand. He indicated that there was no question as to McLachlan's responsibility for publication of the document; the distribution of the letter to the union locals "in itself was a publication"; in the case of the appearance of the letter in Halifax — where there were no union locals — Mellish suggested the following reasoning: "I don't think it unreasonable to say that when a document of that kind once became distributed in the way McLachlan intended it should be distributed that he would naturally expect it would be published all over Nova Scotia and get into the newspapers also." As to the question whether the document was seditious under the definition provided, Mellish had few doubts: "it is capable of a seditious construction, I may tell you, gentlemen; and the next question for you is, whether it was intended that the construction should be put upon it." In considering that issue, Mellish continued, it was relevant to consider the reasons why it was being urged that the military and the police be withdrawn from Sydney:

You are told by counsel for the defence that the police were there to break the strike. Was that the purpose for which the police were there? Or were the police there to maintain order? What interest had the Glace Bay miners in having the police removed from Sydney? ... Was it to give the strikers a free hand to do as they had been doing before? That is a question for you to consider, as to whether this document was intended to operate and incite people against law and order, — the orderly government of the community by the executive of the people.

[32]The King vs. McLachlan, 67-8.

It was also relevant, to "consider his opinions, and those of the party whom he represents"; for the benefit of the jury he quoted excerpts from the radical resolutions of June 1922 and drew attention to the "seditious literature" in McLachlan's possession.[33]

Thus instructed, the jury retired to consider their verdict and returned one and a half hours later to pronounce the prisoner guilty on all three counts. It was hardly a surprising result. The attorney general had seen the case as a personal crusade against the man he regarded as the personification of Cape Breton Bolshevism. In his conduct of the case and in his charge to the jury, the trial judge had virtually directed a verdict of guilty; moreover, Judge Mellish, "who ruled over his court as would an emperor," was well-known as "an outstanding corporationist on the bench" and on previous occasions had displayed his judicial prejudices against the coal miners' union.[34] For their part, the defence lawyers had presented no coherent line of defence in the course of the trial. Their strategy seemed to be based largely on technical objections and perhaps the hope of a successful appeal. Harrington seemed surprised by the judge's decision to admit evidence of the Sydney disturbances and, probably unreasonably, accepted the argument that truth was no defence in a case of seditious libel. Although Harrington himself had drawn the parallel with the trial of Joseph Howe, he failed to recognize that one of the lessons of that case had been that this restriction could be easily evaded in the process of clarifying the defendant's intentions. The failure to present a single witness or to hear from the accused must surely have seemed curious to the jury, twelve citizens of Halifax and Dartmouth whose knowledge of conditions in industrial Cape Breton was no doubt limited. There we face another contrast with the trial of Howe, for although Howe addressed the jury at extraordinary length and with exceptional skill, it has also been pointed out that Howe faced a jury of peers and acquaintances who might be expected to be sympathetic to his position.[35] It may be excessive to claim

[33] *Ibid.*, 68-70.

[34] Opinions of Mellish are included in R.A. Kanigsberg, *Trials and Tribulations of a Bluenose Barrister* (Halifax 1977), 36, and in an incomplete letter from Sydney to J.S. Woodsworth, 9 February 1924, in PAC, J.S. Woodsworth Papers, MG 27 III C7, vol. 11. He had in 1918 tried a case in which the Dominion Coal Company and several officials were charged with manslaughter as a result of a notable mine disaster (a case in which he directed the jury to deliver a not guilty verdict without leaving the box), and in 1922 Mellish had given a controversial interpretation of the Industrial Disputes Investigation Act which allowed Besco to implement an immediate wage reduction; "Mine Explosion in New Waterford, 1917," *Cape Breton's Magazine*, 21 (1978), 1-11; PANS, Records of the Supreme Court of Nova Scotia, "Opinion of Mellish, J., UMW *et al.* vs. Dominion Coal *et al.*," 10 January 1922; *Maritime Labor Herald*, 11 February 1922.

[35] Joseph A. Chisholm, "The King vs. Joseph Howe: Prosecution for Libel," *Canadian Bar Review*, XIII (October 1935), 584-93; J.M. Beck, "'A Fool for a Client': The Trial of Joseph Howe," *Acadiensis*, III (Spring 1974), 27-44. The jury included the following: one accountant, two truckmen, two farmers, one grocer, one butcher, one messenger, one porter, one waiter, one barber and one carpenter.

that Harrington exploited the case to promote the fortunes of the Conservative party and prove the iniquity of the Liberal government, but nevertheless the defence was an ineffectual one.

The legal aftermath of the case continued for several months. The prisoner appeared for sentencing on 31 October. On his behalf, Walker made a strong plea for leniency and urged that the prisoner be given a suspended sentence; the attorney general replied that McLachlan had been fairly convicted of "a very serious offence against the law of Canada" and reminded the court that a conviction, "generally speaking, was designed for the purpose of impressing the community." Mellish pronounced a sentence of two years in Dorchester Penitentiary on each of the three offences, the sentences to run concurrently.[36] Walker immediately applied for bail pending an appeal on behalf of the prisoner. Chief Justice R.E. Harris — a former president of the Nova Scotia Steel and Coal Company — denied the application, and McLachlan remained in the Halifax county jail until the appeal was decided on 8 January 1924.

The appeal was heard on 17 December 1923 before the province's newly established court of criminal appeal. The defence presented arguments based on eleven points of law, including errors on the part of the trial judge, defects in the indictment, an irregularity in the constitution of the jury, the improper admission of evidence, the court's lack of jurisdiction, and the prisoner's inability to make a full defence. With the concurrence of the four other judges sitting on the appeal, Chief Justice Harris delivered the judgement. In the light of Merkel's direct evidence on how the document reached the Halifax *Chronicle*, the conviction on the charge of publication in Halifax was set aside; on the other two counts the conviction was upheld. The judgement overlooked the fact that the Halifax charge had determined the unfavourable venue and ruled that the Supreme Court did have the jurisdiction to try McLachlan in Halifax on all three charges.[37] There was one further legal step in the case. On 29 January Walker presented a motion for leave to appeal the case to the Privy Council, and on 16 February 1924 this was granted. Justice Russell noted that at least one significant issue was at stake: "the use that may be made of books or documents found in the library of a suspected person presents a question of 'great general and public importance.'" However, the matter never was submitted to the Privy Council, and the case passed on into the untapped obscurity of legal history.[38]

Despite the legal issues raised in the case, there was little doubt in the minds of contemporaries that this was above all a political trial. While coal miners in Cape Breton passed resolutions protesting the outcome of the trial, Besco president Roy

[36] *Sydney Post*, 1 November 1923.
[37] *Nova Scotia Law Reports*, 56 (1924), 413-31; *Canadian Criminal Cases*, XLI (1924), 249-62. The first of these states, incorrectly, that Judge Mellish served as a member of the appeal court on this case.
[38] *Dominion Law Reports*, 1 (1924), 1109-12; *Crankshaw's Criminal Code of Canada*, 7th edition, 577.

Wolvin was telegraphing his congratulations to Attorney General O'Hearn.[39] Soon after the conviction was announced, a flood of telegrams, letters and petitions began to arrive in the offices of the Minister of Justice in Ottawa, many of them inspired by appeals from the Nova Scotia Workers' Defence Committee.[40] From Cape Breton there were protests from local unions and public meetings, and, following the failure of the appeal, resolutions from the town councils in the coal towns and in Sydney requesting McLachlan's release. Most of the protests from across the country were from trades and labour councils and local unions, appealing not only for the release of McLachlan or for a new trial but also in some cases for the repeal of all the sedition laws. From his retirement in Oakville, Phillips Thompson wrote directly to the Prime Minister, warning his old acquaintance, "it would be much to be regretted should Canada follow the bad example of the degenerate republic across the border, with its judicial frame-ups, its scores of political prisoners and its brutal suppression of free speech...."[41] In the House of Commons and on speaking tours, J.S. Woodsworth took a close interest in the case and also pressured the government to release McLachlan.[42] Similarly, the executive council of the Trades and Labour Congress of Canada made a case on McLachlan's behalf at their annual meeting with the Dominion cabinet in January 1924.[43]

As it became clear the government might take action to release McLachlan, there were also counterprotests. The Employers' Association of Manitoba, supported by the Winnipeg Board of Trade, warned against such action: "it would have a most injurious effect on this country and result in further acts of sedition and lawlessness and disobedience to the authority of the State."[44] Two Nova Scotia Liberal MPs expressed concern at the possible consequences of McLachlan's release, and Attorney General O'Hearn met with the solicitor general to explain his view that "it is not in the interests of peace and order in the community that he

[39]*Sydney Post*, 22 and 24 October 1923; Nova Scotia, Royal Commission on Coal Mining Industry [Duncan Commission, 1925], "Minutes of Evidence," 1085.

[40]The Nova Scotia Workers' Defence Committee, which may be considered a precursor of the Canadian Labour Defence League, raised more than $12,000 between July 1923 and January 1924 on behalf of McLachlan and others arrested in the industrial conflicts in 1923; Wade, "History of District 26," chapter IV.

[41]PAC, Records of the Department of Justice, RG13 C2, vol. 1233, file 25777, Phillippe [sic] Thompson to W.L. Mackenzie King, 5 December 1923 (copy).

[42]*Maritime Labor Herald*, 29 December 1923; PAC, Woodsworth Papers, vol. 2, O.D. Skelton to Woodsworth, 28 March 1924; then Dean of Arts at Queen's University, Skelton expressed surprise at the "mediaeval interpretation" of seditious libel which appeared to prevail in the case; also, he wondered why it was that strong statutory declarations prepared on behalf of the defendant regarding the disturbances in Sydney had not been offered in evidence.

[43]PAC, Trades and Labour Congress of Canada, Executive Council Minutes, MG 28 I103, 11 and 12 January 1924; *Sydney Post*, 15 January 1924.

[44]PAC, Records of the Department of Justice, RG13 C2, vol. 1233, file 25777, Charles Roland to Sir Lomer Gouin, 18 December 1923.

should receive any clemency while he maintains his present defiant attitude."[45] Besco president Roy Wolvin also wrote to the Prime Minister to express his views:

I have had much experience with this man's activities and I consider him a dangerously clever "Red." He has cost the coal mining companies of Nova Scotia many millions of dollars and the miners an equal amount. Some leaders in this district today will say with bravado to let him come back but I do not agree with them. He is the concentrated cause of past unrest in this district and with him away for a few years, possibly, his teachings may be forgotten.[46]

McLachlan was released from Dorchester Penitentiary on 5 March 1924 on a ticket-of-leave which required him to report regularly to the local chief of police until his sentence formally expired on 30 October 1925. When he reached New Glasgow late on a rainy evening, he received a "triumphal reception" from the Pictou County miners. The Academy of Music was packed to the doors when McLachlan appeared on the platform, "and the building fairly rocked with applause." The cheering coal miners found his fighting spirit undiminished by his time in jail. Entertaining the audience at length with the details of his trial, ridiculing the attorney general's statements, McLachlan explained the nature of his crime:

Sedition, said Mr. McLachlan, is when you protest against the wrongs inflicted on working men; when you protest against the resources of the province being put in the control of men like Roy Wolvin; when wage rates are forced on you without your consent. These things will be given back to the working class and their wrongs will eventually be redeemed. If you say that strongly enough, you are liable to get into jail for sedition.[47]

Obviously unrepentant, McLachlan left on the midnight train for another hero's welcome in Cape Breton. In Glace Bay he would be asked to take on the editorship of the *Maritime Labor Herald*, and through this newspaper and later the *Nova Scotia Miner*, his remained a powerful voice in industrial Cape Breton. Yet the events of 1923 had marked a turning point in McLachlan's public career. Removed from union office, convicted on criminal charges, he had passed the peak of his influence among the coal miners.

In this the prosecution had enjoyed some success, and the conviction of McLachlan would be remembered as one of the major achievements of O'Hearn's stint as attorney general. For O'Hearn, however, it was a shortlived triumph; within a month the incorrigible McLachlan was soon repeating the same "seditious libel" which had resulted in his conviction, and these were by no means the most inflammatory of his public declarations over the following years. The arrest and conviction of McLachlan had not ended the influence of the radicals, nor resolved Cape Breton's industrial problems. It was the intervention of John L. Lewis, rather

[45] *Ibid.*, T.L. Kelly to W.L.M. King (copy), 10 January 1924; G.W. Kyte to E.J. McMurray, 18 January 1924; E.J. McMurray, "Memorandum for Mr. Clarke," 8 January 1924.
[46] PAC, King Papers, R.M. Wolvin to King, 10 January 1924.
[47] *The Workers' Weekly* (Stellarton), 7 March 1924.

than the arrest of McLachlan, which broke the sympathetic strike in July 1923. When the UMWA restored the district's independence in September 1924, the coal miners immediately installed a slate of officers well-known as McLachlanites, and in most cases also members of the Workers' Party. The long struggle against Besco continued, and the final confrontation came in 1925. Like most of the Liberal MLAs, O'Hearn went down to defeat in the Liberal rout in July 1925; he later became a judge of the Halifax county court. For Gordon Harrington, though he lost the case, the trial helped confirm his reputation as a friend of labour's cause and that in turn helped the Conservative party sweep to victory in 1925; Harrington and the Conservatives carried all the seats in industrial Cape Breton in 1925, he and Walker both entered the new cabinet, and Harrington became premier of the province in 1930.

"Listen, my children, and you shall know/ Of a crime that happened long ago." In the narrative verse of Dawn Fraser, "The Case of Jim McLachlan" easily entered the popular culture of industrial Cape Breton.[48] Elsewhere, however, the case of The King vs. James B. McLachlan subsequently attracted little notice. One of the few writers to refer to the case considered that, even under the Supreme Court of Canada decision in the Boucher case in 1951, which tended to narrow the scope of seditious offences, McLachlan might still have been convicted.[49] Yet the history of this case surely reminds us that there is a need for greater attention to the establishment of historical context in studying issues in the history of Canadian law. While it is customary to scrutinize the intentions of the accused, in political trials such as McLachlan's it is necessary to examine other factors as well. "Depending on the questions asked," David Flaherty has rightly noted, "legal history can find itself closely allied with political, social, economic, or intellectual history."[50]

In this case the law of sedition had been used not only to curtail freedom of speech and to punish labour radicalism. In a day when the law allowed easy access to armed force in industrial disputes and offered no support for workers seeking union recognition, the arrest and prosecution of McLachlan came as a challenge to the growth of labour organization in the industrial community and particularly to the legitimacy of the sympathetic strike. Finally, let us also consider that the case belongs to a transitional moment in Canadian labour history, a period when the rule of force was gradually being supplanted by the rule of law. The use of military aid to the civil power, for instance, was being abandoned in labour disputes, largely as a result of the discreditable Cape Breton experiences of 1922 and 1923; in the meantime, the laws which could be used against radicals and unionists had undergone a considerable broadening in the wake of the Winnipeg General Strike and other anxieties of 1919. It was the misfortune of industrial Cape Breton and James

[48]The first version of Dawn Fraser's "The Case of Jim McLachlan" appeared in the *Maritime Labor Herald*, 16 February 1924; see Fraser, *Echoes from Labor's War*, 48-60.
[49]Schmeiser, *Civil Liberties in Canada*, 206-7 and 211.
[50]David Flaherty, "Writing Canadian Legal History: An Introduction," in Flaherty, ed., *Essays in the History of Canadian Law*, I (Toronto 1981), 4.

Bryson McLachlan in 1923 to stand at the intersection of the old and the new; the sympathetic strike was challenged both by the rule of force and by the rule of law, leaving behind a legacy of considerable bitterness. All of this was closely observed by one of Walter O'Hearn's assistants in the McLachlan case, a young lawyer by the name of Angus L. Macdonald. As premier of Nova Scotia in 1937 he would introduce the Trade Union Act which promised to bring the steelworkers across the great divide separating the era of "labour's war" from the age of "industrial legality."[51]

---

[51]"The Coming of the Trade Union Act (1937)," *Cape Breton's Magazine*, 23 (August 1979). For subsequent national developments, see Laurel Sefton MacDowell, "The Formation of the Canadian Industrial Relations System During World War Two," *Labour/Le Travailleur*, 3 (1978), 175-96.

Part Four
The Rights of Labour

The Labour Question entered a new phase in the 1930s and 1940s. Instead of revolution there was reform, and there were several advances in Canadian social and economic democracy. As the chapters by E.R. Forbes and Sean Cadigan show, in response to demands for relief during the Great Depression, governments began slowly and reluctantly to accept greater responsibility for the welfare of the unemployed and destitute. The arrival of the welfare state, symbolized in federal policy by the adoption of unemployment insurance and family allowances in the 1940s and medicare in the 1960s, was accompanied also by a recognition of the legitimate role of organized labour within the world of work. The 1937 Trade Union Act in Nova Scotia was an example of the new kind of legislation that recognized the right of workers to join unions and required employers to accept them as representatives of their employees for the purposes of collective bargaining. These principles provided the basis for federal policy in 1944 and then, included in postwar provincial legislation, became the basis for the modern industrial relations system. The postwar settlement amounted, in Eugene Forsey's view, to the achievement of responsible constitutional government in the world of work. His own brief contribution sheds light on two episodes which demonstrated the limits of the new system of industrial legality as it worked out in Prince Edward Island and Newfoundland. These were early episodes, but the frequency of governments' recourse to exceptionalism, especially in the context of public-sector employment, raises important questions about the adequacy of the currently existing industrial relations system. One of the new features of organized labour in this period was the emergence of public sector unionism. In this section Anthony Thomson introduces the special problems affecting the growth of workers' organizations in the public sector, where the rights of unionism and collective bargaining were much slower to arrive and did so in less complete form than in the private sector. Martha MacDonald and Patricia Connelly examine the working world of women in the Atlantic fishery, an approach that requires us to appreciate first of all the significance of household labour for understanding this part of the regional economy and secondly the pervasive influence of government policy on the options available to workers and their families. Finally, Harry Glasbeek and Eric Tucker, in a thoughtful reflection on the Westray mine disaster, have provided a critical perspective on some of the underlying assumptions about the world of work and its dangers at the beginning of the 1990s.

Additional Reading

Battiste, Marie. "Different Worlds of Work: The Mi'kmaq Experience," in Dorothy E. Moore and James H. Morrison, eds., *Work, Ethnicity and Oral History* (Halifax 1988), 63-70.

Calhoun, Sue. *A Word to Say: The Story of the Maritime Fishermen's Union* (Halifax 1991).

_____. *"Ole Boy": Memoirs of a Canadian Labour Leader, J.K. Bell* (Halifax 1992).

Cameron, Silver Donald. *The Education of Everett Richardson: The Nova Scotia Fishermen's Strike, 1970-71* (Toronto 1977).

Comish, Shaun. *The Westray Tragedy: A Miner's Story* (Halifax 1993).

Earle, Michael, ed. *Workers and the State in Twentieth Century Nova Scotia* (Fredericton 1990).

Gilson, C.H.J., ed. *Strikes in Nova Scotia, 1970-1985* (Hantsport 1986).

Inglis, Gordon. *More Than Just a Union: The Story of the NFFAWU* (St. John's 1985).

Ladd, H. Landon. "The Newfoundland Loggers' Strike of 1959," in W.J.C. Cherwinski and G.S. Kealey, eds., *Lectures in Canadian Labour and Working-Class History* (St. John's 1985), 149-64.

McFarland, Joan. "Changing Modes of Social Control in a New Brunswick Fish Packing Town," *Studies in Political Economy*, 4 (Autumn 1980), 99-113.

McKay, Ian. "Springhill 1958," in Gary Burrill and Ian McKay, eds., *People, Resources and Power: Critical Perspectives on Underdevelopment and Primary Industries in the Atlantic Region* (Fredericton 1987), 162-85.

Ommer, Rosemary. "One Hundred Years of Fishery Crises in Newfoundland," *Acadiensis*, XXIII, 2 (Spring 1994), 5-20.

O'Neill, Brian. *Work and Technological Change: Case Studies of Longshoremen and Postal Workers in St. John's* (St. John's 1981).

Overton, James. "Economic Crisis and the End of Democracy: Politics in Newfoundland During the Great Depression," *Labour/Le Travail*, 26 (Fall 1990), 85-124.

Parenteau, Bill. "'In Good Faith': The Development of Pulpwood Marketing for Independent Producers in New Brunswick, 1960-1975," in L. Anders Sandberg, ed., *Trouble in the Woods: Forest Policy and Social Conflict in Nova Scotia and New Brunswick* (Fredericton 1992), 110-41.

Strong, Cyril W. *My Life as a Newfoundland Union Organizer, 1912-87* (St. John's 1987).

Sutherland, Duff. "Newfoundland Loggers Respond to the Great Depression," *Labour/Le Travail*, 29 (Spring 1992), 81-115.

E.R. Forbes   12

'Cutting the Pie into Smaller Pieces': Matching Grants and Relief in the Maritime Provinces during the 1930s

The Maritimes in the 1930s was for many a grim place to live. The documents give
a picture of an often repressive society in which governments were slow to try to
bridge the gap between the comfortable and the desperately poor. The three
provinces were among the last to adopt such social programmes as old age pensions
and mothers' allowances and they were on record as opposing unemployment
insurance. They were the meanest of all the provinces in their aid for the unemployed. All levels of government attempted to avoid responsibility for relief,
sometimes at the expense of the health and lives of their citizens. The record
abounds with examples of elderly and destitute refused assistance, deaf and blind
cut off from their schools, seriously ill denied hospitalization, and moral offenders
savagely punished.

Maritime governments were unique neither in the nature of their problems nor
in their responses to them; they shared in the broad ideological currents of the day.[1]
If their attitude towards those in need seemed harsher than governments in other
provinces, it was primarily because of their more limited economic resources and

[1]For general perspectives on relief policy see James Struthers, *No Fault of Their Own:
Unemployment and the Welfare State 1914-41* (Toronto 1983); J.H. Thompson with Allen
Seager, *Canada, 1922-1939: Decades of Discord* (Toronto 1985); Christopher Armstrong,
The Politics of Federalism: Ontario's Relations with the Federal Government, 1867-1942
(Toronto 1981); L.M. Grayson and Michael Bliss, eds., *The Wretched of Canada: Letters to
R.B. Bennett* (Toronto 1971); Michiel Horn, ed., *The Dirty Thirties: Canadians in the Great
Depression* (Toronto 1972); and John Taylor, "Relief from Relief: The Cities' Answer to
Depression Dependency," *Journal of Canadian Studies*, XIV, I (Spring 1979), 16-23.

Published with permission of the editor. From *Acadiensis*, XVII, 1 (Autumn 1987), 34-55.

their inability to participate effectively in the federal government's relief programmes. The matching grant formulas in the federal programmes would have been fair, if all the provinces had possessed equal wealth. But since their resources varied dramatically, the poorer provinces had either to commit a much greater percentage of their funds to a given programme or to deny to their citizens the benefits conspicuously available elsewhere.[2] In discouraging the expansion of relief programmes at federal-provincial conferences, Maritime governments were expressing the frustration and political embarrassment which the inequities of the relief structure created for them. As the political pressure mounted locally for greater participation in federal relief programmes, they became more adept in cutting their meagre share of the pie into smaller pieces.

This problem was compounded by the poorer provinces' inability to alleviate economic disparity among the municipalities within their borders. As the percentage of uncollected taxes mounted and the proportion of future budgets committed to servicing the municipal debt increased, ratepayers' representatives became increasingly mean in their definition of relief need. With revenues dwindling and debt service charges mushrooming, provincial governments could only urge further restraint. Thus, residents in the poorest municipalities in the poorest provinces became the victims of a process which at two stages reduced the assistance which should have come their way.

The statistics show just how little the Maritimes obtained from the federal relief programmes. Of the total of $463,667,018 which the central government distributed among the provinces from 1930 to 1939, residents of the Maritimes received only $15,151,475 or 3.3 per cent. Calculated on a per capita basis, this works out to just over a third or 33.5 per cent of the national average. If one includes federal relief loans to the provinces of $175,839,121, the Maritimes' share drops to less than a quarter or 23.7 per cent.[3] The disparity in federal funding was also reflected in the smaller amount actually paid the recipients of direct relief. In the winter months, from January to May 1935, for example, the three levels of government spent an average of $2.84 for each relief recipient in the Maritimes, an amount less than one half of the $6.18 spent in the remaining six provinces.[4]

[2]For surveys of matching grant programmes in Canada see D.V. Smiley, *Conditional Grants and Canadian Federalism* (Toronto 1963), 1-6 and J.A. Maxwell, *Federal Subsidies to Provincial Governments in Canada* (Cambridge 1937), part II.

[3]Calculated from Department of Finance, "A Summary of Net Loans to Western Provinces under Relief Legislation by Fiscal Years," and "Dominion Relief Expenditures Since September 1930," 13 June 1940, J.L. Ralston Papers, MG27 111, vol. 50, file "Loans to Provinces Gen. (Secret)," Public Archives of Canada [PAC].

[4]The monthly rates for those receiving relief in the individual provinces were P.E.I., $1.93; N.S., $4.38; N.B., $1.67; P.Q., $5.40; Ont., $8.07; Man., $6.58; Sask., $3.58; Alb., $6.49; B.C., $6.96. Calculated from J.K. Houston, "An appreciation of Relief as Related to Economic and Employment Tendencies in Canada," 31 October 1936, Department of Labour Papers, RG27, vol. 2096, file Y 40, PAC.

The contemporary explanation for the discrepancy was the apparent difference in need. The Maritimes required less because they suffered less severely from the depression. This myth was widely accepted at the time and has persisted in the literature from the period. The myth was partly created by defenders of the region. In the late 1920s politicians, board of trade leaders, and newspapermen embarked upon a campaign to counter the negative image of their economy projected by the earlier Maritimes Rights propaganda and to attract investment in a period of economic expansion.[5] When their tactics appeared to pay dividends in new investment in pulp and paper and in tourist facilities, Maritime leaders met renewed depression by increasing the urgency of their campaign. No group of evangelists could have more zealously proclaimed the message of imminent salvation or more vigorously denounced the sin of unbelief. The Halifax *Herald* greeted the new year of 1930 with a list of reasons for regional optimism and exhorted all Maritimers to keep their faith. The Moncton *Times* stated flatly that "business and labour conditions are better in the Maritimes than in any other part of the country." The Kings County *Record* printed an open letter from the editor of *MacLean's* Magazine congratulating the Maritime people on their new-found prosperity and urging them to maintain their positive approach; "1930 will be what sound thinking makes it." The *Record* itself went on to explain why local industries would not be "retarded by any temporary depression" and in 1931 offered an editorial analyzing the "happy situation in which the Maritimes find themselves." The Ottawa *Journal*, the *Telegraph Journal* noted in the spring of 1930, had stated that "while the rest of us have all become querulous and pessimistic the Maritimes have all become optimists." The Vancouver *Sun* attributed the transformation to the Duncan Report which "has changed the Maritimes from a section of despondency and decadence into a live section of optimism and growth" and hailed the regional defenders as "economic statesmen." By 1932, when the orchestrated optimism of regional leaders had begun to peter out, the impression remained throughout the country that the Maritimes was somehow better off.[6]

The statistics of the period do not support the myth that the Maritimes suffered less from the depression than did the rest of Canada. Indeed, it was often contradicted in the data compiled for the Rowell-Sirois Commission. But the commission scholars did not confront the myth head on and at times seemed to encourage it. S.A. Saunders, for example, gave the decline in per capita income in the Maritimes in the first three years of the depression as four to five percentage points smaller

[5] E.R. Forbes, *The Maritime Rights Movement, 1919-1927: A Study in Canadian Regionalism* (Montréal 1979), 180.
[6] Halifax *Herald*, 3, 6, 7 January 1930; Moncton *Times*, 2 June 1930; Kings County *Record*, 3 January 1930 and 2 January 1931; Saint John *Telegraph-Journal*, 14 April 1930. See also K.G. Jones, "Response to Regional Disparity in the Maritime Provinces, 1926-1942: A Study of Canadian Intergovernmental Relations," MA thesis, University of New Brunswick, 1980, 45-7.

than in Ontario and Québec and far behind that of the West.[7] But if one considers the actual figures instead of percentages, which were skewed by the region's incomplete recovery from the recession of the early 1920s, the Maritimes' per capita personal income of $185 in 1933 was only marginally above the Prairies' $181 and very substantially below the Canadian average of $262.[8] The impact of the depression was more directly indicated by the only complete employment survey of the period. The 1931 Census reported 19 per cent of regular wage-earners not working in the Maritimes on 1 June 1931 compared with 16.6 per cent for Ontario, 16.9 per cent for Québec and 18.4 per cent for the country as a whole. Only in the devastated West were the numbers higher, ranging from 19.9 per cent in Saskatchewan to 24.7 in British Columbia.[9] Of course, more Maritimers did live in rural areas (62.2 per cent compared with a national average of 47 per cent), where fuel and shelter tended to be cheaper. But the discrepancy in relief granted remains even when one compares urban communities of similar size. A report of relief in ten cities with populations of less than 100,000, compiled by the Welfare Council of Canada in 1935, showed the average monthly cost per relief recipient for the three Maritime cities, Halifax, Saint John and Sydney, to be $3.77. The average for the other seven was $9.47.[10] The lower cost of living can not explain the discrepancy, since in 1930 the Department of Labour reported that the average weekly cost of food, light, heat and rent in the Maritimes was just 7.4 per cent below the national average.[11] Nor does James Struthers' theory of "less eligibility," *i.e.* the perceived need to keep relief low enough to prevent it from competing with local wages, in itself account for such large gaps in relief levels. New Brunswick's average wage of $3.82 per

[7]S.A. Saunders, *The Economic History of the Maritime Provinces* (Fredericton 1984), 49-51 and *Report of the Royal Commission on Dominion-Provincial Relations* (Ottawa 1940), 150; W.A. Mackintosh, *The Economic Background of Dominion-Provincial Relations* (Ottawa 1939), 70-1.

[8]Dominion Bureau of Statistics, *National Accounts Income and Expenditure 1926-1956* (Ottawa 1958), 64.

[9]The other provincial figures were Manitoba, 21.4 and Alberta, 21.6. Calculated from *Canada Year Book 1933* (Ottawa 1933), 778.

[10]The other cities ranged from a high of $11.47 in Calgary to a low outside the Maritimes of $5.78 in Hull. Calculated from "Relief Trend Report No. 2," Papers of the Canadian Council on Social Development (before 1935 this was the Canadian Council on Child and Family Welfare), MG28, 110, vol. 125, file 1935-37, PAC. The Halifax entry was compiled from "The Direct Relief Report ... Nova Scotia," January 1935, RG27, vol. 2096, file Y 40-0 "Nova Scotia Statistics," PAC. This is not to suggest that amounts paid elsewhere for relief were excessive. Indeed, studies of relief in Ottawa and Montréal argue the contrary. See Judith Roberts-Moore, "Maximum Relief for Minimum Costs: Coping With Unemployment and Relief in Ottawa During the Depression, 1929-1939," MA thesis, University of Ottawa, 1980; June MacPherson, "'Brother Can You Spare a Dime?,' The Administration of Unemployment Relief in the City of Montréal, 1931-1941," MA thesis, Concordia University, 1976.

[11]The Maritime figure was $19.68 (P.E.I., $19.74; N.B., $19.87; N.S., $19.74) and the Canadian $21.25. Calculated from Department of Labour, *Prices in Canada and Other Countries 1930* (Ottawa 1931), 7.

person per day was 30 per cent below the national average of $5.47, but Nova Scotia's $5.62 was marginally above it.[12] If total relief costs in the Maritimes were reduced by lower wages and cheaper living expenses, they were also raised by the inclusion of destitute elderly and single mothers, who in Ontario and the West were treated separately under old age pension and mothers' allowances programmes.[13]

The striking disparity between the Maritimes and the other regions is explained in large part by the inability of the Maritimes to participate in the federal matching grants on which the relief programmes were based. The process of metropolitan consolidation which led to the concentration of manufacturing, wholesaling and financial institutions in southern Ontario and Québec also hived much of the taxable resources of the nation within the two central provinces.[14] Ontario and Québec were the only provinces readily able to match large federal grants for relief. The western provinces were in a weaker position — their need greater, their finances impaired by the depression and their credit limited by past borrowing and reputations for less than financial orthodoxy. But what the westerners did retain was the confidence that however severe the existing depression, their ultimate growth was assured. They also believed that, with their increased population and political influence, they would eventually be able to redress injustices in the federal system which discriminated against them. Their problem was to obtain the money to deal with immediate relief needs. This they initially did by borrowing their share of the funds from the federal government in the form of relief loans and, as this source threatened to dry up, by developing a variety of expedients to extort more.[15] The Maritimes, though no poorer in circumstances, were much poorer in future prospects. Without the West's option of borrowing against the expectations of future growth, they could only marginally participate in the shared cost relief programmes.

[12]Department of Labour, *Wages and Hours of Labour in Canada 1929, 1934, and 1935* (Ottawa 1936), 93; Struthers, *No fault of their Own*, 6-7.

[13]Kenneth Bryden, *Old Age Pensions and Policy Making in Canada* (Montréal 1974), 98 and Veronica Strong-Boag, "'Wages for Housework': Mothers' Allowances and the Beginning of Social Security in Canada," *Journal of Canadian Studies*, XIV, I (Spring 1979), 24-33.

[14]See L.D. McCann, "Metropolitanism and Branch Businesses in the Maritimes, 1881-1931," *Acadiensis*, XIII, 1 (Autumn 1983), 112-25 and T.W Acheson, "The Maritimes and 'Empire Canada,'" in D. Bercuson, *Canada and the Burden of Unity* (Toronto 1977), 87-114.

[15]As Minister of Finance Rhodes' correspondence with the western governments on relief was voluminous. See especially Memoranda dated 30 May and 13 July 1932, Rhodes Papers, MG2, 47947 and 47134, Public Archives of Nova Scotia [PANS]. For British Columbian and Saskatchewan perspectives on relief administration see J.D. Belshaw, "The Administration of Relief to the Unemployed in Vancouver during the Great Depression," MA thesis, Simon Fraser University, 1982; Blair Neatby, "The Saskatchewan Relief Commission, 1931-34," in Donald Swainson, ed., *Historical Essays on the Prairie Provinces* (Toronto 1970); P.H. Brennan, "Public Relief Works in Saskatchewan Cities, 1929-1940," MA thesis, University of Regina, 1981; Alma Lawton, "Urban Relief in Saskatchewan during the Years of the Depression, 1930-1939," MA thesis, University of Saskatchewan (Saskatoon), 1969.

The inverse relationship between poverty or need and the participation in federal relief was also apparent within the Maritime region. New Brunswick's greater problems were reflected in a per capita income figure of $174 and an unemployment rate of 20 per cent compared with Nova Scotia's $202 and 19.6 per cent. Yet Nova Scotia received 15 per cent more on a per capita basis for relief purposes and an additional $3.2 million for their destitute elderly before New Brunswick joined the old age pension programme.[16] The gap appears more severe in the amounts actually given relief recipients. In 1934, for example, recipients in New Brunswick received an average of $2.27 per month compared with $3.72 for those in Nova Scotia or 39 per cent less, while Prince Edward Island whose per capita income was just $133 paid out an average of only $2.21 per recipient.[17]

The onset of the depression found the three Maritime governments already struggling with problems arising from the matching grants formula. The old age pension scheme by which the federal government paid half the cost of $20 monthly pensions to the needy elderly posed a serious problem for Maritime governments. Already burdened with debt charges as a percentage of revenue far above the national average (26 per cent for Nova Scotia and 28 per cent for New Brunswick compared with 15 per cent for all provinces), they could ill afford a programme which might consume an additional 15 to 20 per cent of annual revenues.[18] Limited finances along with a disproportionate number of potentially eligible aged seemed to put the pension scheme out of reach. Yet the pressure on the governments to establish pensions mounted as national funds were directed to the elderly in Ontario and the four western provinces while denied to those in the Maritimes. The failure to provide old age pensions was a factor in the discontent which almost defeated the Conservative government of E.N. Rhodes in the Nova Scotia election of 1928.[19] In the late 1920s elderly Maritimers sent their often pathetic letters to federal politicians requesting assistance from the national pension scheme, but the latter

[16]See footnotes 3 and 9 above and W. Eggleston and C.T. Kraft, Dominion-Provincial Subsidies and Grants (Ottawa 1939), 104 and 115.

[17]P.E.I.'s unemployment rate was 6.8 per cent in 1931.

[18]Royal Commission on Dominion-provincial Relations, Public Accounts Inquiry, *Dominion of Canada ... and Provincial Governments: Comparative Statistics of Public Finance* (Ottawa 1939), 95; *Final Report of the Commission Appointed to Consider Old Age Pensions* [Fredericton 1930] in New Brunswick Cabinet Papers, RG....RS29, 1930, Provincial Archives of New Brunswick [PANB]. Prince Edward Island's debt was relatively low at 10 per cent of revenues, but Premier A.C. Saunders estimated that pensions for 20 per cent of those 70 years of age or older would require "about 18% of the total revenue." A.C. Saunders to J.L. Ballon, 7 January 1930, Premier's Office Papers, Provincial Archives of Prince Edward Island [PAPEI]. H.E. Mahon in the "Interim Report of the Commission ... to Consider Old Age Pensions" estimated the cost of the pensions in Nova Scotia at $2.2 million at a time when provincial revenues totaled just under $7 million. Appendix #31, *Journals of the House of Assembly*, 1929.

[19]E.R. Forbes, "The Rise and Fall of the Conservative Party in the Provincial Politics of Nova Scotia, 1922-33," MA thesis, Dalhousie University, 1967, 112-4 and 129-30.

disclaimed any responsibility and referred them to provincial governments. In the federal election of 1930 Mackenzie King claimed that pensions were a provincial responsibility; the problem was constitutional. Campaigning in the Maritimes, R.B. Bennett gave the constitutional argument short shrift: "I will see to it that old age pensions are paid to every province.... it is a national obligation.... If the Dominion can pay fifty per cent of the Old Age Pensions why cannot it pay 99 per cent?"[20]

After the federal election, the provincial spokesmen cited Bennett's statements as constituting a promise of a new pension scheme and urged the elderly to write to the federal government. As the months passed without any word on the pensions, individual and provincial appeals for federally-funded pensions became increasingly strident.[21] Finally, in the summer of 1931, the long-awaited announcement arrived. But it brought neither a federally administered scheme nor 99 per cent funding for those run by the provinces. The matching grant formula was still intact with the federal government's contribution raised to 75 per cent. For the Maritime provinces this change merely tantalized. Since their revenues were further impaired by the depression, having to find even a quarter of the cost seemed to leave the pensions as far out of reach as ever.

Nonetheless, as the political pressure for old age pensions continued, the three provinces eventually found a way to introduce them. In 1933 Prince Edward Island led the way. After conversations with the federal bureaucracy, the Islanders decided that, if they could not raise their revenues sufficiently to participate in the federal programme, they could scale down the programme to fit their revenues. Moreover, smaller pensions would conform more closely to their other relief payments. The government set the maximum pension at $15 rather than $20 and developed a means test stricter than those employed in the other provinces. It passed legislation making it obligatory that children provide for their parents. The support of children was given an arbitrary value and added to the theoretical total capital wealth of the individual. This "capital" was assumed to yield an income of 5 per cent per year and if a person's income was calculated to be in excess of $125, the excess was subtracted from the pension. Of the approximately 6000 residents of 70 years or more on the Island, only 1200 were ruled eligible for any portion of the pension. Many of these were simply shifted from the direct relief rolls, for which the province paid 50 per cent or 33 1/3 per cent if they lived in Charlottetown, to the pension rolls for which the province paid just 25 per cent.[22]

It was an astute political move whose advantages were not lost on the Liberal oppositions in Nova Scotia and New Brunswick. In the former Angus L. Macdonald

[20]Yarmouth *Light*, 3 July 1930 (clipping in Ralston Papers, vol. 15). See also E.N. Rhodes' speech in Moncton in the Moncton *Times*, 21 July 1930.
[21]See file #13 "Old Age Pensions" in Nova Scotia Provincial Secretary-Treasurer's Papers, RG7, vol. 225, PANS. See J.A. Macdonald to J.S. Gallant, 18 October 1930, J.A. Macdonald Papers, PAPEI.
[22]*Canadian Annual Review*, 1934. See also Bryden, *Old Age Pensions and Policy Making in Canada*, 84-97 and 101.

promised old age pensions in the election of 1933 and introduced them soon after taking office. In New Brunswick Allison Dysart made the government's failure to provide old age pensions an issue in the 1935 campaign and established them the next year. The provincial governments were careful to prevent the municipalities from taking advantage of money saved from the care of the elderly to expand relief services. A Nova Scotia spokesman at the Dominion-Provincial conference of 1935 told how the new government had intervened at the municipal level to place its own nominees on local relief committees and boasted that through "rigid administration" and "more stringent regulations" it had reduced the numbers on relief from about 50,000 to about 16,000.[23] In New Brunswick in 1936 Premier Dysart accompanied his pension scheme with an attempt to curb relief at the municipal level. The government persuaded the municipality of Gloucester, for example, to accept a system of relief quotas which reduced the allowance for those on relief to just $.70 a month.[24]

Moreover, neither province admitted that they were introducing pensions that paid substantially less than other provinces. In New Brunswick government spokesmen obscured initial complaints with a discussion of means test regulations. Confronted with the opposition's charge that even "almshouse residents" did not receive more than $15, the government suggested that the pensions would rise once the programme became better established.[25] The federal report for 1936-37 listed the average monthly pension paid under the act as $10.58 in Prince Edward island, $13.39 in New Brunswick and $14.49 in Nova Scotia compared with an average of $18.24 in the other six provinces.[26]

The technical education programme was another which taxed the ingenuity of Maritime governments to participate and created additional political problems for them. Nova Scotia, which had pioneered technical education in Canada, had concentrated its expenditures at the university level. The federal act of 1919 was designed to encourage technical programmes in high schools. By 1929 Nova Scotia and Prince Edward Island governments had failed to obtain even half of the federal grant allotted to them.[27] New Brunswick participated more fully, channelling funds into vocational schools in Saint John, Woodstock and Sussex, only to be embarrassed by the federal government's decision to terminate the programme in 1929. Under intense pressure from the municipalities to take over the federal share of funding, New Brunswick urged the Bennett government to resume its contribu-

---

[23]Minutes of the Dominion-Provincial Conference, 9 December 1935, Provincial Secretary-Treasurer's Papers, RG7, vol. 231, file 8, PANS.

[24]"Report of the Direct Relief Committee," 31 December 1936, Minutes of the Municipal Council of Gloucester, RG18, RS149, PANB.

[25]*Synoptic Report of the Proceedings of the Legislative Assembly of New Brunswick*, 1937, 23-5 and 1938, 8.

[26]*Labour Gazette*, XXXVII, 5 (May 1937), 513.

[27]Janet Guildford, "Coping with De-industrialization: The Nova Scotia Department of Technical Education, 1907-1930," *Acadiensis*, XVI, 2 (Spring 1987), 79 and Maxwell, *Federal Subsidies and Provincial Governments in Canada*, 211.

tion.[28] Although federal legislation was passed in 1931 to do so, it was not implemented. In 1930 H.P Blanchard of Colchester County warned Premier Rhodes to consider carefully the perils of entering another federal programme lest the senior government "back out ... and leave the whole 100% on the province as they did with the main highways, technical schools etc."[29]

Given these difficulties, it was not surprising that the three provinces greeted the federal relief programmes of the 1930s with something less than enthusiasm. As early as 1928 the three Maritime premiers voiced their exasperation in response to federal labour minister Peter Heenan's proposal for unemployment insurance. They simply could not, they argued, commit provincial funds to a new programme when they were already unable to participate in existing programmes. Rhodes took pains to make clear that their quarrel was not with unemployment insurance, since they were "sympathetic to all modern measures of similar character." J.B.M. Baxter of New Brunswick noted both his province's inability to initiate pensions and the added burden of the "probable withdrawal ... of assistance to technical education" in explaining why the proposed unemployment scheme was "utterly impossible" for a province "of such limited means."[30]

The new matching grants programmes of the 1930s again promised to increase the strain on provincial finances, they offered no guarantee of permanency, and they threatened to awaken expectations among municipalities and individuals for a degree of provincial participation which these provinces could not afford. The three provincial governments therefore tried to keep their participation in relief programmes to a minimum. They sought to portray their role as essentially that of intermediaries between the municipalities, who were responsible for relief, and the federal government, which wished to come to their aid. Nova Scotia warned its local governments of the limited nature of its commitment which would end with the termination of federal funds.[31] New Brunswick went further, scaling down the requests for assistance from the municipalities and cutting off its contribution in the summer months.[32] At the Dominion-provincial conferences Maritime representatives spoke out against further extensions of relief programmes, criticized the

[28]J.D. Palmer and W.K. Tibert to C.D. Richards, 8 December 1931 and C.D. Richards to F.M. Sclanders, 19 February 1932, NB Cabinet Papers, RG1, RS9, PANB.

[29]H.P. Blanchard to E.N. Rhodes, 9 April 1930, Rhodes Papers, 40930, PANS.

[30]Copies of the three letters, E.N. Rhodes, J.B.M. Baxter and Saunders to Peter Heenan, dated 3 August 1928, are in Rhodes Papers, 47338, PANS.

[31]Circular letter from R. Gordon to the Nova Scotia municipalities, 21 April 1931, Provincial Secretary-Treasurer's Papers, RG7, vol. 225, file 12, PANS.

[32]C.A. Ferguson, "Responses to the Unemployment Problem in Saint John, New Brunswick, 1929-1933," MA thesis, University of New Brunswick, 1984, 109-13 and D.P. Lemon, "Public Relief Policy in Moncton: The Depression Years, 1929-1939," MA report, University of New Brunswick, 1977, 15-6.

other provinces for their extravagance and emphasized the primary responsibility of the municipalities for relief.[33]

The three provinces found more attractive the relief proposals involving highway construction — particularly the trans-Canada highway projects for which the senior government initially paid half of the cost. These offered political patronage, much-needed employment, and progress towards realizing the provinces' strong aspirations for a tourist industry. Indeed, they suggested another aspect of the provinces' dilemma. Should responsible leaders concentrate scarce resources on the direct relief of individuals while the provincial infrastructure, including roads and electrical development, fell so far behind the rest of the country as to impair future development? Yet, after 1932, the federal government abandoned its highway programmes and shifted to a policy of direct relief because it was less costly.[34] At the nadir of the depression the provinces were left to complete construction largely with their own resources. They obtained the money for both roads and direct relief by borrowing and, by the end of 1933, debt charges consumed respectively 35 and 55 per cent of Nova Scotia and New Brunswick revenues. The financial problems of New Brunswick, in particular, remained acute throughout the decade as its governments had difficulty in selling bonds and faced tough negotiations with chartered banks.[35]

The relations between the provinces and the municipalities often paralleled those of the provinces and the Dominion. A few of the wealthiest municipalities were able to participate in the federal programmes to the extent that their provincial governments would let them. But the gap in economic resources among the municipalities left the poorest without the finances to obtain more than a fraction of the assistance available. Moreover, like the provinces, the municipalities were already embarrassed by their enforced participation in programmes which took little account of their straitened circumstances.

In Nova Scotia Premier Harrington noted in the spring of 1931 that the "financial condition" of some of the municipalities seemed to be "in very bad shape."[36] Guysborough county, already suffering from rural depopulation, general out-migration and pockets of chronic poverty in the 1920s had no reserves with

---

[33]See statements by A.P. Paterson, Walter Lea and Mr. Paul in the Minutes of the Dominion-Provincial Conference, 9 December 1935, Provincial Secretary's Papers, RG7, vol. 231, file 8, PANS; Charlottetown *Guardian*, 21 March 1934, quoted in L.J. Cusack, "The Prince Edward Island People and the Great Depression, 1930-1935," MA thesis, University of New Brunswick, 1972, 135.

[34]E.N. Rhodes to J.F. Fraser, 10 November 1931, Provincial Secretary-Treasurer's Papers, vol. 225, #5, PANS.

[35]R.W. Gouinlock to P.S. Fielding, 21 May 1937, Premier's Office Papers, PAPEI. See copy of telegram for the Premier of New Brunswick from "the four banks who lend money to that province" in G.T. Towers to J.L. Ralston, 15 April 1940, Department of Finance Papers, RG19, vol. 2697, PAC.

[36]G.S. Harrington to John Doull, 17 July 1931, Provincial Secretary-Treasurer's Papers, RG7, vol. 225, PANS.

which to cushion the effects of a new depression on its fishing and lumbering industries. Failing to collect more than 36 per cent of its taxes by the spring of 1931, the municipality found itself unable to pay bank overdrafts and debts to the province. A bitter county clerk protested that the escalation of costs in municipal estimates was due almost exclusively to the items of the budget over which the municipality had no control, including education, care for the insane and the indigent ill, and child welfare. The Hospital Act, in particular, forced the municipality to "pay for every seeming affliction anybody may imagine he has."[37] Faced with reports of widespread destitution, the county council sought permission to distribute whatever money it did obtain, in the cheapest way, as direct relief.

In New Brunswick the difficulties of the poorest municipalities followed a similar pattern. The northern counties suffered from the problems of the forest industries, especially lumber, and the fisheries. With the closure of sawmills the parish officers of Northumberland county rapidly exceeded the amounts assessed their parishes for assistance to the poor. Their appeals for provincial help brought reminders that the parishes were a municipal responsibility and legislation authorizing the municipalities to borrow to meet parish obligations.[38] The Northumberland Council secured loans to cover their overseers' deficits but carefully assigned responsibility for both principal and interest to the parishes which had incurred them. Early in 1933 the provincial and federal governments recognized the special nature of Northumberland's difficulties by increasing their share of relief in the county to 80 per cent. Even this assistance was not sufficient to keep the county solvent. With an estimated one third of the county requiring relief and tax revenues shrunk to 40 per cent of "normal," the bank cut off credit.[39] The province then provided guarantees for temporary relief loans until the county's new bond issue. But only a portion of the bonds could be sold and by 1934 the long-suffering merchants who were unable to collect the more than $10,000 owing for past relief orders refused further credit.[40] The county's appeal to their famous native son, R.B. Bennett, reporting "large numbers destitute to danger of starvation" brought the standard reply that there was "no contact between Dominion and municipalities." Faced with predictions of "serious disorders imminent," the province finally agreed to make loans to the municipality while accepting its bonds as security.[41] The neighbouring counties of Gloucester and Restigouche were likewise refused bank loans in 1934. Gloucester too had to be bailed out by the province but Restigouche,

[37]J.A. Fulton to John Doull, 2 April 1931, *ibid.*

[38]22 George V, 1932, c. 6.

[39]Minutes of the Municipal Council of Northumberland, 17, 21 January 1933, RG 18, RS153, PANB.

[40]*Ibid.*, 13 February 1933.

[41]Minutes of the Municipal Council of Northumberland, 17, 18 January 1934; Order in Council, 3 April 1934, New Brunswick Cabinet Papers, PANB.

with a stronger economy, launched a collection drive, resolutely cut back on expenditures and managed to re-establish its credit with the bank.[42]

The New Brunswick municipalities protested what their Union spokesman T.H. Whalen called the province's "continually unloading things on the municipalities." They particularly resented the charges for hospitalization which the province increased during 1931.[43] With so many of their people unable to pay for their health services, the three northern counties appealed to the province to assume the responsibility and became increasingly reluctant to commit the indigent to long term hospitalization.[44] The denial of hospital services, particularly to the victims of tuberculosis, may have been reflected in changes in the provincial death rate. The number of deaths per 100,000 declined throughout the 1920s, leveled out in the early 1930s, and rose again in Gloucester and Northumberland at mid-decade. In the year ending October 1935, deaths from tuberculosis in Gloucester municipality jumped from a previous annual average of less than three to 40 and the following year to 50.[45] In presenting Northumberland's submission before the Rowell-Sirois Commission D.K. Hazen stated that "the Municipality, owing to lack of funds is unwilling to pay the expenses of hospital treatment if it can be avoided and the treatment, therefore, is not generally given in the advanced stages when it is most effective."[46] In 1937 a Red Cross worker from Chatham included in her report to the cabinet a snapshot of a tubercular woman convalescing in a room which had been hastily created for her by neighbours closing in a verandah.[47] A proposal to give health officers the authority to commit indigent patients to hospitals was successfully resisted by the municipalities who required formal approval of admissions by parish representatives. Restigouche also refused to accept doctors' bills not signed by the overseers of the poor.[48]

The position of the parish officers directly responsible for relief was not an enviable one. For a consideration of perhaps $10 a year the poormasters were

[42]Minutes of the Finance Committee of the Municipality of Gloucester, 4 April 1935, Gloucester County Minutes, PANB; Minutes of the Municipality of Restigouche County, 22 May 1934, RG18, RS155, A1, PANB and "Auditor's Report" in *ibid.*, 1 January 1936.

[43]Royal Commission on Dominion-Provincial Relations, Report of Proceedings, 23 May 1938, 9069. (Copy in stacks at Harriet Irving Library, UNB.)

[44]Minutes of the Municipal Council of Gloucester, 20 January 1932; Minutes of the Municipality of Restigouche County, 18 January 1934, PANB.

[45]The Annual Reports of the Sub-Health District of Gloucester were included with the county minutes, 31 October 1935 and 31 October 1936. For expenditures on tuberculosis care see *Submission by The Municipality of Gloucester to the Royal Commission on Dominion-Provincial Relations* (April 1938), 15. (Copy in stacks at Harriet Irving Library.)

[46]Royal Commission on Dominion-Provincial Relations, Report of Proceedings, May 23, 1938, 9085.

[47]Mrs. E.T. McLean to J.B. McNair, 17 January 1938, New Brunswick Cabinet Papers, PANB.

[48]Minutes of the Municipality of Restigouche, 18 January 1935 and 22 January and 17 July 1936 and Minutes of the Municipality of Gloucester, 24 January 1936.

expected to investigate the needs of hundreds or even thousands of relief recipients and take the steps necessary for their survival. During their financial crises, the municipal councils tended to divide whatever money they collected among their most pressing creditors and to distribute what was left among the parishes for relief. When the money ran out, the poormasters often tried to secure loans on their personal credit for which the municipality might eventually take responsibility. On one hand was the constraint imposed by the difficulty of borrowing money and, on the other, the pressure of watching their friends and neighbours go hungry. An investigation of Restigouche finances in 1934 revealed several thousands of dollars in unrecorded liabilities incurred by individual poormasters.[49] It is not surprising that the harried poormasters reacted angrily towards those who inadvertently increased the number of mouths they had to feed. Sentences of nine months to a year became customary for males prosecuted by the poormasters for the crime of bastardy.[50]

The problems of Prince Edward Island were similar to those of the rural municipalities. In the 1920s, the province faced rising expectations in education, roads, health and welfare with hopelessly inelastic revenues and a longstanding tradition of popular resistance to direct taxation. Of greatest urgency was the need to provide better public health services. National anti-tuberculosis campaigns had considerable appeal when upwards of one per cent of the population (estimates ranged from 700 to 1000) were infected by the disease.[51] Pressure from Women's Institutes, Red Cross and other groups for the construction of a sanitorium drove Premier A.C. Saunders to desperate pleas for additional funds from the federal government. As he told the Young Men's Commercial Club in 1928, in resisting their petition for a sanitorium, there are "only two sources of revenue," the federal government and the farmers, and the latter "do not feel disposed to stand for any additional taxes."[52] Specifically Saunders called on the federal politicians for the province's share of additional funds which might come from the general rationalization of provincial subsidies recommended by the Duncan Commission. The King government had used a vague promise of a new investigation to detach Prince Edward Island from the Maritime Rights campaign, but the anticipated settlement failed to materialize. At the beginning of the 1930s A.C. Saunders and his successor, W.M. Lea, diverted appeals for improved services, including higher salaries for teachers and old age pensions, with the plea that these must await the additional funds from Ottawa.[53] The province did contribute $30,000 to the building of a small

---

[49]"Auditor's Report," Minutes of the Municipality of Restigouche, 3 July 1934.

[50]J.W. Farth to J.B. McNair, 20 August 1935 and A.W. Bennett to A.J. Leger, 13 March 1931, New Brunswick Cabinet Papers, PANB.

[51]A.C. Saunders to Rev. T. Constable, 26 November 1928, Premier's Office Papers, PAPEI.

[52]A.C. Saunders to G.S. Buntain, 1 March 1928, *ibid.*

[53]E.R. Forbes, *The Maritime Rights Movement*, 186-7; A.C. Saunders to Agnes Murnaghan, 27 March 1929, and W. Lea to R.B. Bennett, 5 February 1931, Premiers' Office Papers, PAPEI.

sanitorium by volunteer groups, but it obtained a portion of this money by cutting back the assistance previously given to enable blind and deaf children to study in the specialized schools in Halifax.[54]

With the onslaught of another depression, successive P.E.I. premiers worked to minimize the popular expectation of relief. Relief, they argued, was largely unnecessary for the Island with an economy based on mixed farming and lacking either the large population of industrial unemployed or the drought which afflicted the West. But as the bottom dropped out of the market for Island potatoes and fish these arguments became less convincing.[55] Lacking rural municipalities, the provincial government was responsible for relief outside of the towns, and in a deliberate policy to discourage those seeking relief, it refused to inaugurate new procedures. It merely extended the traditional paupers' list by which indigents were aided at the rate of $5 per family per month after a case had been made for them by local clergymen, doctors or neighbours. It also encouraged volunteer agencies to greater efforts in succoring those in difficulty. In 1932 it did persuade the federal government to pay for a portion of the paupers' list and the customary third for relief administered through the municipality of Charlottetown.[56]

The letters to the premiers documenting individual cases for relief reveal unpleasant features of rural poverty. They tell of farmers lacking seed for crops, of animals slowly starving in their stalls, of children suffering malnutrition, and of a long waiting list for the sanitorium.[57] Moreover, as the depression worsened, its impact became cumulative and apparently irrevocable. In a 1936 letter to the Dominion commissioner of relief, Prince Edward Island's Deputy Provincial Treasurer, P.S. Fielding, explained that unemployment conditions on the Island had failed to respond to improved markets because "a large proportion of our farming population has ... degenerated into circumstances where the conditions of market have very little effect on their general living conditions. They ... have reached the stage where they are unable to cultivate their land, which has consequently ... deteriorated. Stock and equipment have been gradually depleted ... during the past winter conditions generally were far more critical than ... in any previous season." Two years later an unemployment committee representing churches, labour unions, the Legion, the Free Dispensary and the Fishermen's Loan Board reported "distress and destitution" in Charlottetown and "employment conditions ... more serious than at any time since the depression set in."[58]

[54]A.C. Saunders to G.E. Saville, 31 October 1939; G.E. Saville to A.C. Saunders, 28 October 1929, and A.C. Saunders to George Bateman, 29 August 1929, *ibid.*
[55]Cusack, "Prince Edward Island and the Great Depression," ch. 2.
[56]J.D. Stewart to Harry Hereford, 9 January 1934, "Direct Relief Files 1935-1941," Records of Dominion-Provincial Affairs, RG21, PAPEI.
[57]P.A. Scully to A.C. Saunders, 27 September 1929, and Dr. R.K. Boswell to T. Campbell, 6 February 1939, Premier's Office Papers, PAPEI. "I know you may be tired of such cases," Boswell wrote.
[58]P.S. Fielding to Harry Hereford, 6 August 1936, "Direct Relief Files 1935-1941," PAPEI; see resolution and collection of statements dated 11 May 1938 in *ibid.*

The direct relief statistics from municipalities reinforce the impression of an inverse correlation between poverty and relief under the matching grants programme. In Nova Scotia one can discern four levels of assistance according to the average monthly payments to relief recipients. The most generous community, Amherst, which before the war boasted more millionaires per capita than any other town or city in Canada, occupies a level by itself.[59] This small manufacturing and commercial centre of about 8,000 maintained almost 2000 people on relief throughout 1933 at an average cost of $5.70 per month.[60] This figure was almost on a par with the national average and more than a quarter above the per recipient contribution of any other Maritime municipality. At a relief conference of Nova Scotian municipalities in 1934, Amherst Mayor Read defended his town's greater largesse by noting that its grant for food worked out to 4 1/2 cents per person per meal for a family of four and invited the other mayors to explain "how anyone can live on less." His challenge was not accepted. Amherst retained and even extended its lead through the remainder of the decade.[61]

Mining towns held three out of four places at the next level. Glace Bay, Springhill, and New Waterford owed their prominence in granting relief less to relative wealth than to the organization and political influence of those demanding assistance. The initial pressure for help came from areas where labour was organized, alert to the funds distributed in industrial centres elsewhere, and determined to obtain their share. Familiar with the co-operative relief activities required by strikes, the leaders of District #26 United Mine Workers of America co-operated with the Corporation in rationing shifts and with the municipalities in appointing investigating committees to apply for and distribute what direct relief was available. The town of Glace Bay borrowed $100,000 in 1930-31 and then, with its credit nearly exhausted, required "donations" to the municipality from relief recipients of one-third of their total assistance as an expedient to keep federal and provincial funds flowing.[62] Although required to abandon this practice, the miners were able to force attention from Conservative provincial and federal governments who regarded the industrial centres as critical to their continued political success.[63]

[59]Nolan Reilly, "The Growth and Decline of Amherst as a Manufacturing Centre, 1860-1930," a paper delivered to the Sixth Atlantic Studies Conference, May 1985.

[60]The monthly "Direct Relief Reports" from Nova Scotia to the Minister of Labour are complete from April 1933 to March 1934 and largely complete from October 1932 until the end of the decade, RG27, vol. 2096, file Y 40-0, PAC.

[61]*Proceedings of ... the Union of Nova Scotia Municipalities*, 1934, 143. For accounts of what it was like to "live on less" see David Frank and Don Macgillivray, eds., *George MacEachern: An Autobiography* (Sydney 1987), ch. 3.

[62]M.S. Campbell, "Re unemployment situation etc. Sydney, North Sydney, Sydney Mines, New Waterford, Dominion, Glace Bay, Louisburg and Springhill," copy enclosed with H.H. Ward to G.S. Harrington, 18 August 1931, Provincial Secretary-Treasurer's Papers, RG7, vol. 226, #7, PAC.

[63]W.J. White, "Left wing Politics and Community: A Study of Glace Bay, 1930-1940," MA thesis, Dalhousie University, 1978, 69-77 and 44-7.

Particularly useful at this time was their reputation for radical militancy. A federal investigator of conditions in the mining communities in August 1931 reported that "the Red element" was "showing signs of liveliness" and there was potential for a strike "worse than anything previous in the history of Cape Breton." This report was followed by the announcement of new relief projects by the senior levels of government. The federal government also increased coal and steel tariffs and coal transportation subsidies.[64]

Most other urban centres, Halifax, Trenton, Westville, New Glasgow, Sydney Mines, Truro, Dartmouth, Sydney, and North Sydney, gave relief averaging in the $3.50 to $3.00 range. Last among the towns which paid relief on a twelve month basis were Inverness, Pictou, and Stellarton at close to $2.00 each. Only two rural municipalities paid relief for the twelve-month period, Pictou County at $3.07 and Cape Breton County at $2.07. At the bottom level were the remaining 17 municipalities who paid relief on an irregular basis often restricted to the winter period. Guysborough County was one of these. In 1934 it cut off relief in May and did not resume it again until February. A check of Guysborough's relief payments in the peak month of March indicate how erratic and limited its assistance really was, even during the few months it was offered. In 1934 the three levels of government distributed through the municipality $3066 to 2696 people for an average of $1.14 per person. A year later they gave 90 people an average of $2.20 apiece for the month.

On Prince Edward Island the gap was sharp between those receiving provincial aid and those assisted through the municipality of Charlottetown. For February 1935 the average payment for the 6466 provincial recipients was $1.90 compared to Charlottetown's $3.20 for 2119 residents of the city. For February 1936 the disparity increased as the respective averages were $2.19 and $5.35. Prince Edward Island's overall figures were reduced by interruptions in relief, usually during the summer months. The combined average of province and city for the year 1935 was just $1.77.[65]

For New Brunswick more fragmentary data suggests a similar gulf between the stronger and weaker municipalities in the amount paid. In the year ending 31 March 1935, Moncton carried an average 1344 people at a monthly rate of $3.35, Saint John paid $2.93 to a monthly average of 4761, and Campbellton assisted 507 people at $1.35 a month for two months.[66] In February 1936, Gloucester municipality gave its 12,234 relief recipients an average of $1.14 apiece. February averages

[64]M.S. Campbell, "Re. unemployment situation etc."

[65]Copies of monthly relief reports to the Minister of Labour are contained in two boxes of papers entitled "Relief to 1940," PAPEI and in RG27, vol. 2096, Y 40-1, "Statistics PEI" (First and Second sections), PAC.

[66]New Brunswick seemed determined to avoid supplying data which could be used for comparisons in the amounts of relief given. Statistics on three communities for one year is given in Department of Labour Papers, RG27, vol. 2096, file Y40, "Classification of Unemployed," PAC.

for the previous year for Moncton and Saint John were respectively $4.35 and $3.21. In Ontario the average paid each relief recipient for the same month was $8.13.[67]

In New Brunswick the low level of relief given even prevented the province's participation in the national programme for encouraging a return to the land. The talk of a "back-to-the-land" movement initially drew responsive echoes from New Brunswick, whose politicians were conscious of its large tracts of uncleared forests, previous failures to attract immigrants, and an earlier interest in colonization by Acadian spokesmen. In 1930 premier J.B.M. Baxter advised the unemployed to "go back to the land and work it," for as long as one has "land and health" a man will not starve.[68] The province announced a new tripartite programme to go into effect in March 1932, appointed a board to administer it, and began surveying lands and building roads for the new settlers.[69] But the New Brunswick government apparently failed to consider the terms of the national programme from the perspective of its municipalities. The programme called for each level of government to contribute $200 per family: $400 for building materials, animals and farm implements and the remaining $200 to provide additional support over the first two years. In Ontario, at these figures, municipalities might expect to recover their investment in the first two years through a saving of direct relief costs. In Nova Scotia, where the programme was inaugurated for "surplus" miners, it at least suggested the possibility of an eventual break-even point.[70] But so much lower were the direct relief totals in New Brunswick that the programme meant only increased costs to the municipalities. Some municipalities were also uneasy about who would be responsible for future relief in the new settlements should they fail to become self-sustaining. New Brunswick municipalities therefore unanimously rejected the scheme. Even Restigouche County, which had rushed to offer Campbellton as a headquarters for the programme, ultimately refused to participate.[71]

It is one of the ironies of the period that the back-to-the-land movement became most popular in a province which could not participate in the national programme. So desperate were many New Brunswickers and so limited their alternatives that they clamoured to take out land with only a fraction of the assistance available elsewhere. In 1932 the number of new families setting out each year to carve new

[67]Report of the Direct Relief Committee to the Municipal Council of Gloucester in Minutes, 31 December 1936, 452. PANB, RG18, RS149 gives the amount spent on relief for the month. The numbers on relief in New Brunswick municipalities for one month only are contained in Papers of the Department of Public Works, RG14, RS128, 4/16, PANB. For provincial figures see J.K. Houston, "An Appreciation of Relief," 25.

[68]Saint John *Telegraph-Journal*, 15 September 1930 and New Brunswick, *Report of the Department of Lands and Mines*, 1930, 53-4.

[69]"Agreement...," 17 May 1932, New Brunswick Cabinet Papers, PANB; *Report of the Department of Lands and Mines*, 1932, 56.

[70]Department of Labour, "Report on Nova Scotia's Unemployed," R.B. Bennett Papers, 477764, Harriet Irving Library, UNB.

[71]Moncton *Transcript*, 17 June 1932; Minutes of the Council of the Municipality of Restigouche, 23 January 1931 and 5 July 1932.

farms out of the New Brunswick wilderness rose from about 150 to more than 300 and after 1936 exceeded 600. By 1939 the department of lands and mines, which was responsible for parcelling out the lands, reported a population of 11,165 in several dozens of new settlements concentrated in the northern counties. Québec with five times the population had 24,666 and Manitoba came a distant third at 5900.[72]

Despite their heroic efforts in clearing and cultivating land, few of the new settlers managed to become economically independent. The provincial government regularly supplied them with seed, allowed pulp-cutting from their 100-acre claims and, aided by federal grants for the relief of unorganized territories, supplied $4.07 worth of groceries four times a year.[73] In 1935 the province circulated additional cash among the colonists through bonuses for land ploughed and brought under cultivation. In the summer of 1939 a federal department of agriculture analysis of the economic progress of 300 settlers in northern New Brunswick revealed that their average total net worth including cleared land, buildings, farm implements, and personal possessions after an average of 4.2 years on their new holdings amounted to just $578. This was about what they might have received at the outset had they resided in most other provinces. Noting their lack of adequate farm implements, machinery for clearing land and sewing machines for their wives, the investigators concluded that, as a result of insufficient capital, their efforts had been largely wasted.[74]

In August 1934 the federal government officially abandoned the matching grants formula in direct relief for a new programme of grants-in-aid to the provinces. These were to be based on "need and the ability of the province to deal with the problem." The grants, which were fixed in advance and paid regularly at monthly intervals, did help the provinces in planning their programmes. They had limited effect, however, on the distribution of federal assistance since the principal indicator of need was taken to be the money spent by each province under the old matching grants system. The timing of the transition was unfortunate for the Maritimes. The new monthly relief grants of $68,000 — $2,125 to Prince Edward Island, $25,000 to New Brunswick and $40,875 to Nova Scotia — were substantially less than the federal share of relief costs paid to the region for 1933. But unlike the country as a whole, whose relief payments continued to rise during the first half of 1934, those

[72]New Brunswick, *Report of Department of Lands and Mines*, 1939, 120; Department of Labour, "Dominion Unemployment Relief Since 1930" (January 1940), 39; see also W.M. Jones, "Relief Land Settlement," in L. Richter, ed., *Canada's Unemployment Problem* (Toronto 1939), 261-95.
[73]E.M. Poirier, "The Founding of Allardville Settlement," MA report, University of New Brunswick, 1973, 21.
[74]A. Gosselin and G.P. Boucher, *Settlement Problems in Northern New Brunswick* (Ottawa 1944), Canada Department of Agriculture Publication No. 764, 24-9. By this time the provincial department responsible was also beginning to doubt the value of the programme. See Department of Lands and Mines, "A Discussion of Land Settlement in New Brunswick," RG10, RS106, box 42, "Correspondence re Reconstruction."

in the Maritimes declined sharply as municipalities ran out of money and provincial governments forced draconian cutbacks in the summer months. In 1933 monthly relief totals varied from $312,422 in February to $164,253 in July. In 1934 the totals were respectively $268,700 and $101,810 for the same two months.[75] Thus, while the new grants-in-aid could be projected as increases over the low summer relief totals,[76] they were in fact reductions of more than 1/4 from the *average* monthly direct relief payments by the federal government to the Maritimes through the calendar year of 1933. The federal payments continued with little variation through 1935 and in December of that year provided the base for a 75 per cent increase to all provinces by a newly elected Liberal government. The increase was intended "to enable the provinces to lighten the burden upon the municipalities."[77]

The matching grants mentality persisted, however. In 1936 the King government commissioned Charlotte Whitton of the Canadian Welfare Council to analyze the existing relief structure and to produce recommendations for reform. Whitton, who emphasized the importance of professional social workers in the distribution of relief and was adept at telling King what he wished to hear, counselled against any additional assumption of relief responsibilities by the federal government.[78] The need for expert supervision was implicit in her charge that, under the grants-in-aid system, the provinces were escaping their relief responsibilities. Whitton chose the Maritime provinces as her prime exhibit of provincial delinquency. In nearly half a page of underlined prose, she reviewed past relief statistics on the Maritimes to suggest prosperity (later she referred directly to "prosperous and pleasant little Prince Edward Island") and gave the startling information that the provincial and municipal governments were together paying only 19 per cent of relief costs on the Island, 12 per cent in Nova Scotia, and eight per cent in New Brunswick. Whitton created her dramatic statistics by reference to a period which did not include the winter months in which most Maritime municipalities concentrated their limited payments. Elsewhere her own tables reveal the anomaly that she was presenting. For the year, 1935-36, they show that New Brunswick, Nova Scotia and Prince Edward Island paid respectively 56 per cent, 39 per cent and 68 per cent of their direct relief costs. The provinces may not have been aware of the attack which had been launched against them. Whitton asked that her 300-page study be kept confidential since there were "a few statistics" of which she was not certain.[79]

[75]Department of Labour, "Dominion Unemployment Relief Since 1930" (January 1940), 97-8, Department of Labour Papers, RG27, vol. 213, PAC and J.K. Houston, "An Appreciation of Relief," 21-3.
[76]See James Struthers, *No Fault of Their Own*, 117 and 242, n. 43.
[77]"Dominion Unemployment Relief Since 1930," 23.
[78]James Struthers, "A Profession in Crisis: Charlotte Whitton and Canadian Social Work in the 1930s," *Canadian Historical Review*, LXII, 2 (June 1981), 169-85.
[79][Charlotte Whitton], "The Organization of Aid to Persons in Distress: Report and Recommendations of the Division on Co-ordination of Aid," March 1937, Department of Labour Papers, RG27, vol. 227, file 617, vol. 2, 65b and 68-9, PAC.

In the next two years the Maritimes tightened their relief offerings still further in a campaign against the "demoralizing effect" of relief and "relief dependency." The federal government provided the incentive by trimming its direct relief payments to the provinces by 15 per cent in April 1936 and another 10 per cent in June. After Whitton's report, total direct relief grants to the provinces were cut by about one third in April and June 1937 and those to the Maritimes by 62.7 per cent.[80] Once again the Maritime governments seem to have been masking adversity in public assertions of optimism. With the return of better economic conditions, they argued, relief was no longer so necessary. New Brunswick went further. In August of 1936 the government of Allison Dysart announced the absolute termination of direct relief in New Brunswick.[81]

There was a certain logic in the government's action. To the degree that its finances would permit, the Dysart government, upon taking office late in 1935, had launched a series of positive programmes including pensions for the aged and the blind and new public works projects.[82] In the poorer municipalities they agreed to pay up to 90 per cent of the cost of the relief of unemployables.[83] The employables thus isolated were expected to find work in expanded highway programmes, a slowly improving forest industry, or by joining the pioneer settlements. The federal cutbacks forced the pace. Rather than undercutting the new programmes to pick up a much larger share of direct relief, the Dysart government apparently decided to reap whatever political and psychological advantage might be derived from posing as the first government in Canada to end "the dole." This decision was easier for New Brunswick than for other provinces since their people received so little in any case, especially during the summer months. Government spokesmen in New Brunswick explained their action as necessary to defend the credit of both province and municipalities and to help those dependent on direct relief which was "sapping

[80]Monthly payments to the provinces are given in "Dominion Unemployment Relief Since 1930," 25-7. More comprehensive annual figures which includes money for work projects and drought relief are available in "Dominion Relief Expenditures," J.L. Ralston Papers, PAC. Total federal relief payments to the Maritimes dropped from $2.8 million in 1935-36 to $2.5 million in 1936-7 and to $1.4 million in 1938-9. Relief payments to the country as a whole for these years were $79.4 million, $78.0 million and $68.5 million. See also J.R. Rowell, "An Intellectual in Politics: Norman Rogers as an Intellectual and Minister of Labour, 1929-1939," MA thesis, Queens' University, 1978, 143-4.
[81]Saint John *Telegraph-Journal*, 13 August 1936. For a collection of statements on relief policy by members of the New Brunswick cabinet from May to August 1936 taken from the Saint John *Telegraph-Journal*, see enclosures J.H. Conlon to Marjorie Bradford, 13 April 1937, Canadian Council on Social Development Papers, MG28, I10, vol. 122, file "1937," PAC.
[82]Positive views from different perspectives on Dysart's administration are contained in R.M. Tweedie, *On with the Dance: A New Brunswick Memoir, 1935-1950* (Fredericton 1986), and Patrick Burden, "The New Brunswick Farmer-Labour Union 1937-1941," MA thesis, University of New Brunswick, 1983.
[83]See New Brunswick Cabinet Papers, 1 December 1936, PANB.

the morale and initiative of our people."[84] As economic conditions again worsened in 1937, this 'cold turkey' cure caused real suffering even among people who had a very limited acquaintance with "relief dependency." The province did relent sufficiently to provide emergency assistance to the city of Saint John and the northern municipalities during the winters of 1937 and 1938.[85]

With the benefit of hindsight one can criticize Maritime leaders on humanitarian grounds for failing to do more to ameliorate the hard circumstances of their people in the 1930s. Throughout the period they seemed to accept, to grant and to rationalize less than the minimum required by their citizens for physical and economic health. So harsh were their policies in all three provinces, even when compared to those of other governments in the period, that they tempt one to attribute them to some distinct trait of regional character, perhaps arising from a different class configuration or a unique aspect of their political culture. But a close examination of the structure and operations of the relief process in Canada reveals logical reasons for the Maritimes' apparently deviant behaviour. Under the system of conditional matching grants the three provinces were forced to play in a relief game whose rules only allowed the effective participation of wealthier players. The additional pressures and more limited choices faced by Maritime leaders largely explain their more draconian treatment of those requiring assistance.

The study of relief policies in the Maritimes suggests yet another perspective on the cumulative development of regional disparity in Canada. In the 1930s with business stagnant throughout the country, federal funds played an important role in the economic survival of individuals and industries. The Maritime region received during the decade approximately $50 million less in relief monies from the federal government than they would have had the money simply been distributed on a per capita basis. In the extreme deflation of the mid-1930s such a sum was not insignificant. One can speculate on the role which it might have played in saving individuals from personal bankruptcy, allowing independent commodity producers to maintain their operations within a market economy, or enabling at least some of the pioneer settlements to emerge as productive communities. One might speculate too on the impact of this sum if it had been available to the provincial governments for the health and education of the regional work force and/or maintaining the region's relative level of infrastructure including roads and electricity.[86] It is ironic that, while emerging as the agent of the welfare state in Canada, the federal

[84]*Synoptic Report of the Proceedings of the Legislative Assembly of New Brunswick*, 1937, 57 and 131.

[85]New Brunswick, "Public Accounts," *Journals of the Legislative Assembly*, 1939, 355-6 and A.P. Paterson's report to the Cabinet 20 May 1937, New Brunswick Cabinet Papers.

[86]Weaknesses in these areas would later be cited as factors in the consolidation of regional disparity during the 1940s. E.R. Forbes, "Consolidating Disparity: The Maritimes and the Industrialization of Canada during the Second World War," *Acadiensis*, XV, 2 (Spring 1986), 3-27.

government, through the inequity of its matching grants formulas, inadvertently became an agent in the development of regional disparity.

The research for this paper was funded by the Social Sciences and Humanities Research Council of Canada. The author is particularly indebted to Murray Young, Eric Sager and Robert Young for advice and criticism and to Carol Ferguson for research assistance in newspapers.

Battle Harbour in Transition: Merchants, Fishermen and the State in the Struggle for Relief in a Labrador Community during the 1930s

In Newfoundland, the historical experience of capital accumulation did not take place predominantly within the context of industrial capitalist development. The labour of a working class, until the mid-twentieth century, remained confined to services ancillary to the fishery in a few urban areas, the railway, some mining, and the early pulp and paper industry. Most Newfoundlanders depended on the fisheries for their livelihoods, yet the struggle between classes in Newfoundland's fishing communities has received, until recently, only scant attention, the most recent statement about social relations in the Newfoundland fishery being that of Gerald Sider. Sider felt truck to be the great exploitative evil in Newfoundland's history — the social and economic form of merchant capital's hegemony over Newfoundland society. Merchants exploited the fishery by impoverishing fishing families through the use of barter to buy salt cod for resale. Families were never given cash, but held accounts in which supplies were balanced against catches; some families' successes balanced against others' losses so that most families remained in constant debt to merchants. Some merchants also used tal qual, paying an average price for all cures provided by fisher families, but setting those prices themselves.

The final result of this truck system, for Sider, was the inhibition of any capitalist productive relations in the Newfoundland fishery from approximately 1840 through 1960. The Newfoundland fishery remained economically dominated by dependent household production, and socially dominated by an autonomous outport, kin-based village culture among fish producers. This culture, a form of

Published with permission of the editor. © Canadian Committee on Labour History. From *Labour/Le Travail*, 26 (Fall 1990), 125-50.

"traditionalism" created by merchant capital's hegemony, ensured that the antagonisms of truck's exploitation were both expressed and obscured in popular customs: telling cuffers, mummering and scoffing.[1] Because the wage, both alienating and solidifying in working-class formation, did not penetrate the greater alienation of outport traditionalism, fish producers could not generate, at the point of production, alternatives to household production dependent on merchant capital. Unable to do without merchant credit, Newfoundland fishing families were powerless to resist exploitation; they could only develop "traditions" to diffuse class antagonisms and thus avoid confrontation.[2]

Historians of truck in other regions of Atlantic Canada, however, already reject such interpretations of truck as a monolithic edifice oppressing the lives of fishermen and their families. Both Rosemary Ommer's and Roch Samson's work on the Gaspé, for example, are sensitive both to the manner in which merchants used truck to profit from the labour of their fishing clients, and also to the manner in which those clients used truck to ensure regular year-round access to credit, even in bad years when either catches or markets were poor. David Macdonald too has found that fishermen on Newfoundland's south coast negotiated the use of merchant credit for their own purposes in the fishery.[3]

---

[1] Instead of challenging truck's exploitation, Sider suggested that Newfoundland fishing families could only cope with the indignities of merchant capital domination in three main forms. At times, people might tell each other half-true stories about the difficulties they experienced with merchants, embellishing the wrongs suffered at merchants' hands and mocking their own acceptance of those wrongs. These stories are cuffers. Families redistributed labour among themselves through mummering — a Christmas tradition whereby people invited each other to visit from house-to-house in disguise, entertaining each other and usually drinking lots of liquor. The invitation and entertainment allowed productive units to be formed and reformed without insult or ever confronting the inequalities among producers which had their origins in merchant capital's domination of marketing. Finally, families coped with the false equality of tal qual by holding scoffs: large feasts in which meals were obtained by some fishing families stealing from each other. In all these traditions, Newfoundland fisher people displayed their own inability to confront merchant capital. They could only develop anthropological blinds to disguise exploitation in the clothing of traditionalism. See Gerald M. Sider, *Culture and Class in Anthropology and History: A Newfoundland Illustration* (New York 1986), 166-9.

[2] *Ibid.*, 4, 22-88, 156.

[3] Rosemary E. Ommer, "The Truck System in Gaspé, 1822-77," *Acadiensis*, XIX (Fall 1989), 109; "'All the Fish of the Post ': property, resource rights and development in a nineteenth-century inshore fishery," *Acadiensis*, X (Spring 1981), 107-23. Ommer had begun the study of early twentieth-century truck in Newfoundland in "Merchant Credit and Household Production: Newfoundland 1918-1928," paper presented to the Canadian Historical Association, Quebec City, June 1989. Roch Samson, *Fishermen and Merchants in 19th Century Gaspé* (Hull 1984), 74-6. David A. Macdonald,"They Cannot Pay Us in Money: Newman and Company and the Supplying System in the Newfoundland Fishery, 1850-1884," *Acadiensis*, XIX (Fall 1989), 145-55.

By attributing to merchants exclusive agency in the shaping of economy and society in Newfoundland fishing communities, Sider's work continues to homogenize the Newfoundland class experience.[4] In seeing Newfoundland history as the story of how merchant capital, supported by the state, exploited producers who participated in their own victimization by culturally accepting truck through cuffers, mummering and scoffs, Sider portrays them as passive and helpless. Such an overreaching and assertive interpretation of life in outport Newfoundland needs to be studied at the level of the community. A series of case studies would determine whether or not fishing families really were helpless to challenge the exploitation of merchant capital. That is what this paper seeks to begin, by examining the outport community of Battle Harbour during the 1930s. In particular, this study will demonstrate that Battle Harbour fishermen's struggles with the firm of Baine, Johnston contributed to the decline of truck and the rise of government relief in that area from 1929 to 1935.

The District of Battle Harbour comprises a string of typical outports (Henley Harbour to Venison Islands) which are isolated from urban, more capitalist St. John's and Conception Bay, and located on the south-east coast of Labrador [see map]. These communities take their collective name from the settlement of Battle Harbour, once the area's most important community, a fishing village which grew up around the merchant station located at the tickle between Great Caribou and Battle Islands. Lying just north of the Strait of Belle Isle, at the entrance to St. Lewis Inlet, it was, in the mid-eighteenth, nineteenth and twentieth centuries an unsurpassed location for Labrador cod, salmon and seal fisheries, as well as fur trapping. The Slade merchant family of Poole, Fogo and Twillingate were the first to establish a seasonal fishing post there. Like other merchants interested in Labrador's resources, they found it most efficient to deal with year-round resident producers, rather than employ wage labour directly in a seasonal fishery. As a result, over the years the Labrador fishery drew thousands of northeast coast Newfoundlanders to the Labrador coast either as stationers (who caught fish in one place) or as floaters (who lived on ships and moved from one fishing ground to another). Many gathered at Battle Harbour to prepare for a fishing season on the Labrador coast. By the end of the nineteenth century the coast of Labrador had several permanent communities of Newfoundland fishing families.[5] At roughly the same time (the 1870s), the Newfoundland fish merchants began to consolidate their enterprises in St. John's.

[4]See J.K. Hiller, Peter Narváez and Daniel Vickers, "Panel Review: Newfoundland's Past as Marxist Illustration," *Newfoundland Studies*, 3, 2 (Fall 1987), 265-9. On the problems of Sider's interpretation see Ian McKay, "Historians, Anthropology, and the Concept of Culture," *Labour/Le Travailleur*, 8/9 (Autumn/Spring 1981/82), 205-11. McKay discussed Sider's "Christmas Mummering and the New Year in Outport Newfoundland," *Past and Present* 71 (1976) and "The Ties That Bind; culture and agriculture, property and propriety in the Newfoundland village fishery," *Social History*, 5 (1980).

[5]No history has yet been written of Battle Harbour. The preceding two paragraphs are based on W. Gordon Handcock, "An Historical Geography of the Origins of English Settlement in

Map
The District of Battle Harbour in the 1930s

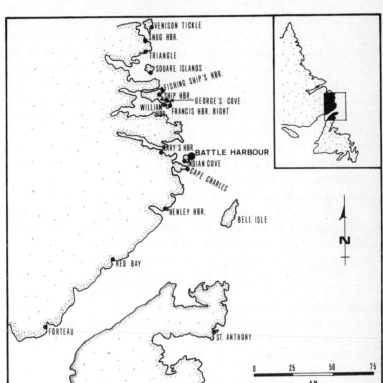

Newfoundland: A Study of the Migration Process," unpublished PhD thesis, University of Birmingham, 1979, 257-305; "Slade, John," *Dictionary of Canadian Biography, IV, 1771-1800* (Toronto 1979), 711-3. Handcock demonstrates that merchants played an essential role in the formation of a resident fishery and settlements. For a more extensive discussion of the transition from a wage-based fishing industry to kin-based fishing communities on the Labrador coast see Patricia A. Thornton, "The Demographic and Mercantile Bases of Initial Permanent Settlement in the Strait of Belle Isle," in John J. Mannion, ed. *The Peopling of Newfoundland* (St. John's 1977), 152-83.

Particular material on Battle Harbour stems from my own research on Battle Harbour for the Labrador Institute of Northern Studies, Memorial University of Newfoundland (MUN). See Lambert de Boilieu, ed. by Thomas F. Bredin, *Recollections of Labrador Life*, [1861] (Toronto 1969), xi-xii, 12-3; *The Carbonear Sentinel*, 24 August 1837, 21 June, 14 July 1838, 15 June, 27 August, 15 October 1839, 25 July 1843; *The Weekly Herald*, Harbour Grace, 16 June 1852, 4 May 1853; Newfoundland, Journal of the House of Assembly, various reports of Labrador fisheries officers and circuit court judges, 1848/9, 1870, located in journal appendices; Newfoundland, *Abstract Census and Return of the Population of Newfoundland 1869* (St. John's 1870), "The Labrador," n.p.

As part of this structural shift, the Slades sold their Newfoundland operations, including Battle Harbour, to Baine, Johnston & Co. of St. John's.[6]

Only fragmentary evidence remains of Battle Harbour District fishing families' experiences with truck. In 1909 a visitor at Battle Harbour reported residents remembering the Slades as a firm which used very exacting truck charges, inflating the prices of provisions obtained on credit by as much as 100 per cent above cash prices for goods. This same observer asserted that Baine, Johnston was less exploitative, acting as a paternalistic "guide, philosopher and friend of the entire community."[7] This view must be tempered by J.P. Alley's earlier view that Baine, Johnston & Co. kept "nearly all of its three hundred inhabitants in debt to it."[8] In 1917, acting on complaints about the truck system by the International Grenfell Association, the Newfoundland government appointed a royal commission to investigate the IGA co-operative movement. Baine, Johnston's agent at Battle Harbour, John Croucher, defended the truck system before the commission. In the process, he gave some idea of how that system worked. Croucher stated that Baine, Johnston took on all the risk of the fishing season by giving fishermen credit before the firm knew what international fish prices would be at the end of the season. If prices proved low, Baine, Johnston stood to lose on its investment, through credit, in fishermen's voyages. Croucher believed that this risk obliged Battle Harbour fishermen to trade all of their fish to Baine, Johnston at the season's end.[9] At the same time as he defended the merchants' side of truck, Croucher stated that any competition that worked against the mutual obligations of truck, any leakage in the system whereby fishermen could deal outside of truck with other merchants, would "unfairly" destabilize the supply merchants' economic base.

Aggregate census data for 1935 suggests that the District of Battle Harbour relied heavily on merchant provisioning for most of its subsistence goods. The entire region produced only 8 bushels of potatoes and 1,650 lbs. of cabbage to help feed 802 people. Some livestock, goats and hens were kept by residents and these produced a little milk, eggs, and perhaps, meat. Every other dietary staple in addition to clothes and the other necessities of life had to be purchased from merchants. Battle Harbour was a community of fishing families: 80 per cent of the households enumerated in manuscript census data (119 out of 149 total) derived most of their

[6]Shannon Ryan, "The Newfoundland Cod Fishery in the Nineteenth Century," unpublished MA thesis, MUN, 1971, 38-58. MUN, Maritime History Archive, Baine, Johnston Collection, 27-A-41, conveyance, Slade-Grieve, 1871.

[7]P.W. Brown, *Where the Fishers Go: The Story of Labrador* (New York 1909), 238-41.

[8]Jonathan Prince Alley, *Bowdoin Boys in Labrador: An Account of the Bowdoin College Scientific Expedition to Labrador led by Prof. Leslie A. Lee of the Biological Dept.* (Rockland, Maine 189?), 1-16.

[9]Provincial Archives of Newfoundland and Labrador, International Grenfell Association Business Office. Copy of the Report of R.T. Squarey, Esq., J.P. Re. IGA Enquiry. Testimony of John Croucher, 27 September 1917. I would like to thank Jessie Chisholm for bringing this document to my attention.

income from fishing. Only three merchant or merchants' agents' households existed on the coast. At Battle Harbour proper a number of residents worked as labourers for Baine, Johnston & Co. The Church of England minister, a constable, and a Justice of the Peace added to the limited social diversity of the settlement of Battle Harbour.[10] In the District of Battle Harbour, one factor dominated the lives of fishing families: such families depended almost completely on fish merchants for provisions, clothing, household goods, and fishing equipment.

The 1930s saw the beginning of the end of such dependent relationships between merchants and fishermen at Battle Harbour, as long-term structural problems matured in the Newfoundland economy. At the end of the nineteenth century, St. John's merchants dominated the economy of Newfoundland. Their continued use of tal qual, along with population expansion and capital impoverishment due to truck, all contributed to the declining quality of the Newfoundland fish product at the same time that world fish prices were falling and supplies of better quality Icelandic fish were increasing after 1919. Through the 1930s, little was done to change the situation. Merchants and governments preferred to follow economic diversification policies through agriculture, railways, rural inland settlement, and domestic manufacturing, and use public works programs to absorb the unemployed, while ignoring Newfoundland's economic base in the salt fishery. The results were, at various times, a weakening of the merchant firms in the fisheries; impoverishment of the Labrador fishery; severe decline in the Bank fishery; deterioration in cure in all fisheries; impoverishment of large sectors of the population as a result of the truck system and low prices offered to fishermen for their fish; further lack of cooperative marketing by merchants; and a decline in suitable local shipping to access markets.[11]

This economic crisis, particularly on Newfoundland's northeast coast, moved many fish merchants to withdraw capital from the fishery, particularly with respect to winter relief and the extension of credit to those repeatedly unable to clear most of their debts. By the first decades of the twentieth century, a process of social differentiation was well underway among fishing families; even outside the Conception Bay area, the "traditional" household-based fishing villages were nowhere

[10]MUN, Maritime History Archive, Baine, Johnston Collection, 27-A-36, Valuation of Sale of Battle Harbour From Slade, 1871; 27-A-93, Summary Inventory transferred to Earles Freighting Service Ltd., Battle Harbour, 14 June 1955. Government of Newfoundland, *Tenth Census of Newfoundland and Labrador* (St. John's 1931), Vol. I, Table 28, Vol. II, sec. I, Table 4, 55. The published census material incorrectly lists the District of Battle Harbour as having 150 families. The manuscript nominal census lists 149, giving only 18 families at Cape Charles, rather than 19.

[11]Rosemary E. Ommer, "What's Wrong With Canadian Fish?," *Journal of Canadian Studies*, 20, 3 (Fall 1985), 125-32. David Alexander, "Development and Dependence in Newfoundland, 1880-1970," in David Alexander, compiled by Eric Sager, Lewis R. Fischer, and Stuart O. Pierson, *Atlantic Canada and Confederation: Essays in Canadian Political Economy* (Toronto 1983), 3-31; and *The Decay of Trade: An Economic History of the Newfoundland Saltfish Trade, 1935-1965* (St. John's 1977), 1-37.

so homogeneous in their structure as Sider suggests. As they tightened credit, merchants increasingly dealt only with fishing families owning capital equipment — like cod traps or motor boats — that could be used as collateral. Families with little or no equipment faced two prospects: pooling resources to buy equipment, or becoming a labour reserve employed by those with equipment. In either case fishing communities produced a number of "trap skippers," linked to their fellow fishermen by family and community ties, but becoming increasingly responsible for the management of production and marketing. These skippers were something more analogous to skilled master craftsmen in relation to journeymen than they were to merchants. Many, in their reaction to mercantile exploitation, provided the Fishermen's Protective Union with its organizational base both on the northeast coast and on the Labrador coast.[12]

The 1935 census of Newfoundland provides evidence of similar differentiation occurring in the District of Battle Harbour. The manuscript census data indicate that 119 families earned their income from the fishery. Most fishing families earned between $200-400 (Can.) in the year from 1 June 1934 to 30 May 1935 (81 out of 119). Only fifteen households earned less than $200, while 20 made between $500-800. The number of families making more than $800 drops sharply to only three out of 119 families. It would not be wise to accept alone differences in income levels for one year as an indication of social differentiation. Earnings in the fishery remain extremely vulnerable to seasonal fluctuations in fish stocks and international market prices.

As the work of Barbara Neis suggests, the early 1900s saw increased differentiation among fishing families arise from increased differences in families' ownership of fishing equipment. While only five fishing families registered no income in 1934-35, 24 indicated that they owned no equipment. The 1935 census lists the heads of all these families as independent fishermen who did not work for wages. In the Battle Harbour District, then, fishing families with little or no equipment must have engaged in some sort of shares arrangement, bearing part of the fishing voyage's expenses and gaining a property right in the catch, with those who did have equipment.[13] Thirty-four families owned small amounts of equipment, valued at less than $500. Twenty-three families owned between $500-1,000 worth of equipment, while twenty-one owned between $1,000-1,500. These numbers drop sharply to only six families owning between $1,500-2,000; and five each owning $2,000-2,500, and $2,500-3,000. Only one fishing family possessed $3,000 worth of equipment — that of Gus Bradley at Indian Cove. Bradley was fortunate enough to own, among other equipment, two motor boats, two cod traps, and ten salmon nets.

[12]Barbara Neis, "A Sociological Analysis of the Factors Responsible for the Regional Distribution of the Fishermen's Protective Union of Newfoundland," unpublished MA thesis, MUN, 1980, 40-2.

[13] This type of arrangement is very well examined in Peter Sinclair, *From Traps to Draggers: Domestic Commodity Production in Northwest Newfoundland, 1850-1982* (St. John's 1985), 43-51.

Unwilling to risk their capital by extending credit to all fishing families, merchants in the northeast coast and Labrador fisheries by the 1930s gave credit only to those with motor boats and cod traps. Yet such equipment was labour-intensive in operation. In the District of Battle Harbour, only 46 out of the 119 fishing families owned cod traps, 65 families owned motor boats, and 73 owned salmon nets [see Table 1]. In the District's four largest communities — Henley Harbour, Cape Charles, Battle Harbour and George's Cove — only 22-25 per cent of the fishing families owned cod traps. This data suggests that social differentiation among fishermen was important. Yet such differentiation did not become class differentiation; the fishing families of Battle Harbour District stood together as family-based communities of domestic commodity producers.[14]

Table 1
District of Battle Harbour:
Fishing Families and Equipment, 1934-35

Settlement	Total # Families	# Fishing Families	# Fishing Families with cod traps	# Fishing Families with motor boats	# Fishing Families with salmon nets
Henley Hr.	10	10	5	6	7
C. Charles	18	14	11	11	12
Battle Hr.	43	27	6	13	10
Indian Cove	8	7	4	4	6
Mary's Hr.	4	-	-	-	-
Fox Hr.	18	17	3	8	15
D.W. Creek	3	3	2	2	0
Seal Bight	2	2	2	2	2
Murray's Hr.	2	2	2	2	2
Wm.'s Hr.	6	6	2	4	6
Francis Hr. Bight	6	5	2	3	3
Fishing Ship Hr.	1	-	-	-	-
Square I.	4	4	0	1	4
Snug Hr.	1	1	0	0	1
Triangle	2	2	1	1	2
Venison I.	7	5	1	1	1
Total	149	119	46	65	73

[14]The census data for the preceding discussion, as well as Table 1, is drawn from Provincial Archives of Newfoundland and Labrador, GN2/39/B, Manuscript Census, Labrador, District of Battle Harbour, 1935, Table 7, F-3; Manuscript Nominal Census, 1935, Labrador, District of Battle Harbour, vol. 36, 22-31, 43-63, Reel A-7-4.

The fishing families of Battle Harbour had to cope with a merchant firm which was experiencing profound structural change within Newfoundland's economy. Like other Newfoundland fish exporters, Baine, Johnston found waning international markets for Newfoundland's fish cure, especially the Labrador product. Baine, Johnston did try to improve quality in the production of cod. The company insisted on higher standards in drying and handling fish. Besides refusing sun-burnt fish, Baine, Johnston's agent, S. Loveridge, instructed his collectors to make sure that fishermen properly cleaned fish. Yet by the early 1930s, the problems of selling fish were out of any one firm's hands. The best markets for Labrador fish — Spain, Italy and Greece — either were disrupted by workers' strikes or undercut by better quality Icelandic fish. In 1930, a revolution in Brazil closed Pernambuco to Baine, Johnston's ships; and Malaga, Spain, the firm's principal market, was closed by strikes. These market conditions forced Baine, Johnston to instruct Loveridge that "Any dealer who is in the habit of making poor fish, it might be advisable to withhold supplies altogether." By 1931, due to worsening markets, the company decided only to give credit to those who could "square up their accounts."[15]

Baine, Johnston responded to such market problems by reducing fishing families' supply of credit. In part, controlling "leakage" lay behind this strategy. The simple fact is that, on the Labrador coast, immense competition existed between merchants for the produce of fishing families. In 1927 Baine, Johnston faced the Hudson Bay Company's attempt to take over Battle Harbour's salmon fishery by introducing fresh fishery technology. All Loveridge could do was to "be tactful with the dealers and please the fishermen" so that they would not abandon Baine, Johnston for HBC.[16] Other merchants, like W.A. Munn at Gunning Island and Harvey & Co.'s dealer Morgan, tried to cut in on Baine, Johnston's Battle Harbour fishery; they proved to be consistent thorns in the company's side throughout the 1930s.[17] Occasionally independent traders appeared on the coast trying to undercut Baine, Johnston's prices in a particular season. For example, Stone at Cape Charles in 1929 and Baggs & Co., Ltd. of Curling in 1930 offered groceries for codfish and herring, but "Needless to mention they are not providing salt nor any supplies on credit for fishery." Baine, Johnston dealt forthrightly with fishermen who went to the competition. The Company instructed Loveridge to "keep an eye ... and any dealer who plays double you can tell him to look to Mr. Stone for supplies." In the Baggs & Co. case ".... should any of the dealers, whom we have helped out, ship

[15]PANL, Baine, Johnston & Co., P7/A/2, Battle Harbour Letters, Box 22B, 1927-32, Correspondence between S. Loveridge and Baine, Johnston & Co., Battle Harbour and St. John's, 14, 16 June 1927; 4 July 1939; 17 June, 11, 15, 21 July, 26 August 1930; 20 August 1931; 14 September 1932.
[16]*Ibid.*, S. Loveridge to Baine, Johnston & Co., Battle Harbour, 24 January, May 1927, 5 October 1929, 9 October 1929, 10 July 1930.
[17]*Ibid.*, S. Loveridge to Baine, Johnston & Co., 24 June, 11 August 1927; 20 August 1931.

their fish to Baggs' Coy., we leave you to deal with them in the best way you think fit, pointing out that we do not intend to be made a convenience of."[18]

In trying to deal with the problem of leakage, Baine, Johnston had to face one basic fact: some of the better-off fishing households, those of people like Gus Bradley, actively challenged Baine, Johnston's desire to maintain its control of Battle Harbour's fish business. The Company had to tread carefully because it did not want to lose its best fish producers. When Bradley decided to produce salmon for a competitor, Allen's at Cape Charles, in 1933, Loveridge reported that Bradley owed Baine, Johnston $391 (for credit towards his purchase of equipment) and that he would have "reliable fishermen" watch over Bradley because he might start buying other Baine, Johnston and Co. fishermen's produce for Allen's. When questioned about this, Bradley stated that he was fed up with Baine, Johnston's new, tighter, credit policies and that in Croucher's day the company was more "forgiving" about fishermen's debts. Baine, Johnston, when Loveridge advised them that he tried to force Bradley to stop dealing with Allen's, quickly cautioned him not to antagonize Bradley because "He is the sort of chap that if you make an enemy of, could do the Firm a lot of harm, use diplomacy, and you might convince him that what he did was not after all to his benefit."[19]

Caution ruled Baine, Johnston's treatment of Bradley because they feared he would attract good fishermen from Baine, Johnston. It galled the Company to restrain itself with regard to Bradley because "we look on this as an unfriendly act."[20] In fact, Bradley kept on dealing with Allen's and, by 1934, had other fishermen, including James Pye, dealing with Allen's as well. Baine, Johnston was aghast, and helpless, because it did not want to lose the more successful fishermen's business:

[18]*Ibid.*, S. Loveridge to Baine, Johnston & Co., Battle Harbour, 8 August 1930; Baine, Johnston & Co. to S. Loveridge, St. John's, 3 June 1929; 14 August 1930.
[19]*Ibid.*, Box 23B, 1933-39, S. Loveridge to Baine, Johnston & Co., 10, 12 July 1933; Baine, Johnston to S. Loveridge, St. John's, 18 July 1933. In Sider's account, trading activity like Bradley's is merely an abstract economic concept: "leakage." Fish merchants, as did Baine, Johnston in the early 1930s, restricted winter credit to families they felt could not make good on their accounts in times of bad prices for fish. This, in turn, forced fishing families to try to escape the obligations of previous debts to merchants by dealing with competitors in the hope, given Newfoundland's lack of alternative subsistence resources in agriculture, of obtaining enough supplies to survive the winter. "Leakage" further eroded merchants' abilities to profit in world fish markets because it deprived them of supplies of fish. In Sider's account merchants alone overcame this block to capital accumulation by dictating to the state the need for government relief to subsidize "the unit cost of labour," thereby halting haemorrhage in the supply of fish to merchants. Again, by this abstraction of fishing households' participation in the development of relief, Sider denies fishermen their place within the historical dynamic of community development. Merchants and their government puppets act, but not producers. Fishing families appear only as the passive recipients of merchant capital's hegemonic dictates. See Sider, *Culture and Class,* 146-7.
[20]*Ibid.*, Baine, Johnston & Co. to S. Loveridge, St. John's, 11 July 1933.

We are surprised to learn that he [Pye] should play a double part. We thought he would at least be loyal to the firm. All you can do is watch the dealers that sold salmon to Allen, and if they do not square up with you in the Fall, tell them we will not stand for it another year. You will have *to be tactful* [emphasis mine] in how you handle them. We presume if we do not supply them, some one else will, we mean for the codfishery.[21]

When Loveridge questioned Pye about his loyalty to the firm, Pye replied that he gave Baine, Johnston half of his catch, the other to Allen's because of their better prices, "and said if we got half we ought to be satisfied."[22] As for Bradley, he continued to deal where, and as, he pleased. As Loveridge told head office in St. John's, as business declined on the coast the Battle Harbour store depended on the business of "independent" men like Bradley.[23] By 1938, Bradley's efforts proved so successful that he began to retail small items at Indian Cove to his neighbours.[24]

Gus Bradley and James Pye, mavericks within the larger group of Baine, Johnston's fishermen-dealers, did not enjoy exceptionally high incomes. Bradley earned a respectable $600 while Pye registered no income in 1934-35. What separated these two fishermen from other family heads was the amount of equipment they owned. In the District, 46 families owned between them 67 cod traps, 65 families owned 89 motor boats, and 73 families owned 410 salmon nets. Bradley's two motor boats and two cod traps meant that he was somewhat better off than even those other families owning motor boats and cod traps. But Bradley's great advantage lay in the ten salmon nets he owned. The average number of these held by fishing families was only between five and six. Despite his lack of income, James Pye owned two each of motor boats and cod traps, but owned seven salmon nets.[25]

Differences in equipment ownership appear to be the only significant factor in allowing Bradley and Pye, the latter unsuccessfully, to challenge Baine, Johnston's claim to their produce. Neither Indian Cove (Bradley's home community) nor Cape Charles (Pye's home community) were far removed from the Company's headquarters at Battle Harbour proper. Bradley's and Pye's attempts to deal with firms other than Baine, Johnston were not facilitated by their being able to use distance as a shelter from the firm's watchful eye.

Bradley and Pye were distinct in the means which they had to catch more salmon than most. At a time when Labrador cod fetched low prices in international markets, Baine, Johnston turned increasingly to the salmon fishery for compensation. While Pye succumbed to Baine, Johnston's pressure, Bradley did not. Little direct evidence exists to suggest that Bradley's equipment, by providing livelihoods to those of his neighbours with less, gave him the influence with other families that the firm so worried about. But there are factors that make this a reasonable inference:

[21]*Ibid.*, Baine, Johnston & Co. to S. Loveridge, St. John's, 16 July 1934.

[22]*Ibid.*, S. Loveridge to Baine, Johnston & Co., Battle Harbour, 10 July 1934.

[23]*Ibid.*, S. Loveridge to Baine, Johnston & Co., Battle Harbour, 17 October 1934.

[24]*Ibid.*, S.D. Grant to Baine, Johnston & Co., Battle Harbour, n.d., 1938.

[25]Government of Newfoundland, *Tenth Census...*, Vol. II, Sec. I, Table II; PANL, Manuscript Census, 1935, Table 7, F-3, Manuscript Nominal Census, Vol. 36, 22-31, 43-63.

Bradley could not operate all of his equipment on his own; Baine, Johnston clearly saw him as being much more independent than his fellow fishermen; and the Company acknowledged explicitly that Bradley was an important community leader. Bradley closely resembles those "trap skippers" Neis suggests were emerging in the northeast coast and Labrador fisheries in this period, using both their community positions and new importance in production and marketing to launch a direct challenge to the hegemony of merchant capital over their lives.

To prevent other fishermen from following Bradley's course, warnings to Loveridge by Baine, Johnston not to give credit to those dealing with other firms were accompanied by the caution "be tactful." The need for this tact can be seen in Baine, Johnston's dealings with another defecting fisherman, Jeremiah Thoms, in 1933. Thoms began to deal with a firm by the name of Moores, also buying other households' fish for that firm. Baine, Johnston instructed Loveridge to handle Thoms "as diplomatically as you can" because, until such time as Thoms had to look to Baine, Johnston & Co. for credit "he would try to hold us up to ridicule [sic] ...." for their attempts to secure Thoms' fish.[26]

Thoms was not able, like Bradley, to escape Baine, Johnston's hold over him. The next year, in 1934, Thoms had to approach Baine, Johnston about "what conditions can we come on as in the regards of something to eat for the winter." Baine, Johnston agreed to supply Thoms if he turned over "all your voyage to the firm."[27] Thoms communicated directly with Baine, Johnston's St. John's office because he felt shabbily treated at Loveridge' hands. ".... Sir I am writing you to See what you can do or the firm of Baine Johnston & Co. not Mr. Loveridge. I am not having any discussion with him whatever ...."[28]

This is important. Even dealers like Thoms who remained subordinated to Baine, Johnston, actively negotiated the terms of that subordination. The year before, in 1933, the firm reprimanded Loveridge for insulting James Pye in a dispute over the latter's dealings with Allen's. Pye wanted, and received, an apology from Loveridge for calling him a "cur" in front of other men on the wharf at Battle Harbour.[29] Head Office was losing its patience with Loveridge. When it earlier had told him to trim expenses, instead of cutting his own, Loveridge cut perks given to fishermen when they came to the store. Anonymous letters arrived in St. John's complaining of Loveridge's stinginess and he was reprimanded by the firm:

Perhaps in your eagerness to make the business a success you have been rather 'nippy,' as we have been told so. This does not pay, especially in a Labrador business, and when we tell you to economise we do not mean you to cut an old custom. What we mean is, when the dealers come from far away places you should give them a cup of tea, or what the fishermen

[26]PANL. Baine, Johnston & Co., P7/A/2, Box 23B, 1933-39, B.J.C. to S. Loveridge, St. John's, 9, 20 September, 1933; S. Loveridge to Baine, Johnston and Co., Battle Harbour, 11 September 1933.
[27]*Ibid.*, Baine, Johnston & Co. to Jeremiah Thoms, St. John's, 18 September 1934.
[28]*Ibid.*, Jeremiah Thoms to Baine, Johnston & Co., Battle Harbour, 28 August 1934.
[29]*Ibid.*, S. Loveridge to Baine, Johnston & Co., 21 October 1933.

call a 'mug-up,' rather than allow them to go away hungry. It may cost the firm perhaps five dollars or a little more to do so, but it is money well spent and we do not want you to stop this practice.[30]

Baine, Johnston's director, T. Collingwood, also instructed Loveridge to stop "charging the fishermen 40 cents for the use of the puncheons .... I do not think it advisable to do this because it seems sort of nippy, and while the charge is small it leaves room for people to talk, and may do more harm than good."[31] After more anonymous complaints through 1934-35, Baine, Johnston fired Loveridge to keep up some appearance of being a firm interested in accommodating the needs of Battle Harbour's residents. Baine, Johnston would rather dismiss its agent than further jeopardize relationships with its fish-suppliers, which already were strained by credit restrictions.[32]

The firing of Loveridge is a strong statement about the role some fishermen played in shaping their own environment. Because they controlled production, and because they enjoyed the intimate familiarity of families linked together in the structure of village communities, these fishermen had power. Its exertion was motivated by the family's well-being, its very subsistence, for, as Loveridge admitted, "Tact will count for nothing and will not appeal to empty stomachs as they see looming before them even ... the Fall months."[33] Baine, Johnston constantly worried about their reputation in the talk of these fishing families because they feared agitation might start against the firm, causing the company to lose its fish business to competitors. To prevent this, occasionally, the firm granted a loyal dealer like Archibald Pye special credit favours because "He is quite a talker and has quite an influence with the fishermen."[34]

By cultivating the support of such fishermen, Baine, Johnston and Co. acknowledged the capacity of a differentiated fishing community to produce leaders

[30]*Ibid.*, Box 22 B, Baine, Johnston & Co. to S. Loveridge, St. John's, 30 May 1931.

[31]*Ibid.*, 5 September 1930. It is not easy to convey the precise meaning of Collingwood's use of the term "nippy." In Newfoundland the expression often is used to describe someone who is being tight-fisted or parsimonious. Story *et al.* gave two definitions which are useful. The first "nip" is a verb meaning "'of ice, to squeeze or crush (a vessel).'" One might say that Baine, Johnston did not wish to appear to be squeezing the fishermen too much by wringing the last cent possible from them by charging for the use of puncheons, or denying a cup of tea. The second definition is "nipper," a noun used to describe any variety of loathsome gnats which, by constantly "nipping," or biting people, suck the lifeblood from their victims. In this sense, Baine, Johnston would not wish to carry too far their own parasitical expropriation of fishing households' produce. Both definitions seem appropriate self-descriptions of Baine, Johnston's relationships with fishing households in the 1930s. See the *Dictionary of Newfoundland English* (Toronto 1982), 348-9.

[32]*Ibid.*, Box 23B, 1933-39; S. Loveridge to Baine, Johnston & Co., St. John's, 5 December 1936.

[33]*Ibid.*, Box 22B, 1927; 1929-32; Loveridge to Baine, Johnston & Co., Battle Harbour, 5 September 1931.

[34]*Ibid.*, S. Loveridge to Baine, Johnston & Co., Battle Harbour, 4 October 1929.

capable of challenging its operations. Baine, Johnston continued to give credit for the fishery to influential dealers, and to those who proved to be good sources of fish. But as fish markets weakened, the Company began to have trouble with families to which it began to restrict winter credit. Yet Baine, Johnston did tighten credit and refused supply to poorer households unable to pay on their debts. The firm's solution was to turn to the Newfoundland government to make provisions for the impoverished's relief. In 1929 the Newfoundland government opened an account with Baine, Johnston at Battle Harbour so that, on the recommendation of Gus Brazil, the J.P. and relief officer, residents might charge goods on relief. Loveridge found that Brazil probably manipulated this account for personal gain, and, at the firm's instigation, the government eventually replaced Brazil with another officer, Reid.[35]

These relief measures by no means were some magnanimous measure taken by either Baine, Johnston & Co. or the government. Relief was the government's response to Baine, Johnston & Co.'s letter to the Colonial Secretary, Dr. Barnes:

.... the following is a copy of the telegram received by us last night from our Battle Harbour agent:

"Several family men facing starvation, rumour around will take goods informed Government today," signed 'Hoffe.'

We may say that we made no provision last year for winter relief, but have ample stocks of provisions on hand to relieve all deserving cases.

Hoffe is our winter agent, and has only one or two assistants, so that in the event of an attempt being made to take the goods forcibly, we could not protect them.[36]

The grand total of government relief allowed for the next year was $68.00 which, combined with a poor seal harvest, led Loveridge to comment "Many very deserving cases in sick and aged were left to mercy of poor friends and relatives, how these existed all through the long season is a mystery."[37]

The more-impoverished fishing households were not submissive victims of Baine, Johnston's winter credit restrictions, nor were they passive recipients of state relief. The 1929 telegram suggests that fishermen, when faced with the prospect of their families' starvation, were quick to take action against the merchants whose restriction of credit violated the historical accommodation of the truck system. Baine, Johnston recognized the power held by these fishermen, and yielded to it by encouraging the state to come to the poor's relief.

[35]*Ibid.*, Baine, Johnston to S. Loveridge, 28 March, (?) September 1927; 15 June, 4, 8 July 1929.
[36]*Ibid.*, Baine, Johnston & Co. to Dr. Barnes, Colonial Secretary, St. John's, 9 February, 1929. Charles Hoffe was Baine, Johnston's winter agent. He lived at Battle Harbour, managing the firm's business after Loveridge returned to his home at Twillingate at the end of October.
[37]*Ibid.*, S. Loveridge to Baine, Johnston & Co., Battle Harbour, 6 June 1930.

The paltry relief allowances of 1929-30 did not diffuse tension at Battle Harbour. The niggardly sums doled out seem to have been determined by Brazil, the relief officer. This caused problems for Baine, Johnston, as Loveridge wrote to Head Office:

> Brazil is very unpopular with the people at Battle Harbour and he knows this, and I rather foresee that he will screw them down to the very smallest allowance per family & their threats of destroying our property would not have any affect on him if it came to their disputing that allowance was not sufficient for families to exist on.[38]

The Company lay between the rock, the popular discontent of Battle Harbour families with relief, and a hard place, government attempts to keep relief expenditures down.

The outcome of the tension imbued in this conflict was another threatened attack on Baine, Johnston's Battle Harbour premises. On 18 January 1930, Charles Hoffe telegraphed Loveridge that two men, Arch Rumbold and Levi Spearing, appeared with axes to break into the Company stores, take winter provisions, and threatened to shoot any who might get in their way.[39] The correspondence between the Newfoundland government, Baine, Johnston, and the agents at Battle Harbour about this incident is worth looking at in some detail because it says much about the potential for conflict between merchants and fishermen in Newfoundland communities.

Baine, Johnston immediately informed the government that ".... the men threaten, when the present food is consumed, to shoot anyone who prevents them from breaking. There is no doubt that the situation is serious ... we have a lot of valuable property there without any protection, and that they should take the necessary steps to protect life and property."[40] The Acting Deputy Minister of Justice responded by wiring Brazil, advising him to hire two local men as constables to deal with Spearing and Rumbold. Brazil replied that it was "Impossible get two men as Constables here owing all relations." Brazil could not turn families against families; the solidarity of family producers at Battle Harbour forced him to give out extra relief rations.[41] As Loveridge informed Baine, Johnston:

> ... S.W. Brazil would not succeed in securing services of even one man much less any number of men who would take responsibility of endeavouring to protect our property from any attack by hungry men who have also their families to keep from starving.[42]

[38]*Ibid.*, S. Loveridge to Baine, Johnston & Co., Twillingate, 21 January 1930.
[39]*Ibid.*, Charles Hoffe to S. Loveridge, Battle Harbour, 18 January 1930.
[40]*Ibid.*, Baine, Johnston & Co. to S. Loveridge, St. John's, 18 January 1930.
[41]PANL, GN13/1/2; Nfld., Dept. of Justice Correspondence, vol. 31, June 1929-February 1930, Reel Aa-1-30, Acting Deputy Minister of Justice to Colonial Secretary A. Barnes, St. John's, 18 January 1930.
[42]PANL, P7/A/2, Baine, Johnston & Co., Battle Harbour Letters, Box 22B, 1927; 29-32; S. Loveridge to Baine, Johnston & C., Twillingate, 21 January 1930.

The isolation of Hoffe and Brazil must have been intimidating. Outside their very door, the nine fishing families of Rumbolds, and the two of Spearings, constituted almost 25 per cent of the total families living at Battle Harbour, and 41 per cent of the village's fishing families. Other communities were even more heavily dominated by family ties, without any apparent links to those who represented Baine, Johnston and the state at Battle Harbour. Gus Bradley's fellow Indian Cove residents were, with one exception, Rumbolds (Bradley was a migrant from Newfoundland, but his wife Clara was a native Labradorian — the 1935 census does not give her former surname). The ten families at Henley Harbour all shared the surname of Stone. At Cape Charles, with one exception, all the families were Pyes. Fox Harbour, like Battle Harbour, shared an assortment of fishing family names with other communities in the District: Chubbs, Curl, Rumbold, Mangrove, and Poole. George's Cove was the domain of the Penny's, Giblunouchs, Burdens, and Wards. The six families of William's Harbour were all Russells. The remaining smaller communities all represented fragments of these families. In short, as Hoffe and Baine, Johnston acknowledged, the ties between District fishing families proved a potent force which, in times of crisis, neither the firm nor the state had easy ways to deal with.[43]

Unable to find support among District fishing families, Baine, Johnston could not turn to the coast's other important presence: the International Grenfell Association. While antagonisms arising out of the 1917 dispute between the firm and the Grenfell organization had lessened, neither had been able to come to terms with the other. Throughout the 1930s Baine, Johnston continued to support the Grenfell Mission's medical presence in a cottage hospital on the island of Battle Harbour. But when the Grenfell Association began to propose another co-operative store in the area, the Company withdrew its support, informing Loveridge that ".... the Mission can go their way and we will go ours;... there must be no more favours, now that Dr. Grenfell has shown his teeth." The Association began to ignore Baine, Johnston as it went about its business on the coast; its correspondence for the 1930s is silent on the relationship between fishing families and Baine, Johnston.[44]

The state could not easily accept yielding its authority to that of Battle Harbour families' notion of what was morally right. Even if families were starving, said Colonial Secretary Barnes, that was no excuse for breaking the law: anyone like Spearing and Rumbold must be warned against breaking into the Battle Harbour store. But, and here is the essential point, the Newfoundland government recognized that it had no choice but to yield extra relief because it could not really protect Baine, Johnston's premises.

[43]PANL, Manuscript Census, 1935, Table 7, F-3.

[44]PANL, P7/A/2, Box 22B, Baine, Johnston & Co. to S. Loveridge, St. John's, 8 August 1932. The relationship between the Grenfell Association and Baine, Johnston is explained in greater detail in Sean Cadigan and Jessie Chisholm, *Understanding a Provincial Historical Resource: A Preliminary Historical Survey of Battle Harbour* (Happy Valley, Labrador 1989), 21-4, 77-90.

As there is not a sufficient force to control the people and to enforce law and order, it appears to the Government that it would not be wise to fight the situation, but, having let the men proceed to an unlawful act, the Justice of the Peace should then meet the situation to the best of his ability by granting such relief as he considers is proper and right.[45]

This final authorization of relief comforted Loveridge, who had begun to panic as the government tried to decide what actions should be taken:

Certainly Gracious the Justice Department are not going to delay action and wait until some desperate means have been resorted to by the heads of some starving families ....
... Hoffe is in great suspense these days and very anxious of what the outcome will be ....
I can foresee that it is only bunkum for the Justice Dept. to talk of getting Brazil to swear in special constables for protection of our property, if the people are demanding food to feed their families.[46]

When asked by Baine, Johnston as to whether or not one of the firm's fishing household clients would come to the Company's aid, Loveridge replied:

There is no sturdy independent man in the vicinity that I could recommend who would act in the event of any trouble. Augustus Bradley would be the only person that would have any influence. He lives three miles from Battle Harbour proper. I repeat again however that if families are destitute especially if on the increase ... then if any sympathy it will be expressed with those who may go so far as to break in the stores to obtain food for the families.[47]

Baine, Johnston could not count on the support of Battle Harbour's most successful fishermen like Bradley because their loyalties lay with their fellow household producers. Yet, luckily for the Company, people directed their hostility against Brazil despite the fact that the two men who started the affair, Levi Spearing and Arch Rumbold, were denied credit by Baine, Johnston. Loveridge felt that Spearing was too lazy, and Rumbold's family had grown so large Loveridge feared Rumbold would never pay for the increased supplies he took on credit.[48]

Baine, Johnston capitalized on popular disgust with Brazil by arranging to have relief administered through Charles Hoffe at the Battle Harbour store. The Newfoundland government ordinarily opposed such arrangements because it feared that merchants would be too liberal in opening the public purse.[49] But in the Baine,

[45]PANL, GN2 12/A; Nfld., Colonial Secretary's Correspondence, vol. 205, November 1929-February 1930; Reel A-10-2; Deputy Colonial Secretary to B.E.S. Dunfield, Acting Deputy Minister of Justice, St. John's, 4 February 1930.
[46]PANL, P7/A/2, Baine, Johnston & Co., Battle Harbour Letters, Box 22B, 1927; 1929-32; S. Loveridge to Baine, Johnston & Co., Twillingate, 4 February 1930.
[47]*Ibid.*
[48]*Ibid.*, S. Loveridge to Baine, Johnston and Co., Twillingate, 29 January 1930.
[49]PANL, GN2/1/A, Nfld., Colonial Secretary's Correspondence, vol. 205, November 1929-February 1930, Reel A-10-2, Deputy Colonial Secretary to Rev. J.A. Reese, St. John's, 13 February 1930.

Johnston case, a new form of government chicanery occurred to Colonial Secretary Barnes, in light of the state's inability to use force to ensure minimum public relief expenditure: the Newfoundland government would arrange with Baine, Johnston to distribute relief without any participation by the Relief Officer.

The people when they are in need will approach ... Charles Hoffe, who will use his discretion and give the people applying such goods only as he thinks they actually need on the understanding that if they have no cash then, they will pay for the same from the process of the seals or fur that they may catch during the Winter Season.

That is, the goods given out will not be understood to be Government goods for the relief by those receiving the same, but will be taken as advances by your firm to men who will pay for the same in due course.[50]

The government assured Baine, Johnston that any accounts not balanced would be paid for by the public account.

Baine, Johnston accepted this arrangement because, in the face of continuing defections by its best fishermen, it allowed the company to appear as if it was honouring old commitments to its dealers by nothing more than good will, when what appeared to be winter credit was guaranteed payment by the Newfoundland government. The Company realized that Hoffe would become the focal point for families' discontent about its strict credit policies "... but it cannot be helped. The [government] realize that relief will be necessary, and all they ask us to do is to be firm, and after investigating to relieve those in need, and to get returns if it is possible. They have no intention of making us scapegoat."[51] Unfortunately for Hoffe, Battle Harbour families expressed much discontent about the new arrangements, and he feared that "much abuse will be hailed against us."[52] Throughout 1931-1934, Hoffe had to fend off complaints about tight credit and surreptitious government efforts to replace traditional white flour with supposedly more healthy, if cheaper, brown flour.[53] In 1932, worried about more threats of violence, Baine, Johnston prevailed upon Battle Harbour's Anglican minister, D.C. Noel, to pressure the government to increase guaranteed payment to the firm from $800.00 to $2,500.00. At this time, Baine, Johnston was only too happy to let Noel play an increased role in doling out relief. The Company could see the end of Dominion government coming as Newfoundland tottered on the brink of financial ruin, and accordingly tightened relief in fear the government would not honour its commitments.[54] By 1933 the government appointed its own official, Neil, to begin taking

[50]*Ibid.*, Deputy Colonial Secretary to Tom Collingwood, Baine, Johnston & Co. Ltd., St. John's, 25 October 1930.

[51]PANL, Baine, Johnston & Co., Battle Harbour Letters, P7/A/2, Box 22B, 1927; 1929-32; Baine, Johnston and Co. Ltd. to S. Loveridge, St. John's, 5 November 1930.

[52]*Ibid.*, S. Loveridge to Baine, Johnston & Co., Battle Harbour, 21 November 1930.

[53]*Ibid.*, Correspondence between Loveridge and Baine, Johnston & Co., 11 June, 2 September, 10-16 October 1931; 3 October 1932.

[54]*Ibid.*, Baine, Johnston and Co. to S. Loveridge, 10 October 1932.

over relief responsibilities, and Rev. Noel took charge of certifying relief cases so that government would pay Baine, Johnston. Through 1934 Neil administered relief and, in 1935, the Commission Government appointed a Ranger,[55] Glendinning, to administer relief, although he would relieve only a small number of the most destitute.[56] No evidence remains to suggest how those families Glendinning would not relieve survived. They probably continued to eke out a living from the fishery as best they could, perhaps even moving off the coast in search of work.

While no other threats of violence appear to have been made, households that either did not receive, or did not ask for relief refused to acquiesce in Baine, Johnston's continued restriction of credit. Local dealers who did not like the Company's low prices offered for fish, or the lack of credit, in Loveridge's words "put the pistol to our heads (so to speak) for to barter some of the remains of fish that were on their hands or otherwise they would barter at Morgans."[57] These fishermen sold salmon to anyone who might pay in cash. Loveridge's successor S.D. Grant charged that these families behaved as they did "to protect themselves for the winter and want us or somebody to feed them this fall. It is coming to a point where the supply system must end or find some means of protection against such treatment."[58]

Baine, Johnston replied that they did not "see why we should carry dealers on, who in the past, and especially this year, shipped their salmon and fish clear of us; in other words those who haven't played the game in the past ...."[59] In fact, Baine, Johnston was "firmly opposed to winter credit because it has proven ... that the fishermen have enough to do to look after their summer accounts ...," but they would supply "thoroughly reliable dealers" who did not carry too much debt on their accounts.[60] Two firms in particular, Morris and Monroe, continued to compete with Baine, Johnston. The firm cautioned Grant not to tolerate competition, but that he

---

[55]In 1935 Hope Simpson, the new British Commissioner responsible for Newfoundland's Justice Department, reorganized the colony's magistracy and police to establish a Ranger Force responsible for all aspects of criminal and civil administration in Newfoundland's outports. A quasi-military force, the Rangers attended almost everything from customs duties, medical services, and implementation of agricultural innovations to policing outport communities. Yet from 1935 to 1940 most Rangers spent from half to three-quarters of their time overseeing government relief programs. After Confederation, the Rangers were amalgamated with the RCMP. See Marilyn Tuck, "The Newfoundland Ranger Force, 1935-1950," unpublished MA thesis, Memorial University of Newfoundland, 1983, 54-60, 74-83, 98-108.

[56]*Ibid.*, Box 23B, Correspondence between Charles Hoffe, S. Loveridge, and Baine, Johnston & Co., 16 February, 16 November 1933; 16 October, 10 November, 10-12 December 1934, 14 November 1936.

[57]*Ibid.*, Box 22B, S. Loveridge to Baine, Johnston & Co. Ltd., Battle Harbour, 22 October 1932.

[58]*Ibid.*, Box 23B, S.D. Grant to Baine, Johnston & Co., Battle Harbour, 18 August 1936.

[59]*Ibid.*, Baine, Johnston & Co. to S.D. Grant, 24 September 1936.

[60]*Ibid.*, 25 September 1936.

must give supplies to keep the firm's potential supply of fish available because they did not "believe the codfishery is done, and some of those who are scared and talking blue ruin, may be next year they will have a different tune, and although I told you to be careful about supplies, I leave you to use your discretion."[61]

In a time of crisis during the Great Depression, then, fishermen did not restrict their response to the increased severity of merchant capital's exploitation by telling self-mystifying cuffers, stealing food from each other, or dressing up during Christmas to go house-to-house and redistribute their anxieties. The fishermen of Battle Harbour did not limit their responses to Baine, Johnston to cuffers, scoffs, or mummering. These customs probably were an important part of the lives of Battle Harbour's fishing families. But such "traditions" must be reinterpreted in light of the more overt manner in which fishing families did challenge merchant capital over the issues of winter credit and relief.

In a society in which differentiation did occur among household productive units, some of the better-off fishermen chose, when Baine, Johnston began to restrict winter credit, to break away from the firm and deal on better terms with other traders. Their actions cannot be seen simply as a passive "leakage" in the merchant credit system, but represented an active rejection of merchant capital's right to dominate fishermen's lives. If the actions of these fishermen were not an abstract economic force, neither should they be regarded merely as profit-maximizing opportunism by proto-capitalist entrepreneurs. The language of conflict between Gus Bradley and Loveridge, between Jeremiah Thoms and Baine, Johnston, were as much about the manner in which the firm reneged on its customary credit obligations, and other no less important, if "smaller" customs, like treating fishermen with respect and not being "nippy" about providing lunches when fishermen came to deal at Baine, Johnston's wharves and stores.

The fishermen of Battle Harbour were no more proletarians than they were capitalists. Despite this, fishing families, as a form of non-industrial labour, could resist the effects of their reliance on a merchant capital-dominated fishery for a livelihood. Fishermen controlled the daily production of fish as a commodity. This control gave fishermen power in society, although as Gus Bradley's case demonstrates, this power was distributed unequally. It consisted in the ability to determine whether or not a merchant might get enough fish to have a good year, and to demand that merchants treat producers with "tact" or respect.

The struggles which developed between fishermen, Baine, Johnston, and the Newfoundland government in themselves constitute a definition of a moral economy as "... a consistent traditional view of social norms and obligations, of the proper economic functions of several parties within the community ...."[62] This is not to argue that Battle Harbour fishermen's efforts restored the edifice of the moral economy. By the 1930s, irreparable cracks in the surface of Battle Harbour society

---

[61]*Ibid.*, Baine, Johnston & Co. to S.D. Grant, St. John's, 3 March 1939.

[62]E.P. Thompson, "The Moral Economy of the English Crowd in the Eighteenth Century," *Past and Present*, 50 (February 1971), 79.

had begun to appear. "Leakage" was the internal contradiction of a cod fishery in crisis. As the winter supply obligations of truck disintegrated, fishermen did turn to Baine, Johnston's new competitors on the Battle Harbour coast; they turned to the marketplace to find a fair return for their labour that Baine, Johnston would no longer concede. But it is in such a break between fishermen and Baine, Johnston that one can find demarcated the boundaries of Battle Harbour's moral economy.[63] The actions of Battle Harbour fishermen like Gus Bradley or James Pye implied that they held traditional notions about *fair* prices for fish, or giving Baine, Johnston a *fair* share of their fish in return for *fair* winter credit allowances. These fishermen, already participating in the production of staple commodities for export markets, were quick to abandon Baine, Johnston, once the firm removed the prospect of fair credit. Baine, Johnston ultimately let go of people like Bradley who could use the market to their advantage; it usually did not offer better prices or credit to recapture lost clients. Instead, when Baine, Johnston broke with tradition by allowing the marketplace to intrude overtly in their relations with fishermen (by restricting winter credit) the firm resisted the defection of their fishermen by a combination of threats *and* tact, using the assistance of the state to buttress Baine, Johnston's apparent return to tradition. To keep up such appearances, Baine, Johnston even went so far as to fire an agent who could not find a place to sit on a fence between merchant profit and fishermen's customs.

When it came to the poor whom merchants and the state thought they could neglect, fishing families took collective action to secure relief on their own behalf. Such actions resembled, on a much smaller scale, the bread riots of eighteenth-century French and English crowds in defence of a moral economy rooted in another pre-industrial context. Like these French and English rioters, fishermen at Battle Harbour did not take kindly to the inroads of capitalist market logic into the custom of winter credit. Like the eighteenth-century rioters, these fishermen found in threats to the subsistence and well-being of their families a powerful motivating force in a united action against the merchant, by threatening Baine, Johnston's agent and store, as well as anyone who might stand in the way of families taking what they needed to survive.[64]

The actions of Battle Harbour fishermen, unlike the food rioters of eighteenth-century France and England, did not pose any challenge to the structure of patriarchal authority within the District's fishing families. The food riots were often led and dominated by women in their roles as managers of the family's consumption

[63] As Peter Sinclair has shown, fishermen on Newfoundland's northwest coast were quite willing to sell fish for cash whenever the opportunity arose. Fishermen's acceptance of truck represented the absence of the alternative of cash sales in the pre-1965 fishing industry. Necessity, not tradition, forced fishing families to accept truck. When alternatives appeared, some families abandoned truck's exploitation, but within the context of a struggle over social customs that were the legacy of a moral economy negotiated around truck at Battle Harbour. See Sinclair, *From Traps to Draggers*, 48-9.

[64] George Rudé, *The Crowd in History 1730-1848* (London 1964, 1981), 19-46.

and reproduction. It was women who began to protest as they arrived at a bakery or market only to find merchants 'unjustly' raising the price of bread, or limiting its availability. For these women, marketing was a facet of their everyday lives.[65]

The families of Battle Harbour, like families in other staple-based societies and economies, differed in that export-oriented production intensified the sexual division of labour within households. Women focused their productive activity on family maintenance throughout the year, while men concentrated on the work associated with the production and export of the staple commodity. In such households, the male family head continued to appropriate all the surplus of the family through his dominance over the market nexus of the staple, and his ownership of the household's property.

The organization of household production in the fishery of a place like Battle Harbour intensified this form of patriarchy. Household production in agricultural societies, such as in nineteenth-century Ontario, eventually gave rise to indigenous markets for much of what had been women's non-waged work within the household.[66] In Newfoundland, even such limited opportunities for women to engage in activities relating to the world outside the household did not exist in a place like Battle Harbour. In such fishing communities, women played crucial roles with their reproductive labour, and, along with other family members, as curers of fish. But in the inshore fishery, men dominated ownership of the means of production more completely than in any other staple-based activity. Only men owned the boats and gear used in the fishery. The fishery did not give rise to local markets on the coast of Labrador, and the region's harsh soil and climate provided no basis for the kinds of indigenous market activity farm women undertook in Ontario. Moreover, fishing boats were the only means of travel among Battle Harbour District communities. At the Village of Battle Harbour, men alone usually dealt with the Company; they were the ones who actually had access to boats so that they might travel to Baine, Johnston's premises.[67]

Among the more desperate of Battle Harbour's families (those like Levi Spearing's or Arch Rumbold's) the threat of violence, the threat of something like a riot, was a blunt sanction against a merchant's unwillingness to play fair in keeping with traditional expectations that it would sustain families throughout the winter. Although it entailed only a solitary threat of violence, the importance of the actions of Spearing and Rumbold should not be underestimated. The two men brought to a boiling point tensions over the restriction of winter credit which had been simmering between Battle Harbour District's fishermen and Baine, Johnston. Anxious to keep a lid on such a difficult situation, both the Company and the state

[65] Louise A. Tilly and Joan W. Scott, *Women, Work, and Family* (New York 1981), 55-6.
[66] Marjorie Griffin Cohen, *Women's Work, Markets, and Economic Development in Nineteenth-Century Ontario* (Toronto 1988), 29-59.
[67] On women's productive and reproductive roles in the Newfoundland fishery, see Marilyn Porter, "'She was Skipper of the Shore-Crew': Notes on the History of the Sexual Division of Labour in Newfoundland," *Labour/Le Travail*, 15 (Spring 1985), 105-22.

reconsidered carefully their position on winter credit. Fishermen did not overturn merchant capital, but they did force it to turn to the state for a relief system to replace what was lost in the winter credit system, without any cost to Baine, Johnston. The actions of Battle Harbour fishermen joined those of people across Newfoundland during the 1930s. As recent work by Jim Overton suggests, riots, or the threat of riots, everywhere forced both Dominion and, later, Commission Governments to either maintain, or increase relief allowances.[68]

It is important to see that family well-being was the fundamental basis of fishermen's conflicts with the state and Baine, Johnston concerning winter relief at Battle Harbour in the 1930s. When merchant capital looked to the state for relief provisions, it did so in the first instance because Baine, Johnston restricted winter credit due to the "leakage" caused by some fishermen trading with the competitors of their old suppliers. This "leakage" represented fishermen exercising their power over the control of the supply of fish to sanction a firm which restricted credit. Fishermen who could not elsewhere find credit, especially for the winter, demanded, with threats of violence, that Baine, Johnston fulfill its customary role in helping their families survive a winter. These demands forced the company to turn to the state. The Newfoundland government had to concede relief because it had to acknowledge that in outport Newfoundland, the state had little actual means of enforcing a rule of law over custom. Government relief at Battle Harbour represented a compromise between the state and merchant capital to protect the latter's interests. But this compromise was essentially a concession to fishermen's claims. Fishermen's "traditions" included the ability to challenge and negotiate the terms of their exploitation by Baine, Johnston. Battle Harbour fishermen, whether they broke away from Baine, Johnston and dealt with other firms, or openly threatened the firm's Battle Harbour premises, when Baine, Johnston tightened winter credit, showed a tremendous capacity to challenge the hegemony of merchant capital over both society and the state.

[68]Jim Overton, "Public Relief and Social Unrest in Newfoundland in the 1930s: an Evaluation of the Ideas of Piven and Cloward," in Gregory S. Kealey, ed., *Class, Gender, and Region: Essays in Canadian Historical Sociology* (St. John's 1988), 153-66.

I would like to thank Rosemary Ommer, Gregory Kealey, Jim Overton, Mark Leier, and the anonymous readers of Labour/Le Travail *for their criticisms of earlier drafts of this paper. Thanks also to the organizers of the Atlantic Canada Workshop at St. Mary's University, Fall 1989, where the first version of this paper was presented.*

Eugene A. Forsey

14

Labour and the Constitution in Atlantic Canada

I can hardly say what an honour and pleasure it is for me to be here, especially in view of my long acquaintance with Sackville. I almost have a feeling of coming home when I come to Sackville because I have so very many happy memories of times spent here, notably with Senator Josiah Wood and his family. Senator Wood was a friend of my grandmother's when she was at Mount Allison Ladies' College in 1861, and the families have been friends ever since, generation after generation. Mount Allison is in my blood. Both of my parents were graduates and I heard about Mount Allison from the word go in my life. I could deliver an entire evening's reminiscences of great Mount Allison figures because I heard so much of them from my mother and from Winthrop Bell, a friend of ours for many years. When Mother would stop, Winthrop would begin, and *vice versa*. However, that is not what I am supposed to be here for tonight.

When I was thinking over what I would say, I reflected that I have really three claims to speak on this subject tonight.

The first is the fact that, though I have spent most of my life in Ottawa and Montréal, I am *not* an Upper Canadian. I am a fifth-generation Newfoundlander born. My ancestors were in Nova Scotia before the American Revolution and immediately afterwards. Some of them were Loyalists, some pre-Loyalists. I am, I always say, a Maritimer *in partibus infidelium*.

The second title that I have to speak on the subject, "Labour and the Constitution in Atlantic Canada," is that I was for 27 years in the labour movement, and I think in that time succeeded in learning something about it. I was especially interested in the Atlantic provinces where, in fact, the Canadian labour movement started. The first union I could discover, when working on my history of trade unions in Canada, was in Saint John, New Brunswick, during the war of 1812-14, and I

Published with the permission of the Centre for Canadian Studies, Mount Allison University. From *Perspective on the Atlantic Canadian Labour Movement* (Sackville 1985), 9-25. This was a speech delivered by the late Senator Forsey.

was determined that in that study the unions of this part of the country should get their due share of attention.

My third reason for having some title to speak on this subject is that for a great many years I have been reading, studying, speaking, writing, and teaching on the Canadian constitution. I may say that my reputation as a constitutional authority is, I think, vastly overblown, but I do know something about the constitution and, in fact, a good deal about certain parts of it.

If the intentions of the Fathers of Confederation had been carried out, however, I should not have had to give this lecture. Although few people realize it, the Fathers of Confederation undoubtedly thought and intended that the whole question of labour legislation and industrial relations should come under the Dominion Parliament. The Trade Union Act of 1872, for example, was passed through Parliament — with scarcely a murmur of opposition — by the government of Sir John A. Macdonald, which contained eight Fathers of Confederation. They included the Minister of Justice, Sir Alexander Campbell, and they knew very well what they were doing. When Sir John came in for the second time, with a government including five Fathers of Confederation, he returned to this broad subject and introduced four successive factory bills, arguing strenuously that they were within the power of the Parliament of Canada. The attempt to pass a Dominion Factory Act did not succeed, and from that time on it was generally considered that the whole question of factory legislation rested with the provinces and not with the Dominion. Yet clearly the Fathers of Confederation had not thought so.

The belief that industrial relations legislation rested with the Parliament of Canada survived much longer. In 1907 the Liberal government, which strongly favoured provincial rights, introduced Mr. Mackenzie King's masterpiece, the Industrial Disputes Investigation Act or Lemieux Act, providing for conciliation and regulation of strikes across the whole country. It lasted until 1925, when the Judicial Committee of the Privy Council — I always call them the wicked stepfathers of Confederation — proceeded with their task of turning the constitution largely inside out. The Judicial Committee threw out the Lemieux Act as being beyond the powers of Parliament. Industrial relations matters were to be within the jurisdiction of the provinces, with the implied exception of the ten per cent of the Canadian workforce which was employed in industries clearly under Dominion jurisdiction, such as interprovincial railways, banking, shipping, later on air transport and international and interprovincial highways. The committee's decision created inconvenience for the provinces and a number of them, notably Nova Scotia and New Brunswick, proceeded almost immediately to provide that the Lemieux Act should apply to purely provincial industries.

The first collective bargaining legislation in the country was the Nova Scotia Trade Union Act of 1937, and it shone for many years as a good deed in a naughty world. Or so it did in the opinion of the trade union movement; this was perhaps not so unanimous an opinion in all classes of society. Then came the war, and for most practical purposes the War Measures Act became the constitution of Canada.

All industries, provincial or otherwise, came under Dominion jurisdiction for the time being, and in 1943 the government of Canada passed an Order in Council making collective bargaining compulsory in all industries across the country. After the war, this was followed up by the Industrial Relations and Disputes Investigation Act, which provided for legalized, compulsory collective bargaining in all Dominion industries. This again raised the question of whether legislation could be devised that would cover some provincial industries as well, and several provinces — notably Nova Scotia, New Brunswick, and Prince Edward Island — proceeded to pass acts of their own in which they inserted a clause saying that by agreement with the government of Canada they could entrust the administration of their Labour Relations Acts to the Canada Labour Board. (This is the well-known device of administrative delegation.) Yet in this case nothing ever came of it, for the clauses have not been put into effect.

That being so, one might ask whether anything more can be said about labour and the constitution in the Atlantic provinces. The provinces have virtually complete jurisdiction over labour legislation, collective bargaining, trade unions, and all the rest of it, and so what is the use of going on? For reasons which I hope will become apparent, it is indeed worthwhile to go on.

One reason is the fact that the matter of the legislative jurisdiction of the Dominion and the provinces does not comprise the whole of the Canadian constitution, despite the tendency of law schools to confine the study of constitutional law to this area.

Another reason lies in the existence of certain special features of the British North America Act which survive even in the supposedly new Constitution of 1982. In reality, nearly all of the Act of 1867 is still in force, including the power of the Government of Canada to disallow provincial Acts within one year of their arrival in Ottawa, and the power of the Lieutenant-Governor to reserve provincial bills for the signification of the Governor General's pleasure. A Lieutenant-Governor may also refuse assent to a bill, outright, and in fact this has been done 28 times in various provinces, the last occasion being in Prince Edward Island in 1945. A reserved bill goes to Ottawa in a state of suspended animation, and does not come into force unless within one year it receives the assent of the Governor General in Council.

That the powers of disallowance and reservation were left in the Act of 1982 is rather surprising, because the Dominion's power to disallow provincial Acts is tied to the Queen's power to disallow Dominion Acts; and the Lieutenant-Governor's power to reserve provincial bills is tied to the Governor General's power to reserve Dominion bills. Both might have been seen as vestiges of colonialism of the kind deplored by the fervidly nationalist government of Mr. Trudeau. Yet in 1982 these provisions were, in effect, deliberately re-enacted. It is quite impossible, therefore, to say that the power of the Dominion to nullify provincial legislation has become obsolete. It still remains, and could conceivably be invoked.

The existence of both powers, reservation and disallowance, became an important issue during what I shall call the battle of Prince Edward Island, 1948. In 1945 the Prince Edward Island Legislature had passed a Trade Union Act which was practically a carbon copy of the Nova Scotia Act of 1937. In 1946 it added a proviso that the provincial government, through the provincial secretary, could set down rules for the formation of trade unions and the election of their officers. This gave a considerable power to the government. In 1947 there was a packinghouse strike across the country. It extended to Prince Edward Island and prompted an annoyed provincial government to decide that the existing law was inadequate to deal with it. The government accordingly passed an amending act in March 1948 which said in effect that, except on the Canadian National Railways, there would be no unions in Prince Edward Island except purely local unions made up of Island residents. Even local unions would be unable to strike without arbitration — to which the provincial government would be a party — and would have to have a licence from the Provincial Secretary. The Provincial Secretary could refuse a licence, or could cancel a licence at any time, thus holding a sword of Damocles over the heads of even the most purely provincial unions.

This of course stirred up the labour movement like an egg-whisk. At that time, there were four major labour bodies in the country. One was the Catholic Unions of Québec, which had no members in Prince Edward Island and did not care much about the issue one way or another. The railway operating brotherhoods, the aristocrats of labour, were not directly affected but were alarmed at the possibility of the legislation being copied elsewhere in Canada. They joined on this matter with the Trades and Labor Congress of Canada — the old and respectable organization founded in 1883 — and with the new Canadian Congress of Labour, which was only eight years old and which the Trades and Labor Congress rather looked down on as an upstart. The first thing that happened was that the Canadian Congress of Labour jumped the gun on the others and tried to get the government of Canada to instruct the Lieutenant-Governor to reserve this bill. The bill had been brought in on March 17th. It received second reading the next day and assent on the 25th. While it was still not yet law, we in the Canadian Congress of Labour thus went after the Dominion government to stop the process. I drew up the memorandum giving our reasons for this. We pointed out that the bill was contrary to Dominion policy, which recognized trade unions as proper and legitimate. We pointed out that the situation was not one of urgency; not even the government was claiming that an emergency existed. We pointed out that the bill was discriminatory. It discriminated against Prince Edward Island workers in comparison with other workers. It discriminated between the Prince Edward Island workers on the railway and the other Prince Edward Island workers. It discriminated among citizens of Prince Edward Island by preventing unions from belonging to national and international organizations while bodies such as the Rotary Club, the Masons, and others could continue to do so.

Yet the Dominion government did not act, despite our arguments. The three union organizations then got together and drew up a petition to the government of Canada to exercise its other major power with respect to provincial legislation: that of disallowance. At least they ordered it to be drawn up. I drew it up. I am afraid I sound rather egotistical in these matters, but I was really in the middle of these affairs. My employers, the Canadian Congress of Labour, knew that I had some interest in the constitution and some knowledge of it. Whenever they faced a crisis involving governments or legislatures they invited me, as it were, to marry my knowledge of the constitution with my knowledge of trade unions. Repeatedly I did so: to their satisfaction, I am glad to say. This time, now that the bill had become law, we set to work to have it disallowed. Despite a legal opinion favourable to our case from the Dean of the Faculty of Law at the University of Toronto, it would have been very difficult to have the law set aside by the courts, especially in view of the time limit of one year within which disallowance must take place. Nowadays, the first thing a union would do would be to appeal to the section of the Charter of Rights and Freedoms which safeguards freedom of association. This did not exist in 1948. The old British North America Act had a very few guaranteed rights, but for the most part you could not get an Act set aside unless you could prove that the enacting authority had invaded the jurisdiction of another authority: that the Dominion had "jumped the fence into the provincial garden," or *vice versa*. To say that a bill was discriminatory or that it denied freedom of association would mean nothing to the courts.

We therefore went on to argue that there were many reasons for disallowance other than the question of the power of the legislature to pass the law. We went into statements by the Fathers of Confederation to this effect, as well as looking at Sir John A. Macdonald's first report on how the power of disallowance should be used, and at court commentaries and the precedents established by a long series of Ministers of Justice in recommending disallowance. The reasons given were manifold. The power of disallowance is not limited in any way, except that it *must* take place within one year of the time the act arrives in Ottawa. Otherwise, the government of Canada can disallow any provincial act for any reason it sees fit. A vast number of reasons had been given in the past, notably that the act in question was contrary to reason, justice, and natural equity; that it was discriminatory; that it was hasty or unwise legislation; that it was an invasion of the rights of property. We rehearsed a long litany of these reasons, given by Ministers of Justice of both political parties down to the last disallowance of 1943. Each province had had acts disallowed except Prince Edward Island, which bore away the palm for the number of bills reserved but had never had any act actually disallowed. We rehearsed this litany of reasons, and argued that the government of Canada should proceed now to disallow this act. We sent a delegation from the three union organizations to interview the Cabinet, and were received by the Minister of Justice, the Solicitor-General, the Secretary of State, and the Postmaster-General. Why, exactly, the Postmaster-General always puzzles me, but anyway there they were. Our delegation included three from the Trades and Labor Congress, five from the Canadian Congress of Labour (of whom I was one), and two from the railway operating brotherhoods.

Despite arguing the case before this committee of Cabinet, we did not get disallowance. Yet we did get what we wanted. This I did not discover for many years, until Professor Frank MacKinnon told me that after this performance had gone on he was down on the Island and he went to see the Premier, Walter Jones. The Premier said to him: "You know that Prince Edward Island Trade Union Act that we passed last year. The Dominion government sent Mr. Ilsley, the senior Maritime minister, down here to tell us that either we repealed it, or we took out the offending sections, or it would be disallowed."

That was 1948, and it is interesting that many people regard disallowance as having been as dead as mutton since the power was last used in 1943. Yet here in 1948, you had the Dominion government threatening its use. The government of Prince Edward Island proceeded in the next session to put through the legislature a bill which took the stuffing out of the act of 1948. Thus, we won a victory, even though it was not immediately obvious why we had won it. Anybody could see that the Act had had the stuffing taken out of it, but the Dominion had not been seen to intervene. The fact was that it *had* intervened, *sub rosa* and behind the scenes, and we had got what we wanted. We were inclined, long afterwards, to feel that we had not done too badly in spite of the fact that our specific requests had been turned down.

So much, then, for the battle of Prince Edward Island, 1948 and on to the much more formidable battle of Newfoundland in 1959. Here there existed a situation where, on the face of it, for most of the unions in the province, the provincial legislature was sovereign. It could do anything it liked, provided it did not invade some field of Dominion jurisdiction, and provided it was not stopped by the process of reservation or disallowance. Most people by that time were inclined to regard reservation and disallowance as obsolete in view of the increased importance of the provinces in Dominion-provincial relations. The government of Canada, they believed, would never dare to use this power. Many were inclined also to believe that the provinces had become more enlightened, and that no province would now do the kind of thing that Prince Edward Island had in 1948. Then took place in Newfoundland in 1959 the passage of legislation dealing with trade unions, beside which the Prince Edward Island Act of eleven years before was commonplace, innocent, harmless.

By that time, the Trades and Labor Congress and the Canadian Congress of Labour had merged to become the Canadian Labour Congress. Some of the operating brotherhoods had stayed out, but for the most part — except for the Catholic or former Catholic unions now composing the Confederation of National Trade Unions — there was now a united labour movement. Early in the career of the new Congress, one of its unions went into Newfoundland and organized the woodworkers. The International Woodworkers of America succeeded in organizing the loggers employed by the two big companies there, or by their contractors: the Anglo-Newfoundland Development Company, and the numerous contractors for the Bowaters Newfoundland pulp and paper mills. Local 2254 was for the Anglo-

Newfoundland employees, and local 2255 for the Bowaters people. Local 2254 went through all the processes prescribed by the Newfoundland Labour Relations Act, including accepting a conciliation report which the company rejected, before it finally took a strike vote and came out on strike. All this had been perfectly legal. Nobody has ever questioned the fact that local 2254 followed to the letter every prescription in the Labour Relations Act. The other local, perhaps discouraged by the failure of local 2254 to make progress through its scrupulous following of legal procedures, then lost patience and struck without going through those procedures at all. The one strike, therefore, was perfectly legal, and the other, illegal.

The government could have proceeded against the second union for breaking the Act. It did not do so. It could have applied, or had the employers apply, for decertification of both unions. It did not apply. No steps available under the law were taken. Yet the employers were incensed by having to deal with a real union, and a strong one. They had never had this experience before, and they now brought pressure upon the government. The government responded by introducing two bills to deal with the situation. One of them — the Trade Union Emergency Provisions Act — simply decertified the two locals. That disposed of both of them immediately. They were dead, finished. But the government had tasted blood, and were not satisfied with this. They wanted to assume the power to make sure that no union, whether national or international, would be able to do anything they did not like. Hence the second act, amending the Labour Relations Act. This applied to all unions, except those in industries under Dominion jurisdiction, and it was an astonishing performance.

The amending act provided in the first place that when it appeared to the Lieutenant-Governor in Council — that is, the provincial cabinet — that a substantial number of the officers, agents, or representatives of any union or body of unions outside the province had been guilty of a heinous crime (such as trafficking in narcotics, perjury, embezzlement, manslaughter, and so on), then the Lieutenant-Governor might cancel the certification of the union. This was an astonishingly sweeping power. If it *appeared* to the Lieutenant-Governor that a substantial number of officers of the union, elsewhere in Canada or more likely in the United States in the case of an international union, had been guilty, then that was enough to decertify the particular local union or unions concerned in Newfoundland. What was a substantial number? The Lieutenant-Governor in Council would decide. Would the persons in question actually have had to be convicted? No. Was there any provision for a hearing? No. The Lieutenant-Governor in Council might cancel the certification by mere fiat and without any legal proof. The thing was so broadly worded that it would have applied to an extraordinary number and variety of individuals and organizations, for even affiliation was enough. Most of the national and international unions were affiliated with the Canadian Labour Congress, for example, so that any *appearance* of guilt on the part of officers of the congress, or even on the part of those of the International Confederation of Free Trade Unions with which the congress in turn was affiliated, would be sufficient for decertification of a local union.

The amending act also had a provision which in effect forbade strikes. It forbade a number of other things as well, such as secondary boycotts and secondary picketing. Some of its other provisions extended not only to officers, agents, or representatives of the union, but also to members. One of them prescribed that the Lieutenant-Governor in Council could decertify a union if an injunction, other than an interim injunction, had been issued against the union or against any officer, agent, representative, or *member* of the union. The injunction did not have to have been violated: the Lieutenant-Governor could step in even if it had been obeyed completely. Another provision made unions sueable for tortious acts in connection with a trade dispute, but gave them no right to sue somebody who committed a tortious act against them: this was clearly discriminatory, and again applied not only to officers, agents, or representatives, but also to individual members. Provision was made, moreover, that if the Labour Relations Board was considering decertification for the perfectly legitimate reasons specified in the original Labour Relations Act — that is if, for example, a union had lost its majority, or some other union came in and got a majority — then the Lieutenant-Governor in Council could intervene and decertify the union by his own fiat, completely setting aside the jurisdiction of the board. If that happened, the union could not be certified in any future proceedings without the express permission of the provincial cabinet. For greater certainty, the Lieutenant-Governor in Council could take possession of the assets of a dissolved union and dispose of them as he saw fit. So that this wretched union, whatever it was, which may have simply *appeared* to have somewhere, somehow, somebody who had been guilty, so the Lieutenant-Governor in Council thought, of certain specified crimes, could not only be decertified but also lose control of its assets. The Lieutenant-Governor in Council could hand them over to the Salvation Army, or to the poor of St. John's, or to the Anglo-Newfoundland Development Company, or simply add them to the consolidated revenue fund of the province. There was absolutely no restriction at all.

Now these things sound rather outlandish. I could use stronger language, and did at that time. The legislation was extraordinary, punitive, and outrageous. It was true that after the two strikes had begun there had been a good deal of violence on the picket lines and a constable had been killed. This was undoubtedly a factor in the reaction of the provincial government to the situation. I still think, however, that it does not justify the particular action that the provincial government and the legislature took. I still think the trouble should have been dealt with by the ample means provided by the existing laws, and that the existing laws should not have been set aside and superseded by two acts that were arbitrary and extreme in a way unparalleled in the history of Dominion or provincial legislation. Nobody had ever seen anything like it before. The Trade Union Emergency Provisions Act decertified both locals of the International Woodworkers of America alike, even though one of them had scrupulously observed every bit of the law relating to trade unions. This discriminated between the local which had behaved itself and the local which had not, and seemed to us an illegitimate way of proceeding. The more general amending act was a very sweeping piece of legislation indeed, and wholly without judicial safeguards.

That, then, was what we were faced with. I was even more in the middle of this affair than in the case of the earlier Prince Edward Island dispute. The government of Newfoundland kept the bills under wraps, except of course from the legislature. It gave no notice and allowed no representations. Nobody, except those in the legislature, knew what was in the legislation. There were reports in the newspapers, but they were not of much use. If we were going to ask the government of Canada to act in the matter, we had to know exactly what the bills said. So I became a sort of animated telephone. I called the union's lawyer in St. John's, and he read the bills to me over the telephone. Then I called the Minister of Justice, Davie Fulton, who was a close friend, and said, "Davie, do you know what's in those Newfoundland bills?" "No," he replied, "we haven't seen them." I had jotted them all down, and so I read them out to him. I think we actually asked the government of Canada to have the bills reserved for the signification of the Governor General's pleasure, a power which the Lieutenant-Governor was supposed normally to exercise upon the instructions of the Dominion government. In any event, the bills went through with lightning speed and did receive assent. I have heard it reported, by people who ought to know, that the Dominion government did instruct the Lieutenant-Governor to exercise his power to reserve. Yet he did not reserve; he gave assent. So then we plunged into the whole business of disallowance.

The request of the Canadian Labour Congress for disallowance of the two acts was based on substantially the same reasoning in each case. We pointed out the history of the whole power of disallowance, and what the Fathers of Confederation had said about it. We pointed out what Sir John A. Macdonald had laid down as criteria for the use of the power in his report of June 18th, 1868, which was intended to guide subsequent Ministers of Justice for the rest of the existence of the country. His report had made it perfectly clear that the issue need not simply concern the power of the province. A thing might be perfectly within the power of the province and still be objectionable: objectionable because it was unconstitutional in the broad sense; objectionable because it was an invasion of private rights; objectionable because it was unjust and inequitable. Macdonald himself had recommended disallowance of particular acts, notably the three Ontario Streams Acts which he disallowed three times over. We pointed out what had been done by Minister of Justice after Minister of Justice in the 112 cases of disallowance. We argued that the Newfoundland acts comprised discriminatory legislation, that they were unjust and oppressive, that they formed part of a scheme of oppression of workers. These phrases were all taken from previous disallowances. We gave a detailed, careful, point-by-point account of the whole history of disallowance with references. There was no question of embroidery. In most of the cases where disallowance had taken place on grounds of invasion of rights, the issue had involved property rights. We suggested that the government of Canada should not seem to give priority to property rights over the rights of workers, in its use of the power of disallowance, for this would enable Marxist critics to portray the government as simply the representative of the employing class. It would be said that the government would staunchly defend the rights of the employing class, but would do nothing when the rights of workers were invaded. We did not ourselves say that, but we hinted that we hoped that no government of Canada would discriminate in favour of property against workers.

We then went on to point out that, while there were theoretically other ways of dealing with this situation — other than through disallowance — they had real disadvantages. One possibility was to let somebody complain to the courts, and thus prompt a test case, but we said that would not do. It would be far too slow, and in the absence of a charter of rights and freedoms it was very doubtful anyway whether the courts would find grounds to set aside the acts. The test case would also be very expensive, and the unions would be compelled to pay considerable sums to defend what was really a public right, not a private one. The further possibility of a reference case by the Governor General in Council, asking the Supreme Court whether this was valid legislation, would have been quicker but would still have been expensive and uncertain as to the result. So we said that this would not be adequate. Indeed, as we pointed out, our ground of objection to the acts was not essentially based on a matter of law or jurisdiction. It was not that the province had exceeded its jurisdiction, not that it had "jumped the fence," but instead it was a matter of public policy. The province was doing something which was contrary to one of the standards that Sir John A. Macdonald and other Justice ministers had laid down, contrary to Dominion legislation and Dominion policy. The Dominion had passed one piece of legislation after another which indicated plainly that trade unions were legitimate and proper. It had passed an amendment to the criminal code which penalized employers for violating certain rights which this legislation destroyed for the workers of Newfoundland. We argued, therefore, that this was a question of the general interests of Canada, that it was not purely a provincial matter even if the legislation had been within the legal power of the province, and that the only effective remedy was disallowance.

We made this case as thoroughly as we could, I think, although I am perhaps a little prejudiced because I drew up the petition. Still, we did not get disallowance. The government was confronted with a situation where it had two courses of action, two different aspects of the situation, presented to it. The R.C.M.P. was doing the policing by contract with the government of Newfoundland. Confronted with the violence that existed, the R.C.M.P. asked for reinforcements — not unreasonably, in my judgment. The Canadian Labour Congress asked for disallowance of the acts. The government then took, in my view, the exact opposite course of action from what it ought to have done on the two requests. It refused to send the reinforcements, and it refused to disallow the acts. So there we are. This Draconian legislation was allowed to stand: this abominably and iniquitously penalizing legislation, this legislation which wiped out rights all over the lot, this legislation which could have crippled the whole trade union movement in Newfoundland and put practically all the unions in Newfoundland at the absolute mercy of the provincial government.

Fortunately, however, this is not quite the end of the story. Apparently our remonstrances produced some effect, little by little. The worst parts of the legislation were gradually eroded. The Trade Union Emergency Provisions Act, of course, was spent the moment it was passed. It decertified the union locals, and that was the end. They were, for all practical purposes, gone, and the International Woodworkers of America finished in Newfoundland. So that was that, as far as that act was concerned; it was too bad, but it was not the worst feature of the situation. The Labour Relations Amendment Act remained on the statute books, unchallenged in the courts — where it would probably have survived anyway — and untouched by any action of the Dominion government. In 1960, however, the provincial legislature amended the Labour Relations Amendment Act, removing or modifying certain of the offensive sections. Most important, it revised section 6a, the one that said "where it appears to the Lieutenant-Governor in Council"; this was changed to read, "where, upon the application of the Attorney General, the Supreme Court of Newfoundland is satisfied that a substantial number of officers, agents, or representatives of any union or body of unions has been guilty ...." That was an improvement, especially as they added that the Supreme Court might direct that the party concerned be entitled to a hearing. Then in 1963, the legislature had another go, and repealed the whole of section 6a. By the time a new comprehensive Act was passed in 1977, all the things we had objected to were gone.

Yet it had taken some time to achieve these happy results, and in the meantime the legislation had achieved its objects in that the two union locals had been destroyed and their parent union for all practical purposes eliminated from Newfoundland, and replaced by a tame union nearer to the heart's desire of the government. Also by 1977, of course, the provincial government responsible for these iniquitous measures had been succeeded by a different government, nearer to the heart's desire of the people of Newfoundland.

Certain comments might be made at this point as to the value of the foregoing discussion. Some might ask, for example, why I picked out two Atlantic provinces for these denunciations. Does this show a prejudice arising from having lived too long in Upper Canada? Well, the first reason for picking out two Atlantic provinces was that it was the Atlantic region I was asked to deal with. But the other thing is that in fact it was only in Prince Edward Island and Newfoundland that the kind of legislation was passed that I have described. The record of Nova Scotia and New Brunswick, incidentally, was perfectly clear in such matters. Prince Edward Island and Newfoundland, alas, were both guilty of legislation which in my judgment can be described — to use a mild term — as highly objectionable.

Another comment that might be made is to the effect that all of this history of strife can now be forgotten, since the Charter of Rights and Freedoms will ensure that such things can never happen again. That is true on the face of it, until you notice that the first section of the Charter says that rights — including the right of freedom of association — are subject to "such reasonable limits prescribed by law as can demonstrably be justified in a free and democratic society." What the courts will make of that, nobody knows. My guess is that they will probably interpret it pretty reasonably; but Sir John A. Macdonald said long ago of elections that they were "like horse races — you know more about them after they're run." Judicial decisions are a little like that too. You know more about them after they have been handed down, and sometimes some get handed down that appear even to competent critics to be rather odd. So you cannot be absolutely sure that some restrictive legislation, passed by a provincial legislature, might not be held by the courts to be protected by section 1 as reasonable and fair in a free and democratic society. Then there is section 33 of the Charter, which provides that either the Parliament of Canada or the legislature of a province, acting within its pre-1982 jurisdiction, can override section 2 of the Charter — the one that contains the right of freedom of association — and sections 7 to 15 simply by saying "notwithstanding section so-and-so." This can be valid for a renewable time period of five years. Some government, imbued with the same venom and animosity against trade unions as Mr. Smallwood's government was in 1959, might in the future avail itself of section 33, and the courts would not be able to do one thing about it.

Then you would be left with either of two courses. You could argue that the government of Canada should exercise its power to instruct the Lieutenant-Governor of the province involved to refuse assent to the legislation or reserve it for consideration by the Governor General in Council. Or, if the bill has already been signed and has become an act, you could petition the government of Canada for disallowance. These would still have to be the recourses of an injured party in these matters. While it would be nice to think that we are now so enlightened, so fair-minded, and so judicious in our attitudes that nothing could ever happen again such as happened in Prince Edward Island in 1948 or in Newfoundland in 1959, I do not think we can count on it. Public opinion is very volatile, and gusts of public opinion can sway the minds of legislators. We all remember what happened to the Japanese-Canadians. We all remember what happened in Québec with the Padlock Act. We all remember the kinds of things, the high jinks, that Mr. Aberhart tried to get on with in Alberta: notably the Alberta Press Bill, which was reserved by the Lieutenant-Governor and never came into effect. What happened before could, I am afraid, conceivably happen again, and this is a matter of importance to all of us in any province. We cannot forget either that we are now living in an age when neo-conservatism — with its exaltation of private rights and sometimes, I fear, its insufficient appreciation of the rule of law in our society — may tempt governments, Dominion or provincial, to do things which a later generation may look back on and deplore.

Now, perhaps the Charter may give governments the necessary nerve and backbone to use their power to deal with nefarious provincial legislation of this kind. It would require high political courage, however, to exercise the power. There would be all kinds of temptations and pressures not to exercise it. I *hope* that any government we may have would, if the circumstances to justify it arose, not be afraid to use its power, first, to instruct the Lieutenant-Governor to reserve a bill of the kind I have been describing, and, secondly, if he gave assent, to use its power to disallow the resulting act. I hope so, but I am afraid that the precedent of 1959 in Newfoundland — a craven precedent — might encourage a government which was anxious to be on good terms with all the powerful forces in society to look the other way. I *hope* we shall have governments which will have a proper respect for traditional British rights and liberties. I know it is not popular now in some places to say anything about British tradition, but I have no shame whatever in invoking it. I *hope* we shall have governments which will have a proper respect for these traditional Canadian liberties, for they are part of our heritage wherever they came from. Both the trade union movement, however, and those of us generally who value our rights and liberties, must keep in the back of our minds the possibility of their being violated. We must stand on guard to preserve the liberties which we all should cherish, whether they are for people we like or people we do not like.

Anthony Thomson   15

The Nova Scotia Civil Service Association, 1956-1967

Public sector unionism has rapidly acquired prominence in Canada in recent years. Although the history of government employee organizations extends back to the end of the 19th century, unionism among civil servants has become increasingly extensive in the last 25 years. Government employment is now the most fully-organized sector of the Canadian workforce, and public service workers are often regarded as being exceptionally militant. In Nova Scotia civil servants, teachers, nurses, federal employees and municipal workers make up the majority of the organized workforce; the unionization of the public sector has made the difference between a declining and an expanding labour movement.[1]

These are, however, new developments. White-collar workers have in the past been generally reluctant to adopt collective strategies in the marketplace, and these feelings have been most pronounced among government employees. Despite great differences between high-ranking professionals in the civil service and lower-level clerical workers, most government employees have enjoyed security of employment and benefits generally superior to white-collar workers in the private sector. Furthermore, public employment has usually been accompanied by a service ethic which encouraged workers to identify their interests with those of management and to perceive unionism as contrary to the neutrality expected of civil servants. Blue collar public employees have been more likely to join unions than white-collar civil servants, but in recent years it has become apparent that white-collar public service

[1] Labour Canada, *Directory of Labour Organizations in Canada, 1980* (Ottawa 1981); three of the four largest unions in Canada represent municipal, federal and provincial employees. For discussions of some aspects of the growth of public sector unionism in Canada, see Anthony Thomson, "'The Large and Generous View': The Debate on Labour Affiliation in the Canadian Civil Service, 1918-1928," *Labour/Le Travailleur*, 2 (1977), 108-136; Joe Davidson and John Deverell, *Joe Davidson* (Toronto 1978); Gil Levine, "The inevitability of public sector strikes in Canada," *Labour Gazette*, LXXVII (March 1977), 117-120.

Published with the permission of the editor. From *Acadiensis*, XII, 2 (Spring 1983), 81-105.

workers have been more likely to organize unions than their counterparts in the private sector. This suggests that there are conditions in government work which are conducive to organization and points up the essential ambiguity of public sector work: the ethic of public service is balanced by the fact of dependent employment.[2]

In a relatively short period of time the civil service has undergone a major transformation. The growth of government activity since the 1940s has resulted in a great expansion in the number of municipal, provincial and federal employees. In Nova Scotia, for instance, there were about 1,900 provincial civil servants in 1953, but by 1966 this figure had doubled, and ten years afterwards the civil service included some 7,300 employees in the province.[3] Beyond the great increase in the number of public employees, there has also been a major change in the work environment. From a small and personal employment setting the civil service has become a large, impersonal bureaucracy. The resulting rationalization of employment tended to break down the paternalistic relationship which supervisors and government officials had with their civil servants, and bureaucratization has emphasized the civil servant's status as an employee with interests apart from those of the employer or manager. These changes have been accompanied by the growth of increasingly pro-union sentiments among public employees.

The modern history of civil servants in Nova Scotia has conformed to this pattern. In 1958 they created an association to protect members' interests as employees. Over the next decade the association progressively evolved towards trade unionism as members gradually recognized the inadequacies of the association and adopted an increasingly oppositional stance towards government. The year 1967 represented a high point in the history of the Nova Scotia Civil Service Association. The establishment of a joint council for association-government negotiations marked the culmination of early efforts to achieve collective bargaining. In retrospect, however, this accomplishment was already an anachronism, for by 1972 new relationships had been established with the government and the labour movement. A study of the first decade of the NSCSA enables us to understand the traditions of civil service employment, the ambiguous status of government employees and the resulting controversies which have shaped the character of the present organization.

In Nova Scotia there was no early pressure from civil servants for employee organization or civil service reform. The service was small and generalist, and historical circumstances had provided provincial employees with a special security

[2]Important discussions of the issues involved in white-collar work and public sector unionism include C. Wright Mills, *White Collar* (New York 1956); David Lockwood, *The Blackcoated Worker* (London 1958); R.M. Blackburn, *Union Character and Social Class* (London 1967); Adolf Sturmthal, *White Collar Trade Unions* (Chicago 1967); A. Stewart, K. Prandy and R.M. Blackburn, *Social Stratification and Occupations* (London 1980); P. Johnston, "The Promise of Public Sector Unionism," *Monthly Review*, XXX, 4 (1978), 1-17; Harry Braverman, *Labor and Monopoly Capital* (New York 1974).

[3] Nova Scotia Civil Service Commission [NSCSC], *Annual Report, 1954*, NSCSC, *Annual Report, 1977*.

of tenure: between 1882 and 1956, with the exception of one eight-year span, the Liberal Party had held a virtual monopoly on formal political power and civil service appointments. In 1934 a royal commission had advocated a policy of further public regulation of the economy and provincial control over natural resources to promote economic and social development. Since the implementation of such a policy required a permanent and efficient civil service, the practice of political patronage was judged an obstacle to economic progress. As one result of this report, a Civil Service Act was passed in 1935, creating a Civil Service Commission to establish a classification of positions and to make appointments by competitive examination.[4] Although removal of the patronage barrier was a necessary condition for employee organization, nearly 20 years were to pass before Nova Scotia civil servants actively pursued organization.

Public sector unionism became significant in Canada after the Second World War. The federal government had granted collective bargaining rights in 1944 to the employees of national boards and commissions.[5] In the provincial and municipal service fields, two principal unions had emerged by the early 1950s — the National Union of Public Employees (NUPE) and the National Union of Public Service Employees (NUPSE). In 1947 the Nova Scotia government responded to this trend by excluding all provincial employees from the provisions of the provincial Trade Union Act. This step was soon challenged. In 1954 Local 311 of the Canadian Union of Stationary Engineers and Allied Workers was formed, representing blue-collar workers at the Victoria General Hospital, the Nova Scotia Technical College and the Vocational Training School.[6] The union affiliated with the Canadian Congress of Labour and in the following year both the CCL and the Nova Scotia Federation of Labour demanded that full collective bargaining rights be extended to all provincial employees.[7] Nova Scotia's labour legislation was also being discussed at Dalhousie University's Institute of Public Affairs, a common meeting ground for businessmen, government officials, academics and trade union leaders. The Institute provided an opportunity to devise policy in an intellectual environment which accepted the principle of organized interest-group participation in pluralist decision-making.

[4]Nova Scotia, *Report of the Royal Commission, Provincial Economic Inquiry* (Halifax 1934), 83-8; "Report on the Civil Service," in Nova Scotia, *Royal Commission on Provincial Development and Rehabilitation* (Halifax 1944), 9-13. Under the Civil Service Act, tenure was still defined as "at pleasure," the commission could exclude any position from the provisions of the act, and deputy ministers were authorized to refuse any appointment. Also, the act did not end the use of patronage: see John Hawkins, *The Life and Times of Angus L.* (Windsor, N.S. 1969), 243.
[5]Both major labour centrals in Canada, the Trades and Labour Congress and the Canadian Congress of Labour, subsequently called for the extension of full collective bargaining rights to all government employees: *Labour Gazette*, LI (May 1951), 637-42.
[6]Kevin Reilly, "A Search for Collective Bargaining — The Nova Scotia Government Employees Association Experience," unpublished paper, 1979.
[7]*Labour Gazette*, LI (May 1951), 637.

As a result of these influences, by the mid-1950s the provincial government was prepared to adopt a more responsive stand on labour-management relations in the public sector. In the Speech from the Throne opening the 1956 session of the legislature, the Liberal government announced its intention to grant recognition to unions of public servants, with the exception of those appointed under the Civil Service Act. Based on a recommendation from Minister of Labour Clyde Nunn, the government issued an order-in-council on 8 February 1956 giving recognition to unions of workers at public boards and commissions, granting them "permission ... to act as bargaining agent," and directing that negotiations between the union and management "shall" take place "with the view to arriving at a mutually agreeable understanding." Under this order the union was granted permission to bargain rather than recognition of its right, and the Minister of Labour was given absolute discretion to grant certification and to define the bargaining unit. While the employing board or commission was instructed to negotiate, no agreement necessarily resulted, although a written agreement, "may be signed" on behalf of the Province, subject to cabinet approval. Since there was no dispute resolution procedure, the employer was not compelled to reach an agreement. A "withdrawal of services" by the employees was declared "incompatible with the basic principles of public service," and a stiff sanction was imposed: "withdrawal of permission to act as agent of the employees in the unit."[8]

However, the largest group of government employees was excluded from these provisions for recognition and bargaining. Legislation divided the public sector into two distinct components. In one category, generally consisting of utility operations such as the Nova Scotia Power Commission, an independent agency was the legal employer, holding independent rights over personnel management and policy formation. This sector was managed in a manner similar to private industry and the bargaining procedures as set out in 1956 restricted bargaining to this set of employees. By 1960, 180 employees of the power commission were organized by the International Brotherhood of Electrical Workers; 50 employees of the Highways Garage and 100 N.S. Liquor Commission employees were organized in locals directly chartered by the Canadian Labour Congress; and 25 members of the cleaning staff of the Provincial Building in Sydney were organized by the Building Services Employees International Union. Only the electrical workers had negotiated a signed agreement.[9]

The largest group of provincial employees — the civil service — consisted of workers who were employed directly by a government department. Unlike the agency employees, who were hired and fired by independent boards, civil servants were hired through the Civil Service Commission and were subject to the Civil Service Act. Management was administered by a staff headed by a cabinet minister.

[8] *Royal Gazette Extraordinary* (Halifax), 14 February 1956; a copy of the order-in-council is included in Box 1, file 1.0, Nova Scotia Government Employees Association Papers, Dalhousie University Archives [NSGEA Papers].
[9] "Arguments Concerning Association Representation," NSGEA Papers, Box 1, file 1.0.

These employees were specifically excluded from the bargaining provisions granted the agency workers. Nor were civil servants demanding such recognition. However, the 1956 throne speech had also given authorization for employees subject to the Civil Service Act to form an association. While the government had maintained a broad framework of control over the recognized public service unions, they clearly desired a more direct influence over the activities of this proposed association; thus it was specified that the proposed association's constitution, rules and by-laws "shall be subject to the approval" of the Cabinet.[10]

Although the official history of the Nova Scotia Civil Service Association notes that this announcement "had been proposed without the prior knowledge of the civil service community,"[11] and thus reflected the entrenched paternalism which informed official civil service policy, the civil service community, or more precisely its higher levels, did play an important role in the process. In the early 1950s some civil servants became concerned about the pay scales and benefits granted to provincial employees. Such feelings were strengthened when in December 1953 the federal government had met the demand of federal civil servants for a substantial general increase in pay.[12] Although few opportunities existed for an organized expression of this sentiment, civil servants did voice concern through the Province House Credit Union (founded in 1937) and also through the Institute of Public Affairs. Through their involvement in IPA discussions, several key career civil servants came to accept labour-management co-operation as a philosophical basis for civil service participation in decision-making. Such co-operation obviously required as a minimum some form of organization among the employees. There was one other consideration: security of tenure. It did not require great foresight to anticipate that after 23 years the Liberals were slipping from power, and an association would help maintain civil service continuity and oppose patronage dismissals.[13]

Two weeks after the passing of the 1956 order-in-council, a meeting of about 40 civil servants, described as "unofficial but representative,"[14] took place in the Department of Mines. Six males from senior positions[15] and one female secretary were elected to a provisional committee which, with the assistance of a personnel manager from the Civil Service Commission, was to organize the association. The chairman of the committee was Gordon Burnham, a securities clerk in the Depart-

[10]Order-in-Council, 8 February 1956, NSGEA Papers, Box 1, file 1.0.

[11]Gordon Burnham, *Civil Servants by the Sea* (Halifax 1977), 23.

[12]NSCSC, *Annual Report, 1954.*

[13]Following the Conservative victory in 1956, former Premier Henry Hicks gave seminars on responsible government and employer-employee relations through the Institute of Public Affairs, which were attended by some high-ranking civil servants.

[14]Gordon Burnham to Premier Henry Hicks, 9 April 1956, NSGEA Papers, Box 1, file 1.0.

[15]A supervisor of school attendance, an assistant deputy registrar general, a supervisor of delinquency services, an assistant chief accountant, a chief clerk, and a securities clerk: "Report of the Provisional Committee," April 1956, NSGEA Papers, Box 1, file 1.0.

ment of Finance who had been active in the Credit Union and IPA discussions. He was subsequently elected to the first presidency of the NSCSA in 1958, serving in this position for four years. In 1962 he became treasurer, and later president, of the Canadian Federation of Government Employee Organizations, a national umbrella organization. Throughout the 1960s he continued to serve on the NSCSA Executive, consistently taking a strong position in favour of collective bargaining. During its deliberations, the provisional committee sought advice from officials in the Departments of Education and Labour, from the IPA, and from other civil service associations. The trade union movement was not a major source of inspiration, although a representative from the Canadian Labour Congress, and the secretary of the Joint Employee Council of Imperial Oil Limited, also met the committee.[16] Early in March 1957 it was announced through the IPA that civil servants would attempt to form the Nova Scotia Civil Service Association.

In April 1957 300 civil servants met in the chambers of the House of Assembly and endorsed the programme of the provisional committee. Believing that the "good will and confidence of our employer must be maintained," the committee proposed first to seek the premier's approval to proceed, and then to draft a constitution to be submitted to the cabinet. Once official approval was obtained, a conference would be held to ratify the constitution and found the association.[17] Anxious to receive the blessing of government, the committee initially worked more closely with the officials than with its own potential membership. Nevertheless, the provisional committee soon won the support of the majority of civil servants. Using the government's pay distribution system, the committee had sent notices of intent to organize to all civil servants with their April salary cheque. In response the majority of employees indicated "interest in the proposed association as a means of fostering high standards of service and maintaining good relations with the government."[18] Receiving 1,500 replies, the association's leadership concluded that the poll had tapped existing attitudes and interests.

Despite the reported near-unanimity concerning the objectives and orientation of the association, the activities of the provisional committee did not proceed in an atmosphere of complete consensus. An alternative conception of the organization apparently existed among a minority of employees. In the organizational meetings, the provisional committee carefully ensured that it had control over the prevailing discussion. Vice-chairman Stanley MacKenzie ordered that the 1956-1958 Progress Report, written by himself and Burnham, and "submitted to the Premier," was the only address to be given to the pre-convention meetings. Any "deviation from the content in principle" was deemed unwarranted, "especially when consideration is given to its source."[19] More explicitly, a second memorandum suggested that

---

[16]*Ibid.*
[17]*Ibid.*
[18]Provisional Committee, "Press Release," 11 January 1957, NSGEA Papers, Box 1, file 1.0.
[19]S.E. MacKenzie, "Some observations respecting two organizational meetings," NSGEA Papers, Box 1, file 1.0.

people should spend more time on their duties and on the functions of their departments rather than basing their discussions "on their relationships as ... civil servants." The memorandum claimed that unspecified individuals had used the organizational meetings for their own aggrandizement and warned that "any remark relating to political parties, or some fields being designated as training grounds, and expressions suggesting over-aggressiveness" should be avoided because such discussion "could result in defeating one of our primary objectives: 'Maintaining good relations with the Government.'" The document concluded clearly enough: "this is an Association ... not a union."[20] Publicly, Burnham did not take such an inflexible stance. In the first edition of the *Newsletter* he wrote: "We are a Civil Service association with ideals and purposes neither purely professional nor yet have they the characteristics of a labour union. It is evident that the popularity of our activities in this quarter or that could ebb and flow depending on which of the three aims receives the most emphasis." The three aims specified in the constitution were to further the interests of civil servants, to maintain good relations with the government, and to develop a higher standard of service for the public. It was assumed that there was no necessary incompatibility between the three and Burnham expected each to receive equal weight, adding that "no effort will be made which will allow any one of the three to suffer from lack of consideration."[21]

The inauguration of the association had originally been planned for the spring of 1957, but this was delayed after the Liberals were defeated in the 1956 provincial election. The new Conservative government was generally less committed to the principle of civil service organization, according to Burnham, and delayed the formation of the association specifically in the interests of making political appointments.[22] However, on 5 December 1957 the cabinet approved the constitution and by-laws of the Nova Scotia Civil Service Association.[23] Beginning in February 1958, meetings were held to organize the founding convention. These were attended by more than 50 per cent of eligible members, indicating considerable support for the organization. The constitution was ratified at a convention held the following spring, when an executive of eight members was elected, including both Burnham and MacKenzie who had served on the provisional committee. The executive and most councillors were drawn from the administrative or supervisory personnel, a situation which continued throughout the first decade. With the exception of 1962, when a new president took office, only two or three changes in the personnel of the

[20]"Nova Scotia Civil Service Association," undated document, NSGEA Papers, Box 1, file 1.0.

[21]Nova Scotia Civil Service Association, *Newsletter [NSCSA Newsletter]*, September 1958.

[22]Burnham, *Civil Servants by the Sea*, 11. The cabinet had excluded many positions from appointment by the Civil Service Commission.

[23]The government also granted the use of public buildings for association meetings, time off for delegates to attend the convention, and other concessions: Order-in-Council, 5 December 1957, NSGEA Papers, Box 1, file 1.0.

executive occurred each year, with the result that it maintained considerable continuity, not only of classification, but of actual membership.

According to the philosophy of the association's executive, the key to success was direct communication with the government. In this view, problems arose out of ignorance or from mistakes, rather than from directly conflicting interests. "The Government," Burnham declared, "is friendly .... We must learn to work together with our fellows, and with Government for our mutual benefit."[24] As middle level supervisors, the association leaders shared with their superiors a similar philosophy of management, but were generally excluded from making major policy decisions. They expected the association, however, would enable them to have access to information about proposed changes, making their task of policy implementation easier and providing some channels for influencing their own work. Although one year after the formation of the association the executive was still claiming that relations with the government had been "gracious" and that "mutual respect has been achieved,"[25] the first crack in this relationship was being formed by a scientific classification study.

In 1958 the government contracted an American management consulting firm, Jerome Barnum Associates, to study the classifications, salaries and grading policies of the civil service. From the outset the civil servants' response to this survey was ambivalent. There were objections to having outsiders, particularly foreigners, prying about and interfering with their jobs. Civil servants also objected to the possibly restrictive effects of the new job descriptions. At the association's fall council meeting it was proposed to prepare a brief, noting inter-provincial salary inequalities as well as the "complexity of the responsibility" shouldered by civil servants in Nova Scotia in contrast to other provinces where civil servants had a "more sharply defined and narrowed responsibility."[26] The Barnum study, however, also held out the expectation of "an upward adjustment in salaries."[27] The association decided to take no formal part in the study and, in place of preparing a brief, formed a committee to record existing classifications and salary scales and monitor any changes recommended by Barnum.[28] Association leaders advised civil servants to comply with requests to outline their job content and responsibilities.[29]

---

[24]*NSCSA Newsletter*, September 1958.
[25]*NSCSA Newsletter*, September 1959.
[26]*NSCSA Newsletter*, February 1959.
[27]*NSCSA Newsletter*, September 1959.
[28]*NSCSA Newsletter*, February 1959.
[29]The Point Method Plan was used, each position being scored on ten factors. Two sets of positions were defined: the professional and general (clerical), and the manual skills and crafts. Seven factors, such as knowledge, experience, physical demand, were common between the two. In addition, the former plan included mental and visual effort, decisions affecting cost, and "contacts," presumably with the public; the latter pay plan included manual skill, responsibility for tools, and responsibility for the safety of others. To implement

The association had thus demonstrated its good will and expected to be informed of the findings and recommendations of the survey. Despite the employees' co-operation the government controlled access to the information, and by delaying for a time the release of the information, demonstrated the weakness of the association's position. Writing to Premier Robert Stanfield, Burnham noted that frustrations were rising among the employees who were "anxious ... to be properly compensated." However, in an effort to reassure the premier that the association deserved both trust and respect, Burnham wrote that the association would "assure the ultimate success of any worthwhile proposal," and was "anxious to assist the employees in their competent understanding of the Evaluation findings."[30] Again, this promise to gather employee support for the proposals was founded on the assumption that the results would generally be in the interests of the civil servants. In response, Premier Stanfield denied that a general salary increase was planned and referred Burnham to the Civil Service Commission, which had been charged with assessing the report and making recommendations to the government.[31] Writing next to Commissioner William Finn, Burnham dropped the deferential tone and claimed the employees' "right to question the intrinsic worth of the 'facts' so described since we ourselves participated in the process."[32]

To the surprise of the civil servants, in February 1960 the Halifax *Chronicle-Herald* predicted a substantial general salary increase for the provincial civil service. The executive of the association was concerned that the media appeared to have access to information which the employees did not. Furthermore, the report contradicted what the premier had written and the limited increase the association had informed its members to expect. They feared the report would create unrealizable expectations which would rebound to the association's discredit, and that the executive would be charged with having agreed to less than was possible. To demonstrate its good faith to the membership, the association published the correspondence in a special edition of the newsletter, warning members that the new salary scale would be lower than anticipated, especially in relation to the rising cost of living.[33]

The first results of the classification survey, released to government departments in February 1960, indicated increases of from zero to six per cent, far below the anticipated average increase of ten per cent.[34] The executive responded by questioning the scientific procedures followed. If the survey did not meet the

---

this rationalization scheme, the Civil Service Commission hired a job analyst responsible for job reclassifications, and a researcher to study compensation rates: NSCSC, *Annual Report, 1960*.

[30] Burnham to Premier Robert Stanfield, 16 December 1959, NSGEA Papers, Box 16, file 10A.

[31] Stanfield to Burnham, 5 January 1960, NSGEA Papers, Box 16, file 10A.

[32] *NSCSA Newsletter*, Special Edition, February 1960.

[33] *Ibid*.

[34] NSCSC, *Annual Report, 1960*. See also Burnham to Finn, 1 March 1960, NSGEA Papers, Box 16, file 10A.

reasonable expectations of the responsible civil service leaders, it was mistaken and was to be queried on the grounds of scientific method. For Burnham, the results were "not what one would expect from a scientific survey."[35] He objected to its failure to establish a "progressive ... forward-looking policy": "the situation has deteriorated so that in some groups the same salary is received by persons who are able to assume responsibility and do not receive immediate supervision, as that received by experienced persons who require immediate supervisors." Failure to establish the appropriate differentials "militates against the continuance in the Service of progressive, ambitious staff" and contributes to a decline in morale.[36] A progressive policy would mean that salary differentials would be determined objectively on the basis of recognized degrees of skill and technical expertise and the sharpening of these skills "through experience in the performance of technical duties or professional practices."

The difficulties experienced over the Barnum study raised the issue of how employees could have a more direct voice in influencing government policy. During the 1959 fall council, when the employees were becoming impatient with the delay in publishing the new reclassification, a resolution was passed calling for the formation of a joint council as the best framework for ensuring good relations with the government.[37] From the beginning the members of the original provisional committee had seen such a council as the ideal forum for influencing their conditions of work. They had anticipated a slow, evolutionary process in which good relations, mutual respect and confidence between the government and the association officials would grow, a "gradual development towards full-fledged representation with the eventual goal being some form of Joint Council."[38] The problem was seen as the need for the association to prove to the government that it was trustworthy and responsible. The executive had no doubt that all interests were reconcilable within the unity of purpose underlying social service. A letter setting

[35]*NSCSA Newsletter*, April 1960.
[36]NSCSA, "Brief to the Government of Nova Scotia," September 1961, NSGEA Papers, Box 5, file 3.1.6. The Barnum Survey formed the basis of the classification scheme followed by the commission, but over the next few years hundreds of new positions were created while only approximately one-sixth as many were deleted. Not until the acceptance of collective bargaining was there a systematic attempt to group them into large occupational components. The inequalities and disruptions caused by the study were still being felt several years after its initial implementation, and it was referred to disparagingly by civil servants as the "Barnum and Bailey Survey."
[37]NSCSA, "A Brief in Support of a Joint Council," January 1960, NSGEA Papers, Box 16, file 10A. The idea of a joint council had originally arisen in a meeting of the provisional committee in 1957, and the model for such a council was provided by the Joint Industrial Council of Imperial Oil Limited; the provincial Department of Labour promoted such joint councils and the principle of labour-management co-operation: "Report of Meeting," (July 1957), NSGEA Papers, Box 1, file 1.0.
[38]NSCSA, "Revision: Argument concerning association representation," n.d., NSGEA Papers, Box 1, file 1.0.

forth this perspective emphasized that all discussions with the government "ought to be within a unified framework .... There will be no need in this type of representative development for the Association to become a conflicting group with motives other than the general welfare."[39]

A formal request for the creation of a joint council was submitted early in 1960. Directing attention to the "they complex," defined as an attitude of "us versus them," the brief noted that this attitude is "particularly prevalent during a time of major change. Many manifestations of this human trait have been observed during recent times in this service." In the context of the Barnum Study, "good relations appear to have broken down." While arguing that it was from the conflict of interests between employers and employees that the opportunity arises for progress in human relations, the brief maintained that the mutual objectives shared by management and employees should be accorded overriding importance. Both sides should pool their efforts in their joint undertaking. The brief also asserted the right of employees to be informed, for access to information would overcome the syndrome of antagonism and would provide "'an incentive for each member to contribute his share to a group output'" thereby improving "the effectiveness of the organization." Besides giving the employees confidence in their employer, it would afford them "'sound reasons for an attitude of loyalty.'" Participation would ensure employee interest and support and give them a feeling of importance as well as a "'sense of proprietorship.'"[40] Despite these arguments and the obvious benefits management would derive from a consultative body, by mid-1960 it was clear that the association had failed to persuade the government to institute a joint council.

Disenchanted with the limited recognition originally granted, the association executive began to realize that it was necessary to exert some added pressure to obtain results. A second brief, submitted in January 1961, was written in a lively question-and-answer format.[41] It was given wide distribution in the media, the public being seen as a potential ally in the campaign for a joint council. The

[39]*Ibid.*

[40]"A Brief in Support of a Joint Council," January 1960: the problems with those joint councils which existed in other provinces were said to be "brought on ... by attempting to apply an industrial private enterprise system [collective bargaining] to a government function." The association's brief quoted industrial relations texts with titles such as "Human Relations in Industry," "Teamwork in Industry," "Instincts in Industry" and "Partners in Production." In addition quotes were taken from a half-dozen booklets published by the American Management Association. The labour-management co-operative approach was not one confined to management and industrial relations experts, but did represent a trend within the North American labour movement of the 1950s, as some unions were able to obtain real improvements in working conditions and wages in the context of general economic prosperity.

[41]NSCSA, "Brief to the government of Nova Scotia regarding Joint Council," *NSCSA Newsletter*, February 1961. The association was becoming disenchanted with the limited recognition received under the order-in-council. With bargaining rights confined to agency employees only, civil servants increasingly came to see themselves as "second class citizens."

ideological frame of reference remained unchanged: the team spirit would be developed in an atmosphere of trust and respect as employers and employees worked together to accomplish the common purposes of the service. While the goal remained the establishment of a joint council, the association's conceptualization of the role of such a council had been, to a degree, altered. Although it would not make final decisions for its constituents, the council would have the responsibility to make recommendations to them — it would be an advisory body. Also, while the first brief had only implied the possibility of a labour affiliation, one alternative to the joint council was now explicitly listed as "Affiliation with labour and ultimately collective bargaining." The words conveyed several meanings. For some executive members they indicated a realization that there were no necessary legal barriers to a collective bargaining position for government employees, and Saskatchewan was cited as a Canadian example. For most members, however, the model of negotiation rights was the limited provision granted the agency workers in Nova Scotia and the threat of labour affiliation was only a bargaining tactic.

The government responded to the 1961 brief with an offer to set up a procedure whereby the Civil Service Commission, the association, and government officials could "meet periodically to consider matters relating to the public service." Although this was not the desired joint council, the executive decided to participate and work for a guarantee of continuity through legislation.[42] In the subsequent meetings Burnham argued that the association was seeking official recognition and the right to deal with "responsible authorities" and to "suggest possible changes in the Civil Service Act."[43] The government, however, considered a joint council unnecessary because the Civil Service Commission was responsible for giving advice on civil service matters. According to Premier Stanfield, such issues as grievance procedure, holidays, travel policy, means to prevent high turnover, job training, temporary employees, and overtime pay were all matters properly dealt with by the Civil Service Commission.[44] By 1963 the association was declaring joint consultation to be an "exercise in futility."[45]

In 1962 the hiring of a full-time executive secretary demonstrated the association's determination to have a more effective voice in influencing government. The new official, A.E. King, was described as an experienced public relations executive who had been "associated in the consulting and corporate public relation's field."[46] He began his tenure by opening the association's campaign to obtain a general salary increase rather inauspiciously. Writing to Commissioner G.E. Perry, he instructed the Civil Service Commission to "institute without delay, an upward revision" of

[42]*NSCSA Newsletter*, June 1961.
[43]"Preliminary report on second joint meeting between Government and the Nova Scotia Civil Service Association," 29 September 1961, NSGEA Papers, Box 16, file 10A.
[44]Stanfield to Burnham, 22 September 1961, NSGEA Papers, Box 16, file 10A.
[45]*NSCSA Newsletter*, May 1963.
[46]Burnham, *Civil Servants by the Sea*, 59. He was also an active member of the Halifax Board of Trade.

civil service salaries.[47] Perry did not reply to this directive, and four months later the new president, Alex Buchanan, wrote a second letter in the customary deferential tone. Noting that the association "had not been favoured with a formal acknowledgement" of its request, and that it would "greatly appreciate knowing the Commission's stand," Buchanan reiterated King's arguments about the cost of living, the adjustments other employees had received, and the threat these posed for recruitment and retention of personnel. There was also reference to members who "were becoming justifiably impatient with the Association."[48] The sense of relative deprivation had increased since provincial highways workers, who were represented by a union, had recently won a general wage increase. Buchanan promised a sympathetic response if the commission would take the association "into the picture."[49]

The request for an across-the-board increase was rejected because it was contrary to the policy that compensation was to be determined scientifically for each classification. According to Commissioner Perry, the only acceptable procedure was "regular and periodic salary reviews" based on the commission's own studies of prevailing rates.[50] This was to be a method of establishing comparisons which would not admit the use of force or change in the face of pressure. This conception did not imply that the association had no role to play: it could be involved in

[47]*NSCSA Newsletter*, October 1962.

[48]Some association members resigned after their demand that the executive secretary achieve a general increase for the service was not met; three of these dissidents had "union backgrounds and were all for leading this group into a union and force their demands": "Resignation of 14 members — Division 5," [1962], NSGEA Papers, Box 7, file 3.7.4A; see also Minutes, Executive Committee, Division 13, 28 November 1962, NSGEA Papers, Box 4, file 2.5.2. There were also other indications of dissatisfaction. Late in 1962 the association commissioned the Institute of Public Affairs to conduct a survey of members' attitudes. Although the 700 replies (28.5 per cent of the membership) agreed that the organization ought not to interfere in areas of management responsibility, there were numerous criticisms, including the view that the association was built from the "top down," objections to the failure to obtain salary increases, and some support for a stronger "union type" of organization. The membership of the association declined from a high of 6 per cent of eligible civil servants in 1961 to 53 per cent in 1965: see Christopher Bailey, "White Collar Unionization: The Case of the Nova Scotia Government Employees Association," MA thesis, Dalhousie University, 1979, 104, 17.

[49]*NSCSA Newsletter*, October 1962. The highways workers had received an additional five to eight cents an hour. The government's standing position on civil service salaries was that government employees should not "expect to receive as high a salary as they might earn outside the service" and in recompense they would receive security of tenure and adequate pension benefits. Salaries, however, should not be so low as to act as a disincentive for "men of solid ambition and high competence"; pay schedules were to be "fair and equitable": *Royal Commission on Provincial Development, 1944*, 10, 44-5.

[50]*NSCSA Newsletter*, October 1962.

informative discussions, it could question the scientific procedures used,[51] and finally it could assist in the propagation of the decisions. Open communication could produce confidence in the government and in commission policy and develop "a sound reason for an attitude of loyalty toward the employer" which would help to increase productivity.[52]

In the early 1960s, battle lines were beginning to take shape on these issues all across the country. Public employees were commonly paid less than prevailing rates for comparable jobs in the private sector, but the advantages that civil servants had in other areas were beginning to disappear as white-collar workers and trade unions negotiated better holidays, pensions and other benefits. Increasingly, civil servants believed the cause of their weakness was the absence of bargaining rights. In the federal civil service, associations demanding bargaining rights were supported by the opposition parties of the day, including the Liberal Party. The Canadian Council of Provincial Employee Associations, which had existed since 1944, was reorganized in February 1962 as the Canadian Federation of Government Employee Organizations, with the basic aim of gaining collective bargaining rights for civil servants in all provinces. The CFGEO claimed that government employees had an "undeniable right" to participate as equals in negotiations. Paradoxically, however, the CFGEO and its member associations were seen as an alternative to trade unionism such as that represented by the Canadian Union of Public Employees.[53]

When the CFGEO circulated a brief to provincial governments in July 1962 outlining its arguments in favour of collective bargaining, the federation declared that unions typified "to many thousands of government employees a sure way of accomplishing improvements in wages and working conditions which their own organizations" had never been able to achieve. Dissatisfactions were growing and pressure was increasing "for some satisfactory form of conducting direct negotiations." Aware of this sentiment the union movement had begun preparations for a massive organizing drive spearheaded by the Canadian Union of Public Employees. In response to this, the CFGEO urged, governments should grant exclusive recognition and a satisfactory negotiating procedure to the existing provincial employee associations, since they were "a last barrier standing between governments and the

---

[51]In his reply, Buchanan questioned the method: the industries chosen for comparison, the samples used, and the results obtained: *NSCSA Newsletter*, October 1962.

[52]*Ibid.*

[53]Elsewhere in Canada, most provincial civil service organizations had obtained some negotiating rights through joint councils. The experience with this form of consultation had been unsatisfactory and the growing militancy of the membership pushed these associations in the direction of collective bargaining. See Saul Frankel, *Staff Relations in the Civil Service* (Montréal 1967) and L.W.C.S. Barnes, *Consult and Advise: A History of the National Joint Council of the Public Service of Canada, 1944-1974* (Kingston 1975). The development of collective bargaining procedures was seen as necessary to undercut the potential appeal of trade unions. CUPE had begun organizing agency employees in New Brunswick, where there was an open jurisdiction, causing concern among association leaders in Nova Scotia: H.B. Hunter to King, 20 March 1963, NSGEA Papers, Box 16, file 10.1A.

union movement. They may well represent a final opportunity for governments to work out, in co-operation with their own employees, the effective means necessary to the conduct of a mutually satisfactory employer-employee relationship in the public services of our province." If the governments were to show some foresight, imagination and "more trust in the responsible leaders of government employee organizations," they could prevent the "potential developments from ... ripening into a bitter fruit." The strike was seen as the most distasteful aspect of trade unionism, and the CFGEO willingly disavowed this sanction in order to convince governments to accept its proposals.[54]

The Nova Scotia association had joined the national organization of civil servants in 1959, and when Burnham left the association presidency in 1962, he became treasurer, and subsequently president, of the CFGEO. Although Burnham had been a consistent supporter of collective bargaining rights including the right to strike, within the Nova Scotia association, this was not the case with his successor, Alex Buchanan. Buchanan, supervisor of the Apple Maggot Control Programme in the Annapolis Valley, had joined the association shortly after it was organized, becoming vice-president in 1961, and president in 1962. In contrast to Burnham who was more intellectual in his approach to organization and more inclined to argue, on principle, that the NSCSA should have bargaining rights equal to any other employee in the province, Buchanan was more pragmatic and less inclined to rock the boat. In his own view, most civil servants at the time were "perfectly happy with their lot in life" and were not union-oriented.[55] Under Buchanan's leadership, the association would take steps which consolidated its position as a consultative body.

In this context, the Nova Scotia association not only continued efforts to obtain an advisory joint council, defined as "a system of bilateral determination," but, to protect their flank from "invasion by outside groups," they also argued for an expanded jurisdiction.[56] The reasons for this were apparent in Halifax, where the

[54]Canadian Federation of Government Employee Organizations [CFGEO], "A Brief to all the Prime Ministers of all the Provinces of Canada," July 1962, NSGEA Papers, Box 5, file 3.3B. Most provincial governments sent representatives to a conference held in Toronto in January 1963. In his confidential report, Chairman E.W. Hinman, the provincial treasurer of Alberta, stressed that the absence of bargaining rights was encouraging labour unions to become increasingly active in the public sector. An immediate matter of concern was the imminent merger of two public sector unions to create the Canadian Union of Public Employees, which was seen as a threat to existing provincial associations. In return for formal certification as bargaining agent, the associations offered insurance against outside control of the civil service associations, recognition of the principle of sovereignty, and agreement on "the undesirability of strike action on the part of government employees"; in place of strike action they requested binding arbitration to resolve disputes: "Chairman's Report to the Prime Minister and the Premiers of the Provinces," February 1963, NSGEA Papers, Box 5, file 3.3C; CFGEO, "Opening Statement," 1963, NSGEA Papers, Box 5, file 3.3B.
[55]Interview with Alex Buchanan, 14 September 1982.
[56]*NSCSA Newsletter*, May 1963.

non-civil service staff in the provincial hospital, the Victoria General, had been organized by the Canadian Brotherhood of Railway, Transport and General Workers. The certification of this union led to dissatisfaction in the NSCSA's Division 11 because the union members appeared "to be gaining benefits which they previously did not have, also wage considerations in a shorter time than it is taking the Association to solve the problems of its members." As a result, according to Burnham, civil servants had "become more concerned as to just what the Association can do for them."[57] To prevent the encroachment of organized labour on other fronts, a formal request for an enlarged jurisdiction was sent to the premier in July 1963. If the unions succeeded in organizing the public employees, the association declared, the government and the people, who held the "biggest stake," would have the most to lose.[58] Also in July 1963 the NSCSA made its third submission requesting a changed relationship with the government. The existing system of consultation was declared to have been "inconclusive" and civil servants were said to have the "inherent right to bargain collectively with their employer." The association disavowed the "strike privilege as a weapon ... provided a system of arbitration is a part of the agreement with our employer."[59]

In response to these initiatives, and following a provincial election in the fall of 1963, the government finally proposed a formal joint council in which the NSCSA would be recognized as the sole negotiating agent for provincial civil servants. Stanfield wrote that the government had come to accept the view that "progressive flexibility in the exercise of government sovereignty, good faith and mutual trust are essential elements in establishing good staff relations."[60] By proposing a council to deal with terms and conditions of employment, the premier had essentially accepted the original 1960 proposal, making no reference to the changes in the subsequent submissions. Upon receipt of the draft proposal from the

[57]Burnham to Pauline MacDonald, 27 January 1961, NSGEA Papers, Box 16, file 10.1A; Division 11 Annual Report, 1963-1964, NSGEA Papers, Box 4, file 2.5.2.

[58]"Draft Report of Joint Council Committee," NSGEA Papers, Box 16, file 10.1A. The CLC had not restricted the public sector jurisdiction to CUPE, and, in the words of the Joint Council Committee, had guaranteed instead "the law of the jungle" and civil servants were "fair game for say, Jimmy Hoffa's boys."

[59]NSCSA, "Submission in support of its right to bargain collectively with the Government of the Province of Nova Scotia," July 1963, NSGEA Papers, Box 7, file 3.6A.

[60]Stanfield to Buchanan, 23 November 1963, NSGEA Papers, Box 16, file 10.1A. There was considerable support outside the civil service for the inclusion of a provision for arbitration. Judge Alexander MacKinnon, who was appointed in 1960 as a one-man commission to investigate labour relations in the province, had advocated that the Trade Union Act be made applicable to civil servants, with the inclusion of a model paragraph withdrawing the right to strike and replacing it with compulsory arbitration: *Labour Gazette*, LXII (May 1962), 508-9. The Halifax press also argued that civil servants should have collective bargaining with arbitration, for without this sanction the government would be both an interested party and an adjudicator: *Chronicle-Herald* (Halifax), 15 August 1962.

government, the immediate response of the NSCSA's joint council committee was to seek inclusion of an additional provision for binding arbitration.

Association opinion was divided on whether to accept the government's offer. At the fall council meeting, Burnham argued that a council without arbitration was unacceptable, first on the grounds that the government could "after all discussion is over say 'no' or 'yes' without laying the full argument on the table" — that is, withhold information — and second, because the government retained power to make unilateral decisions. Furthermore, without arbitration as a "weapon," the jurisdiction of the association would be put at risk in the face of raiding unions.[61] On the other side of the argument, President Buchanan's position was that the association should accept the government's offer, and that attempts to secure more reforms could continue within the new framework. A unanimous motion instructed the joint council committee to "go back and intensify their efforts" to get collective bargaining with arbitration.[62] Differences remained, however, and the second day of fall council produced a clarification. Several members of council understood that the motion to renegotiate had been an implicit rejection of the government's proposal, and this interpretation was released to the press. Buchanan argued, however, that the motion had implied working within the proposed council to change its terms of reference to include binding arbitration. Whether the outcome indicated a clarification, or whether a change had been engineered between sessions, a majority voted to accept the joint council as offered and to inform the media that the original press release had not reflected the association's position.[63] Shortly thereafter, Burnham resigned from the joint council committee.[64]

Formation of the new council was announced by the provincial government and the NSCSA in February 1964. Given a wide scope to discuss matters relating to terms and conditions of employment, the council would have "power, upon reaching agreement, to transmit its decision to appropriate authorities for implementation."[65] No provision was provided to resolve disputes if agreement could not be reached, but since agreement was necessary for implementation, there would be pressure on the association to accept even minimal offers on the grounds that these were better than nothing. Like most civil service associations in Canada, the NSCSA adopted the view that the use of strikes was not an acceptable weapon for

[61]Burnham, "Paper on collective bargaining," presented to NSCSA fall council, November 1963, NSGEA Papers, Box 7, file 3.6A.
[62]Minutes of NSCSA Fall Council Meeting, 18-19 November 1963, NSGEA Papers, Box 16, file 10A. This motion was moved by Alex MacRea, who believed that the association may have committed a "blunder by telling government we would withhold strike action." He understood the motion to be one of rejection of the offer rather than provisional acceptance.
[63]Minutes, 1963 Fall Council. The vote was 14-6.
[64]"Report of the Joint Council Committee," April 1964, NSGEA Papers, Box 16, file 10A.
[65]"Joint Release from the Offices of the Premier of Nova Scotia and the Nova Scotia Civil Service Association," ibid.

public service workers.[66] The Nova Scotia association, in rejecting the strike, exaggerated the role of strikes in the private sector while minimizing their potential effectiveness for public employees. The strike was called the "great equalizer" in private industry, but it was deemed unworkable in the public sector for two reasons. First, orderly government activities were essential to the public and a strike would be seen as "disproportionately disruptive if not intolerable" to the public.[67] Second, any contest of economic strength between "stable government and a section of its community — its employees" would be so unequal that the employees would necessarily lose more than they could potentially gain.[68] In any case, the government would declare a strike by civil servants to be against the public interest and therefore illegal.

It took a dramatic illegal strike in the federal civil service to indicate that the power of the government was not absolute and that the disruption of a public service could be regarded sympathetically. The 1965 national postal strike, brought about by the government's refusal to implement a pay award recommended by the Civil Service Commission, was generally seen by the NSCSA as a justifiable response to the government's provocation. It was argued in the association's *Newsletter* that the strike produced "prompt and beneficial results" which impressed civil servants elsewhere. This increased legitimacy of the strike, as a last resort in the most extreme situation, added a new element to the discussions. Without the "distasteful prospect of a strike" as a sanction, it was argued, civil service salaries would continue to lag two years behind the private sector. However, the Nova Scotia government was assured that once granted this right, the civil servants would no longer feel oppressed, and would be no less responsible in bargaining than in the past.[69]

For the Nova Scotia association, arbitration was still seen as the appropriate equalizer, but the main problem was the government's power to veto an award. Both

[66]The principal argument used by civil servants in their rejection of the strike was the public service ethic. The ambiguity of this argument, however, is that in many cases those occupations which have a direct public service component, such as police, firefighting, hospital work, have often been granted the right to strike, while white-collar civil servants, more removed from the immediately essential services, have not. With the exception of the CCF government elected in Saskatchewan in 1944, Canadian governments had been unwilling to grant the right to strike to civil servants up until the mid-1960s. The Conservative government's view was that any agreement to bargain with federal employees was conditional on their agreement to renounce the right to strike: John G. Diefenbaker to the Federal Employee Associations, n.d., NSGEA Papers, Box 16, file 10.1A. The Heeney Report (1965), which recommended a collective bargaining procedure for federal employees, included only binding arbitration as a sanction for employees: *NSCSA Newsletter*, February 1965.
[67]S.J. Frankel, "Address to the Interprovincial Conference on Employer-Employee Relations in the Public Service," Halifax, 25 September 1963, NSGEA Papers, Box 5, file 3.3C.
[68]*NSCSA Newsletter*, August 1963.
[69]*NSCSA Newsletter*, October 1965.

parties were expected to use "common sense," the civil servants having no intention of "making outrageous demands and ruining their advantage," while the government side was "to treat reasonable demands with proper respect." The association hoped that the public would recognize a refusal by government to implement "an award won through a fair and legal bargaining procedure" as an injustice and be sympathetic to the employees.[70] Yet in the joint council formed in Nova Scotia in 1964, even this limited sanction of binding arbitration was absent. By July of that year the government had delimited the role of the council, deeming it incompetent to deal with matters concerning the application of the Civil Service Act, such as promotions or work organization, and listing those matters which were to be handled at the departmental level. Automatic membership, for example, was not a "proper matter" for discussion while the distribution of Service Pin Awards to faithful civil servants was considered proper.[71] While the premier was expressing the desire to give joint consultation a further trial period,[72] the association was asking, rhetorically, whether the results of council consultation were a foregone conclusion.[73]

Meanwhile, provincial associations in Western Canada were receiving exclusive jurisdiction rights, signed contracts and binding arbitration. The success of the postal strike was instrumental in the decision to alter the proposed federal legislation to include the option of choosing the right to strike. In Nova Scotia the provincial government amended the Trade Union Act in 1965, giving agency workers employed by boards or commissions the right to come under this act. As the civil servants were informed by their executive at their annual convention, "these people, many of them in your own classifications, have all the rights under present labour legislation, including the right to strike."[74] The expansion of the rights of other workers in the public sector exacerbated the perceived union threat of trade union organizing campaigns. Unless it secured full negotiating rights, including the ability to go on strike, warned the NSCSA executive secretary in 1965, the association could be deserted by its membership and the civil servants would fall "like a ripe plum into some union basket."[75] The main speaker at the 1965 convention, CLC vice-president William Dodge, underlined this jurisdictional threat. Tactfully expressing a desire to see the association become a competitor for the agency sector, he added that if this did not happen, these employees would become "in the not too

[70]H.B. Hunter to King, 20 March 1963, NSGEA Papers, Box 16, file 10.1A.

[71]Memorandum, "Civil Service Joint Council," 28 July 1964, NSGEA Papers, Box 16, file 10A.

[72]Buchanan to Stanfield, 9 March 1965, NSGEA Papers, Box 7, file 3.6A.

[73]NSCSA Newsletter, October 1965.

[74]NSCSA Newsletter, June-July 1965. On achievements in the west, see Hunter to Buchanan, 5 February 1965, NSGEA Papers, Box 16, file 10.1A.

[75]Hugh MacLeod to Buchanan, 27 January 1965, NSGEA Papers, Box 16, file 10.1A.

distant future, members of a strong labour organization competing for the present membership of the Association."[76]

The union threat was put most forcefully within the association executive by Hugh MacLeod, who replaced King as executive secretary when the latter resigned in 1965 to take a post with the provincial government. MacLeod had some trade union experience in the Halifax Dockyard Council and later became secretary of the Nova Scotia Federation of Labour. His support for full bargaining rights for civil servants was an important factor in his selection for the position and, in conjunction with the Institute of Public Affairs, he initiated an educational programme on bargaining procedures.[77] In the aftermath of the amendment to the Trade Union Act which gave public agency workers union rights, MacLeod anticipated the full extension of rights to the civil service. While unions had not been interested in government employees because of "past frustrations in trying to deal with an employer who was immune to the general rules of collective bargaining," he believed that when this situation changed, unions would renew their interest.[78]

There was an alternative possibility: the jurisdictional threat could be undercut if the right to organize civil servants was confined legally to the association. The government could be persuaded to concede this special relationship if it could see the benefits to be derived — and the association promised responsible demands and the renunciation of the strike. The problem that the success of the unions would widen the disparity between the two sections of government employees, leading to more militant demands from civil servants which would overturn the special relationship, could be solved in advance by procedural improvements to ensure that the relative positions of the civil servants were not eroded. Given an economic climate of general prosperity in the mid-1960s, this was a potentially successful strategy. Neither the government nor the civil servants would be required to renounce their ingrained attitudes of paternalism.

Several developments shaped the realization of this alternative relationship. Elsewhere in Canada the revival of public sector militancy, influenced by the settlement of the postal dispute, was meeting with determined opposition. In Ontario, the government withdrew the right to strike from hospital workers and substituted compulsory arbitration,[79] and a strike at the provincial power corpora-

---

[76]*NSCSA Newsletter*, June-July 1965. Certain agency groups in the public sector, such as the employees of the Amherst School for the Deaf, had petitioned for association membership. These requests could not be granted within the terms of the existing constitution, which could be amended only with the government's approval.

[77]Buchanan to Hunter, 15 January 1965, NSGEA Papers, Box 7, file 3.6A. Buchanan reported that the association had received a "shot in the arm" with MacLeod, who appeared to get on well with the membership.

[78]MacLeod to Buchanan, 15, 27 January 1965, NSGEA Papers, Box 7, file 3.6A, Box 16, file 10.1A. Demands for collective bargaining rights were made by Division 1 (Cape Breton) at the 1965 convention, and by Division Ten (Halifax Provincial Building) at the fall council that year: Minutes of Fall Council, 1965, NSGEA Papers, Box 7, file 3.6A.

[79]*NSCSA Newsletter*, July-August 1966.

tion in Saskatchewan prompted the government to pass emergency legislation imposing penalties on the unions and requiring them to submit to arbitration.[80] The association executive watched these events with considerable interest, for they appeared to prove that the right to strike was unworkable in a situation where the government could simply legislate settlements.[81]

Within the association internal developments led to the ascendancy of an accommodationist trend. When MacLeod resigned later in 1965 to accept a position with the government as Director of Labour Standards, an important individual supporter of collective bargaining was removed from an influential position. The individual who was most important in developing the new trend within the association was the new executive secretary, Tom Shiers. Recommended by MacLeod, Shiers had impressive trade union credentials. He had been president of the Nova Scotia Quarry Workers Union and led them through a long and difficult 14-month strike in 1955-56, an experience which had impressed upon him the value of conciliation and arbitration to resolve disputes. Subsequently he became treasurer and then vice-president of the Nova Scotia Federation of Labour and then worked as a representative of the Newspaper Guild in Ontario. Shiers came to the NSCSA at a low point in its brief existence. Membership numbers were stagnating. Some divisions had not met for several years. The executive was dominated by a number of supervisory civil servants with little organizational experience and little knowledge of collective bargaining. Trade union sentiment was very low among members. The existing joint council was a powerless instrument without provision for compulsory arbitration. There was a minority position within the association in favour of full collective bargaining rights, but Shiers believed the strike weapon had been proven unworkable in the public sector.[82] Shiers quickly established himself as the bargaining representative for the association, striking up a personal relationship with Civil Service Commissioner Perry. The first fruit of this relationship, coming in September 1965, less than two months after Shiers' appointment, was an automatic dues check-off, which placed the association on a more solid financial basis.

Shiers' contribution to the association would be very ambiguous. The association edged in the direction of trade unionism as Shiers negotiated a better grievance procedure and opened discussions with the Civil Service Commission and the government for a more formal bargaining relationship. On the other hand, Shiers' influence was instrumental in consolidating the co-operative labour-management approach which was successful in the short-run in obtaining benefits for the members, but proved unsuitable in the more antagonistic labour relations of the 1970s. Although President Buchanan tended to be greatly influenced by the phi-

[80]Minutes of CFGEO Executive Council Meeting, 22-23 September 1966, NSGEA Papers, Box 6, file 3.3D.
[81]Interview with Thomas Shiers, 19 January 1983.
[82]*Ibid.*

losophy of the executive secretaries who worked during his tenure,[83] he was most sympathetic to Shiers' approach because it was more compatible with his own conservatism.

Members of the association executive were also realizing that the implications of collective bargaining were not in their own interests. As part of its national campaign for the extension of negotiation rights, the CFGEO organized a seminar on bargaining procedures which was attended by Buchanan and Shiers. Buchanan reported that "the matters discussed were a revelation" and that he had been "almost completely unaware of the many ramifications of" collective bargaining.[84] Rather than preparing the association executive for the inevitability of bargaining, the seminar had inadvertently consolidated their opposition to it. While the western associations argued that in their experience it had been beneficial to exclude bona fide management from their membership, these observations worried the association's leadership, most of whom were themselves in supervisory positions. Another issue, the union principle of seniority, was regarded as contrary to the civil service expectations of promotion on merit. In the middle levels of the service — the supervisory positions and the steps immediately below them — there was considerable individual competition for advancement, and only those in positions of immediate succession on the basis of seniority were liable to approve of the union principle. From the point of view of middle management personnel who had some influence over which internal candidate would be promoted, any seniority clause would reduce even further their capacity to make decisions on personnel matters. With these implications in mind association leaders began to turn away from collective bargaining towards the establishment of a special relationship with the government.

The two points of view within the executive were debated at length during an enlarged session of the executive in August 1966. Buchanan raised the issue of "what the people who are talking collective bargaining mean." He was concerned that exclusions would leave supervisory staff with no organization to bargain with the government, and that coming under the Trade Union Act would open the association for raiding by unions. In response, Alex MacRae, an executive member from Division 1 (Sydney district), indicating the ambivalence of the collective bargaining group within the executive, replied that bargaining meant a written agreement, but "wondered if this would wear so well in the Civil Service." He added that, with exclusions, the association "would lose the people who are capable of bargaining for us." Burnham, who had arrived late, spoke more directly, declaring the two issues raised to be "red herrings." "Maybe it would be better," he argued, "if some of the people who elect the supervisors to the executive should be on the executive themselves." Rather than request "special protection from the trade unions," he urged the association to "work harder because of the competition."[85]

[83]Reilly, "A search for collective bargaining," 16.

[84]*NSCSA Newsletter*, July-August 1966.

[85]"Discussion on collective bargaining," 20 August 1966, NSGEA Papers, Box 7, file 3.6A.

Burnham's arguments were not persuasive. J.H. MacKenzie raised the crucial issue: "supposing as of May '67 we get collective bargaining with the exclusion of everyone around this table, all the members of committees and maybe half the Councillors, then where is the Association?" Exclusions "would wreck us totally as we stand today." The leading spokesman opposed to Burnham at this meeting was Tom Shiers. He endorsed the view that the strength of the association lay "in the top brackets." It was "the respect afforded the top people by government that has obtained the things" that the association had won.[86] There was some limited opposition to the consolidation of this viewpoint among the members. In the *Newsletter* one member objected to the renunciation of full collective bargaining which had occurred in "behind the scenes dealings without the proper authorization of the membership," but there was no evidence the membership would support the minority sentiment in the executive.[87] During the fall of 1966 Buchanan and Shiers undertook a systematic campaign to carry the executive's point of view to divisional meetings throughout the province. The existing relationship between the association and government was declared to be the best in Canada, while talk of the right to strike had "no place in public service."[88]

While the special relationship with government, which was the essence of this strategy, existed formally in the joint council and informally in joint consultations between Shiers and Commissioner Perry, it was also necessary to establish security of jurisdiction and some machinery to ensure that civil servants maintained their relative position. The first provision was satisfied when the association was certified by an order-in-council as the negotiating agent for employees appointed under the Civil Service Act, thus erecting a barrier against the potential threat from the trade union movement. Negotiations to satisfy the second requirement between Shiers, W.E. Moseley, chairman of the joint council, and Tom McKeough, the Minister of Labour, led to the proclamation of a legislative basis for joint council, Bill 111.[89]

In an early meeting between Shiers and Moseley there had been agreement that in return for arbitration there would be no right to strike. But the arbitration clause in the bill did not appear to be binding on the government, since awards "seriously prejudicial to the public interest" would not be implemented until the next prorogation "unless the House of Assembly otherwise determines."[90] Moseley reported to McKeough that Shiers "had receded from his stand on the right to strike." Shiers agreed that there should be no strikes but he was reluctant to agree to taking away

[86]*Ibid.*

[87]*NSCSA Newsletter*, September-October 1966. Of more immediate concern to the members was the closed nature of association dealings. During the 1966 convention several sharp exchanges occurred between the executive and spokesmen from the floor. To obtain an increase in dues the executive prepared an Extraordinary Resolution which "was sprung on the Council," narrowly missed defeat, and provoked "uncontrollable rudeness" and talk of a walkout: *NSCSA Newsletter*, September-October 1966.

[88]Minutes, Division 4 Meeting, 24 November 1966, NSGEA Papers, Box 3, file 2.5.2.

[89]Buchanan to Stanfield, 9 March 1965, NSGEA Papers, Box 7, file 3.6A.

[90]NSCSA to R.A. Donahoe, 20 March 1967, NSGEA Papers, *ibid.*

the right[91] and demanded that section ten, explicitly denying the strike sanction to civil servants, be withdrawn. This was less a point of principle and more a bargaining tactic, for Shiers agreed that civil servants would not strike. The clause stating that decisions of the new joint council would "be transmitted to the appropriate authorities for implementation," had been inserted in the 1964 order-in-council establishing joint consultation, but it had been "utterly confusing in its application," and the association was able to obtain a stronger guarantee that decisions and awards won through arbitration would be implemented as a matter of routine.

Meanwhile, official pronouncements from the association were reminiscent of the perspectives adopted in the earliest requests for joint consultation. Stanley MacKenzie, a member of the provisional committee in 1956, described the goal of the association as one of fostering high standards of service and maintaining good relations with government.[92] The staff side of joint council reported that "so long as fair and reasonable demands are presented, supported by full and detailed facts, progress to the benefit of our membership and the people of Nova Scotia will be forthcoming."[93] In the words of the Civil Service Commission, informal meetings with the executive secretary, conducted in a spirit of good faith, "successfully served the purpose for which they were intended and proved the value of joint consult-ation."[94]

The Joint Council Act of 1967 marked the apex of the labour-management approach in the NSCSA. Throughout the 1960s developments within the provincial civil service were strengthening the pro-union forces within the association. Between 1962 and 1968 the number of civil servants in Nova Scotia doubled; these younger employees did not have a history of a paternalistic relationship with the government and entered the civil service at a point where it was becoming increasingly bureaucratized. The appearance of stability in the two years following the enactment of Bill 111 was temporary. The grievance procedure proved inadequate; there was no signed agreement; membership did not have direct control over the acceptance or rejection of negotiated settlements; and the structure of the association favoured a self-perpetuating leadership. Beginning in 1969 changes were instituted in the association, including the creation of a system of shop stewards and a component bargaining framework complete with signed contracts; members began to ratify or reject negotiated agreements; and the executive was enlarged.

[91]Memorandum to T.J. McKeough from W.E. Moseley, 23 November 1966, *ibid.*
[92]*NSCSA Newsletter*, December 1965.
[93]Quoted by Burnham, *Civil Servants by the Sea*, 83.
[94]NSCSA, *Annual Report, 1965*; see also reports for 1966 and 1967. Some agency employees were asking to be represented by the NSCSA, a decision which the association claimed indicated their "reluctance to become members of Trade Unions." Here the identical perspective on the nature of the associations was expressed in the same terms as a decade previously.

The jurisdiction was expanded to include non-civil servants, and the name of the organization was changed to the Nova Scotia Government Employees Association.

These internal developments were given an additional impetus by a changed relationship with the employer. By 1970 governments across Canada were feeling the pinch of financial constraint and consequently were adopting tougher bargaining positions with their own employees. In Nova Scotia the Liberal government imposed a five per cent limit on increases in provincial employees' salaries. The acquiescent response of many association leaders, including executive secretary Shiers, precipitated a wholesale change in the leadership. Pockets of exceptional militancy surfaced among members, particularly those employed in the Victoria General Hospital in Halifax. For its part, the new executive pressed for the right to strike and encouraged affiliation with the Canadian Labour Congress. With the Civil Service Collective Bargaining Act of 1979 and a further change in its name, the Nova Scotia Government Employees Union has now adopted all the formal attributes of unionism, but it remains to be seen to what extent the civil servants have abandoned their traditional attitudes in favour of an unambiguous union consciousness.

M. Patricia Connelly and Martha MacDonald

16

State Policy, The Household and Women's Work in the Atlantic Fishery

In this paper we examine three types of policies and the way in which they apply to the Atlantic fisheries: subsidies to the private sector, income maintenance of individuals (UI), and fishery regulatory policies. The aim is to show the pervasiveness of these general social and economic policies in the lives of women and men, how women and men act and react both as individuals and as household members to the policies as they are implemented, and how women and men are differentially affected by both policies and household strategies. The policies examined apply to the Atlantic region as a whole. The major focus, however, is on Nova Scotia and the case study material used is from research done in six Nova Scotia fishing communities.[1]

The Atlantic region has long been characterized as less developed than the rest of Canada.[2] Wages and incomes are lower, unemployment is higher, out migration

---

[1] In each community we did oral histories with older residents, interviews with key informants, a survey of employers, a survey of a ten per cent random sample of households, and secondary data collections. Data was collected from 1984-1987. In this paper we use the non-sexist term fishers for ease of writing. In the communities we use the terms of fishermen, fisherwomen or crew members; these are terms to which the people relate.

[2] See Henry Veltmeyer, "The Capitalist Underdevelopment of Atlantic Canada," in *Underdevelopment and Social Movements in Atlantic Canada*, ed. R.J. Brym and R.J. Sacouman (Toronto 1979), 17-35; James Sacouman, "Semi-proletarianization and Rural Underdevelopment in the Maritimes," *Canadian Review of Sociology and Anthropology* 17/3 (1980), 232-45; James Bickerton, "Underdevelopment and Social Movements in Atlantic Canada: A Critique," *Studies in Political Economy* 9 (Fall 1982), 191-202; Michael Clow, "Politics and Uneven Capitalist Development: The Maritime Challenge to the Study of Canadian Political Economy," *Studies in Political Economy* 14 (Spring 1984), 117-40; Ralph Mat-

Reprinted with permission of the *Journal of Canadian Studies*. From *JCS*, 26 4 (Winter 1991-2), 18-31.

is high, and the industry structure is skewed toward traditional primary resource industries and services — many of which are government funded. In particular, opportunities for women in the region are severely limited, and this is reflected in lower labour force participation rates and higher rates of unemployment and seasonal work.[3] However, the fact that the region is underdeveloped does not mean that it is a static economy. Regional underdevelopment is a process whereby change and growth occur, but in a way that is distorted by processes and interests outside the region, that does not create a balanced, integrated economy, and that does not keep pace with growth in the centre of the economy. The Atlantic region has not been a centre for self-sustaining capitalist development for the better part of a century.

In the context of underdevelopment, the role of the state comes into sharp focus.[4] The state attempts to deal with what is referred to as "regional disparity" through policies aimed at creating the conditions for successful capital accumulation in order to attract industry to the region. The Canadian government and the Atlantic provinces have spent millions over the years creating infrastructure and providing subsidies and tax incentives to draw to the region companies such as Michelin, Pratt & Whitney, and Clairtone. In one case, to increase the attraction, the province of Nova Scotia also passed special legislation to regulate the conditions under which workers can unionize.[5] The state's role in facilitating private capital accumulation takes place in the context of the national/international capitalist system — not in the context of maximizing locally based or locally controlled capital accumulation.

In addition to making conditions attractive to industry, the state must be concerned with the large numbers of people unable to find work to support themselves and their families in the region. Maintaining some semblance of social

thews, "Class Interests and the Role of the State in the Development of Canada's East Coast Fishery," *Canadian Issues*, 3, 1 (Spring 1980), 115-24; and Peter Sinclair, "Why Canadian Fisheries Policy Hinders Regional Development: The Case of Newfoundland and Labrador," paper presented at the Ninth International Seminar on Marginal Regions, Skye and Lewis, July 1987.
[3]M.P. Connelly and Martha MacDonald, *Women and the Labour Force, Statistics Canada Focus on Canada Series* (Ottawa 1990).
[4]Our major points of reference for this discussion of the state are: Ralph Miliband, *The State in Capitalist Society* (London 1969); Nicos Poulanatzas, *Political Power and Social Class* (London 1973); James O'Connor, *The Fiscal Crisis of the State* (New York 1981); Leo Panitch, ed., *The Canadian State: Political Economy and Political Power* (Toronto 1977); Zillah Eisenstein, *The Radical Future of Liberal Feminism* (New York 1981); and Mary McIntosh, "The State and the Oppression of Women," in *Feminism and Materialism: Women and Modes of Production*, ed. Annette Kuhn and Ann Marie Wolpe (London 1978), 254-89.
[5]The so-called Michelin Bill made it impossible for workers at individual Michelin plants to unionize separately. The bill specified that all Michelin plants must form one bargaining unit and therefore must be organized within a limited time period. This legislation was passed after a unionization vote had been taken by one of the Michelin plants and the bill was made retroactive.

harmony requires the state to provide monies, through unemployment insurance, welfare and other policies. It is only federal government transfers to the region which have kept it from falling even further behind in terms of incomes.[6]

Nowhere is the role of the state more obvious than in the region's major indigenous industry, the fishery. In the Atlantic region one-quarter of the population lives in small fishing communities where most people are dependent on the fishery for their livelihoods. Since the early 1970s the Canadian state has intervened in a significant way in an attempt to create a viable industry and an adequate social and economic environment for these communities. But by the early 1980s a sizable majority of full-time fishers had total incomes below the poverty line, plant workers earned very low wages, and the processors were near bankruptcy and in need of an economic bail-out by the state. A period of prosperity followed the state "restructuring" of the industry but by 1989 the industry faced yet another crisis. The latest crisis has so far resulted in the closing of several plants and the direct unemployment of hundreds, with more indirect unemployment to follow as communities try to adjust to the loss of their major source of employment.

It is in this context that we examine the role of state policies and their effects on the family household and women's work. Most of the literature on state policy in the fishery focuses on the processing and harvesting sectors. Seldom is the family household and rarely are gender issues mentioned. When the household is addressed it is seen as a cohesive unit with homogeneous interests.[7] The differential impact of policies on women's and men's work inside and outside the household is always ignored. In this paper we argue that policies aimed at particular issues are, in fact, experienced and interpreted as a whole by women and men within households. Even though policies may not be directly aimed at the family household, it is in the household that policies come together in their effects; moreover, these effects are different on women and men. Policies often have unintended consequences since, to the extent possible, households and individual household members develop strategies to use policies in their own interests. People respond and act to influence the direction of change and the development of policy not just as individuals or groups of workers, but also as household members. Household strategies have different effects on women and men.[8]

---

[6]For example, from 1961-76 the annual growth rate of earned income per capita was only 4.81 per cent in Nova Scotia whereas the growth in transfers to persons per capita was 7.86 per cent and transfers to the provincial government grew by 9.8 per cent. Atlantic Provinces Economic Council, *The Atlantic Vision — 1990* (Halifax 1979), 33.

[7]A good example of this can be found in Ottar Brox, *Newfoundland Fishermen in the Age of Industry: A Sociology of Economic Dualism* (St. John's 1972) where he spends an entire chapter on the outport household and never discusses the gendered division of labour or the differential impact of adaptation on family members.

[8]We see this as a contribution to the body of literature on social policies and the way they affect women. See, for example: Monica Boyd, "The Status of Immigrant Women in Canada," *The Canadian Review of Sociology and Anthropology*, 12, 4 (1975), 406-16; Ruth

Subsidies

The state has always played an important role in the fishing industry and it has been especially significant since the 1970s. Gene Barrett has shown historically that the state has been supportive of the growth and development of large-scale fishing capital and since 1974 has strongly supported the establishment and growth of vertically integrated firms.[9] Since the early 1970s, the Atlantic fishery has been in crisis. A low point was reached in 1974. The stated reasons were over-fishing by both Canadians and foreigners, rising costs of catching and processing fish (partly as a result of the oil crisis), and the softening of markets. Between 1974 and 1977 the federal government provided millions to salvage the industry from the crisis. Most of this money went to the large processing companies. In general, the corporate sector with its integrated harvesting (offshore) and processing industry has been supported at the expense of inshore fishers, small processors and fishery-dependent communities. For example, one of the communities we studied had a community owned co-op processing plant. In the early 1970s the co-op expanded its plant out of retained earnings. When the crisis was at its worst the co-op had no back-up resources and went into receivership. The state refused to help: it ran the plant for one year and then sold it to a private owner for a very low price, leaving community members very bitter over losing the plant and their investment of time and money. Another community saw its independent plant go bankrupt while the state supported the National Sea Products plant in that community. The bankrupt plant eventually came under new ownership but it did not resume groundfish processing and as a result the fishers had fewer options and the number of plant jobs fell from over 200 to 55. National Sea gained a stronger bargaining position in its

Pierson, "'Home Aid': A Solution to Women's Unemployment after the Second World War," *Atlantis*, 2, 2 (1977), 85-97; Kathleen Jamieson, *Indian Women and the Law in Canada: Citizens Minus* (Ottawa 1978); Veronica Strong-Boag, "Canada's Early Experience with Income Supplements: The Introduction of Mother's Allowances," *Atlantis*, 4, 2 (1979), 35-43; Veronica Strong-Boag, "Working Women and the State: The Case of Canada 1889-1945," *Atlantis*, 6, 2 (1981), 1-9; Pat Armstrong, "Women and Unemployment," *Atlantis*, 6, 1 (1980), 1-17; Brigette Kitchen, "Women and the Social Security System in Canada," *Atlantis*, 5, 2 (1980), 89-99; Brigette Kitchen, "The Family and Social Policy," in *The Family: Changing Trends in Canada*, ed. Maureen Baker (Toronto 1984), 178-97; Louise Delude, *Pension Reform with Women in Mind* (Ottawa 1981); Canadian Advisory Council on the Status of Women, *Love, Marriage and Money ... An Analysis of Financial Relations Between Spouses* (Ottawa 1984); Margrit Eichler, *Families in Canada Today: Recent Changes and Their Policy Consequences* (Toronto 1983); Margrit Eichler, "The Familism-Individualism Flip-Flop and its Implications for Economic and Social Welfare Policies," in *Social Change and Family Policies, Key Papers*, Part 2, of the 20th International CFR Seminar (Melbourne 1984), 431-72.
[9]Gene Barrett, "Capital and the State: The Structural Content of Fishery Policy Between 1939 and 1977," in *Atlantic Fisheries and Coastal Communities Fisheries Decision Making Case Studies*, ed. C. Lamson and A.J. Hanson (Halifax 1984), 77-104.

relations with both fishers and plant workers, most of whom were women.

Also during the 1970s, the unemployment insurance benefit period for fisher-men was extended and the federal government began seriously to manage and regulate the fishery. Internationally, they negotiated the 200-mile limit with the object of phasing out the foreign fleet; nationally, they developed quota and licensing regulations with the object of holding the Canadian fleet stable until the fish stocks recovered. By 1979 the stocks had begun to rebuild; Canadian catches steadily increased and markets recovered. In the years that followed the estab-lishment of the 200-mile limit, banks provided loans to fishers and processors and the state passed out large subsidies to processors for buying new vessels, for expanding plan facilities, and for building new plants.[10] The Fisheries Loan Board also extended large loans to fishermen.[11] Improved conditions in the fishery had a different effect on women and men as family members rearranged their labour. In one community we learned that fishers who had kept their boats through the bad times began to earn higher incomes, as did the inshore and offshore crew. Fish-plant wages, however, remained relatively low, and families with both husband and wife in the plant had combined incomes that were lower than most fishers. With the increase in the fishers' income, it no longer made economic sense for their wives to work for low wages in the plant. Under these conditions fishery households rearranged their work patterns but plant worker households did not. Fishers' wives in this community decided to return to the home even though many preferred to continue earning a wage. This decision was made in the interest of the household since, given their husbands' income and the wage level in the plant, their full-time domestic labour would make a greater contribution than their wage labour. With the withdrawal of fishers' wives from the plant, the owner had the option to raise wages, to substitute capital for labour, or to find a more marginalized labour supply. The latter option was taken. With the opening of a state-funded ferry service, women from a community across a small bay, who had previously had no employment opportunities, were happy to have the jobs at low wages. This example illustrates several points. First, the fisher/plant worker household strategy involved the real-location of women's, not men's, labour and in some cases involved women putting the household's interest over their own interests. Secondly, the household's strategy overrode the needs of capital: that is, the employers' need for cheap labour. And finally, the ferry is an example of the state providing the conditions for capital accumulation through the provision of infrastructures, when needed.

By 1981 the industry was once again in crisis. Specific reasons given for the crisis were: increased foreign competition for United States markets (from countries with currencies lower than Canada's against the American dollar); the sudden softening of the American fish market; and high interest rates which led to the

[10]Michael Kirby, *Navigating Troubled Waters: A New Policy for the Atlantic Fisheries, Report of the Task Force on Atlantic Fisheries* (Ottawa 1982).
[11]During the 1981 crisis many fishers were unable to meet their loan payments and there was an extremely high rate of boat repossessions.

reduction of Canadian fish inventories in external markets. Over-capitalization and over-expansion in relation to a vulnerable resource was also recognized as a reason for the crisis. The federal government responded by appointing a Task Force to determine how a viable fishing industry could be achieved and maintained. A year later the Task Force presented their objectives and recommendations for an Atlantic fisheries policy and these clearly pointed to the state's role in fostering capital accumulation and social harmony. The first major objective was to develop policies to help create a viable industry that would not require government assistance. The second pointed to maximizing employment and providing reasonable incomes, including fishery-related income-transfer payments.[12] However, according to the recommendations, if economic viability were to conflict with employment then economic viability should be given priority.[13] This decision was readily made in the 1990 crisis as we shall see below.

To prevent immediate collapse of the industry, the Task Force recommended that it be restructured. In Nova Scotia this took the form of a new amalgamated company, National Sea Products Ltd. (amalgamation of National Sea Products Ltd. and Nickerson and Sons Ltd.). The deal resulted in paying off the banks, leaving the private sector in control for the smallest investment, giving the federal government a small amount of equity and control for the largest input of capital, and giving the province no equity for the second largest amount of financial support. Rick Williams sums it up nicely:

By any standards, the crisis in the Nova Scotia fishing industry has been "resolved" by an outrageous scandal. The banks have been bailed out. The Nickersons received $3 million cash for their National Sea shares, so they're OK. The people of Nova Scotia, whose government is already $500 million in debt, have handed over $50 million more to the private sector with no equity position. The people of Canada have handed over $90 million with no meaningful control over the use of the investment. No changes in the overall direction of the company have been announced. There has been, in a word, no "restructuring."[14]

With this arrangement the government once again reaffirmed its development direction. Despite the fact that this strategy had failed in the past to provide stability in the industry, the government continued to consider a highly concentrated, capital-intensive, vertically integrated fishery as the way of the future. Because the strategy was well-entrenched, attempts to reorganize or restructure the industry on a large scale would have resulted in serious short-run adjustment costs for the entire

---

[12]There are three major objectives outlined in the Kirby Task Force Report. The third objective is that fish within the 200-mile Canadian Zone should be harvested and processed by Canadians in firms owned by Canadians wherever this is consistent with objectives 1 and 2 and with Canada's international treaty obligations.

[13]See Kirby, *Navigating Troubled Waters*.

[14]Rick Williams, "The Restructuring that Wasn't: The Scandal at National Sea," *Canadian Dimension*, 19, 1 (March/April 1985), 10-13.

industry. For that reason most sectors of the fishery supported the bail-out of the large corporations.

What did "restructuring" mean for women's and men's work in fish plants? After the "restructuring" the pressure on National Sea to show a profit increased significantly. Attempts to increase productivity in all of their plants was a step in that direction. One of the communities had a brand new modern plant and there was some feeling that it was to be treated as a test case. Time-management people were brought in, new computers were used to measure individual productivity and strictly to enforce individual performance levels of output. Previously, individual performance levels were more difficult to measure for both quality and quantity and they were only loosely enforced. The emphasis had been on average production levels and workers who trimmed the fish earned average bonuses for the line.

Under the new system, the performance level was based on the amount of fish processed in a given time period and the quality of the product obtained. While each worker had to meet a performance level, the complexity of measurement differed by job. Cutters (who were all men) knew approximately how many pounds they had to cut and packers knew approximately how many packs they must do. The greatest change was for the trimmers (who were all women), whose expected output varied depending on the quality of fish being processed. Only the most experienced trimmers knew at the end of the day whether they had made the required performance level. Under these new conditions the turnover rate skyrocketed. Women quit because they couldn't stand the pressure or were let go for not making "performance." Although the basic bonus and performance level system was not new to the workers, it was applied and experienced in a totally new way. Conditions were somewhat better for men, since they did the jobs that were not only better paying but also allowed for freedom of movement and a more varied workload.

The increased pressure in the plant made women's second job in the home more onerous and in response the household strategy changed. Women worked for wages as long as they could stand the pressure, then quit and went on unemployment insurance. This allowed them time to rest, to spend time with their children, and to get their housework "under control," as they put it. This forced the plant to widen the radius from which they hired their labour force. The new employees were not used to the hard work of fish processing and often had to travel long distances to the plant. High turnover was affecting productivity. Although the plant had informed women in the community that they would not be rehired if they quit, in fact they were usually hired back because they were the best workers. The new household strategy involved the rearranging of women's work so that they could continue to do both their wage and domestic labour. It did not involve women continuing to do their paid work while sharing the household and childcare work with their husbands. As this example shows, the policy of "restructuring" meant changes in the labour process in the plant and changes in household strategies, both of which differentially affected women's and men's work.

By 1990, after a period of prosperity in the industry and expansion and high profits for National Sea, the fishery was once again in crisis. The policies of the 1980s did not create the much needed stability in the industry. The reasons given for the latest crisis are declining fish stocks and increasing fishing capacity.[15] The Department of Fisheries and Oceans announced that many fish stocks were depleted and fish quotas would be drastically cut. The response by the large companies was to close plants. For example, National Sea announced the closure of five fish plants. Two of these are in Nova Scotia, unemploying 1,200 workers. These two communities have been based on the fishing industry for over two hundred years and there are no employment alternatives in these one-industry towns. The communities have asked National Sea to keep all of their plants operating at full capacity on a seasonal basis rather than close some plants and maintain others at full capacity year round. The company argues that this is too inefficient and too costly. The choice between the economic concerns of the company and the employment needs of people in the fishing communities was made with little difficulty it seems. All of the communities have appealed to the provincial and federal governments to help keep their plants open. How will the state respond? Will there be another bail-out of National Sea?

With the Free Trade Agreement in place, the state is constrained in the type of subsidies that it can provide in the fishery without triggering countervailing action by the United States. In February 1990 a deal was announced whereby the federal and provincial governments would spend several million dollars to prevent one of the Nova Scotia plants and one of the Newfoundland plants from closing permanently. The deal for the Nova Scotia plant included a nine-month shutdown, job-sharing to maintain part of the workforce (300 out of 750), and replacement of the plant's refrigeration system. The trawler fleet and the crew of 150 men were to be moved from the community and fish would be trucked in from other ports. The plan was for 150 people to work 20 weeks, followed by another 150 for the same period, allowing 300 of the workforce to qualify for UI benefits. This would eliminate the need for severance pay, saving the company more than $500,000. The federal and provincial governments have agreed to cover part of the losses National Sea incurs by operating the plant next year at reduced capacity.[16] Community and union leaders, who were not consulted, were highly critical of the plan. In effect, the National Sea plant gets to continue plant specialization, its strategy through the 1980s, using government money. Again, the subsidies fit in with corporate plans, not community needs and potential. This plan was ultimately rejected, and a buyer has been found for the two plants in question; this purchase, of course, is also to be heavily subsidized by the state. The province of Nova Scotia will assume $17.5 million in debt for the Canso plant. This debt was part of the $20 million loaned to National Sea in the 1984 "restructuring" deal. In addition to being relieved of this debt, National Sea gets $3.5 million upon signing the deal and another $8.5 million

[15]J.E. Hache, *Report of the Scotia-Fundy Groundfish Task Force* (Ottawa, December 1989).
[16]Brian Ward, "Fish plant jobs to be 'time-shared'" and "NatSea workers cheated opposition," *The Chronicle Herald*, February 7 and March 21, 1990, respectively.

in payments (after three years at a nine per cent interest rate) from the buyer who is listed as putting into the deal $6 million in equity, including $3 million for a fish plant bought for $100,000. The federal and provincial governments are also investing in a new refrigeration system at a cost of $5.5 million. The new deal will mean employment for 500 people for ten months a year, and some trawlers (and quota) will stay with the plant. National Sea, the new owners and the community of Canso benefit from the deal but everyone else in the industry resents it.[17]

It seems clear that the state's support over the years for increasing concentration in the industry has not led to the objective either of an economically viable industry without government assistance or of maximum employment for people in fishing communities as outlined in the Kirby Task Force. There are some voices calling for a more diversified, medium-size plant, community-based fishery. Given the powerful corporate sector's view that only large capital can be internationally competitive, and the state's support of that view through its policies, a shift in the direction of development within the fisheries is highly unlikely.

Insuring Incomes

As indicated above, income insurance is an integral part of the strategies of both households and corporations. Plant workers have always been eligible for unemployment insurance (UI) provided they have enough weeks of work to qualify; however, this has not been the case for fishers. Until the late 1950s, when a special amendment to the UI Act was passed to cover them, fishers were considered to be self-employed or co-adventurers and therefore ineligible for UI. In 1976 the benefit period was extended to cover a longer period of time for all fishermen. Wives who fish with their husbands were not eligible for UI until the Act was challenged in 1979 by a woman who set and hauled nets and gutted and cleaned fish on her husband's boat. She had the weeks to qualify, had paid Canada Pension and a UI deduction, and in addition had paid $60 a week for a babysitter, but what she earned was considered "joint income" and this meant that only her husband was eligible for UI. In 1980 she won her case and fisherwomen became eligible.[18]

The incomes of fishers vary considerably but a sizeable majority of full-time fishers have total incomes below the poverty line. In 1981, 83 per cent of full-time fishers received unemployment insurance, which averaged 16 per cent of total income.[19] Fish-plant hourly wage rates are significantly lower than those in other manufacturing industries in the region and fish-plant work is highly seasonal which means that plant workers' earnings are not high and unemployment insurance is an important income supplement. UI has also become increasingly important as subsistence activities like cutting firewood are no longer profitable options. Cash

[17]Rob Gorham, "The Seafreez Shuffle," *The Chronicle-Herald*, October 6, 1990.
[18]*Awareness for Women in the Fishery Project Report* (Cape Breton, funded by Secretary of State, 1985), 12.
[19]See Kirby, *Navigating Troubled Waters*, 54, 61 (see #11 above).

needs have increased as the rural economy becomes more integrated into the market economy.

In our research we found that UI has had an effect on household labour allocation decisions. UI has facilitated the breakdown of male occupational plural-ism in favour of more family members participating in the labour market and thus becoming eligible for its benefits. Occupational pluralism for men has been replaced by family pluralism. When we examined patterns of work and UI use in our sample of households, we found that 42 per cent of wives were working and on average they contributed 34 per cent of family income (ranging from 9 per cent to 45 per cent in different communities). Of these women, 28 per cent were in fish plants and the rest were in the service sector. Of the men, 42 per cent were in fishing or plant work. For fisher families, UI represented on average 11 per cent of family income (ranging from 5 per cent to 26 per cent in different communities). UI was more important for women plant workers than for male plant workers who tended to have the steadier jobs in the plants. Given the decline of subsistence activities and the increasing need for cash to meet household maintenance needs, UI has affected individual and household labour allocation decision-making. As fish stocks decline, dependence on UI increases.

The effect of UI is very controversial. Generally, UI is viewed as improving conditions for households in the short run, thus fulfilling its "social harmony" role. However, UI is often viewed as detrimental in the long run. Typical arguments include that it creates work disincentives, keeps incomes from rising in the fishery (by encouraging too many people to fish), and prevents "regional adjustment." The latter is generally understood to mean out-migration from the region. Thus, the critique of UI is usually based on its interference with capital accumulation.

Although UI is generally presented as supporting labour, it can also be seen to have a capital accumulation function in that it underwrites the cost of labour in seasonal industries such as fish processing. UI maintains a pool of labour to be used in these communities, a pool to which the employer is thus able to pay lower wages. Furthermore, UI (like the public sector as a whole) serves to help maintain a capitalist system (or region) when the private sector is unable to provide jobs for the increasing labour reserve — as in the present crisis.

There is an ongoing controversy about UI. In 1986 the Forget Commission Report recommended dropping regionally extended benefits; it also recommended phasing out UI benefits for fishers (over a five-year period), arguing that they were self-employed and would be better served by an income stabilization/supplemen-tation program.[20] Forget also proposed an annualization scheme, basing benefits on average weekly earnings over a year. This was a particular threat to seasonal workers, be they employed in fish processing or tourism. Forget's reforms would

[20]See *Commission of Inquiry into Unemployment Insurance: Final Report* (Ottawa 1986); Canada, House of Commons Issue No. 28. *Minutes of Proceedings and Evidence of the Standing Committee on Labour, Employment and Immigration. Respecting: A Study of Unemployment Insurance. Including: The First Report to the House* (1987).

have made UI benefits for such workers less than welfare payments. The labour representatives on the Commission filed a minority report, supporting the interests of recipient groups such as fishers and seasonal workers. Both the Minority Report and the report of the House of Commons Standing Committee on Labour Employment and Immigration rejected the key features of the Forget Commission's recommendations. They also argued for the retention of fishers' UI.

There was intense public opposition to the Forget Report in the Atlantic region. Opposition came from the affected groups, like fishers, but it also came from the provincial governments which, as we have seen, are very dependent on transfer income. In May 1987, the Minister of Employment and Immigration ended the immediate controversy by recommending that the UI system remain unchanged. This, of course, meant rejecting reform notions from all sides — those who wanted to expand the benefits, as well as those who wanted to reduce them. Politically, it seemed too costly to move in either direction. The response to the Forget recommendations underscores the tension between the state's role in capital accumulation and social harmony. The social harmony aspect of UI and the failure of private-sector capital accumulation to create jobs for significant numbers of Canadians make it extremely difficult to change the *status quo* although the federal government continues to try. In 1989 the Conservative government introduced new unemployment insurance legislation that would result in people in the Atlantic region needing to work a greater number of weeks to qualify for UI and making them eligible for fewer weeks of benefits. In this legislation as well UI money would be used for job-training, a factor which is irrelevant in communities with few job options. The federal government, which had been funding regionally extended benefits and fishers' UI, would under the new legislation drop this funding. Indeed, it was proposed that the whole UI program would be funded by employee/employer contributions, thus generating the fear that the change would undermine the political will to maintain these programs. In response, the Liberal-dominated Senate has delayed legislation in order to get public input by means of hearings held across the country.

Income-maintenance policies like UI that help to legitimate the system by "helping" people are not necessarily in the long-term interests of people. This point was strongly made in the Newfoundland Royal Commission on Employment and Unemployment Report.[21] Its authors showed that UI propped up centralized capitalism and undermined local independence, initiative and development. They argued for massive reform of social security, but not of the punitive type recommended by Forget. They argued for a system that encourages local initiative, development and skill rather than one that escalates a psychology of dependence. At the same time, their recommendations were designed to provide income guarantees for people.

[21]Royal Commission on Employment and Unemployment, *Building on Our Strengths* (St. John's 1986).

UI is a policy aimed specifically at individuals. People are generally eligible, regardless of gender or family status. However, such policies do impact differently on men and women. We have seen how in the case of UI for fishers, fisher wives were originally ineligible. The UI program is also gender-biased in its discrimination against part-time workers, most of whom are female. We have also pointed out how household labour allocation decisions are affected by UI. UI facilitated the shift from male occupational pluralism to a labour market in which more family members participated, thus becoming eligible for UI. To the extent that UI encourages the "ten-week worker," it is argued that so-called secondary earners in families (i.e., women) will be more likely to respond in this way. A background study for the Newfoundland Royal Commission undertaken by Douglas May and Alton Hollett argued that UI may thus partly explain the increased participation rate among rural women.[22] The findings from our research show that it is women who mainly reallocate and readjust their labour as conditions change, in order to maintain the family household. Women's work decisions seem to be dependent on their husbands' situations whereas the men's decisions remain independent. It is the women, therefore, who adjust their work to the economic rationality of UI. Thus we found, for example, where male fishing incomes (including UI) were high, wives were discouraged from labour-force participation.

In their Newfoundland study, May and Hollett also note that UI has forced households to alter their non-market work due to regulations defining "availability for work." They use the example of people having to do household economy work (such as boat repairs) outside of the hours of nine to five in order to conform to UI regulations. They also suggest that some people "buy" stamps — paying an employer to put them on the payroll and to pay benefits on their behalf. This may not be common, but it shows the extent to which UI does affect individual and household decision-making; it also shows the extent to which "people have adapted the UI system to meet their very real needs."[23]

Regulating the Industry

Since 1974 the government has taken a major role in regulating the fishery. This role became even stronger once the 200-mile limit was introduced in 1977. Regulation of the industry was done, in large part, by creating fish quotas for various fleets and by limiting entry to the fisheries through licensing. These regulatory measures are meant to match the fishing effort to the available resource, thereby creating stability in the industry. Having created these regulations the government was put in the position of having to mediate between the needs and demands of fishermen and processors. Who would get what licences? How would the quotas be distributed? These issues are the source of conflict, especially between inde-

---

[22]Douglas May and Alton Hollett, *The Causes of Unemployment in Newfoundland* (St. John's 1986).
[23]*Ibid.*, 193.

pendent inshore fishermen and the vertically integrated processing companies that operate offshore trawlers.

In 1984 Enterprise Allocations (EAs), which gave each company that owned groundfish trawlers a guaranteed share of the overall quota, became a permanent feature of managing the fishery. Unlike the inshore/midshore fleet these companies no longer have to compete for their share of the quota. National Sea, for example, can now make decisions on when, where and how much of particular species should be harvested. This policy was created in order to allow processing companies to fish according to market demand, thereby preventing over-fishing by their offshore trawlers. In 1986 and 1987 National Sea had large profits which they indicated were due, at least in part, to Enterprise Allocations. Clearly, Enterprise Allocations were an enormous gain for the processors over the independent fishers who still had to compete with one another to survive.

EAs may have provided more stability for the company, but did they provide more stability for the household and the community? Our research showed that EAs have significantly altered patterns of how/where fish is caught and when/where it is processed. In the case of the offshore trawler fleet, National Sea now carefully directs and co-ordinates the fishing of each vessel from head office. Whereas the captain of a trawler traditionally had considerable control over where to fish and what to catch in order to catch as much of the quota for the company as possible, under the new system the company directs the vessel as to where to fish, for what species, and in what amounts. Now a trawler is sent to a particular zone to catch a particular species (and nothing else), and may come back with a catch that only earns broker pay for the captain and crew. Captains object to the loss of control and trawler crews are worried about falling incomes. The new approach to planned fishing has also had a negative impact on family life.

Our data show that trawler-crew wives do not work outside the home. Until recently, crew incomes were good and crew schedules left them in port for short periods of time. As a rule men are at sea for up to fourteen days and at home for forty-eight hours. Given these schedules trawler crews do almost no work in the household, not even the routine outdoor tasks typically done by men. The entire household responsibility rests on the women's shoulders. With men's incomes decreasing and their jobs becoming more precarious, women now have to look for paid work, a household strategy that will have a negative impact on women's workload and well being.

When the present crisis developed, National Sea announced plans to move an entire trawler fleet from one community to another, totally disrupting trawler-crew households. In fact, according to government regulation the company is allowed to take their Enterprise Allocation away from the community. The quota belongs to the company, not to the plant or community. As already noted, National Sea is also closing plants and laying off workers. As a result, affected communities must now fight for their survival. They have also been asking the government not to allow the company to take the Enterprise Allocation out of the community. An unintended consequence of the policy is that communities are losing not only their quotas but also their jobs. In the latest deal to reopen the National Sea plant in Canso, special arrangements have been made to give some quota to the purchasing company, a move which solves one problem but makes the quota system arbitrary and *ad hoc*, thus causing other conflicts and problems.

Another regulatory issue of concern has been the matter of whether to allow factory-freezer trawlers. For many years National Sea had been requesting factory-freezer trawler licences (FFT) from the government. National Sea argues that this is a more profitable way to harvest and process fish. For its part the government has refused to grant such licences because of concern over loss of onshore employment. However, with EAs in place, the government decided that an FFT would probably operate efficiently and profitably; thus, National Sea was awarded one licence. The government was well aware of the consequences of the FFT for the community since their own discussion paper indicated that there would be a net loss of shore-based employment.[24] In addition, the pattern of women working in the plant in order to contribute to household incomes and to become eligible for UI benefits in the off-season would have to change, since FFTs meant long periods at sea for the workers, a condition which women with families would find difficult. In fact, the introduction of FFTs resulted in a shift from female to male and from older to younger workers.

Like EAs, limited-entry licensing policies were aimed at conserving the resource and promoting the stability and economic viability of the fishery. But as Ralph Bannister argues, not only have these policies not reached their goal, they have also had some unintended and very negative consequences.[25] These policies attempt to promote equitable access to the fisheries and to control the harvesting capacity of vessels by limiting the number, size, and type of new vessel. However, as Bannister shows, they only encouraged those who could afford it to buy the latest, very expensive technology for their existing boats in order to increase their harvesting capacity. Equipped with the new technology, these boats have specialized in harvesting only the most marketable fish, thus disrupting the historical fishing patterns and increasing conflict between fishers. Unlike the traditional multi-use vessel that could change operating patterns as biological and market conditions varied, these new, highly specialized boats are vulnerable to changes in the availability of resources and in market conditions since there are no alternative uses for them. In the scramble to catch the biggest share of the quota, these boats fish away from their home ports, thus further disrupting family life and putting an additional workload on women. In response, families, as well as boats, have become more specialized and hence more vulnerable. When the Department of Fisheries

[24]Canada, Department of Fisheries and Oceans, *Discussion Paper on Factory Freezer Trawlers* (Ottawa 1985).

[25]Ralph Bannister, "Orthodoxy and the Theory of Fishery Management: The Policy and Practice of Fishery Management Theory Past and Present," MA thesis, Saint Mary's University, 1989.

and Oceans announced that many fish stocks were depleted and that quotas would be drastically cut, these boat owners responded by asking for higher quotas. The processors, as we have seen, responded by laying off workers and closing plants. Clearly, these policies have not created the stability necessary to maintain workers, their households or their communities.

Conclusion

Until recently, literature examining the impact of social policies on the family has treated the family as a cohesive unit with homogeneous interests, ignoring the fact that it consists of women and men whose individual interests may differ. New work by feminist researchers has corrected this focus by examining family policies and the way they specifically affect women. In this paper, we add to this research by examining how several more general (i.e., not obviously family-related) social and economic policies affect women and men in households under specific political and economic conditions of regional underdevelopment. We examine three types of policies in the Atlantic fishery: subsidies to the private sector; income maintenance of individuals (UI); and fishery regulatory policies. At one level these policies are aimed at fostering capital accumulation and social harmony; at another level they seek to solve specific problems faced by employers and workers in the industry. The family household and gender relations are not taken into account in the policy-making process; they are also ignored by analysts of the state. By integrating the family household and its women and men members, we feel that we have added an essential dimension to an analysis of what appear to be non-family-related policies.

We have shown that while policies are developed to deal with particular issues, such as the problem of stock depletion, and to address the needs of particular groups, such as fishers or plant workers, these specific policies are, in fact, experienced and interpreted as a whole by women and men within households. Even though policies may not be directly aimed at the family household, it is in the household that policies come together in their effects, and these effects are different on women and men. We have also shown that household members do not simply react to policies; they also act by developing strategies to use policies in innovative ways to serve the household's interest. People respond and act to influence the direction of change and the development of policy, not just as individuals or groups of workers but also as household members. Our data show that a major component of the household strategy is the reallocation and rearrangement of women's domestic and wage labour. Because of unequal gender relations in the household, women often pay the highest price as households respond to changing conditions and policies.

We would like to thank the people in the communities we studied and the members of our research team, Joyce Conrad, Linda Gallant, Suzan Ilcan, Beth McIsaac, Kathy Moggridge, and Daphne Tucker, for their contributions. This research was supported by a grant from the Canadian Donner Foundation and a SSHRC Women and Work Strategic Grant. All papers out of this joint research are co-authored with alternating order of names.

Harry Glasbeek and Eric Tucker

17

Death by Consensus: The Westray Mine Story

I. Introduction

At about 5:20 on the morning of May 9, 1992, an explosion ripped through the Westray coal mine in Pictou County, Nova Scotia, killing 26 miners. A 10-day search and rescue operation led to the recovery of only 15 of the miners' bodies. The horror and anxiety of the families and friends can only be imagined. Politicians and the mine owner expressed their condolences in sonorous tones and praised the herculean efforts of the unsuccessful rescue workers.

In a sense, all of this is humdrum. Mining disasters involving mass deaths are familiar events. In Pictou County itself, 246 miners already had been killed in a series of explosions which occurred between 1838 and 1952. Most miners killed on the job, however, die in less spectacular circumstances. Another 330 Pictou miners suffered accidental deaths from other causes (that is, falls of stone, crushed by coal cars, mangled by mining machinery) between 1866 and 1972. In addition, an unknown number of miners were killed between the time commercial mining began, 1809, and the year record-keeping began, 1866. Also unknown is the number of workers who died prematurely from occupational diseases.[1] In short, it is routine

[1]Table of Recorded Coal-Mining Explosion Fatalities Pictou County, 1838-1952

Year	Number Killed
1838	2
1858	2
1861	3
1872	60
1880	44
1885	13
1914	2
1918	88
1924	4
1952	19

Source: James M. Cameron, *The Pictonian Colliers* (Halifax 1974), 163-253.

for miners to be killed, maimed, or made ill by their work.[2]

The responses to these recurring mining catastrophes also are routine: doleful mourning, expression of anger followed by the setting up of an inquiry. Westray is only exceptional in the number of inquiries it has spawned: no less than four have been initiated.[3] Invariably, these inquiries reveal that the deaths and injuries are attributable, at least in part, to violations of existing mining regulations.[4] This finding inexorably leads to statements of firm resolve that there will be no recurrences, no more violations, no more disasters. But, as the record shows, these oft-asserted goals are never realized. The reason why this dreary sequence — accidents, inquiries, recommendations — does not bring about much amelioration is that whatever changes in practices are sought to be implemented, both the broader political economic and some specific operative assumptions about occupational health and safety regulation remain unexamined, leaving the improved practices subject to the same weaknesses as the preceding standards of operation.[5]

These recurring episodes only came to an end when the incidence of coal mining declined sharply during the 1960s. Almost all of the coal mining which led to these "accidents" in Pictou County took place as investors sought to take advantage of a particularly rich deposit sited there, known as the Foord seam. Westray was the most recent adventurer to seek to extract profit from that treacherous seam.

[2]Miners have the third highest fatality rate in Canada, after forestry and fishing. It is over seven times the average. Labor Canada, *Employment Injuries and Occupational Illnesses, 1985-87* (Ministry of Supply and Services 1990), Table 6.

[3]The government of Nova Scotia has appointed a judge to head a commission of inquiry; the Royal Canadian Mounted Police (RCMP) has begun a police investigation; the minister responsible for mine safety in the province has ordered his own department to investigate its performance and the causes of the disasters; and the owner of Westray Mine has hired its own investigation team.

[4]John Braithwaite, *To Punish or Persuade* (Albany 1985); Andrew Hopkins, "Blood Money? The Effect of Bonus Pay on Safety in Coal Mines," *Australia and New Zealand Journal of Sociology*, 20, 1 (1984), 23; and Harry M. Caudill, "Manslaughter in a Coal Mine," *The Nation*, 23 April 1977. As the text will show, such violations had preceded the explosion at Westray.

[5]For similar analyses of accident inquiries, see W.G. Carson, "Occupational Health and Safety: A Political Economy Perspective," *Labor & Industry*, 2 (1989), 301, esp. 310-15, and Kit Carson and Cathy Henenberg "The Political Economy of Legislative Change: Making Sense of Victoria's New Occupational Health and Safety Legislation," *Law in Context*, 6 (1988), 2, esp. 3-8. A recent Canadian example of this approach to the investigation of occupational health and safety disasters was the Royal Commission on the Ocean Ranger Marine Disaster. For a critique, see W.G. Carson, "Ocean Ranger. Still More Questions to Come," *At the Center*, 7, 4 (1984), 15. Ironically, these academic critiques are substantiated by an explosion in nearby Cape Breton on 24 February 1979. Twelve coal miners were killed at the federally operated mine. The ensuing investigation and report recommended changes in safety practices and investigations to prevent the recurrence of conditions which led to the explosion. These recommendations were accepted. The conditions which were sought to be prevented bear a striking resemblance to the ones which prevailed at Westray only 13 years later and only a few miles away.

It is these assumptions on which we focus in this paper. We want to explore how the Canadian, and more particularly the Nova Scotian, political economic context creates an environment in which the protection of workers from harm is only a minor consideration in the decision-making and behavior of government officials and private investors.

An especially important aspect of that context is the dominance of staple extraction in the economy. It has coloured relations between capital and the state as well as between labor and capital. From the beginning, the exploitation of Canada's abundant natural resources has been seen as the engine of growth. This has required the state to be more directly supportive of private capital than is the case in economies whose growth is more tied to its manufacturing base. Governments have had to subsidize resource extraction through huge investments in infrastructure. The hope is that the returns on the sale of resources will lead to the development of domestic industry which will supply local markets. For this strategy to succeed, much depends on the international market for the resources. Because the government cannot control those markets, it has very few tools with which to manage the economy. Its reliance on capital's willingness to invest becomes a profound dependency.[6] Over time, this creates an ideological climate in which governments openly advocate that they should do everything in their power to create a favourable climate for investment. This makes close links between elected politicians, government bureaucrats, and capitalists the norm rather than the exception. In regions where the staple-led growth strategy has failed to produce any kind of industrial development, potential employers are able to have governments create particularly attractive conditions for them. Nova Scotia — and Pictou County, Nova Scotia, especially — is such a region. Michelin Tire, for example, was able to have the basic, well-established labour laws re-drafted so that it could avoid unionization. The government's incentive was to retain the jobs created by Michelin Tire. It succeeded. One of Michelin's factories is in Pictou County; indeed, it is the county's largest employer.[7]

Linked to, and reinforcing, this kind of political economy are a number of assumptions to the following effect:

1) as risk is a natural and unavoidable consequence of productive activity in general, and staple extraction in particular, any given set of social relations of production is not determinative of the level of risk created;

2) private economic activity is preferable to public activity;

3) occupational health and safety is an area in which workers and employers share a common set of interests and objectives. While a shared ideology does not prevent workers and employers from having disputes over the distribution of their joint productive efforts — requiring them to engage in adversarial bargaining from

[6]The literature on staple-led growth is extensive. For an overview, see Janine Brodie, *The Political Economy of Canadian Regionalism* (Toronto 1990).
[7]Brian Langille, "The Michelin Amendment in Context," *Dalhousie Law Journal*, 6 (1981), 523.

time to time — health and safety issues do not give rise to the same kind of disputes and, therefore, problems should be resolved as much as possible by consensus;

4) legal forms, such as the contract of employment and the corporate form, are neutral and facilitative.

The events at Westray call into question the validity of all of these assumptions and, unless an inquiry finally faces up to these more fundamental issues, it is likely that history will repeat itself again, not as farce, but as tragedy. The paper will proceed as follows. We will tell the Westray story in two parts, first, the decision to set up the mine and, second, the operation of the mine. These events illuminate the salience of the broader political economic context to an understanding of what happened. Further, the story gives the lie to the assumptions which underpin health and safety regulation. Next, we detail the implications of the political economy and the prevailing ideology for the enforcement of health and safety regulation. We then critically examine a component of, or prop for, the consensus theory which postulates that workers and capitalists share, in some roughly comparable way, the risks of production. In part, this is done by examining the proposition that the corporate form is a neutral, facilitating device.

II. The Making of a Disaster

A. The Decision to Mine

Underground coal mining in Pictou County virtually ceased by the end of the 1950s as a result of the loss of markets to fuel oil, aging facilities, and deep seams which were expensive to mine.[8] But, the local Foord coal seam has some particularly attractive features, which made it likely that there would be someone new coming forward to resume mining in the area. The coal seam is unusually thick, varying from 2 to 8 metres, its sulphur content is below one per cent, and it is a high energy producer, generating between 10,000 to 12,000 British Thermal Units per pound. Reserves are estimated at approximately 45 million tons. But, as its history has shown, the seam also presents some significant problems for profitable and safe mining. The area in which the seam is located is widely known to be gaseous, exuding significant quantities of methane, and is highly geologically faulted. This increases the risk that the roofs of the underground rooms will collapse. Spontaneous combustion also had been a problem in previous mining operations in the area. The ash content of the coal seam varies significantly.[9]

Although investors are always on the look-out for new opportunities which might arise as a result of changing market conditions and new technologies, none could contemplate coal mining in the Pictou area before 1982. The federal government had set up the Cape Breton Development Corporation (Devco) as a crown

---

[8]On the history of mining in Pictou County generally, see James M. Cameron, *The Pictonian Colliers*.

[9]Ash is an impurity which may have to be removed, increasing the cost of coal production.

corporation to mine coal in Cape Breton in 1967. When it did so, it extracted an agreement from the province not to issue new coal mining licences on the mainland for a 15-year period.

As the end of the ban approached, Suncor was the first resource company to express interest in resuming underground mining in the Pictou coalfield.[10] It began intensive feasibility studies in 1981, acquired coal rights and exploration licences from the province, and purchased and optioned land above the contemplated mining site. But, Suncor decided not to exploit its leases. In February 1987, Placer Development Ltd. took an option on Suncor's interests and conducted its own feasibility study which was completed in July of that year.

An examination of the four volumes produced by that study discloses a remarkable lack of direct and explicit concern for the health and safety of miners. To the extent that hazards are considered, they are discussed in the context of whether they would render mining technically and economically infeasible. The health and safety of miners is not identified as an independent factor in the study. For example, the second volume considers the mining operations. It begins by setting out the parameters which were used in developing a mine design proposal. There is no express statement to the effect that the mine should be designed to minimize the risk of harm to workers. Indeed, of the 11 parameters set out, only two or three relate to safety, and then only indirectly.[11] Existing health and safety regulations are discussed briefly in the report, but this amounts to little more than a description of the statutory requirements regarding certified personnel and training.[12] This lack of concern does not stem from ignorance.

The report reveals an awareness of the geological faults, the dangerous roof and floor conditions to which this may lead, the potential for spontaneous combustion, and the dangerous presence of methane. These are not, however, identified as health and safety problems. Rather, they are considered primarily as problems which go to technical and economic feasibility. At best, health and safety is subsumed within these engineering and profit-maximizing calculations.[13]

[10]George E. Wimpey of Canada Ltd. explored the option of open pit mining in 1979 and the Nova Corporation conducted tests between 1979 and 1987 to determine whether methane extraction was commercially viable. See Placer Development Limited, *Pictou Project Feasibility Study*, Vol. 1, Geology (July 1987), Table 1.2. [*PPFS*] (released by federal government, available on request).
[11]*PPFS*, Vol. 2, Mining, 2. One parameter is that there should be isolation of units to permit sealing off of worked-out areas to minimize the risk of spontaneous combustion.
[12]*Ibid.*, 43-6.
[13]This approach is widespread. A study of American mine engineers found that "the mining engineer was compelled to subordinate whatever technical considerations might create conflicts to more comprehensive and commanding economic considerations ... But it would be wrong to presume that many mining engineers found this to be a particularly stressful situation, for in the past, as at present, they largely accepted the industry on its own terms"; Arthur L. Donovan, "Health and Safety in Underground Coal Mining, 1900-1969: Professional Conduct in a Peripheral Industry," in Ronald Bayer ed., *The Health and Safety of*

This relegation of the value of human life to a lesser concern when engaged in planning permits the designers to feel comfortable about their belief in the capacity of modern mine technology and management to solve problems as they might arise. This faith suffuses the entire report. For example, in the first few pages of the report there is a brief discussion of mining history in the Pictou coalfield. After noting that the records "include references to fires and explosions associated with the mining industry," the report continues, "technological advances in underground coal mining and more stringent regulations have decreased the frequency of such occurrences."[14] So much for the lessons of history. Later on, in the context of discussions of the potential for roof collapses, confidence is expressed that problems will be detected and that appropriate adjustments will be made.[15] Had the risk to the lives of the miners who might be killed or injured been squarely before these planners, they might have been less sanguine about their implicit assumption that nothing would go wrong.

In the event, Placer Development merged with two other mining companies and it chose not to proceed with the Pictou project.[16] It was at this point that the people who were to be the Westray mine operators came forward. They commissioned their own feasibility study from Kilborn Limited in November 1987 and, in December 1987, purchased Suncor's interests. Kilborn's study closely paralleled Placer's. Again, there was virtually no expression of concern over mine workers' health and safety. For example, the criteria used to choose the most appropriate

---

Workers [:] Case Studies in the Politics of Professional Responsibility (New York 1988), 100. Also see William Graebner, "Private Power, Private Knowledge, and Public Health: Science, Engineering, and Lead Poisoning, 1900-1970," *ibid.*, 26, who concludes, "engineers, no less than owners and managers, were profit — and production — conscious."

[14]*PPFS*, Vol. 1, Mining, 6. This kind of "neutral" expertise serves players and governments very well when making plans and, even more so, when confronted with disaster. For instance, when Westray mine manager Gerald Phillips was asked about the risk of methane explosions prior to the opening of the mine, he said that the history of deaths in the Pictou coalfields had "more to do with the old mining methods" and that the mine would use "modern monitoring systems ... [so] you can detect a problem [methane gas] before it comes a real problem." *Chronicle-Herald*, 9 May 1989, 2. As for the way in which this kind of faith in expertise was used after the explosion, see within.

[15]*Ibid.*, 129. One of the techniques they expected to be satisfactory was roof and pillar mining, something which would necessitate skilled and experienced miners who could exercise a good deal of on-the-spot judgment. Typical of technology enthusiasts, they assumed away the problem of finding the right workers and ignored any pressures which might affect workers' judgment calls.

[16]Later, Westray, in the business plan prepared by it for the purposes of obtaining financing for the mine, asserted that Suncor and, then, Placer did not proceed with the development of the mine because each had decided to concentrate their activities in other resource sectors (oil and precious metals respectively). See Loan Insurance Agreement, Schedule "B," 3 (released by the federal government; available on request). There is no independent confirmation of this.

mining method made no mention of the need to protect worker safety and health.[17] Statutory health and safety requirements are dealt with essentially by indicating that "[t]he mine will be managed and operated in accordance with the statutory requirements of the Coal Mines Regulation Act ... [t]hese [A]cts require that the mine be safely operated by properly qualified, trained and experienced personnel." A one-page description of the statutory requirements follows.[18]

While it is not surprising that private resource companies and their mine consultants do not consider occupational health and safety a central question to be addressed before a decision is taken to develop a mine, it should be expected that governments would. After all, they have regulatory responsibility and they may be held politically accountable in the event miners are hurt. The available record indicates that, although some federal and provincial government officials expressed concern about the issues, they were not taken seriously by those with decision-making authority.

When the federal government was asked to contribute financially to the Westray project, a study was conducted by the Canada Centre for Mineral and Energy Technology (CANMET) in 1989. It was admittedly a "limited and somewhat superficial" review, based on eight hours of meetings with various officials in Halifax and a 10-hour review of the Kilborn and earlier studies.[19] The CANMET review raised a number of concerns, including some which were health and safety related. But, they were not the focus of the study. A few examples will suffice. "The planned roof support is the minimum and will likely need up-grading in places. Whether this is included in the cost is unclear."[20] "Room and Pillar mining forces face workers to make frequent value judgments (particularly in depillaring) that impact coal recovery, safety and the like. To initiate such mining in a new set of site-specific conditions you must expect to have a lengthy learning curve even with experienced people."[21] While this last remark suggests a real safety concern, the predominant technical and economic focus is clarified when the author returns to this point in the general comments of the report. "The real question is whether this property can bear the cost of the learning curve to get to a routine development/extraction practice."[22] At best, it seems, human lives are reduced to a cost factor.

The federal government review was largely concerned with technical and economic questions because it only became involved with the Westray project when Curragh Resources was seeking federal loan guarantees and other subsidies. The direct cost of poor health and safety practices (that is, the cost of compensating

[17]Kilborn Limited, *Technical and Cost Review of the Pictou County Coal Project Nova Scotia*, Volume I, 3-5 (available on request).
[18]*Ibid.*, 3-18-3-19.
[19]CANMET, *Westray Coal Incorporated Pictou County Coal Project: Technical Review*, n.d., 1 (available on request).
[20]*Ibid.*, 3.
[21]*Ibid.*, 5.
[22]*Ibid.*, 8.

injured workers and/or their families) was neither a substantial concern to private investors, nor to federal government officials reviewing the project. Moreover, the federal government did not have jurisdiction over mine safety in the province. Therefore, it could take the position (as it did both before and after the explosion) that the safe operation of the mine was to be left to the province and, as long as the federal government had undertakings on the part of Westray that it would comply with the applicable provincial law and orders made by the provincial government, the matter could be ignored.

The provincial government could not pass the health and safety buck so readily. It has jurisdiction over coal mine safety. But, there is no requirement for a would-be mine operator to get permission from the government to start a mine. There is a requirement that notice be given where any work is about to be commenced for the purpose of opening a mine.[23] From that point on, the Department of Labor can insist that the operations be conducted in accordance with provincial health and safety law. The point, however, is that the decision to mine does not have to be cleared in advance with provincial health and safety authorities.

There was, then, no governmentally or legally mandated reason to consider workers' health and safety when deliberating as to whether or not to mine. Yet, the issue was not completely ignored during the Westray decision-making. However, the few voices that were raised attracted little attention at the time. The Development Corporation of Cape Breton was one such voice. It was concerned about the possible development of the Westray mine because of the negative impact it might have on its operations. In a confidential submission to the federal and Nova Scotia governments, Devco pointed to the safety risks in the Pictou coalfields arising from the geological fault structure, gaseousness, and the potential for spontaneous combustion of coal dust. This, however, was something of a makeweight argument in a document much more concerned with the economic impact of the development of Pictou coal.[24] Another person, Trevor Harding, a Pictou County native who, when he was quoted, was the grievance chairman for United Steelworkers of America, Local 1051, which represented the miners at Curragh Resources' lead and zinc operations in Faro in the Yukon, warned of that company's atrocious safety record there. He said there had been 39 reported accidents in April 1989 and a dozen dust fires in late February and early March which caused workers to walk off their jobs.[25] No one seemed to think this to be relevant to the mining to be done in Nova Scotia, although Curragh Resources Inc. was now the Westray mine owner.

[23]Coal Mines Regulation Act, Royal Statutes of Nova Scotia 1989, c. 73, s. 104(1)(b).
[24]The former chair of Devco, Ms. MacNeil, has been quoted as saying that Devco's opposition "was around economics, not safety. We would all like to think today that we were all preaching safety. Safety was a factor, it was mentioned (only) [sic]." *Canadian Press*, 13 May 1992. *Canadian Press* entries will hereinafter be cited as *CP*. These righteous statements must have had a macabre ring to insiders given Devco's own disaster in 1979; see note 5.
[25]*Chronicle-Herald*, 9 May 1989, 35. The refusing workers were disciplined; see *Curragh Resources v. U.S.W.A., Local 1051, Canadian Occupational Health & Safety Cases*, 5 (1990), 81.

Curragh Resources Inc.'s lack of experience in operating an underground mine also was raised by Derek Rance, a private mine consultant. In addition, he pointed to the gas problem and the difficulty of properly ventilating when conducting room and pillar mining. The depth at which this technique was to be used was also troubling: "When you start getting towards the limit of the technology, it is not as safe as if you were mining comfortably inside the envelope of technology. It's like pushing something to the limit all the time. In order for that mine to be safe, everything is going to have to work right all the time."[26]

The failure to heed these warnings or to take health and safety seriously as an independent concern may be linked to the pervasiveness of consensus theory presumptions regarding health and safety. The starting point is that, while risks are inevitable, they have been set at levels which governments, employers, and workers agree are tolerable. If particular workers want to reduce the risk further, they are free to bargain for this at their own cost. Given the assumed confluence of interests, there is no reason for government to insist in advance that the proponents of a risk-creating enterprise should demonstrate that health and safety issues are adequately considered. An acceptable risk level has already been set and the parties can be assumed to have no interest in avoiding it. All they need is a guiding hand.

This makes for an interesting contrast with the way in which environmental concerns are treated in the approval process. In principle, mining cannot take place before the environmental impact of that activity has been assessed. Nor can federal assistance be given until that has been done.[27] As a result, the question of environmental impact was part and parcel of all of the feasibility studies conducted by, and for, the resource companies interested in mining in Pictou county. As early as November 1985, Environment Canada and the Nova Scotia Department of the Environment jointly prepared elaborate guidelines for an environmental impact assessment of what was then Suncor's coal mining project. In January 1990, Acres International Limited submitted to Industry, Science and Technology Canada a detailed and lengthy environmental evaluation of the Westray coal mine development. It recommended that federal funding be contingent on the satisfaction of 17 environmental protection conditions.

Why do we insist, as a matter of law, that careful consideration of the external environment must go into the decision to mine while no such consideration is to be given to the internal environment? Obviously, different legal requirements reflect different politics. The politics of the environment are different, at least in part, because there is no perception that the interests of the company in making a profit from its investment and the interests of the public in protecting the environment are coincidental. Nor is there any assumption that contract is an instrument through which conflicts will be negotiated. And, finally, there is no assumption that members of the public have voluntarily accepted the risk of being harmed by

[26]*Chronicle-Herald* (Halifax), 18 August 1989, 1-2.

[27]For Nova Scotia, see Environment Assessment Act, S.N.S. 1988, c. 11. The federal Environmental Assessment Review Process (EARP) was created by Cabinet directives.

environmental degradation. In other words, once the presumptions central to consensus theory are removed, a different regime of regulation seems appropriate. Employers respond to this different political climate by making great efforts to be seen as environmentally friendly.[28] It is because of the unchallenged nature of a presumed consensus in respect of occupational conditions that governments could be involved in the development of the Westray mine without feeling the need to concern themselves too much about workers' health and safety, that is without considering whether there should be any mining at all given the risks this would create for workers. And this is crucial because it is exceedingly unlikely that the Westray mine would have been developed without extensive government involvement.

Placer Development's feasibility study was not premised on such government assistance and this may have been a factor in the decision not to proceed.[29] By contrast, the project was attractive to Curragh Resources Inc. precisely because its moving force, Clifford Frame, had political connections which enabled him to put together a sweetheart deal with the responsible governments.

Frame convinced the Nova Scotia Power Corp., a publicly owned utility, to commit itself to buy 700,000 tons of coal annually at about $74 a ton (a very generous rate, given these production costs were estimated to be $29 a ton[30]) for a coal-fired power plant being constructed in Trenton, Nova Scotia. The reason given by the government for entering into this agreement to purchase a set amount of Westray coal was that the Foord seam mine coal was low in sulphur, thereby reducing the cost of the pollution controls which would have to be installed by the government at its power plant.

Even with this guaranteed sale at this high price, Frame and his companies which owned the leases were finding it difficult to get private financing for the operation. Further government assistance was sought and obtained. The federal government guaranteed 85 per cent of a $100 million loan obtained from the Bank of Nova Scotia. In addition, it turns out that the federal government provided up to $8.75 million by way of interest subsidies. Another hand-out of $3.6 million to this private risk-taker was provided by the federal government by way of a development subsidy to start the mine.[31]

The provincial government also was asked to do its bit, and it did. It lent $12 million to Curragh Resources Inc., the principal of which was not to be begun to be repaid until 1995. To further secure the financing of the mine, the provincial

---

[28]For instance, see Curragh Resources Inc., *1990 Annual Report*, where it is stated, "For the mining industry, protection of the environment is a priority .... At Curragh, we are always searching for new technologies to help us minimize impact on the ecology" (no page number).
[29]*PPFS*, vol 4, 8.
[30]CANMETs reviewer described the arrangement with Nova Scotia Power Corporation as "particularly attractive," 9.
[31]*CP*, 8 June 1992.

government also entered into a deal whose details it has refused to disclose,[32] but whose outlines are known. The agreement requires the provincial government to guarantee the sale of an additional 275,000 tons of Westray coal annually. The bottom line is that Westray has a guaranteed market for 975,000 tons of coal annually.

One question which these arrangements raise is why, if various levels of government were to take virtually all the risk of financing the mine and to purchase virtually all of its output, did they not decide to own and run the mine and reap the profits, if any, on behalf of the citizens? The answer, at bottom, is to be found in the logic of the staple-led economic growth model and the depth of the free enterprise ideology it has generated.

It is scarcely controversial to assert that our governments favour private economic activity over public enterprise as a means to create the welfare which needs to be maintained to legitimate them and to keep any particular government in power. In this context, politicians who feel the need to demonstrate to their constituents that they are promoting economic prosperity, are willing, maybe even eager, to enter into cozy deals with private entrepreneurs who promise to create jobs if their conditions are met. Of course, in any private enterprise economy some would-be entrepreneurs will be in a better position to influence politicians and policy-makers than others and sometimes the political will to do a deal for instrumental reasons will be more obvious than at other times. Clifford Frame was, apparently, a person with special influence and some federal and provincial politicians were very keen for reasons of their own to take advantage of his blandishments. What made the Westray mine situation particularly ripe for this kind of collaboration was the fact that the mine was located in the provincial riding of Donald Cameron, now the Premier of Nova Scotia. While negotiations for federal support were still underway, Cameron was a provincial development minister and campaigning to hold his seat in a fiercely contested election. Although he had hoped to announce that a deal had been reached days before the election, some details had not yet been agreed upon. This did not prevent Clifford Frame from announcing that the development of the Westray mine would go ahead.[33] Four days later, Cameron was re-elected by a slim margin of 753 votes. Cameron was subsequently appointed Minister of Industry, Trade and Technology. Although an agreement still had not been reached on the federal government's support, funds were released to Westray by Cameron's ministry to allow construction of the mine to commence in

---

[32]Many of the dealings are shrouded in secrecy. The Nova Scotia Power Corporation, with the support of the government, refused to disclose the details of its contract with Westray to the Public Accounts Committee of the legislature; *CP*, 3 and 31 May 1989. The details of the government's "take or pay" deal with Westray are the subject of a freedom of infomation action brought in court by Mr. Boudreau, a member of the Liberal opposition in the Nova Scotia legislature. Curragh Resources Inc. has joined the government in fighting disclosure; *CP*, 5 November 1991, 17 February 1992.

[33]*CP*, 2 September 1988.

April 1989.[34] Later, when Cameron decided to run for the leadership of his party
in 1990, he quickly raised $41,600 in campaign contributions in November,
including $4,450 from Maritime Steel and Foundry and $3,500 from Satellite
Equipment. Both companies had been awarded work on a $5-million contract with
Westray to build a spur line to the mine. No other candidate could come close to
matching Cameron in campaign contributions, the nearest being then Tourism
Minister Roland Thornhill, who raised $16,600 during the same period.[35] On
February 9, 1991, Cameron was elected leader of the party at its convention and
became Premier. On the face of it, it had been good for him to be seen as the creator
of wealth and jobs. Indeed, the Liberal provincial opposition alleged that the
Westray deal was a case of crude pork-barrel politics. That argument was made all
the more vehemently by it because it had been federal Liberals who had set up the
now-threatened Cape Breton mine and it was provincial Liberals who held most of
the seats in the Cape Breton electoral ridings.

There was more fuel for the Liberals' fire because Pictou County is located in
the federal riding known as Central Nova. This was the very riding in which the
then new leader of the Progressive Conservative Party, Brian Mulroney, chose to
run for his first federal seat in 1983. At the time, it was judged too dangerous or
impractical for him to run in his native Québec. Central Nova was selected because
it was a safe Conservative seat, then held by Elmer McKay, a senior Conservative
Nova Scotia politician. In the next election, Brian Mulroney switched to the riding
he now holds in Baie-Comeau, Québec, and Elmer McKay re-took Central Nova
and became a cabinet minister in the newly elected federal Progressive Conservative government. He was to be a main protagonist of the development of the Westray
mine, fighting hard to maintain the federal government's support when it began to
waver in the face of public pressure mounted by Devco, aided by a federal Liberal
Member of Parliament from Nova Scotia, David Dingwall. The fact that Donald
Cameron has acknowledged that he spoke with Brian Mulroney to seek his support
for the Westray project[36] only adds to the perception that the decision to open the
Westray mine, after giving very favorable terms to a friend of the ruling party élite,
was taken because it advanced the immediate needs of that political élite.

The point being made here is not that there was a particularly ugly and unusual
kind of conspiracy. It was not just a case of crass self-advancement. To the contrary,

[34]*CP*, 11 April 1989. The failure to reach an agreement with the federal government subsequently
caused construction of the mine to be halted in late July. It did not resume until January 1990;
CP, 31 August 1989, 4 January 1990.
[35]*CP*, 14 December 1990. The links between Eric Barker, the owner of Satellite Equipment,
and Don Cameron and the fact that the contract with Westray was awarded without tender
became the subject of an exposé on the Canadian Broadcasting Corporation's national
investigative news show, *The Fifth Estate*, aired on 11 December 1990. Clifford Frame, in
defending the contract, was quoted as saying, "I'd give a contract to the devil if he would do
the job cheaper than somebody else." *CP*, 11 December 1990.
[36]*CP*, 19 May 1992.

the argument is that, in a political economy where government sees itself as a facilitator of private development and dependent on its success, there is a strong tendency for this kind of decision-making to become the norm. Indeed, Frame was able to structure a similar deal, with an NDP-led territorial government, in order to re-open the Cyprus Anvil zinc-lead mine in Faro in the mid-1980s.[37] The dangers to political democracy posed by this tendency are so great that conflict-of-interest rules are continually being made and revised, all without great success, precisely because government actors and private capitalists need each other. All that is peculiar about this situation, then, is who the actors were and how they came together. Clifford Frame's career as a professional mining engineer and his company's non-involvement in coal mining should not have given him an advantage over a corporation such as Suncor. Perhaps his personal ingenuity made the difference, but perhaps also his contact with a former Progressive Conservative cabinet member from Nova Scotia, Robert Coates, helped him out. Frame had hired a lobbyist who was on Coates' staff. Coates has been quoted as saying that he acted as the effective marriage broker between Frame and the two levels of government.[38]

For our purposes, the most significant point is that in this kind of staple extraction model of development, occupational health and safety becomes a secondary consideration for the decision-makers. This was manifestly true in the Westray case. In the absence of a legal requirement to assess the health and safety consequences of this project and to develop a design which minimized risk to workers as a condition of granting it the permits and funding it required, government officals were not inclined to raise obstacles which might complicate and delay the political dealmaking.

In sum, the way in which these decisions are made means that there is a bias towards a kind of economic cost-benefit calculation in which the benefits of realizable profits are given great weight while the costs of occupational health and safety harm are discounted severely. Property owners and politicians, that is, non-workers, assume that productivity, especially in coal mines, entails risk and that there is nothing unusual about that. Those risks are worth taking if profit is likely to be made. The risks can be dealt with by good monitoring and adept technological adjustments. Indeed, CANMET's report was later used by the Minister of Energy, Jake Epp, when he was asked to defend the federal government's decision to involve itself in this kind of mining. Epp noted that while the "memo recommended that it was feasible to open the mine ... we were all aware of the mine having high methane deposits, and that with the new technology there would have

---

[37]If anything, Curragh did even better there. In addition to financial guarantees, it obtained huge environmental concessions, subsidized power and transport and wage and work-practice concessions from the workers; see Bruce A. Lourie, "Northern Resource Decision-Makers: A Case Study of the Faro Mine, Yukon Territory," in Peter Adamo and Peter G. Johnson, eds., *Student Research in Canada's North: Proceedings of the National Students' Conference*, November 1986 (Ottawa 1988).

[38]Stevie Cameron, *Globe and Mail*, 8 June 1992, A4.

to be a learning curve."[39] Nothing could be more explicit: whatever learning had
to be done was to come at the expense of workers' bodies. Basically, workers' major
role in helping to develop better health and safety standards is by the provision of
a body count.

B. Operating the Mine: The Learning Curve in Action

As we noted earlier, construction of the mine commenced in April 1989 with federal
backing promised but not in place. Because it had not materialized, construction
halted at the end of July 1989. Extensive lobbying by the provincial minister,
Donald Cameron, and by Elmer McKay, now the federal Public Works Minister,
eventually was successful in opening up the dam blocking the flow of federal
monies. Construction resumed in January 1990. But the delay increased the difficulty of meeting the scheduled opening date of September 1991, a crucial date. It
was at that point of time that the Trenton generating station, which also was under
construction, was expected to need its first supply of Westray coal. Not surprisingly,
this pressure to construct quickly was linked to safety problems.

On December 12, 1990, the Department of Labor issued its first order to
Westray. The inspectorate found that the Westray mine had been conducting
underground blasting without qualified people being present. As was to be the case
with future orders, work was not stopped until the order was complied with, and no
charges were laid. Rather, the company was advised that a failure to comply with
the order would constitute a breach of the law which might lead to a prosecution.
The violation which gave rise to the order in the first place apparently did not, in
the department's view, merit a sanction.

On May 23, 1991, 24 metres of roof fell in. Fortunately, no miners were injured.
An independent engineering company was hired to investigate the cause of the
collapse. No orders were issued in respect of this collapse. The department did,
however, issue an order on June 24, 1991, to forbid any more electrical arcing in
the mine, a highly dangerous practice in a site with so much inflammable gas. Again,
no charges were laid.[40]

On July 29, 1991, there had been a report to Nova Scotia's Chief Mine
Inspector, Claude White, to the effect that the levels of both fine coal dust on the
mine floors and methane concentration readings in the air were relatively high and
presented a risk. A similar warning had been sounded by Westray's private
consultant, Associated Mining Consultants Ltd., on July 3, 1991.[41] No government

---

[39] As quoted in *CP*, 11 May 1992. The same language was used in the CANMET review.

[40] Earlier that month, thousands of fish were killed when Satellite Construction discharged a
chlorine-based solution it had used to flush out water pipes at the Westray mine into a nearby
river. The work had been approved by Westray. In contrast to the way in which violations
of health and safety laws were handled, Satellite was charged and convicted of offences under
the Nova Scotia Water Act and Environmental Protection Act; *CP*, 4, 7, 12 June 1991, *CP*,
2 April 1992.

[41] *CP*, 13 May 1992.

action to enforce better standards seems to have been taken.

The question of the safety of the Westray mine was now beginning to attract the attention of those who had previously expressed opposition to the undertaking based on their interest in protecting the Devco mine in Cape Breton. Bernie Boudreau, the provincial Liberal industry critic, raised the issue of the May 23 roof collapse in the legislature at the beginning of July. He argued that "[b]ecause of the fault structure and gas contained in the formation of coal seams in Pictou County, Westray mine is potentially one of the most dangerous mines in the world." He alleged that Leroy Legere, the Minister of Labour, was ignoring safety standards because the mine was located in the riding of the Premier, Donald Cameron. Legere denied the charge: "I would assume that my department and the mine safety people are doing as good a job at Westray as they are doing at all the other mines in Nova Scotia."[42]

The Westray mine opened on schedule in September 1991. In October there was more public questioning about the safety of Westray. In the two weeks leading up to October 20, 1991, there had been three more rock falls at the mine. The ministry and Westray officials met. All in all, the government found, there had been seven such rock falls since the development began in 1989. The report of the meeting shows that the ministry officials came away satisfied with the precautionary means taken by Westray. Apparently, the owners had implemented a geomechanics program and hired a geotechnical engineer to assess ground conditions on a daily basis.[43] The inspectorate's willingness to accept Westray's assurances that safety was being taken care of was to repeat itself.

On November 4, 1991, the Minister of Labor issued an order directing Westray to develop written rules to ensure that mine workers should not work in areas where the roof was not supported and it required the corporation to keep records of the rock falls which had occurred and of any which might occur in the future.[44] Clearly, there was by then a recognition within the ministry of the dangerous conditions created by Westray's mining activities. But this alertness did not lead to precautions capable of averting further problems. Indeed, a miner by the name of Ryan has now told the press that, in February of 1992, there was another cave-in.[45]

On March 28, 1992, there was yet another cave-in which caused ministry officials to visit the mine. While there, they found that the air sample taken for testing contained four per cent methane. The scientific assumption is that, when the methane concentration reaches five per cent, it becomes explosive if ignited. As a precaution, the law requires work to be halted and miners to be removed when the methane level reaches a level of 2.5 per cent of the ambient air. When it reaches

[42]*CP*, 3 July 1991.
[43]Memorandum from Claude White, Director, Mine Safety to Executive Director, Ministry of Labour, 21 October 1991 (available on request).
[44]*CP*, 28 May 1992.
[45]*CP*, 23 May 1992.

concentrations above 1.25 per cent, electricity to the area is to be shut-off.[46] But, on March 28, 1992, production was not halted. Indeed, the Nova Scotia Department of Labour's safety officer, Albert McLean, indicated that he was satisfied that Westray management had the situation under control.[47] Throughout the period, the amount of coal dust on the floors of the mine had been a constant concern. The coal dust is explosive. To combat this danger, a standard precaution is to put down limestone dust to cover it. The law requires 20 bags of stone dust to be stored near every working section and, where there is room and pillar mining, that a "suitable amount" of stone dust be kept nearby.[48] Between February and April 1991, that is, during the preparatory construction before the mine opened, inspectors pointed out the need for more limestone dust to be put down on at least nine occasions. As already noted, a similar report was issued in July 1991. When the mine did open in early September 1991, McLean declared himself satisfied by the Westray's management plan to put a coal dusting plan in place by the end of September. Apparently, the plan was not implemented because, on April 29, 1992, only 10 days before the explosion, the Ministry of Labour issued formal orders to Westray requiring it to comply with the statutory requirements. In addition, management was to design a plan for spreading the stone dust in an efficient manner. As is now known, the ministry's inspectorate had not checked to see whether there had been compliance with these orders when, on May 10, the explosion occurred.

What this officially documented record of breaches of existing safety standards and procedures makes clear is that, as in other mining disasters, violations preceded the disaster. Moreover, the almost unrelenting flow of health and safety problems is a clear indication that the Westray operation remained firmly situated at the bottom of the steep learning curve its promoters had said they would climb. Indeed, alarming evidence which shows that no steps were taken to climb the curve has emerged as miners have come forward to tell about their experiences.

Two such employees, Evans and Taje, tell horror stories. They have spoken of the use of a cutting torch in the mine, and how this had led to a fire. They have said that there was no firefighting equipment or rock dust nearby, although the regulations promulgated to prevent fires in mines required this. On one occasion, they said, the roof gave way and a big red flash was seen. The workers were alarmed. These two former employees also spoke of poor training and supervision. Taje claims that, on a number of occasions, he had reported his concerns to his supervisors and once to the provincial authorities, but that he had been ignored. He, Evans, and one other person had quit two weeks before the explosion, because of the danger to health and safety. They were all experienced miners.[49] Dwight House, Randy Roberts, and Don Wentzel also had quit their employment because the mine was

---

[46]Kevin Cox, *Globe and Mail*, 30 July 1992; Coal Mines Regulation Act, n. 23, ss. 72 and 85.
[47]Kevin Cox, *Globe and Mail*, 30 July 1992.
[48]Coal Mines Regulation Act, n. 23, s. 70(5).
[49]*CP*, 11 May 1992.

too dangerous. In House's words, the mine was "a disaster waiting to happen," "the methane levels were so high that at times we had to stop work." He has spoken of one particularly traumatic incident when he was operating his scoop with two men in the bucket. He pulled the bucket back just a minute or two before there was a cave-in. "If I hadn't moved within those two minutes, me and those other two guys probably would have been buried." Randy Roberts has told the Corner Brook *Western Star* that he left his Westray employment in February because "it was the only mine in where I never felt sleepy. I was too scared of the mine's working conditions to ever get sleepy."[50] Another miner, Wayne Gosbee, has said that he and his fellow workers often talked about the mine's safety problems. In his view, "as far as the company doing all they could do to make it safe ... on the scale of 1 to 10, I would rate them about a 2."[51] Walter Ryan, a miner who quit because of his anxiety about safety only to return to Westray because he needed the money, is now apparently second-guessing himself as to whether he ought to have spoken up more. He has said that there were tractors in the mine with no jackets to prevent sparks, that there were poorly covered batteries, that oil containers and oil rags were left lying about in the mine, and that he saw an acetylene torch used underground. He recounts how experienced miners were aware of the presence of methane because they suffered from light-headedness; they commented on the staleness and the rankness of the air. The workers suffered from dizziness and headaches. In addition, Ryan claims that there were at least 16 cave-ins, one of which had caused him to quit.[52] Other miners have reported that, while work was to be stopped when levels of methane reached 2.5 per cent of the air, levels of 3.5 and 3.75 per cent were common. They said methane monitors were defective.[53]

As these miners' stories made the news, Westray management countered them with stout denials. Colin Benner, the executive vice-president, operations, of Curragh Resources Inc., has rejected any arguments that the company allowed flagrantly unsafe practices in the mine such as smoking, the use of acetylene torches or the employment of machines with electrical starters. He has argued that it is unreasonably prejudicial to look for human agents (especially if these agents are said to be corporate managers!) as the cause of the accident. Reflecting the conventional wisdom about risk creation, he has argued that "some people are assuming that human error is the only possible cause of such a tragedy ... Nature cannot always be predicted or controlled ..."[54]

But the inspectors' reports support the workers' allegations, not the contentions that human agency may have had little impact. They reveal that, on two occasions, open containers of oil were detected in working areas and that, on two other occasions, unauthorized vehicles, that is, vehicles which had no devices fitted to

[50]*CP*, 12 May 1992.
[51]*CP*, 25 May 1992.
[52]*CP*, 23 May 1992.
[53]*CP*, 18 May 1992.
[54]*CP*, 11 May 1992.

prevent sparks, were found to be in use underground.[55] And, as has been noted, the inspectorate had issued at least one order forbidding further dangerous electrical arcing in the mine.

In sum, there were many warning signals. Inasmuch as attention was paid to them, they were treated as a series of unrelated, even natural, events. There seems to have been no concerted effort to follow-up on the promises to provide the best possible equipment and technology. While there was a good deal of monitoring — 56 inspector reports were issued — there was no vigilant enforcement. At no stage did the ministry exercise its enforcement power directly, preferring polite request and consultations to penalties. This is the norm.

III. Enforcement — 'Sticks and Stones May Break My Bones But Words Will Never Hurt Me'

A. The Norm of Non-Enforcement

The roots of the norm of non-enforcement go back to the beginnings of direct state health and safety regulation in the mid-19th century. From the time inspectors were first appointed to enforce statutory minimum standards, they have relied upon gentle persuasion rather than vigorous enforcement through prosecution to obtain compliance. The approach, which typified the enforcement of this first wave of legislation, was premised on a number of assumptions.

The first was that employers who violated the statutory requirements were not, by and large, guilty of criminal misconduct. This was true because illegalities were graded. Only some were serious enough to be treated as criminal. They would be so characterized if the conduct served no useful purpose and/or offended society's norms. Any other kind of violation was deemed to be quasi-criminal at worst.[56] In respect of occupational health and safety, the activity being regulated — the private production of goods and services — was socially useful. Hence it was simply not appropriate to treat the wrongdoing of the private capitalist engaged in such activity in the same way as the misconduct of a common criminal. Moreover, there was a deeply held belief that workers voluntarily assumed risks in the workplace and, even if the market could not be relied upon exclusively to determine the permissible level of risk, the seriousness of exposing workers to risks in excess of stipulated levels was attenuated by their apparent willingness to incur them. The fact that the illegal employment of under-age children in unhealthy conditions was viewed as a more serious wrong than the violation of existing health and safety standards was a reflection of the fact that the perception of consent influenced the categorization of the misconduct in question.

[55]Kevin Cox, *Globe and Mail*, 30 July 1992.
[56]In Canada, the constitutional boundary between federal and provincial jurisdiction is drawn on the basis of this distinction: true crime falls within federal jurisdiction, regulatory offences are within the provincial domain.

A second related assumption was that employers' violations were not the result of intentional wrongdoing. Rather, employers were perceived to be socially responsible citizens who, through ignorance or organizational incompetence, had failed to observe the law. Inspectors firmly believed that safety paid; that rational, profit-maximizing employers would find it was in their self-interest to comply with the law. After all, the law itself did not require uneconomic safety measures. It stipulated that employers were only required to take measures "reasonably required in the circumstances" to protect workers' health. Economic feasibility was always a pivotal consideration when deciding what was reasonable. Moreover, because workers were assumed to have an interest in their employers' economic viability, it could be concluded that there was a common interest between employers, workers and the state in matters pertaining to health and safety. It followed, therefore, that health and safety was not an issue of conflict which needed to be addressed through the industrial relations system. Rather, the internal self-monitoring system of the employer could be relied upon to achieve compliance, subject to occasional supervision, instruction, reminders, and gentle prodding, by the state.[57]

Beginning in the 1970s, a second wave of occupational health and safety legislation swept through much of the English-speaking industrialized world. In part, the inspiration for this legislation was rooted in the failures of the old model of regulation. The old internal responsibility system which had, by and large, excluded worker participation was no longer seen to be apposite. This was not because the architects of the new legislation were willing to acknowledge that there was a fundamental conflict between labour and capital over health and safety. Rather, it was because the failure to include workers had encouraged apathy on their part, leading them to be careless at work, and had denied them the "natural right" to participate in decisions affecting their own health and safety. To some extent, the reformers were also concerned about the deficiencies of the existing external responsibility system. The aim of the reforms they offered in this respect was to rationalize and modernize the bureaucracy. In particular, the reformers sought to overcome the fragmentation of authority over health and safety regulation and they also saw that the capacity to deal with occupational health problems, as opposed to more traditional safety hazards, needed to be expanded.[58]

[57]For a sampling of the literature which explores the historical development of the ideology and practice of occupational health and safety regulation from this perspective, see W.G. Carson, "The Conventionalization of Early Factory Crime," *International Journal of the Sociology of Law*, 7 (1979), 37 (England); Eric Tucker, *Administering Danger in the Workplace: The Law and Politics of Occupational Health and Safety Regulation in Ontario, 1850-1914* (Toronto 1990) (Ontario); and Neil Gunningham, *Safeguarding the Worker* (Sydney 1984) (Australia).

[58]The views of these influential reformers were expressed in reports of various government inquiries in comparable jurisdictions. For example, *Safety and Health and Work*, U.K Cmnd. 5034 (Robens Report), 1972; Ontario, *Report of the Royal Commission on the Health and Safety of Workers in Mines* (Attorney General of Ontario 1976) (Ham Report); Report of the Joint Federal-Provincial Inquiry Commission into Safety in Mines and Mining Plants in

The net effect of these changes was, on the one hand, to create new opportunities for workers to contest health and safety issues on the shop floor, and, on the other hand, to further entrench the traditional practice of enforcement on the basis that the new improved internal responsibility system could now be relied upon as the primary means through which compliance would be achieved. The role of the inspectorate as a support system for the internal responsibility system was emphasized. Formal sanctions were still only to be used as a last resort or in the event of a fatality or serious injury. Thus, the practice of external enforcement changed little, although there were many more standards to enforce.

The opportunities created for workers to better their lot through the new internal responsibility system, however, were carefully circumscribed. Workers were given a right to know about hazards present in the workplace (including the right to have a worker-delegate conduct periodic inspections), a right to be consulted and a right to refuse unsafe work. Only the last right provided workers with the means to take direct action for their own protection, but it was carefully defined as an individual right. Health and safety strikes were not permitted (although groups of workers might refuse if each person felt endangered individually) and worker health and safety representatives could not order dangerous operations shut down pending a state inspection. What workers could get out of such a scheme depended, to a significant degree, on their relative power resources. Clearly, the opportunity to make gains was greater for unionized workers in relatively secure industries than it was for non-unionized workers whose employers were operating at the margin. In addition, workers could make only limited use of what was potentially a very useful resource, the state inspectorate. Because inspectors were instructed to be facilitators first, workers calling upon them to back their claims were likely to be told to be reasonable in their demands and to resolve their differences with their employers through the internal responsibility system.[59]

Thus, the dominant assumptions regarding health and safety were not questioned at all. The view that criminal law and/or external enforcement had little if any role to play and that health and safety was a realm of consensus, not conflict,

Ontario, *Towards Safe Production* (1981) (Burkett Report) and *Report of the Commission of Inquiry into Occupational Health and Safety*, 1981 (New South Wales, Australia) (Williams Report).
[59]For critical appraisals of the reforms, see Robert Sass, "A Critique: Canadian Public Policy in Workplace Health and Safety," *New Solutions* (Fall 1991), 39, and "The Implications of Work Organization for Occupational Health Policy: The Case for Canada," *International Journal of Health Services* 19 (1989), 163; Vivienne Walters and Ted Haines, "Workers' Use and Knowledge of the 'Internal Responsibility System': Limits to Participation in Occupational Health and Safety," *Canadian Public Policy* 14 (1988), 411, and Eric Tucker, "Worker Participation in Health and Safety Regulation: Lessons from Sweden," *Studies in Political Economy* 37 (1992), 95. For a more positive evaluation, see Katherine E. Swinton, "Enforcement of Occupational Health and Safety Legislation: The Role of the Internal Responsibility System," in Kenneth Swan and Katherine E. Swinton, eds., *Studies in Labor Law* (Toronto 1983), 143.

remained firmly entrenched in the health and safety bureaucracy.[60] Needless to say, the enforcement of mine safety was not significantly different from the model described here.[61]

B. The Case of Nova Scotia

Nova Scotia was a leader in regulating coal mine safety in the 19th century. Largely this was the result of the efforts of the Provincial Workmen's Association, the province's first colliers' union, formed in 1879. It lobbied hard to improve health and safety regulation in the mines and met with some successes, especially in the aftermath of disasters. A flood in October and an explosion in November 1880 at the Foord seam killed 60 workers in total. These disasters led to the enactment of legislation which strengthened the external responsibility system. It authorized the appointment of deputy inspectors and it made special provision for gas-related inspections. The internal responsibility system was also reformed. The law empowered workers at each colliery to form two-men committees which were allowed to inspect the mine at least once a month and to file official evaluations. In 1884, legislation was enacted which established qualifications and staffing requirements. A further legislative victory was won in the aftermath of the Springhill mine disaster of 1891. That Act gave miners' committees the right to visit scenes of accidents and miners the right to begin prosecutions of management by affidavit. Despite these legislative innovations, mine owners fiercely resisted their effective implementation, especially when it impinged on managerial prerogative. As a result, enforcement remained generally lax.[62]

[60]This is not to say that such a scheme could not be administered more vigorously. This happens when labor-friendly political parties can generate this kind of pressure, as occurred in Saskatchewan from 1974 to 1982 when, under NDP government, Bob Sass served as Director of the Occupational Health and Safety branch of the Department of Labour and introduced many progressive reforms, and in Ontario when the New Democratic Party was able to influence a minority Liberal Party government. But the underlying assumptions remain the same and the more usual slack enforcement is likely to return as soon as the pressure is reduced. This does not require formal changes in the regulatory mechanism. The example of Saskatchewan in the period following the defeat of the NDP is instructive. See Robert Sass, "The Tory Assault on Labor in Saskatchewan," *Windsor Yearbook of Access to Justice*, 7 (1987), 133, esp. 143-7.

[61]See Andrew Hopkins and Nina Parnell, "Why Coal Mine Safety Regulations in Australia Are Not Enforced," *International Journal of the Sociology of Law*, 12 (1984), 179-94; Andrew Hopkins, "Crime Without Punishment: The Appin Mine Disaster," in Peter Grabowsky and Adam Sutton, eds., *Stains on a White Collar* (Sydney 1989), 160, and Daniel J. Curran, "Symbolic Solutions for Deadly Dilemmas: An Analysis of Federal Coal Mine Health and Safety Legislation," *International Journal of Health Services*, 14 (1984), 5.

[62]S.N.S. 1881, c.5, ss. 1, 2, and 8; c. 21; and S.N.S. 1891, c. 9, ss. 12 and 14. On the background to these legislative changes, see Donald Macleod, "Colliers, Colliery Safety and Workplace Control: The Nova Scotia Experience, 1873 to 1910," *Historical Papers* (1983), 226, and Ian McKay, "The Provincial Workmen's Association: A Brief Survey of Several

Nova Scotia's position as a leader in health and safety law, at least on the books, has not been sustained. The Coal Mines Regulation Act, although periodically updated, has not been amended to increase workers' control rights over the operation of the mine and, although additional rules have been enacted, today the maximum fine for most violations is a paltry $250. As well, the government must lay charges within six months of the occurrence of the violation.[63] In regard to occupational health and safety law generally, Nova Scotia was one of the last two provinces (the other being Prince Edward Island) to enact second-wave legislation of the kind described above. It did so only in 1985.[64] The maximum fine for a violation of that act is $10,000. This is at the medium to low end of the spectrum of maximum fines provided for in similar legislation in other provinces.[65]

Although there are deficiencies in the available data on health and safety enforcement in the province, making categorical statements difficult, what evidence there is suggests that persuasion is still the primary strategy and that prosecutions are rare events indeed. For example, from 1985 to 1990, a total of 14 companies were charged with offenses under the Occupational Health and Safety Act and the maximum fine imposed appears to have been $2,500. No mining companies were prosecuted, however, despite the fact that, according to another tabulation, between fiscal years 1987-88 and 1991-92, 1037 directives were issued to mining companies. The fact that directives never result in charges does not mean there is much compliance, as the Westray saga shows.[66]

Viewed in this light, the (non-)enforcement of safety at Westray was unexceptional. Sadly, then, Leroy Legere, the Nova Scotia Minister of Labor, was likely correct when, in response to charges of favouritism made prior to the disaster, he declared that "the people in the Department of Labor are not treating the Westray Mine any differently than they are treating any other mine in the province."[67]

While there is a close fit with the general pattern, the specific conditions at Westray which influenced health and safety practices at the mine and the state's

---

Problems of Interpretation," in W.J.C Cherwinski and Gregory S. Kealey, eds., *Lectures in Canadian Labor and Working Class History* (St. John's 1985), 127-34.

[63]R.S.N.S. 1989, c.73, ss. 142 & 146.

[64]S.N.S. 1985, c.3, s.49 and S.P.E.I 1985, c.36.

[65]The highest fine, $500,000, is set in Ontario. Alberta is next at $150,000. Manitoba is closer to Nova Scotia with a maximum fine of $15,000.

[66]Compiled from Nova Scotia, Department of Labor, *Annual Reports*, 1985-86 to 1989-90. In the 1988-89 report, only the total amount of fines levied was reported ($8,700 from four convictions), making it impossible to ascertain the highest fine. In another tabulation of prosecution data, a total of 97 charges were laid between the fiscal years 1987-88 and 1991-92, resulting in 42 convictions and fines totaling $69,750. (Letter from Jim LeBlanc, Director, Occupational Health/Safety Training, Nova Scotia Department of Labor, to Eric Tucker, 19 August 1992.) The discrepancy between the number of companies charged and the number of charges may result from the fact that any one company may be charged with a number of offences at the same time.

[67]Nova Scotia, *Assembly Debates*, July 1991.

response to them nonetheless merit closer consideration. First, there is some question as to the technical capacity of the mine safety branch at the time Westray opened. It had little recent experience regulating underground coal mines since the large Devco operation was under federal jurisdiction. The only underground coal mine it was then overseeing was a rather small operation conducted by Evans Coal Mines Ltd. in Inverness County. As a result of this lack of experience, the inspectors may have been unusually reticent to take strong measures in regard to enforcement.[68]

A second consideration is that Curragh Resources Inc., the owner of the Westray mine operation, was indebted in 1991 and needed both a good cash flow and profits from the Westray mine. Its primary business was the mining of lead and zinc concentrates.

Depressed world prices for those concentrates, heavy investment in a new project, the Stronsay lead and zinc mine in British Columbia, a failed attempt to diversify, and a 10-week strike by workers at its Faro mine in Yukon (motivated in part by health and safety concerns)[69] had caused Curragh to lose $98 million on revenues of $225 million in 1991.[70] In an attempt to raise money, Curragh Resources Inc. tried to interest institutional investors in buying convertible debentures from it. The security offered these potential institutional creditors was the Westray mine. Curragh Resources Inc. was expecting the cash flow from the mine to repay the debt it proposed to undertake. In the event, institutional investors were uninterested. Curragh then announced that it would put the Westray mine up for sale as a way of raising cash for its sputtering enterprises. The sale never took place.[71]

In this context there was a pressing need to get Westray going. The rock falls in October and the ensuing public pressure to do something about this kind of risk must have been a real nuisance to a company which was keen to get on with intense production. But the corporation's problems only got worse. By October 30, 1991, it was apparent that Westray could not meet its obligation to supply the coal it had contracted to furnish the Trenton power plant. That plant cannot use coal with ash levels which exceed 20 per cent. Much of the coal Westray mined had a 40 per cent ash level. The excess ash had to be washed out. This took time and cost a great deal of money. The Westray management was hopeful that, as the digging went deeper, the ash level would drop.[72] The investment was no longer looking so good. Westray

---

[68]These speculations have been confirmed by a report commissioned by the Ministry of Labor of Nova Scotia from the independent firm of Coopers and Lybrand. It found that the responsible department was poorly organized and managed and, consequently, routinely failed to follow up on safety orders at work sites (*Toronto Star*, 30 April 1993, A12).

[69]*Financial Times of Canada*, 15 April 1991, 20.

[70]Allan Robinson, "Won't Gamble Again, Curragh Head Says," *Globe and Mail*, 6 May 1992, B6.

[71]*CP*, 5 September, 29 November 1991.

[72]*CP*, 30 October 1991.

sought to alleviate some of the pressure by obtaining rights to strip-mine at the nearby Wimpey site (see below), but it had to continue to dig underground in order to meet its contractual commitments. The miners were offered production incentives and the opportunity to work unlimited overtime.[73]

These kinds of pressures on operations are likely to accentuate the conflict between profit and safety. Firms under a great deal of pressure to meet production deadlines may cut corners to do so.[74] The Westray case exemplifies this. The violation of regulations controlling coal dust and the frequency of rock falls suggest that production was being given priority over safety. Here it is apposite to note that there was at least one other major cave-in in February and that conditions were highly dangerous during 1992, as the April 29, 1992 orders indicated.

Third, Westray may have had a particularly cozy relationship with politicians in the province. The staple model of development made the region dependent upon Westray's success to improve its economic well-being. Moreover, important politicians, led by the Premier, Donald Cameron, and Elmer McKay, federal Minister of Public Works (both of whom represented the riding in which Westray was located), not only invested provincial and federal money in the project, but also their political capital. The inspectors could not have been oblivious to this and may very well have understood that an even softer approach to enforcement than usual would be appropriate. This cannot be proved, of course, but the possibility is real and the initial handling of Westray's application to strip-mine certainly is suggestive of the impact these relations can have on regulatory regimes.

C. The Wimpey Strip-Mine

When Curragh Resources Inc. could not sell its Westray mine or operate it profitably, at least in the short term, it looked for relief elsewhere. Again, the Nova Scotia government came to the party. On or about January 6, 1992, the government announced that it would permit Westray to do some strip-mining, that is, above-ground mining at the undeveloped Wimpey mining site near Stellarton. This kind of mining presents environmental problems. The Nova Scotia government exempted Westray from having to go through an environmental assessment. Its

---

[73]Kevin Cox, *Globe and Mail*, 16, 17 May 1992, and interviews with Cox and Mr. Ronald Pink, the lawyer representing the U.S.W.A. at the judicial inquiry into the disaster. There is some controversy over the effect of production bonuses on safety, many believing it to be adverse but, for a skeptical view, see Hopkins, "Blood Money?"

[74]On the general relationship between productivity pressure and accidents, see Leon Grunberg, "The Effects of the Social Relations of Production on Productivity and Workers' Safety: An Ignored Set of Relationships," *International Journal of Health Services*, 13 (1983), 621. In the context of coal mining, see Michael Wallace, "Dying for Coal: the Struggle for Health and Safety Conditions in American Coal Mining, 1930-82," *Social Forces*, 66 (1987), 336 at 343. For a similar analysis in other work contexts, see Chris Wright, "Routine Injury Risks in the Canadian Meat Packing Industry," *International Journal of Health Services*, 20 (1990), 281.

justification for this exemption was that it was only giving a permit to allow Westray to take a sample for testing purposes. Having been informed of this, the federal government decided that, even though strip-mining would normally be subjected to a fisheries' department review, it would not be necessary to do so in this case.

The sample which Westray was permitted to take was actually to be 100,000 tons. It was crystal clear that the Nova Scotia government was giving Westray an opportunity to meet its commitments under its contract to supply the Trenton power plant. This raised a storm of protest. The intensity of the protest was increased when, on January 17, 1992, it was revealed that Westray actually had obtained a permit to take out 200,000 tons if it needed it. The anger was further fuelled because mining at the Wimpey site began before the Stellarton residents had been advised that a permit had been granted. Curragh's management — Westray's owners — came to Stellarton to say that it was all a sad misunderstanding and it helped establish a committee which included local residents to monitor the strip-mining.[75] But, as it turns out, this is not all that Westray got.

As is now known, on November 28, 1991, the Nova Scotia government, by executive order, granted Westray a 20-year lease over the Wimpey strip-mine. Westray was not required to pay anything for this grant. The province is to get 27 cents for every ton of coal dug out. The enormity of the secretly made grant can be gauged from the fact that Suncor had sought the Wimpey mine rights but had been refused them after Novaco, a provincial crown corporation established to regulate open pit mining in Nova Scotia, had suggested that there was enough underground coal to meet the existing demand and that Wimpey could be developed quickly, if necessary. Suncor was only given strip-mining rights above the ground of its underground mining zone. Novaco assumed that Suncor would not easily be able to develop both strip-mining and underground mining in the same site.

The November 1991 executive order had given Westray a potential pot of gold. Shortly after the disaster, Westray applied and lobbied for permission to extract 900,000 tons per year from the Wimpey mine to permit it to meet its obligation to the Nova Scotia Power Corporation. Potentially, the profit was enormous. The cost of extraction at Wimpey is much lower than it is at the Westray coal mine site. The cost at Wimpey has been estimated at between $14 and $20.[76] If the selling price to Trenton remained at $74, as is stipulated under the original Westray contract, or even something close to it, a handsome yield would be obtained by the Westray coal mining operation.[77] Unsurprisingly, Curragh's management was willing to move heaven and earth to get permission to mine at Wimpey.

[75]Dave Glenen, *New Glasgow Evening News*, 12 January 1992, 16 January 1992; Randy Jones, *The Mail-Star*, 15 January 1992; Rob Roberts, *The Daily News*, 17 January 1992.

[76]Interview with B. Boudreau, Liberal member of the Nova Scotia Legislative Assembly and an early critic of the Westray project.

[77]Stevie Cameron, *Globe and Mail*, 29 June 1992; Nova Scotia, *Assembly Debates*, 24 June 1992, 10524-10527.

Curragh hired a firm of environmental consultants, Nolan Davis & Associates. This firm submitted a report to the Nova Scotia government and presented it to the aggrieved residents in Stellarton. This report concluded that the strip-mining poses no environmental danger. Nonetheless, Curragh offered the local people, in addition to some royalties, clothes driers, vinyl siding, and air conditioners to help them cope with whatever coal dust might be floating around. If developed, the strip would have operated within a few yards of 20 to 30 homes in the town of Stellarton and the people inhabiting these homes, as well as many other members of their community, were very upset at the prospect of the strip-mining. In the result, after much public controversy, the Nova Scotia government has refused Curragh Resources Inc. a permit to strip-mine without first going through a thorough environmental assessment impact.[78]

IV. Consensus at Work — The Myth of Equivalent Risk-Taking

A central pillar of consensus theory, and the regulatory approaches justified by it, is that labour and capital share a common set of goals. In part, this is so, it is argued, because there is some rough equivalence between them. One aspect of this equivalence is in relation to risk-taking. Employers risk their capital, workers their lives and health. On its face, the notion that these risks are equivalent is absurd. Yet, in capitalist economic theory, all values, including the value of life and health, are monetized and, therefore, comparable.[79]

Support for the idea of a shared ideology also derives from the belief that workers voluntarily assume the risks present in the workplace. This belief is widespread. For example, some might say that, if the danger of working at Westray was as obvious as some of the miners have now said it was and as the record compiled by the Department of Labour's inspectors show it to have been, the fact that miners continued to work and did not exhibit more resistance suggests that they were willing to incur the risk.

The idea that workers and employers voluntarily incur roughly equivalent risk not only has influenced legal doctrine in the past,[80] but it continues to serve as a

[78]*Globe and Mail*, 16 July 1992; *Toronto Star*, 4 September 1992. This turn-around is illustrative of the argument made earlier that environmental concerns can be more readily mobilized than occupational health and safety ones. An investigative television report, *The Fifth Estate*, broadcast by the Canadian Broadcasting Corporation on 6 April 1993, produced evidence that Curragh Resources asked bereaved families to help them in their efforts to get access to the strip mine. The alleged bargain was that, if they did so, Curragh would make efforts to recover the bodies of the missing miners.
[79]For example, see W. Kip Viscusi, *Risk by Choice* (Cambridge 1983). For a recent effort to re-calculate the implicit monetary value workers place on life and limb, see Michael J. Moore and W. Kip Viscusi, *Compensation Mechanisms for Job Risks* (Princeton 1990).
[80]See R.C.B. Risk, "'This Nuisance of Litigation': The Origins of Workers' Compensation in Ontario," in David Flaherty, eds., *Essays in the History of Canadian Law*, Vol. 2 (Toronto

rationale for not intervening to protect workers from harm. It justifies reliance on the internal responsibility system and the gentle persuasion approach to enforcement; that is, it justifies the very practices which led up to the Westray disaster. For that reason it is important to subject these ideas to critical analysis.

A. Workers as Risk-Takers

There is no doubt that workers at the Westray mine put their lives and health at risk. The question here is: did they assume the risk voluntarily? The simple idea that miners are a self-selected group of workers who spontaneously develop a taste for risk does not stand up to scrutiny.

The list of victims and the stories told by miners who have been interviewed reveal a pattern. Some of the miners at Westray were professional miners who moved around the country following employment opportunities, from Newfoundland, Alberta, Saskatchewan, Northern Ontario, and other parts of Nova Scotia. They needed jobs. They understood the dangers of mining. This is clear from the statements of the miners and their friends. They adverted to the risks they were taking, but it seems that an adaptive culture has evolved among them which enables them to live with the terror of it all. One journalist, Tom McDougall, after a series of interviews with miners, wrote: "There's a certain mystique about it — a soldier-like pride in sticking with a job that would scare lesser folk witless. There's also a spirit of brotherhood — part old-soldier camaraderie and small-town solidarity."[81]

These personal observations find resonance with the results of more formal studies of the formation of male working-class identity. For example, Paul Willis, in a study of the education of working-class boys in England, came to the following conclusion: "The brutality of the working situation is partially re-interpreted into a heroic exercise of manly confrontation with the task. Difficult, uncomfortable or dangerous conditions are seen, not for themselves, but for their appropriateness to a masculine readiness and hardiness. They are understood more through the toughness required to survive them, than in the nature of the imposition which asks them to be faced in the first place."[82]

In addition to this complex cultural articulation of sexual and class identities, other psychosocial processes also shape and constrain workers' perceptions of, and decisions about, risks at work. It has been noted that workers develop "experience-based" standards which often depart markedly from official ones. In part, this occurs because the risk of harm is relatively remote and, in the absence of recent experience of its materialization, there is a tendency to discount its probability excessively.

1983), 418, and Eric Tucker, "The Law of Employers' Liability in Ontario 1861-1900: The Search for a Theory," *Osgoode Hall Law Journal*, 22 (1984), 213.

[81]*CP*, 11 May 1992.

[82]Paul Willis, *Learning to Labor* (New York 1981), 150. Also see Cynthia Cockburn, *Brothers* (London 1983), 132-140 and Jack Haas, "Learning Real Feelings," *Sociology of Work and Occupations*, 4, 2 (1977), 47.

Moreover, there may be immediate costs to workers if they comply with safety rules, including physical discomfort and increased workload because of poorly designed safety equipment, as well as loss of production bonuses. Because safety and productivity often conflict, management may endorse, implicitly or explicitly, experience-based practices if they result in increased productivity.[83]

Also, processes of cognitive dissonance play a role here. Workers faced with objectively risky conditions may adjust, even if only temporarily, their beliefs about the safety of the activity in order to avoid feelings of constant fear and uncertainty.[84] Thus, although there were miners at Westray who quit because it was too dangerous, others stayed put but now say that they were always anxious and afraid. What this suggests is that, when they speak bravely about the dangers they face every day, they may be making the most of necessity. To vulgarize Jung, an exercise in free will is no more than doing willingly what one knows one has to do anyhow. In short, if going underground is the only realistic option which these workers believe they have, normal emotions like fear must be repressed, at least partially. As Alvin Jahn, an uncle of a Westray victim and a former miner himself, said about mining, "It's an eerie feeling, but it's a matter of daily bread."[85]

It is important, therefore, to understand how the socio-economic environment of Pictou County constrains workers' choices. Population in the county declined by 1.1 per cent between 1981 and 1986 and was disproportionately comprised by young and elderly people. This indicates a pattern of out-migration among people of potential working age. The reason for this is that local employment opportunities are limited. Unemployment in the county rose from 9.2 to 17.6 per cent during this period, an increase of 88.2 per cent. Average annual family income in the county for 1986 was $30,913, equivalent to 93.9 per cent of the provincial average. However, the percentage of low-income families was increasing. Employment in manufacturing was declining rapidly, from 32.2 per cent of the workforce in 1981 to 22.8 per cent in 1986. Put differently, the number of manufacturing jobs decreased by 28.3 per cent in five years.[86]

These conditions not only help us to understand the behaviour of miners before the disaster, they also illuminate the reasons why some miners, survivors, and family members, as well as community leaders in the area, have been calling for a re-opening of the mine.

Curragh Resources Inc. has had no trouble in having a petition signed by former mine workers, the unions, as well as by local churches, supporting its efforts to start mining in another spot. In short, what is true in coal mining in depressed economic

---

[83]See Hopkins, "Blood Money," 31-4. In our view he discounts the influence of bonuses a little too much.

[84]George A. Ackerlof and William T. Dickens, "The Economic Consequences of Cognitive Dissonance," *American Economic Review*, 72 (1982), 307, esp. 308.

[85]Michael MacAfee, *CP*, 11 May 1992.

[86]These data, derived from Statistics Canada, are presented in Acres International Limited, *Westray Coal Mine Initial Environmental Evaluation*, Final Report, January 1990 (Industry, Science and Technology Canada), 4-18-4-26.

regions, such as Pictou County, is really a marked manifestation of a general truth. Workers are so dependent for their welfare on private investors that they seem almost oblivious to risk. They are likely to develop rationalizations for their actions, creating a culture which inures them to daily fears. In short, they develop what might be described as false consciousness.[87]

A more mundane, but nonetheless important, reason for the apparent willingness to put up with bad conditions is that employers can use their powers to still resistance. This is why statutory regimes, such as Nova Scotia's Occupational Health and Safety Act, provide that workers should not be penalized for exercising their rights under the Act.[88] Certainly, it seems as if Westray management was not backwards in repressing obstreperous workers' demands. Robert Chisholm, the labour critic for the provincial NDP in Nova Scotia, released copies of Westray's health and safety policy. In part this policy recited that "Under no circumstances may information be released to any other person without the express authority of the Vice-President, General Manager of Westray Corporation." This is in violation of the Occupational Health and Safety Act. It goes some way towards explaining why complaints made by some workers got no action and, more importantly, why so few workers came forward with health and safety issues, though it seems clear that many were anxious about their conditions.[89] One Piche, a union organizer, has said that workers approached supervisors with health and safety problems but "you can only go to the sink so many times before you realize you are not going to get any water." He said that if workers tried to improve safety they were told "you can go down the road and look for another job."[90] Intimidation was made all the more effective in the Westray case by the fact that the Westray operation was one of the few mines in the country which was not unionized.[91]

Under conditions such as these, the internal responsibility system, which is premised on the notion of common interests, could not, and did not, work. Randy Facette, an experienced coal miner, was an employee representative on the joint health and safety committee at Westray. In his words, "It was a joke. We never got any help at all from the company ... having actual health and safety committee

[87]In addition to the problems discussed here, there is a large literature which critically evaluates the assumption economists make that workers rationally calculate risk and behave accordingly. These relate to issues such as imperfect information, improper understanding of probability relationships, etc. For a sample, see John Dennis Chasse and David A. LeSourd, "Rational Decisions and Occupational Health: A Critical View," *International Journal of Health Services*, 14 (1984), 433; W.L.F. Felstiner & Peter Siegelman, "Neoclassical Difficulties: Tort Deterrence for Latent Injuries," *Law and Policy*, 11 (1989), 309.
[88]S. 25, Occupational Health and Safety Act, 1985, c. 3, s. 1.
[89]Allan Jeffers, *CP*, 28 May 1992; s. 25(2)(d) Occupational Health and Safety Act.
[90]*CP*, 22 May 1991.
[91]It is worth pointing out that when Curragh Resources began its endeavours in the Yukon, again with federal government guarantees and territorial hand-outs, one of the attractions for it was that the work force was not unionized. Eventually it did become a unionized enterprise, as did Westray in the aftermath of the disaster.

meetings, having a chairman, there was nothing like that." Moreover, he said, the company seldom acted on complaints he passed on from other miners.[92]

At the same time that Westray was being tough with its workers in respect to health and safety complaints, it was holding out to the public that, despite the occasional glare of publicity caused by the questions raised in the legislature, it was running a safe mine. Indeed, it was reported that, only two weeks or so before the explosion, Westray was awarded a John T. Ryan safety award. The award was granted by the Canadian Institute of Mining, Metallurgy, and Petroleum which based its award on the frequency of reportable injuries in any one year. This must be set in context.

The earlier quoted miner, Ryan, has stated that the company paid workers to avoid reporting injuries to the Workers' Compensation Board. Workers would be paid for doing light duties. Ryan said that he himself had been put on such duties on this basis.[93] This hiding of injuries is reported to be a common tactic used by employers who are trying to minimize the workers' compensation premiums.[94] A sad irony about the John T. Ryan Award given to Westray is that the company sent one of its workers to get it. The worker was to become one of the victims of the May 10 explosion.[95]

B. Employers as Risk-Avoiders

Before we begin this section, we note again, because it is so important, that attempts to compare the risks run by employers and workers in respect to health and safety are grossly distorting. At the very worst, the employing classes can only lose money; the workers can actually lose their lives. But, even if health and safety harm is calculated only in dollar terms, the employing classes bear much less of the risk than do workers.

First, the economic costs of the harm caused by occupational health and safety debilitation is primarily borne by the workers, secondarily by the government and taxpayers, and only thirdly and, to a much lesser degree, by the employing classes. Each accident leads to both direct and indirect costs. Obvious direct costs include compensation for lost earnings and pensions for the victims and their dependents. Indirect costs include those associated with lost work-time, equipment replacement and upgrading, record-keeping related to the accident, expenses incurred to accom-

[92]Nancy Robb, "The History of Westray," *Occupational Health and Safety Canada* (July/August 1992), 43.
[93]*CP*, 28 May 1992.
[94]Again we want to underscore that what happened at Westray was normal. Two independent studies in two jurisdictions have found that the ratio of unreported to reported claims is 3:1. See Keith Harpur, "Work accidents 'three times reported rate,'" *Guardian*, 12 December 1991, 6 (reporting on HSE study), and Stephen Brickey and Karen Grant, "An Empirical Examination of Work-Related Accidents and Illnesses in Winnipeg" (paper presented at Manitoba Federation of Labor Conference on Workplace Health and Safety, 27 April 1992).
[95]*CP*, 28 May 1992.

modate returning workers and to recruit and train new people. Some of these losses are borne by employers in the first place, for example, lost productivity, increased compensation, premiums, penalty assessments, training and accommodation. But, some may be passed on by them later. For instance, workers' compensation policies, in the end, are paid out of workers' wages; increased costs of production can be passed on by employers in monopolistic or oligopolistic positions, a common circumstance in Canada. More important, perhaps, is the fact that taxpayers (mostly workers) bear many of the costs. They fund the medical care system, public pension regimes which include disability schemes, welfare, and charitable organizations which look after the victims of accidents and their dependents.[96]

Second, as has been clearly demonstrated by the particular circumstances of the Westray case, private property owners are not shy when it comes to feeding at the public trough. As much as it is possible to do so, they will seek to have governments underwrite their costs. In various liberal democracies, capitalists are able to pursue this goal more successfully than in others. Canada presents one end of the spectrum, the end at which it is quite possible — and becoming ever more possible — for private entrepreneurs to get governments to underwrite their ventures. Again, we emphasize that it is not just the political chicanery of Nova Scotia politics which is at issue. For instance, Curragh Resources Inc., was able to obtain almost an identical deal to the one it got for the Westray venture at its Faro Mine operations in the Yukon. The federal government guaranteed 85 per cent of its borrowings and the territorial government, run by the NDP, chipped in with an undisclosed public grant.[97]

Displacement of costs by wealthy owners is no more than to-be-expected behaviour in a class-divided society: inevitably, the dominant class will try to socialize the costs at the same time as it privatizes the profits of production. One of the great triumphs of the hegemony established by the employing classes in Canada is that this strategy is acceptable because it dovetails with one of the cornerstones of working capitalism in a staple-led growth economy, namely, that the state should help promote the unmediated pursuit of self-interest as much as it possibly can. While there are occasional expressions of concern about the efficiency of public hand-outs,[98] overall they are seen as necessary concessions to private capitalists whose willingness to take risks must be bolstered to foster general economic and

[96]For a more extended discussion, see H. J. Glasbeek, "A Role for Criminal Sanctions in Occupational Health and Safety," in Meredith Memorial Lectures 1988, *New Developments in Employment Law* (Cowansville, Québec 1989).

[97]Matthew Fisher, *Globe and Mail*, 1 September 1986, B6.

[98]K. Murty and Y. Siddiqi, "Government Subsidies to Industry," *Canadian Economic Observer*, 4 (May 1991) (subsidies by three levels of Canadian government amounted to $10.5 billion in 1986, $12.5 billion in 1987, $11.3 billion in 1988, $11 billion in 1989); John Deutsch Round Table on Economic Policy, *Tax Expenditures and Government Policy*, proceedings of a conference held at Queen's University, 17-18 November 1988 (Queen's University 1988); M. Trebilcock, *The Political Economy of Business Bailouts* (Toronto 1985).

social welfare. Not only does this line of argument provide a justificatory frame-work for the socialization of costs by employers as a class, it also serves to hide the effectiveness of another important set of risk-diluting stratagems, namely that employers, as individuals, can use the corporate form as a risk-avoidance mecha-nism. That is, the reasoning also supports the deployment of a facilitating device which has some surprising effects.

Most for-profit activity is carried on through corporations. Inasmuch as a corporation's investment may be lost, it makes sense to say that the market can be relied upon to exercise discipline over the behaviour of corporations. In the aggregate, therefore, the impact of the invisible hand on individuals and corpora-tions will lead to efficient wealth production. If the corporation is an appropriate surrogate for individual risk-taking investors, the use of this organizational form does not distort the private economic ordering model favoured in our kind of political economy. But, this is not the case.

The corporation has been given the legal standing it has to facilitate profit-mak-ing activities. In particular, it is designed to permit the pooling of small, discrete holdings of capital into aggregates which can be deployed more efficiently. In a similar way, diverse human resources and skills can be put together in one envelope to make their combined efforts more effective, in large part by a reduction of the transaction costs involved in contracting with a myriad of suppliers, purchasers and component part producers which would otherwise be necessitated. To achieve these goals a number of legal devices have been generated:

(i) Individuals are inveigled to invest some of their capital in a corporate venture by a rule which ensures that only that amount of their capital is at risk. The remainder of their assets are safe from the corporation's creditors. Investors have the luxury of limited liability. This also entails the ability to diversify the investment of their remaining assets. As if this were not enough protection, they are free to take their investment out of any one corporation at any time and sell it to a willing buyer.

This contrasts sharply with the position of the worker who invests in the same corporation. All of the capital she invests is at risk because she cannot safeguard some of her body from the physical dangers of the job. Moreover, as a practical matter, she cannot get out from under anywhere as easily if she does not like her work/investment situation. Aside from the rule which requires employees to give their employers reasonable notice of their intent to quit, the labour market rarely has as many willing buyers for her services as does the capital market for shares held in viable corporations.

(ii) The corporation becomes the legal owner of all the little capitals invested in it by individual investors. As a legal property-owning person, the corporation has the juristic standing to invest, sell, lease, buy, and so forth. It is responsible for the debts of the enterprise and to make good losses caused by it.

To engage in these business activities, however, the corporation needs humans to act for it. Managers and employees are hired to carry out the necessary tasks under the supervision of a directing board. This arrangement takes the private investor off the hook. He is not directly responsible for the way in which the corporation, a manager, or an employee acts. Adverse results are the corporation's and/or the managers' and/or the employees' problem. Needless to say, there is no equivalent way for the worker to pass on the risk of injury on the job. The best that she can hope for is that some measure of compensation be awarded her for the injury she has suffered as a result of her investment. A shareholder not only has a different kind of risk to the worker engaged in the co-operative productive activity, but the shareholder can also dilute the risk in a way the worker cannot.

Right from the beginning of modern incorporation law it was seen that limited liability, added to the ability of investors to alienate shares, would lead individual investors not to care much about what, and how, the corporation did things (provided that it continued to yield adequate returns). *The Law Times* referred to the proposal for limited liability as a Rogues' Charter.[99] Nothing in modern corporate law is aimed at blunting the incentive to human beings who are shareholders to be willfully oblivious to the harm corporate profit-maximization activities might cause. Individual property owners are induced to be passive investors because their apathy allows a large part of the risks created to satisfy their profit-seeking goals to be displaced to others. This is particularly odious when the displaced risk is the maiming and killing of workers.

Not only are the rules of corporate law such that shareholders can profit from their passivity, they also inexorably lead to the kind of positive manipulation which makes a mockery of the claim that individual investors take risks of any magnitude. In particular, shareholders exploit the fact that the corporation in which they invest has a separate legal personality. This means that, in a large number of situations, an investor can be any or all of the following: (i) a major shareholder with limited financial responsibility for debts and materialized risks; (ii) a senior manager who can create risks which might cause harm to third parties and, perhaps, to the corporation, but which enure to his benefit as a shareholder; and (iii) a controlling shareholder and manager who can cause the corporation to enter into transactions with a business in which he has a direct interest as an owner or as a shareholder. There are rules which require that persons in controlling positions within a corporation must disclose their material interests in a transaction or dealing. This gives the appearance that the corporation is entering into arms'-length transactions with others but, by and large, these are procedural hurdles, easily cleared. They do not seriously impede this kind of self-interested dealing. Virtually the only people who can effectively object to these gyrations are other shareholders.[100] This counter-

[99]*The Law Times*, 21 June 1856.

[100]Shareholders may cause the corporation to bring an action because it (notice the reification) is being inequitably treated. This is the derivative action. Shareholders may bring an action in their own right if they can show that their interests have been prejudiced in a discriminatory manner. This is the oppression remedy. It is also available to other interested persons, perhaps even workers. But, thus far, amongst non-shareholders, only a handful of creditors and officials appointed to supervise the administration of corporate law statutes have availed themselves of this extraordinary remedy.

weight has little effect where there are no other shareholders but the exploiting ones. This is a common circumstance. One of the more remarkable aspects of corporate law is that the corporate form is available where neither the aggregation of lots of small capital, nor the savings on transaction costs, are realities. These situations (one-person companies, or not very widely held companies) are the ones in which investors are most likely to profit by the legalized manipulation of rules. This is what happened in the Westray mine affair.

The story of how C.H. Frame used his capacities as an individual promoter, an investor, a management consultant, as well as a shareholder in a number of closely related businesses, to create a web of corporate connections and dealings which seem to have left him secure and well-off — regardless of how the Westray affair plays itself out — is told in the pages of Curragh Resources Inc.'s Annual Report 1990 and in the statement registered with the U.S. Securities and Exchange Commission on November 6, 1989.[101]

The beginning point is the incorporation of an Ontario company on April 29, 1987. It was named 715914 Ontario Inc. On May 20, 1987, its name was changed to Curragh Resources Inc. The day it was formed — April 29, 1987 — the numbered company acquired all of the resource properties and other assets and liabilities of a business called Curragh Resources. This was a firm which had been established by C.H. Frame and two partners. Because Curragh Resources had been a partnership, its members had been, as a matter of law, jointly and severally responsible for the debts and obligations of the firm. The firm had been established to acquire the Faro division and other mining properties of a company called Cyprus Anvil Mining Corporation. It had done so. In order to acquire the Curragh Resources partnership's business, 715914 Ontario Inc. had to raise $50 million. That sum allowed 715914 Ontario Inc. to acquire all the assets of Curragh Resources and to undertake all of its liabilities. In addition, 715914 Ontario Inc. borrowed $7 million to operate the business. In short, C.H. Frame and his partners in the Curragh Resources firm were paid in full for the investments they had made.

Two years later, in December 1989, Curragh Resources Inc. (the former 715914 Ontario Inc.) bought a 90 per cent interest in the mining leases and options known as the Westray Coal Property. This interest was bought from a company known as 630902 Ontario Inc. 630902 Ontario Inc. was a wholly-owned subsidiary of a company called Frame Mining Corporation. In turn, 74 per cent of the shares in Frame Mining Corporation were owned by a company called the Westray Mining Corporation.[102] Seventy per cent of Westray Mining Corporation's shares were

[101] This was when Curragh Resources Inc. became a public company.

[102] The other 26 per cent of the shares in Frame Mining Corporation were divided equally between a Swedish company called Boliden Canada Ltd. and Mitsui and Co. (Canada), Ltd., a Japanese company. The former was to be responsible for marketing of lead and zinc concentrates in Europe, the latter in the Far East, on behalf of Curragh Resources Inc. The pre-existing links between Curragh Resources, Curragh Resources Inc., C.H. Frame, and the Westray coal project are manifest.

owned by C.H. Frame, the man who was the promoter of the Westray coal project. As we know, it was he who had concluded the dealings which led to the very favourable conditions for extracting coal at the Westray site.

When Curragh Resources Inc. bought 90 per cent of the Westray coal project, it paid $9 million in cash to the then owner, 630902 Ontario Inc., and assumed $13 million of the liabilities which had been incurred in the promotion of the project. Once again, it appears that C.H. Frame had recouped his investment. Yet, stated in legal terms, nothing unusual had occurred: one mining development corporation had bought the interest which had been owned by another corporation. But, when Curragh Resources Inc. entered into an agreement to buy the Westray Coal Project operations from a C.H. Frame-controlled set of corporations, the same C.H. Frame controlled Curragh Resources Inc.

Curragh Resources Inc.'s list of significant shareholders is now part of the public record. As of March 1, 1991, the corporation had issued 16,406,302 subordinate voting shares and 15,719,737 multiple voting shares. Each subordinate voting share gave its holder one vote, whereas each multiple voting share gave its owner 10 votes. C.H. Frame beneficially owned, directly or indirectly, 100 per cent of the multiple voting shares. In a company report issued in March 1991, Frame indicated that he intended to use his voting control to ensure that all his nominees for directorships would be appointed. The legal governing body of Curragh Resources Inc. was to be his creature.[103]

Not only was Frame the principal engineer of the coal mining project, he was, at the same time, the very well-paid chief executive officer of Curragh Resources Inc. The legal ability to act in various capacities and guises obviously was exploited to the full by Frame. There was also a company called C.H. Frame Consulting Services. Among its businesses was the supply of executive officers and personnel to Curragh Resources Inc. In 1987 and 1988, Curragh Resources Inc. paid $.9 million and $1.2 million respectively to C.H. Frame Consulting Services for this supply. C.H. Frame Consulting Services also provided management services to the Westray coal project in connection with the planning and development of the Westray coal mine. It was to get $6 million for this when the mine was in full production. Curragh Resources Inc., managed by a board of directors associated with Frame and with Frame as C.E.O., bought out C.H. Frame Consulting Services for $1.5 million, that is, paid its owners $1.5 million. For this, Curragh Resources Inc. obtained the benefits of the management services contract for the Westray coal

---

[103]The Westray Mining Corporation (70 per cent of whose shares were owned by C.H. Frame) owned 519,737 of the multiple voting shares in Curragh Resources Inc. At the same time, Frame Mining Corporation (in which Westray Mining Corporation held 74 per cent of the shares) held 678,887 of the multiple voting shares in Curragh Resources Inc. Finally, 630902 Ontario Inc., wholly owned by Frame Mining Corporation, held 14,521,113 of the multiple voting shares in Curragh Resources Inc.

project: a Frame-created business obtained benefits from its links with another Frame corporation.[104]

It is, of course, quite likely that many of the payments made to Frame and his associates for the projects which he had developed and sold to Curragh Resources Inc. were made by way of shares in Curragh Resources Inc. In this sense, Frame, as a shareholder in Curragh Resources Inc., still runs some of the risks arising out of the enterprises which it runs. But his other personal assets are not at risk. The corporation itself, Curragh Resources Inc., is not directly responsible for most of the monies owed on the Westray coal project. The government of Nova Scotia's loan is secured by the assets at the Westray mine and is only collectable after the loan obtained from the Bank of Nova Scotia — guaranteed by the federal government — has been satisfied. In terms of satisfaction of the debt to the bank, Curragh Resources Inc. is only required to indemnify the bank and/or the federal government for $25 million of the $100 million borrowed. All in all, the position of Curragh Resources Inc. shareholders is not much less secure than it was because of the Westray disaster. Since then, however, its position as a corporation has deteriorated because of the poor world market for zinc and lead. It has been forced into the condition equivalent to Chapter 11 bankruptcy to hold off its creditors and it has given the keys to the Westray mine site to the government of Nova Scotia, leaving it with the mess.

The story makes it clear that, inasmuch as the dominant model of occupational health and safety regulation assumes some equivalence of risk between capital investors and labour power investors, the assumption is a distortion of reality. Employers, as a class, pay relatively little towards compensating victims and are not exposed to the same kind of risk as are workers. More importantly, by clever use of the corporate form, individual investors are able to displace the economic costs of injury and death to workers and to society at large.

V. Conclusions

The Westray story demonstrates that the assumptions which underlny health and safety regulation in Canada are inimical to the goal of providing adequate protection for workers. This is because, at bottom, they are wrong.

Employer-employee relationships in a capitalist economy are inherently conflictual, not consensual. A truly shared ideology is an illusion; it can only be

[104]When Curragh Resources Inc. bought an interest in the Westray Coal Project by dealing with 630902 Ontario Inc., it bought only 90 per cent of the holdings, leaving 630902 Ontario Inc. with the option of retaining a 10 per cent interest in the mining lease and exploration licences and to enter into a joint venture with Curragh Resources Inc. to further develop the property or to convert its interest into a five per cent cash flow royalty totalling approximately $15 million which would be paid before any other royalty was paid out. This is known as a back-in deal and is relatively common in the industry. It is not the unusual nature of the deal, then, to which attention is drawn, but the fact that, once again, an arrangement was made which would profit a major promoter and shareholder in this web of dealings.

maintained by artifice and with great effort. Health and safety issues in particular are likely to undo these efforts. Only workers get hurt at work, not employers. Because of this the notion of shared risk is, on its face, unbelievable. This is why so much effort is put into creating the image of mutual concern about physical working conditions and why there are repeated assertions that responsible employers, governments, and employees enjoy a shared ideology. It also partially explains why influential industrial relations and health and safety experts insist that health and safety problems should not be resolved in the same way as other industrial relations problems are when there is an impasse, that is, by controlled employer-employee confrontations. To allow them to be settled in this way would undermine the carefully constructed myth of common interest.[105]

To date, the effort to uphold this myth has been largely successful and it permits profit-oriented employers to build risks into production processes on the basis of cost-benefit calculations which suit them, subject only to whatever constraints are imposed by government or by workers through the internal responsibility system. Historically, health and safety standards have been set at levels which do not seriously infringe on employer profitability or prerogative. Workers effectively participate in setting these standards principally in an historic sense: governments have reacted to previous disasters, body counts and undeniable evidence of workers being harmed from commonly followed practices (for example, unguarded machinery). Workers' struggles for improved health and safety are much less likely to succeed when graphic evidence of their losses is not readily available.[106]

Now, as capital's mobility is enhanced and global competition intensified, it becomes more difficult both for workers to mobilize and for the state to regulate on their behalf. These conditions also restrict the opportunities for workers to influence employer-risk creation through the internal responsibility system. The superior economic power of employers who may withdraw their capital if they deem conditions unfavourable imposes clear limits on what any particular group of workers can hope to achieve. Contrary, then, to another of the assumptions which underlie health and safety regulation in Canada, particular social relations are determinative of the level of risk. At any level of productivity, different political and social structures, and the balance of forces within those structures, will produce

[105] Another reason for denying that health and safety as an industrial relations issue is that employers and state officials wish to contain any erosion of managerial prerogative resulting from the extension to workers of weak rights to participate in production decisions affecting their physical well-being. By insisting that these rights are bestowed in a sphere which falls outside "normal" industrial relations, the standard exclusion of workers from decision-making in general can be sustained. See Breen Creighton and Neil Gunningham, "Is there an Industrial Relations of Occupational Health and Safety?" in Creighton and Gunningham, eds., *The Industrial Relations of Occupational Health and Safety* (Sydney 1985), 4-5 and Vivienne Walters, "State Mediation of Conflicts over Work Refusals: The Role of the Ontario Labor Relations Board," *International Journal of Health Services*, 21 (1991), 717.

[106] On the role of worker protest in the development of U.S. mine safety legislation, see Daniel J. Curran, "Symbolic Solutions," and Michael Wallace, "Dying for Coal."

different levels of risk. The degree of danger at work is not just simply related to natural conditions or technical capacity.

In this context, the Westray story is illuminating precisely because the particular conjuncture of unequal power and the near-total acceptance of the need to please private capital made the working of the health and safety regulatory machinery so fraught with danger. But it need not be this way. Because risks and regulatory regimes are socially constructed, a range of mediations are possible within an untransformed social system. The history of health and safety regulation attests to this. We have already described three stages in the historical development of health and safety regulation in capitalist economies: market regulation, weak command and control regulation, and weak worker rights regulation. Worker struggles and changing economic, political, and ideological conditions made these developments possible.

Comparative studies provide further evidence that a range of mediations is viable. For example, in Sweden where workers' political and economic resources are highly developed, stronger worker rights and more protective standards have been legislated. At the other end of the spectrum, workers in the United States enjoy fewer participatory rights.[107] Moreover, even within a particular jurisdiction, the actual operation of the regulatory regime is responsive to changes in the balance of forces. We have already mentioned the strengthening of enforcement in Ontario which began during the NDP-Liberal Accord in the mid-1980s. Developments in Sweden and the United States also are instructive. The retreat of the Swedish social democrats on the issue of economic democracy, the move toward integration with Europe and the recent electoral defeat of the social democrats, all impact adversely upon the administration of health and safety and the ability of workers to make use of their legal rights.[108] In the United States, the election of Reagan led to a gutting of the health and safety administration without any formal change in the law whatsoever.[109] In sum, because a range of mediations is possible within any one set of social relations, the regulation of health and safety can be improved in Canada without waiting for transformation.

[107]See Vicente Navarro, "The Determinants of Social Policy — A Case Study: Regulating Health and Safety at the Workplace in Sweden," *International Journal of Health Services*, 14 (1983), 517.
[108]Eric Tucker, "Worker Participation in Health and Safety Regulation: Lessons from Sweden," *Studies in Political Economy*, 37 (1992), 95.
[109]Charles Noble, *Liberalism at Work: The Rise and Fall of OSHA* (Philadelphia 1986) and Andrew Szasz, "The Reversal of Federal Policy Toward Worker Safety and Health," *Science and Society*, 50 (1986), 25. The sensitivity of fatality rates in coal mining to the level of government spending on enforcement of strong coal mining safety laws has been demonstrated by Charles S. Perry, "Government Regulation of Coal Mine Safety," *American Politics Quarterly*, 10 (1982), 303.

At a minimum, the political struggle must begin from the perspective that, "There is nothing subtle, refined, genteel or courtly about this struggle. This IS war. This IS life and death."[110] This war, however, can only be fought one step at a time.

We have written the Westray story before the reports of the formal inquiries have been handed down because we believe that our analysis of events already clearly points to several viable strategies and goals, unlikely to be identified by a commission which does not question the underpinnings of current health and safety regulation. In particular, we believe that the dominant class's insistence that it is truly concerned about workers' health and safety may be exploited to advantage. There are limits, of course, to the gains which can be made by seeking to take advantage of employer and government hypocrisy. But it may be possible to get a better level of mediated regulation, setting the stage for further struggles until the structural limits of change are reached.[111]

To this end, much more vigorous and frequent criminal prosecution, posited on the reckless disregard for human life exhibited by employers when they willfully ignore existing standards or engineer unacceptable risks into an enterprise, would help focus attention on the fact that employers make all the important decisions on health and safety and workers take all the risks. Such anti-democratic practices fit poorly with the portrayal of a shared ideology and of consensual relations. Hoisted on their own petard, employers and governments may accept, or even initiate, measures which strengthen workers' participatory rights, giving them greater control over their work environment.[112]

In the same vein, there should be a concerted effort to de-mystify the corporate form. The thrust of this endeavour should be to show that real flesh and blood human beings profit from the maiming and killing which goes on in the corporate-owned enterprise. This will make it more difficult for governments, even conservative ones, to hold fast to the view that there is no question but that economic welfare should be produced primarily by the private sector rather than the public one. The notion that the private sector must be supported at any cost, even at the expense of the lives of people like those of the miners at Westray, may have to be addressed more explicitly than it is at the moment.[113]

[110]James Clancy, president of NUPGE, *National Union News*, May 1992 (writing about the Westray disaster).

[111]Erik Olin Wright, *Class, Crisis and the State* (London 1978).

[112]H. J. Glasbeek, "A Role for Criminal Sanctions in Occupational Health and Safety," and Tucker, "Worker Participation."

[113]In this regard, it is interesting to note that the Cape Breton Development Corporation Act, R.S.C. 1985, C-25, which created Devco as a crown corporation for the purpose of conducting mining in Cape Breton, states (at s. 15) that the object of the Coal Division is "to conduct coal mining and related operations in the Sydney coalfield on a basis that is consistent with efficient mining practice and good mine safety." This inclusion of safety as an independent objective stands in marked contrast to the approach we saw earlier by private coal developers. Of course, as the explosion referred to in note 5 reveals, statements of legislative intent do not necessarily get translated into action, but the possibilities for better health and safety regulation are greater in a publicly run enterprise than in a private one.

These tactics can be employed from within the existing scheme and its harmful assumptions. If purposefully engaged in, they may yield some positive results. It may be that the Westray body count will not lead to yet another instance of self-righteous posturing and band-aid solutions offered by complacent élites who have not been forced to change their beliefs. Rather, these tactics may help generate a political and ideological climate in which the radical surgery which is required will be on the agenda, one in which the workers will be the chief surgeons.

Postscript

The events surrounding the Westray disaster continue to unfold. The provincial Ministry of Labour laid 52 charges against the company and four mine managers arising out of the sorts of violations of health and safety laws discussed in the paper. The timing of the charges was dictated by the approaching end of the limitation period. Meanwhile, the Royal Canadian Mounted Police (RCMP) investigation into possible criminal wrongdoing was continuing, but met resistance from Curragh Resources Inc., the mine's owner. Curragh successfully brought an action in court forcing the RCMP to return a large number of documents it had seized on the basis that they were protected by solicitor-client privilege. The provincial inquiry also ran into legal obstacles. Four of the mine's managers brought an action in the Nova Scotia courts to put the inquiry on hold until after any and all charges either under provincial health and safety law or the Criminal Code have been dealt with. This is a common strategy. It is based on the claim that if the inquiry were to be held first, people could be compelled to give evidence which may be used against them in subsequent proceedings. It is argued that this would violate the constitutional right against self-incrimination. Also, it is claimed that the publicity generated by an inquiry would prejudice the right of the accused to an impartial hearing. In this case the Nova Scotia Court of Appeal determined that the provincial commission of inquiry could go on, but only after the processes which might lead to the imposition of quasi-criminal and criminal sanctions had been completed.

This not only suspended the inquiry, but led to the abandonment of the 52 charges belatedly laid under the provincial health and safety legislation in respect of the violations discussed in the text.

The RCMP has now laid charges of manslaughter and criminal negligence against Curragh Resources Inc., Gerald Phillips, the former Westray mine manager, and Roger Parry, the former underground manager of the mine. While this is to be welcomed because it underscores the seriousness of the events, it does not negate the need for a more open-ended political inquiry into the systemic failures of the regulation of occupational health and safety outlined in this paper. If this is not done, we can expect more tragedies.[114]

[114]DEATH BY CONSENSUS: The Westray Story was originally published in November 1992 by the Centre for Research on Work and Society, York University, Suite 201, 4700 Keele Street, North York, M3J 1P3, Canada; telephone: (416) 736-5612; FAX: (416) 736-5916. It was No. 3 in its Working Paper Series.

The Centre addresses the issues arising for labour out of the present, volatile transformation of the Canadian world of work. It links the labour movement and academics in research, education, and policy formulation. It also publishes a newsletter. The director of the centre is Carla Lipsig-Mummé.

ISER BOOKS

10 **Politically Speaking: Cross-Cultural Studies of Rhetoric** —Robert Paine (ed.)

9 **A House Divided? Anthropological Studies of Factionalism**—M. Silverman and R.F. Salisbury (eds.)

8 **The Peopling of Newfoundland: Essays in Historical Geography**—John J. Mannion (ed.)

7 **The White Arctic: Anthropological Essays on Tutelage and Ethnicity**—Robert Paine (ed.)

6 **Consequences of Offshore Oil and Gas—Norway, Scotland and Newfoundland**—M.J. Scarlett (ed.)

5 **North Atlantic Fishermen: Anthropological Essays on Modern Fishing**—Raoul Andersen and Cato Wadel (eds.)

4 **Intermediate Adaptation in Newfoundland and the Arctic: A Strategy of Social and Economic Development**—Milton M.R. Freeman (ed.)

3 **The Compact: Selected Dimensions of Friendship**—Elliott Leyton (ed.)

2 **Patrons and Brokers in the East Arctic**—Robert Paine (ed.)

1 **Viewpoints on Communities in Crisis**—Michael L. Skolnik (ed.)

Mailing Address:

ISER Books (Institute of Social and Economic Research)
Memorial University of Newfoundland
St. John's, Newfoundland, Canada, A1C 5S7

FAX (709) 737-7560 Telephone (709) 737-7474

imprimerie gagné ltée

PRINTED IN CANADA